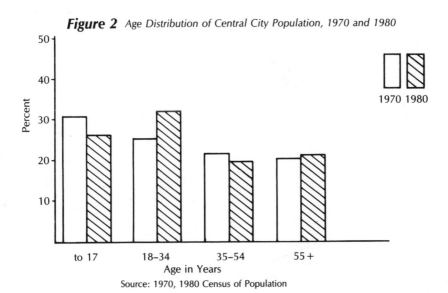

Figure 2 *Age Distribution of Central City Population, 1970 and 1980*

1970 1980

Percent

to 17   18–34   35–54   55 +
Age in Years
Source: 1970, 1980 Census of Population

The postwar baby-boom generation, followed by the 1970s baby-bust generation, moves through the age distribution. In the 1960s and 1970s our cities were burdened with children in need of education. By 1980, the postwar babies had become young adults, the return-to-the-city generation. By 2000 they will be middle-aged parents—the prime age group for suburban living.

URBAN ECONOMICS

Fourth Edition

URBAN ECONOMICS

Fourth Edition

Edwin S. Mills
Northwestern University

Bruce W. Hamilton
Johns Hopkins University

Scott, Foresman and Company
Glenview, Illinois   Boston   London

Acknowledgments are found on page 439, which is a legal extension of the copyright page.

Library of Congress Cataloging-in-Publication Data
Mills, Edwin S.
    Urban economics.

    Includes bibliographies and index.
    1. Urban economics.   I. Hamilton, Bruce W.,
II. Title.
HT321.M53   1988   330.9173'2   88-18625
ISBN 0-673-38323-7

    2 3 4 5 6–KPF–89

Preface

This book is primarily the offspring of Edwin S. Mills's text, *Urban Economics,* and Bruce W. Hamilton's urban economics course offered for the past several years at Johns Hopkins University. As will be seen, however, the book claims several other parents as well.

We have preserved almost intact the theoretical section from *Urban Economics, Second Edition,* as well as the new chapters from the third edition that contain a critical examination of the theoretical model and urbanization in developing countries. In the fourth edition, we have significantly expanded discussion of the historical context in which cities and cities' systems developed. This edition also contains new material on the changing economic function of central cities, particularly the dramatic recent shift from manufacturing to high-tech services. Although the book remains a text on urban—rather than regional—economics, we have substantially increased the depth of treatment of interactions among cities and among regions.

As this book is intended for use as a core text in urban economics, a reasonably solid foundation in microeconomic principles is a prerequisite. We found it necessary to describe the results of regression analysis at a few points in the book. The discussion is fairly basic, and we believe it is accessible to students who are unfamiliar with regression techniques. However, we have included an Appendix on the rudiments of regression to help students with these passages.

A final observation about the flavor of the book is this: We hope it represents the state of the discipline as it is, warts and all. We believe that economics contributes greatly to an understanding of how cities function and hope students will share this view after studying the book. But at the same time, there are poorly understood phenomena and facts that are at odds with our theoretical predictions. We discuss many of these uncomfortable facts. This ought not to leave the students confused; rather, we hope to convey the message that there are important questions that remain to be studied.

As is always the case in such a venture, we have received generous help from many quarters. Foremost among these is Molly Macauley, who served in the multiple roles of research assistant, consultant, and first reader of draft chapters for the third edition. She and Robert Schwab, the other reader of draft chapters, provided invaluable help in all parts of the book. For the fourth edition, Mohamed Elhage provided excellent research assistance.

We extend our thanks to several reviewers who provided many useful suggestions:

Ralph M. Braid, *Columbia University*
Louis P. Cain, *Loyola University of Chicago*
Mark Dynarski, *Mathematica Policy Research*

Gerald Goldstein, *Northwestern University*
Vernon Henderson, *Brown University*
Irving Hoch, *University of Texas*
Robert Inman, *University of Pennsylvania*
Theodore Keeler, *University of California at Berkeley*
Richard Muth, *Emory University*
Robert M. Schwab, *University of Maryland*
Stephen Sheppard, *University of Virginia*
William Vickrey, *Columbia University*
Ann Witte, *University of North Carolina*

In addition, we owe special thanks to Kenneth Small of the University of California, Irvine, whose help on the transportation chapter went far beyond that of a normal reviewer.

Many people also provided us with unpublished information:

Ronnie Davis, *National Association of Realtors*
William Geppart, *Geppart Demolition Contractors of Philadelphia*
Nelson James, *Society of Industrial Realtors*
Macy Whitney, *Knott Remodelling, Washington, D.C.*
Richard P. Davis, *Baltimore City Department of Housing and Community Development*

George Lobell of Scott, Foresman has been extremely helpful in several phases of our revision. Anne Whitmore provided invaluable assistance in the preparation of the manuscript.

Edwin S. Mills

Bruce W. Hamilton

Table of Contents

Part One

Basic Ideas and Historical Background

1

The Nature of Urban Areas

☐ The city is one of humanity's earliest and most productive inventions. The first true cities arose along the Nile, the eastern Mediterranean, and the Fertile Crescent, approximately 5500 years ago. By 2000 B.C. cities had spread throughout the Mediterranean basin and the Arabian peninsula, and on to the Indus River valley in India and the Yellow River valley in China.

Since that time, the advances and declines of civilization have been intimately connected with advances and declines in urbanization. The episode of urbanization that began along the Nile and the Fertile Crescent reached its apex with the Roman Empire. With the sacking of Rome in A.D. 476, both urbanization and the quality of life went into a steep decline throughout southern Europe. Recovery from this decline began in approximately the tenth century, with the emergence of the medieval city. With some setbacks, urbanization and economic progress proceeded slowly until the beginning of the nineteenth century and the Industrial Revolution.

At this point it is useful to ask two questions: first, what conditions are necessary for the formation of cities, and second, what is to be gained from urban life? The answers to these questions cannot be arrived at without an understanding of the types of economic activities that always take place in cities.

From earliest times onward, the city has been the home of specialists—in particular, specialists in nonagricultural activities. Dating from these earliest times, these specialists could not survive without the produce of the land, so the first prerequisite for a city was the presence of an agricultural sector which produced a surplus—more than enough food to sustain itself. Second, urban dwellers had to induce farmers to part with their surplus—either by exchange or by force.

Both before and after the initial formation of cities, one of the crucial requirements for urbanization was the improvement of agriculture.

Techniques of irrigation and metal implements were among the first such innovations.

In order to thrive in an economy based on exchange rather than force, cities had to be productive—to provide something for the agricultural sector which the latter could not provide as well for itself. This ability of cities to provide something with which to trade for produce is dependent on scale economies, for *large scale* is a city's unique attribute. In other words, a city is distinguished from its *hinterland* (the rural region served by the city) in that a city concentrates large numbers of people, and large amounts of physical capital, in a confined area. As will be seen, this concentration has proved to be a most productive way of providing many of the fruits of civilization; but it also has created problems that are virtually absent in rural areas and small villages.

This book is concerned with the economic opportunities which cities present to people. In addition, attention is focused on the economic problems which arise with the existence of cities, and possible ways of handling these problems.

Most people make intuitive distinctions between urban and rural areas and between big cities and small towns. For many purposes, the intuitive distinctions are adequate. Nevertheless, it is worthwhile to start with some careful definitions and distinctions, because data sources depend on them.

☐ WHAT ARE URBAN AREAS?

There are many urban concepts: town, city, urban area, metropolitan area, and megalopolis are examples. Some have legal definitions: *towns, municipalities,* and *cities* are built-up areas designated as political subdivisions by states, provinces, or national governments. Practices in designating urban government jurisdictions vary greatly from country to country and, in the United States, from state to state. What one country or state designates a city, another may designate a town. More importantly, the part of an urban area included in a city or other political subdivision varies from place to place and from time to time. In 1980 the city of Boston contained only 20 percent of the 2.8 million people in its metropolitan area, whereas the city of Austin contained 64 percent of the 537,000 people in its metropolitan area. In America's metropolitan areas, the largest city contains, on average, less than half the residents of the metropolitan area. Other countries tend to expand city boundaries as the metropolitan area expands so that the city includes all or nearly all of the metropolitan area.

To the political scientist studying local government, the legal definitions of local government jurisdictions are of primary importance. They are also important to the economist studying economic aspects of local government. Much of Chapter 13 is about the causes and effects of arrangements of local government jurisdictions. These jurisdictions, however, were chosen largely for historical and political reasons, and they have little to do with the economist's notion of an urban area. They are therefore of secondary concern in urban economics.

Much more fundamental for urban economists than legal designations is variability in population and employment density from one place to another. A country's **average population density** is the ratio of its population to its land area. In 1980 the average population density in the United States was about sixty-four people per square mile. It is conceivable that every square mile in the country might have about the same number of residents. The study of urban economics begins with the observation that population density varies enormously from place to place.

In 1980 there were about 300 places in the United States where the population density reached extremely high levels relative to the average level and relative to levels a few miles away. In New York City, to take the most dramatic example, the population density was more than 23,000 people per square mile. Fifty miles away, in Sussex County, New Jersey, it was 160. A less dramatic, but instructive, example is Wichita, Kansas. In 1980 its population density was 2754 people per square mile. The remainder of Sedgwick County, which contains Wichita, had a population density of 56. The adjoining county of Kingman had a density of only 10. New York City and Wichita are clearly urban areas. Such places contain more than half the country's population and constitute the popular image of a metropolitan area, but they do not exhaust the list of urban areas. There are hundreds of small cities and towns, many with population densities exceeding those of surrounding rural areas by factors of 50 or 100. These are also urban areas.

Thus the fundamental and generic definition of *urban area,* or *metropolitan area,* is a place with a much higher population density than elsewhere. At least a few urban areas have existed since the beginning of recorded history, and they now are found in every country in the world. For some purposes, this crude definition is adequate. For purposes of data collection and analysis, however, more careful definitions are needed.

The generic definition of an urban area is a relative concept. A place with a high population density relative to the average density in one region or country might not be high relative to the average density in another region or country. To take an extreme example, the average population density in Japan in 1980 was 811 people per square mile. This is higher than the densities of many metropolitan areas in the United States. Thus a minimum density that would define an urban area needs to be higher in Japan than in the United States. Similar situations arise within the United States. The average population density in the Phoenix metropolitan area is just slightly more than one-third that of the entire state of New York. Thus urban areas cannot be defined exclusively by population density.

To be designated urban, a place must have not only a minimum population density but also a minimum total population. An isolated half-acre lot lived on by a trapper's family in Alaska may have as great a density as many urban areas, but no one would call it a one-family urban area. Many small places have densities that are high relative to surrounding areas. Official statistics necessarily employ an arbitrary population cutoff in defining urban areas, usually between 2500 and 25,000 people.

A final problem arises in counting urban areas. As urban areas grow, they frequently come to encompass places that were formerly separate urban areas. Metropolitan areas encompass what were formerly separate small towns. On a larger scale, metropolitan areas gradually grow together. The New York-northeastern New Jersey area encompasses several metropolitan areas, and the Chicago-Gary area encompasses two metropolitan areas. Such amalgamations create no problems in counting the urban population, but they do cause problems in counting the number of urban areas. When metropolitan areas grow together, the U.S. Census Bureau wisely presents data separately for each metropolitan area so that users can put the data together as they please. The Census Bureau also uses its criteria to determine which metropolitan areas are integrated sufficiently to be considered one large area, and it publishes the combined data. For example, several metropolitan areas across the Hudson River from New York City are closely related to the New York metropolitan area, although they are in some ways distinct.

☐ NOTE ON STATISTICAL DATA

Most of the U.S. data available to the urban economist, as well as most data used to compare urban areas nationwide, come from the censuses of population and housing, manufacturers, businesses, and government. Every student of urban economics should get to know these data sources. Despite their many inadequacies, there are no better sources.

Most federal government data pertaining to urban areas now are based on the same set of definitions regarding the area covered. The federal government distinguishes between several urban concepts, however, depending on the way data become available and the purposes for which measures are intended.

An **urban place** is any concentration—usually in an incorporated town, borough, or city—of at least 2500 people. Since an urban place is usually defined by political boundaries, it does not correspond to the economist's notion of an urban area. Data pertaining to urban places are therefore of relatively little value to the urban economist. In fact, an urban area usually contains many urban places. In the 1980 U.S. census of population, there were 8765 urban places containing 154 million people, about 68 percent of the country's population of 226.5 million at that time.

The concept that corresponds to the economist's notion of an urban area is called an *urbanized area* by the federal government. An **urbanized area** consists of one central city (or sometimes two) of at least 50,000 residents, as well as the surrounding closely settled area. Thus an urbanized area is the physical city, defined without regard for political boundaries. In 1980 the census identified 366 urbanized areas in the United States. They contained 139 million people, or 61 percent of the country's population.

Mainly to facilitate data gathering, the government defines various categories of **metropolitan statistical areas** (MSAs). The boundary of an MSA is always a legal boundary—typically a county boundary. The most frequently discussed type of MSA is the *standard* metropolitan statistical area (SMSA), which consists of one central city (or possibly two) of at least 50,000 residents, as well as one or more *contiguous counties that are metropolitan* in character, as determined by the percentage of the labor force that is nonagricultural and by the amount of commuting between the county or counties and the city. Thus SMSAs do not include parts of counties. Although the list of SMSAs is virtually the same as the list of urbanized areas, the SMSAs include nonurbanized parts of contiguous metropolitan counties. Not surprisingly, SMSAs have somewhat greater populations than urbanized areas, along with much more land. In 1980 around 169 million people, or 75 percent of the country's population, lived in 323 SMSAs—21.6 percent more people than in urbanized areas. The SMSAs, however, contained about eleven times as much land. Some SMSA counties, particularly in the West, contain large amounts of land, although their nonurbanized parts contain few people. A dramatic example is the San Bernardino SMSA in California, which extends through the desert to the eastern boundary of the state.

There are several instances in which two or more SMSAs have grown together to such a degree that they are really one urban agglomeration. Such agglomerations—really aggregations of SMSAs—are called CMSAs (consolidated metropolitan statistical areas). The individual SMSAs within a CMSA are sometimes referred to as PMSAs, where *P* stands for "primary." For example, the Los Angeles CMSA is made up of four PMSAs—Anaheim-Santa Ana; Los Angeles-Long Beach; Oxnard-Ventura; Riverside-San Bernardino. In 1980 the government recognized seventeen CMSAs.

The urbanized area corresponds much more closely to the generic concept of an urban or metropolitan area than does the SMSA. Why then should an economist be interested in SMSA data? The answer is easy: more data are available for SMSAs than for urbanized areas, because some data become available by county and therefore can be put together for SMSAs, but not for urbanized areas.

The term *megalopolis* sometimes is applied to the part of the eastern seaboard from Boston to Washington or Richmond. It also is applied to the Pacific coast of Japan from Tokyo to Osaka and to the stretch of England from London to Manchester. The term is popular and some-what descriptive, but it is unofficial. It is also inaccurate. The three megalopolises do indeed contain many people. The Japanese megalopolis is the largest of the three, with more than 40 million residents. Yet the metropolitan areas within these megalopolises are not united by the usual criteria of people commuting from one to another. The term is also inaccurate in that each of the three megalopolises, especially the American one, contains large amounts of rural land.

Overall density data indicate that the urbanized area is a significant urban concept. In 1980 population density for the United States was sixty-four people per square mile. In urbanized areas it was 2675. By contrast, in SMSAs it was 299.

In this book the term *urban area* refers generically to places of high population density. The term *city* refers to the legal city. The terms *urban place, urbanized area, SMSA,* and *CMSA* refer to the concepts used in federal government data sources.

☐ WHY URBAN AREAS?

If an urban area is defined by dramatically high population densities relative to those found elsewhere, the next question is the following: why are there urban areas? There is no single answer. Historians, geographers, sociologists, political scientists, and economists tend to emphasize different sets of causes in explaining why urban areas exist. The fundamental proposition is that urban areas exist because people have found it advantageous to carry on various activities in a spatially concentrated fashion.

Most of the differences of opinion about the reasons for urban areas' existence result from the fact that these activities may be of very different kinds: military activities, religious practice or religion administration, government activities, and private production and the distribution of goods and services. At various times in history, many urban areas had defense as their major function. It was simply more economical and effective to defend a large group of people if they were spatially concentrated. (The word *was* is used intentionally, because weapons technology in the nuclear age may make it easier to defend a dispersed population than a concentrated one.) In such urban areas, people commuted out of the city to carry on the predominant economic activity, farming. Colonial North America provides one interesting example of this phenomenon. During the first several decades after the original settlement of English North America, the fraction of the population which was urban actually declined, because of the gradual reduction in fear of attacks by natives.

Some urban areas began as cathedral towns or centers for religion administration. Other cities grew because they were seats of civil government. Washington, D.C., is the most obvious example.

Most urban areas today, however, do not owe their existence or size to military, religious, or governmental activities. In countries where economic decisions are mainly private, *the sizes of most urban areas are mainly determined by market forces*. Households have found that income and employment opportunities, as well as prices and the availability of consumer goods, are more favorable in urban than in other areas. Businesses have found that investment returns are higher in urban areas than in rural areas.

In the United States, seats of government are almost the only major exceptions to the determination of urban sizes by market forces. Washington, D.C., is a clear exception. To some extent, most state capitals also are exceptions. Most of them were intentionally located in small towns away from major centers, and many have remained small towns. European national capitals, such as London, Paris, and Rome, are harder to classify. They certainly owe part of their size to their being seats of government. The opposite is also true: they were made seats of government partly because they were major cities.

People unsympathetic to *economic location theory* sometimes claim that historical, rather than economic, forces have determined the locations of major urban areas. They claim, for example, that a certain urban area is where it is because some settlers happened to land there first. This idea assumes that settlers or other founders were unresponsive to the advantages and disadvantages of alternative locations. More importantly, the map is dotted with places where settlers happened to settle. Some became major urban centers, but most remained just dots on the map, despite elaborate local plans and efforts to make them metropolitan centers. Those that developed into major centers did so in large part because their economic potential induced thousands of people and institutions to decide to work, live, and produce there. But as will be seen in Chapter 2, forces other than simple economic superiority of one site over another have at times played crucial roles in urban locations. The best assumption is that economic factors affect location decisions to about the same extent that they affect other types of decisions, such as pricing by firms and demand for goods and services by consumers. Employers who locate in wrong places find that they cannot compete for employees or customers. Workers who make poor locational choices find that their living standards suffer.

Scale Economies

How do market forces generate urban areas? It has already been pointed out that most urban areas arise because of the economic advantages of large-scale activities. The economist's term for this phenomenon is **indivisibilities**, or, more generally, **scale economies**. General price theory says that a firm's production function displays scale economies if a proportionate change in all inputs leads to a greater proportionate change in output. Scale economies exist at any level of output at which, with all input prices constant, the long-run average total cost is falling. Thus **diseconomies of scale** exist if the long-run average cost is rising.

What is the relationship between scale economies and spatial concentration? Economists usually assume that most scale economies are realized within a plant, which is usually a contiguous set of production facilities. Even if they are contiguous, however, they may be more or less concentrated; that is, the ratios of capital or other inputs to land may be high or low. Which ratio entails lower costs?

In some cases, the mechanism by which proximity provides scale economies is clear. When a raw material is subject to several processing stages, greater spatial separation of the stages entails more movement of the material. This is particularly significant when material must be at extreme temperatures during processing: to move molten steel over substantial distances would be highly impractical. Contiguity does not always seem to be a requirement for scale economies, however. It is easy to imagine that a firm with two plants might find it economical to provide a service facility, such as maintenance, for its plants, and that it therefore might have lower average costs than a firm with one plant that either bought maintenance services from another firm or produced them itself. Although examples are easy to come by, economists to date have paid relatively little attention to the spatial aspects of scale economies.

Scale economies are important for the existence of urban areas. Consider a simple model of a country in which there are no scale economies. In the economy a finite, but possibly large, number of different goods is produced. Inputs in each industry include the outputs of other industries; several kinds of labor, which are mobile; and a single, nonproduced natural resource, which is distributed uniformly over the land. Suppose all input and output markets are competitive, and that there are neither economies nor diseconomies of scale at any output in any industry. Thus, production can take place on however small a scale is necessary to meet local demands. There is no loss of efficiency, and therefore no need for transportation from one area to another. Each small area contains the same mix of production and the same mix of people with different tastes. Markets are in equilibrium, because population and employment densities are uniform, with all demands satisfied by local production.

The density of population or employment in any one area is not greater than elsewhere: competition for land in a high-density area drives its land values above the land values in areas of lower density, so households and businesses in the high-density area move to an area of lower density with lower land costs. They are not held back by lower production costs or lower prices of consumer goods and services resulting from economies of scale in the high-density area.

The crux of the argument is that without scale economies, production can take place on a very small scale near each consuming location, and population and production density—and land values—thus will be uniform.

Now change the model by supposing that one industry (S) does have scale economies, at least at small outputs. It now pays for a firm to spatially concentrate the production of Industry S in a large plant in order to obtain a lower average cost. The amount produced in one place depends on the extent of the scale economies, on the nature of demand, and on transportation cost. In addition, workers in Industry S live near their place of work to avoid commuting costs. Moreover, it is advantageous to other industries—without scale economies—to locate nearby if they sell their products to Industry S or to its employees. It is also advantageous to their employees to live nearby. Again, the same advantages apply to industries selling to these industries and their employees, and so on.

The process produces a spatial concentration of economic activity that legitimately can be called an urban area. Although the description of the process makes it appear that everything might end up in one urban area, at some size the advantages of proximity are balanced by high transportation costs, and the urban area's growth ceases. Thus, there will be several urban areas, each of which has one firm of Industry S. In addition, the urban areas do not trade with one another, although Industry S may export its output to the surrounding countryside. Each urban area satisfies its own demands for the product of Industry S and for the products of all industries without scale economies, so there is as yet no specialization among urban areas.

The foregoing description is perhaps the simplest model of urban areas. Such models, based on scale economies, are referred to as *central place theory,* which has had a long and distinguished history. (One of the curiosities of that history is that, until after World War II, most contributions were made by German-speaking writers, and central place theory was practically unknown to English-speaking economists. August Lösch, the father of modern location theory, was the most important contributor. The English translation of his *Economics of Location,* published in 1954, did a great deal to familiarize English-speaking economists with central place theory.)

The relationship between pricing and transport cost in the presence of scale economies can be seen in Figure 1.1. The horizontal axis depicts distance from the plant, whose location is shown on the vertical axis labeled I.[1] The vertical axis measures cost. Suppose the unit cost of producing Good S is A if a scale economies technique is not employed and B if a quantity sufficient to capture scale economies is produced. Regardless of where consumers live, they can acquire the good at price A. If a firm sets up a large plant, it will be able to sell its output at price B and still cover costs. Not all consumers will find this cheaper than A because of the transport cost involved.

Suppose that it costs $\$t$ per mile to transport the good from the factory to the home. This is depicted by the upward-sloping lines la-

1. The vertical line labeled II is the site of a competing plant. Ignore it for now.

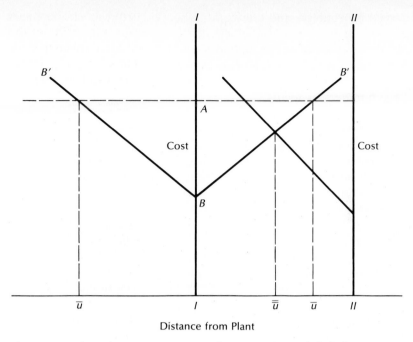

Figure 1.1 *Relationship Between Pricing and Transport Cost with Scale Economies*

beled B' emanating from the plant, with a slope of t. The height of the line, at each distance, now represents the price of the good *inclusive of transport cost*. Transport cost obviously rises with distance from the factory until finally, at distance $\bar{u}$, transport cost has eaten up all the scale economies. Beyond this point, consumers are better off producing the good locally, at cost A. Thus, everyone who lives inside the circle whose center is the scale economies plant and whose radius is $\bar{u}$ will purchase from the plant rather than produce locally or do without. This circle is called the firm's *market area*.

It is important at this point to note two features of the model. First, the scale-economies producer might charge a price above the average cost in an attempt to extract some monopoly profit. Second, consumers living close to the plant are better off than those living far from the plant, because they get the good more cheaply. Thus consumers can be expected to compete with one another for sites near the plant. This competition would be expected to make land value higher for sites close to the plant. This basic relationship between accessibility and rent pervades the study of urban economics. The price of land varies geographically to offset other advantages of location.

Spatial competition. If a firm is able to charge a price above the average cost, it makes a profit. This example attracts imitators, and like the original, imitators carve out market areas limited by transport cost. Eventually, all the land from which circular market areas can be carved is occupied, and the world, when viewed from above, might look like Figure 1.2, with each circular market area tangent to the four adjacent market areas and with interstices between the circles that are too remote to be served. Each plant is indifferent to the existence of the others; in no sense does competition exist, even though there are large numbers of agents.[2]

It is possible (although not certain), however, that genuine competition could spring up. Consider point a in the middle of an unserved region in Figure 1.2. Suppose an entrepreneur opens a plant there, at the same scale (and therefore at the same cost) as the existing plants in the circle centers. The entrepreneur attracts all customers who live closer to point a than to their former shopping centers, and carves out the market inside the dashed square.[3] The market area is smaller than the original circles, but it still may be large enough to earn the entrepreneur a positive profit. This entry shrinks both the market area and the profit of competitors. The most efficient outcome of this spatial competition is a world filled with hexagonal market areas, with the size of the hexagons just sufficient to permit each entrepreneur to cover costs,[4] as shown in Figure 1.3.

Returning to Figure 1.1, there is now a competing plant at II, and the edge of the market area is no longer the point at which home production is cheaper; instead, it is the point at which purchasing from a competing, large plant is cheaper ($\overline{\overline{u}}$ in Figure 1.1).[5]

This is a complete description of the organization of economic activity in a world in which there are scale economies in one industry. The land is dotted with self-sufficient cities, each trading its specialty good for the agricultural products in its hinterland, but no city trading with another. The size of a city is limited by the degree of scale economies, by transport cost, and by competition from other cities.

Specialization of a kind results from the next step toward reality in this model. Economists tend to think of scale economies mainly in manufacturing. In terms of absolute scale, that may be appropriate. In

2.   Actually, there is some dispute over the strength with which market forces would cause these circular market areas to be tightly packed, as in Figure 1.2. They might arise with bigger gaps between the circles.

3.   All the points inside the square are closer to the plant at point a than to any other plant.

4.   The hexagonal packing, in addition to being efficient, is an equilibrium in the sense that if the world should happen to find itself in such a configuration, no agents would have an incentive to change their location or other behavior. However, the world might not find itself in such a configuration, as will be seen.

5.   This spatial competition model is essentially that of Lösch (1954), who has a relatively readable discussion in Friedmann and Alonso (1964). His model is much richer and more flexible than the one discussed. For example, an L-shaped average cost curve is assumed—average cost is either A or B in Figure 1.1, depending upon whether the plant does or does not have scale economies. In Lösch's work, average cost curves are smoothly downward sloping. His model, in fact, is essentially the Chamberlain monopolistic competition model, with spatial separations providing the product differentiation.

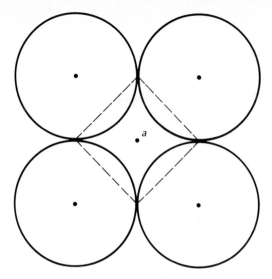

Figure 1.2 *Market Areas*

a manufacturing plant, scale economies may not be exhausted until employment numbers in the hundreds. Scale economies are pervasive in all industries, however, at least at low levels of output. In retailing, wholesaling, and services, scale economies also exist, but they may be exhausted when employment reaches only a dozen or a few dozen people. It is not the absolute scale at which economies are exhausted, but rather *the scale relative to market demand,* that determines whether there can be 1, 2, or 100 firms in an industry. Many service industries, for example, are highly specialized and have extremely low per capita demands. Scale economies may prevent such industries from locating in towns and small cities or may permit so few firms that those that exist have substantial monopoly power. Thus, large urban areas provide specialized cultural, legal, medical, financial, and other services that are not available in small urban areas.

The fact that scale economies exist in all industries rather than in just one, and that scale economies may be exhausted at different levels of output or employment in different industries, greatly enriches this hypothetical landscape. All industries tend to concentrate spatially to some extent, and transportation costs can be kept low if the industries concentrate near one another. Thus, it is now possible to account for variety among urban area sizes, as well as for a certain kind of trade between large and small urban areas. The small urban areas contain only those industries with scale economies exhausted by the demands of small populations. The larger urban areas contain, in addition to small-scale industries, industries with scale economies exhausted only by the demands of a larger population. The larger urban areas supply such products not only to their own residents, but also to residents of small

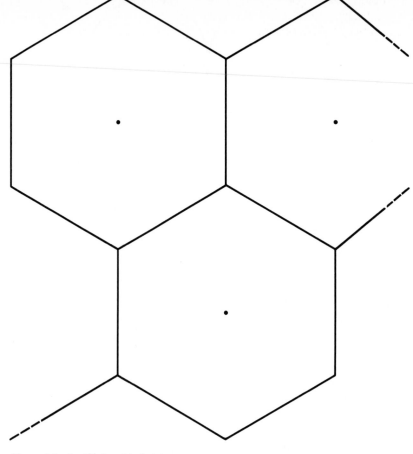

Figure 1.3 *Equilibrium Market Areas*

urban areas. The largest urban areas contain all types of industries and are the only urban areas containing those industries whose scale economies require the demands of the largest population to exhaust them.

Thus, urban areas of a given size would export to urban areas of smaller sizes, but there would be no other kind of trade between urban areas. In particular, it is not yet possible to account for mutual trade, in which one urban area both exports to and imports from another.

In this model big cities export to small cities but do not import anything in return. Thus, it appears that some balance-of-trade principles are violated. If small cities have nothing big cities want, how do they pay for their purchases? The answer is that small cities' exports to big cities are roundabout—via the rural sector. Small cities export their output to the agricultural sector, which exports to the big cities, which export to the small cities. This completes the circular flow of trade. Superimposed upon this, of course, are direct-trade circles involving only farms and small cities, as well as farms and large cities.

An interesting implication of this hierarchical view of cities is that there are many small cities and few large cities. A bit more formally, the number of cities of a given size is inversely related to city size. The theory does not tell us how rapidly the number of cities declines as city size increases; that depends upon empirical details of the degree of scale economies in various industries, the density of demand, and transport costs. Chapter 4 will show that the empirical relationship between the number of cities and city size is remarkably stable.

Export base.   According to this scale economies-based theory, a city arises because scale economies enable it to produce a good or goods that can be exported profitably to a hinterland. The demand for the export good and the ability of a city to supply it through scale economies production are the reasons for the existence of a city. Initially, this prototype city can be thought of as populated only by people who work in the scale economies plant. These people subsist on imports of agricultural goods from the hinterland.

Of course, these workers can be expected to consume something besides food imports. For example, they also demand services and manufactured goods. The existence of a labor force with these demands, concentrated in a city, attracts suppliers of services and manufactures for home consumption. Thus, a city ultimately will be substantially larger than the export sector that gave rise to its existence in the first place.

Employment in a city's scale economies export sector frequently is called *basic,* or *export base, employment,* and the remainder of employment (that which satisfies local demand) is called *nonbasic employment.* As cities (or regions or nations) get bigger, the ratio of nonbasic to basic employment tends to rise. If some of the home-consumption goods are produced subject to scale economies (which is surely the case), then, as a city gets bigger, it finds itself able to substitute home production for imports of these goods. This is known as *import substitution;* it will play an important role in the discussion of regional shifts in Chapter 2. The result of import substitution is that large cities are more self-reliant than small cities.

Space in microeconomic theory.   It is interesting at this point to note how standard microeconomic theory must be modified to accommodate the existence of space and transport cost. First, however, notice that most economic models are completely spaceless. Even the theory of international trade pays little attention to the friction of space and distance. In very advanced treatments of theory, in which consideration of time is basic, economists typically assume that space can be overcome costlessly or that all economic activity takes place at the same point.

The introduction of space creates some nasty problems for economists, but it also clears up a few. First, in a spatial world, plant size under constant returns is no longer indeterminate—it is zero (or rather, just big enough to satisfy one household's demand). Without increasing returns, there is no reason to incur transport cost. Casual observation reveals that this finding is correct—activities that can be done as cheaply at home as in a factory, such as brushing teeth and washing dishes, are done at home to save the transport cost. Firms that produce for more than one household have scale economies, at least over some range.

Second, a spatial model clears up the problem of pricing under increasing returns. In the absence of a spatial model, increasing returns and efficient pricing are incompatible, because marginal cost is less than average cost. Furthermore, the existence of competition is in doubt both as a descriptive and a normative model, because bigger is always better, both socially and privately. With the introduction of space and location, however, increasing-returns firms take on a different look. Even if production cost falls with output, average transport cost generally rises with output, since the only way to increase output is to ship the increment a greater distance. Hence the existence of transport cost is likely to give firms a "normal" U-shaped average cost curve, with the upward-sloping average transport cost curve eventually outweighing the downward-sloping average production cost curve, even if there are increasing returns in production.

The introduction of space and transport cost also causes problems for microeconomic theory. The most important is that the equilibriums that emerge might not be optimum or unique.

The first case in which spatial competition does not lead to an optimum was analyzed by Hotelling (1929). To understand this model, suppose there is a beach along which sunbathers are evenly distributed, and on this beach there are two ice cream vendors, each of whom wants to locate to maximize sales. Every sunbather buys one ice cream cone per day (that is, demand is perfectly inelastic), walking to the nearest vendor. The optimum location is obvious—the vendors should locate respectively one-fourth and three-fourths of the way from one end of the beach (at points a and b in Figure 1.4). Even if they start at these locations, however, each will have an incentive to move toward the other. To take an extreme case, the vendor at point a might move to point a' next to point b, thus capturing all the market to the left of point b, which is three-fourths of the beach. The vendor at point b, of course, would hop over the vendor at point a', and this leapfrogging would

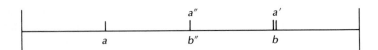

Figure 1.4 *Competition Along a Line*

continue until the vendors were next to one another at the midpoint of the beach (points a'' and b''). This is the only stable equilibrium, yet the average trip length is twice as long as at the optimum.

The Hotelling model has been applied to a wide range of problems, some of which have nothing to do with geographic space. It has been cited, for example, as the reason both major political parties tend to stake out platform positions near the political center.

There is some dispute over the practical importance of the Hotelling finding. The presumption of a nonoptimum equilibrium is greatly weakened when there are more vendors (in particular, when there are at least four). When there are many vendors on the beach, a move toward one competitor is a move away from another, so a vendor's optimum location is midway between the neighboring vendors. This is also the socially optimum location, since it minimizes average transport cost. The model is most appropriate when large numbers are precluded for some reason (as in the case of political parties), but even in this context the model contains some assumptions which are odd from an economist's perspective. First, demand is perfectly inelastic with respect to price (the customers at the end of the beach do not curtail their demand when the vendors move toward the middle). Second, it apparently never occurs to the vendors that they can compete with one another on price as well as location. The reader may want to think about what happens to the model's results when one or both of these assumptions is relaxed.

Some technical considerations. * Even in the case of a large number of competitors, in the spirit of the central place theory model previously discussed, there is some dispute as to whether an economy will tend to arrive at the optimum hexagon configuration of Figure 1.3. Consider the world of Figure 1.3, in which hexagonal market areas represent an optimum. Now suppose that the plants are oriented in such a way that the actual market areas are squares. It is easy to see that this is not an optimum. If a market area of the same size were served by a hexagon, average transport cost would be lower. A hexagon more closely approximates a circle than does a square, so the average distance from a point in the polygon to the center is less for a hexagon than for a square. The corners are less remote.

The configuration of square market areas might be an equilibrium, however. To see this, note that a new entrant would establish a plant at a point like a in Figure 1.5. In the original configuration, the side of a market square is 1, so the market areas are also 1. The new entrant,

* The technical material presented in this section, up to "Agglomeration Economies," is not central to material in the remainder of the book. Some readers may wish to skip this section.

at point a, carves out a market square with a side of 0.7 and therefore has an area of 0.5. It is possible that the area will be too small to generate positive profit, even if the original (unit) market area is profitable. If this is indeed the case, there will be no new entrants (because they would make a loss). The original participants in the market have no incentive to change their behavior, so the configuration of squares is an equilibrium. Profit has not been eliminated; market areas have not achieved their optimum (transport-minimizing) shape. Whether the world is carved up into optimum hexagons or nonoptimum squares, rectangles, or triangles appears to be a matter of historical accident, rather than the efficient direction of an invisible hand.[6]

In the configuration of square market areas, no firm has an incentive to move, or to enter or leave the industry. Thus, the outcome appears to be an equilibrium, even though it is not an optimum. The result is that freedom of entry and spatial competition do not necessarily yield an optimum location pattern.

Some economists dispute this result. The new entrant, at point a in Figure 1.5, carves out an unprofitable market area of 0.5 and therefore decides not to enter only if the entrant fails to recognize that his or her entry might drive an established producer out of business. It is plausible, however, that the potential new entrant, recognizing that this is a profitable industry, might enter at point a, set a price below cost, and thus carve out a market area bigger than 0.5. This bigger market area exists at the expense of the established merchants adjacent to the entrant. If the entrant's price were low enough, he or she might drive all neighbors out of business and then be able to charge a high enough price to recoup early losses. Only when the world is carved into efficient hexagons is this predatory behavior definitely unprofitable.

This analysis can shed light on location patterns within urban areas. Customer densities vary greatly within an urban area, so market areas cannot be expected to be perfect hexagons or other polygons. Some urban activities, however, do appear to have spatial patterns roughly in accord with the analysis. Supermarkets and shopping centers are good examples. What about drugstores, doctors, and lawyers? You can plot the locations of these activities on a street map using the Yellow Pages as a data source.

Other activities tend to concentrate near one another instead of spreading themselves out to be near customers. Most garment manufacturers and wholesalers in the New York City area are concentrated in a small area below midtown Manhattan. This is because they produce fashion goods, and customers—mostly retail buyers—like to do comparison shopping. In many cities, especially New York City, stockbrokers are also concentrated. Doing business by phone and mail reduces their need to be near customers, but it does not explain why they are close to one another.

6. These arguments are fully developed in Eaton and Lipsey (1976). This paper is very interesting and not as difficult as it appears to be.

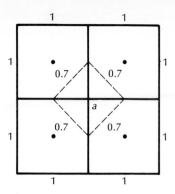

Figure 1.5 *Inefficient Equilibrium Market Areas*

Agglomeration Economies

So far, the existence of urban areas has been explained entirely in terms of scale economies in production, a concept economists understand relatively well. Urban economists also often refer to the **agglomeration economies** of urban areas. In part, they mean by the term the advantages of spatial concentration resulting from scale economies. Of course, it must be remembered that scale economies exist not only in the private sector, but also in mixed public/private or regulated sectors, such as transportation, communications, and public utilities. Also, scale economies may exist in such public sector activities as education, police protection, water supply, and waste disposal.

Urban economists also use the term *agglomeration economies* to refer to the advantages of spatial concentration that result from the scale of an entire urban area, but not from the scale of a particular firm. The most important of such agglomeration economies is statistical in nature and is an application of the law of large numbers. Sales of outputs and purchases of inputs fluctuate in many firms and industries for random, seasonal, cyclical, and secular reasons. To the extent that fluctuations are imperfectly correlated among employers, an urban area with many employers can provide more nearly full employment of its labor force than can an urban area with few employers. Likewise, a firm with many buyers whose demand fluctuations are uncorrelated will have proportionately less variability in its sales than a firm with few buyers. It therefore can hold smaller inventories and employ smoother production scheduling.

A second such agglomeration economy is complementarity in labor supply and in production. Different kinds of labor are to some extent supplied in fixed proportions. For example, industries with large demands for female workers are attracted to areas where women live because of their husbands' workplaces (though as women gain equality in the labor force, this is becoming progressively less true). Complementarity in production works the same way. If two commodities can be produced more cheaply together than separately, users of both commodities will be attracted to areas where they are produced.

A third agglomeration economy has been emphasized by Jane Jacobs (1969). Although her argument is complex, it is based on the contention that spatial concentration of large groups of people permits a great deal of personal interaction, which in turn generates new ideas, products, and processes. She views urban areas generally as the progressive and innovative sector of society. Hers is a fascinating theory that ties in with economists' interest in sources of technical progress, and it deserves careful attention. Other types of agglomeration economies have been claimed, but on analysis they usually turn out to be special cases of the mechanisms just described. The final major economic rationale for the existence of cities—comparative advantage, or inherent differences in attributes of different regions—is taken up in Chapter 2.

☐ LIMITS TO URBAN SIZE

To be viable, a city must be able to produce one or more products more cheaply than its hinterland, after accounting for the cost of transporting the export good or goods to the hinterland and agricultural products to the city. Throughout history, city size has been constrained by transport cost. The size of cities that owe their existence to market forces also is constrained by the degree of scale economies relative to market demand. Another constraint on city sizes and configurations is the cost of carrying on activities within the city itself—special costs that arise as a result of urban life. Most important among these is commuting to work, which is unnecessary in agriculture. Other such costs, not uniquely urban but much higher in cities, are the delivery of water and the disposal of waste and sewage. An important portion of the history of urban areas in the last two centuries is the history of the progressive relaxation of these constraints on viable city sizes through a series of inventions and innovations. What follows is a brief summary of this history, emphasizing the constraint relaxations that have permitted the dramatic changes in urban form.

Preindustrial United States Cities

Buildings in early nineteenth-century cities were frame (though not of the modern style; see "Construction Innovations" section ahead), brick, or stone, with residential structures generally limited to two or three stories. Overland transport, both in commuting and trading with the outside world, was either by foot or horse (either on horseback or by some form of conveyance). The cheapest form of bulk transport was by water (overland transport by horse and wagon was perhaps 100 times more costly than ship or barge travel). Water was provided to urban residents largely through private wells, and sewage was carried away on the (generally dirt) surfaces of streets or in the streams that ran through the cities. (Prior to the development of concrete and asphalt around 1900, the only way to hard-surface a street was with cobblestones. For most streets the cost of laying a cobblestone surface was prohibitive.)

Since almost all commuting was by foot, it was impractical for workers to live more than about 3 miles from their jobs (about a one-hour walk, at a moderate pace). Employment was almost necessarily centered along a navigable waterway to reap the cost advantage of water versus overland bulk transport. Thus, cities could extend no more than about 3 miles inland. Given the relatively low construction density that was feasible, it was not possible to house a very large labor force within commuting distance of a central employment district.

The technology for the underground delivery of water and disposal of sewage was available, though expensive, at this time.[7] Typically, other constraints prevented cities from reaching sufficient size to require their use. In any case, a lack of pure water and efficient sewage disposal was a major contributor to health problems and above-average mortality in nineteenth-century cities. Well-water was particularly contaminated in low-lying areas, where it was more seriously exposed to the runoff of sewage from higher elevations. It was well known at the time that mortality was high in these low-lying areas (though it was thought that the cause was the quality of the air rather than the water), with the result that almost all upper-class housing was built on high ground. The causes of such epidemic diseases as yellow fever, malaria, cholera, and tuberculosis were not widely understood until approximately 1900, but the effects were quite apparent during the early phases of urbanization. New York's death rate almost doubled from 1810 to 1859, surely due to increases in density without adequate facilities for providing water or removing waste.[8]

At the beginning of the nineteenth century, the real constraint on city size was not the limit on the infrastructure of cities. Rather, it was the cost of trade with the hinterland. Output was exported and food was imported over dirt roads by horse and wagon. Water transport, as noted, was much cheaper, but only a tiny hinterland had access to water. In fact, water transport was so cheap that most American manufactured goods came from Europe (especially Britain). Manufacturers in the United States frequently could not compete with British manufacturers, even after accounting for the cost of transatlantic shipping.

---

7. Colonial New York City had a rudimentary water delivery system, with hollowed-out logs for pipes.

8. Glaab and Brown quote the editor of the *New World:* "The offal and filth, of which there are loads thrown from the houses in defiance of an ordinance which is never enforced, is scraped up with the usual deposits of mud and manure into big heaps and left for weeks together on the sides of the street."

In fact, the major American cities in 1800 were not manufacturing centers at all, but commercial centers. They were largely collection points for agricultural products bound for export and distribution points for imported manufactures. For this reason, most cities of consequence were located on or below what is called the *fall line*—basically, the farthest upriver point that can be reached by oceangoing vessels. This provided access to the maximum amount of land while still preserving access to the ocean.

Preindustrial Cities Elsewhere

It was not impossible to build large cities with preindustrial technology, though cities of more than 100,000 population were very rare before 1800. From the time of Christ to approximately A.D. 300, Rome's population ranged from 500,000 to one million, but this size was not achieved again in the West until London reached one million in 1800. And it is clear that Rome achieved this size only at great cost to its inhabitants. Streets ranged in width from about 6 to 20 feet; they were apparently used all night by wagoneers and cattle drovers (who were excluded from the streets during the daytime). Dwelling units were about five stories high (apparently somewhat beyond safe limits, since there are many accounts of buildings collapsing). The standard method of disposing of human waste was to pitch it out the window (sometimes chamber pot and all). Juvenal wrote, "Anyone who goes out to dinner without making out a will is a fool. You can suffer as many deaths as there are open windows to pass under." Population density was approximately 185 people per acre (118,400 per square mile), though the figure would be much higher if it were possible to properly deduct for the land which was occupied by public buildings and temples. By comparison, Athens at its peak had a population of only about 40,000.

Rome was able to achieve this population because of a combination of technical advances (primarily engineering) and willingness to suffer. Foremost among the technical advances were aqueducts and roads to the hinterland, and the system of artificial harbors at Ostia.

In Europe, both cities and civilization went into general decline after the fall of Rome, with the recovery of both beginning in approximately the tenth century. By the late Middle Ages, the biggest cities in Europe were Palermo (300,000) and Cordoba (500,000), which were still at this time under Moslem domination. Of cities which were later to attain prominence, Paris and Milan each had populations of about 200,000.

Infectious diseases played a role in keeping urban populations in check. In the light of this observation, it is interesting to examine the case of Rome, and of the subsequent decline and slow recovery of urban Europe. The average age at death among adults (that is, for those who survived childhood) was apparently just under thirty years in Rome (McNeill, p. 286), and this mortality record existed before the arrival of the major killer epidemic diseases in Europe. Smallpox and measles apparently arrived in the second or third century A.D. (about the time the decline of the empire began), and bubonic plague first appeared in Europe in 1346. According to McNeill, the emergence of modern urban Europe had to await society's accommodation—part immunological and part behavioral—to these epidemic diseases.

Industrialization

On the eve of the Industrial Revolution the technology of city-building was not much advanced over what it had been in Roman times. Industrialization fundamentally altered both the demands upon cities and the means of building cities. As will be seen, with industrialization the benefits of large cities grew enormously. At the same time the technical progress which underlay the Industrial Revolution offered new solutions to the fundamental problem of how to crowd so much activity into so little space.

Industrialization in the United States

Manufacturing became big business in northern cities during the first half of the nineteenth century, after the initial establishment of cities as commercial centers and also after the first major innovation in this story—a swift and dramatic improvement in overland bulk transportation.

Canals and railroads, as well as steamboats on the Mississippi and Ohio rivers (and somewhat later on the less-navigable Missouri), reduced the cost of overland bulk transport by well over 90 percent, on average, between 1800 and 1850 (Tolley and Krumm, 1983). These innovations transformed the United States from a coastal society to a nation with a genuine, integrated heartland. Eastern cities now could trade profitably with areas hundreds of times larger than those previously accessible. With the geographic expansion of viable markets, it became possible for East Coast cities to profitably reap the advantages of scale economies in industrial manufacturing. The keys to the Industrial Revolution were specialization and scale, and these could only be exploited by a city with a large market. Once a region began to industrialize it would also gain population. With this larger population the local economy can support larger-scale manufacturing, replacing imports with domestic production. This process is called *import substitution,* and it is one of the fundamental themes which will be covered again in the discussion of regional shifts within the United States (Chapter 2). Basically, import substitution occurs when the domestic market reaches sufficient size to support scale-economies manufacturing.

With the opening of the Erie Canal in 1825, New York City could trade by water with upper New York State, as well as with the northern part of Ohio bordering on Lake Erie. Philadelphia, via the Delaware

River Canal, had access to the upper Delaware valley, and Baltimore, with the B&O Railroad, was linked with the Ohio valley.[9]

The significance of these changes in overland transport is apparent from Table 4.1 in Chapter 4. In 1790 New York City had a population of just under 50,000 and Philadelphia, the second largest American city, just under 30,000. No other city had as many as 20,000 people. By 1850 New York City housed over half a million people, and six cities had populations over 100,000. The methods of building cities and of transporting goods and people within cities were not very different from what they had been in 1790. New York City, by this time, had water and sewer lines. Baltimore, however, was not to have generally available water until the 1880s, nor a sewer system until 1906 (Olson, 1980).

The growth of cities, fostered by improved access to the hinterland, placed great strain on the urban infrastructure and environment and led to improvements in the efficiency of conducting urban functions. Walking was no longer an adequate means of commuting. In a city of 200,000 people, with employment still concentrated along a small section of waterfront, a commute would have required something like a two-hour walk each way.

The 1830s saw the introduction of the omnibus, a horse-drawn vehicle carrying twelve passengers. It was not much of an improvement over walking, however. The fare was somewhere between an eighth and a half of the average daily wage, and it traveled only about 50 percent faster than a pedestrian. In short, the omnibus served only the rich. The same was true of commuter railroads (also introduced in the 1830s), which also were expensive and were banned in several major cities because of smoke and noise. The first breakthrough for the masses was the two-horse streetcar, which ran on rails in the streets and was introduced in the 1850s and 1860s. A streetcar could haul three times more passengers, at speeds one-third greater, than the omnibus. (The streetcar was successful because friction is almost 75 percent less on rails than on a well-paved street, but rails were too expensive until the development of cheap smelting of iron and steel around the middle of the century.) This substantially increased the radius of feasible development. For a given time spent commuting by streetcar (say, an hour), the radius of the city could be twice as great as under the walking mode, and therefore the area could be almost four times as great.[10] Except in New York City, Boston, Philadelphia, and Chicago (all of which built subways around 1900 or shortly thereafter), the streetcar (and walking) remained the dominant modes of commuting until the arrival of the automobile and the bus. The source of power changed from horse

9. Washington, D.C., also was linked with the Ohio valley via the C&O Canal, but the canal was costly to maintain and subject to flooding and damage. It never competed successfully with the B&O Railroad.

10. The reason for the "almost" modifier is that it was not practical to serve every point with trolley lines.

to electricity (see "Subways and Electric Trolleys" section ahead), but the mode remained the same.[11] Interestingly, the horse-drawn street-car was adopted much more quickly in the United States than in Europe, in part because American streets were more primitive, and in part because American land was more plentiful (and therefore cheaper). This meant that expansion of the urban radius was a more attractive option in the United States.

In addition to facilitating great expansion of cities, streetcars had a profound effect upon the shapes of cities. Because of the fixed-rail, mass transit nature of streetcars, they were relatively good at only one thing—collecting people along "spokes" and dropping them off at the "hub." The system was well suited, in other words, to delivering a large labor force to a small area—a *central business district* (CBD). It was not suited to the crosstown or reverse direction commuting possible with an automobile-based system. Any tendency firms already had to locate at the central node—access to the port, to interurban rail lines, or to other firms—was enhanced by the obvious tendency to locate at the one place in the city to which the transport system could deliver the labor force.

Steel

After the introduction of the streetcar, many urban-form innovations relied heavily upon steel, which is considerably stronger and lighter than iron. The first economical steel-making process was developed by Bessemer in England in 1856, and was quickly adopted by the Carnegie Company of Pittsburgh. Prior to the adoption of the Bessemer process, steel was so expensive that some firms attempted to produce and market iron railroad rails with a steel cap, thus providing a steel surface for contact with the wheels.

The advantages of steel can perhaps be seen most clearly in bridge-building. The maximum length of an iron span is approximately 500 feet; a steel span, 1500. Since cities tend to be built on the water, the ability to span bodies of water with long bridges considerably increased the potential for building large cities. In addition, without bridges across the great rivers of the interior, the railroad network of the second half of the nineteenth century would have been much less efficient at tying the nation together.

Construction Innovations

The second half of the nineteenth century also saw crucial innovations in the construction of both commercial and residential buildings. The breakthrough for commercial buildings was the development of

---

11. The discussion and data from this paragraph draw heavily on LeRoy and Sonstelie (1983).

the high-rise building, and the key innovations underlying the high rise were structural steel (developed in the 1880s) and elevators (first installed in New York in 1857). The replacement of brick with a steel skeleton[12] made it possible to build higher buildings more quickly and cheaply, and to reduce the lower-floor space devoted to thick supporting walls. The high rise essentially substituted vertical for horizontal transportation and expanded the population limits of cities for a given transportation network. Even though high-rise construction is more costly, it became worthwhile in big cities because of the savings in commuting that could be realized. The emergence of viable high-rise construction was stimulated by the transport system, which specialized in delivering people to a CBD. This transit system raised the value of CBD sites, and encouraged the substitution of capital for land (as will be seen in more detail in Chapter 6). The development of the high rise contributed to another crucial change in urban form—a change whose implications are still being worked out today. The high rise has made it possible for office activity to outbid manufacturing for valuable downtown land. (This topic will be covered in Chapter 15.)

The big advance in residential construction took the form of balloon (today known as frame) construction. This is the now-familiar method whereby $2'' \times 4''$ (or larger) rafters, studs, and joists are nailed together to form the shell of a house. Prior to this, wood construction required a mortise-and-tenon system of carefully fitting beams into one another. This method was slow and intensive, in terms of both wood and skilled carpenters. The balloon technique made it possible to put up a large number of houses quickly.[13] It was on the strength of balloon construction that Chicago grew from virtually nothing to a city of one million between 1830 and 1880. (This is surely the most rapid episode of city-building anywhere in the world prior to the twentieth century.)

Subways and Electric Trolleys

Probably the most important constraint on city size in the latter quarter of the nineteenth century, even with the existence of the streetcar, was urban transit. In the absence of rapid mechanical transit, it was difficult for cities to spread out, either to relieve crowding or to expand population. The importance of the transport constraint can be inferred by reading contemporary accounts of these cities. A reporter for the *New York Tribune* counted the number of horse-drawn conveyances going up and down Broadway over a 13-hour period in 1867.

---

12. This method was first employed in Chicago, in 1884, in the aftermath of the 1881 fire. One of the motivations for using steel instead of brick was apparently a desire to break the bricklayers' union, which was on strike at the time.

13. The crucial component of the balloon method, absent before about 1830, was the mass-produced steel nail.

One such vehicle went by, in each direction, every 1.3 seconds.[14] In London in 1820, merchants complained that their produce rotted in the sun while they were trying to transport it across town.

Mechanical transit, to be viable, had to await the development of electric traction. Coal-fired locomotives were banned from most city streets and were even more impractical in subways. The London underground, opened in 1863, was for a time powered by coal-fired locomotives, and the air was so bad that many deaths from asphyxiation were reported.[15] Underground, the problem of effluents is compounded by the fact that the coal fire depletes the supply of oxygen.

Electric traction, a product of the last decade of the nineteenth century, permitted the running of clean subways and trolley cars. The electric trolley represented the first truly radical departure from the methods of city-building which had existed for centuries. (The only competitor for this honor would be the high-rise building.)

America's first electric trolley line opened in Cleveland in 1884. This was followed by a period of rapid innovation and experimentation, as developers searched for the most efficient technology. The real problem was how to deliver the electricity to the trolley. Early experiments included batteries and at-grade cables. Batteries were too heavy and at-grade cables delivered nasty shocks to people and lethal shocks to horses (the difference in severity apparently due to horseshoes). The overhead power line, which became ubiquitous in American cities in the first half of the twentieth century, was developed by Frank Sprague, a former Edison employee. His first installation of this system was in 1887 in Richmond. The speed with which electrification was adopted is almost beyond belief. By 1890 20 percent (914 miles) of American trolley lines were electrified. Within another decade total mileage had increased to 30,000, with 98 percent electrified. The rapid adoption is due to the fact that service was approximately twice as fast, and half as costly, as horse-drawn trolley service. In addition, electric trolleys could negotiate grades between two and three times as steep as horses could manage.

The electric trolley was adopted with much less speed or enthusiasm in Europe than in the United States, largely because of public concerns over the aesthetics of overhead wires. Europe lagged behind the United

14. This was a dramatic increase over traffic volume fifteen years earlier, when a vehicle passed the same intersection, in each direction, every 13 seconds. (These numbers are cited in Bobrick, 1981).

15. Incredibly, the first New York City subway was constructed and operated clandestinely for a time. The infamous Boss Tweed would not permit a subway franchise to be issued on the pretext that it was infeasible, but in fact because a substantial portion of his income was extorted from ferry and omnibus franchises. In 1870, therefore, Alfred Ely Beach built his subway at night. Only 312 feet long, it used pneumatic power provided by a reversible fan at one end of the tunnel (thus, the tunnel was pollution free). He had hoped that popular demand would force the legislature to grant him a franchise for a line all the way to Central Park. A combination of political intrigue and the Panic of 1873 ultimately did in the project, however.

States by some fifteen years, but the trolley wave ultimately swept Europe's cities as well.

If the trolley was the innovation which permitted small cities to become big, the subway was the revolution which permitted big cities to become giants. New York City opened its first subway line in 1904.[16] This mechanism of fixed-rail transit greatly expanded the reach of commuting networks, but it was still best suited to delivering a large number of workers to a fixed point—a CBD.[17]

The primary economic distinction between the subway and the trolley is in the degree of scale economies. Subways require massive capital investments, with the result that they are viable only with very high traffic volumes (see Chapter 12 for more detailed discussion).

With the mechanization of commuter traffic, the remaining major bottleneck in urban travel was the delivery of materials—goods (both finished and in process) and solid waste. As recently as 1910 almost all such materials were moved by horse and wagon. In addition to the cost consideration, this method is very space intensive. The transport revolution wrought by electric traction was almost exclusively to the benefit of personal transport. The next major transport innovation— the internal combustion engine—revolutionized freight transit.

Electric Power

Before discussing the internal combustion engine, one other urban consequence of the development of electric power transmission should be noted—the first major wave of manufacturing decentralization.

As already seen, the urban innovations of the nineteenth century greatly expanded the ability of the city to (1) deliver a large labor force to a CBD, and (2) export goods to a far-flung hinterland. Manufacturing was still tied to a CBD location, in part because of the presence of the port or railhead, in part because of the presence of the labor force, but in large measure because of its reliance on steam power—and therefore its reliance on coal. Access to the railhead was valuable in part because it meant access to coal. With the advent of electric power transmission toward the end of the nineteenth century, however, power could be delivered anywhere. In particular, power could be delivered to sites on the outskirts of the city where land was cheap and regulation of smoke and noise was nonexistent. Largely on the strength of electric power, the suburban rings outside central cities were the manufacturing growth centers beginning as early as 1900.[18]

16. The Boston subway opened earlier, on a smaller scale, in 1897. Also New York City had elevated trains in the last two decades of the nineteenth century.

17. A more complete discussion of the history of the New York subway and Beach's clandestine pneumatic tube can be found in Bobrick (1981).

18. From 1899 to 1904, suburban manufacturing employment increased by 32.8 percent, as opposed to 14.9 percent for central cities. For the next five-year period the numbers were respectively 48.8 percent and 22.5 percent (see Glaab and Brown, p. 277).

Internal-Combustion Engines

Compared with the steam engine, the internal-combustion engine is very small. It can be used to power much smaller vehicles such as cars and trucks. With this innovation, mechanized transport no longer had to be mass transport, which in particular meant that it was no longer necessary that everyone be going to or coming from the same place. Automobile transport is both faster (generally) and more flexible than the fixed-rail mass transit systems powered by steam or electricity.[19]

The automobile substantially expanded the feasible range of the city, both by increasing the range of commuting and by permitting residential location in places unserved by rail transit. Initially, of course, the automobile was available only to the rich, so the initial wave of automobile-spawned suburbanization was largely upper-class.

To some extent, the automobile eased constraints upon firm location as well. With automobiles, cities have a transit system that can deliver labor to virtually any point. Thus, firms no longer are tied to central locations because that is where the labor force gets dropped off every morning. For some types of firms, the truck may have been equally important. With the advent of the truck, materials transport was no longer tied to railheads and ports. Material inputs and outputs now can be shipped from almost anywhere. Railheads and ports still may have a cost advantage for some firms, but it is generally not the overwhelming advantage it was fifty years ago. Many firms may find that the advantages are outweighed by the high land rents of prime locations.

Thus the invention of the automobile and the truck did two things. First, it increased the feasible size of cities by reducing transport cost and expanding the range of the transport network, both for commuters and materials. Second, by introducing flexibility in the pattern of origins and destinations, it reduced the center orientation of cities and gave an impetus to the decentralization that had begun well before these inventions.

☐ Summary

An urban area is a place in which economic activity is highly concentrated. Both population and employment density are much higher than in surrounding areas. A major benefit of this concentration is the realization of scale economies, and a major cost is the necessity of transporting materials both to and from the urban area. With the technical progress of the past two centuries, the benefits of urbanization have increased, and the costs have been reduced.

---

19. See Chapter 12 for a discussion of the relative speeds and costs of the various modes of transport.

Questions and Problems

1. Suppose there are economies of large-scale production so that large urban areas export to small urban areas, but not vice versa. How can small urban areas pay for their imports?

2. In the central place theory analysis embodied in Figures 1.1 and 1.3, how would you expect each of the following to influence the distance between production sites?
   a. A rise in income (an outward shift in the demand curve for the output)
   b. A decline in the cost of transporting the good

3. Commuting times and distances are greater in large urban areas than in small urban areas. Is this evidence of diminishing returns in large urban areas?

4. Suppose urban areas produce just one commodity, X. Each urban area produces $x = AN^a$ units, where N is the labor force in an urban area and A and $a > 1$ are constants. Thus, there are increasing returns in producing a large amount of Commodity X in each urban area. However, each urban area must supply Commodity X to the rural residents who live closer to it than to another urban area. Rural residents have a fixed density (D), and each consumes a fixed amount (x) of Commodity X. If urban areas are too small, the advantages of large-scale production are missed; if they are too large, scale economies will be more than offset by the costs of transporting Commodity X from urban areas to rural consumers. Find the optimum size of each urban area. (Assume each unit-mile of transportation of Commodity X requires γ workers. The optimum-sized urban area minimizes the sum of workers needed to produce and ship units of Commodity X.)

References and Further Reading

Beckmann, Martin. *Location Theory* (New York: Random House, 1968). A short and elementary, but very abstract, statement of modern location theory.

Blinder, Alan. "The Economics of Brushing Your Teeth." *Journal of Political Economy* (1974): 887–91. A clever spoof on the tendency of economists to describe everything in terms of economic models. Blinder forgot to discuss the location patterns of toothbrushing establishments.

Bobrick, Benson. *Labyrinths of Iron: A History of the World's Subways* (New York: Newsweek Books, 1981). A very good popular book on the history of subways, subway construction and engineering, and the character of cities during the period when subways were built.

Eaton, B. Curtis, and Richard G. Lipsey. "The Non-Uniqueness of Equilibrium in the Löschian Location Model." *American Economic Review* 66 (1976): 77–93. A discussion of the possibility that some configuration other than efficient hexagons might be a location equilibrium.

Friedmann, John, and William Alonso, eds. *Regional Development and Planning: A Reader* (Cambridge, Mass.: MIT Press, 1964). Contains a very readable chapter by Lösch (Chap. 5, 107–15) on his spatial theory, entitled "The Nature of Economic Regions."

Glaab, Charles N., and A. Theodore Brown, *A History of Urban America* (New York: Macmillan, 1967). This is an excellent discussion of the history of the development of Urban America. It is an excellent companion to Chapters 1 and 2.

Hotelling, Harold. "Stability in Competition." *Economic Journal* 39 (1929): 41–57.

Jacobs, Jane. *The Economy of Cities* (New York: Random House, 1969). A wise and perceptive essay by a noneconomist on economic aspects of urban life.

LeRoy, Stephen, and Jon Sonstelie. "Paradise Lost and Regained: Transportation Innovation, Income, and Residential Location." *Journal of Urban Economics* 13 (1983): 67–89. A very good theoretical discussion of what happens if different income groups use different transport modes, backed by a nice historical discussion of technical changes in urban transport. The theoretical section should not be attempted before reading Chapter 7 of this book.

Lösch, August. *The Economics of Location* (New Haven: Yale, 1954). Probably the most important contribution ever made to location theory. The book can be very difficult in some places.

McNeill, William H. *Plagues and Peoples* (Garden City, New York: Doubleday, 1976). A fascinating account of the role of infectious disease in history.

McKay, John P. *Tramways and Trolleys* (Princeton, Princeton University Press, 1976).

Olson, Sherry. *Baltimore: The Building of an American City* (Baltimore: Johns Hopkins, 1980). A history of the development of Baltimore from colonial to modern times.

Perloff, Harvey, E. S. Dunn, E. E. Lampard, and R. Muth. *Regions, Resources and Economic Growth* (Baltimore: Johns Hopkins, 1960). An influential study of the causes and consequences of differences in economic growth rates among regions of the United States.

Tolley, George, and Ronald J. Krumm. "On the Regional Labor-Supply Relationship." *The Urban Economy and Housing*, ed. Ronald Grieson (Lexington, Mass: D.C. Heath, 1983): 203–37. A good, readable survey paper.

U.S. Census Bureau. *Census of Population* (Washington, D.C.: Government Printing Office). Published for every year ending in zero. It presents the most complete urban data available anywhere and provides careful definitions of concepts.

2

Comparative Advantage and Regions

☐ Chapter 1 describes a system of cities that emerge as a result of scale and agglomeration economies. In the model there are no interregional differences in resource endowments, and there is no trade among cities of equal size. Once the fiction of the featureless plain is dropped, however, and the notion of interregional differences in endowments (comparative advantage) introduced in its place, the world becomes more interesting and more realistic.

The first part of this chapter lays out the principles governing interregional firm location decisions. The second part presents a brief history of regional shifts in the United States.

☐ THEORETICAL PRINCIPLES OF INTERREGIONAL FIRM LOCATION DECISIONS

The *principle of comparative advantage* states that if two different regions (or workers, or nations, or machines) differ from each other in their *relative* abilities to produce two goods, the value of output is maximized if the region that is relatively good at (that is, has a comparative advantage in) producing one good specializes in producing that good. Adherence to this rule is equivalent to being on, rather than inside, the nation's production possibilities curve. As Chapter 8 will explain, competition and profit maximization induce factors to pursue their comparative advantages.

The principle of comparative advantage is illustrated in Figure 2.1. Panels *a* and *b* are respectively the production possibilities curves for regions 1 and 2 (note that region 1 is better at producing *both* goods than is region 2). The aggregate production possibilities curve is in panel *c*. As can be seen, efficient production requires that region 1 specialize in x_1 and region 2 specialize in x_2, to the extent the mix of demands permits this. Ignoring transport cost, it is in the interest of region 1 to

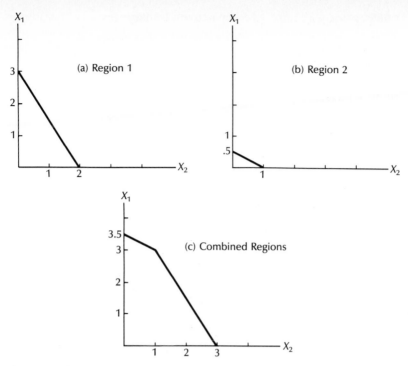

Figure 2.1 *Illustration of Comparative Advantage*

import its x_2 from region 2, even though region 1 is actually better at producing x_2 than is region 2.

As can be seen from Figure 2.1, specialization improves aggregate production possibilities only when the shapes of the region-specific production possibilities curves differ. This in turn happens only when regions have different mixes of inputs. Thus trade among regions would be expected to occur when the regions have different mixes of inputs, though even when the input mixes differ, trade will only occur if the gains from trade are sufficient to overcome transport cost.

Comparative advantage and the specialization that follows from it give an economic rationale for trade between regions or between cities of different or equal size. As in the case of scale economies, trade occurs only if comparative advantage is strong enough to justify the transport cost.

Economists frequently argue that comparative advantage is a rationale for the existence of cities. This is not true: it is a rationale only for trade among regions. If there were no scale economies in transportation, interregional trade could take place between the individual agents in the various regions without the intervention of cities.

There are scale economies in transport, however—in vehicles, rights-of-way, and facilities for loading and unloading. These scale economies, along with regional comparative advantage, give rise to transport-node, or port, cities. The location of port cities is governed largely by the technology of freight transport. Two principles basically characterize this technology: (1) water transport is much cheaper, but slower, than any other mode, and (2) loading and unloading are substantial portions of total transport cost; hence, shipping cost per ton-mile declines with distance.

Determinants of Firm Location When Regions Differ

If regions differ from one another, in either natural or man-made aspects of their economic environments, the differences affect locations of economic activities. This section lays out some principles governing these location decisions.

Cost considerations. A profit-maximizing firm is also a cost-minimizing firm, but in the spatial context it must be remembered that cost includes both production and transport cost. Furthermore, transport cost includes the cost of transporting both inputs, if they are not locally available, and outputs. Generally, there are geographic variations in both transport and production costs, so a profit-maximizing firm must look at both these sources of interregional cost variation. What follows is a rough taxonomy of firms based upon the types of cost considerations that most heavily influence their optimum locations.

The first step is to dichotomize firms into either production cost or transport cost orientation. A production cost-oriented firm bases its location decision upon regional differences in production cost, largely ignoring transport cost. The reverse is true for a transport cost-oriented firm. A firm is likely to be production cost oriented if both of the following are true:

1. Transport cost is a small fraction of total cost—generally because inputs and outputs are light in weight relative to their value or because inputs are available everywhere (ubiquitous) and outputs are light in weight.
2. The production process is intensive in some input for which there is substantial geographic variation in cost—such as labor or, more recently, energy.

The textile industry is production cost oriented. Textiles are light in weight per dollar of value, so total cost is not very sensitive to the transport component. The industry is intensive in unskilled labor, so a low-wage region offers a large cost saving. Thus, the textile industry moved from New England to the South when the development of steam power (used in the operation of power looms) freed it from water power. (For the same economic reasons, the textile industry has more recently moved to the developing countries of the Pacific rim.)

At the opposite end of the spectrum is transport orientation. For such firms, the following are true:

1. Transport is a large fraction of cost—generally because either an input or an output is heavy and bulky relative to its value.
2. Interregional differences in input prices are relatively less important.

Examples are steel and beer. In the case of steel, the raw material inputs—iron ore, coal, and lime—are heavy relative to the value of the final product, and it is worthwhile to locate to economize on transportation of these inputs. This means it is most economical to smelt steel at sites to which it is relatively cheap to transport the inputs. In the case of beer, the heaviest input is water—also costly to transport relative to its value. In this case, it is most economical to brew beer near the market to avoid trucking water all over the country.

In one of the previous examples, transport cost considerations induced the firm to locate at an input source; in the other, the firm located at the market where the output was to be sold. These represent two subcategories of transport orientation, known respectively as *materials orientation* and *market orientation.* A firm is materials oriented if it is cheaper to ship the output than the input; hence, the output is produced at the input site. The catchword for "cheaper to ship the output than the input" is *weight losing,* although, as will be seen, not all materials-oriented firms are technically weight losing. The opposite case is called *weight gaining.* If the production process begins with an input available only at certain sites (a localized input, such as coal or iron ore) and yields a relatively lightweight output (steel is light in weight compared with the amount of coal and ore required to produce it), transport cost is minimized by locating the plant at the site where the localized input is available.[1] Other products are weight gaining, such as beer. In the most straightforward cases, a ubiquitous input (water, in the case of beer) is added to raw materials or an intermediate product to yield the final product. Transport cost is minimized by shipping the localized inputs to the market and then adding the ubiquitous input.

As noted, *weight losing* is a catchword for "cheaper to ship the output than the input." It does not necessarily mean "weight losing" in the literal sense, as the history of livestock slaughtering demonstrates. Prior to about 1960, the majority of hogs and cattle raised in Indiana, Illinois, and Iowa were shipped to the Chicago stockyards for slaughter. Chicago, in Carl Sandburg's famous phrase, was "hog-butcher to the world." Slaughtering, however, is not weight gaining—only about

---

1. In the case of more than one localized input, such as in the case of steel, the optimum site minimizes the total cost of shipping inputs. This generally will be at the site of the heaviest localized input.

60 percent of live weight is dressed out as meat. Why, then, did farmers ship live animals to Chicago, rather than the meat only? Until the invention of the refrigerated truck, the meat would have spoiled in transit. With refrigerated trucking, however, the shipment of meat to market became cheaper than shipping livestock. Soon the Midwest was dotted with small slaughterhouses, and Chicago is no longer hog-butcher to the world. Indeed, it is no longer hog-butcher to Chicago; its last stockyard closed in 1971. Thus, with the change in technology, slaughtering shifted from market orientation to materials orientation.

As a rough characterization, the historical trend in the United States has been away from materials orientation in particular (contrary to the pattern noted above for beef slaughter) and transport orientation in general. The reason for the shift away from materials orientation is simply that with the more complicated production processes that have come with technical progress, fewer processes are weight losing. Transport orientation in general has declined because of rapid declines, over the history of the United States, in the cost of transport.

An example: The steel industry.   The history of the steel industry illustrates well the decline in the importance of materials and transport orientation. The transport orientation of the steel industry has been greatly reduced over the past century, first, because of improvements in bulk transport, and second, because of dramatic technical improvements in steel production. Between 1879 and 1919 the coal requirement per ton of steel fell 67 percent, from 3.93 to 1.31 tons. Over the same period, ore requirements fell 45 percent, from 2.11 to 1.16 tons (Harper, 1976). By 1980 coal and ore requirements had fallen to 0.57 and 0.104 tons, respectively.[2] The reduction in coal use came from more efficient use of heat in mills; the reduction in ore use resulted partly from the discovery of richer ores in Minnesota and partly from the increased use of scrap iron as an ore substitute.

Another way to see the decline in the importance of transport cost is to note that Japan, with neither coal nor ore deposits, is a major steel exporter. Indeed, when the World Trade Center was built on the Baltimore waterfront in 1977, the structural steel was imported from Japan, despite the fact that Bethlehem Steel's Sparrows Point mill is less than 5 miles away by barge.

Technical progress in steel manufacture is only part of the story. In 1879 railroad rails constituted 44.8 percent of steel mill output (in tons). By 1919 the rails' share had fallen to 9.5 percent, and by 1980, to 2.1 percent. Structural steel took up much of the slack, with its share rising from 8.3 percent in 1879 to 22 percent in 1919 (and down to 15 percent in 1980). Rails are finished products, but the overwhelming

---

2.   The 1980 data come from the *1981 Annual Statistical Report* of the American Iron and Steel Institute. The ability to produce a ton of steel from a tenth of a ton of ore results from the use of scrap- and iron-bearing by-products of mining and smelting.

bulk of steel output in 1980 was intermediate products (14.5 percent of output went to the auto industry and 14.2 percent to construction). In 1879, in other words, most of the value added to iron ore took place at the steel mill. Today, however, because more complicated things are done with steel, the bulk of value added takes place after the steel leaves the mill. The location of most production, even if it uses steel as a major input, is independent of the fact that steel smelting is a weight-losing industry.

The production of steel is more footloose (a term which will be explained in the following section), both because technical progress has reduced its input requirements and because of improvements in bulk transport. Furthermore, the manufacture of steel *products* is more footloose than in the past because the steel itself has become a smaller part of the value of final products.

Footloose Industries and Amenity Orientation

If transport orientation has declined, is it necessarily true that production cost orientation has increased? The secular decline in transport cost has left firms more able to seek locations where production cost is low. One side effect of firm movement to areas of low production cost, however, is the raising of production costs in the receiving area and the reduction in them in the sending area. If firms move from a high- to a low-wage area to take advantage of cheap labor, wages are driven up in the low-wage area and depressed in the high-wage area.

This gradual reduction in interregional input price differentials (which will be documented for labor in the next section) implies that production cost orientation is declining. When interregional production cost differences are small, they should not have a big effect upon firm location.

What does it mean to say that both transport and production cost orientation have declined historically? Basically, it means that, for a large range of firms, interregional cost differences are very small, and location decisions are of less importance than they were several decades ago. Increasingly, according to this view, firms are *footloose*—largely free from traditional location constraints. This state of being footloose has led to *amenity orientation*, a firm location criterion based upon pleasant locational attributes—say, climate or culture—rather than upon transport or production cost.

In fact, however, amenity orientation is production cost orientation in another guise. As will be discussed more fully in Chapters 7 and 14, most interurban wage differences appear to be directly related to interurban amenity differences. Basically, labor can be attracted to a high-amenity environment more readily (and hence, for a lower wage) than to a low-amenity environment. Thus, even in a world of perfect mobility, wage differences persist as compensation for amenity differences. Firms now may be attracted to high-amenity sites because labor there is cheaper, because workers are attracted to high-amenity sites. This trend may continue until high-amenity regions begin to suffer amenity declines with rising population. Such declines might be the result of pollution and congestion or, in the case of the Southwest, water shortages.

☐ REGIONS AND REGIONAL SHIFTS IN THE UNITED STATES, 1790 to 1980[3]

At the time of the founding of the United States, most manufactured goods consumed in this country came from Europe. A few small iron foundries, which had been established during the Revolution, continued to operate, but these were the major exception. Cities formed along the North-Atlantic seaboard to serve as collection points for grain exports and manufactured imports. The market initially was not sufficiently dense to support much local manufacture.

Manufactured goods tended to be imported from Europe rather than produced domestically because of scale economies (coupled with the fact that ocean transport was cheap). The American population was not large enough to support home production.

With the growth of cities and the decline in overland transport cost in the first half of the nineteenth century (see Chapter 1), the economic feasibility of domestic manufacturing emerged. Manufacturing developed initially in the North—but not the South—because of higher concentrations of people, which in turn was in part because of the difference between the technologies for exporting grain and tobacco. Grain, produced in the North, was transported overland from farms to port cities, where it was loaded onto ships. (This costly overland transport was justified because of the high value of grain relative to its weight.) By contrast, tobacco produced in the South was loaded directly onto ships at the plantation wharf. In part this was due to the high bulk-to-value ratio of tobacco and in part to the fact that southern rivers are generally navigable farther inland (the fall line is farther inland) than northern rivers.

Geography played another important role in determining the differences between northern and southern development. Most of the Carolina coast is bounded by barrier islands, which prevent oceangoing ships from reaching the coast. Carolina produce was sent up the coastal waterway in special shallow-draft barges to Norfolk, Virginia, where it was loaded onto oceangoing vessels.[4] On the eve of the Revolution Nor-

---

3. This discussion relies heavily upon Mieszkowski (1979), to which the reader can turn for a fuller treatment of these topics.

4. The inland Carolina waterway was also the home of the pirate Blackbeard, so for a considerable period transit of produce to Norfolk was quite hazardous.

folk was one of the major colonial cities, but it was virtually destroyed during the war. For reasons to be given, it did not regain its former prominence during the nineteenth century. The early emergence of northern cities was also influenced by the wider availability of water power, which enabled it to take advantage of the manufacturing opportunity presented by its colonial growth.

Northern colonial cities flourished as a result of exploitation of some exportable resources. Boston exported fish from off Cape Cod; New York exported furs from the Hudson Valley; Philadelphia and Baltimore exported wheat from nearby land. Until approximately 1750 all were primarily import-export depots—commercial rather than manufacturing centers. Contact among colonial cities, particularly until about 1850, was probably less significant than contact with England.

By the beginning of the nineteenth century, many northern cities had become large enough to support home production of manufactured goods, thus replacing some imports. This process, known as *import substitution*, is one of the central themes of this chapter. The self-feeding process works as follows: population rises sufficiently to permit home production of some goods, causing population to rise more, causing more import substitution, and so on. This process was well under way in the cities of the eastern seaboard by 1810, and by 1850 the Northeast had not only replaced many European exports with its own production, it had also become a major exporter of manufactured goods to the South and the emerging Midwest. As will be seen, this process of import substitution was repeated in the Midwest, the Far West, and more recently in the South.

Finally it should be noted that the emergence of northern cities as manufacturing centers was stimulated in part by the cutoff of British goods during the Revolution and again during the War of 1812. Indeed, the War of 1812 seems in some ways to have been connected with New York City's emergence as America's premier city (before the war, it was a tossup between New York City and Philadelphia). As the war ended, British manufacturers saw the threat from American manufacturing, and set out to flood the American market, through New York, to bankrupt American manufacturers. Many were bankrupted, but with the flood of goods New York realized an era of prosperity in its old role as a commercial center. Part of the fruit of this prosperity was invested in the Erie Canal. At almost the same time (1817) a group of merchants offered the first *scheduled* transatlantic shipping service (the so-called "packet service"). These two innovations placed New York in the lead among eastern cities as a commercial center, from which base manufacturing soon reemerged.

Import substitution can be seen clearly in the growth of Pittsburgh. Founded as Fort Duquense by the French, it was renamed Fort Pitt after the French and Indian War. It became a commercial center after the Revolution by supplying the needs of migrants into the Northwest Territory. Pittsburgh purchased all manner of manufactured goods from

Baltimore and Philadelphia, and resold them to homesteaders. The road from Philadelphia to Pittsburgh saw a steady stream of Conestoga wagons hauling this material.[5]

As the trade down the Upper Ohio increased it became economically feasible to replace the imported manufactured goods with home production. As early as 1820, Pittsburgh began to sprout foundries, glass factories, and machine shops.[6]

Chapter 1 already noted a series of innovations which reduced intracity transport costs by an order of magnitude. The initial innovations came in approximately 1850, but the most dramatic progress was made between about 1890 and 1940, with the adoption first of electric and later internal-combustion power. These innovations were preceded by approximately fifty years by a series of innovations which marked an absolute revolution in interregional transport. The development of cities, and the changing location pattern of cities, is intimately connected to these innovations.

The first of these innovations—the Erie Canal and rail links between eastern cities and the Ohio valley—have already been noted. The Erie Canal not only vastly expanded New York's hinterland, it also pushed the effective fall line to Detroit, and ultimately to Chicago. By bypassing Niagara Falls, all the Great Lakes except Superior became essentially coastal.[7] Like New York before it, Detroit began as a commercial and transshipment center. And once again the process of import substitution allowed Detroit to gradually replace New York manufactures with home production, and ultimately to become a manufacturing exporter itself.

The big boom town was Chicago. The Erie Canal gave it access to the Atlantic, and by 1847 Chicago had a canal connecting Lake Michigan with the Illinois (and therefore the Mississippi) River. Chicago quickly emerged as the preeminent city of the heartland.[8]

What the Erie Canal did for Detroit and Chicago the steamboat did for New Orleans and St. Louis. New Orleans was not established as a commercial or manufacturing city, but rather as part of a grand French design to dominate North America. The plan was to have an empire which ran up the St. Lawrence River, through the Great Lakes basin, and down the Mississippi, thus isolating the English colonies on the east-

---

5. The Conestoga wagon was built with a watertight box so that it could stay afloat while fording a deep stream. When railroads replaced the wagon trains, these Conestogas became surplus, available for recycling into their better-known use, for trips across the Great Plains.

6. For an excellent discussion of the early development of Pittsburgh, see Glaab and Brown.

7. With the opening of the Soo locks in 1855, Lake Superior also gained access to the coast. This gave the American steel industry access to the rich iron mines of Minnesota.

8. Glaab and Brown give a vivid description of land-value escalation in Chicago, including a 100-fold increase between 1834 and 1837. They state, "As the real estate boom neared its climax, early in 1837, daily advances in land values of twenty to twenty-five percent were not unusual."

ern seaboard. New Orleans was established for this military purpose in 1721.

Even before the advent of the steamboat in about 1820, New Orleans was a major commercial center. Goods were floated down the river on rafts, then loaded onto oceangoing vessels. But trade, of course, is two-way, and upriver travel was costly.

The steamboat cut the cost of river travel by perhaps 90 percent, and its advent assured the emergence of New Orleans. Between 1810 (seven years before the first steamboat) and 1860, New Orleans grew from 17,000 to 168,000. In 1840 it was the third largest city in the nation.

St. Louis was founded in 1764, under orders from France, for the purpose of developing trade on the Missouri River. Located on the first high ground south of the confluence of the Missouri and Mississippi rivers, this is precisely the role it served for the next century.[9]

The first steamboat arrived from New Orleans in 1817. From this time on, St. Louis had direct and inexpensive access to the great water routes of the world. For the first half of the nineteenth century the major product St. Louis offered to the world was furs. The fur traders left St. Louis every spring with provisions and barter material[10] for the trappers and Indians, returning in the fall with furs. The Missouri is considerably more treacherous than the Mississippi, with the result that steamboat navigation was delayed until the late 1840s. Early travel up the Missouri was by keelboat, powered by poles and ropes. A round trip from St. Louis to the fur-yielding regions of the upper Missouri required a full season—depart St. Louis in the early spring and return in late fall. The steamboat not only reduced cost but also increased the probability of returning at all.

The importance of St. Louis was further enhanced by the opening of navigation between the Mississippi and Chicago, enabling it to send and receive goods from that direction as well. Without the steamboat, however, river travel would not have been sufficiently economical to permit St. Louis to become more than a minor regional center.[11]

A city's ability to flourish was primarily determined by its ability to develop a trading hinterland and access to the outside world; until the Civil War this success depended upon water navigation routes. The railroad, which came into widespread use in the decades after the Civil

9.   The French founded St. Louis just at the time they were losing their North American empire, so the city was originally governed by Spain. It came into U.S. possession, as did New Orleans, with the Louisiana Purchase.

10.   As a lesson in economics, it is fascinating to read Chittenden's account of the disdain the Indians and traders felt for one another, and each for the same reason. In the exchange of furs for beads, blankets, metalware, and other manufactured goods, each party to the trade thought the other side was giving up something of great value in exchange for something almost valueless.

11.   For an excellent and colorful discussion of this material on New Orleans and St. Louis, see *The American Fur Trade of the Far West*, by Chittenden. See in particular the chapters on Louisiana and St. Louis.

War, significantly weakened the advantage of water as a medium for bulk transport. In prerailroad days, overland transport was perhaps a few hundred times more costly than water transport, but the railroad reduced this gap to something considerably less than 10:1.

With the railroad, east-west transport across the country became feasible. In addition, within fairly broad limits railroads could be built anywhere. The location of cities, at least in detail, became less tied to the accidents of geography and more tied to the locations of railroad lines. Particularly in the West, many cities are where they are in large measure because of effective boosterism on the part of city fathers.

A prime example is Kansas City. The confluence of the Missouri and Kansas rivers is hardly the stuff of which locational advantage is made, yet it became a major meat-packing center shortly after several business leaders persuaded (bribed) the Hannibal and St. Joseph Railroad to build its connection with the Union Pacific through Kansas City rather than Leavenworth. This was the first bridge across the Missouri, completed in the late 1860s. Similar stories, with approximately equal parts geographical imperative, chance, and hucksterism, surround the locations of many other western cities, including Denver, Omaha (another bridge across the Missouri), and Los Angeles. In each instance the existence of an exportable surplus ensured that a city would arise, but the location of the city, up to a radius of sometimes 100 miles or more, was a matter of choice.

The element of choice added considerable color to the development of the West. The location of future cities lay in considerable measure in the hands of the railroad barons. Given that the value of urban land is up to several hundred times greater than that of rural land, landowners from all over the West went to great lengths to secure the railroad links which held the hope, if not the promise, of great wealth.

The rise of the railroads reduced the significance of the Mississippi and its main tributaries as the only viable transport link to the Great Plains. Of the water-based cities of the first half of the nineteenth century, the ones which flourished in the second half were those which developed important rail links. Thus Chicago, not St. Louis, became the hub of the upper Midwest. New Orleans, which had been the fifth largest city in 1860, fell to fifteenth by 1910.

The railroads did much more than determine the details of location of western cities. The railroads reduced overland transport cost sufficiently to make trade between these regions and the rest of the world viable.

Until about 1940 the South did not challenge the Northeast in manufacturing, nor did many low-paid, low-skill workers migrate to higher-paying jobs in the North. The failure of industry to move south, where incomes and, presumably, wages were lower, may have resulted from scale economies and the larger initial population in the North, as well as from the more fully developed railroad network in the North. (See Figure 2.2, which shows the gradual convergence of real incomes

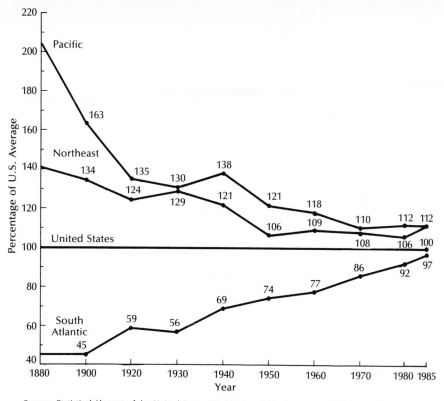

Source: *Statistical Abstract of the United States.* Washington, D.C.: Government Printing Office, 1981, 1987.

Figure 2.2 *Regional Per-Capita Income, 1880 to 1985 (Selected Regions, Percentage of U.S. Average)*

among regions.) The failure of southern low-skill workers to migrate to the high-wage North surely resulted in part from racial barriers in the North. In addition, the jobs in the North that might have been claimed by migrating southerners were claimed, for several generations, by European immigrants.

Although the South did not compete with the Northeast, the Far West did. From the start, the Pacific (and later the Mountain) states were a high-wage area for both supply and demand reasons. Initially the population was small, so manufactured goods had to be imported from Europe or the Northeast. Wages had to be high to compensate for the high cost of living. Employers were willing to pay high wages, however, because labor was scarce relative to the abundant supply of resources (largely lumber and minerals). Indeed, the wage premium offered by employers was apparently more than sufficient to compensate for higher prices. The high wages induced migration, and eventually the population of the Far West began to grow. By 1910 the population of the West was growing faster (in absolute numbers, not just in percentage) than the Northeast. Figures 2.3, 2.4, and 2.5 document these population shifts

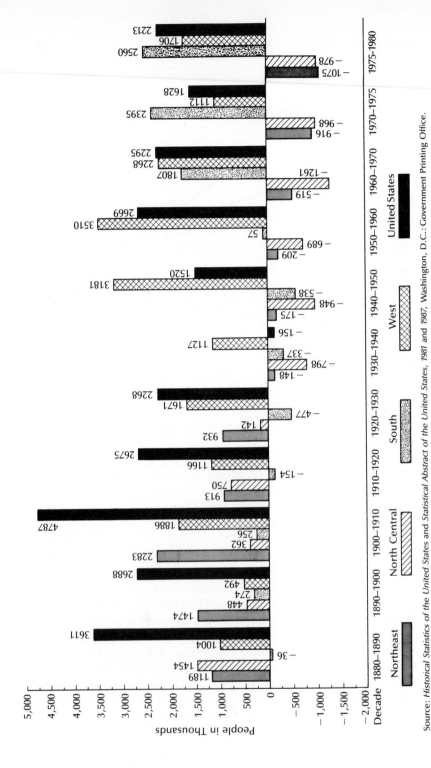

Source: *Historical Statistics of the United States* and *Statistical Abstract of the United States, 1981* and *1987*, Washington, D.C.: Government Printing Office.

Figure 2.3 *Net Interregional Migration: Whites, 1880 to 1980, including Foreign-born*

for U.S.-born whites, blacks, and foreign-born whites. With population growth came the ability to take advantage of scale economies locally and substitute home production for imports from the Northeast. This process fed on itself in the West, as it had earlier in the Northeast—up to a point. The more home production, the larger the population that can find jobs. The larger the population, the more it is possible, because of scale economies, to substitute home production for imports.

The export base continues to be the rationale for the West's economy, as in the Gold Rush days. With today's larger population, however, the region is more nearly self-sufficient, and the ratio of nonbasic to basic (export) employment has risen. The result of these forces is that the West's wage premium over the Northeast has been eroded gradually, first, because migration has reduced the labor shortage and second, because the gradual substitution of home production for imports reduced the West's cost-of-living premium.

The increasing local production of the West gradually has robbed the Northeast of one of its export markets. A substantial portion of the Northeast's comparative advantage throughout the history of the United States has been derived from both its access to Europe and its size (population). The gradual erosion of both advantages began almost with the founding of the nation.

It is important to note that the flight from the Northeast to the West, which has received so much attention over the past few years, has been going on for two centuries. There are two differences between the period from 1970 to the present and the previous 194 years. First, until about 1970, the emigrants from the Northeast always were replaced by immigrants—from Europe until about 1930 and then, beginning with the Great Depression and World War II, by southern blacks.

Beginning in the early 1970s, however, the wave of black migration from the South to the Northeast stopped, and in fact reversed. As can be seen in Figure 2.4, the out-migration of blacks from the Northeast began in the first half of the 1970s (and apparently accelerated in the second half). About one-third of the 1960s migration of blacks to the Northeast was undone by migration from the Northeast (basically a return to the South and a move west) in the 1970s. At this time, the long-standing pattern of migration from the Northeast to the West began to result in population declines for the Northeast.

The second difference is that over the past two decades, the West has achieved sufficient size (population) to be roughly comparable to the Northeast. In short, the Northeast no longer has its initial advantage—scale—as compared with the rest of the country. Also, it no longer serves as a major processing region for immigrants.

While much of this shift between the Northeast and the West was in progress, the South was languishing in the aftermath of the Civil War and Reconstruction. As late as 1940, 40 percent of the southern population worked in agriculture (as compared with 23 percent nationwide).

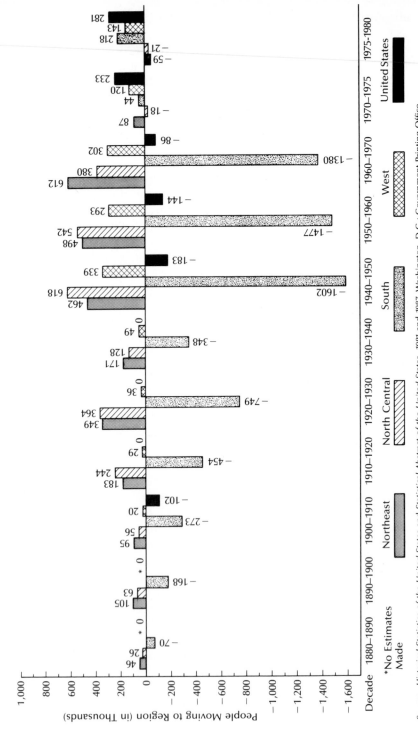

Figure 2.4 Net Interregional Migration: Native-born Blacks, 1880 to 1980

Source: *Historical Statistics of the United States* and *Statistical Abstract of the United States, 1981* and *1987*, Washington, D.C.: Government Printing Office.

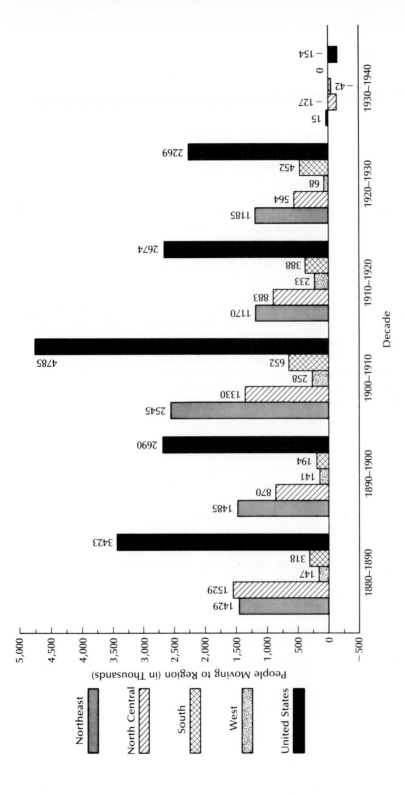

Source: Historical Statistics of the United States and Statistical Abstract of the United States, 1981. Washington, D.C.: Government Printing Office.

Figure 2.5 Net Interregional Migration: Foreign-born Whites, 1880 to 1940

The failure of the South to show much economic growth before World War II, even though its low wage structure should have attracted industry, resulted from a number of causes. First, the Northeast continued to dominate the South in terms of size and transport network. Thus, the Northeast continued to be the location of choice for market-oriented firms with scale economies (it is cheaper to ship a small amount of output to the South than a large amount to the North). Second, although this is hard to document, regional prejudice may have played a role in industries' locating in the North rather than the South.

Until the development of modern sanitation and medicine, disease may have been a more serious impediment to southern urbanization than to northern. The drier summers and colder winters of the North provided a check on the spread of infectious diseases, and mosquito-borne diseases (most notably yellow fever) took a heavy toll in the South in the nineteenth century. There is no reason to believe yellow fever was much worse in urban than rural areas, but the same would not be true for diseases carried by air- or water-borne germs.

The industrial awakening of the South began with a dramatic shift out of agriculture—partly a shift to southern manufacturing, but largely a migration of southern blacks to the Northeast. By 1970, only 6 percent of the southern population was in agriculture (compared with 4.8 percent nationwide). Interestingly, the migration of southern blacks to northeastern cities began after the flow of European immigrants had almost halted. The massive migration of blacks (3.4 million between 1940 and 1970) was caused by a combination of push and pull. The mechanization of southern agriculture forced many low-skill workers off the farm, and, at the same time, wages were higher in the North (and for the first time since Emancipation, these jobs were not being taken by European immigrants).

Almost simultaneous with this out-migration of blacks from the South was a substantial net in-migration of whites, largely from the Northeast. Between 1950 and 1970 there was a net in-migration of 1.9 million whites to the South followed by another 2.3 million in the first half of the 1970s. These generally highly skilled whites apparently were attracted to the South by its manufacturing boom. The manufacturing boom may have resulted in part from the availability of a low-wage, nonunion work force (although the boom was not sufficient to absorb all the people released from agricultural work).

All the flows of labor described are expected—from low-wage regions to high-wage regions. The continual flow of people from the Northeast to the West follows this pattern, as does the earlier flow of blacks from the South to the Northeast. Figure 2.2 shows America's per capita income, by region and decade, as a percentage of the national average. The figure reveals that the West always has been a high-wage region and the South, a low-wage region relative to the Northeast. The most striking feature of the figure is the convergence of incomes over the past century. This convergence, according to Mieszkowski, is even more nearly complete if regional difference in living costs is taken into account.

This characterization of the economic interactions among regions leads to a number of observations regarding cities and urban economics:

1. The flight from the Northeast to the Sunbelt is of long duration and was driven in part by predictable interregional wage differences. These wage differences had been largely eliminated by 1980, leading to the prediction that migration will slow.
2. The major reason for the increased visibility of the flight to the Sunbelt is the lack of replacement migration to the Northeast. With the cessation of black migration from the South in about 1970, gross outflows have been net outflows.
3. The emergence of the modern southern urban sector has been in progress since at least 1950. The rapid out-migration of blacks in the 1950s and 1960s tended to conceal from view the almost equally rapid in-migration of highly skilled whites.
4. The rapid migration of blacks into northeastern cities, which began after World War I, reached its peak in the 1940s, 1950s, and 1960s, and completely stopped shortly after 1970. Few blacks (or whites, for that matter) live in rural areas of the South, so another such wave of migration cannot be expected. This leads to the question of whether some of America's urban racial problems are due in some part not to race per se, but to the disruptions and tensions associated with the one-shot, massive migration.[12]

☐ Summary

When regions differ in terms of their resource endowments, the world becomes more interesting than the world described in Chapter 1 in two important ways. First, the profitability of firms varies with location; hence, different types of firms will locate at different types of sites. Second, both profitability and efficiency dictate that regions trade with one another, because they tend to produce different types of goods.

This chapter began by exploring the determinants of firm location in a world with geographic variety in endowments. Next, it used this theory to examine the economic history of the development of regions in the United States.

---

12. Absorption of waves of migrants, and problems associated with this absorption, is hardly a new phenomenon for American cities. Through the second half of the nineteenth century New York was dominated by immigrants. In 1890, for example, 80 percent of the residents of New York were either foreign born or the offspring of foreign born.

Questions and Problems

1. This chapter explained that transport-oriented firms tend to locate either at sources of raw materials or at markets. Would it ever pay a firm to locate midway between its materials sources and markets? Why?

2. Name cities whose location is explained by the following:
    a. Materials-oriented firms
    b. Production cost-oriented firms
    c. Market-oriented firms

3. First in the Northeast, then in the West, and most recently in the South, industrialization and urbanization progressed quite slowly for a while and then accelerated. Can you think of a reason for this pattern?

4. From 1950 to 1970, most of the rapidly growing American metropolitan areas were near the edges of the country, with easy access to ocean transportation (this includes the Great Lakes ports). How do you explain this in a country in which international trade is relatively unimportant?

References and Further Reading

American Iron and Steel Institute, *1981 Annual Statistical Report* (Washington, D.C.: American Iron and Steel Institute, 1982).

Chittenden, Hiram M. *The American Fur Trade in the Far West* (Lincoln: University of Nebraska, 1935).

Fogel, Robert, and Stanley Engerman, eds. *The Reinterpretation of American Economic History* (New York: Harper & Row, 1971). A collection of essays by several scholars on various aspects of U.S. economic history.

Glaab, Charles N., and A. Theodore Brown. *A History of Urban America* (New York: Macmillan, 1967). This is an excellent discussion of the history of the development of urban America. It is an excellent companion to Chapters 1 and 2.

Harper, Ann. *The Location of the American Iron and Steel Industry: 1879–1919*. Ph.D. dissertation, Johns Hopkins University, 1976.

Isard, Walter. *Location and Space Economy* (New York: Wiley, 1956). A technical discussion of location theory.

Mieszkowski, Peter. "Recent Trends in Urban and Regional Development." *Current Issues in Urban Economics*, eds. Peter Mieszkowski and Mahlon Straszhein (Baltimore: Johns Hopkins, 1979). An excellent and highly readable discussion of regional shifts, as well as the basis for much of the discussion in this chapter. Other survey papers in this volume are also very good and frequently will be referred to at the appropriate places.

Temin, Peter. *Iron and Steel in 19th Century America* (Cambridge, Mass.: MIT Press, 1964).

Weber, Alfred. *Alfred Weber's Theory of Location of Industries.* Translated by Carl Friedrich (Chicago: University of Chicago Press, 1929).

3

Urbanization and Economic Growth in the United States

☐ Very poor countries, without exception, are largely agricultural, since food is the primary requirement for life. Economic development consists in part of the transfer of labor and other inputs from predominantly rural agriculture to predominantly urban manufacturing and service industries. Thus, economic growth everywhere is associated with urbanization. During the nineteenth century, rapid economic growth in Europe and North America resulted in rapid urbanization. The United States, having industrialized somewhat later than western Europe, also lagged in urbanization. Much of Europe was highly urbanized by the early decades of the twentieth century. Since about 1925, even more rapid industrialization and urbanization have taken place in some countries in Asia and South America. (Urbanization in developing countries will be discussed in Chapter 16.)

One prerequisite for the urbanization of the past two centuries was technical progress in various aspects of urban life, discussed in Chapter 1. Equally important, however, was technical progress in agriculture, which enabled a small farm population to feed an urban population many times its size. The effects of this change are documented in Table 3.2.

☐ A DIGRESSION ON DISEASE

The nature of the agricultural revolution that facilitated modern urban growth need not concern us here, though it is interesting to note that advances in agriculture have been behind previous waves of urbanization. Indeed, until modern times the rural sector had to produce not only a surplus of food but also a surplus of people. Until the advent of modern sanitation, urban death rates were sufficiently high that cities were demographically unable to sustain themselves. In some parts of the world, rural populations were sufficiently disease-ridden that they could not produce this surplus of either food or people. According to McNeill (1976) the unhealthy environment in tropical Africa is one of the major reasons why cities did not emerge there. Rather, urbanization had to await the migration of humans from their apparent birthplace in east Africa to less humid, more temperate regions. This migration gave man a respite from the killing and debilitating diseases of the tropics. This respite, in turn, allowed the rural sector sufficient health to produce its surplus of food and babies, thus allowing cities to grow with at least some hope that they would not be wiped out by epidemics.

To a degree, this respite was only temporary. The major debilitating parasitic diseases of the tropics have never effectively penetrated the temperate regions, since the parasites require warmth and humidity in order to travel from host to host. Nevertheless, infectious diseases ultimately caught up with humanity's northward migration.

Europe appears to have been free of epidemic diseases such as measles, smallpox, and bubonic plague throughout classical times.[1] The first epidemic disease to reach Europe was apparently smallpox, probably carried by Roman troops, in about A.D. 165. This outbreak of smallpox, and other epidemic diseases which were to follow, ushered in an era of European population decline and deurbanization which was to last 500 years (McNeill, p. 103). In the city of Rome, it is said that 5000 people per day died at the height of the original epidemic. Even before the arrival of bubonic plague, there are many recorded instances of a single epidemic killing 90 percent of a city's population.

A new infectious disease more severely damages a population than an established disease, for a variety of reasons, including that after a few generations populations tend to adapt. So it was with smallpox and measles. Then came bubonic plague in the fourteenth century, which reportedly reduced the population of Europe by 35 percent. These infectious diseases were apparently more severe in cities than in rural areas, simply because of the density of people and the consequent ease of transmission.

During the period when these infectious diseases were establishing themselves in Europe and China, it became virtually impossible to build and sustain cities of anything approaching the size of classical Rome or Hangzhou, China, which achieved a population of approximately one million in the twelfth century (before the fourteenth-century arrival of plague in China).

Thus the modern era of urbanization owes a large measure to humanity's ability to accommodate the killer diseases of the past. Part of this accommodation is immunological and was well underway before the beginning of the nineteenth century. The last major outbreak of plague in London occurred in 1665, a year before the great fire. (There

---

1. Even without these killers, the average age at death in Rome, for those who survived childhood, seems to have been just under thirty years.

is some speculation that the fire killed many of the rats harboring disease, and that the methods used during rebuilding were less hospitable to rats than previous construction methods.) The real breakthrough came with the understanding of the causes of diseases, which understanding began in the middle of the nineteenth century. This ultimately led to sewer systems, attention to clean water and chlorination, and the development of vaccinations and antibiotics. All told, the taming of disease is one of the most important prerequisites to modern urban society.

☐ LONG-TERM TRENDS

Although the pattern of urbanization and economic growth in the United States has not differed greatly from that observed in Europe, its scale and speed have been as dramatic here as anywhere. During a period of less than two centuries, the United States was transformed from a rural and agricultural society into an urban and industrial society. Urbanization has been one of the most prominent, widely studied, and controversial trends throughout America's history. This chapter and the next discuss the broad trends of urban growth and the sizes and structures of urban areas. These chapters present a historical context, begun in Chapters 1 and 2, for the analytical chapters that follow in Part 2 and for the policy chapters in Part 3.

The simplest statistical picture of the growth and urbanization of the American population is presented in Table 3.1, which shows the growth of both urban and total population from 1790, the time of the first U.S. census, to 1980.[2] The urban population consists of people living in urban places. Chapter 1 pointed out that most urban areas consist of many urban places, so the population of an urban place is not an indication of the size of an urban area. Nevertheless, the population of all urban places is the proper measure of the urban population of the entire country. Remember that an urban place can contain as few as 2500 people; urban places therefore include many villages and small towns.

Total U.S. population grew from 3.9 million in 1790 to more than 238.7 million in 1985. In 1790, only 5 percent of the country was urban, even under the inclusive measure used in Table 3.1. In 1960, 63 percent was urban. Since 1950 the Census Bureau has used a new and somewhat broader definition of urban places that increases the urban percentages for 1950 and 1960 in Table 3.1 by about 7 percentage

---

2. Interestingly, the percent urban apparently declined from early colonial times until about 1790. Glaab and Brown (1967) report that in 1690 almost 10 percent of the population was urban. There are two reasons. The first was safety. Only after the Indians were pushed beyond the Alleghenies could farmers live in relative safety. Second, the Crown apparently encouraged urban living, possibly thinking urban colonists would be easier to control.

Table 3.1 *Urban Population of the Coterminous United States, 1790 to 1980 (Population in millions)*

Year	Total Population	Urban Population	Urban Percentage
1790	3.9	0.2	5.1
1800	5.3	0.3	5.7
1810	7.2	0.5	6.9
1820	9.6	0.7	7.3
1830	12.9	1.1	8.5
1840	17.1	1.8	10.5
1850	23.2	3.5	15.1
1860	31.4	6.2	19.7
1870	38.6	9.9	25.6
1880	50.2	14.1	28.1
1890	63.0	22.1	35.1
1900	76.2	30.2	39.6
1910	92.2	42.1	45.7
1920	106.0	54.3	51.2
1930	123.2	69.2	56.2
1940	132.2	74.7	56.5
1950	151.3	90.1	59.6
1960	179.3	113.1	63.1
1970[a]	203.2	149.3	73.5
1980[a]	226.5	166.9	73.7

[a]Based on new urban place definition; not comparable with earlier data. See the source for definitions.
Source: Data from U.S. Department of Commerce, Bureau of the Census. *Census of Population.* Washington, D.C.: Government Printing Office, 1972 and 1982.

points. Only data based on the new definition are available in the 1970 and 1980 U.S. censuses.

The urban percentage of the U.S. population grew steadily from 1790 to 1980, with the exception of an insignificant drop between 1810 and 1820. The country's total population has grown fast enough that the number of people in rural areas also has grown each decade, even though its percentage of the total population has declined. Indeed, the number of rural residents in 1960 exceeded the country's entire population in each census year up to 1900.

Table 3.1 also suggests the close historical relationship between urbanization and industrialization. Historians place the beginning of rapid American industrialization at about 1840. Table 3.1 shows that between 1790 and 1840, the urban percentage of the population increased by about 1.1 percent per decade. Between 1840 and 1930, the increase averaged about 5 percent per decade. Urbanization thus proceeded very rapidly during the second half of the nineteenth century and the early part of the twentieth century, when industrial employment and output also were increasing rapidly.

It is not widely appreciated that *urbanization has decelerated since about 1930.* Between 1930 and 1960 the urban percentage of the population increased by an average of only 2.3 percent per decade. Industrialization has become more widespread, and the growth rate of employment in manufacturing has slackened relative to that in other sectors. Also, despite the massive urbanization of society, rural areas are by no means drained of people. Even under the new *urban place* definition, almost 60 million people still live in rural areas. Another popular misconception is that most rural people live on farms. In 1980 the U.S. farm population was 7.2 million (3 percent of the U.S. population).

In the early years of America's history, the cities and towns in which the urban population lived were very small. In 1790 only 62,000 people lived in the only two cities (New York City and Philadelphia) whose populations exceeded 25,000. By 1840 three cities (New York City, Baltimore, and New Orleans) had populations in excess of 100,000, but the three cities together contained little more than one-half million people. In 1840 Chicago had fewer than 5000 people. Statistics on the growth of cities during the last half of the nineteenth century are difficult to interpret because of the common tendency to annex suburban areas to the central city. For example, between 1890 and 1900, New York City's population increased from 1.5 million to 3.4 million, mainly due to the consolidation of the five boroughs that now constitute the city. By 1900, however, six cities (New York City, Chicago, Philadelphia, Baltimore, St. Louis, and Boston) had at least one-half million people each. Los Angeles, now the nation's second largest metropolitan area, had little more than 100,000 people.[3]

Employment data are fragmentary for the early years of the nation's history, but they make it possible to trace the rough outlines of the industrialization process. Table 3.2 shows the number of gainful workers in the total labor force and in agriculture and manufacturing for selected years from 1820 to 1980.

Table 3.2 also vividly shows the transformation of the American economy. Farm workers fell from 71.9 percent of all workers in 1820 to a mere 3.6 percent in 1980. Manufacturing workers increased from 12.2 to 27.1 percent in 1960. Even in 1820, many rural people did not live on farms. In that year, as seen in Table 3.1, 92.8 percent of the population was rural but only 71.9 percent of the workers were on farms. Table 3.2 also shows that the period of rapid industrialization was between 1840 and 1920. During that period, the percentage of all workers employed in manufacturing increased by an average of 1.4 percent per decade. Between 1920 and 1960, however, the percentage of all workers in manufacturing hardly changed. By 1970 it had fallen be-

3. All statistics in this paragraph are from the U.S. Department of Commerce, U.S. Bureau of the Census. *Census of Population.* Washington, D.C.: Government Printing Office, 1960. For a more complete list, see Table 4.1.

Table 3.2 *Industrial Distribution of Gainful Workers, 1820 to 1980 (Employment in thousands)*

						Workers	
Year	Total	Agriculture		Manufacturing		Other and Not Allocated	
1820	2,880	2,070	71.9%	350[a]	12.2%	460	16.0%
1840	5,420	3,720	68.6	790[a]	14.6	910	16.8
1860	10,530	6,210	59.0	1,930[a]	18.3	2,390	22.7
1880	17,390	8,610	49.5	3,170	18.2	5,610	32.3
1900	29,070	10,710	36.8	6,340	21.8	12,020	41.3
1920	41,610	11,120	26.7	10,880	26.1	19,610	47.1
1940	45,070	8,449	18.7	10,650	23.7	25,951	57.6
1950	56,435	6,909	12.2	14,685	26.0	34,841	61.7
1960	64,639	4,257	6.6	17,513	27.1	42,869	66.3
1970	78,627	3,462	4.4	19,369	24.6	55,796	71.0
1980	93,770	3,364	3.6	20,285	21.6	70,121	74.8

[a]Includes construction.

Sources: 1820 to 1920 data from *Historical Statistics of the United States*. Washington, D.C.: Government Printing Office, 1976; 1940 to 1960 data from U.S. Department of Commerce, Bureau of the Census. *Census of Population*. Washington, D.C.: Government Printing Office, 1972 and 1982.

low its 1920 level. By 1980, manufacturing absorbed a smaller fraction of the labor force than it had in 1900. (The 1940 figure is strongly influenced by the large amount of unemployment that still existed that year.) The figures in Table 3.2 are workers, not labor force, and employment fell much more in manufacturing than in agriculture during the Great Depression. Therefore, the 23.7 percent of the workers in manufacturing in 1940 would be closer to the 1920 and 1970 percentages had there been full employment in 1940.

Table 3.2 shows the magnitude of the agricultural revolution that has been in progress for the last century. As a result of mechanization and other changes, productivity per farm worker has risen at an unprecedented rate. Despite the fact that food consumption has increased substantially, agricultural workers have decreased, not only as a percentage of all workers, but also in numbers. Between 1950 and 1980 about half the agricultural jobs disappeared. Since the rural population grew or, under the new definition, remained about constant during the period, nonfarm people have become an increasingly large percentage of the rural population.[4]

The provision of food has the highest priority in every society. A poor society must devote most of its labor force to the production of food, or of exports to get the foreign exchange needed to import food.

---

4. The agricultural revolution is far from complete. It appears that farm workers may fall by half again by the turn of the century. But even if this does happen, the effect on the urban sector will be trivial since the total number of people involved is very small.

In wealthy societies, however, high productivity in agriculture and low income elasticities of demand for food free much of the labor force to produce other goods and services. In such societies, increases in agricultural productivity come from technical progress in both agriculture and industry. In the United States, large increases in agricultural productivity have resulted from technical progress in the design and production of farm machinery, part of the manufacturing sector. The process of freeing workers from food production has gone much farther in the United States than in other countries that produce enough food for their population, and the United States is a large net exporter of agricultural products.

Nonagricultural workers can, and often do, find rural employment in manufacturing and other sectors, however. Rapid urbanization has occurred because manufacturing and other employers found it increasingly advantageous to locate in large population centers. Since about 1920 there has been a deceleration of growth in manufacturing employment. One consequence has been a deceleration in the growth of urban areas. Another consequence has been that urban employment has grown more rapidly in other sectors.

☐ RECENT TRENDS

National Employment

As seen in Table 3.2, the fraction of the labor force in manufacturing grew steadily from 1820 to 1960, and then began a fairly steep decline. As Table 3.3 shows, this decline has continued in the 1980s. In the 1980–85 period, manufacturing employment fell in absolute numbers (by 4.8 percent), not just as a percent of the total. Simple calculations from Tables 3.2 and 3.3 reveal that manufacturing's share of total employment was down to 19.2 percent in 1985. Table 3.3 also shows that the major growth industry in the early '80s was service. The service sector of every region of the country registered at least a 15 percent growth in employment. Manufacturing was stagnant virtually everywhere except for healthy growth in the Pacific states. Manufacturing declined most severely in the mid-Atlantic and east North Central states. The shift from manufacturing to service, and the regional bias associated with this shift, are important forces shaping the destinies of individual cities. In later chapters these trends will be noted several times, culminating with a discussion in Chapter 15.

SMSA Population

Much more accurate and comprehensive data regarding urbanization are available for the period since 1940. Most important has been the publication by the Census Bureau of comprehensive demographic

Table 3.3 *Growth of Population and Selected Employment Categories, United States and Regions. Percent Change 1980 to 85.*

	Population	Employment		
		Total	Manufacturing	Service
United States	5.4	8.0	−4.8	22.8
New England	2.5	10.7	−3.6	23.7
Mid-Atlantic	1.1	5.9	−12.7	22.1
E. North Central	−0.1	0.5	−10.1	16.1
W. North Central	2.2	3.7	−4.8	16.0
South Atlantic	8.8	14.2	1.2	32.1
Mountain	12.5	10.2	−6.4	26.9
Pacific	10.2	13.5	8.7	26.2
W. South Central	11.6	9.8	1.9	20.7

Source: Data from *1987 Statistical Abstract of the United States*. Washington, D.C.: Government Printing Office, 1987.

and economic data for SMSAs (see Table 3.4). These data confirm the observation that the populations of urban places and SMSAs are of similar magnitude. Some urban places are outside SMSAs, and some parts of each SMSA are rural. There is a large overlap between SMSAs and urban place populations, however, and the two nonoverlapping groups approximately cancel each other out.

The SMSA data provide the best picture of the metropolitan character of the American population. Table 3.4 shows that in 1985 over three-fourths of the population lived in metropolitan areas. This places the United States among the world's most urbanized countries. Almost certainly, the percentage of the population living in SMSAs will increase only slowly during the coming decades.

SMSA Employment

By and large, SMSAs are labor market areas. Most people who work in an SMSA also live there, and vice versa. There is some commuting between SMSAs, however. For instance some people live in Gary and work in Chicago; some people live in Newark and work in New York City. For this reason the Census Bureau designates certain areas as CMSAs. There is, however, relatively little commuting between SMSAs and non-SMSA areas. The number of workers employed in SMSAs is therefore about the same as the number of workers living in SMSAs. That is, it is not necessary to distinguish workers by place of employment from workers by place of residence, although the distinction is crucial in discussing data on suburbanization (see Chapter 4).

Table 3.5 shows U.S. and SMSA employment in 1950, 1970, and 1980 for twelve major industry groups. For 1950 and 1970, the SMSA entry refers to employment in SMSAs larger than 100,000. For 1980,

Table 3.4 *Population of the United States and SMSAs; 1940 to 1985 (Population in millions)*

Year	United States	SMSAs	Percentage in SMSAs
1940	132.2	72.8	55.1
1950	151.3	89.3	59.0
1960[a]	179.3	112.9	63.0
1970	203.2	139.4	68.6
1980	226.5	169.4	74.8
1985	238.7	182.5	76.5

[a]1960 and subsequent data include Alaska and Hawaii.
Sources: U.S. Department of Commerce, Bureau of the Census. *Census of Population.* Washington, D.C.: Government Printing Office, 1982, and *1987 Statistical Abstract of the United States.*

the figure is more inclusive—all SMSAs. In addition to those included for 1950 and 1970, the 1980 tabulation includes small SMSAs with populations ranging from 50,000 to 100,000. The expansion of the definition adds about 5 percent of the labor force to the urban total. Thus the 1980 numbers show more urbanization of employment in part because of an expanded definition of the urban sector.

Aside from those people not reporting the industry in which they were employed, the groups are exhaustive; that is, they include all workers. The names of the groups are self-explanatory.

For each year, Table 3.5 shows the percentage distribution of total U.S. and SMSA employment by industry. The table also shows the percentage of all workers found in SMSAs in each industry. For any industry and year, the percentage figure in the last column of Table 3.5 exceeds the national total at the bottom of the table if, and only if, the percentage figure in the SMSA column exceeds the percentage figure in the U.S. column. In other words, if the percentage of the workers in a certain industry who are in large SMSAs exceeds that for all workers, then that industry's workers must constitute a larger percentage of SMSA than of U.S. workers.

This is easiest to see by considering an example, such as manufacturing. Table 3.5 reveals that in 1950 the United States had 14,685,000 manufacturing jobs, which constituted 26 percent of total employment. There were 10,021,000 SMSA manufacturing jobs, making up 30.5 percent of the SMSA jobs. The next column shows that 68.2 percent of manufacturing jobs were in SMSAs. Going to the bottom of this column, note that 58.2 percent of all jobs were in SMSAs. Thus manufacturing was more urbanized than overall employment in 1950. (Note that by 1970 this was not true, nor was it true in 1980, even with the expanded definition of *urban*.)

It should be expected that some industries are located predominantly in SMSAs, whereas others are predominantly outside SMSAs. In 1970 the percentage of workers living in large SMSAs ranged

Table 3.5 Industry Groups of Employed Persons: United States and SMSAs (Employment in thousands)

	1950					1970					1980				
	United States		SMSA		Pct. in	United States		SMSA		Pct. in	United States		SMSA		Pct. in
Industry	No.	Pct.	No.	Pct.	SMSAs	No.	Pct.	No.	Pct.	SMSAs	No.	Pct.	No.	Pct.	SMSAs
Agriculture, forestry, and fisheries	7,034	12.5	826	2.5	11.7	2,840	3.7	782	1.5	27.5	2,913	3.0%	1,194	1.5%	40.9%
Mining	931	1.6	251	0.8	26.9	631	0.8	240	0.5	38.0	1,028	1.1	460	0.6	44.7
Construction	3,458	6.1	2,004	6.1	57.9	4,572	6.0	2,978	5.6	65.1	5,740	5.9	4,193	5.5	73.0
Manufacturing	14,685	26.0	10,021	30.5	68.2	19,837	26.0	13,722	25.8	69.1	21,915	22.4	16,613	22.0	75.8
Transportation, communication, and utilities	4,450	7.9	2,911	8.9	65.4	5,186	6.8	3,832	7.2	73.8	7,087	7.3	5,653	7.5	79.7
Wholesale and retail	10,507	18.6	6,834	20.8	65.0	15,373	20.1	11,026	20.7	71.7	19,934	20.4	15,677	20.0	78.6
Finance, insurance, and real estate	1,920	3.4	1,508	4.6	78.5	3,838	5.0	3,129	5.9	81.5	5,898	6.0	5,057	6.7	85.7
Business and repair services	1,308	2.3	888	2.7	67.8	2,395	3.1	1,904	3.6	79.4	4,018	4.1	3,482	4.6	86.6
Personal services	3,465	6.1	2,154	6.6	62.1	3,537	4.6	2,356	4.4	66.6	3,076	3.6	2,327	3.0	75.6
Entertainment, recreation	493	0.9	382	1.2	77.4	631	0.8	492	0.9	77.9	1,007	1.0	855	1.1	84.9
Professional and related services	4,826	8.6	2,899	8.8	60.0	13,511	17.6	9,606	18.0	71.0	19,812	20.3	15,509	20.0	78.2
Public administration	2,514	4.5	1,727	5.3	68.6	4,202	5.5	3,175	6.0	75.5	5,147	5.3	4,103	5.4	79.7
Not reported[a]	843	1.5	435	1.3	51.6	—	—	—	—	—	—	—	—	—	—
Total	56,434	100.0%	32,840	100.1%	58.1%	76,553	100.0%	53,242	100.1%	69.5%	97,575	100.4%	75,123	97.9%	76.9%

[a]"Not reported" category not applicable to 1970 and later years.
Sources: Data from U.S. Department of Commerce, Bureau of the Census. Census of Population. Washington, D.C.: Government Printing Office, 1951, 1972, and 1982.

from less than 28 percent in agriculture, forestry, and fisheries to more than 81 percent in finance, insurance, and real estate. By 1980, agriculture, forestry, and fisheries remained the least urbanized sector, but even this sector was 41 percent within SMSAs. Mining was next with 44 percent. Finance, insurance, and real estate remained the most urbanized in 1980, at 85.8 percent.

Although manufacturing is the largest employer in both the United States and in large SMSAs, it is not among the most highly urbanized industries by the measure in Table 3.5. In both 1970 and 1980, seven industries had larger percentages of their employment in large SMSAs than did manufacturing. Manufacturing was slightly less urbanized than total employment.

If 1950 is compared with 1970, the percentage of total employment in large SMSAs rose from 58.2 to 69.6. Manufacturing employment fell from 30.5 percent of SMSA employment in 1950 to 25.8 percent in 1970 and 22 percent in 1980. The percentage of manufacturing employees who were in SMSAs rose slightly from 68.2 to 69.2, however. The increased urbanization of manufacturing from 1970 to 1980 (75.9 percent urbanized in 1980) is due almost entirely to the expanded definition of the urban sector.

In percentage terms, the largest growth in both national and SMSA employment was in service industries: finance, insurance, and real estate; business and repair services; personal and professional and related services; and public administration. Together, these industries grew from 25.8 percent of the work force in 1950 to 40.3 percent in 1980. (As noted in Table 3.3, this trend accelerated between 1980 and 1985. By 1985, 45.8 percent of employment was in the service sector.) Not only did these industries grow rapidly; they also became increasingly urbanized. It is now clear what is suggested by the data presented in the foregoing section on "Long-Term Trends": since 1950 the service sector has been the major growth industry in urban areas, and since 1980 manufacturing has actually declined.

The major lesson of Table 3.5 is that manufacturing and other industrial jobs (construction, transportation, communication, and utilities) are no longer the major sources of SMSA employment growth. A secondary lesson is that highly urbanized service industries are not only major sources of increased SMSA employment; they also are becoming more urbanized. The shift of SMSA employment toward services parallels the national trend and results mainly from high income elasticities of demand and the slow growth of productivity in service industries, as well as rapid labor-saving technical progress in manufacturing. One reason for the increased urbanization of service industries is that they find it increasingly advantageous to locate near hospitals, medical laboratories, law courts, financial markets, and other institutions found mainly in large population centers. Another reason is that improved transportation and communication have increased the ability of service industries to provide services to customers whose residences are far away.

An anomaly in Table 3.5 is that the percentage of agricultural, forestry, and fisheries employment in large SMSAs rose from 11.7 percent
in 1950 to 41 percent in 1980. Only a relatively small part of this increase is due to the expanded urban definition, as can be seen by noting the growth between 1950 and 1970. There was a smaller drop in
SMSA than in total employment in this sector, probably because of three
factors. First, land prices in the rural parts of SMSAs probably increased
relative to prices of other factors of production in agriculture, so SMSA
agriculture became increasingly labor intensive. Second, there was probably a tendency near population centers to substitute production of
labor-intensive agricultural products. Third, nurseries are part of agriculture, and the rise in SMSA employment in agriculture probably reflects
the growth of nurseries in suburbs. Indeed, approximately 10 percent
of agricultural employment takes place in central cities, and another
10 percent in the urbanized portion of suburban rings. Surely this is
almost exclusively nursery and other specialty activities.

Note also that mining is 44.8 percent urban. Like agriculture, approximately 10 percent of mining employment takes place within central cities. This is apparently just an artifact of small numbers; only 1
percent of total employment, and 0.6 percent of SMSA employment,
are in mining.

SMSA Manufacturing Employment

In 1950, manufacturing was by far the largest employer of SMSA
workers, employing 30.5 percent of the urban workforce. In second
place was wholesaling/retailing, employing 20.8 percent. In a virtual
tie for third place were transport, etc., (8.9 percent) and professional
and related services (8.8 percent). By 1970 professional and related services had grown substantially to 18 percent, and manufacturing had
shrunk to 25.8 percent. Manufacturing continued to be the leading urban employer, but its lead over both wholesaling/retailing and professional services was very modest. Nevertheless, the dominance of
manufacturing indicates that it is worth special attention. In this section the manufacturing sector of Table 3.5 is broken down into the various components reported by the census.

Most U.S. federal government industrial statistics now are based on
a consistent industrial classification scheme. The data in Table 3.5 are
based on what is called the *one-digit standard industrial classification* (SIC) *code*. The next level of detail is the two-digit level. For example, all manufacturing industries are in one-digit Groups 2 and 3.
Two-digit numbers are numbers from 20 to 39 that represent 20 more-
detailed categories of manufacturing industries.[5] These two-digit groups
are successively divided into three-, four-, five-, and seven-digit groups.

5. In 1963 a new two-digit industry (ordinance, with SIC Code 19) was added, but
it is not included in the data discussed in this section.

For example, food processing is the two-digit manufacturing industry bearing the SIC Code 20. Within the food-processing category are several three-digit industries, including meat products, given the three-digit Code 201. Within the three-digit meat products category are several four-digit industries, including slaughterhouses, given the four-digit Code 2011. Altogether there are 149 three-digit industries and 427 four-digit industries. There are also five- and seven-digit codes. Disclosure rules limit the detail government agencies can publish. In addition, most five- and seven-digit data are too detailed for economists' purposes. Only at the two-digit level are comprehensive data available for large SMSAs, and even at this level of aggregation the data are not broken down between urban and rural after 1972.

Table 3.6 provides complete two-digit data for manufacturing. The table shows U.S. and large-SMSA employment data for all two-digit manufacturing industries for 1947 and 1972, as well as the national totals for 1982. The set of SMSAs included consists of those with at least 40,000 manufacturing employees. The set contains only about one-third of the SMSAs included in Table 3.5.

It should not be surprising to find that some two-digit manufacturing industries are much more urbanized than others. In 1972 large-SMSA employment ranged from a low of 6.1 percent of total employment in tobacco products to a high of 70.7 percent in printing. Generally, the figures in Table 3.6 confirm what would be predicted based on the location theory described in Chapter 2. Materials-oriented industries would be expected to be less urbanized than market-oriented industries, since markets almost invariably are concentrated in urban areas, while localized materials frequently are available only in rural locations. Of course, to some extent cities would be expected to grow up around materials-oriented manufacturing plants, so a dramatic difference would not be expected in urbanization between materials- and market-oriented industries. The industries starred in Table 3.6 are less urbanized than the average of all industries; with the sole exception of transportation equipment, they are all either definitely or plausibly materials oriented. The more urbanized industries generally are those that process intermediate goods rather than raw materials.

In going from 1972 to 1982 it is not possible to trace the degree of urbanization of the various manufacturing industries. Overall employment trends can be noted, however. Total manufacturing employment fell by 1.2 percent over this period,[6] but there is striking variation across industries. Ten industries suffered more than a 10 percent decline: tobacco; textiles; apparel; lumber products; leather; stone, clay, and glass products; primary metals; and transportation. Seven industries recorded growth: printing, chemicals, petroleum refining, rubber products, nonelectrical machinery, electrical machinery, and instruments. In general, employment shifted to later stages of processing. In

6. The 1982 figure is depressed somewhat by the severe 1981–82 recession.

Table 3.6 *Manufacturing Employment by Industry Group (Employment in thousands)*

Industry	1947 Employment United States	SMSA	Pct. in SMSAs	1972 Employment United States	SMSA	Pct. in SMSAs	1982 United States	1972–82 Pct. Change
Food*	1,442	717	49.7	1,569	764	48.7	1,488	−5.2
Tobacco*	112	33	29.5	66	4	6.1	58	−12.1
Textiles*	1,233	384	31.1	953	327	34.3	717	−24.8
Apparel*	1,082	759	70.1	1,386	721	52.0	1,189	−14.2
Lumber products*	636	87	13.7	691	143	20.7	576	−16.6
Furniture*	322	158	49.1	462	219	47.4	436	−5.6
Paper*	450	207	46.0	633	300	47.4	606	−4.3
Printing	715	511	71.5	1,056	747	70.7	1,291	22.3
Chemicals	632	370	58.5	837	482	57.6	872	4.2
Petroleum refining*	212	133	62.7	140	68	48.6	151	7.9
Rubber products	259	176	68.0	618	342	55.3	682	10.4
Leather*	383	159	41.5	273	84	30.8	200	−26.7
Stone, clay, and glass products*	462	203	43.9	623	305	49.0	531	−14.8
Primary metals	1,157	839	72.5	1,143	727	63.6	854	−25.3
Fabricated metals	971	698	71.9	1,493	1,001	67.0	1,460	−2.2
Nonelectrical machinery	1,545	1,018	65.9	1,828	1,107	60.6	2,189	19.7
Elect. machinery	801	614	76.7	1,662	974	58.6	1,915	15.2
Transportation equipment*	1,182	901	76.2	1,719	747	43.5	1,596	−7.2
Instruments	232	184	79.3	454	257	56.6	624	37.4
Miscellaneous	464	339	73.1	446	296	66.4	383	−14.1
Total	14,292	8,490	59.4%	18,052	9,615	53.3%	17,818	−1.3%

Sources: Data from U.S. Department of Commerce, Bureau of the Census. *Census of Manufactures.* Washington, D.C.: Government Printing Office, 1947, 1973, and 1983.

part this is due to the tendency to do more complicated things with primary materials (noted in Chapter 2); in part it is because earlier production stages have increasingly been carried out in other countries. The United States, with its literate and skilled labor force, has a comparative advantage in the later, more complicated stages of production.

Table 3.6 shows a drop of 6 points in the percentage of manufacturing employment in large SMSAs from 1947–1972. This finding is in contrast to Table 3.5, which shows a slight increase in the percentage of manufacturing employment in large SMSAs. Neither the years nor the SMSAs are the same in the two tables. Table 3.5, which represents the larger set of SMSAs, shows that the percentage of manufacturing employment in SMSAs has been stagnant, whereas the percentage of the population in SMSAs has grown. The contrast between Tables 3.5 and 3.6 shows a dramatic shift of manufacturing from large to smaller SMSAs.

If changes in urbanization among particular two-digit industries are considered, an interesting pattern emerges. The percentage of employment in large SMSAs fell in most two-digit industries and in those employing most manufacturing workers. The percentage fell in 16 of the 20 two-digit industries. In 1947, the 16 industries employed 89.6 percent of manufacturing workers in large SMSAs and 80.5 percent of manufacturing workers in the United States. Furthermore, the percentage decreases are much larger in the industries that became less urbanized than in the industries that became more urbanized.

How did most manufacturing industries become substantially less urbanized at a time when the total changed relatively little? This apparent paradox occurs frequently in economics statistics and merits exploring. Although it did not happen, it is logically possible for urbanization to decrease in every manufacturing industry at a time when urbanization increases in total manufacturing employment. An example will make this phenomenon clear. Suppose a country has two industries, A and B, and that SMSA and total employment data for Years 1 and 2 are as shown in Table 3.7. Between Years 1 and 2, urbanization decreased from 80 to 71 percent in Industry A and from 20 to 7 percent in Industry B. Yet urbanization of total employment increased from 50 to 52 percent. This peculiar pattern is made possible by a shift in employment in the direction of the more highly urbanized industry. Thus, even though a smaller percentage of workers is in SMSAs in Year 2 than in Year 1 in each industry, the percentage of all workers in SMSAs has increased, because the more urbanized industry employs a larger percentage of all workers in Year 2 than in Year 1.

A less extreme form of the phenomenon is illustrated in Table 3.6. In 1947, 39.7 percent of manufacturing employees were in two-digit industries whose urbanization was below the national average of 59.4 percent. By 1972 these particular industries employed only 33.9 percent of manufacturing employees. Thus, as in Table 3.7, manufacturing employment has shifted in the direction of relatively urbanized two-digit industries.

So much for the apparent statistical paradox. Why did employment shift toward the more highly urbanized industries? Once again, this is predictable based upon the location theory presented in Chapter 2. Technical change is pervasive and rapid in manufacturing. An inevitable characteristic of technical progress is an increase in the number of processing stages through which raw materials go before they reach the final consumer. Indeed, the Industrial Revolution itself imposed the factory between the farmer as producer and the farmer as consumer. Current technical change continues to create further stages of raw material processing. The greater the number of processing stages, the greater the number of workers who will be found in those two-digit

Table 3.7 *Increasing/Decreasing Urbanization*

	Year 1			Year 2		
Industry	National Employment	SMSA Employment	Percentage in SMSA	National Employment	SMSA Employment	Percentage in SMSA
A	25	20	80%	35	25	71%
B	25	5	20	15	1	7
Total	50	25	50%	50	26	52%

industries representing later processing stages. As has been seen, however, industries engaged in later stages of processing are precisely those that are not tied to locations near predominantly rural sources of raw materials.

Increased fabrication of raw materials explains the shift of employment toward urbanized two-digit industries, but it does not explain the decreased urbanization of these industries. All two-digit industries have substantial employment outside urban areas. There is no reason to expect that the percentage of employment in large SMSAs will remain constant in any industry. Nevertheless, the particular pattern of decreased urbanization of the most highly urbanized industries calls for study and explanation.

There are, of course, special explanations for changes in particular industries. The decreased urbanization of the textile industry is part of the migration of that industry from New England to predominantly rural parts of the South. This movement has been extensively studied. Decreased urbanization in the apparel industry is explained partly by the movement of that industry out of New York City. There undoubtedly are reasons peculiar to other industries, but it would be interesting to know the importance of factors that are common to most industries.

The pattern observed in this section is one of rather modest increases since World War II in the percentages of population, total employment, and manufacturing employment found in SMSAs. However, there is evidence in all three categories of a slowing down in urbanization. At the same time, there has been a dramatic trend away from manufacturing, particularly at early stages of production, and toward service employment. No one knows what future censuses will show, but it seems likely that the trends since 1940 will persist during the remainder of the twentieth century.

☐ Summary

In less than 200 years, the United States has been transformed from a country in which 95 percent of the population is rural to one in which three-fourths is urban. In broad outlines, the transformation has been associated with dramatic decreases in agricultural employment and with industrialization of the economy. Since about 1920 urbanization has proceeded steadily, even though the percentage of the labor force in manufacturing has remained roughly constant.

There is great variation in the extent of urbanization among industries. Manufacturing is more urbanized than most industries but less urbanized than many service industries. Within manufacturing, industries that process raw materials are the least urbanized, whereas those that process materials previously processed are more urbanized. Since World War II there has been a shift in manufacturing employment toward more highly urbanized industries but a decrease in urban location in most manufacturing industries.

Questions and Problems

1. Do you think manufacturing will be less urbanized in 2000 than it is now? Why?

2. What part of the population do you think will live in SMSAs in 2000? Do you expect the service sector to urbanize more rapidly than the total population during the remainder of the century?

3. In the late 1970s about two-thirds of the population of industrialized countries was urban, whereas only about one-third of the population of less-developed countries was urban. How will these figures change by the end of the century?

4. In many industrialized countries, a larger fraction of the nonfarm population is urban than in the United States. How would you explain that fact?

References and Further Reading

Davis, Kingsley. "The Urbanization of Human Populations." *Scientific American* 213, no. 3 (1965): 41–53. A provocative survey of long-term trends in urbanization in industrialized and less-developed countries.

Handlin, Oscar, and John Burchard, eds. *The Historian and the City* (Cambridge, Mass.: MIT, 1963). Papers by historians and other scholars on urban history.

McNeill, William H. *Plagues and Peoples* (Garden City, N.Y.: Doubleday, 1976). This fascinating book discusses the role of disease (particularly communicable and epidemic disease) in shaping world history. The book makes a compelling argument that the process of urbanization was profoundly influenced by the relationship between man and disease-causing microorganisms.

Perloff, Harvey, et al. *Regions, Resources and Economic Growth* (Baltimore: Johns Hopkins, 1960). An influential study of the causes and consequences of regional shifts in population and production.

Thernstrom, Stephan, and Richard Sennett, eds. *Nineteenth-Century Cities* (New Haven: Yale, 1969). Fascinating historical essays on life in nineteenth-century cities.

4

Trends in Sizes and Structures of Urban Areas

☐ The first three chapters presented the broad outlines of trends in the urbanization of people and jobs during 200 years of American history. This chapter completes the historical survey by discussing two other important characteristics of urbanization: the sizes of urban areas and suburbanization.

Urban areas vary enormously in total population. Many millions of people live in the largest metropolitan areas; only a few hundred inhabit each of dozens of small towns. Documenting and explaining the facts has been a favorite pastime of urban specialists for decades. With significant qualifications, the facts are easy to obtain. Total populations of cities are published by more national censuses and for more years than are almost any other data except for national population totals. The important qualification is that the most common data are populations of legal cities, and it has been seen that these often do not include the entire urban area. Persuasive explanations of the observed data are much more difficult to find. This chapter concentrates mainly on the data; comments on explanations are reserved for Chapter 15.

Also important, but outside the scope of economics, is the effect of the size of the urban area on attitudes and lifestyles. Life in New York City or Los Angeles differs in many ways from life in Broken Bow, Nebraska, or Monroeville, Alabama. Anyone raised in one place or the other is forever stamped by the experience. In terms of economists' measures, however, such differences are less important than they once were. Incomes are lower in small towns than in metropolitan areas, but living standards vary less by size of urban area than they did in earlier times. The kinds and brands of products purchased and the work done also differ much less from place to place than in the past.

Suburbanization refers generically to the dispersion of population from the centers to the peripheries of urban areas. People in the United States associate the phenomenon with the outward movement of people across central-city boundaries. This is indeed an important aspect of the phenomenon. It profoundly affects the ways local governments function in urban areas. This public finance aspect of the issue will be analyzed in Chapter 13. The generic notion of suburbanization, or dispersion of population, however, does not depend on the locations of central-city boundaries. Careful measurement of the phenomenon will be discussed in Chapter 15. This chapter relies on jurisdictional data.

However measured, suburbanization is one of the most pervasive and important urban phenomena of the twentieth century. It is pervasive in that it has been important in all industrialized countries and has proceeded since at least the beginning of this century—and since well before that, at least in countries where the phenomenon is documented. Thus, the first lesson about suburbanization is to stop thinking of it as exclusively a post-World War II American phenomenon resulting from racial turmoil, high taxes, and poor public schools in central cities. The phenomenon also occurs when and where these causes are absent. They are undoubtedly important in the American context, but are hardly fundamental causes.

Nevertheless, suburbanization has proceeded far in postwar urban areas in the United States. The final task of this chapter is to trace this process and to point out some of its implications.

☐ SIZES OF U.S. URBAN AREAS

The two most important measures of the size of an urban area are its total population and its total land area. The former is more important and better documented than the latter. In this section, the size of an urban area always refers to its total population.

The primary characteristic of the sizes of urban areas is diversity. In most countries large enough to have more than a few urban areas, the largest urban areas are 100 or 1000 times (two or three orders of magnitude) as large as the smallest. In the United States, the largest urban area is the New York City CMSA, with about 17 million inhabitants. It is approximately ten times as big as the twentieth-ranked SMSA, San Diego, and fifty times as big as the one-hundredth-ranked SMSA, Little Rock. The world's largest urban area is the Tokyo metropolitan area, with about 25 million residents, half again as big as New York.

Table 4.1 provides data on sizes of selected American cities at twenty-year intervals from 1790 to 1970, plus figures for 1980 and 1984. The table contains data for the ten cities that were largest in 1980 and for a few other cities. The left-hand column shows each city's rank in 1980. The data refer to legal cities, not urban areas, but the distinction is generally unimportant before World War II. Even with the restricted number of cities included in the table, the great range of sizes can be seen. The tenth-largest city in 1980, Baltimore, is just over 10 percent as large as the largest city, New York City.

Although all cities in the table grew a great deal during the country's history, there is great persistence in rankings. New York City was the nation's largest city in 1790 and has been ever since. Chicago, the nation's second-largest city until 1984, occupied that rank for about 100 years. Ranks do change, but slowly. Philadelphia was the second largest city in 1790, but it fell to third place about a century ago and to fourth place after World War II. In 1790 Baltimore was the fourth-largest city (it moved up briefly to second in 1840); it was seventh in 1970 and tenth in 1980. Los Angeles, Dallas, Houston, and Miami are relative newcomers to the ranks of large cities and have moved up in rank rapidly during the twentieth century. San Diego moved from fourteenth to eighth position between 1970 and 1980, and Phoenix, from twentieth to ninth.[1] The only cities to move up a rank between 1980 and 1984 were Houston, which overtook Philadelphia for fourth place, and Los Angeles.

Although cities change ranks only slowly, there is even greater persistence in the relative sizes of cities of particular ranks. The largest city may continue to be twice as large as the second-largest city, even though the ranks come to be occupied by different cities. In fact, New York City was 2.28 times as large as the second-largest city in 1870 and 2.34 times as large as the second-largest city a century later in 1970, although a different city had come to occupy second place. More will be said about the relative sizes of cities of different ranks at the end of this section.

The final important observation about the data in Table 4.1 is that a majority of the cities included had population declines between 1950 and 1980; the decade of the 1970s accounted for most of the decline. Note that most of the cities which suffered population decline in the 1970s continued to do so during the early 1980s, though for almost all of these cities the rate of decline was much smaller than during the '70s. (Note that the rate of decline for 1980–1984 is for only a four-year period; to compare these rates with those reported for the 1970s, multiply by 2.5.) It is also worth noting that population decline during the 1970s was concentrated in the Northeast and North Central regions. Though this pattern continued in the early 1980s, New York and Boston bucked the trend. Chapter 15 discusses the economic causes and consequences of these facts.

---

1. Chapter 1 emphasized that historical accident is an inadequate explanation for the location and growth of urban areas. Nevertheless, accident does play some role, as can be seen by looking at the population figures for Baltimore and Philadelphia in 1850 and 1870. In 1850 the Baltimore and Ohio Railroad had put Baltimore well ahead of Philadelphia in the race to be the leading mid-Atlantic port. During the Civil War, however, pro-South Baltimore was occupied by federal troops and Philadelphia moved ahead and has remained so ever since.

Table 4.1 Population of Selected Cities for Selected Years, 1790 to 1984 (Population in thousands)

	Rank 1980	Rank 1970	Population 1790	1810	1830	1850	1870	1890	1910	1930	1950	1970	1980	Percentage Change 1970–80	Population 1984	Percentage Change 1980–84
New York City	1	1	49	120	242	696	1,478	2,507	4,767	6,930	7,892	7,895	7,071	−10.4	7,165	1.3
Chicago	2	2				30	299	1,100	2,185	3,376	3,621	3,367	3,005	−10.8	2,992	−0.4
Los Angeles	3	3				2	6	50	319	1,238	1,970	2,816	2,967	5.4	3,097	4.4
Philadelphia	4	4	29	54	80	121	647	1,047	1,549	1,951	2,072	1,949	1,688	−13.4	1,647	−2.4
Houston	5	6				2	9	28	79	292	596	1,233	1,594	29.3	1,706	7.0
Detroit	6	5		2	2	21	80	206	466	1,569	1,849	1,511	1,203	−20.4	1,089	−9.5
Dallas	7	8						38	92	260	434	844	904	7.1	974	7.7
San Diego	8	14										697	876	25.7	960	9.6
Phoenix	9	20										582	790	35.7	853	8.0
Baltimore	10	7	14	47	81	169	267	434	558	805	950	906	787	−13.1	764	−2.9
Washington, D.C.	15	9		8	19	40	109	189	331	487	802	757	638	−15.7	623	−2.4
Cleveland	18	10			1	17	93	261	561	900	915	751	574	−23.6	547	−4.7
Boston	20	16	18	34	61	137	251	448	671	781	801	641	563	−12.2	571	1.4
Pittsburgh	30	24		5	13	47	86	239	534	670	677	520	424	−18.5	403	−5.0
Miami	41	42							5	111	249	335	347	3.6	373	7.5

Sources: Data from U.S. Department of Commerce, Bureau of the Census. *Census of Population.* Washington, D.C.: Government Printing Office, 1972 and 1982; and *1987 Statistical Abstract of the United States.*

Population decreases in central cities have been common during the postwar period, reflecting in part massive suburbanization and interurban migration. Even metropolitan areas that have grown rapidly throughout the postwar period have had declining central cities. Chicago is an example. In fact, many central cities that have recorded postwar growth have done so by annexing land adjacent to the city as population grows. Annexation is especially common in southwestern states (for example, Texas). The tendency to annex land in certain regions of the country makes comparisons difficult. The subject of suburbanization and its measurement will be discussed at the end of the chapter. Central-city population loss will be examined in Chapter 15.

As has been pointed out, comprehensive SMSA data are available only since 1940. Table 4.2 shows rank and population of each of the ten largest SMSAs for 1950, 1970, 1980, and 1985. Ranks of SMSAs are of greater interest than are ranks of central cities, since SMSAs correspond more nearly to the notion of the generic urban area. Table 4.2 also indicates considerable stability of ranks, at least during the relatively brief period covered. New York City was the largest SMSA throughout the period. Chicago and Los Angeles switched places between 1950 and 1970. Philadelphia and Detroit retained their ranks. Four of the five smallest SMSAs in 1950 lost rank by 1980. One—San Francisco—rose. Cleveland dropped out of the ten largest SMSAs by 1970, whereas Washington, D.C., entered. By 1980 Houston and Dallas were among the top ten. Between 1980 and 1985, only two of the SMSAs lost population—New York and Detroit. In the case of New York, the population loss occurred outside New York City.

What Table 4.1 showed for cities, Table 4.2 shows for SMSAs: there is greater persistence in the relative sizes of SMSAs of given ranks than in the identities of the SMSAs that occupy those ranks. New York City was 1.85 times as large as the second-largest SMSA in 1950 and 1.65 times as large in 1970. By 1980, however, it was only 1.21 times larger than the second largest. The regional shifts underlying this convergence were discussed in Chapter 2. Likewise, the fifth-largest SMSA was 1.78 times as large as the tenth largest in 1950, 1.65 times larger in 1970, and 1.58 times larger in 1980. In fact, these ratios suggest that the largest SMSAs have grown less rapidly than somewhat smaller SMSAs during the postwar period. In particular, New York City lost ground to its nearest competitors during the 1970s. The SMSA data understate the size differences between the top three metropolitan areas (most particularly, New York City and Los Angeles) on the one hand and the others in Table 4.2 on the other. Each of the top three SMSAs is part of a larger urban area, designated a *CMSA* (see Chapter 1). The New York City CMSA includes Jersey City, Newark, and their suburbs; the Chicago CMSA includes Gary; and the Los Angeles CMSA includes Long Beach. Whenever the CMSA population differs from the SMSA population, the latter figure is also given for 1985.

Table 4.2 Rank and Population of the Ten Largest SMSAs, 1950 to 1985 (Population in thousands)

Rank	SMSA	1950 Population	SMSA	1970 Population	SMSA	1980 Population	1985 Estimated Population	Percentage Growth 1980–85	1985 CMSA Population
1	New York City	9,556	New York City	11,572	New York City	9,120	8,466	−7.2	17,931
2	Chicago	5,178	Los Angeles	7,032	Los Angeles	7,478	8,109	8.4	12,738
3	Los Angeles	4,152	Chicago	6,979	Chicago	6,060	6,177	1.9	8,085
4	Philadelphia	3,671	Philadelphia	4,818	Philadelphia	4,717	4,784	1.4	5,776
5	Detroit	3,016	Detroit	4,200	Detroit	4,488	4,319	−3.8	4,581
6	Boston	2,414	San Francisco	3,110	San Francisco	3,241	3,464	6.9	5,809
7	Pittsburgh	2,213	Washington, D.C.	2,861	Washington, D.C.	3,251	3,490	7.4	–
8	San Francisco	2,136	Boston	2,754	Dallas	2,931	3,512	19.8	–
9	St. Louis	1,755	Pittsburgh	2,401	Houston	2,736	3,222	17.8	3,623
10	Cleveland	1,533	St. Louis	2,363	Boston	2,806	2,832	0.9	4,051

Sources: Data from U.S. Department of Commerce, Bureau of the Census. *Census of Population.* suppl. report P180-S1-5. Washington, D.C.: Government Printing Office, 1972 and 1982; and *1987 Statistical Abstract of the United States.*

☐ ESTIMATES OF SMSA SIZE DISTRIBUTIONS

The best way to think systematically about sizes of urban areas is to think of them as a frequency distribution. Urban area sizes can be arrayed in various categories, just as a frequency distribution of incomes or of almost any economic variable can be displayed. Such frequency distributions are published in every population census. It has been shown that the size distribution of cities or SMSAs is characterized by a small number of very large cities or SMSAs and a much larger number of small cities or SMSAs. In other words, the frequency decreases continuously as sizes of urban areas increase. Such distributions are said to be "skewed to the right." They contrast with the more familiar normal, or Gaussian, distribution, which is symmetrical around its highest point. Many economic variables have been found to follow distributions that are skewed to the right: incomes, firm sizes, and urban area sizes. Statisticians and economists have studied carefully the properties of several such distributions.

The distribution most commonly employed to study urban sizes is the **Pareto distribution.** It can be written as follows:

$$G(x) = Ax^{-a}, \tag{4.1}$$

where $G(x)$ is the number of urban areas with at least x people, and A and a are constants to be estimated from the data. Thus, $G(x)$ is the rank of an urban area with x people. For some reason, the Pareto distribution usually is written as in Equation (4.1), a cumulative distribution, cumulated from the top. That is, $G(x)$ is the number of observations *at least as large as x,* whereas the usual way to write a cumulative distribution is the number of observations *at least as small as x.*

Scholars in many disciplines have estimated Equation (4.1) from data on urban populations taken from American and many other national censuses. Frequently, a is estimated to be about 1. Then the Pareto distribution can be written as follows:

$$G(x) = Ax^{-1}, \tag{4.2}$$

which is known as the **rank-size rule.** Putting $G(x) = 1$, we see that $x = A$; that is, A is the population of the largest urban area. Multiplying both sides of Equation (4.2) by x,

$$xG(x) = A. \tag{4.3}$$

That is, the product of an urban area's rank and population is a constant equal to the population of the largest urban area. Thus, the rank-size rule implies that the second-largest urban area is half the size of the largest, that the third-largest urban area is one-third the size of the largest, and so on. There is no theoretical reason to expect the rank-size rule to hold with precision for urban sizes. However, it is such a simple distribution that it is remarkable how close the fit is for urban area sizes in very different countries and at many different times in history.

An indication of the accuracy of the rank-size rule can be obtained from the data in Table 4.3. The table shows the population, rank, and rank times population for every tenth entry in the census list by size of urbanized areas for 1980. Do those data confirm or refute the rank-size rule? Of course, no theory in economics is exactly confirmed by significant bodies of evidence. The most that can be hoped for is that deviations of actual from theoretical values are small and random.

There is a tendency for the product of rank and size of urbanized areas in the table to cluster, and the average of the entries in the last column is 18,411. There are also substantial and apparently systematic departures. The smallest entries are at the top and bottom of the column. Entries rise smoothly from the top to the third entry, and they fall almost continuously after the sixth entry. The best way to test the rank-size rule is to return to the Pareto distribution, Equation (4.1). Take logs of both sides:

$$\log G(x) = \log A - a \log x. \tag{4.4}$$

The Pareto distribution can be estimated by computing the least squares regression of Equation (4.4).[2] Equation (4.5) presents an estimate of Equation (4.4) calculated, not from the data in Table 4.3, but from the full census list of ranks and populations of the 366 urbanized areas:

$$\log G(x) = 6.833 - 0.905 \log x. \qquad R^2 = 0.99.$$
$$(0.025) \quad (0.005) \tag{4.5}$$

The numbers in parentheses are estimated standard errors of the coefficients above them. In a sample as large as this one, the probability is less than 0.05 that the true and estimated coefficients differ by at least as much as twice the standard deviation. R^2 in Equation (4.5) is the squared correlation coefficient between $\log G(x)$ and $\log x$. The reported R^2 means that the regression equation explains 99 percent of the variance of $\log G(x)$.

Two important observations should be made about Equation (4.5). First, the Pareto distribution provides a very accurate description of the distribution of population sizes of urbanized areas. An R^2 of 0.99 means that the data all lie very close to the estimated Pareto distribution. It is remarkable that, in country after country and in decade after decade, the Pareto distribution fits urban area size distribution data so well. Second, the rank-size rule (the special case of the Pareto distribution where $a = 1$) can be rejected for the U.S. 1980 data. The previous paragraph implies that the true value of a is unlikely to be above 0.915, or $0.905 + 2(.005)$. That is still well below the unit value of a implied by the rank-size rule.

---

2. Least squares regression means using as estimates of $\log A$ and a values that minimize the sum of squared differences between values of $\log G(x)$ calculated from Equation (4.4) and those in a sample of data. See Appendix B for a more detailed discussion of regression analysis.

Table 4.3 *Population and Rank of a Sample of U.S. Urbanized Areas, 1980*

Urbanized Area	Rank	Population (thousands)	Rank × Population
New York-Northeastern New Jersey	1	15,590	15,590
St. Louis, Missouri	11	1,849	20,335
Denver, Colorado	21	1,352	28,394
Indianapolis, Indiana	31	836	25,932
Salt Lake City, Utah	41	674	27,642
Omaha, Nebraska	51	512	26,132
Las Vegas, Nevada	61	433	26,407
Oxnard, California	71	378	26,817
Wichita, Kansas	81	306	24,770
Des Moines, Iowa	91	267	24,315
Fort Wayne, Indiana	101	236	23,887
Lawrence, Massachusetts	111	211	23,465
Eugene, Oregon	121	182	22,083
Winston-Salem, North Carolina	131	172	22,467
Aurora, Illinois	141	159	22,405
Amarillo, Texas	151	149	22,529
Poughkeepsie, New York	161	137	21,993
Topeka, Kansas	171	126	21,529
Lakeland, Florida	181	114	20,706
Gastonia, North Carolina	191	107	20,418
Asheville, North Carolina	201	102	20,582
Laredo, Texas	211	95	20,024
Kingsport, Tennessee	221	90	19,846
Fort Walton Beach, Florida	231	85	19,704
St. Joseph, Missouri	241	80	19,256
Steubenville, Ohio	251	78	19,503
Jacksonville, North Carolina	261	73	19,027
Fairfield, California	271	69	18,780
Monessen, Pennsylvania	281	66	18,518
Parkersburg, West Virginia	291	63	18,362
Bismarck, North Dakota	301	61	18,391
Visalia, California	311	59	18,318
Santa Maria, California	321	57	18,361
Warner Robins, Georgia	331	55	18,172
Redding, California	341	53	18,039
Janesville, Wisconsin	351	52	18,112
Rock Hill, South Carolina	361	51	18,339

Source: Data from U.S. Department of Commerce, Bureau of the Census. *Census of Population.* Washington, D.C.: Government Printing Office, 1982.

The estimated value of a of 0.905 in Equation (4.5) means that populations of urbanized areas far down in the size distribution are smaller than is indicated by the rank-size rule. This is a reflection of the fact that, in moving down most of the final column in Table 4.3, the product of rank and population falls. Unfortunately, few countries have measures of urban size as good as those provided by the U.S. urbanized area data. In a recent study employing data on legal cities, Rosen and Resnick (1980) estimated Pareto distributions of city sizes for all countries in the world that had a substantial number of cities and published the needed data. Their estimated value of a for the United States was somewhat above the average estimated a in the worldwide sample, indicating that city sizes are somewhat more evenly distributed here than in most countries. Nevertheless, the most important of Rosen and Resnick's findings from the U.S. data was that America's city sizes are distributed in a manner typical of many countries.

Chapter 1 discussed the gradual relaxation of technological and economic constraints on the sizes of urban areas. The skewed size distribution of urban areas revealed in Table 4.2 and Equation (4.5) indicates that only a small number of urban areas have fully exploited the possibilities for urban growth that were created by this technical progress. This is to be expected. One of the improvements that has permitted growth of cities has been in long-distance goods transport. As long-distance transport (both of city exports and of food from farms) became cheaper, it became feasible to concentrate some activities in only a small number of widely dispersed urban areas. Urban areas vary in size because variations in scale economies, density of demand, and transport cost mean that the optimum market area is larger for some goods than others.

☐ SUBURBANIZATION

Despite its familiarity, suburbanization is not really a simple concept. As has been stated, people in the United States tend to think of it in terms of numbers or percentages of people living or working in central-city and suburban jurisdictions of urban areas. The concept, however, is more basic than locations of jurisdictional boundaries. A basic definition is that an urban area is more *suburbanized* the more dispersed are residences and jobs around the center of the urban area. This definition does not rely on jurisdictional boundaries but still admits of several possible quantitative measures of the concept.

Jurisdictional measurements of suburbanization are unavailable in most countries because central-city boundaries are moved out as population expands, thus keeping all or nearly all the urban area within the boundaries of the central city. During the period of rapid urban growth in the nineteenth century, it was common to expand central-city boundaries as population expanded, even in the United States. In the twentieth century, the process of boundary movement stopped in much of this country, thus permitting the measurement of suburbanization by concentration of people and jobs in central-city and suburban jurisdictions. By this measure, an urban area is said to have suburbanized between Years 1 and 2 if a larger percentage of the urban area's residents lived or worked in suburban jurisdictions in Year 2 than in Year 1. That measure will be exploited in this section. Data are easily available and, for that reason, jurisdictional measures of suburbanization almost always are used in popular discussions of the subject in newspapers and magazines. More sophisticated measures will be introduced in Chapter 15 after their theoretical basis has been laid in intervening chapters.

It is important to keep in mind several limitations of jurisdictional measures as they are discussed in this section. First, jurisdictional measures do not permit careful cross-sectional comparisons. If one urban area has a larger percentage of its population living or working in the central city than another, it may indicate no more than where central-city boundaries happen to have been drawn many decades ago. Second, even time-series comparisons are imprecise, because some central-city boundaries still are moved outward as population and employment expand, especially in the South and Southwest. Each census presents population data within central-city boundaries as they existed at the time of the previous census, but making the comparison among several decades is laborious and approximate.

Table 4.4 contains some comprehensive data on postwar suburbanization, making use of jurisdictional data. Keep in mind that the data understate postwar suburbanization, since they do not take into account boundary movements. The problem of differing central-city boundary locations was avoided by basing Table 4.4 on the same set of SMSAs for each year included. The SMSAs included are the 168 SMSAs defined by the census in 1950, less the SMSAs in the three CMSAs that had been defined by 1970. The reason for eliminating the CMSAs is that one SMSA may in a sense be a suburb of another SMSA within a CMSA. The exclusions leave 135 SMSAs, which contained nearly two-thirds of the total SMSA population in 1970. The 1980 numbers are based on a subsample of eighteen of the SMSAs that make up the sample for the previous years.

Despite the limitations of the data, Table 4.4 shows the massive suburbanization that has taken place in the United States since World War II. In 1950, 57.3 percent of the residents of the metropolitan areas included in the table lived in central cities. The percentage fell to 49.2 in 1960, 43.1 by 1970, and 39.9 by 1980.

The employment data included in Table 4.4 are incomplete. Some private service jobs are excluded from the service category included in the table, but the most important exclusion is government service employment. Government employment is probably more concentrated in central cities than total employment, so its exclusion may give an

Table 4.4 Suburbanization of Population and Employment in Selected SMSAs, 1950 to 1980

	1950		1960		1970		1980	
	Central City	Suburban Ring	Central City	Suburban Ring	Central City	Suburban Ring	Central City	Suburban Ring
Population	57.3%	42.7%	49.2%	50.8%	43.1%	56.9%	39.89%	60.11%
Employment[a]								
Manufacturing	63.3	36.7	56.5	43.5	51.0	49.0	46.15	53.85
Retailing	74.4	25.6	65.3	34.7	52.2	47.8	46.64	53.36
Service	80.8	19.2	75.2	24.8	64.2	35.8	58.25	41.75
Wholesaling	87.1	12.9	80.4	19.6	65.5	34.5	57.33	42.67
Total	70.1%	29.9%	63.1%	36.9%	54.6%	45.4%	49.54%	50.46%

[a]Employment data are from 1977 for a random sample of 18 SMSAs. Employment data are averages of data for census years from the relevant employment census.
Sources: Data from the following publications of the U.S. Department of Commerce. Bureau of the Census, Washington, D.C.: Census of Population, 1950, 1960, 1972, and 1982; Census of Manufactures, 1947, 1954, 1958, 1963, 1967, 1972, and 1977; Census of Business, 1948, 1954, 1958, 1963, and 1967; Census of Retail Trade, 1972 and 1977; Census of Selected Service Industries, 1972 and 1977; and Census of Wholesale Trade, 1972 and 1977.

exaggerated impression of employment suburbanization in the table.

Employment is less suburbanized than population, as expected. Like population, employment has become much more suburbanized during the postwar period. In 1950, 70.1 percent of jobs in the metropolitan areas included in Table 4.4 were in central cities. By 1970, the percentage fell to 54.6. By the 1977 census, employment was almost evenly divided between central cities and suburbs.

In employment sectors, manufacturing and retailing are the most suburbanized, with services and wholesaling being much less suburbanized. None of the employment sectors is as suburbanized as population, however. All four employment sectors have suburbanized a great deal since 1950. By one measure, the four employment sectors have come to be more nearly equally suburbanized since 1950. In 1950 almost 24 percentage points separated the percentage of jobs in central cities in the wholesaling and manufacturing sectors. By 1977 the range was just over 11 percent. This implies that postwar suburbanization has been most rapid in the employment sectors that were least suburbanized in 1950.

A final point worth noting regards the suburbanization of jobs and people. Between 1950 and 1980 the fraction of people living in suburbs increased by 17.4 percent. Over the same period, the fraction of jobs in the suburbs increased by 20.5 points. The suburbanization of jobs has been modestly faster than that of people, suggesting a slight reduction in central-city jobs per capita over the postwar period.

There are two crucial aspects of employment decentralization which are not evident from Table 4.4. First, note that manufacturing fell from 63.3 percent in the central city (1950) to only 46.2 percent in the central city in 1980. Since manufacturing is the largest urban sector, this represents a massive loss of central-city jobs. Second, concealed within the service sector is an industry which has enjoyed extremely rapid growth in central cities. This industry can be categorized as "information processing."[3] It includes legal, financial, banking, and other professional services. As can be seen in Table 4.5, this industry has grown so fast that it is by far the leading employer in each of the sample cities (bear in mind that these cities are old-line *manufacturing* cities). For these central cities, manufacturing and construction together are only about half as big as information processing. During precisely the time when manufacturing has been fleeing to the suburbs, information processing has been racing to central cities (and to central business districts in particular).

The reasons for these moves are not hard to find. Before the days of trucks and electricity, manufacturing was tied very tightly to railheads (the city core). Neither coal nor the steam power produced from it could

---

3.   In the accompanying Table 4.5, "information processing" is defined as service industries excluding government, for which more than half of the employees hold executive, managerial, professional, or secretarial positions.

Table 4.5 *Central-City Employment in Three U.S. Cities, by Sector, 1953, 1970, and 1980 (Figures in thousands)*

Central City and Sector	Number of Jobs			Percentage of Total		
	1953	1970	1980	1953	1970	1980
New York						
Total employment[a]	2,977	3,350	2,866	100	100	100
Agriculture and mining	5	5	5	*	*	*
Manufacturing and construction	1,176	971	650	40	29	23
Retail and wholesale	805	779	596	27	23	20
Selected services						
Information processing[b]	646	1,172	1,302	22	35	45
Other services	344	424	314	12	13	11
Philadelphia						
Total employment[a]	788	772	628	100	100	100
Agriculture and mining	0.7	0.7	0.5	*	*	*
Manufacturing and construction	398	291	171	50	38	27
Retail and wholesale	206	180	134	26	23	22
Selected services						
Information processing[b]	98	220	271	12	28	43
Other services	85	81	52	12	10	8
Boston (Suffolk County)						
Total employment[a]	402	465	437	100	100	100
Agriculture and mining	2	0.9	0.5	*	*	*
Manufacturing and construction	130	105	77	32	22	17
Retail and wholesale	132	111	82	32	24	19
Selected services						
Information processing[b]	87	194	232	22	42	53
Other services	51	55	46	13	12	10

*Less than 1.
[a]Total classified employment and industry subcategories, excluding government employees and sole proprietors.
[b]Service industries (excluding government, retail, and wholesale) in which more than one-half the employees hold executive, managerial, professional, or clerical positions.
Source: U.S. Bureau of the Census, *County Business Patterns*, selected years, and 1970 and 1980 *Occupation by Industry* statistics. Figures are rounded.

readily be transported from the railhead; in addition the nineteenth-century transport network was designed to deliver the workforce to the railhead. All of this changed with the advent of electric power, the auto, the truck, and the declining energy intensity of manufacturing.[4] These changes weakened the advantages of central locations for manufacturing, and allowed manufacturing to take advantage of some real benefits offered by suburban locations, the most important of which were cheap land and an escape from narrow streets which were laid

4. Energy intensity has declined due to technical progress and also because we do more complicated things with raw materials, which require more processing but less energy. See the discussion of steel production in Chapter 2.

out before the era of the car and truck. Cheap and plentiful land is important because with modern manufacturing techniques one-story plants offer tremendous advantages.

Suburbanization has been among the most dramatic and widely discussed phenomena of recent history. Analyzing its causes and consequences will occupy a large part of both the theoretical and applied chapters of this book. This section has presented only the crudest measures of suburbanization, but they are adequate to show that it has occurred on a large scale.

☐ Summary

This chapter has reviewed trends in the sizes and structures of urban areas. There is great persistence in the ranks of metropolitan areas and even more persistence in the relative populations of metropolitan areas that occupy particular ranks in the metropolitan size distribution. The Pareto distribution closely approximates the metropolitan size distribution for many countries and times in history. Furthermore, the exponents of the Pareto distribution cluster around 1.

The decentralization of residences and employment around the centers of metropolitan areas is also characteristic of many countries and many times in history. Metropolitan dispersion has proceeded especially far and fast in post-World War II American metropolitan areas, which by 1970 were probably as dispersed as metropolitan areas anywhere in the world.

Questions and Problems

1. Find out what government data are available on incomes, prices, and consumption patterns for particular metropolitan areas. What additional data do you think the government should collect and publish?

2. Would you expect greater persistence in relative sizes of central cities or of SMSAs of particular ranks?

3. Would you expect the exponent in the Pareto distribution of metropolitan populations to become larger or smaller as time passes? Why?

4. Do you think employment suburbanization has caused population suburbanization or vice versa? What do you think has caused whichever movement you think caused the other?

5. Which regions of the country do you think have the most suburbanized metropolitan areas? Why? Check your guess with census data.

6. What industries would you expect to be most concentrated in big urban areas? Why?

References and Further Reading

Beckmann, Martin, and John McPherson. "City Size Distributions in a Central Place Hierarchy: An Alternative Approach." *Journal of Regional Science* 10 (1970): 25–33. A theory of city size distributions based on the work of Lösch. It provides an explanation of why the distribution is approximately Pareto.

Chinitz, Benjamin. *City and Suburb* (Englewood Cliffs, N.J.: Prentice-Hall, 1965). A collection of essays on the causes and consequences of suburbanization.

Kasarda, John. "Urban Change and Minority Opportunities." *The New Urban Reality,* ed. Paul E. Peterson. (Washington, D.C.: Brookings, 1985). Kasarda discusses the effects of employment shifts on the availability of various types of jobs in the central city. Other essays in this book are also excellent.

Lösch, August. *The Economics of Location* (New Haven: Yale, 1954). A classic on location theory; parts are highly technical.

Moses, Leon, and Harold Williamson. "The Location of Economic Activity in Cities." *American Economic Review* 57 (May 1967): 211–222. A fine empirical study of employment suburbanization in Chicago.

Rosen, Kenneth, and Mitchel Resnick. "The Size Distribution of Cities: An Examination of the Pareto Law and Primacy." Vol. 8, No. 2 *Journal of Urban Economics* (1980): 165–86. An analysis of city size distribution for many of the world's countries.

Part Two

Theoretical Foundations

5

Introducing Land and Land Rents Into Price Theory

☐ Chapter 1 showed that urban areas are places where market activities result in much higher production and employment densities than are observed elsewhere. Tall, closely spaced buildings and crowded streets and sidewalks are visible manifestations of high densities. To the urban economist, however, urban land, buildings, and human labor are inputs in producing commodities and services. The observation that population and employment densities are high in urban areas translates into the economic statement that ratios of capital and labor to land inputs are high in these areas. Thus the key observation in urban economic model building is that input proportions in urban areas are systematically and dramatically different from those elsewhere.

Analysis of input proportions and input prices is part of the microeconomic theory of production and supply.[1] Modern price theory textbooks, however, hardly mention land, land prices, or land rents except in the context of agriculture. Hence, the first task is to incorporate land into production theory. This chapter carries out that task. The second task is to use the theory of production, modified by the inclusion of land, to analyze the particular spatial relationships that characterize urban areas. Chapter 6 carries out this task. Together with the discussion of welfare economics in Chapter 8, these chapters provide a broad theoretical framework within which urban problems can be analyzed in Part 3.

Just as the wage is the price of labor services, so land rent is the price of land services, and just as a large part of labor market theory is concerned with wage determination, so much of land market theory is concerned with land rent determination. Prices are, of course, instruments for rationing the uses of inputs and outputs in a market econ-

---

1. For review, Mansfield (1979) offers a good discussion of production theory.

omy. This is no less true of land than of any other commodity or service, yet the special character of land rent as the price of a nonproduced input has stimulated some of the most interesting scientific and political controversy in history. Some comments on this controversy are made later in this chapter.

☐ SOME TERMS

It is necessary here to define carefully several closely related terms. *Land value* and *land rent* are related in the way that the price of any asset is related to the price of the service it yields. Stocks of physical assets are valuable because they yield flows of services during many years. **Land rent** is the price of the services yielded by land during a specific time period, as well as of the unit in which land is measured. For example, land is the present value, or capitalized value, of the rent the asset will yield during its useful life. That is, if a tract of land will yield a rent of R dollars per year in perpetuity, and if the appropriate interest rate to use in discounting is $100i$ percent per year, the price (V) of the land is as follows:[2]

$$V = R/i. \qquad (5.1)$$

The asset price (V) has the dimension only of the unit in which the asset is measured (for example, dollars per acre).

Man-made assets, such as buildings and machinery, inevitably deteriorate with time and use, and they eventually cease to be valuable. Land used—or rather, abused—in agriculture also may deteriorate. Most urban land uses, however, do not cause physical deterioration, and the land therefore yields a perpetual stream of services, as Equation (5.1) assumed.

The second set of terms to define are *unimproved land value* and *improved land value*. Most urban land uses require that structures be built on the land. In other words, urban production of goods and services normally requires both land and capital, among other factors of production. **Unimproved land value** means the price of the land with no structure on it, whereas **improved land value** means the price of the land and the structure on it. Since structures are usually expensive to move or demolish, it is often difficult to estimate the unimproved value of land that has a structure on it. Furthermore, in many urban areas very little unimproved land appears on the market, especially near

---

2. The present value at Time 0 of a stream of R dollars per year in perpetuity, discounted at interest rate i, is as follows:

$$V = \sum_{i=1}^{\infty} \frac{R}{(1 + i)^i} = \frac{R}{i}.$$

city centers. There are therefore few transactions from which to estimate unimproved land values, which are among the scarcest and poorest of the data needed by urban economists.

There are also many ways to improve land in addition to building on it, if the term *improve* is taken literally. Land can be drained and graded, provided with pipes for water supply and waste disposal, and planted with or cleared of trees. These are simply different kinds of capital investment in land, and like buildings, they can affect its market value. Some of the ambiguity of unimproved land value data results from the fact that various amounts of nonbuilding capital may have been invested in it.

Although nonstructural land improvements present real problems in applied research, as well as in real estate tax assessment, they are not important in this book. The terms *land value* and *land rent* refer here to the prices and rents of unimproved land, that is, before any capital has been invested in it. *Improved land value* includes the value of buildings and other capital invested in the land. Much of the analysis here is concerned with equilibrium situations in which land values and land rents are proportionate to each other, as in Equation (5.1).

☐ THEORY OF LAND RENT AND LAND USE

In this section and throughout much of the book *it is assumed that input and product markets are perfectly competitive,* that is, that each market participant can buy and sell unlimited quantities without affecting the price set by the market. There are two compelling reasons for this assumption. First, most urban phenomena and problems can be best understood and analyzed within the competitive framework. Although monopoly and oligopoly may worsen some urban problems, they are not important *explanations* of most urban phenomena. Racial discrimination, poverty, poor housing, congestion, and pollution would hardly be less serious problems in competitive than in noncompetitive markets. (The analysis to support this claim is presented in Part 3.) Second, spatial models, such as those used to analyze urban markets, are usually much simpler to formulate and analyze if perfect competition is assumed than if other market structures are considered. There are basic difficulties (discussed later on) that economists have not yet solved in formulating spatial relationships in noncompetitive markets.

It is also assumed, as it is in other branches of economic theory, that people own productive land and capital assets because of the return they yield. Owners therefore seek the use of the asset that yields the greatest return available.

These are powerful assumptions, and they yield many insights. Among them is the inference that, in equilibrium, *all equally productive units of land command the same price*—which does not imply that all urban land has the same price or rent. Productivity may vary greatly from one unit of land to another within an urban area.

Suppose a firm in a competitive industry produces a single commodity with the aid of several inputs—land, labor, and capital. The firm can vary its production continuously by appropriate variations in its inputs. The firm's production function represents input combinations that can be used to produce each output volume. Input and output prices are given to the firm, so it need only find the input and resulting output volumes that maximize its profit level at those prices. Intermediate price theory textbooks show that profit maximization requires input quantities that equate the *value of the marginal product (VMP)* of each input to its price or, in the case of an asset, to its rental rate. This important result can be established as follows.

The *marginal product (MP)* of an input is the change in output that results from a small change in the input quantity employed. The *VMP* is the product price multiplied by the *MP* of the input. It shows the change in the firm's revenue resulting from a small change in the employment of an input, holding constant the amounts of other inputs. The input price shows the change in the firm's cost resulting from a one-unit change in the employment of the input. If the *VMP* exceeds the input price, it means that the employment of additional units of the input adds more to revenue than to cost. Profit therefore increases. If the *VMP* is less than the input price, a decrease in employment of the input reduces cost by more than revenue. Profit therefore increases. It follows that profit is largest when an amount of the input is used that equates the *VMP* and the input price.

The result is illustrated in Figure 5.1. The term n stands for the amount of the input—say, labor—employed. S_n is the perfectly elastic supply curve of labor, and w is the competitive wage rate. VMP_n decreases as n increases, because the labor MP falls as more labor is employed with fixed amounts of other inputs. The term $\bar{n}$ shows the profit-maximizing employment of labor for the firm, in that it equates VMP_n to w.

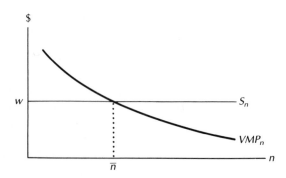

Figure 5.1 *Determination of Equilibrium Wage and Employment*

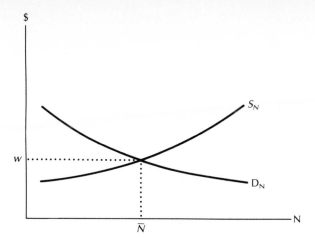

Figure 5.2 *Equilibrium with Rising Supply Curve*

The result in Figure 5.1 also can be stated algebraically. Suppose three inputs—land, labor, and capital—are used to produce a product. Then the conditions for profit maximization can be written as follows:

$$p \times MP_l = R, \qquad p \times MP_k = r, \qquad p \times MP_n = w,$$

or

$$MP_l = R/p, \qquad MP_k = r/p, \qquad MP_n = w/p, \qquad (5.2)$$

where p is the price of the product, R is the rental rate of land, r is the rental rate of capital, w is the wage rate, and the MPs are the marginal products of the inputs indicated by the subscripts. By the assumption of perfect competition, the product price and each input price are given to the firm. Each MP depends not only on the quantity of the input designated, but also on quantities of the other two inputs. Thus, each of the equations involves all three input quantities, which must be solved simultaneously to ascertain the profit-maximizing input levels, as shown in Figure 5.1[3].

Until now, the discussion has been concerned entirely with the firm. In a competitive input market, input price is given to the firm and is determined by industry supply and demand. To understand land rent determination, it is necessary to discuss the industry as a whole. Industry demand is computed by adding the demands of all firms for the input at the fixed input price. The industry input demand schedule is obtained by repeating the procedure at each input price. Like the firm's VMP curve, it is downward sloping. Although the input supply curve is horizontal for the firm, it is normally upward sloping for the indus-

3. As Figure 5.1 indicates, the VMP is the firm's demand curve for the indicated input. It shows the profit-maximizing input quantity at each input price.

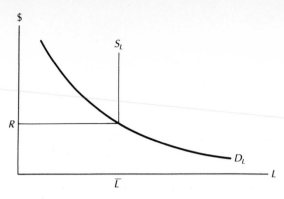

Figure 5.3 *Supply and Demand for Land*

try. The input price is determined by the equality of demand and supply for the input in the industry as a whole.

Input price determination is illustrated in Figure 5.2. N refers to labor employment in the entire industry. S_N and D_N are the labor supply and demand curves for the entire industry, w is the equilibrium wage rate, and $\overline{N}$ is total employment of labor in the industry. The term w equals the common value of VMP_n in all the firms in the industry.

The only peculiarity of land is that, being a nonproduced input, its total supply is fixed. Therefore, its supply curve to the industry is vertical, or perfectly inelastic. Nevertheless, the competitive supply to the individual firm is horizontal, or perfectly elastic. Thus, the foregoing analysis applies in full, and the appropriate diagram is Figure 5.3. L is land used by the entire industry, D_L is industry demand for land, and S_L is the vertical industry supply curve. R and $\overline{L}$ are the equilibrium land rent and land employed in the industry, respectively. As with labor or any other input, land rent equals the common value of its VMP in all land-using firms.

☐ WELFARE AND ETHICAL ASPECTS OF LAND RENT

During the nineteenth century, some economists and social philosophers held passionate views about land rent. Many people still feel that land is basically different from other inputs and should be treated differently by governments. Two basic considerations account for these views. First, David Ricardo (1821), Henry George (1879), and others thought land rents would absorb all the fruits of economic progress. Second is the view that land, not having been produced by people's efforts, should yield no return to its owners. Each view should be analyzed with care.

Ricardo's view rested on Thomas Malthus's population theory and on an inadequate appreciation of the importance of technical change. Ricardo believed that high birth rates would increase the labor supply and keep wage rates at the subsistence level in the long run. Land rent, being a residual, would absorb all revenues left over after paying workers—and perhaps capital owners—the input prices necessary to induce their supply. Thus, Ricardo believed, land rents would become an increasing share of total revenue as technical progress occurred. However important Malthusian theory may be for some parts of the world, it is not a threat for the foreseeable future in western Europe, North America, and certain other parts of the world. Birth rates there have fallen secularly for many decades, and many countries now have virtually stationary populations. Thus, *wage rates have risen rapidly in real terms as capital accumulation and technical change have occurred.*

On the conceptual level, the relationship between land rents as a residual and land rents as a return to the owner of a productive input proceeds as follows. Suppose the production function has constant returns to scale and that input and output markets are competitive. Then Euler's theorem[4] shows that all combinations of inputs and outputs satisfy the following identity:

$$x \equiv MP_l \times l + MP_k \times k + MP_n \times n. \qquad (5.3)$$

Here, x is the output level, and l, k, and n are amounts of land, capital, and labor, respectively, employed by the firm. Eliminating the MP terms from Equation (5.3) by substituting from Equations (5.2) and multiplying both sides by p yields this result:

$$px = R \times l + r \times k + w \times n. \qquad (5.4)$$

Equation (5.4) shows that the sum of competitive payments to the three inputs is equal to total receipts from the sale of the product in a competitive market. Thus, *the land rent that pays landowners the value of land's marginal product is precisely the amount left over after paying owners of other inputs the values of their marginal products.* This remarkable result shows that there is no conflict between the notion of land rent as a residual and the notion of land rent as a payment based on input productivity in the conditions stated. The result does not depend on the number of inputs.

The result also does not depend on the restrictive assumption of constant returns to scale in the firm's production function. Suppose that input and output markets are competitive and that fixed competitive input prices yield a conventional U-shaped long-run average cost (*LAC*) curve, as Figure 5.4 shows. The term *LMC* represents the firm's long-run marginal cost curve, p is the industry's long-run equilibrium price, and $\bar{x}$ is the firm's long-run equilibrium output. Thus, price equals both average and marginal cost, and competitively priced payments to

---

4. Euler's theorem is proved in many calculus and mathematical economics textbooks.

inputs therefore exhaust revenues. Once again, land rent, or any other input payment, can be viewed as a productivity-based payment or as a residual.

Equation (5.4) makes no distinction between land and the other inputs; each is paid the value of its MP, and each could be regarded as receiving the residual after other factors are paid the value of their MPs. Total land rent is the box inscribed under the lines originating at R and $\bar{L}$ in Figure 5.3. Similar equilibrium supply-and-demand diagrams for the other inputs determine equilibrium prices and total payments to these inputs. For the United States, the supply curve of labor is probably nearly vertical. As in the case of land, an outward shift in the demand curve raises wages but brings forth, at most, a modest increase in labor supply. The fact that land rent can be thought of as either the value of the MP or the residual after other inputs have been paid will be of some importance in this book. Sometimes we will calculate rent one way, and sometimes, the other.

Constant returns to scale and U-shaped average cost curves by no means exhaust the market situations that interest economists. They exhaust those that are consistent with perfect competition, however. In recent decades, economists have considerably sharpened their tools for analyzing land rents in noncompetitive markets, but they appear to have lost interest in the subject. In fact, the best evidence is that the share of land rents in American national income has been between 6 and 8 percent since the middle of the nineteenth century (Keiper, 1961). The share probably fell slightly from 1850 to 1950. Thus, even if the Ricardo-George theory of a rising share of land rents were conceptually sound, it would be refuted by the facts.

Turn now to the second concern about land: why should there be a return to landownership? Unlike labor and capital, land supply does not result from forgone leisure or consumption. No resources are used to produce land. Thus, many writers have felt that landowners should not receive a return on this asset.

George (1879) proposed a "single tax" on land. Since land supply is perfectly inelastic, he argued correctly that a tax equal to its entire rent would have no effect on its supply or use. He called it a *single* tax because he thought its yield would be sufficient to finance all government activity, making other taxes unnecessary. He was probably right in 1879, the time he wrote, but the government now spends and taxes a much larger part of national income than the 6.4 percent that goes to land rent. Nevertheless, many economists believe that a very high tax on land rent would be a good idea and that it should replace other taxes to the extent that its yield would permit.

An analogy between land rent and wages may help clarify the issues. Labor supply is more complex than land supply; it depends on choices between work and other activities and, in the long run, on birth and death rates. However, labor, like land, is supplied quite inelastically even over long time periods. Thus taxes probably have little dis-

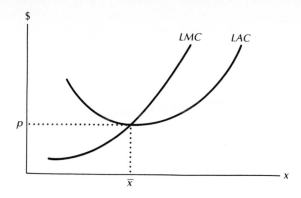

Figure 5.4 *Cost Curves and Competitive Pricing*

torting effect on supplies of either input. Should income from land be taxed differently from income from labor? Not necessarily.

First is the equity issue. Income from land and other assets is more unequally distributed than income from labor. Thus a 100 percent tax on land rent would fall more heavily on high-income people than would an 8.5 percent tax on wages, which would yield government about the same income. The object of a progressive tax, however, should be to tax at higher rates those with higher incomes. The best way to levy a progressive tax is to tax high incomes at higher rates than low incomes. Income from land is by no means perfectly correlated with total income, so a high tax on land rent is a poor substitute for a progressive income tax.

Second, a large part of what we call *wage income* is really a return on investment in human capital, such as education and training. Taxes on wages reduce the return on investment in human capital, and hence discourage it. It is also difficult to separate the return on land from the return on capital investment, or improvements, on it. Thus, in principle, land and labor are similar. Both are typically "improved" by investments, which should not be discouraged. It is much easier to separate the return on improved and unimproved land than the return on improved and unimproved labor. The same kinds of problems are present in both cases, however.

Third, a major justification for competitive pricing of any input is to provide its owner with an incentive to use it efficiently. A central result of modern welfare economics (demonstrated in Chapter 8) is that if all inputs are priced competitively, and if their owners use them where the return is greatest, goods and services will be produced efficiently. Thus, if wages are taxed heavily, owners of labor (that is, workers) lack incentive to find the occupation with the highest return. Again, the situation is nearly symmetrical with respect to land and labor. If central planners knew the best use for each plot of land and each unit of labor, they could allocate both without the help of market transactions. Central planners, however, do not know the best use of each unit of each input. Market prices, therefore, are used as rewards to encourage input owners to find the best uses. An important difference between land and labor is that people are much more bothered by bureaucratic controls over the use of labor than over the use of land. The former violates a human right, whereas the latter violates a property right.

The problem with the single tax remains. To levy the right tax, the assessor must know the best use and the resulting rent for each plot of land. If the assessor levies an excessively high tax, resource misallocation will result. Thus, *the single tax would assign to the tax assessor the task now assigned to real estate markets.* This is a serious matter, because urban land is a valuable resource, and it is important that it be used efficiently. Whatever the deficiencies in the ways competitive markets allocate land (discussed in Chapter 11), it is clear that the job should not be given to the tax assessor. Tax assessors are skilled at tax assessment, not at urban land allocation.

A final point is that a 100 percent tax on land rent is, economically speaking, the same as land confiscation. It is not desirable public policy in the United States to institute such a tax without the compensation of landowners at fair market values. If government and landowners held the same expectations of future land rents, however, compensation would equal capitalized future land rents, and the government would be in no better financial position with the single tax than without it.[5]

The theoretical merits of the single tax seem slight. Most concern with land rents probably is based on concern with the distribution of asset or wealth ownership. If that is the case, asset redistribution is the appropriate reform, and one less drastic than the adoption of the single tax.

Although the single tax may not be desirable, higher tax rates on land than on improvements may be justifiable. In the United States, real estate taxation is mainly the preserve of local governments. They now tax both land and improvements at high rates, especially in urban areas. It can be argued that less distortion of resource allocation would result if land were taxed at higher rates and improvements at lower rates than they are at present. This practical policy issue is discussed in Chapter 10.

☐ Summary

Chapter 6 will use the basic theory of land rent and land allocation to develop the theory of urban structure. It is worth emphasizing here that land rent and allocation theory are tools to help people understand other urban phenomena and are not themselves of primary concern. Reasons for direct concern with land rents were discussed in this chap-

---

5. This statement assumes that the government's discount rate equals the landowners' discount rate less the marginal income tax rate. It may be quite true, because public and private risk premiums may differ.

ter. Otherwise, land is merely one of several inputs used in urban production, and its remuneration certainly accounts for less than 10 percent of total incomes.

The theory and social implications of land rent were among the most hotly debated subjects in economics during the nineteenth century. David Ricardo, the father of land rent theory, believed that land rent equals residual revenues remaining after other inputs are compensated at competitive prices. Modern economic theory shows that land rents, like other input prices, are set by marginal productivity. Marginal productivity and the residual theory are equivalent in competitive equilibrium.

Questions and Problems

1. Would you expect land rents to be a larger share of national income in the United States or in Japan? Why?

2. What would be the effect of a single tax in Iowa on Iowa land values and corn prices?

3. Property income is more unequally distributed than earned income. Do you think landownership is more unequally distributed than ownership of other property?

4. Can you generalize Equation (5.4) to the case of a monopoly output market?

References and Further Reading

George, Henry. *Progress and Poverty* (republished New York: Robert Schalkenbach Foundation, 1954). George's basic exposition of his theory of land rents and his defense of a single tax.

Keiper, Joseph, et al. *Theory and Measurement of Land Rent* (Philadelphia: Chilton & Co., 1961). A fine survey of land rent theories and estimates of land rents in American economic history.

Mansfield, Edwin. *Microeconomics* (New York: Norton, 1979). A good undergraduate microeconomics textbook that explains input price determination in detail.

Ricardo, David. *Principles of Political Economy and Taxation.* 3rd ed., 1821 (republished 1886, London: John Murray). A definitive statement of the views of the famous nineteenth-century economist.

6

Theoretical Analysis of Urban Structure

☐ The goal in theorizing about urban structure is to understand how the urban economy ticks. Why are certain goods and services produced in urban areas? Why are some produced downtown and some in suburbs? Why do suburbs grow more rapidly than central cities? Why are certain areas much more intensively developed than others? Most important, what are the causes and cures of problems that afflict urban areas?

As Chapter 1 showed, urban areas are places where large amounts of labor and capital are combined with small amounts of land in producing goods and services. Intensive development of central cities is another way of saying that the ratio of nonland to land inputs is greater there than in suburbs. A major determinant of production location within an urban area is the extent to which large amounts of capital and labor can be combined economically with small amounts of land. Other things being equal, goods and services are produced downtown if their production function permits the substitution of capital and labor for land. If not, they are produced in suburbs or, as in the case of agriculture, outside urban areas altogether. Furthermore, goods and services produced both downtown and in suburbs are produced with higher ratios of nonland to land inputs downtown than in the suburbs. Therefore, understanding how the urban economy ticks is mainly a matter of understanding how markets combine land with other inputs in varying proportions at different places to produce goods and services. This chapter presents the basic ingredients of models of urban structure and puts them together in models of increasing complexity and realism.

☐ URBAN AREA WITH A SINGLE INDUSTRY

Suppose there is a region with a comparative advantage in the production of a certain commodity. The commodity is exported from the region at a certain point, which may be a port or a railhead. Wherever the commodity is produced in the region, it must be shipped to the point of export. Production of the commodity as close as possible to the point of export is therefore an advantage. Indeed, needed material input probably can be brought to the production site by the same mode that carries exports to the other places.

A circle of radius u has a circumference of $2\pi u$ and an area of πu^2. Therefore, within u miles of the point of export, there are πu^2 square miles of space. Some of the space may be covered by water or have other topographical features that make it unusable for production. Some space may be needed for intraurban or interurban area transportation. Obviously, however, the greater the distance from the point of export, the more space is available for production. Quite generally, the supply of such space can be represented by a function showing the square miles of land within u miles of the export point. For simplicity, suppose that ϕ radians of the circle are available for production at every distance from the point of export. The supply of land for production within u miles of the point of export, then, is $(\phi/2)u^2$ square miles. Of course, ϕ cannot exceed 2π.

Production Conditions

Labor inputs and the production of housing services play no role in this model. They are introduced in the next section. It is assumed that only one commodity is produced in the urban area. Equivalently, it can be assumed that all commodities have the same production functions. The commodity can be sold locally as well as exported, but all units of the commodity are assumed to be shipped to the point of export for distribution in all cases. The demand for the commodity is a function of price at the point of export.

The commodity is produced with land and capital. The production function has constant returns to scale and permits substitution between capital and land. Suppose a building has a certain number of floors and a certain number of rooms. The inputs and the output of usable floor space then can be doubled by constructing an identical building adjacent to it.[1] This is the meaning of *constant returns to scale*. Now suppose the building is extended up rather than out to economize on land. Suppose, for example, that an identical second floor is added to a one-story building. The land input is unchanged, but the amount of capital has more than doubled; although the second story requires the same amount of materials as the one-story building, the walls of the first story and the foundation must be strengthened to hold the second story, as well as the first. In addition, the output of usable floor space is less than double, because part of each story must be used for stairs to provide vertical transportation between the floors. Similar con-

---

1. This is not quite true. Some economy is made possible by sharing common walls. However, this economy becomes unimportant in a building with a modest number of rooms.

siderations apply to additional floors in the building. Thus *capital can be substituted for land, but with diminishing returns to the use of additional capital with a fixed amount of land.*

It is assumed that input and output markets are perfectly competitive. A *competitive output market* means that all units of the commodity must be sold at the same price at the point of export, wherever they are produced. *Competitive input markets* mean that producers take rental rates on land and capital as given at each location. It is assumed that the supply of capital is perfectly elastic to the urban area as a whole, as well as that the rental rate on capital is the same throughout the urban area. Land rent, in contrast, is determined by the model and depends on distance from the point of export.

Finally, it is assumed that shipment costs of the commodity to the point of export depend only on the straight-line distance between the location of production and the point of export. This is an approximation, since shipments must follow the road network. Studies have shown, however, that actual transportation time and distance are strongly correlated with straight-line distance in urban areas. Thus, transportation cost per commodity unit per mile is assumed to be constant— independent of the distance shipped and the point of origin.

The dependent variables in the model are the amounts of capital employed on different plots of land, the rental rates on the various plots, and the total output and price of the commodity. Since transportation cost to the point of export depends only on distance and not on direction, it follows that all the land available at a distance u from the export point has the same rent; that is, land rent also depends only on distance and not on direction.

As Chapter 5 showed, in any place that production of the commodity occurs, producers use amounts of capital and land inputs that equate the *VMP*s of the inputs to their rental rates. We can write these equations as follows:

$$MP_{K(u)}(p - tu) = r. \qquad (6.1)$$

$$MP_{L(u)}(p - tu) = R(u). \qquad (6.2)$$

$MP_{K(u)}$ and $MP_{L(u)}$ are the marginal products of the amounts of capital and land used at a distance u miles from the point of export. Each *MP* depends on the amounts of both factors used. The term p is the price of the commodity at the point of export, and t is the unit-mile shipment cost to the point of export. The term $p - tu$ is therefore the price at the point of production for units of the commodity produced u miles from the point of export, that is, the price net of shipment cost to the point of export. The terms r and $R(u)$ are the rental rates per unit of capital and land.

The analysis leading to Equation (5.4) that showed a rent function $R(u)$, that satisfies Equations (6.1) and (6.2), also makes profit exactly zero at each u. In fact, for given values of p, t, u, and v, a unique R

makes average total cost equal to p. Thus, the competitive equilibrium rent function $R(u)$ makes profit just zero at each u when producers employ capital and land inputs that minimize average cost. It is worthwhile to investigate carefully the shape of the rent function. If no input substitution were possible, the inputs of land and capital per unit of output would be constants, independent of input prices and of u. Equations (6.1) and (6.2) would not need to be solved simultaneously. The rent that equated profit to zero at each u would increase linearly as u decreased—just enough to offset the lower transportation cost as u decreased. In the model here, however, input substitution is possible. It is then easy to show that $R(u)$ must rise faster than linearly as u decreases; that is, $R(u)$ must have the general shape shown in Figure 6.1. The curve in Figure 6.1 is referred to as the *land rent function*. We will discuss the related housing price and residential density function later.

To establish the result on the curvature of the rent function, suppose the contrary. Specifically, suppose $R(u)$ is at a level that makes profit just zero at some large value of u and that, as u decreases, $R(u)$ increases by just enough to keep profit zero at the input proportion that was most profitable at the initial value of u. The previous paragraph showed that the resulting rise in $R(u)$ would be linear, yet the input proportion that was optimum at the large value of u would not be optimum at smaller values of u. At small values of u, land is more expensive relative to capital than at large values of u. This means that at small values of u, production cost is lower if a larger capital/land ratio is used than the ratio appropriate at a large u. Therefore, if $R(u)$ increases linearly as u decreases, profit will be positive at small values of u. Thus $R(u)$ must increase faster than linearly as u becomes small, if profit is to be just zero at each u. Of course, the more rapidly $R(u)$ rises at small u, the more capital is substituted for land. The urban area is in equilibrium when the capital/land ratio at each u is appropriate for $R(u)$, and $R(u)$ makes profit just zero at each u. To be a solution of Equations (6.1) and (6.2), $R(u)$ must satisfy both properties.

Thus $R(u)$ must increase faster than linearly as u becomes small. Of course, the ratio of capital to land inputs is an increasing function of the ratio of land rent to capital rent. Therefore, *as land rent rises rapidly and u decreases close to the city center, the capital/land ratio also rises rapidly.* The expression *rising capital/land ratio* is a graphic one, since it is apparent by the rising height of buildings.

The result is important, because if it were not possible to substitute capital for land, urban rent functions would be linear, and land used for each purpose would be used with the same intensity in all parts of the urban area. However, *land rent, population density, and capital/land ratios fall very rapidly with distance close to city centers and flatten out in the suburbs.* The pattern is a consequence of input substitution, and the precise form of the rent function depends on the ease with which capital can be substituted for land. Nonlinear rent functions

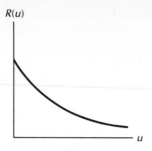

Figure 6.1 *The Relationship Between Rent and Location*

sometimes appear to be mysterious in models with linear transportation costs. Why should land rent increase more with a move from 3 to 2 miles toward the city center than with a move from 9 to 8 miles? After all, the saving in transportation cost is the same in the two moves. The answer, as will now be seen, is input substitution.

Market Equilibrium Conditions

So far, only the marginal productivity conditions of Equations (6.1) and (6.2) have been discussed. The model is completed by several additional equations. First, all the land available within the urban area must be used to produce the commodity. It would never pay to use land at a certain distance from the point of export if closer land were unused. Thus, for each u within the urban area, we must have $L(u) = \phi u$.

Second, the production function tells us how much of the commodity is produced by the land and capital employment at each u.

Third, overall demand and supply for the commodity must be equal for the urban area as a whole. Overall supply is the sum, or integral, of the amounts produced at each u within the urban area. The overall demand equation shows the amount that can be sold, both locally and for export, at each p. Although each competitive producer in the urban area takes p as given, p depends on the total amount produced by the entire area. A decrease in p increases exports in two ways. The commodity is then cheaper in the area in which it was previously exported, and customers there buy more. In addition, a decrease in p increases the area in which the urban area's exports are competitive.

Finally, urban areas compete for land with nonurban users, such as agriculture. Suppose, for simplicity, the nonurban land surrounding the urban area commands a rent of $\overline{R}$. The urban area then includes only the land that can be bid away from nonurban users. The edge of the urban area occurs at a distance $\overline{u}$ miles from the export point, where urban land rent falls to the level $\overline{R}$. The urban area has a radius of u miles where $R(\overline{u}) = \overline{R}$.

This completes the model. The two marginal productivity conditions, the equation relating land use to land available, and the production function give us four equations to determine land and capital inputs, output, and land rent at each u in the urban area. Then the equation of overall demand and supply and $R(\bar{u}) = \bar{R}$ determine the price of the commodity at the export point and the radius of the urban area.[2]

The model here cannot in any sense be thought of as a realistic model of urban structure. Its purpose is to introduce the use of land rent and allocation theory into models of urban structure. It is possible, however, to deduce from the model the single most pervasive characteristic of urban structure—namely, high land rents and intensive land use near the urban center, both falling rapidly near the center and much less rapidly in distant suburbs. Although there are many unrealistic simplifications in the model, the most significant is that the urban area has no people in it. Labor does not appear as an input, and households do not appear as consumers of housing and other outputs.

☐ HOUSEHOLDS IN AN URBAN SPATIAL CONTEXT

There are important similarities between the foregoing model of industrial location and the theory of household location. Firms are assumed to maximize profits by choosing a location for production and shipping the commodity they produce to the urban center. Households are assumed to maximize their utility or satisfaction in choosing a residential location (among other goods and services). It is the workers themselves who get shipped, or rather commute, to the urban center. Hereafter, this urban center, or transport node, will be called the *central business district,* or CBD. Thus the production of housing services is analogous to industrial production, and commuting is analogous to the shipment of commodities. (Of course, not all workers actually work in the CBD, any more than all goods are really shipped to the CBD. More realistic assumptions along this line are introduced later. It is assumed that all commuting is to the CBD in order to maintain parallelism of the model with the model of industrial location.)

Housing services, like other goods and services, are produced with land, labor, and capital inputs. The provision of housing services bears the same relationship to the housing construction industry that the downtown provision of legal services bears to the office construction

---

2. Despite its drastic simplifying assumptions, computations with the model discussed here can be cumbersome. Nevertheless, you can develop a clearer understanding of it by working through the calculations of the more complex model in Appendix A and then returning to this model and the other models in this chapter and working out some examples, using production and demand functions of your own invention or that you have studied in other courses.

industry. In both cases, the construction industry produces a capital good that is used as an input in the production of a service to consumers. The cost of housing services includes labor cost for maintenance and repairs, plus the rent on the land and capital used. Provided that competitive markets supply the inputs to everyone on the same terms, the cost of a given amount of housing services at a given location is the same to all, and the distinction between ownership and rental of housing is immaterial. Real estate mortgage markets are highly competitive, and mortgages are highly secure loans in that land and houses are durable, easily insured, and, unlike cars, virtually impossible to steal (in a physical sense). This chapter focuses on the price per unit of housing services, which is a rental rate analogous to the rental rate on land.

In the United States there are only two important reasons for the cost of a particular house in a particular location to vary from person to person. First and most important is racial discrimination. In many parts of most urban areas, whites sell or rent real estate to blacks only at premium prices, if at all. Second, for federal tax reasons discussed in Chapter 10, housing services are provided on more favorable terms to owners than to renters. (This is most important to people in a high marginal income tax bracket.) More is said about racial discrimination and tax considerations in housing markets in Chapters 10 and 11. At this point it is assumed that the cost of housing services is independent of *tenure status* (that is, whether a household owns or rents its dwelling).

Capital and land can be, and are, substituted for each other in the production of housing services in the same way as for commodity production. A downtown high-rise apartment has a high capital/land ratio. There is, however, an additional consideration that is more important in the production of housing services than it is in commodity production: *the value of housing services is affected by the amount of uncovered land surrounding the house.* Presumably, householders are as well off with a big house surrounded by a small amount of uncovered land as with a somewhat smaller house surrounded by a larger amount of uncovered land. That is, exterior and interior space can be substituted for each other. Although suburban industrial buildings sometimes have considerable amounts of uncovered land around them, it is usually held for parking, future expansion, or speculation.

Assumptions of the Model

A theory of household location choice as an extension of consumer behavior theory can be formulated. Suppose a household has a utility function or set of indifference curves for its tastes or preferences for housing services and for nonhousing goods and services. As is true of nonspatial consumer behavior theory, the theory presented here depends in only minor ways on the number of goods and services available. To facilitate diagrammatic exposition, however, it is assumed that only one nonhousing commodity, called *goods* for short, is available.

The most general way to introduce location choice into the model would be to include u in the utility function. It then could represent all the subjective costs of commuting, such as time forgone from other activities, fatigue, strain, and boredom. Although little is known about some of these factors, it is reasonable to assume that the marginal disutility of additional time spent in commuting increases with the time spent commuting, at least beyond some number of minutes. (Some interesting research has been done on commuters' valuation of travel time; it is discussed in Chapter 12.) Almost no results can be demonstrated unless restrictions are placed on the way commuting affects utility. In this section, a very special assumption is used; it is assumed that commuting costs enter linearly into the budget constraint but do not otherwise affect utility. The important restriction implied by this assumption is that the marginal disutility of additional time spent commuting is a constant. Appendix A shows that the disutility of a given amount of commuting nevertheless may increase with income.

Households maximize their satisfaction with respect to the consumption of housing, goods, and commuting, subject to a budget constraint. The budget constraint says that expenditures on housing, goods, and commuting must not exceed income. In this budget constraint, *income* must be interpreted as "potential income," that is, it must include money income forgone as a result of commuting. Part of this potential income is "spent" on commuting. It is assumed that a household can buy as large a quantity of goods and housing services as it wants without affecting their prices. The price of goods is assumed not to vary with residential location, but the price of housing services depends on u, since the price depends on land rents, which in turn vary with u. In addition to subjective costs, commuting entails monetary costs in the form of fares or vehicle operating costs. The money cost per mile of commuting is assumed to be a constant, and commuting cost, like the cost of commodity shipment, is assumed to depend on the straight-line distance from the residence to the urban center. The coefficient of distance in the budget equation (t in Equation (6.4) in the next section) includes both money and the subjective, or time, costs of commuting.

Wherever a household decides to live, it consumes the amounts of housing services and goods that yield the greatest satisfaction at that location. Figure 6.2 illustrates the equilibrium choice for a household located u miles from the center. The term $x_1(u)$ is the consumption of goods, and $x_2(u)$ is the consumption of housing services. The solid straight line is the budget line for a household living u miles from the center. The curve I is the highest indifference curve that can be reached, attained by consuming $\overline{x}_1(u)$ units of goods and $\overline{x}_2(u)$ units of housing services. The equilibrium condition is the familiar equation between

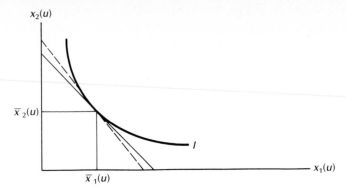

Figure 6.2 *Household's Equilibrium Consumption*

the marginal rate of substitution, or the slope of the indifference curve, and the ratio of the prices of the two consumer goods. If we write Δx_1 and Δx_2 for small changes in the consumption of x_1 and x_2 that keep a household on the indifference curve, the slope of the indifference curve is $\Delta x_2/\Delta x_1$, and equilibrium requires the consumption of amounts of x_1 and x_2 such that

$$\frac{\Delta x_2}{\Delta x_1} = -\frac{p_1}{p_2(u)}. \tag{6.3}$$

A household also must decide how far from the CBD to live. If its residence is close to the center, housing services are expensive,[3] but commuting is cheap. If its residence is far from the CBD, housing services are cheap, but commuting is expensive.

Now suppose that the workplaces in an urban center occupy a space that is small compared with the rest of the urban area, which is occupied by residences. Approximate the area occupied by workplaces with a point at the urban center. Suppose also that $(\phi/2)u^2$ square miles of land are available for housing within u miles of the urban center. Finally, suppose that all households have the same tastes or indifference curves and the same money income. Then an equilibrium location pattern requires that households achieve the same satisfaction level wherever they live. If they did not, some households would move, and the system would be out of equilibrium.

Suppose, for example, that households living 5 miles from the urban center could achieve a higher indifference level than those living 10 miles from the center. By moving closer in, those living 10 miles

---

3. It may seem counterfactual to talk about housing's being more expensive close to the CBD than in more remote locations, since everyone knows that the more expensive houses tend to be in the suburbs and the more modest ones in the central city. As Chapter 10 will discuss more fully, the price of housing refers to the price of a given "amount" of housing. Suburban homes are more expensive because they have bigger yards, more floor space, better appliances, and so on. However, any specified type of house is generally cheaper in the suburbs than close to the CBD.

away could achieve the same satisfaction as those 5 miles away, since they have the same tastes and income and face the same market prices. Thus, some households at the more distant location would move in. This would increase land and housing prices at the closer location and reduce them at the more distant location. Thus, satisfaction levels would fall at the closer location and rise at the more distant location. Movement ceases only when equal satisfaction levels are achieved at all distances from the center.

Implications of the Model

What land rent function shape is implied by this model? It is an interesting and important fact that *the model has a land rent function steeper close to the city center than in the suburbs,* as did the model in the previous section. This can be seen as follows. The household budget constraint can be written like this:

$$p_1 \Delta x_1(u) + p_2(u)x_2(u) + tu = w. \tag{6.4}$$

Here p_1 is the price of goods, which does not depend on u, and $p_2(u)$ is the price of housing services, which does depend on u. The term t is the cost per 2 miles of commuting. A worker who lives u miles from work must commute $2u$ miles per day. The term w is income. Now consider the effect on p_2, x_1, and x_2 of a small change (Δu) in u. Since the budget constraint must be satisfied at both values, Equation (6.4) implies that

$$p_1 \Delta x_1(u) + \Delta p_2(u)x_2(u) + p_2(u)\Delta x_2(u) + t\Delta u = 0. \tag{6.5}$$

Here Δx_1, Δx_2, and Δp_2 are the resulting small changes in x_1, x_2, and p_2. If the Δ terms are sufficiently small, the cross-product ($\Delta p_2 \Delta x_2$) is nearly zero, so it has been ignored in Equation (6.5).

Now Equation (6.3) can be written

$$p_1 \Delta x_1(u) + p_2(u)\Delta x_2(u) = 0.$$

Subtracting it from both sides of Equation (6.5) yields

$$\Delta p_2(u)x_2(u) + t\Delta u = 0.$$

Rearranging terms, this equation can be written as

$$\frac{\Delta p_2(u)}{\Delta u} = -\frac{t}{x_2(u)}. \tag{6.6}$$

Equation (6.6) is known as the **location equilibrium condition;** it is important to understand it and to understand why it is intuitively appealing. This equation will be used several times in this and the next chapter to derive important results on the structure of cities. To see the intuition behind the equation, rearrange it once again:

$$\frac{x_2(u)\Delta p_2(u)}{\Delta u} = -t.$$

Let Δu equal 1 mile. Now the left-hand side represents the benefit of moving 1 mile away from the CBD; it is the change in housing expenditure associated with the housing price decline:

$$\frac{x_2(u)\Delta p_2(u)}{1}.$$

The cost of moving 1 mile away from the CBD is the increase by t in commuting cost. Clearly, if the benefits of moving toward the suburbs exceed the costs, a household will do so. In the reverse case, it will move toward the CBD. Only when the costs and benefits of a move are equal will the household be in location equilibrium. Satisfying the location equilibrium condition, as shown in Equation (6.6), simply means that the costs and benefits are equal.

Equation (6.6) helps clarify how substitution leads to curvature of the housing price function. The slope of the housing price function is equal to $t/x_2(u)$. Assume t is constant; if $x_2(u)$ is also constant, the slope of the price function will be constant as well. Moving up the function (that is, toward the CBD), however, housing gets more expensive. As this happens, people reduce their consumption of x_2; that is, they substitute away from x_2. With a smaller x_2, however, the function must be steeper in order to preserve location equilibrium. The more readily households can substitute away from x_2, the more quickly $t/x_2(u)$ grows. Thus more substitution leads to more curvature of the function.

The left-hand side of Equation (6.6) is the slope of the housing price function. The minus on the right-hand side shows that the slope is negative; that is, housing is more expensive close to the urban center than in the suburbs.

Equation (6.6) implies that the housing price function is steep wherever x_2 is small. Therefore, the housing price function is steeper close to the urban center than in the suburbs if suburban residents consume more housing than those living closer in. Suburban residents must consume more housing, however, or they could not achieve the same utility level as those living closer in. Therefore, in Figure 6.2, the budget line of a suburban resident must be steeper than that of a close-in resident, since the housing price is lower for the suburban resident. A suburban resident also spends more on commuting, however. Since equilibrium requires that suburban and close-in residents achieve the same indifference curve, the combined effect of increased commuting cost and lower housing prices must make a suburban resident's budget line tangent to the same indifference as is that of a close-in resident. Thus, the broken line in Figure 6.2 is the budget line of a suburban resident, and the solid line is that of a close-in resident. It is clear from Figure 6.2 that *a suburban resident consumes more housing than a close-in resident.*

The foregoing result can be stated in terms of income and substitution effects. As people move farther from the urban center, the price of housing falls, though the increased commuting cost exactly offsets the income effect of the decline in housing price. Thus, the new budget line is tangent to the indifference curve achieved before the move. It follows that the only effect of the move on housing consumption is the substitution effect of the decrease in housing price. It is a basic theorem of consumer behavior analysis that the substitution effect on the consumption of a product whose price falls is to increase the consumption of the product.

It is easy to see that the assumption that u does not appear directly in the utility function is crucial in the foregoing demonstration. If u did appear in the utility function, a move away from the urban center would shift the indifference curve in Figure 6.2, and it would not be possible to predict the effect on housing demand.

It has now been shown that suburbanites consume more housing than close-in residents in equilibrium. It follows from Equation (6.6) that the housing price function must be steeper close to an urban center than in the suburbs. If nonland input prices do not vary with distance, housing prices can be steep only where the land rent function is steep. Thus, the land rent function becomes steep close to an urban center in the consumer model, just as in the producer model.

The consumer model has two very realistic implications. First, suburbanites consume more housing than residents close to the urban center. Second, since land is cheaper relative to other housing inputs in the suburbs than it is close to the urban center, suburban housing uses lower capital/land ratios than downtown housing. These two implications entail lower suburban population densities than those near the urban center. (None of this implies that suburbanites are better off than those living close to the urban center. In this model, all households have the same income, and all achieve the same satisfaction level. This assumption is dropped in the next section.)

☐ SEVERAL URBAN SECTORS

Two one-sector models in which an urban area contains only producers or only households have now been considered, thus developing the basic location theory of firms and households. In this section, the theory is extended to explain the location pattern of several sectors in one urban area. A *sector* is defined as a set of institutions that have the same rent functions. Firms' rent functions are affected by their production functions, prices of nonland inputs, and product demand functions. Households' rent functions are affected by their incomes, their tastes for housing, commuting, and other goods and services, as well as by the prices of consumer goods other than housing. Thus, there are many distinguishable sectors in even a fairly small urban area. For theoretical purposes, the number of sectors makes little difference; for applied research and for ease of exposition, however, it is important to keep sectors to a manageable number. This necessitates the group-

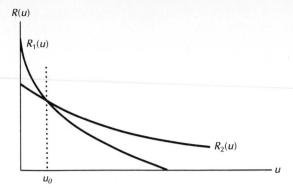

Figure 6.3 *Rent Functions for Different Sectors*

ing of similar, but not identical, institutions as an approximation of a sector. In applied research, the way data are collected and published usually dictates the definition of sectors.

The key to understanding the location pattern of several sectors in an urban area is the notion, introduced in Chapter 5, that land owners want the largest return possible from their asset and hence allocate their land to the institution that offers the highest rent.

Two Industries

Suppose that two industries bid for land in an urban area. The rent that firms in each industry can offer for land at each distance from the center is found using the method discussed at the beginning of the chapter. From here on, the rent that each industry can pay at each u will be referred to as the industry's **rent offer curve.**

Designate the industries as 1 and 2, and suppose that their rent offer curves are as shown in Figure 6.3. At values of u less $u_0 m$ Industry 1 can offer higher rent than Industry 2, and at values of u greater than u_0, the opposite is true. Land close to the urban center is used by Industry 1, and land beyond u_0 is used by Industry 2. At each u, the rent actually paid is the higher of the two rent offer functions. That is, the rent function is the **envelope** of the rent offer curves.

Why should firms in Industry 1 pay much more for land than $R_2(u)$ at small values of u? After all, Industry 1 firms can rent the land if they offer just a little more than Industry 2 firms. The answer is that Industry 1 firms are competing not only with Industry 2 firms, but also with one another. Remember that the entire analysis here rests on the assumption that firms enter each industry until profit is just zero. Thus, the complete set of equilibrium conditions for our two-industry urban area is as follows:

1. Wherever firms in each industry locate, they must make zero profit.
2. Each plot of land goes to the highest bidder.

3. Supply and demand for land must be equal.
4. Supply and demand for the product of each industry must be equal.

There is a very simple rule for the urban location pattern of industries with linear rent offer curves. Imagine an arbitrarily large set of industries, each of which is able to bid successfully for land somewhere in an urban area, and each of which has a linear rent offer curve. The industries are ranked by the steepness of their rent offer curves. The industry with the steepest rent offer curve is closest to the urban center, followed by the industry with the next steepest curve, and so on. This is illustrated in Figure 6.4. The heavy line is the rent function, constructed as the envelope of the industries' rent offer curves. It is easy to see that in an urban area with a large number of sectors, the rent function would be nearly smooth and would become flatter the greater the distance from the center, even if each industry had a linear rent offer curve.

Although Figure 6.4 shows the shape of the rent function, it does not indicate which industries will locate in an urban area. It is not necessarily true that Industry 1 will locate in an urban area at all. This possibility is illustrated in Figure 6.5, in which $R_1(u)$ is steeper than $R_2(u)$, but $R_1(u)$ is nowhere above $R_2(u)$. Industry 1 therefore does not locate in the urban area.

As already seen, inputs and product substitution mean that industry and household rent offer curves are typically not straight lines. Thus, no simple rule indicates the locational pattern to be expected in an urban area. The locational pattern, however, must satisfy the four equilibrium conditions listed previously.

Figure 6.6 illustrates a realistic possibility. The Industry 1 rent offer function is steep at the beginning and flattens as it moves out, whereas the Industry 2 function is more nearly linear. The result is that Industry 1 locates at values of u less than u_0 and at values of u greater than u_1, whereas Industry 2 locates at distances between u_0 and u_1. There

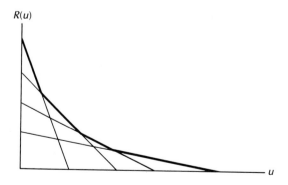

Figure 6.4   *Rent Function as Envelope of Sector Curves*

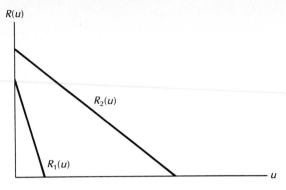

Figure 6.5 *Rent Functions for Different Sectors*

are, however, some reasonable sets of assumptions that preclude multiple intersections. Suppose that each industry has a Cobb-Douglas production function (discussed in detail in Appendix A). Suppose further that the two industries differ only in that their production functions have different land intensities. Then their rent offer functions cannot intersect twice. Alternatively, if the industries differ only in the demand elasticity for their products, their rent offer functions cannot intersect twice. There are situations, however, in which multiple intersections can occur.

Households and Industries

An industry's rent offer function is unique, because zero profit is a well-defined notion. In considering the rent offer functions of households, however, zero utility is not a sensible notion. In fact, in modern

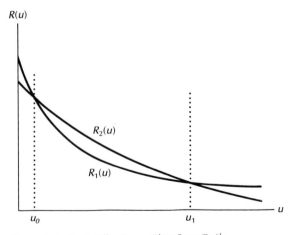

Figure 6.6 *Rent Offer Curves That Cross Twice*

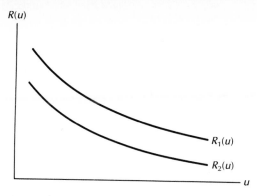

Figure 6.7 *Rent Offer Curves for Different Utility Levels*

ordinal utility theory, any "bundle" of goods and services whatsoever can be assigned zero utility. All that matters is whether one bundle yields more or less utility than another. For a sector of households with given tastes, income, and prices for nonhousing goods and services, a rent offer curve exists for each utility level. The lower the rent offer curve, the higher the utility level, since paying less land rent leaves more money to spend on housing and other goods and services. This is illustrated in Figure 6.7, where $R_1(u)$ is the rent offer curve corresponding to a low utility level for the set of households, and $R_2(u)$ corresponds to a high utility level.

Which rent offer curve is relevant? The relevant rent offer curve is the one that equates supply and demand for labor provided by these households. Figure 6.8 illustrates this notion. $R_1(u)$ is the rent offer curve of an industry that employs labor. $R_2(u)$ is a rent offer curve for the households that supply labor to the industry; it represents a high utility level and a small supply of labor. $R_3(u)$ is another household rent offer curve representing a low utility level and a large supply of labor. If labor demand and supply are equal when the household rent offer curve is $R_2(u)$, it is relevant. If labor demand exceeds supply, however, and if the wage rate is high enough to attract more workers to the urban area from elsewhere, the household rent offer curve rises to one like $R_3(u)$, the labor supply expands, and utility falls. Thus, the equilibrium conditions for households' location are similar to those for industrial location:

1. Wherever households with given tastes and income reside, they must achieve the same utility levels.
2. Each plot of land goes to the highest bidder.
3. Supply and demand for land must be equal.
4. Supply and demand for labor provided by the households must be equal.

Condition 4 implies that household utility levels in this urban area must

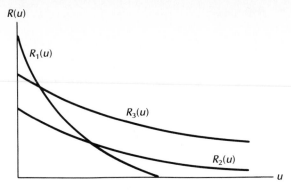

Figure 6.8 *Rent Offer Curves for Interacting Sectors*

be equal to those that can be achieved elsewhere. For some kinds of labor, the lowest rent offer curve that commands land anywhere in an urban area may be so high that the households to which the labor belongs achieve lower utility levels than those that can be achieved elsewhere. Households of this type simply do not locate in this urban area. Farmers rarely reside in large urban areas, and highly specialized workers, such as eye surgeons, are rarely found in small towns. This topic will also be covered in the discussion of the open city model.

As Figure 6.6 showed, not all the firms in an industry necessarily locate in a contiguous area. The same is true of households. In Figure 6.8, $R_1(u)$ is the rent offer curve of a production and employment sector, and $R_2(u)$ and $R_3(u)$ are rent offer curves of residential sectors. In this example, the production sector locates at values of u between 0 and u_0. Residents of type 2 locate at values of u between u_1 and u_2, but residents of type 3 locate both in close-in neighborhoods between u_0 and u_1 and in suburban neighborhoods beyond u_2.

☐ FIRM AND HOUSEHOLD LOCATION WITH DECENTRALIZED EMPLOYMENT

The models of this chapter are built around the notions that access to the CBD is valuable and that the market for land arbitrates the competing desires for this access. In the case of households, access reduces commuting.[4] What about firms? The discussion of household location began with the assumption that all firms were located at the CBD, because it is an export node, though if all firms are not arbitrarily assigned to the CBD, what can be said about the determinants of their location decisions?

The first thing that can be said is that access to the CBD is valuable even to a non-CBD firm. If this access were not valuable, firms would

4. This observation needs some elaboration now that the fact that some employment is located away from the CBD is being discussed. However, it will be seen that the basic properties of consumer equilibrium are unchanged by this fact.

be unwilling to endure the cost of locating anywhere on the flanks of the rent function. Willingness to endure urban land rent means that either directly or indirectly, access to the CBD must be valuable. For non-CBD firms, just like CBD firms, there are two basic reasons why such access might be valuable. The first is agglomeration economies, and the second (already discussed at the outset of the chapter) is access to the CBD export facility.

Suppose a manufacturing firm realizes agglomeration economies because of a financial and legal community in the CBD. These services are more costly to obtain the farther away the firm is located. There is no reason to believe that agglomeration economies are lost entirely if firm locations are not contiguous. The more rapidly agglomeration economies decline with distance, however, the steeper the firm's rent offer curve and the more central its location.

Now suppose the same firm exports its output through the CBD port. It can locate at the CBD, incurring high land rent. In exchange, its output is already at the CBD port and does not have to be transported downtown for export. By moving to the suburbs, the firm saves on land rent but suffers an increase in output shipping costs.

The firm saves on more than land rent by locating away from the CBD, however. The wage rate it must offer its workers is lower at a suburban location than in the CBD. Workers do not have to commute as far to get to a suburban as to a CBD job site; thus, they accept a lower wage. To see this, consider a firm located 5 miles from the CBD, at point F in Figure 6.9. Any household living on the ray between F and G (the suburban side of a line going through both F and the CBD) would save a 5-mile commute by working at F instead of at the CBD. So long as there are more workers living on this segment than the firm at F wants to employ, it can attract workers by offering a wage as much as $5t$ less than the CBD wage (recall that t is the cost of 1 mile of *round trip* commuting). That is, with this wage discount, workers living on the line segment FG are indifferent as to whether they work at F or the CBD. Thus, in addition to the rent function, the city displays a *wage function*, whose slope equals $-t$.

Also notice that jobs at F are most attractive to households living on the segment FG. For anyone else, the commute saving is less than $5t$. For some people, F is farther from home than is the CBD.

The introduction of wage function, leaving appropriately located households indifferent between CBD and non-CBD jobs, preserves the applicability of the monocentric model in the face of decentralized employment. Many people feel that the monocentric model of household location is inappropriate given that only a small fraction of the typical urban area's employment is located in the CBD.[5] However, the description of household equilibrium is unaltered by decentralized employment. Workers still commute up the rent gradient every morning, some

5. As Chapter 4 showed, in 1980 only about half of urban employment was located in central cities, and of even this figure, only a small fraction was in the CBD.

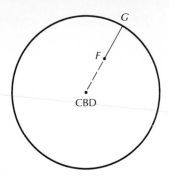

Figure 6.9   *Commute to a Non-CBD Job*

all the way to the CBD and some only as far as their suburban jobs. The location equilibrium condition in Equation (6.6) still holds and still determines the shape of the rent function. The fact that the same location equilibrium condition holds in a world with decentralized employment leads to a somewhat counterintuitive result: *the shape of the rent function is completely unaffected by the decentralization of employment.* It might seem that a city's rent function would get progressively flatter as employment became more decentralized; that is, as the dominance of the CBD was eroded. That is wrong, however; if the rent function had any shape other than that which preserves the equality of Equation (6.6), it would not represent an equilibrium.

Returning to the firm's location problem, the firm is attracted to the suburbs because of cheap labor and land, and it is attracted to the CBD because of agglomeration economies and access to the CBD export node. Here is another way of expressing the decision facing the firm: it can locate in the suburbs (where the workers are and hence where labor is cheap) or in the CBD (where the export terminal is and hence where output shipment is cheap).

This can be expressed formally with an equation similar to the location equilibrium for the household.* The firm's location equilibrium condition is

$$x_2(u)\frac{\Delta p_2(u)}{\Delta u} + L(u)\frac{\Delta w}{\Delta u} = -t, \tag{6.7}$$

where $x_2(u)$ and $L(u)$ are usages of urban land and labor per unit of output. The term t is the extra cost of producing and shipping a unit of output associated with a 1-mile increase in distance from the CBD; it includes both the extra cost of goods shipment and the reduction of agglomeration economies associated with a move 1 mile farther from the CBD. The derivation of this result is similar to that of Equation (6.6) and will not be discussed here. However, it is apparent that it is indeed the firm's location equilibrium condition. The left-hand side is the bene-

---

* This material is fairly difficult. Some readers may want to skip to "Equilibrium with Other Cities: The Open City Model."

fit (reduced land and labor costs) from moving 1 mile away from the CBD; the right-hand side is the cost. The firm locates where the benefit equals the cost. Rearranging Equation (6.7) gives

$$\frac{\Delta p_2(u)}{\Delta u} = -\frac{t}{x_2(u)} - \frac{L}{x_2(u)}\left(\frac{\Delta w}{\Delta u}\right). \tag{6.8}$$

The left-hand side is the slope of the firm's rent offer curve; the steeper this slope, the more strongly the firm is attracted to the CBD. Looking at the first term on the right-hand side, we see that a rise in t increases the slope—increases the attractiveness of the CBD.

A rise in L, however, decreases the slope (since it is multiplied by $\Delta w/\Delta u$, which is negative). The rise in L reduces the attractiveness of the CBD; it pulls the firm toward cheap labor, which is in the suburbs. The steeper the wage function, the stronger the pull is. This makes sense; recall that the slope of the wage function is equal to commuting cost. Thus, steep $\Delta w/\Delta u$ means high commuting cost, and this is just the case where the firm should locate in the suburbs.[6]

The outcome of this process can be characterized as follows: if it is cheaper to ship the workers than their output to the CBD, the firm locates in the CBD; in the reverse case, the firm locates in the suburbs. Empirically, the cost of shipping freight has declined much more dramatically than has the cost of commuting (faster commuting has been largely offset by increases in the value of time), so this shift in relative prices has led to an increase in the tendency for firms to decentralize during the past several decades. This, of course, is just the pattern that has been observed, although it is impossible to say how much firm decentralization has resulted from rapid improvement in freight transport.[7]

☐ EQUILIBRIUM WITH OTHER CITIES: THE OPEN CITY MODEL

So far attention has focused on one city, but the possibility of migration among cities always has been in the background. Interurban migration equalizes supply and demand for labor in a city. The effects of interurban migration will now be examined.

After taking account of any wage, rent, and commuting cost differences, anyone who concludes that City A is preferable to City B can be expected to move to City A. Thus, in considering the interaction of a city with the rest of the country, the following equilibrium condition is needed: no household could achieve a higher utility by moving to a different city.[8] This is known as the **open city model** because

---

6. The advanced reader might puzzle over the fact that a rise in x_2 has an ambiguous effect; it depends upon whether t or $L(\Delta w/\Delta u)$ is larger.

7. Mills (1972, Chap. 5) has a model of firm location which works basically along the lines just presented.

8. As will be shown, this is the same as Assumption 4 in the "Households and Industries" section, which states that the supply and demand for labor must be equal.

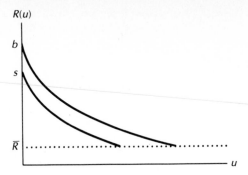

Figure 6.10 *Rent Functions for Large and Small Cities*

of the assumption that the city is open to migration to or from the rest of the country.

An important prediction emerges from the open city model: wages vary among urban areas as compensation for intercity differences in land rent, commuting cost, and other amenities. Chapter 14 will discuss the other amenities; in this section attention is limited to rents and commuting costs.

Begin with the observation that rent is higher in big cities than small.[9] The steepness of the function should not be affected by city size, since there is nothing in Equation (6.6) that varies with city size.[10] Since the rent functions of both big and small cities must start at the agricultural rent at the rural-urban boundary, and since they both have the same shape, the big-city rent function lies everywhere above the small-city rent function, as depicted in Figure 6.10.

Now consider workers deciding whether to live adjacent to the CBD of the big City B or the small City S. In City B they must pay rent b, and in City S they must pay rent s. To induce them to choose City B, the big-city employer must offer them a wage premium sufficient to compensate them for the difference between rents b and s. The same wage premium must be paid to all workers in City B, since the land market in City B insures that all households in the city earn the same utility level as a worker living adjacent to the CBD.

Note an implication of this result for firm location. If a firm finds big-city locations advantageous, perhaps because of agglomeration economies, it must endure both high big-city land rents and big-city wages. These are the signals that big-city production is costly and should be undertaken sparingly.

Chapter 7 will explore the statistical evidence showing the relation-

9. Although this result does not rest on the open city assumption, it is the starting point for the discussion on compensating wage differences.

10. This is not quite right; commuting cost may rise with city size, since congestion would be expected to be greater in big than small cities.

ship between wages and city size, and Chapter 14 will look at the relationship between wages and amenity levels.

☐ COMPARATIVE STATICS: THE EQUILIBRIUM EFFECTS OF CHANGES IN INCOME AND TRANSPORT COST

Changes in income (w) and transport (commuting) cost (t) bring about changes in the equilibrium shape of a city. First, a change in w or t brings about a change in the shape of the housing price function, and a shift in the function induces entrepreneurs to alter their land use decisions. Thus, this section begins by examining the effect of changes in w or t on the housing price function. For both effects, the starting point is the household's location equilibrium condition, Equation (6.6).

Rise in Income

To determine the effect of a rise in income, begin by dividing both sides of Equation (6.6) by $p_2(u)$:

$$\frac{\Delta p_2(u)/p_2(u)}{\Delta u} = -\frac{t}{p_2(u)x_2(u)}. \tag{6.9}$$

The left-hand side expresses the *percentage rate* of housing price decline per mile that preserves households' location equilibria at every location. In other words, this is the percentage rate of decline in the household's rent offer curve. If a city contains only one type of household, Equation (6.9) also gives the percentage rate of decline in the equilibrium rent function.[11] The question to be answered now: does the percentage rate of decline in the price of housing increase or decrease as income rises; that is, does the price function get steeper or flatter?

A change in income affects the right-hand side of Equation (6.9), because consumption of housing (x_2) rises with income. If this were the only effect, the right-hand side of Equation (6.9) would get smaller with a rise in w, and the left-hand side, to preserve location equilibrium, would have to do the same. That is, the price function would get flatter. For reasons that will be given, the land rent function also gets flatter. So does the density function, because the substitution to high density is induced by high rent.

Income affects t as well as x_2, however; a rise in income causes a rise in the opportunity cost of time (a rise in the wage rate). This raises

11. It has been noted that the absolute rate of decline, $\Delta p(u)/\Delta u$, should get smaller as distance increases, due to substitution. As can be seen in Appendix A, however, reasonable assumptions about the degree of substitution lead to the prediction that the percentage rate of decline in the price of housing will be constant, or roughly so. Under certain conditions it follows that the percentage rate of decline in density also will be constant. Chapter 7 will examine evidence on both of these questions.

the time cost of commuting, which raises the overall cost of commuting. The increase in t tends to offset the increase in x_2 in Equation (6.9). Thus it is not known whether the right-hand side gets bigger or smaller. This, of course, means it is not known whether the rent function gets steeper or flatter and whether the city becomes more or less dense.

Quantitatively, the question hinges on whether the cost of transport or the demand for housing rises more rapidly with income. In particular, if the elasticity of transport cost with respect to income is greater than the income elasticity of demand for housing, a rise in income makes the price function steeper (and the reverse in the opposite case). The best available evidence suggests that the income elasticity of commuting cost is only modestly smaller than the income elasticity of demand for housing. If time cost is roughly half of commuting cost, a 10 percent rise in income brings about a 5 percent rise in commuting cost (out-of-pocket costs are unaffected). Thus, the income elasticity of commuting cost is 0.5. Direct estimates of the demand for housing give income elasticities of around 0.7 (see Chapter 10). These two figures together suggest that the rent offer curve gets slightly flatter as income rises. However, the margin of error in these estimates is sufficiently large that it would be unwise to place too much weight on this prediction.

Wheaton (1977) has estimated rent offer curves directly for various income groups and has found no evidence that rent offer curves get flatter as income rises. In summary, a rise in income may be associated with a flattening of the housing price gradient, but the evidence is mixed and the effect, if any, is small.

This observation is important for another subject: income segregation. It was previously noted that the land market tends to segregate economic activities, with sectors with steep rent offer curves locating closer to the CBD than sectors with flat rent offer curves. The past few paragraphs have asked the question: does the rent offer curve get steeper or flatter as income rises? If high incomes are associated with flat rent offer curves, this would at least partially explain the tendency for the rich to live farther from the CBD than the poor. In fact, however, it is impossible to make a definitive prediction as to whether the rich or the poor have steeper rent offer curves. Thus, the explanation for income segregation must lie elsewhere (a topic to which the next chapter will return).

Transport Cost

A decline in transport cost (t) has a direct impact upon the rent function; it makes it flatter. Again, this is clear from Equation (6.9). If the numerator of the right-hand side gets smaller, the whole term gets smaller, and so must the rent function in order to sustain location equilibrium. Indeed, this result is apparent even without recourse to Equation (6.9). The cost of urban transport gives rise to urban land value in the first place, and a reduction in commuting cost reduces the premium a household is willing to pay for a central location. In fact,

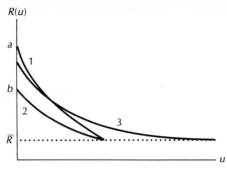

Figure 6.11 *Response of Rent Function to a Transport Cost Decline*

if urban transport became free, urban and rural land values would be uniform.

If the rural-urban boundary does not move in response to the decline in t, the rent gradient shifts from Curve 1 to Curve 2 in Figure 6.11. In fact, however, the rural-urban boundary is expected to shift out, thus giving a rent gradient like Curve 3. To see why this is so, consider the open city effects previously discussed. Consider workers who live adjacent to the CBD (who incur no commuting cost but pay high land rent). Before the decline in t, their rent was equal to rent a in Figure 6.11. When the rent gradient shifts to Curve 2 (before the boundary shift), their rent has fallen to rent b. It is known that the workers were indifferent as to whether they lived in this city or another before the rent gradient declined, since location equilibrium between cities had been achieved. With the decline in City A's CBD rent, however, this equilibrium is disturbed. Now more people prefer to live in City A; at every location the sum of transport cost and land rent is lower than before. Thus, outsiders bid up the price of land in City A, and developers rebuild the city at higher density.

The rent function is not likely to shift all the way back up to rent a (at the CBD), however. As the work force in the city expands, the money wage offered by employers declines (employers have a downward-sloping demand curve for labor in any given city). This chokes off expansion of the city before the intercept of the rent function is driven up to rent a, leaving an equilibrium function like Curve 3.

Thus, the effect of a transport cost decline is the generation of a new rent function in which central-city rents are lower and suburban rents are higher than before. The economic reason for this is straightforward. The value of suburban sites rises because they have obtained an increase in valuable accessibility to the CBD. Central-city sites have declined in value because the total supply of land accessible to the CBD has increased, so the value of any given "amount" of access has been eroded.

It is important to note that the change in land value is *not* an indication of the value of the reduction in transport cost. Whether total land value has increased or decreased cannot even be determined, since

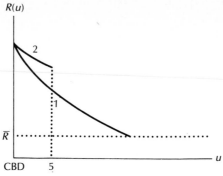

Figure 6.12 *Effect of Transport Improvement for Distances Less than Five Miles from the CBD*

in general it increases in the suburbs and decreases in more central locations. The reason land value changes cannot be used as measures of the value of transport improvements lies in the offsetting effects on land values previously discussed. First, transport improvements improve accessibility of individual sites, increasing their value. If this were the end of the story, land value changes would be a good measure of the value of transport improvements. However, since transport improvements also increase the total supply of accessible sites, the value of access is diminished. It is this diminution of the value of access that breaks the link between changes in aggregate land values and the value of transport improvements. The most extreme case has already been noted: by some act of magic, urban transport becomes costless. Clearly (assuming we do not have to pay the magician), this would be beneficial. Equally clearly, urban land value would drop, since access would be free.

There is one case in which land value changes do reflect the value of transport improvements: the case in which the transport improvement does not extend to the edge of the urban area and hence does not increase the supply of accessible sites. Figure 6.12 depicts such a case. The new gradient, Curve 2, is an equilibrium after a transport improvement, which is available only to the people who live less than 5 miles from the CBD.

Finally, note that there may be differences among households in transport cost. Most obviously, two-worker households incur more commuting cost (per house) than do one-worker households; other things being equal, two-worker households should be expected to have bid rent curves that are much steeper than those of one-worker households. Many two-worker households are also childless. Since children increase the demand for space (and for access to suburban schools), the difference between one- and two-worker households' gradients may be greater still.

☐ REALISTIC URBAN LOCATION PATTERNS AND URBAN SIMULATION MODELS

The model of urban land use developed in previous sections (frequently referred to as the *monocentric model*) is important. This model, and many generalizations of it, has been developed by many scholars during the past two decades. It provides valuable insights, showing how and why land is used, why virtually all land very close to urban centers is used for employment instead of housing, and how and why population density decreases away from urban centers. It provides a possible reason why high-income people live farther from urban centers than low-income people. Finally, it provides a basic explanation for the urban decentralization that was shown in Chapter 4 to have been occurring for several decades. The next chapter will show that it also yields remarkably accurate quantitative predictions on the behavior of density, land rent, and house prices.

The monocentric model has severe limitations as a description of reality, however. Some of the limitations can and will be removed by further research, but some are inherent in the model. One is the fact that all employment is assumed to be concentrated in the urban center. As was shown, the model can be extended to the case where there is a concentration of employment at the CBD and a diffusion of other employment scattered throughout the urban area, although there does not appear to be any way to extend the model to cover the realistic case of large concentrations (subcenters) of employment some miles removed from the CBD. The problem arises because the model contains only a one-dimensional description of location; that is, it contains distance but not direction from the urban center. It might be possible to introduce a two-dimensional description of location into the model, but that would make it extremely complex.

Such complex models yield few analytical results. It generally is necessary to estimate or assume numerical values for the elasticities and other parameters of the model and solve them on a computer. The idea of using large, modern computers to solve or simulate urban models has opened up a large area of research since the 1960s.[12] Computers have an enormous capacity to solve large systems of equations and inequalities. Since the late 1960s, several urban models have been published that make use of this capacity and are closely related to the urban models discussed in this chapter.[13]

All computer simulation models start with a discrete description of locations in urban areas. A set of locations is defined (each might be a census tract), and the computer keeps track of where each location is in relation to all the others. Typically, the computer records a

---

12. "Simulation" means repeated solution of a model with different parameter values to test the effects of parameter changes on the model's solution.

13. For information on these urban models, see Ingram et al. (1972), deLeeuw and Struyk (1975), and Kain and Apgar (1985). For a different approach, see Mills (1972).

great deal of information about housing and employment at each location. Important characteristics of the existing housing stock might include the numbers, kinds, and ages of dwellings at each location. Employment information might include numbers, industries, and occupational descriptions of jobs. Housing demand equations relate residents to desired housing, making use of such information as family size, income, race, and education. The model takes account of considerations that induce people to move: their present dwelling is unsatisfactory, employment changes, or there is a change in family status. New construction is brought into the picture via a supply curve of new housing. Then the movers are matched up with the available housing supply according to a market-clearing equation.

The great advantage of computer simulation models is the detail they can employ regarding housing demand and supply in relation to locations of housing and workplaces. A major purpose of such models is to analyze the effects of alternative national housing policies. Suppose, for example, that a national program is proposed to subsidize housing of low-income people in a specific way. What will be the effect of the program on the amounts and qualities of housing they inhabit? What will be the effect on housing inhabited by those with incomes too high to be eligible for the program? Existing simulation models are designed to answer such hypothetical questions.

The most important limitation of existing simulation models is their limited success in making amounts and locations of employment endogenous to the model. Usually, the models' solutions are conditional, depending on forecasts of exogenous amounts and locations of employment.[14] Simulation models thus have not yet succeeded in incorporating one of the important determinants of the speed and direction of urban growth or decline.

Urban simulation models are expensive. A small team of experts and at least two years are required to formulate the model, collect the data, estimate the parameters in the model, program a computer to solve it, and simulate alternative government programs. Gradually, however, available models become more sophisticated, so they can analyze not only housing programs, but also transportation investments; local government taxation, spending, and regulatory programs; national environmental protection programs; and so forth.

☐ Summary

This chapter has shown how to extend theories of consumer and producer behavior to an urban spatial context. The result is an urban

---

14.   Birch et al. (1974) and Mills (1972) are partial exceptions to this conclusion. An endogenous variable is determined within a theoretical model, whereas an exogenous variable is determined outside the model.

land-use model that provides important insights into urban spatial characteristics.

Most analytical models assume that everything produced in an urban area must be shipped to the urban center for sale inside or outside the urban area. Spatial production theory then shows how production is distributed around the urban center. Spatial consumer theory shows how employees and their families distribute their residences around the employment locations. Such models can provide results that show how land values, land uses, input ratios, and population density vary with distance from the urban center.

Such analytical models are simplified and long-run in character. Computer simulation models have been formulated to analyze in detail the way households distribute themselves among the available housing stock in an urban area. Simulation models can incorporate much locational detail, many demand determinants, and many characteristics of the housing stock.

Questions and Problems

1. How would you introduce real estate taxes into an urban land-use model?

2. Is it possible in equilibrium that land rent might increase with distance from the urban center?

3. Evaluate the argument that employment has moved to suburbs because CBD land values have become so high that employers can no longer afford to locate there.

4. Consider the model in Appendix A, with one household sector. What does your intuition tell you should happpen to $\bar{u}$, the radius of the urban area, if t falls? Can you check your intuition mathematically?

5. Some urban areas (for example, Indianapolis) have essentially a full circle of land surrounding the CBD available for urban development. Others (for example, Chicago) have only a half-circle available because the CBD is on the lakefront. How would you expect these topographical differences to affect rent and density gradients? (Some students might want to look at the estimated density gradients in Mills (1972) or Muth (1969) to see whether their predictions are confirmed.)

6. Suppose lakefront land adjacent to the Chicago Loop is worth $1 million per acre. The city proposes to dump nontoxic garbage into the lake to create more land and sell it. The cost of dumping and grading is only $200,000 per acre of made land, leaving the city with a net profit of $800,000. Would you recommend that the city do this? Why or why not?

References and Further Reading

Birch, David, et al. *Patterns of Urban Change* (Lexington, Mass: Lexington Books, 1974). A complex urban simulation model that determines not only housing location and consumption, but also employment location.

deLeeuw, Frank, and Raymond Struyk. *The Web of Urban Housing* (Washington, D.C.: Urban Institute, 1975). A computer simulation model designed to investigate alternative national policies to subsidize housing for the poor.

Kain, John and William Apgar. *Housing and Neighborhood Dynamics* (Cambridge: Harvard University Press, 1985). A large computer simulation model to investigate a variety of government housing programs.

Mills, Edwin S. *Studies in the Structure of the Urban Economy* (Baltimore: Johns Hopkins, 1972). A research monograph in which congestion is introduced into an urban land-use model.

————. "Planning and Market Processes in Urban Models." *Public and Urban Economics,* ed. Ronald Grieson (Lexington, Mass.: Lexington Books, 1976). An urban simulation model based on linear and nonlinear programming.

Muth, Richard. *Cities and Housing* (Chicago: Univ. of Chicago Press, 1969). A modern classic in urban economics.

Wheaton, William C. "Income and Urban Residence: An Analysis of Consumer Demand for Location." *American Economic Review* Vol. 67 (September 1977): 620–31.

7

A Critical Examination of the Model

☐ Urban areas are obviously much more complicated than the monocentric models of the last chapter. In fact, urban areas are too complicated to describe fully; that is the reason for developing an abstract model. As with all models, the hope is that the abstraction captures important features of reality. The purpose of this chapter is to see how well this hope has been realized. The first part will examine the monocentric model's predictions of the characteristics of urban areas and compare the predictions with evidence. The second part will examine some of the model's specific assumptions and ask whether more realistic assumptions might lead to different results.

☐ STATISTICAL EVIDENCE

The monocentric models developed in the previous chapter yield a number of predictions about urban form. Checking how well the predictions agree with the facts will provide a better idea as to whether the model is a good mimic of reality. This section discusses evidence on geographic variation in density, the price of housing, and land rent to see whether the density and rent gradients of the last chapter really exist. It also calculates the predicted magnitude of the wage gradient and compares our prediction with estimates. It then examines the question of interurban wage variation. Finally, it examines the model's predictions of commuting behavior and compares these with actual commuting patterns.

Housing price gradient. The starting point for these calculations is the household's location equilibrium condition, as shown in Equation (6.6). Here it is written with the percentage rate of decline in the price of housing on the left-hand side:

$$\frac{\Delta p_2(u)/p_2(u)}{\Delta u} = -\frac{t}{p_2(u)x_2(u)}. \qquad (7.1)$$

By filling in reasonable numbers on the right-hand side of Equation (7.1), a predicted value for the percentage rate of decline in the price of housing can be calculated. Consider a household earning $10 per hour, giving an annual income of about $20,000 (close to the national average for 1986). Supposing it spends 20 percent of its income on housing, $4000 is the value for $p_2(u)x_2(u)$.[1] Now assume transport cost is $0.75 per round-trip mile (including the value of time used up in commuting).[2] The next step is to calculate the *annual* cost of a round-trip mile, since the housing expenditure term is in annual units. Assuming 220 workdays per year, t is 220 × $0.75, or $165. Then consider the following:

$$\frac{\Delta p_2(u)/p_2(u)}{\Delta u} = -\frac{\$165}{\$4000} \cong -0.04.$$

Thus, if the model of the last chapter is basically right and the numbers used in this calculation are correct, one should *expect the price of housing to decline roughly 4 percent per mile of distance from the CBD.* This percentage rate of decline is referred to as the *gradient.*

Land rent gradient. Housing is constructed from land and capital with the use of labor. The price of capital (bricks and boards, for example) does not vary much by location in an urban area. Furthermore, although it has been argued that the price of labor varies, its variation is not nearly sufficient to bring about the variation in the price of housing just predicted. If the price of housing is to vary over space, then, the reason must be that the price of the land input varies. According to most estimates, the value of land is between 10 and 20 percent of the value of housing (typically, a person builds an $80,000 structure on about a $20,000 lot and sells the property for $100,000). This means that 80 to 90 percent of the cost of housing does not vary with location, and the entire geographic variation in the price of housing is due to variation in the price of land. If 20 percent of house value is due to land value, a 4 percent per mile decline in the price of housing must be generated by a *20 percent per mile decline in the price of land.*[3] In contrast, if the land's share were 10 percent, a land rent gradient of 40 percent per mile would be predicted.

Even a 20 percent per mile change in the price of land is extremely rapid, as Table 7.1 shows. This table shows CBD land value for various urban area sizes, assuming that land value at the periphery of the urban

---

1. If the price elasticity of demand for housing is − 1, the fraction of income spent on housing does not vary with $p_2(u)$; hence, it does not vary with u. Thus, we do not need to worry about the effect of a change in $p_2(u)$ upon the calculations.

2. See Chapter 12 for a discussion of the cost of commuting.

3. To see this, consider the $80,000 structure on the $20,000 lot. The price of the house (including the lot) declines from $100,000 to $96,000 if it is moved one mile farther from the CBD. The cost of the structure does not change, so the price of the lot must decline from $20,000 to $16,000.

Table 7.1 *Calculated CBD Land Value as a Function of Urban Area Radius*

$\bar{u}$	$R(0)^a$	Area
10	15,000	314
15	40,000	706
20	109,000	1,256
25	297,000	1,962
30	807,000	2,826
35	2,193,000	3,846

[a]CBD land value per acre.

area is $2000 per acre and that land value rises 20 percent per mile until the CBD is reached. Columns 1 and 2 show, respectively, the radius of the urban area, or $\bar{u}$, and the derived CBD land value per acre, or $R(0)$. Column 3 shows the amount of land contained within the urban area, assuming it is a full circle. To put this in perspective, an urban area with a 15-mile radius generally has a population slightly in excess of 2 million people. An urban area with a 30-mile radius has four times as much land as an urban area with a 15-mile radius and might house as many as 15 million people due to its higher density.

Density gradient. As noted in Chapter 6, a city would display a downward-sloping rent function even if it were impossible to substitute away from the use of expensive land. If this substitution were impossible, however, density would be uniform. Density rises as the CBD is approached only because rising land values induce developers to substitute away from land in the production of housing and because households substitute away from housing in their consumption bundles. Thus, the steepness of the density function depends on the steepness of the rent function and on the ability of producers and consumers to substitute. The willingness of consumers to substitute away from housing as it gets more expensive is measured by the price elasticity of housing demand, and the ability of housing producers to substitute away from land is measured by another elasticity, called the *elasticity of substitution*.[4]

Appendix A shows that under reasonable assumptions regarding these elasticities, the density function has the same steepness as the land rent function.[5] It has already been argued that the rent function should

---

4. The elasticity of substitution is a measure of the curvature of the producer's isoquant (see Layard and Walters 1978).

5. This is embodied in Equation A.17, which says that density at distance u is just a multiple of rent at u, so long as $\beta = 0$ (which it will be if the price elasticity of demand for housing is -1).

fall about 20 percent per mile or possibly more, so the simple model predicts that the *density function also falls about 20 percent per mile.*[6]

Wage gradient. Suburban employers can offer lower wages than CBD employers because the suburban job location reduces the required commute. For any given occupation, the wage rate is expected to fall at the rate t per mile, where t is the commuting cost per mile. With the numbers stated at the beginning of this chapter, t is $165 per year; at an average annual wage income of $16,000, a *wage decline of about 1 percent per mile* is expected.

Summary. The proper way to read the predictions made so far is this: the price of housing should decline a few percentage points per mile; a function flatter than, say, 1 to 2 percent per mile or greater than 6 to 7 percent per mile is inconsistent with the model. The land rent function surely should be between five and ten times steeper than the housing price function, since land value is from 10 to 20 percent of house value. The density gradient should be in the same range as the rent gradient, although uncertainty regarding substitution possibilities means that considerable uncertainty surrounds this prediction. The wage gradient should be quite small—no more than about 25 percent of the housing price gradient, or about 1 percent per mile.

Evidence

To compare reality with prediction, a rent, price, density, or wage gradient must be estimated; this generally is done via regression analysis. Under reasonable assumptions (see Appendix A), both rent and density decline by roughly a constant percentage per mile. Such a pattern can be expressed by either of the following two (equivalent) equations:

$$X(u) = X_0 e^{-\gamma u}.$$

$$lnX(u) = lnX_0 - \gamma u. \tag{7.2}$$

$X(u)$ is the density, price, rent, or wage rate (as the case may be) at distance u, and γ is the percentage rate of decline per mile. These observations, which could be plotted in a scatter diagram like Figure 7.1, form the basis for a regression equation like Equation (7.2).

Taking the case of density, suppose there are many observations on density at different distances from the CBD, as plotted in Figure 7.1. Two questions about this scatter diagram must be answered. First, what is the average rate of decline in density? Second, on the average, how well does Equation (7.2) predict the actual variation in density? Regres-

---

6. Actually, a somewhat steeper density gradient than this should be expected. Rich people tend to live farther from the CBD than do poor people, and the rich also consume more housing. Thus, in addition to the forces already discussed, density declines with distance because income rises with distance. This probably adds about five percentage points to the gradient, leaving a prediction that density declines at about 30 percent per mile.

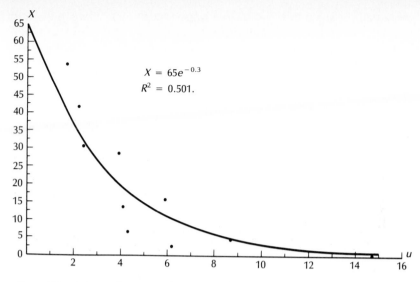

Figure 7.1 A Scatter Diagram with a Least-Squares Log-Linear Regression Curve

The curve in the figure is labeled:

$$X = 65e^{-0.3}$$
$$R^2 = 0.501.$$

sion analysis answers both these questions. First, it finds the curve that best fits the scatter, subject to the restriction that the equation for the curve satisfy Equation (7.2). Technically, the regression finds the parameter values X_0 and γ that minimize the sum of the squares of the distances of points from the curve (see Appendix B for a more complete discussion). Second, the R^2 statistic indicates the percentage of the variation in density that is "due to" the variation in distance. By way of illustration, the scatter diagram in Figure 7.1 yields an R^2 0f 0.501. Thus, the first step in estimating the gradients previously described is to gather observations on density, land rent, and the price of housing or wages, as the case may be.

Density gradient.   The most thorough study of residential density was carried out by Muth (1969) using 1950 Census Bureau data. For a sample of U.S. metropolitan central cities, he used a regression equation like Equation (7.2) and found that density declined by an average of 41 percent per mile.

Using the same regression technique, Mills and Ohta (1976) found that density gradients had become much flatter by 1970, averaging 20 percent per mile. Evidence from 1980 is discussed in Chapter 15. For a sample of Japanese cities, where transport cost is much higher (largely due to congestion), the average population density gradient was 64 percent—3.2 times as steep as for the sample of American cities.

The evidence indicates that density declines with distance at essentially the rate that would be predicted (about 20 percent per mile) when reasonable numbers are put into the monocentric model of the last chapter. The steeper density gradients for Japanese cities are what would be predicted based on higher commuting cost in Japan.

In all these studies, the R^2 (see Appendix B) was between 0.4 and 0.6, indicating that about half the variation among observations in density is due to distance.[7] It is not surprising that there is substantial variation in residential density that is unassociated with distance from the CBD. Cities, after all, are more complicated than the models of Chapter 6 indicate. For the observations used in these studies, residential density is measured by dividing the number of people living in a **census tract** (a small segment of an SMSA with about 4000 people) by the land area of the tract. One reason tracts vary in density—not corrected for in these studies—is that tracts vary in the fraction of land used for housing. On the average, about 59 percent of urban land is residential,[8] but even casual observation reveals substantial geographic variation in this fraction.

At least qualitatively, another prediction of the monocentric models is borne out by looking at residential density patterns. Chapter 1 noted that commuting cost has fallen substantially over the history of the United States. Looking at Equation (7.1), this leads to the prediction that density gradients also would get flatter with the passage of time. Mills (1972) has estimated density gradients for four cities as far back as 1880[9]; the average gradient for selected years is shown in Table 7.2. Density gradients have been getting flatter for at least a century in these cities. The well-known post-World War II suburbanization of American cities is merely a continuation of the little-known suburbanization of at least the previous seventy years.

Housing price gradient. As will be shown later in the book, the price of housing can be expected to vary according to many variables other than distance from the CBD. Property taxes, school quality, air quality, and neighborhood racial mix, to mention a few, all are factors found to influence the price of housing. As Chapter 10 will show, it is inherently difficult to measure the price of housing.[10] The result of these problems is that it is difficult to get a scatter diagram like Figure 7.1, which would be the basis for estimating a housing price gradient.[11]

7. By way of visual reference, the exponential curve through the scatter diagram in Figure 7.1 gives an R^2 of 0.5.

8. The remainder of urban land is divided as follows: open space, 7.5 percent; public/semi-public, 13.5 percent; industrial, 10.2 percent; commercial, 5.1 percent; and transportation and utilities, 4.6 percent.

9. The cities are Baltimore, Philadelphia, Milwaukee, and Rochester, NY.

10. The readily observable value of a house is in units of total expenditure, or price times quantity. The tendency for house values to be higher in the suburbs than in the central city arises from the fact that the nicer houses are in the suburbs, not because the price of a house of constant quality is higher in the suburbs.

11. When the dependent variable (the price of housing, in this case) is influenced by more than one variable, the appropriate statistical technique for estimation is not simple regression analysis (as depicted in Figure 7.1), but rather a slightly more complicated analogue, multiple regression analysis (discussed in Appendix B). The analogue between the scatter diagram and the regression line differs, although the intuition is the same.

Table 7.2 *Averages of Gradients for Population-Density Functions of Four Metropolitan Areas*

Year	Average Gradient
1880	1.22
1890	1.06
1900	0.96
1910	0.80
1920	0.69
1930	0.63
1940	0.59
1948	0.50
1954	0.40
1958	0.35
1963	0.31

Many researchers have tried to overcome these difficulties, with mixed results. Most have found the predicted downward-sloping gradient, but some have found upward-sloping gradients, and others have found no variation with distance. It is likely, although far from certain, that these mixed results are due to the inability of the researchers to hold constant other determinants of the price of housing. In fact, a recent study (Jackson, 1979) that took extreme care to hold other price determinants constant found a downward-sloping gradient of about 2 percent per mile.[12]

Wage gradient.   Wage gradients are difficult to measure, because the predicted variation in wages is small and because it is difficult to get data on wages that give the location of the employer. In other words, there are few samples available from which to plot the scatter diagram of Figure 7.1.

Eberts (1981) solved the latter problem by using data on public sector wages paid by various jurisdictions in the Chicago metropolitan area. Essentially, he obtained a scatter diagram like Figure 7.1 by observing the wage and location (distance from the Chicago Loop) for each of five different occupations (for example, police and firefighters) for each of the jurisdictions in his sample. For each of these occupations he was able to estimate a wage function. He found a wage decline of between 0.95 and 1.6 percent per mile for four of the five occupations studied

---

12.   The gradient Jackson found is considerably more complicated than the simple negative exponential. The peak is slightly off-center from the CBD, and the equal rent contours bend away from the peak along freeway routes. This seems to indicate that the housing market incorporates information on differences in commuting costs along different corridors.

(Eberts 1981, pp. 57–58).[13] This compares very well with the predicted rate of decline of about 1 percent per mile.

Land rent gradient. Data on land rent (or land value) in urban areas are difficult to obtain because there are very few transactions in undeveloped land. Very few studies exist in which a researcher has gathered the data for a scatter diagram of land value versus distance from the CBD like that in Figure 7.1, because adequate samples are so rare. The reason for the scarcity of adequate samples is simply that the vast majority of urban land is already built upon, so there are very few sales of uncovered land. Nevertheless, a few of the bigger metropolitan areas in the United States have yielded samples large enough to warrant careful statistical work. The earliest careful work, on Chicago, was done by Hoyt (1933). Hoyt found Loop land values of about $1 million per acre in 1892 and about $1.9 million by 1928. Recent statistical analyses of his data by Mills (1969) and Kau and Sirmans (1979) yielded estimated rent gradients of about 40 percent per mile in 1836 and just over 20 percent per mile in 1928. By the 1960s, according to an estimate by Mills, the land rent gradient had flattened sufficiently that the rate of decline was only 11.5 percent per mile.

Chicoine (1981) examined sale prices of farmland at the periphery of the Chicago metropolitan area using multiple regression analysis to explore simultaneously a large number of determinants of land value. This analysis showed that the sale price per acre fell 41.3 percent per mile of distance from the Chicago Loop. Since the observations are all of farmland, they are far from the CBD; this study does not indicate whether this steep gradient persists as the CBD is approached. This 41.3 percent gradient is at the upper end of the range predicted at the outset of this chapter.

The monocentric model also predicts that for any given distance from the CBD, land will be more valuable in large metropolitan areas than in small ones. The anecdotal evidence in favor of this prediction is overwhelming; everyone knows that land values are very high in New York and Tokyo. In 1970 the most expensive land in the United States—prime sites in Manhattan—was worth over $50 million per acre. The most expensive land in Tokyo was worth around $100 million per acre. The world's highest land prices apparently occur in Hong Kong, with some sites commanding over $200 million per acre. However, it is almost impossible to make firm quantitative statements because of the difficulty of getting comparable data on land values for different cities.

Table 7.3 gives sale prices (per acre) for prime industrial sites in 1982. Industrial sites generally are located some distance from the CBD, so these figures do not very accurately indicate CBD land values (that is, values of prime commercial sites). Nevertheless, the figures confirm

---

13. The fifth occupation, firefighters, also displayed a downward-sloping gradient, but it was smaller and statistically insignificant.

Table 7.3 *Sale Price Per Acre of Central-City Prime Industrial Sites (Improved Land, Less Than Two-Acre Site)*

1	Seattle	479,000	19	Indianapolis	87,000
2	East Los Angeles	392,000	20	Albuquerque	87,000
3	New Orleans	305,000	21	Atlanta	70,000
4	Portland (Oregon)	283,000	22	Charlotte	65,000
5	Miami	261,000	23	Des Moines	65,000
6	New York City	261,000	24	Baltimore	59,000
7	Houston	196,000	25	Little Rock	59,000
8	Pittsburgh	196,000	26	Orlando	59,000
9	Los Angeles (Riverside–		27	Philadelphia	59,000
	San Bernardino)	185,000	28	St. Louis	59,000
10	Cleveland	163,000	29	Fort Worth	54,000
11	Denver	142,000	30	Memphis	54,000
12	Dallas	122,000	31	Detroit	44,000
13	Cincinnati	120,000	32	Columbus (Ohio)	37,000
14	El Paso	105,000	33	Omaha	37,000
15	Wichita	100,000	34	Milwaukee	35,000
16	Chicago	98,000	35	Syracuse	22,000
17	Minneapolis	98,000	36	Akron	17,000
18	Charleston	87,000			

Source: Data from Society of Industrial Realtors. *Industrial Real Estate Market Survey* (Washington, D.C.: Society of Industrial Realtors, Spring 1982).

that high-proximity urban land values are hundreds of times higher than nearby rural land values. There is also a tendency (with some marked exceptions) for large-city sites to have higher site values than sites in smaller cities.[14]

Interurban wage differences. Chapter 6 noted that wages are predicted to be higher in large metropolitan areas than in small ones. The argument already given is that a worker who lives adjacent to the CBD has to pay higher rent in the large urban area and must be compensated. Workers who live at the edges of the large and small urban areas also might be compared. Viewed this way, large-city workers must be compensated for the fact that their commutes to the CBD are longer than if they lived in a small metropolitan area. It is difficult to establish a firm prediction of the magnitude of the relationship between the wage rate and urban area size, so for this section the procedure previously followed will be reversed; the statistical findings will be described, then the question of whether the magnitude is reasonable or not will be addressed.

14. The reader should not make too much of the comparison among cities; there is no presumption that the sites in the various cities are equally distant from the CBD. For example, Chicago industrial sites are surely farther from the CBD than are Portland sites due to the massive commercial district in the Chicago CBD and the large concentration of industrial plants around O'Hare International Airport.

In a study described more fully in Chapter 14, Rosen (1979) estimated the relationship between (among other things) wages and urban area population, as well as between wages and population density. He found that a 10 percent increase in population leads to an average $48 increase in annual wages, and that a 10 percent increase in population density (holding population constant) leads to a $120 reduction in wages (Rosen, 1979, Tables 3.4 and 3.5). Although this discussion concentrates on the Rosen findings, other researchers have found the same pattern.

Is it plausible that these wage differences are due to the intercity equilibrium conditions discussed in Chapter 6? Consider a metropolitan area with a population of 2 million and a radius of 15 miles (roughly the correct numbers for Baltimore). Now suppose the population increased by 20 percent to 2.4 million. According to Rosen's estimates, this would lead to a wage increase of just under $100. The estimated annual round-trip cost of a 1-mile increase in the commute is $165, so the observed $100 wage increase would be reasonable if the population increase from 2 million to 2.4 million were associated with about a 1-mile increase in the radius of the metropolitan area.

In fact, the area of a circle (or partial circle—it makes no difference) with a radius of 16 miles is 13.8 percent greater than that of a circle with a 15-mile radius. As the metropolitan area grew to the 16-mile size, its average density also would increase somewhat, so it seems reasonable that a 13.8 percent increase in land area, achieved by a 1-mile expansion of the radius, would be associated with a 20 percent increase in population. Also, this 1-mile expansion in radius should lead to an annual wage increase of about $165—close to the observed $100.

An increase in population density is associated with a wage reduction, according to Rosen's findings. Qualitatively, this also makes sense. The higher the density for a given population, the smaller is the radius of the city and the shorter the commute of the worker who lives at the edge.[15] To see if this can explain Rosen's findings, return to the previous example. Shrinking the radius of a city from 16 to 15 miles reduces land area (and therefore increases density) by 12.1 percent. The reduced radius should reduce wage demands by about $165 (the annual cost of a 1-mile round trip); from Rosen's estimates it can be calculated that it actually reduces the average wage by $145 ($120 × 1.21). Thus, the observed pattern of interurban wage variation agrees remarkably well with predictions based on the theory of Chapter 6. Overall, the density, land rent, house price, and wage patterns conform very nicely to the predictions coming from the monocentric model of Chapter 6.

No model is a perfect characterization of reality, however, and it is not surprising to learn that some aspects of reality are very much at

---

15. Higher average density does not necessarily mean smaller average lot size. It also can result from more "orderly" development, with little leapfrogging and leaving rural land uses within the area of urban development.

odds with the predictions of the model. For example, consider the troubling findings detailed in the next section.

Commuting patterns.   The monocentric model predicts that all workers commute straight toward the CBD, even if they work at a suburban job. The reason is simple: workers are willing to commute because housing is cheaper at the home end of the commute. In fact, it is the cheap housing that compensates workers for their commutes. (This situation is depicted in Figure 6.9.)

With a modest amount of statistical information it is possible to calculate how far workers commute, on the average, in any metropolitan area, assuming everyone commutes straight toward the CBD. To see this, begin by calculating the mean commute if everyone works at the CBD. The mean commute is the mean distance of residences from the CBD, and this can be calculated from the residential density gradient.[16] Hamilton (1982) has estimated this number for a sample of medium-sized and large urban areas; the average over the sample is 8.70 miles. This means that for these urban areas, if all jobs were in the CBD, the mean one-way commute would be 8.70 miles.

However, not all jobs are at the CBD, as Chapter 4 noted. Using the same technique used for home sites, Hamilton estimated the mean distance of jobs from the CBD. For the same sample urban areas, the average distance was 7.58 miles. Jobs, on the average, are therefore almost as decentralized as population, so jobs, on average, are not far away from workers' homes. Since jobs are, on the average, 7.58 miles from the CBD, the average commute length should be reduced by this amount, compared with the mean commute of 8.70 miles that people would have to make if all jobs were in the CBD. This means that, for this sample of urban areas, it would be possible for all workers to commute to their jobs—given the current locations of homes and jobs—with a mean commute of only 1.12 miles (8.70 − 7.58). It is possible to convert all the movement of jobs to the suburbs into commute savings. Furthermore, if everyone commuted straight toward the CBD, as the monocentric model predicts, all these potential savings would be realized. In other words, the monocentric model predicts an average one-way commute of 1.12 miles for this sample of urban areas.

In fact, the average commute for these metropolitan areas is 8.70 miles, the same as it would be if all jobs were at the CBD. None of the potential commute savings resulting from job decentralization has occurred. By this calculation, about 85 percent of commuting in the sample metropolitan areas is wasteful.

---

16.   Basically it works like this:

$$\text{Mean distance} = \frac{[N(1) \times 1] + [N(2) \times 2 + \ldots + [N(\bar{u}) \times \bar{u}]}{N},$$

where $N(1)$ is the number of people living one mile from the CBD, $N(2)$ is the population two miles from the CBD, and so on). N is the sum of the $N(u)$ variables in the numerator, and is the total population. The integration (basically taking the sum depicted in the equation) of the density gradient multiplied by u yields this mean distance from the CBD.

In fact, the simple logical extension of the monocentric model that implies that all workers can commute directly toward the CBD is unrealistic. Non-CBD jobs tend to be concentrated in specific places, as are CBD jobs. In addition, the urban transportation network is not ubiquitous. Recently, White (1988) has reestimated the amount of wasteful commuting for Hamilton's sample of metropolitan areas, and concluded that only about 11 percent of commuting is wasteful.

Both Hamilton's and White's studies show that the simple model is inadequate to describe commuting patterns, and that is the key issue here. Underlying that issue is the following question: what model would adequately explain metropolitan commuting patterns, and would it imply waste? The jury is still out on that deeper issue.

Conclusion

This section began by noting that no model fits reality perfectly; the monocentric model is no exception. The gradients with respect to density, housing price, land rent, and wages conform remarkably well to predictions generated by the model and reasonable assumed numbers. In particular, no other model has predictions for these patterns so close to reality. Actual patterns of commuting, however, appear to be at odds with the predictions of the model. This suggests the need for more sophisticated models in which the cost of commuting toward the CBD is not responsible for the entire shape of the urban landscape. The commuting findings show that residential and job locations are more complicated than those described in the models of Chapter 6. However, despite the obvious need for further research on the determinants of home and job locations, the monocentric model of Chapter 6 correctly predicts many important features of urban form.

☐ CRITICISMS AND EXTENSIONS

The models of the previous chapter are static; by assumption, the urban area has no history. Today's circumstances determine the shape of today's urban area. To put it a bit differently, the models deal (properly) only with urban areas in which everything has achieved equilibrium. This is obviously false, however; urban areas have durable inventories of housing, office, and manufacturing structures, as well as transport networks. The rapid declines in transport cost over the past several decades have led to declines in the steepness of *equilibrium* density gradients for American cities. The best available evidence indicates that actual gradients have become flatter, as already shown, though the process of converting to lower central-city density is far from instantaneous; it can take decades.

The conversion process frequently necessitates the demolition of buildings. The full cost of this demolition is greater than the fee that must be paid to the wrecking company; it also includes any income the building would have generated if it had been allowed to stand. It is worthwhile to incur this cost only if the value of the vacant land exceeds the demolition cost plus the present value of forgone rent (net of current costs such as repairs and maintenance) on the demolished building. Thus, even if the equilibrium density has declined, a market economy may achieve this density reduction only very slowly. Also, it is economically more difficult to convert from high to low density than the other way around for two reasons. First, demolition of low-density structures is cheaper than demolition of high-density structures. Second, the reason people would want to convert from high to low density in the first place is that raw land value has fallen. However, if the cleared land is not worth very much anyway, the payoff to demolition is low. Thus, conversion from high to low density has high costs and a low payoff. This means that high-density urban areas are likely to persist long after they are economically and technologically obsolete.

Demolition cost can be a serious impediment to redevelopment, as the figures in Table 7.4 indicate. Demolition costs about $0.15 per cubic foot for brick buildings one to three stories tall and about $0.30 per cubic foot for taller buildings.[17] Column 2 of Table 7.4 shows demolition cost per acre of cleared land for various building heights, assuming that 70 percent of the land is covered by the structures. If raw land is worth less than this amount, demolition is not worth the cost, even if the buildings currently occupying the land are worthless.

To add perspective, Column 3 in Table 7.4 gives the "critical distance." Assume as before that rural land is worth $2000 per acre and that urban land value rises 20 percent per mile from the edge of the metropolitan area. The critical distance entry in Table 7.4 gives the distance from the edge of the urban area at which land value is just sufficient to justify the demolition of unwanted buildings. Take the case of two-story buildings. Urban land value achieves a level of $91,476 per acre 19 miles from the edge, meaning that the land to be cleared must be at least this far from the edge if proceeds from the sale of vacant land are to cover the demolition cost. Five-story buildings must be at least 27 miles from the edge. For an urban area whose radius is smaller than this critical distance, demolition is not justified even at the CBD. In such circumstances it is cheaper to abandon structures than to demolish them and sell the vacant land. The numbers in Table 7.4 reveal that abandonment is economically preferable to demolition in many actual conditions.

As noted, the demolition contractor's fee is typically only part of the cost of demolishing a building. Demolition also involves forgoing the income the building could have earned; even for buildings that have fallen on hard times, this impediment can be more serious than the demolition charge. Consider a standard 18 × 50-foot row house oc-

---

17. These figures were supplied by William Geppert of Geppert Demolition Contractors of Philadelphia. The figures assume an entire block is demolished. The cost is much higher if a single building is demolished while surrounding buildings are protected. The cost rises for buildings four or more stories high, because these buildings typically have steel reinforcing rods and thicker walls.

Table 7.4 *Demolition Cost Per Acre as a Function of Building Height*

Building Height (Stories)	Demolition Cost per Acre[a]	Critical Distance (Miles)[a]
2	$ 91,476	19
3	137,214	21
4	365,904	26
5	457,380	27

[a]See text for assumptions.

cupying 1286 square feet of land (assuming 70 percent coverage). Suppose the building yields income after operating and maintenance (but excluding interest) of $25 per month, or $300 per year. At a 10 percent discount rate the discounted value of this stream is nearly $3000 if maintenance and repair expenditures give the house a long useful life, so the market price of the row house is $3000. Thus, the current use of the land has a present value of $2.33 per square foot ($3000/1286), or $101,600 per acre. In other words, an acre of row houses worth $3000 each has an aggregate market value of $101,600. When this must be added to a demolition cost of $100,000 or more, the decision to demolish is not to be taken lightly. Even when the current buildings are worth little or nothing, the cost of adjusting to the new equilibrium land use can be prohibitive. It is readily apparent that in most of the cities listed in Table 7.3 it would not be profitable to tear down an acre of row houses and sell the land on the prime industrial site market, even if the acre were a prime site.

It would be wrong to infer that this analysis provides justification for government programs to demolish slum housing. Demolition cost and forgone rents are net costs, and markets value them correctly in the analysis here. There may be other costs of slums not yet included in the analysis that would justify government intervention. This issue will be further explored in Chapter 11.

A second observation that emerges from considering an urban area's past concerns residential location patterns. It has already been noted that income tends to rise with distance from the CBD. As the last chapter noted, the static monocentric model can explain this observation provided the income elasticity of demand for housing is greater than the income elasticity of transport cost. Modern evidence suggests that these two elasticities are quite close to one another, however, casting doubt on the static model explanation of income segregation.

Nevertheless, once it is realized that urban areas have histories and that, to a good approximation, they are built from the middle out, there is at least a partial explanation of segregation patterns that is straightforward. Low-income housing tends to be old housing (because it was built at a time when incomes in general were lower than they are today and because quality and rents fall as time passes), and old housing tends to be located in the central parts of American cities. According to one recent study (Cooke and Hamilton, 1982), these forces are more than adequate to explain the existing pattern of income segregation.[18]

Rural-Urban Boundary

According to the models presented in Chapter 6, urban development extends out to the point at which urban land users no longer can outbid rural land users. The standard interpretation of this observation is that urban expansion should take place along a thin line, like an advancing glacier. In fact, however, the edges of most urban areas are characterized by a band up to several miles wide in which rural and urban uses commingle. Judging by census data on the locations of houses of various ages, this appears to have been the pattern at least as far back as the 1930s.

There are three important reasons for this thick, fuzzy boundary between rural and urban uses (sometimes referred to as *urban sprawl*). The first two are discussed here and the third in the next section. The first reason arises from a careful, rather than a casual, interpretation of the monocentric model. Agricultural land is not homogeneous; its productivity varies dramatically from one plot to the next, depending on soil conditions, topography, drainage, and the like. Peterson (1979) has found that parcels with low farm productivity tend to be converted to urban use first. This means that some farmland is skipped over—at least temporarily—because of its high farm productivity.

The second reason for the fuzzy boundary is that farmland tends to come on the market at specific times in the lifetime of the farmer (particularly if the farm is occupied by the owner). A farmer is much more interested in selling at retirement than ten years before, for example. Also, there are tax advantages to selling to a developer at the time of the death of the owner. Finally, of course, farmers simply vary in their desire to remain in business. Thus, not all parcels in the path of urban development are for sale at the same time and price. This means that at any given time, developers have a limited number of sites to choose from. The result is that urban land uses extend far into the countryside, or agricultural uses extend far into the urban area.

Speculation

Many parcels of developable land are held back from urban use not because a farmer does not want to retire yet, but because a speculator is holding the land in anticipation of future capital gains. Many downtown parking lots, suburban farms, and vacant lots are examples. This speculative withholding of land from the market means that today's development must take place at a more remote location than would otherwise be the case. This, in turn, increases many of the costs associated with urban life. The provision of water, sewers, roads, and other services is more costly when development is scattered than when it is con-

---

18. Chapter 11 will cover this topic in more detail.

centrated. Personal travel (commuting, shopping, and the like) probably increases as well. These social costs of scattered development and the speculation that helps bring it about are well known.

What is less well known is that often there are important benefits associated with speculation. It was shown that the full costs of demolition (the demolition contractor's fee plus the forgone income from the old structure) easily can be prohibitive when compared with the value of the cleared land. The decision to develop a parcel of land is frequently irreversible. An efficient development criterion will recognize this fact; if optimum current and future uses of a parcel of land are different, it is necessary to consider the trade-off between present and future development.

The following example illustrates this point. The present density function for an urban area is depicted by the solid curve in Figure 7.2a. The optimum density function 20 years hence also includes the segment AC. The right-hand tail (BC) of the dashed function represents rich people who demand large lots and are willing to live at remote locations. The adjacent section (AB) represents middle-income people who demand smaller lots and more access. Suppose the middle-income demanders (the AB segment) are predicted to arrive in the urban area in ten years but that the rich people (segment BC) are already there demanding housing. Developers could build rich people's housing on the innermost vacant land, beginning at A. This would mean that when the middle-income people arrived ten years hence, their housing would be relegated to the BC segment. The density gradient would look something like Figure 7.2b, with the higher-density housing more remote than the lower-density housing.

Chapter 6 showed that this pattern is not optimum. Among other things, total commuting is greater under the Figure 7.2b configuration than under the Figure 7.2a pattern. To see this, note that high density at remote locations means a large number of commuters at remote locations. Under the Figure 7.2a pattern there are more people close to the CBD and fewer far from it than under the Figure 7.2b pattern. The cost of housing the rich people on the innermost vacant land is this: after the arrival of the middle-income people ten years hence, the pattern of land use will not be optimum. The benefit of housing the rich people in the example on the innermost land is that, in the ten years before the arrival of middle-income demanders, the city will be more compact. This, in turn, will reduce such costs as urban travel, streets, and water and sewer mains.

This example indicates the possibility (although not the certainty) that efficiency is enhanced by initially scattered development and subsequent infilling. Given the timing of development demands, scattered development may be the only way to insure that the ultimate shape of the city is efficient.

A strong case can be made that land speculators cause developers to make efficient decisions regarding the timing and location of development. In the previous case, consider the parcel of land at A, just at the

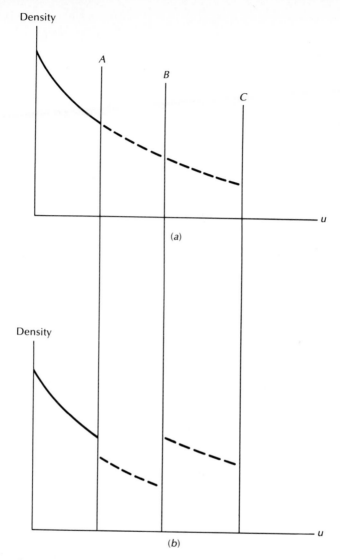

Figure 7.2 *Density Functions with Growth: (a) with Speculation;*
(b) without Speculation

edge of current development. The owner of this parcel (the speculator) can sell immediately to a developer, who will construct low-density,
high-income housing. The owner also can refuse to sell today, in anticipation of a higher price when the middle-income people arrive ten years
hence.[19] Of course, the speculator who sells today can earn interest on
the proceeds of the sale. It is profitable to hold out for future capital
gains only if the expected appreciation is sufficient to cover this forgone interest. In other words, the speculator faces both costs and

19. The land will appreciate, because it no longer will be at the urban periphery;
it therefore will command a location premium over land at the edge.

benefits of withholding central land from production; in a perfect market, these costs and benefits correspond to the social costs and benefits previously discussed.

Note that the speculation and timing-of-development problem arises only because of the durability of capital and the costs associated with changing from one land use to another. If everyone lived in mobile homes, the rich in the example would locate on the AB segment until the arrival of the middle-income people; they then would move costlessly to the BC segment, having been outbid for the AB land.

It should now be clear that the optimum timing of real estate development is a complex and interactive process; an optimum temporal sequence of development does not necessarily occur at sequential distances from the center of an SMSA. The final point to be made is that real estate development decisions are among the most complex economic decisions. Real estate is the longest-lived major capital investment. Industrial capital may last ten to twenty-five years; much real estate capital lasts at least fifty years. Modern high-rise structural steel office buildings may still be around after one hundred years. That implies that real estate development decisions must be based on the longest forecasts of technical and market developments now made. Inevitably, judgments differ as to optimum timing and nature of development. One reason that there are parking lots on land surrounded by properties worth a million dollars an acre is that owners of adjacent properties simply make different judgments about optimum timing of development.

Topography

Another assumption underlying the monocentric models presented in Chapter 6 is that so long as there is land it is possible to build cities upon it. The effect of variations in the character of the land itself upon cities is virtually never given serious consideration by urban economists. Two examples will help to illustrate the importance of considering the underlying terrain when attempting to describe the shapes of cities.

New York. According to the models of Chapter 6, a city should have a single high-density CBD, with density falling off gradually in all directions. But anybody who has viewed the skyline of Manhattan knows that Manhattan has two CBDs—one around 34th Street (the Empire State Building), and the other around Wall Street (the World Trade Center). Between the two, looking like a mountain pass, is Greenwich Village. At least in a casual way, many urban economists have tried to discover the explanation for "what went wrong" with the models in Chapter 6. It turns out that the answer lies not in economics but geology.

The bedrock underlying Manhattan lies close to the surface from about 30th Street north. But south of 30th Street it sinks to several hundred feet (deep enough that the builders of Brooklyn Bridge eventually gave up looking for bedrock and rested the pilings on sand). At the south end the bedrock again rises to only about 100 feet below the surface. The entire surface is composed of former New Jersey land deposited during the last Ice Age. This material is not a suitable substrate for high-rise buildings; hence Greenwich Village. (See McPhee, 1982 for a fuller discussion.)

New Orleans. Until recently New Orleans had considerably fewer high-rise buildings than one would predict for a city its size. The reason again has to do with the substrate. For all practical purposes there is no bedrock under New Orleans; rather, the city is built over a layer of Mississippi river silt some 20,000 feet thick. The instability of this material precluded high-rise construction until the last two decades.

☐ Summary

The monocentric model presented in Chapter 6 accurately predicts geographic patterns of land value, housing prices, residential density, and wages. For poorly understood reasons, however, it and its natural extension do a poor job of predicting commuting patterns.

Many assumptions underlying the basic model in Chapter 6 are unrealistic. Most notable among these is the assumption of continuous (static) equilibrium with no adjustment costs. The recognition of adjustment costs alters and enriches the perception of urban form, but the original model remains the frame of reference.

Questions and Problems

1. How would you expect fees at parking lots to vary with distance from the CBD? Would the rate of variation depend on whether the facilities were street-level lots or multistory parking structures? See whether you can test your prediction by gathering data on parking fees.

2. The 1970s witnessed a rise in the proportion of two-worker, childless households. How do you think this would affect an urban area's housing price and density gradients?

3. In many developing countries the rich live close to the CBD and the poor live at the periphery. What do you think explains this pattern?

4. Many states have "use-value" property taxation for agricultural land. Taxes are based not on market value of the property, but rather on the estimated value of the property in its *current use.* They are designed to make it easier for farmers to remain in business even if their farms are in the path of urban development and hence would command high sale prices to developers. Discuss the distributional and efficiency aspects of use-value taxation. Would you expect urban areas in states with use-value taxation to look different from those in other states? How would you test your hypothesis?

References and Further Reading

Chicoine, David L. "Farmland Values at the Urban Fringe: An Analysis of Sale Prices." *Land Economics* Vol. 57 (1981): 353–362.

Cooke, Timothy, and Bruce W. Hamilton. "Evolution of Urban Housing Stocks: A Model Applied to Baltimore and Houston." *Journal of Urban Economics* Vol. 12 (November, 1984): 304–323. A model of urban form that takes into account the fact that housing is highly durable and thus cannot be readily changed in character when economic conditions change.

Eberts, Randall W. "An Empirical Investigation of Intraurban Wage Gradients." *Journal of Urban Economics* Vol. 10 (1981): 50–60.

Hamilton, Bruce W. "Wasteful Commuting." *Journal of Political Economy* 90 (1982): 1035–58. A comparison of "optimal" and actual commuting behavior in a sample of American and Japanese cities.

Hoyt, Homer. *One Hundred Years of Land Values in Chicago* (Chicago: University of Chicago Press, 1933). A classic study of the behavior of land values.

Jackson, Jerry R. "Intraurban Variation in the Price of Housing." *Journal of Urban Economics* Vol. 6 (1979): 465–479.

Kau, J., and C. Sirmans. "Urban Land Value Functions and the Price Elasticity of Demand for Housing." *Journal of Urban Economics* Vol. 6 (1979): 112–21.

Layard, P. R. G. and A. A. Walters. *Microeconomic Theory* (New York: McGraw-Hill, 1978). A good microeconomics textbook, cited here for its discussion of the elasticity of substitution. It would also be excellent background for Chapter 8.

McPhee, John. *In Suspect Terrain* (New York: Farrar, Straus, and Giroux, 1982). Describes the formation of Manhattan and the geological problems associated with building there.

Mills, Edwin S. "The Value of Urban Land." *The Quality of the Urban Environment,* ed. H. Perloff (Washington, D.C.: Resources for the Future, 1969). One article from an important collection of theoretical and empirical studies.

Mills, Edwin S. *Studies in the Structure of the Urban Economy* (Baltimore: Johns Hopkins, 1972). A theoretical section develops several models of urban form, and an empirical section estimates population and employment density gradients for a sample of American cities, some as far back as the late nineteenth century.

Mills, Edwin S., and Ohta Katsutoshi. "Urbanization and Urban Problems." Chapter 10 of *Asia's New Giant,* Hugh Patrick and Henry Rosovsky, eds. (Washington, D.C.: Brookings, 1976): 673–752. A discussion of urbanization and urban form in Japan, with interesting comparisons to America.

Muth, Richard. *Cities and Housing* (Chicago: University of Chicago Press, 1969). An exhaustive study of the ability of models like those in Chapter 6 to explain actual patterns of urban land use.

Peterson, George E. *Federal Tax Policy and Urban Development* (Forthcoming) (Washington, D.C.: The Urban Institute). An investigation of several features of federal tax policy on urban form.

Rosen, Sherwin. "Wage-Based Indexes of Urban Quality of Life." *Current Issues in Urban Economics,* eds. Peter Mieszkowski and Mahlon Straszheim (Baltimore: Johns Hopkins, 1979). A theoretical and empirical discussion of the relationship between a city's wage rates and the various costs and amenities associated with life in the city.

Wheaton, William. "Urban Residential Growth Under Perfect Foresight." *Journal of Urban Economics* Vol. 12 (July 1982): 1–21. An estimation of the shapes of rent-offer curves for various income groups.

White, Michelle J. "Urban Commuting Journeys Are Not Wasteful." (Forthcoming) *Journal of Political Economy* (1988).

8

Welfare Economics and Urban Problems

☐ The preceding chapters have built a theoretical and empirical framework within which to analyze urban processes and trends. Part 3 focuses on the analysis of urban problems and alternatives open to society to solve them. Welfare economics is the link between the positive analyses and the normative, or policy, analyses. A brief discussion of this field is included here to emphasize certain topics that are important in urban policy analysis. Fuller treatment can be found in a good intermediate price theory textbook.

☐ WHAT IS WELFARE ECONOMICS?

Welfare economics is a branch of economic theory concerned with evaluating the performance of the economic system. To decide whether the system is performing well and whether a change in government policy would improve its performance, a yardstick is needed to measure performance. Such a yardstick is called a *value judgment*. Some people feel that economics becomes unscientific, or at least less scientific, when value judgments are introduced into analysis, but the feeling is misplaced. Economic theory is the deduction of implications from assumptions or axioms. There is no reason for economists not to include value judgments among their assumptions, and hence judgments about the performance of the economy among their conclusions. It is important for economists to make their value judgments as clear and explicit as possible so that others can decide whether to accept the value judgments and hence the concluding evaluation of performance. A major element of progress in welfare economics during recent decades has been to make value judgments explicit rather than implicit in the analysis. This has been part of an important trend in economics to make all assumptions as explicit as possible.

The other side of the coin is that it is not possible to judge the performance of the economy without value judgments. Whenever someone judges that an economy is performing well or badly, that person is explicitly or implicitly using a value judgment as to what constitutes good or bad performance. The implication is that if economics did not involve value judgments, it would be an entirely academic discipline incapable of advising society on the appropriate solutions to economic problems.

What value judgments should economists use in evaluating the economy's performance? In a free society, people can make whatever value judgments they wish. Economists have spent enormous amounts of time and effort discussing and clarifying value judgments that would be interesting and acceptable to many people, or at least to many thoughtful people. The value judgments underlying modern welfare economics are the result of decades of thought and analysis. Nevertheless, they are value judgments, and the conclusions of analysis can be no more persuasive than the value judgments and other assumptions from which they follow.

Welfare economics begins with the idea that the purpose of economic activity is to produce goods and services for people to use. It leads to the broad judgment that *the economic system should be evaluated by the efficiency with which it produces goods and services as well as by the efficiency and equity with which it distributes them for people's use.* For many purposes, goods and services can be defined narrowly as inputs and outputs traded on markets. For some purposes, however, it is desirable to broaden the definition. To take the most important example, suppose the production and consumption of traded goods and services affect the environment in undesirable ways. Then the definition of goods and services can be broadened to include the quality of the environment, and this can be included in the analysis. Of course, the broader definition may require a somewhat different and more complex analysis than the narrow definition.

The foregoing value judgment is not sufficiently precise for purposes of analysis. A crucial step toward precision is the assumption that each individual has a set of preferences for goods and services that leads to indifference curves that have the properties postulated in consumer behavior theory, as well as the assumption that a person's welfare is measured by the indifference or utility level attained. This value judgment usually is expressed by the assumption that each individual is the best judge of his or her welfare. No one accepts that value judgment without qualification. Everyone makes mistakes, and a few people are persistently incapable of judging their self-interest. For many people, however, the attractiveness of this value judgment as a broad guide to government policy is clinched by the following consideration. People make mistakes in choosing which car to buy, play to see, or person to marry, but who is qualified to make such decisions for another? *The value judgment that each person is the best judge of his or her welfare underlies all the subsequent analysis in this book.*

☐ CRITERIA OF ECONOMIC PERFORMANCE

The foregoing consideration leads economists to two specific criteria for evaluating the performance of an economy. The economy is said to perform well if, given the productive resources and technology available to it, (1) no reallocation of inputs and outputs can improve the welfare of some without worsening the welfare of others, and (2) income and wealth are equitably distributed. Criterion 1 is known as the **efficiency criterion,** or the **Pareto efficiency criterion,** after the economist who first proposed it. Criterion 2 is known as the **equity criterion.**

Most people find these criteria easy to accept. Objections come from the fact that Criterion 2 does not specify what distribution of income and wealth is equitable. Utilitarian economists of the nineteenth century believed that a society's welfare was the sum of the utilities of its members. Add the assumptions that all people have the same utility functions and that marginal utility decreases with income, and it is easy to derive the utilitarian conclusion that social welfare is maximized if income is equally distributed. Modern theory of consumer behavior does not attach any meaning to the sum of people's utilities, however. Specifically, if a utility function that represents a person's preferences can be found, any utility function that is an increasing function of the first one will represent that person's preferences equally well. In particular, the sum of all people's utilities can be made any number by choosing appropriate individual utility functions.

Despite this, everyone has strong feelings about the distribution of income. At present, however, economics provides little help in forming or evaluating such feelings. About all that can be said is that each person's evaluation of government policy proposals should depend on the effect of the proposals on income distribution. Of course, a citizen can unhesitatingly support a policy proposal that improves the economy's efficiency without worsening its income distribution, given the citizen's feelings about income distribution. Likewise, a citizen can support a proposal that improves the income distribution without worsening efficiency. The difficult choices involve proposals that would improve efficiency at the expense of equity or vice versa.

However, disagreement about equity issues should not be exaggerated. Nearly all American citizens agree that government should raise the living standards of society's neediest people by taxing those with substantial incomes. Nearly all Americans also agree that high-income people should pay a larger percentage of their incomes in taxes to support government than should middle-income people. A great deal of disagreement exists on the specifics of these matters, but it occurs mainly within a broad consensus on the basic issues. How societies do or should make equity evaluations is the subject of advanced expositions of welfare economics (see Mueller).

The assumption that each person is the best judge of his or her welfare has an important and controversial implication: *government programs to improve equity by raising living standards of the poor should provide them money, not commodities or services.* You cannot make people worse off by providing them with the money value of commodities or services instead of the commodities or services. Most people probably accept this general principle, yet the political process continues to provide or subsidize food, health care, housing, and other things for the poor instead of providing them with money. Direct provision of commodities and services for the poor is justified only if there is **market failure** in private provision of the commodities or services. An important task of this and subsequent chapters will be to analyze arguments for the direct provision of commodities and services to the poor.

The first task is to lay out criteria for market efficiency.

☐ CONDITIONS FOR ECONOMIC EFFICIENCY

The efficiency criterion has implications for the allocation of both outputs and inputs. The basic ideas are most easily understood by considering the simplest situation in which a problem of resource allocation can be posed—a model of pure consumption.

Pure Consumption Model

Suppose a society must allocate fixed amounts of two consumption goods per unit of time between two members. Shortly it will be assumed that the commodities are produced with scarce inputs, but for the moment it is assumed that they simply appear in fixed amounts. X units of one good are available and Y units of the other. Designate the two people A and B and the amounts of the two goods allocated to each by X_A, X_B, Y_A, and Y_B. The allocation of the goods must satisfy the following conditions:

$$X_A + X_B = X, \text{ and } Y_A + Y_B = Y,$$

and all the allocations must be nonnegative.

Individuals A and B have indifference maps representing their tastes for the two goods, as shown in Figure 8.1. Society's allocation problem is usually represented as in Figure 8.2. The horizontal and vertical axes of the indifference diagrams in Figure 8.1 have been extended to lengths X and Y, and the indifference diagram for B has been rotated so that its origin is in the upper right-hand corner of the rectangle. Each point in Figure 8.2 corresponds exactly to one of the possible alloca-

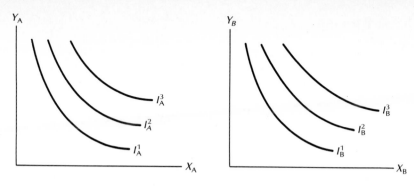

Figure 8.1 *Indifference Maps for Two Consumers*

tions of X and Y between A and B. Society's problem is therefore to choose a point in the rectangle that satisfies the efficiency criterion.

Unless the tastes of A and B differ greatly, there will be some allocations at which the indifference curves for A and B have the same slope. Assume that such allocations exist and can be represented by a continuous curve, designated cc in Figure 8.2. The cc curve represents all the allocations such that

$$MRS_A(X_A, Y_A) = MRS_B(X_B, Y_B),\qquad(8.1)$$

where MRS stands for one person's marginal rate of substitution between the two goods. The **basic welfare theorem** in the pure consumption model is that the set of allocations that satisfies the efficiency criterion is precisely the set that satisfies Equation (8.1).

To prove the theorem, consider an allocation P_1 not on cc in Figure 8.2. There must be exactly one of the indifference curves for A and one for B passing through P_1, but they cannot be tangent. Then any reallocation from P_1 to a point like P_2, which lies between the indifference curves passing through P_1, must place all individuals on higher indifference curves than they were on at P_1. Thus, each person is better off at P_2 than at P_1. Repeating the argument shows that reallocation from P_2 to a point between the two indifference curves passing through P_2 makes both individuals still better off. The argument can be repeated until an allocation is reached on cc. This proves the theorem.

Note that nothing in the argument rests on the assumptions that there are only two people and only two goods in the society. If it consists of any finite number of people and the problem is to allocate among them fixed amounts of any finite number of goods, an efficient allocation must satisfy Equation (8.1) for every pair of goods and every pair of people.

All points on cc are efficient, but they are by no means all equitable. At allocation P_4, A has practically all of both goods and B has almost nothing, whereas at P_3 the opposite is true. Thus, a person who felt that A was relatively deserving would prefer P_4 to P_3, whereas a person who felt that B was relatively deserving would prefer P_3 to P_4. The

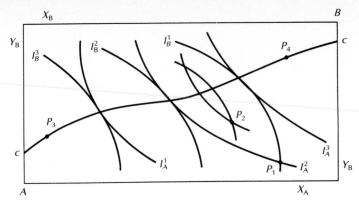

Figure 8.2 *Edgeworth Box with Two Consumers' Indifference Maps*

efficiency criterion narrows society's choice from the set of points in the rectangle in Figure 8.2 to the set of points on *cc*. The equity criterion narrows the choice from the set of points on *cc* to one or a few of those points.

What kinds of institutions might society develop to solve its allocation problem? If someone knew each person's indifference map, that person could compute the set of efficient allocations. Of course, no one has the required information. Recall from price theory that if goods are allocated on markets and if the price each person pays for each good is independent of the amount bought, all individuals maximize their welfare by buying amounts of goods that equate their marginal rates of substitution to the price ratios of pairs of goods. Thus, all buyers who face the same prices choose amounts of goods that equate to each other every person's *MRS* for a particular pair of goods. Competitive markets, in particular, will allocate goods to satisfy Equation (8.1) and hence allocate efficiently. In the pure consumption model, monopoly is also efficient, but it will be shown that only competitive markets, among all market allocations, satisfy the efficiency conditions when input allocations are included in the model.

Are competitive markets equitable as well as efficient? They are not necessarily, since competitive markets insure only that the allocation will be on *cc*, not that it will be at any particular point on *cc*. Equity depends on how much purchasing power or income *A* and *B* bring to the market. Suppose, for example, that *A* and *B* each inherit amounts of the two commodities. Their inheritances put them at a point like P_1, and they then trade the commodities on competitive markets and end up on *cc* between I_A^2 and I_B^1. The point P_1 is entirely determined by the legacies, and the amounts *A* and *B* inherit determine where on *cc* they end up after trading. Thus, competitive markets can guarantee only to get the society to *cc*, not to an equitable point on *cc*. In this simple example, society could insure equity as well as efficiency by enacting inheritance laws that reallocated purchasing power in an equitable way and then letting individuals trade on competitive markets.

Production-Consumption Model

The model now can be enriched by recognizing that X and Y are produced with scarce inputs. Suppose there are two inputs, labor and land, with fixed amounts of each available to society. There are N units of labor and L units of land. Both inputs can be used to produce each output. The amounts of the goods produced are related to the amounts of the inputs used by two production functions:

$$X = F(N_X, L_X), \quad Y = G(N_Y, L_Y),$$

where F and G are different functions. Subscripts indicate the amounts of the inputs used to produce the commodity indicated, so the use of inputs is limited by the following:

$$L_X + L_Y = L, \quad N_X + N_Y = N.$$

Society now has two problems. First, it must allocate the inputs to production of the two commodities. Second, it must allocate the commodities to the two individuals. The production function can be represented by their *isoquants,* as shown in Figure 8.3. An isoquant shows all the combinations of two inputs (here, land and labor) that produce the same amount of output. A representation of the input allocation problem can be formed from Figure 8.3 in precisely the same way that Figure 8.2 was formed from Figure 8.1. The result is Figure 8.4, where the horizontal sides of the rectangle have length L and the vertical sides have length N. The origin for the production of Y is at the upper right-hand corner of the rectangle.

Given an understanding of the proof of the theorem in the pure consumption model, it is easy to see how inputs must be allocated in the production-consumption model to satisfy the efficiency criterion. Any allocation of the two inputs between X and Y corresponds to a point in Figure 8.4. The curve dd connects all the points of tangency between pairs of isoquants. Price theory texts show that the slope of an isoquant is the ratio of the marginal products of the two inputs. Thus, dd is the set of input allocations such that the ratio of the marginal products of the two inputs is the same for the production of both commodities at a given point; that is, dd is the set of input allocations such that:

$$\frac{MP_{LX}}{MP_{NX}} = \frac{MP_{LY}}{MP_{NY}}. \tag{8.2}$$

The basic efficiency theorem in the production-consumption model is that the set of input and output allocations that satisfies the efficiency criterion is precisely the set that satisfies Equations (8.1) and (8.2). The theorem and its proof are analogous to those in the pure consumption model. Suppose that the input allocation is at a point like P_1 in Figure

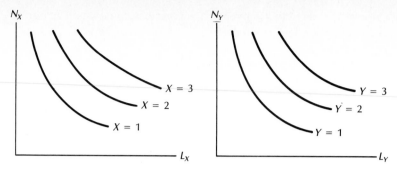

Figure 8.3 *Isoquant Maps for the Production of Goods X and Y*

8.4, not on *dd*. Then the same amounts of the two inputs can be real-located so as to produce more of both X and Y by moving from P_1 to a point like P_2, which is between the isoquants passing through P_1, since P_2 is on higher isoquants for both X and Y than is P_1. Clearly, P_2 represents more output of both X and Y than P_1 does. Thus, it is possible to improve the welfare of both individuals (A and B) by moving from P_1 to $P_2$1, since each can receive more of both goods. Repeating the argument shows that reallocations of inputs can improve the welfare of both individuals as long as the input allocation is not on *dd*.

The set of efficient input allocations is the set on *dd*. Given the total outputs of X and Y, however, efficiency also requires that the outputs be allocated efficiently between A and B. Thus, Equation (8.1) is also a condition for efficiency, just as in the pure consumption model. Therefore, input and output allocations are efficient only if Equations (8.1) and (8.2) are both satisfied. Once again, it is easy to see that the argument applies if there are more than two inputs or outputs. If more than two inputs are used to produce X and Y, Equation (8.2) must hold for each pair of inputs taken separately. There then would be many equations like Equation (8.2). If there are more than two outputs, input allocations must satisfy Equation (8.2) for those outputs as well as for X and Y.

The conditions for efficient allocation of inputs and outputs have been derived without reference to social institutions that might undertake production and distribution. It now can be shown that allocations of inputs and outputs by competitive markets do satisfy the efficiency conditions. Price theory textbooks and Chapter 6 show that the necessary conditions for profit maximization for producers who deal in competitive input and output markets are the following:

$$MP_{LX} \times p_X = R \text{ and } MP_{NX} \times p_X = w \qquad (8.3)$$

for an X producer, and

$$MP_{LY} \times p_Y = R \text{ and } MP_{NY} \times p_Y = w \qquad (8.4)$$

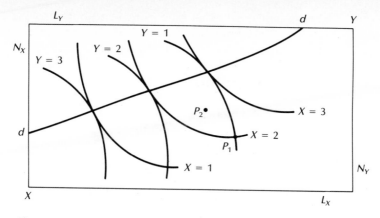

Figure 8.4 *Edgeworth Box with X and Y Isoquant Maps*

for a Y producer. MP is the marginal product of each of the two inputs in producing the two outputs; p_X and p_Y are the prices of X and Y; R is the rental rate of land; and w is the wage rate.

It only remains now to show that Equations (8.3) and (8.4) imply Equation (8.2). Divide the first equation by the second in Equations (8.3) and (8.4). The result follows:

$$\frac{MP_{LX}}{MP_{NX}} = \frac{R}{w} \text{ and } \frac{MP_{LY}}{MP_{NY}} = \frac{R}{w}.$$

Thus, the two ratios of marginal products are equal to the same input price ratio, and hence to one another. This shows that competitive profit-maximizing firms employ inputs in amounts that satisfy the efficiency criterion of Equation (8.2). The pure consumption model showed that competitive output markets satisfy Equation (8.1). Thus competitive input and output markets satisfy both sets of efficiency conditions.

A corollary to the foregoing discussion is that efficiency requires outputs of both X and Y to be such that their marginal costs are equal to their respective prices. This condition, of course, is satisfied by competitive (but not by monopoly) markets.

The efficiency criterion tells society that, among all the points in Figures 8.2 and 8.4, it should choose input and output allocations on cc and dd. As in the pure consumption model, there are many efficient input and output allocations, but not all of them are equitable. Suppose (to stay within the two-input model) that every worker is equally productive, and thus in competitive markets receives the same earned income. Suppose further that ownership of land is determined by inheritance. Then each unit of land receives the same rental rate, but the overall distribution of income or purchasing power is affected by the distribution of land ownership. In this model, society can obtain efficient and equitable input and output allocations by using an inheritance tax to produce an equitable distribution of land ownership and by permitting competitive markets to allocate inputs and outputs. The inheritance tax might, for example, tax those whose incomes exceed the average and distribute the proceeds to others.

Variable Input/Output Model

The pure consumption model assumed that the amounts of the two consumer goods available to society were fixed. The assumption was relaxed in the production-consumption model and replaced by the assumption that the amounts of inputs were fixed. In the model here, the assumption of fixed input quantities is relaxed. It is replaced by the assumption that workers can vary their supplies of labor freely, within limits.

This assumption is, of course, an approximation, since many jobs require more or less rigid hours of work. Hours of work, however, are more flexible than is sometimes realized. Over a period of ten to twenty years, hours of work change substantially, falling as incomes rise. Even within short periods of time, however, there are many ways to vary hours of work. Moonlighting, overtime, and part-time jobs are available. Many professional and self-employed workers have flexible hours of work, as do, to some extent, many commission and piece-rate workers.

Leisure, a catchall for whatever is done during nonwork hours, is valuable, just as consumer goods are valuable. Assume that each individual has a set of indifference curves between leisure and each commodity, as illustrated in Figure 8.5. $\overline{N}_A$ represents hours of leisure for A per unit of time, just as X_A represents the amount of X consumed by A per unit of time. If N_A is hours of work for A, $N_T = N_A + \overline{N}_A$ is the total hours available to A for work and leisure. The indifference curves in Figure 8.5 depend only on the tastes of individual A. Now introduce the production side by supposing that A produces X at work. The output of X depends on A's hours of work, and therefore it varies inversely with the amount of leisure he or she takes. The relationship is shown by bb in Figure 8.5. Since bb shows how the production of X by A varies with his or her hours of leisure, its slope is minus the marginal product of an extra hour of work by A in producing X. If bb is concave, as in Figure 8.5, it means that the marginal product of A falls as he or she works more hours producing X.

The final criterion for efficient resource allocation now can be derived. It states that the hours of work by A should equate his or her marginal rate of substitution between X and leisure to his or her marginal product in producing X; that is,

$$MRS_A(X_A, \overline{N}_A) = MP_{AX}. \tag{8.5}$$

The curve bb is like a budget constraint for A, showing the combinations of leisure and X available to him or her. Individual A achieves

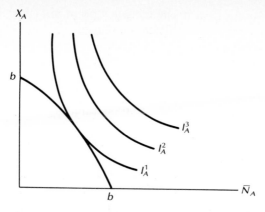

Figure 8.5 *Household's Production-Possibilities Curve and Indifference Map*

the highest possible indifference curve by choosing a combination of X and leisure that places him or her at the point of tangency between bb and an indifference curve. A's wage w may be higher in one sector than another. If so, A should work in the sector in which his or her wage is greatest and work a number of hours in that sector such that his or her production possibility curve is tangent to an indifference curve. Since the movement of A to the point of tangency from another point on bb does not affect the welfare of other members of society, the move satisfies the efficiency criterion; that is, it makes A better off without making anyone else worse off. Going up bb means working more hours, and concavity implies that each additional hour results in a smaller increase in production of X.

It only remains to show that competitive markets satisfy this efficiency criterion, as well as those already discussed. If A sells his or her labor and buys X and Y on markets, the budget constraint is

$$p_X X_A + p_Y Y_A = w(N_T - \overline{N}_A) \tag{8.6}$$

where $N_T - \overline{N}_A$ is the number of hours A chooses to work, and w is the hourly wage rate. If the labor market is competitive,

$$w = MP_{Ax} \times p_X.$$

Substituting for w in Equation (8.6) and rearranging terms, the budget constraint can be written as follows:

$$X_A = (MP_{Ax} N_T - \frac{pY}{pX} Y_A) - MP_{Ax} \overline{N}_A. \tag{8.7}$$

Thus, in a competitive labor market, the slope of the budget constraint of A is MP_{Ax}, the same as that of bb. It follows that the market choice by A will lead him or her to the tangency point in Figure 8.5 that has been shown to satisfy the efficiency criterion.

The production-consumption model showed that society could obtain an efficient and equitable resource allocation by choosing an appropriate initial distribution of input ownership and permitting exchange of inputs and outputs on competitive markets. In the model, input supplies were fixed, therefore redistribution of their ownership did not affect resource allocation decisions. Matters are more complicated in the model with variable inputs, however. In this model, only a wage rate equal to the value of the worker's marginal product results in an efficient allocation of labor resources. If there are many workers with a variety of skills and abilities, the wage of each must be equal to the value of the worker's marginal product. Thus, in the variable input model, the efficiency conditions imply a distribution of earned income, which will be referred to as an *efficient distribution of income.*

Some characteristics that affect worker productivity are innate, but some result from education and training, now referred to as accumulation of human capital. To a considerable extent, workers acquire human capital on the basis of employment and earnings considerations. Thus, a long run characteristic of competitive markets is that they provide strong incentives for human capital accumulation. Returns to human capital are designated as earned income even though they are really property income. Physical assets also provide returns to their owners in the form of profit, interest, dividends, and rents. Such returns are referred to as property or unearned income. Nevertheless, physical assets are accumulated as a result of people's economic decisions, and competitive markets also provide incentives for optimum physical capital ownership.

Thus, the most general concept of an efficient distribution of income depends on the pattern of competitive input and output prices. It also depends on the pattern of inheritance of physical capital and on the extent to which parents finance human capital accumulation of their children. In the United States, labor income is about 80 percent of total income. Most of the labor income is a return to human capital, which careful research concludes exceeds the stock of physical capital.

Is the overall efficient distribution of income also equitable? It can hardly be. Some adults have no salable skills at all because of physical or psychological disabilities. Even among adult males without severe disabilities, earnings vary by more than a factor of 1000, say from $5 thousand to $5 million per year. Adding in property income, the range is much greater. Almost no one doubts that governments should attempt to narrow this range at least somewhat. Most people believe that high income people should be taxed at higher percentages of their incomes than are low income people and that some government revenues should be used to provide transfers and human capital accumulation (especially education) to low income people.

☐ SOME CAUSES OF RESOURCE MISALLOCATION

The discussion of the social efficiency of competitive markets is now complete. There are several reasons to believe that markets are less efficient than the preceding discussion has indicated. This chapter concludes with a general classification and analysis of reasons for resource misallocation. Succeeding chapters will analyze specific problems of efficiency and equity in the urban economy. Each problem requires facts and analysis specific to that problem, and they are presented in the appropriate chapters.

Monopoly and Monopsony

It is easy to show that *monopolists and monopsonists misallocate resources.* A monopolist maximizes profits by employing input quantities that satisfy equations similar to Equations (8.3) and (8.4), but with product prices replaced by marginal revenues. Since a monopolist's marginal revenue is less than price, profit maximization requires that marginal products be greater for the monopolist than for the competitive firm for given input prices, and the monopolist therefore employs smaller input quantities and produces less output than is efficient from society's point of view. Similar reasoning shows that Equation (8.7) also is violated if the employer is a monopoly, and therefore inefficient amounts of labor are supplied. (As an exercise, it should be possible to show that monopsony power also leads to inefficient resource allocations.)

The quantitative importance of resource misallocation from monopoly and monopsony is a subject of debate among specialists in industrial organization economics. If misallocation is substantial, it must be substantial in urban areas, since most economic activity occurs there. It is claimed in following chapters, however, that monopoly is unimportant in understanding most serious urban problems; poverty, poor housing, congestion, pollution, and inadequate public services result only to a minor extent from monopoly power. They would be serious problems even if all markets were perfectly competitive. Many people resist this conclusion, in part because they use the term *monopoly* more broadly than economists do, and in part because of the human tendency to search for villains to blame for problems.

External Economies and Diseconomies

For decades economists have analyzed a closely related set of considerations that entail resource misallocation, even in competitive markets. Despite important recent progress in clarifying the concept, there is still considerable disagreement among economists about the causes and effects of **externalities.** The result is that the term tends to be used somewhat loosely in applied studies. Especially in urban economics, the term is badly overused and abused.

The basic idea behind the notion of an **external effect** is that *the actions of one person or institution may affect the welfare of another in ways that cannot be regulated by private agreements among the affected parties.* As has been discussed, if a firm buys and sells on competitive markets in certain assumed circumstances, market prices and profit maximization induce the firm to behave efficiently from society's point of view. It employs just the inputs and produces just the output that are in society's interest. Now suppose that one of the firm's activities affects people's welfare in a way not based on agreement or market transaction. The classic example, used by generations of writers, is smoke emission. Suppose a certain fuel is among the firm's inputs and that burning the fuel creates smoke that spreads over the neighborhood and reduces residents' welfare. If the fuel is an important input and its smoke is not too harmful, some smoke may be worth its cost to the firm and to the public. However, there is no market on which to register the advantages of smoke production to the firm and its disadvantages to the neighbors. If the smoke maximizes profits, it fails to take into account the cost that its smoke imposes on others. Even though some smoke may be worth the cost, too much is produced. The smoke is then said to be an **external diseconomy.** The resulting resource misallocation—too much smoke—is no less serious just because the firm buys inputs and sells outputs in competitive markets.

In fact, smoke is a less serious problem than it used to be, but nearly all economists agree that air pollution is a serious public problem because of its external effects. In a general way, almost everyone would agree on the underlying explanation that private agreements cannot allocate resources to abate air pollution efficiently. Disagreement comes when people try to establish exactly why private agreements do not work.

The basic reason that private agreements do not work is that *private transaction costs sometimes exceed the potential gain from the agreement.* The reason is not hard to understand in the smoke example. Many people suffer more or less harm from the smoke, and many sources may be more or less responsible for the smoke damage to each person and to each person's property. Thus a private agreement to abate smoke discharges would require negotiations among large numbers of people and factories, and the public would have complex and poorly understood interests in abatement by particular sources. Obviously, a private agreement on such an issue would be extremely difficult and costly to specify and negotiate. That is the meaning of the statement that the transaction costs of such an agreement are high.

Exactly what circumstances entail transaction costs so high as to prevent otherwise desirable agreements? There is no satisfactory answer at present, and the result is that many studies of externalities are merely anecdotal. About all that can be said is that transaction costs may be high regarding agreement about an activity if the activity affects large numbers of people in complex ways. Nevertheless, any study of an apparent externality should include a careful investigation of the kinds and amounts of transaction costs that prevent agreement.

Once an important externality has been identified, the next question is what to do about it. The usual answer is that the government should tax or subsidize so as to create an appropriate market, or it should regulate so that private activity approximates the missing market. In the smoke example, the government can tax emissions, subsidize abatement, or regulate emissions. The first question that needs to be asked, however, is whether transaction costs will be lower if the government intervenes than if private parties try to reach agreement. If not, the transaction costs are unavoidable, and the agreement is not worth having. In the smoke example, the disadvantage of the smoke may be smaller than the cost of doing something about it. In many cases, however, the government can adopt policies that at least approximate the results of private agreements, and with relatively small transaction costs. In each case, however, the facts must decide the issue. Sometimes government programs become cumbersome because the government must bear exactly the transaction costs that prevented the private sector from undertaking the transactions in the first place.

If transaction costs are low enough to justify government intervention, the appropriate policy is easy to specify in principle. In the smoke example, the efficient amount of smoke is the amount such that the cost to the neighbors of a little more smoke equals the cost to the factory of a little more abatement. In other words, the amount of smoke should be such that marginal costs and marginal benefits of abatement are equal. The goal might be achieved by an appropriate tax on smoke or by regulation of smoke discharges. The policy choice is based on the transaction costs of the policies and on the extent to which they approximate efficient resource allocation. Of course, in practice, the benefits of abatement may be difficult to estimate.

Externalities in an Urban Context

What are the important externalities in urban areas? There is no agreement on this matter in the relevant economics literature. Environmental pollution commands the greatest agreement. Almost all economists agree that polluting discharges to air and water result in resource misallocation and that government should tax or regulate such discharges. Consensus probably also could be reached on housing. Most people's welfare is affected by the quality of housing in the neighborhood where they live. Also, most economists probably would agree that government interference in housing markets is justified. There is little agreement as to the best kind of government interference, however. In fact, there is a panoply of taxes, subsidies, codes, and controls on housing markets.

What about urban transportation? Most economists would agree that a street or subway system must be planned as an integrated whole in an entire urban area. This justifies government ownership or regulation of the basic infrastructure. But how should the use of the streets or tracks by vehicles be controlled? Chapter 12 will show that congestion is an external diseconomy that might justify government intervention in the use of rights-of-way by vehicles.

These and other resource allocation problems raise complex issues about whether and how government should intervene. Many of the issues will be discussed in subsequent chapters. The logical sequence of the argument is the same with every issue. What is the justification for government intervention? What is the best kind of intervention? Both questions are important.

Taxes

Governments must raise large amounts of money by taxing citizens to finance the public services and transfers demanded of them. In fact, total tax payments to all levels of government are almost one-third of GNP in the United States. An important goal of tax policy should be to employ taxes that cause as little resource misallocation as possible.

Price theory texts show that a change in the price of a consumer good has an income effect and a substitution effect. Almost all taxes are directly or indirectly taxes on particular kinds of goods and services. They therefore alter the prices of the taxed items relative to untaxed items. The income effect is the desired effect of the tax, and it represents no misallocation of resources. The purpose of a tax is to transfer resources from the private to the public sector, and the income effect measures the value of the resources transferred. If the resources are less valuable in the public sector than in the private sector, there should be no tax and no transfer. If the resources are more valuable in the public sector, however, the transfer should be made, and the income effect of the tax is the desired reduction of private purchasing power. The income effect may reduce demands for private goods and services by varying amounts, but it represents the least costly way of transferring the purchasing power represented by the tax.

The substitution effect of a tax on the demand for the taxed goods and services represents a loss of welfare to consumers beyond that which is necessary to transfer purchasing power. The substitution effect leads to what is called the *excess burden* of the tax, that is, the excess welfare loss over that necessary to transfer the purchasing power to the public sector. *Among all the taxes that have a given income effect in transferring given resources to the public sector, the best is the one with the smallest excess burden,* or substitution effect.[1]

1. See Schitovsky (1971) for a complete discussion of the issue in this and the preceding paragraph.

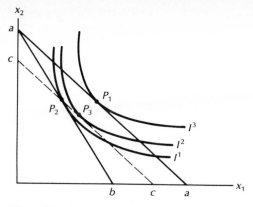

Figure 8.6 *Consumer Response to a Price Change*

These ideas can be illustrated with the property tax (discussed in detail in Chapters 10 and 13). It is necessary to note only that the property tax is a high sales tax on housing services. Figure 8.6 shows a household's set of indifference curves between housing services (x_1) and another commodity (x_2) for a given amount of a public service provided by the government. Suppose that x_1 and x_2 are produced by competitive firms and that *aa* would be the household's budget line in the absence of any tax. Then P_1 would be the household's equilibrium, and it would be efficient. P_1 is not available, however, because it does not provide resources to the government necessary to produce the public service. Suppose then that the government finances the public service with a property tax and that the entire tax is paid by the consumer of housing services. The household's budget line is shifted to *ab*. Its new equilibrium is P_2. Budget line *cc* is drawn parallel to *aa* and passes through P_2. P_3 is the household's equilibrium position for budget line *cc*. The movement from P_1 to P_3 is the income effect of the tax; that is, it represents the household's loss of welfare if the government had taken the resources it needed without affecting the relative prices of x_1 and x_2. The movement from P_3 to P_2 represents the substitution effect of the tax. The fact that the property tax has a substitution effect causes an excess burden of the tax on the household that reduces its welfare from I^2 to I^1.

What kinds of taxes would have no excess burdens? In principle, the answer is that the only taxes with no excess burdens are those that do not affect relative prices. *A "head" tax, which simply charges the same amount of tax to each person, is probably the only tax that has no excess burden.* The property tax is presumed to have a large excess burden, since it is a high tax on a narrow range of activities, namely, housing consumption. A broadly based sales tax is probably somewhat better. A sales tax that taxed all consumer goods and services at the same rate would be a flat-rate consumption tax. It would leave unaffected the relative prices of goods and services. Most sales taxes fall far short of this ideal, however. Most are levied on a narrow set of consumer goods, excluding almost all services and some commodities. Some also are levied on a few intermediate goods, which entails double taxation of the final goods they are used to produce.

Some economists take a more generous view of the property tax to the extent that it is levied uniformly on business real estate as well as on housing. In that case it is a tax on all, or nearly all, kinds of capital. Then, distortion arises only to the extent that the property tax increases current consumption at the expense of capital accumulation, that is, savings. Many economists believe that savings are insensitive to modest taxes on capital or on capital income. Existing real estate taxes are poor approximations to uniform taxes on property, however. They vary greatly by local government jurisdiction and from one kind of real estate to another. Finally, the Tiebout hypothesis, to be discussed in Chapter 13, is germane to the controversy about distorting effects of real estate taxes.

An income tax, like a broadly based sales tax, leaves relative prices of goods and services unchanged, which accounts in part for the strong preference of most economists for income taxes over other taxes. An income tax and a broadly based sales tax do have an excess burden, however. An income tax is a tax on the result of hours spent working but not on hours of leisure. In Figure 8.5, an income tax changes the relative prices of goods and leisure, and, therefore, the slope of the budget line *bb*. The substitution effect of an income tax is an inefficiently large amount of leisure. The total effect that an income tax has on hours of work and leisure depends on the relative sizes of the income and substitution effects.

Is the excess burden of an income tax large? The best study on the subject, by Harberger (1964), concludes that it is substantial, but probably small relative to the excess burdens of existing sales and property taxes. Sales and property taxes, like income taxes, affect the relative prices of goods and leisure. Unlike income taxes, however, they also affect the relative prices of goods and services.

It should be emphasized that this entire discussion has been about the efficiency aspects of taxes. Taxes, like other public policies, also have important equity effects. A major goal of government tax policy is to redistribute income, specifically to reduce income inequality. That goal requires progressive taxes on transfer payments, and the income tax is almost the only tax that can be made to be progressive. Thus, *if equity considerations require progressive taxes, they are an important reason for the use of income rather than other taxes.* It is also possible that equity considerations indicate the desirability of one kind of tax, whereas efficiency considerations indicate the desirability of another. In such cases, a compromise between equity and efficiency is necessary.

☐ Summary

Welfare economics is a branch of economic theory concerned with evaluating the performance of the economic system. Economists evaluate the system's performance by its efficiency and equity in meeting people's economic wants.

An elaborate system of conditions for economic efficiency has been worked out by economists in recent decades. A major result obtained in welfare economics is that competitive markets allocate resources so as to satisfy the efficiency conditions, if strong assumptions are made. Competitive markets, however, may not produce distributions of income and wealth that meet people's senses of equity.

Monopolies and monopsonies misallocate resources, although neither is likely to be an important source of urban problems. External economies and diseconomies imply that even competitive markets misallocate resources. Pollution and congestion are examples of external diseconomies in urban areas.

Governments raise large sums of money by taxes to finance public services and transfer payments. Taxes should be equitable and should cause as little resource misallocation as possible. Most economists believe that sales and property taxes are both less efficient and less equitable than income taxes. There may well be conflict between efficiency and equity in the tax policy, however.

Questions and Problems

1. Show that price discrimination violates the requirements for efficient resource allocation.

2. Economists tend to argue that activities causing external diseconomies should be taxed, whereas government officials tend to regulate such activities. Which strategy is better on equity and efficiency grounds?

3. The do-it-yourself movement, which involves homeowners repairing and maintaining their houses instead of hiring craftspeople, has blossomed since World War II. Do-it-yourself labor is not subject to income tax, whereas a craftsperson's wages are. Do you think the do-it-yourself movement is a distortion in resource allocation resulting from high income tax rates?

4. Governments tend to provide or subsidize goods and services to the poor, despite economists' advice that money transfers are preferable. One reason for this may be that taxpayers prefer to provide goods and services instead of money. Another possibility is that interest groups determine the form of transfers. For example,

farmers like food stamps and builders like housing subsidies. What do you think the real reason is?

References and Further Reading

Harberger, Arnold. "Taxation, Resource Allocation, and Welfare." *The Role of Direct and Indirect Taxes in the Federal System,* ed. John Due (Princeton: Princeton University Press, 1964): 25–70. A thorough study of distorting effects of taxes.

Just, Richard E., Darrell Hueth, and Andrew Schmitz. *Applied Welfare Economics* (Englewood Cliffs, N.J.: Prentice-Hall, 1982). A fine modern text covering every aspect of the subject.

Mishan, E. J. *Cost-Benefit Analysis,* 2nd ed. (New York: Praeger, 1981). A classic study of the use of welfare economics to analyze the benefits and costs of proposed government projects.

Schitovsky, Tibor. *Welfare and Competition* (Homewood, Ill.: Richard D. Irwin, 1971). A microeconomics text with a strong welfare economics orientation.

Part Three

Urban Problems and the Public Sector

9

The Problem of Poverty

☐ Poverty is among the most urgent and widely discussed domestic problems of modern times. The 1960s witnessed a vast outpouring of literature on the subject, much of it written as though poverty had been invented or discovered in about 1960. Although the subject has not been, and should not be, the exclusive preserve of economists, they have made their share of contributions to the subject. Many of the great nineteenth-century economists were deeply concerned with the most fundamental issues related to poverty. Beginning about 1900, some of the best applied economic research was on demand and family budget studies, motivated by a concern with poverty and related nutritional problems. During the 1930s, much of the profession's effort was devoted to public and private measures to alleviate poverty, especially that caused by the massive unemployment that dominated the decade.

Nevertheless, there was a rapid growth of concern with poverty during the 1960s among economists, public officials, and the general public. Both a cause and an effect of this concern was a rapid improvement in the data available about poverty. As the 1970s progressed, the subject of poverty became gradually less fashionable. Serious study has continued, however, and it is now possible to present the dimensions of the subject in a way that was impossible even in 1970. Poverty has not disappeared as a subject of public debate. Successive presidents have proposed reforms in national programs to aid the poor, and successive Congresses have increased federal appropriations to raise living standards of the poor. Although the subject now appears less frequently in the headlines than it did a decade ago, there is more than ever to be said about poverty.

One thing to remember when considering poverty (or any other urban problem) is that the appropriate solution varies enormously according to the nature of the problem. For example, slum housing may be caused by poverty, or it may be caused by market failure. The urban economist therefore must use analytical tools such as those developed in Part 2 to identify urban problems and determine the true cause-and-effect relationships before proposing any solutions.

☐ MEASURES OF POVERTY

What is poverty? The easy answer: it is a lack of money income. Like most easy answers, this one points in the right direction but is inadequate. Many undergraduate and graduate students have relatively low money incomes, but most are not poor in the sense that many blacks and Puerto Ricans in places like the South Bronx in New York City are poor. Most college students know they are preparing themselves for a status that will give them the option of making a good income (whether they choose the option or not), as well as that in an emergency they can obtain money from parents, spouses, or their work. *To be poor requires not only that people have little money income, but also that they have no prospect of substantially greater income,* at least in the near futuure. Unfortunately, official data sources are hardly able to ascertain the extent of voluntarism among the country's low-income population. It is an important issue, however, which will be taken up again.

Furthermore, *money income is only one means to a high living standard,* although it is the most important means. Many poor people receive some income "in kind" in the United States. *In-kind income* is income in the form of commodities or services that are provided directly—especially by governments—instead of money that recipients can spend as they choose. Most of the commodities and services provided—food, housing, and health care—are valuable, and recipients would have purchased some amounts of them if they had been given money. The commodities and services may not be worth as much to recipients as their money cost to taxpayers, however. This issue must also be taken up again.

Finally, *assets must be taken into account.* A family with a temporarily low income can maintain a high living standard by drawing down assets. More importantly, many elderly people with low incomes own a house, furniture, and a car. Such assets provide services and contribute to living standards, although they are not included in income as ordinarily measured. The notion of welfare recipients driving Cadillacs is largely fanciful, yet some people with low money incomes are able to maintain higher living standards than their incomes would indicate because of assets that yield direct services. Again, government data generally do not include such services.

However it is measured, poverty is a matter of degree. A family with an income of $3000 per year would be better off if it had $4000, and still better off if it had $6000. *There is no natural dividing line such that people below it can be said to be poor, and people above it can be said not to be poor.* In terms of the substance of the problem, no poverty line is needed. Data should be available on the entire size distribution of incomes, and society should decide through the democratic process what groups it wants to tax and to whom it wants to give the proceeds.

In fact, great controversy surrounds the notion of an official poverty line and where it should be drawn. The main reason government is urged to draw a poverty line is political: raising everyone's income to the government's poverty level inevitably becomes a social goal. Thus, those who favor a great deal of redistribution of incomes from rich to poor want a poverty line to be established at a high income level. Those who favor little income redistribution want it established at a low income level.

In the early 1960s, the federal government adopted an official poverty line, and raising low incomes to at least that level has been a quasi-official government goal ever since. The official poverty income level is computed in a relatively simple way. The Department of Agriculture computes the annual cost of a nutritious diet for low-income families of various compositions. The food budget then is multiplied by three, because studies have shown that poor families spend about one-third of their incomes on food. As food prices change, the poverty income is adjusted accordingly. In 1960 the poverty income for a family of four was $3022 per year; in 1970, $3968; and in 1985, $10,989.

The poverty income in the United States is about one-third the country's median income. By a worldwide standard it is high—ten times the average income in some of Asia's and Africa's poorest countries—though that should be little comfort for people in the United States. Presumably, the living standard to which all Americans should aspire to bring the poorest Americans should be defined by average American living standards, not those standards in much poorer countries. A more relevant comparison is with countries in northern Europe, where average living standards are roughly the same as in the United States. Although exact comparisons are difficult, the poorest people in the United States likely have lower living standards than the poorest people in several northern European countries. That fact alone does not imply that Americans should have more income redistribution, but it does make the subject worth discussing.

☐ DEMOGRAPHY OF POVERTY

How many people in the United States are poor? The numbers below the official poverty line have been computed only back to 1959 and are shown for selected years in Table 9.1. Approximate poverty measures for much earlier years can be calculated. Allowing for changes in the price level, 1929 income per capita was about the same as the present official poverty level. Thus, roughly half the country was poor in 1929, by the current official poverty standard. By a somewhat bet-

Table 9.1 *Poverty in the United States, 1959 to 1985*

	Poor Population		Poverty Cutoff	Median Income
	Number (Millions)	Percentage	Family of Four (Dollars per Year)	Per Family (Dollars per Year)
1959	39.5	22.4	2,973	5,417
1969	24.1	12.1	3,743	9,433
1974	24.3	11.6	5,038	12,836
1977	24.7	11.6	6,191	16,009
1979	25.3	11.6	7,412	19,715
1985	33.1	14.0	10,989	27,735

Source: Data from U.S. Department of Commerce, Bureau of the Census. *Statistical Abstract of the United States.* Washington, D.C.: Government Printing Office, 1978, 1981, 1987.

ter measure, about one-third of the country was poor in 1947. Table 9.1 indicates that the number of poor decreased from 22.4 percent of the population in 1959 to 11.6 percent in 1979, with no decline since.

Not only the percentage but also the number of poor decreased during the half-century since 1929. Half the 1929 population was about 60 million people, and one-third of the 1947 population was 48 million people. Table 9.1 shows that the number of poor decreased from about 40 million in 1959 to about 25 million in 1979.

The data show remarkable progress in reducing poverty during the period from 1929 to 1969. From 1959 to 1969, the percentage of the population below the poverty line fell about 1.5 points per year. From 1969 to 1979, however, there was a slight increase in the number of people below the poverty line and only a slight decrease in the percentage of the population below the poverty line. Both the number and percentage of people below the poverty line increased during the early 1980s. Both numbers peaked in 1983 and declined in 1984 and 1985.

What happened? Part of the answer is cyclical. Poverty inevitably worsens during recessions, and the number of poor rose during the recession of 1980 and during the much more severe recession of 1982. A more fundamental answer is that the entire economy has grown more slowly since the mid-1970s than it had previously. The shares of various income groups in total income changed only slowly from one decade to the next. Thus, when the overall growth rate slows, income growth slows at least as much for poor and near-poor people as for higher income people. But even that does not explain why the percentage of the population in poverty in the mid-1980s was as great as it had been in nearly twenty years. National government sentiment for antipoverty programs became less favorable during the 1980s, but actual expenditures on programs that favor the poor did not decline enough to account for the retreat in the war against poverty. The failure of the poor to benefit much from the strong recovery after 1982 remains something of a mystery.

Who are the poor? Table 9.2 presents basic demographic data concerning poverty. The column headed "Incidence of Poverty" shows the percentage of people in the groups in each row that are poor. The incidence should be distinguished from the percentage of the poor in each group. For example, the first numerical column shows that about 69 percent (22.9 million out of 33.1 million) of the poor were white, but the second numerical column shows that the incidence of poverty among whites was little more than one-third its incidence among nonwhites (11.4 percent compared with 31.3 percent).

Table 9.2 shows the uneven incidence of poverty among various demographic groups. The data under "Family Status" show that 20.1 percent of children are in poor families. Why is the incidence of poverty among children greater than among the entire population? In part, it is because low-income parents tend to have more children than high-income parents. In part, it is because women with many children cannot undertake paid work; hence, income is low in families with many children. In part, however, it is simply that, for a given family money income, having many children makes the family poor, since poverty depends both on the amount of income and on the number of people the income must support. Table 9.2 shows that the incidence of poverty among the elderly is less than that among the population as a whole. In fact, the most remarkable trend in poverty statistics during the last two decades is a dramatic decrease in the incidence of poverty among the elderly in contrast with a dramatic increase in the incidence of poverty among children. Private pensions and savings available to the elderly have improved as an increasing fraction of the elderly have had most of their working lives during the prosperous postwar years. In addition, social security and medicare benefits have improved greatly. By contrast, children have suffered from rising birthrates to unwed mothers and from rising divorce rates. Yet it remains surprising that support for the elderly has improved even though they have been an increasing share of the population, whereas support for children has deteriorated even though they have become a decreasing share of the population.

The data under "Race" show the crushing burden of poverty borne by nonwhites in the United States. About 90 percent of nonwhites are black. Although there are more than twice as many poor whites as nonwhites, the incidence of poverty is almost three times as high among nonwhites as among whites. Nonwhites also suffer disproportionately when the economy performs weakly.

The data on residence in the table show that poverty is by no means entirely a phenomenon of large cities. Taking metropolitan areas as a whole, income levels are higher and the incidence of poverty is lower than elsewhere in the country. Within metropolitan areas, however, the poor are strongly segregated. The incidence of poverty is more than

Table 9.2 *Number of Poor and Incidence of Poverty in the United States, 1979 and 1985*

Characteristics	1979 Number of Poor (Millions)	1979 Incidence of Poverty (Percentage)	1985 Number of Poor (Millions)	1985 Incidence of Poverty (Percentage)
Total	25.3	11.6	33.1	14
Family status				
Family head	5.3	9.1	7.2	11.4
Family members under 18	9.7	16.0	12.5	20.1
Other family members	4.3	6.0	6.0	7.7
Unrelated individuals	5.6	21.9	6.7	21.5
Race				
White	16.8	8.9	22.9	11.4
Nonwhite	10.7	36.8	8.9	31.3
Residence				
SMSA central city	9.5	15.7	n.a.	n.a.
SMSA suburb	6.2	7.2	n.a.	n.a.
Non-SMSA	9.6	13.7	n.a.	n.a.

Source: Data from U.S. Department of Commerce, Bureau of the Census. *Statistical Abstract of the United States.* Washington, D.C.: Government Printing Office, 1981 and 1987.

twice as great in metropolitan central cities as in suburbs (15.7 percent compared with 7.2 percent).

Many of our commonly identified urban problems are directly linked with poverty. The main explanation for the existence of slum housing is the poverty of its inhabitants. Violent crime is closely linked with poverty. Children of poor families are at a disadvantage in school and in labor markets. Poverty was not invented in urban slums, however, and it is a mistake to focus public policy entirely on the urban poor.

As Chapter 2 discussed, during the late 1940s, the 1950s, and the 1960s, there was a rapid migration of poor people and blacks from the rural South to cities in all parts of the country. Migrants left desperately poor and, for blacks, oppressive rural areas to seek better lives for themselves and their children in the cities. Agricultural employment was declining and urban employment was expanding. This massive movement of people succeeded in increasing living standards for many poor people, and it was a crucial step in the struggle of blacks in the United States to attain political rights and recognition. It also moved some of the nation's poverty from rural areas to metropolitan central cities. The result is that during the 1970s the incidence of poverty in central cities for the first time exceeded that in rural areas.

Many people are concerned about the concentration of the poor in metropolitan central cities. Concentrations of the poor certainly cause problems, which will be discussed in subsequent chapters. The poor are highly visible in city slums, and many people are appalled at the sight. It must be remembered, however, that the poor have come to the cities for good reasons. Poverty was worse, although less visible to others, in the rural South. Urban migration has increased job opportunities for the poor and their children. It has enabled them to organize to demand political rights. Also, it has enabled society to increase their living standards by government transfer payments in ways that are not possible if the poor are scattered in rural areas.

The incidence of poverty is much lower in SMSAs than elsewhere. It is only in central cities that the incidence is high. It is much more constructive to show concern about the discrimination and exclusion that keep the poor concentrated in central cities than it is to be concerned about the movement of the poor from rural to urban areas.

☐ RACE AND POVERTY

In his 1944 classic, Myrdal described American race relations as "an American dilemma." It is no exaggeration to say that race relations became "the American trauma" during succeeding decades. The elemental and brutal fact is that blacks in the United States have been forced into demeaning and subservient status by legal and extralegal means since they arrived in the holds of slave ships. As with the broader issue of poverty discussed in the last section, however, the rapid postwar urban migration of blacks has made their status better, not worse. Black urbanization has made racial disparities much more visible to both blacks and whites and has increased the tension and conflict between blacks and whites. Nevertheless, it has indisputably raised the economic and political status of blacks.

Table 9.3 shows the magnitude of postwar black urbanization. By 1950, 59 percent of blacks lived in metropolitan areas, compared with 63 percent of whites. By 1980, the black percentage had grown to 81 (up from 75 as recently as 1977), whereas the white percentage had grown only to 73. Thus, by 1980, blacks were much more concentrated in metropolitan areas than were whites. Blacks were and are much more concentrated in central cities than whites. The percentage of blacks in the United States who lived in central cities increased from 44 in 1950 to 58 in 1980. The percentage of blacks living in metropolitan suburbs also increased, from 15 to 23. The increase was concentrated in the 1970s and indicates that blacks were beginning to acquire suburban housing in at least a few places.

Living standards of both blacks and whites are higher in metropolitan areas than elsewhere. Table 9.4 shows the incidence of poverty by race in metropolitan and nonmetropolitan areas. Blacks have a much higher incidence of poverty than whites in all areas. For both blacks and whites, however, the incidence of poverty is between one-third and one-half greater outside than inside metropolitan areas. Within metropolitan areas, the incidence of poverty is higher for both blacks

Table 9.3 *Racial Composition of Metropolitan and Nonmetropolitan Areas, 1950 and 1980 (Percentage)*

	1950		1980	
	Black	White	Black	White
Metropolitan areas	59	63	81	73
Central cities	44	35	58	25
Suburbs	15	28	23	48
Nonmetropolitan areas	41	37	19	27
Total	100	100	100	100

Source: Data from U.S. Department of Commerce, Bureau of the Census. *Statistical Abstract of the United States.* Washington, D.C.: Government Printing Office, 1981.

and whites in central cities than in suburbs. Even in central cities, the incidence of poverty among blacks is less than outside metropolitan areas.

Thus poverty is much more common among blacks than among whites everywhere, but urban migration from the rural South has helped blacks reduce their incidence of poverty. Table 9.5 shows that racial disparities in income pervade the income distribution. The table shows family incomes of whites and blacks in 1985 dollars for 1975 and 1985. In both years, blacks' incomes were much more concentrated toward the low end of the distribution than were whites' incomes, and blacks' incomes declined somewhat relative to whites' incomes during the ten years covered by the table. In 1975 the median income of black families was 61.1 percent of the median income of white families; in 1985 it was 59.5 percent. Most social and economic statistics tell the same story: blacks started the postwar period with large disadvantages compared with whites; during the postwar period they have made substantial absolute and moderate relative gains. In 1950 life expectancy was 69.1 years for whites and 60.8 years for blacks, a difference of 8.3 years. In 1985, the figures were 75.3 and 71.2 years, a difference of 4.1 years. In 1950 the median educational attainment was 9.6 years for whites

Table 9.4 *Incidence of Poverty by Race: Metropolitan and Nonmetropolitan Areas, 1979 (Percent)*

	All Races	White	Black
Metropolitan areas	10.4	7.8	28.3
Central cities	15.7	10.7	31.1
Suburbs	7.2	6.2	21.1
Nonmetropolitan areas	13.7	11.2	39.5

Source: Data from U.S. Department of Commerce, Bureau of the Census. *Statistical Abstract of the United States.* Washington, D.C.: Government Printing Office, 1981.

Table 9.5 *Percentage Distribution of Family Income, 1975 and 1985 (1985 dollars)*

	Under $5,000	$5,000–$9,999	$10,000–$14,999	$15,000–$19,999	$20,000–$24,999	$25,000–$34,999	$35,000+	Median
1975								
White	6.0	12.2	11.3	11.1	10.1	19.0	29.8	$24,665
Black	15.0	22.0	14.0	12.3	10.6	13.5	13.0	$14,807
Hispanic	9.3	16.6	16.8	13.9	11.4	17.5	14.4	$17,719
1985								
White	6.4	11.7	11.2	10.8	10.1	17.5	32.3	$24,908
Black	17.6	18.8	14.0	12.4	8.5	12.9	15.7	$14,819
Hispanic	10.8	17.9	14.7	12.2	10.8	15.2	18.3	$17,465

Source: Data from U.S. Department of Commerce, Bureau of the Census. *Statistical Abstract of the United States.* Washington, D.C.: Government Printing Office, 1987.

and 6.8 years for blacks, a difference of 2.8 years. In 1985 the figures were 12.7 and 12.3 years, a difference of only 0.4 years. During the postwar period, black unemployment rates have consistently averaged about twice those of whites, and the disparity has increased during the 1980s.

The most encouraging statistics about the progress of blacks pertain to young and well-educated people. In 1975 the ratio of black to white earnings of male college graduates twenty-five to twenty-nine years old was 93 percent, up from 67 percent in 1949. For high school graduates twenty to twenty-four years old, the ratio was 90 percent, up from 74 percent (Freeman, 1981). These figures are consistent with the low ratios of overall median income previously quoted because relatively few blacks are in the highly educated groups. But as noted in Chapter 13, there has been dramatic improvement in high-school completion among blacks since World War II.

The statistics presented in this section can be either encouraging or discouraging. That there has been progress toward racial equality cannot be denied. However, it also cannot be denied that there are many blacks—concentrated among older and poorly educated groups—who have hardly been touched by the progress. The explanation for the progress is extremely controversial. Part of the explanation is certainly a reduction in discriminatory attitudes by the white majority. Another part is the efforts by blacks to break down barriers in education, employment, and political representation. A third part is the federal civil rights acts and expenditure programs that have helped blacks. A final part is court decisions that have extended constitutional protections to blacks. Sorting out the importance of these explanations will be a complex and controversial activity.

☐ PUBLIC PROGRAMS FOR REDUCING POVERTY

Macroeconomic Policies

By far the most important factor in the gradual reduction of poverty in the United States has been the overall growth of the economy. It has already been stated and will be shown in more detail in the next section that the percentage distribution of income has changed little during the postwar period. Poverty has been reduced rapidly when the economy has prospered and slowly when economic growth has faltered. For example, poverty increased during the recession of 1981–82.

The most obvious beneficiaries of economic growth are the employed and their families, yet economic growth also reduces poverty among the retired and others not in the labor force, because it is easiest to save for retirement and contingencies during working years if income is high and rising and unemployment rates are low. Finally, economic growth increases revenues received by governments at fixed tax rates. Governments thus have more money to finance public services such as education and transfers such as unemployment compensation, welfare, and social security, all of which help reduce poverty.

Thus the most important weapon in reducing poverty is monetary and fiscal policies that promote full employment and economic growth. Such policies are beyond the scope of this book but are discussed in macroeconomics textbooks.

Income-Maintenance Policies: Theory

The best way to organize thinking regarding income redistribution programs is to consider the often-proposed *negative income tax* (NIT). The NIT works just like the ordinary income tax except that below some cutoff level of income, a household receives a payment from the government. The size of the payment depends on pretax income (just like the size of a household's income tax liability depends on pretax income) and is depicted in Figure 9.1. Aftertax income is plotted on the vertical axis against pretax income on the horizontal. In the absence of any income taxation, pretax and aftertax income would be the same, as depicted by the 45-degree line. The ordinary income tax alters the relationship to make aftertax income less than pretax income above some point determined by the tax schedule, exemptions, and deductions. The NIT makes aftertax income greater than pretax income below that point. Of course, the relationship need not be linear, but these are the easier cases to analyze, so this section will focus mainly upon linear tax laws.

The equation for the line A is

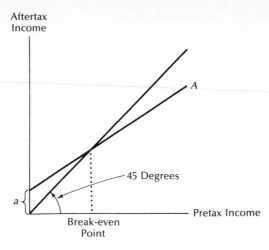

Figure 9.1 Negative Income Tax

$$Y_{at} = a + (1 - t)Y_{pt} \qquad (9.1)$$

where Y_{at} is aftertax income, Y_{pt} is pretax income, a is the lump sum given to a household with no pretax income, and t is the tax rate. The equation simply states that aftertax income is a plus the fraction $(1 - t)$ of pretax income that is left after paying income taxes.

According to the standard proposal, the tax-and-grant law embodied in Figure 9.1 and Equation (9.1) would replace all existing income redistribution programs and the federal income tax. In other words, tax revenue, (tY) would have to be sufficient to finance the grants and other activities of the federal government.

A critical observation regarding the NIT (or, as will be seen, any redistribution program) can be made by plugging numbers into Equation (9.1). Suppose $a = \$4000$, indicating that a family with no pretax income has aftertax income of $4000. Now suppose the tax rate is 25 percent. It readily can be seen that under such a program, aftertax income would be higher than pretax income for everyone with less than $16,000 of pretax income. This point (the intersection of the 45-degree line with line A, where pretax income equals aftertax income) is called the *break-even point*.[1] Notice that under the program just outlined, which sounds reasonable, the break-even point is very high—in fact, it is nearly half the mean per-household income in the United States.

Aside from the fact that taxpayers may not want to subsidize households whose incomes are as high as $16,000, this high break-even point indicates that the NIT might be a very expensive program. In fact, for the linear tax structure considered here, the following result can be es-

---

1. The break-even point is that income level at which $Y_{at} = Y_{pt}$ and can be solved for by setting $Y_{at} = Y_{pt}$ in Equation (9.1). This yields $Y_{at} = a + (1 + t)Y_{at}$ (since $Y_{at} = Y_{pt}$). Solving this, $Y_{at} (= Y_{pt}) = a/t$.

tablished: if the break-even point is equal to mean household income, the entire proceeds from the federal personal income tax are required to finance the program of grants. Clearly, if the NIT is to be financially viable, either the tax rate must be larger or the maximum grant smaller. Neither is an attractive option; the maximum grant in the example is already quite low for a household with no income, and a tax rate too far above 25 percent could have serious effects upon incentives. At all levels of income, a high income tax rate reduces incentives to work and to purchase productivity-enhancing training and education. The inescapable fact is that an NIT program must have either a tax rate sufficiently high to distort incentives seriously or a maximum grant level sufficiently low to redistribute income only modestly.

Some recent experiments provide evidence on the cost and incentive effects of the NIT. The NIT was most recently tested in Seattle and Denver. To mitigate the disadvantages previously discussed, participants received guaranteed payments based on family income prior to the experiment; were reimbursed for federal, state, and local taxes; and were not allowed to receive other transfers, such as food stamps. The results indicated that a nationwide NIT with a guaranteed payment equal to 50 percent of the poverty level and a tax rate of 70 percent would cost $5.3 billion (in 1978 dollars) less than current welfare programs (an expenditure savings of about 41 percent).[2] In contrast, an NIT with a guaranteed payment of 100 percent of poverty income ($9287 for a family of four in 1981) and a tax rate of 50 percent was projected to increase welfare expenditures by $40.5 billion (about a threefold increase over current expenditure).

Interestingly, congressional debate over the NIT has focused on its surprisingly negative effect on marital stability. Unlike Aid to Families with Dependent Children, for example, which accrues only to households without a father present and hence has been criticized as encouraging family breakups,[3] the NIT applies to households regardless of family status. Nevertheless, marital dissolution was about 60 percent higher (and significantly so) among NIT participants than among the control group in the Seattle/Denver experiment. Researchers hypothesize that the NIT causes marriage partners to feel less bound by nonpecuniary family ties, because the administration of the NIT is more impersonal and its nonwage income less stigmatized than other, often locally administered, welfare sources. Ironically, then, the NIT's administrative efficiency reduces not only explicit transactions costs of welfare, but implicit costs of family separation, too, with net effects that Congress, at least, considers undesirable.

2. Current welfare programs accounted for here are Aid to Families with Dependent Children and food stamps.

3. A newer program bases eligibility on the father's employment.

Redistribution Programs in the United States

Detailed discussion of the NIT may seem like a waste of time; the United States does not have such a program, and there seems little prospect that one will be enacted. Still, the theory of the NIT is an ideal vehicle for discussing real-world redistribution programs for the following reason: every income redistribution program specifies a (legal) relationship between preprogram and afterprogram income,[4] and thus the redistributive aspect of the program can be plotted in a graph like Figure 9.1. This means that a tax rate, a maximum grant level, and a break-even point are inherent in any redistribution program or, by extension, in the whole constellation of redistribution programs.

However, if all income redistribution programs have the basic properties of the NIT (the maximum grant level, the tax rate, and the break-even point), all are subject to the same trade-off between generosity to the very poor on the one hand and tax rate-induced distortion or expense on the other. The dilemma of the NIT is that (1) it is extremely expensive or (2) the tax rates on income are so high that they do grave damage to incentives. Note that this is not the dilemma of the NIT per se, but rather the dilemma of any package of income redistribution programs in general.

Income-Maintenance Policies: Facts and Institutions

Government expenditures are either purchases of goods and services or transfer payments. Many goods and services, such as national defense and highway construction, are for the general public, and it is almost meaningless to estimate the extent to which they benefit the poor. This is not the case with transfer payments such as unemployment compensation and social security, as well as goods and services such as public housing and medicare, which are provided by governments for identifiable groups of people. In principle, it is possible to estimate the income classes of the beneficiaries of such programs.

In practice, the number and complexity of such programs make accurate imputation to particular income groups difficult. Some programs, such as the welfare and food stamp programs, were designed to aid particular groups of needy people. Others, such as social security and veterans' benefits, were designed to aid groups thought to be worthy, regardless of need. It is possible, however, to identify programs that are *means tested.* To be eligible for a means-tested program, people must meet a test of need—usually some measure of income. The particular test varies from program to program, but tests invariably require that recipients be quite poor, although not always poor enough to meet the official poverty criterion.

---

4. Many income redistribution programs do other things as well, such as specifically encourage the consumption of food, housing, or medical care.

Table 9.6 *Federal Expenditures for Income-Security Transfer Programs (Billions of Dollars)*

Program	1960	1977	1986
Cash programs	22.0	140.9	249.5
Means tested	2.1	12.3	20.2
Aid to Families with Dependent Children	0.7	6.3	9.9
Supplemental security income	1.4	6.0	10.3
Not means tested	19.9	128.6	229.3
Old Age, Survivors and Disability Insurance	12.9	87.2	179.6
Federal Civil Service retirement	0.9	10.1	11.6
Veterans compensation pensions	3.4	8.4	14.4
Unemployment compensation	2.7	18.4	17.8
Coal miners' "black lung" benefits	–	1.2	1.0
Public service employment	–	3.3	4.9
In-kind programs	0.6	42.1	123.3
Means tested	0.6	21.6	53.1
Food stamps	0.1	6.0	11.6
Medicaid	0.2	9.4	25.0
Child nutrition	0.2	3.1	3.8
Housing assistance	0.1	3.1	12.7
Not means tested	–	20.5	70.2
Medicare	–	20.5	70.2
Total	22.6	183.0	602.1

Source: 1960 and 1977 data from *Setting National Priorities: The Next Ten Years*, eds. Henry Owen and Charles Schultze. Washington, D.C.: Brookings, 1976. Reprinted by permission. 1986 data from *The Budget of the United States*, Washington, D.C.: Government Printing Office, 1987.

Table 9.6 shows transfer program expenditures, classified according to whether or not they are means-tested and by whether they provide cash or services, for 1960, 1977, and 1986. Most program names are self-explanatory. Aid to Families with Dependent Children and supplementary security income are our important welfare programs. "Old Age, Survivors, and Disability Insurance" in the table is the social security program. The public service employment program provides government jobs for the unemployed. Medicaid and medicare are government health care programs for the poor and elderly. The child nutrition program provides food for the children of poor people. Many programs are cooperative federal-state undertakings. The table shows only federal expenditures, but they are much larger than state expenditures.

Three things are remarkable about the data in Table 9.6. The first is the rapid growth in total expenditures. During the twenty-eight-year period, expenditures on income-security transfer programs grew from 4.5 to 14.3 percent of the GNP. The 1977 expenditures were 8 times those in 1960, and the 1986 expenditures were 3.3 times those in 1977. The second is that means-tested programs have grown faster than other programs. In 1986 expenditure on means-tested programs was 27.1 times 1960 expenditure, whereas that on programs not means tested was only 15.1 times its earlier level. Thus, transfer expenditures are becoming better focused on the needy. Third, in-kind program expenditures have grown much faster than cash-transfer programs. The 1986 expenditures on cash programs were 11.3 times their 1960 level, whereas those on in-kind programs were 205.5 times their 1960 level. Thus, we have moved away from the notion of helping the needy by giving them money and toward the notion of providing them with particular goods and services.

Including state government contributions, total government expenditures on income-security transfers cannot be less than 15 percent of the GNP. Opinions certainly differ as to whether the total is too much or too little. No one should believe, however, that America's effort is negligible. Ongoing efforts to help people are substantial and have increased rapidly since the early 1960s. Those who believe that further efforts should be made to help the needy have two options. The easy option is to continue to expand transfer programs. That is the option followed for two decades, and taxpayer resistance to it is increasing. The hard option is to focus transfer programs more accurately on the needy. In 1977 less than 20 percent of the transfers in Table 9.6 were means tested. Of course, much of the remainder nevertheless goes to the needy. Much does not, though. The large programs that are not means tested are social security, medicare, and unemployment compensation. Introducing means tests would be controversial in all three programs, yet if transfers to the needy are to be increased, either middle-class and upper-middle-class workers must bear a larger tax burden or these programs must be reformed. Notice that increasing the focus of these programs on the poor involves a reduction of benefits as income rises—either a gradual reduction of benefits or a termination of eligibility above some cutoff point. This tying of benefit levels to income is precisely the income tax rate previously discussed in relation to the NIT. The more rapidly benefits are reduced as income rises, the more heavily program benefits are concentrated on the poor. The same rapid benefit reduction also represents a very high income taxation rate (in fact, approaching 100 percent over some income ranges). Without question, tax rates of the magnitude that currently exist seriously diminish the incentive to work and engage in training and education.

There can be no doubt that federal government expenditures tend to reduce income inequality in the United States. There is much more doubt about the effects of state and local government expenditures, and state and local government expenditures have increased relative to federal government expenditures during the postwar period. Furthermore, along with government expenditures, government taxes also affect the distribution of income. The more progressive taxes are, the greater the government's effect in mitigating poverty. Thus, the basic question is raised: what is the net effect of government taxes and expenditures on the distribution of income?

The issue is complex. Government taxes and expenditures affect the income distribution in many complex and poorly understood ways.

Table 9.7 *Income Shares of Quintiles, 1950 and 1970*

Percentile Share	Factor Income		Postfisc Income	
	1950	1970	1950	1970
Share of lowest 20 percent	3.6	2.9	6.4	6.7
Share of middle 60 percent	48.5	46.5	53.7	54.2
Share of highest 20 percent	48.0	50.6	39.9	39.1

Source: Data from Morgan Reynolds and Eugene Smolensky. *Public Expenditures, Taxes, and the Distribution of Income* (New York: Academic Press, 1977).

Nevertheless, some very high quality research has been done on the subject in recent years. Table 9.7 summarizes the results of a study by Reynolds and Smolensky (1977). It shows the percentage of total income received by the lowest and highest income quintiles of the population, as well as by the 60 percent between the extreme groups. If each quintile had 20 percent of total income, everyone would have the same income. In fact, the richest quintile has much higher income than the poorest quintile, as the table shows. As Table 9.1 showed, 20 percent was about the same as the poverty group in 1959, but the poverty group was much less than 20 percent in 1969. The first numerical columns of Table 9.7 show income percentages before taxes and government expenditures are taken into account (the factor income). The last two columns show income percentages after effects of taxes and government expenditures have been allowed for—the *postfisc income* (income after accounting for taxes and transfers).

Two facts stand out from Table 9.7. First, *the distribution of income before taxes and government expenditures are taken into account became somewhat less equal between 1950 and 1970.* The income of the lowest quintile dropped from 3.6 to 2.9 percent of the total. Table 9.5 shows much the same trend for a shorter period, but it is restricted to families. The most important reason for this was an increase in the percentage of people in traditionally low income groups (female-headed households, for example). Such demographic changes account for only a part of the observed shift, however. Both Table 9.5 and 9.7 suggest that the rapid growth of transfers shown in Table 9.6 may have reduced the incentive of the poor to earn income. Second, *government taxes and expenditures greatly reduced the inequality in the income distribution.* For example, government taxes and expenditures more than doubled the income share of the lowest quintile in 1970, increasing it from 2.9 to 6.7 percent. Contrary to some popular belief, the postfisc income share of the middle 60 percent increased between 1950 and 1970. Thus, income redistribution has been at the expense of the highest income quintile, not the middle class.

The income share of the poorest group depends very much on how government transfers to them are valued. The official poverty statistics in Table 9.1 include only some transfers in the measure of income of the poor. The data in Table 9.7 include estimates of all transfers received by people in each quintile. Paglin (1979) claims that careful valuation of transfers implies that only 3.8 percent of the population was below the poverty line in 1974, rather than the 11.6 percent reported in Table 9.1.

☐ FURTHER POSSIBLE STEPS FOR REDUCING POVERTY

Where does the United States stand in the national effort to eliminate poverty? What additional steps should the government take? These are complex questions requiring answers based on detailed notions of equity as well as economic analysis. The variety and complexity of government tax and expenditure programs is enormous. Some are federal, but increasing numbers are federal-state or state programs. The intended beneficiaries, the rules of eligibility, and the amount and kind of help provided vary greatly from program to program. Each program, as well as the total effort, is controversial. Specific program evaluations cannot be attempted here, but several general comments can be made.

First, although people can differ in their evaluations of attempts to redistribute income in the United States, no one should sneer at the effort. Redistributive expenditures are now large, and they have grown rapidly since the beginning of the national effort in the early 1960s. The result has been a clear and substantial increase in living standards of the poor, although exact measures are not available.

Second, programs vary greatly in the extent to which they help the poor. Means-tested programs, such as welfare and food stamps, are targeted accurately on the neediest people. Other programs, such as unemployment compensation and social security, benefit unemployed and elderly people with little regard to need.

Third, many programs have become extremely complex. Successive Congresses modify programs to take into account new circumstances or to increase assistance to particular groups. In some cases, programs have become so complex that legal assistance is required to establish eligibility. An excessive burden is placed on prospective beneficiaries, especially those who are poorly educated. Administrative costs of some programs are far too high, opening the door to manipulation of programs by experts on particular programs, both within the administrative agency and within recipient groups. Social security, housing programs, and welfare programs are examples of programs that have become extremely complex.

Self-help has been at the center of traditional ways to reduce poverty in the United States, yet the white majority has used discriminatory obstacles to block efforts of the black minority to lift themselves from poverty. Gradually and painfully a national consensus has emerged that discrimination is unconscionable. The consensus was embodied in the civil rights bills of the 1960s. Evidence has been presented that discrimination indeed has been reduced, yet it still exists in public service provision, housing, employment, and union membership. It is still true that one of the most important antipoverty measures is reduction of racial discrimination, yet the most important obstacle to self-help by the poor during the 1970s and early 1980s has been the instability and slow growth of the macroeconomy. The elimination of poverty will take much longer, and will be much more painful, if the economy continues to grow slowly.

The current political mood suggests that the percentage of the GNP devoted to income-security transfers during the 1980s will not be much larger than it was in the 1970s. If so, the most important antipoverty program—next to increasing the growth rate of the entire economy— will be to simplify and focus transfer programs. *Poverty, as officially measured, could be eliminated by a moderate improvement in the focus of transfer programs on the poor.* Unemployment compensation, medicare, and social security payments are the important candidates for such reform.

☐ Summary

Poverty is a matter of degree. Although the United States has virtually no poverty of the kind widespread in poor countries, many people here are poor by reasonable standards in an affluent society. The incidence of poverty is especially great among blacks. Poverty decreased rapidly during the 1960s but more slowly during the 1970s. Since the early 1960s the federal government has mounted an elaborate, complex, and expensive set of programs to redistribute income. The effect has been to increase the income share of the lowest quintile and reduce the income share of the highest quintile, but the magnitudes of the redistribution are subject to debate.

Attention focused on reform of transfer programs during the late 1970s. Many economists favor substitution of an NIT for many present income-security transfer programs.

Questions and Problems

1. To what extent do you think the poor would benefit from a wage-price freeze that curtailed inflation without raising the unemployment rate?

2. Calculate the cost of an NIT proposal of your choice, and compare it with the cost of recent transfer expenditures. Make explicit your assumptions about incentive effects of the NIT and the present transfer programs you propose to abolish.

3. Do you think local real estate taxes are progressive or regressive?

4. What contribution would the elimination of racial discrimination in housing make to eliminating poverty among blacks?

References and Further Reading

Freeman, Richard. "Black Economic Progress After 1964; Who Has Gained and Why." National Bureau of Economic Research Conference Volume: *Studies in Labor Markets,* ed. Sherwin Rosen (Chicago: University of Chicago Press, 1981). A survey and analysis of trends in incomes of blacks and whites since the passage of the civil rights laws in the 1960s.

Kain, John, ed. *Race and Poverty* (Englewood Cliffs, N.J.: Prentice-Hall, 1969). A collection of essays on the relationship between race and poverty in the 1950s and 1960s.

Myrdal, Gunnar. *An American Dilemma* (New York: Harper & Row, 1944). A classic study of American racial problems by the Swedish economist.

Owen, Henry and Charles Schultze, eds. *Setting National Priorities* (Washington, D.C.: Brookings, 1976). An annual volume by the Brookings Institution staff analyzing the president's budget proposals to Congress.

Paglin, Morton. "Poverty in the United States: A Reevaluation." *Policy Review* (Spring 1979): 7–24. An attempt to include in-kind transfers in measuring income of the poor.

Reynolds, Morgan, and Eugene Smolensky. *Public Expenditures, Taxes, and the Distribution of Income* (New York: Academic Press, 1977). A careful statistical study of the effects of government taxes and expenditures on the distribution of income.

Robins, Philip K., Robert G. Spiegelman, and Samuel Weiner, eds. *A Guaranteed Annual Income: Evidence from a Social Experiment, 1980.*

U.S. Department of Commerce, Bureau of the Census. *Statistical Abstract of the United States* (Washington, D.C.: Government Printing Office, 1987). A useful compendium of government statistics.

10

The Market for Housing

☐ Chapter 6 and other chapters referred to the price and the quantity of housing. In particular, the quantity demanded and supplied was assumed to depend on the price (it also was assumed that the price varies with accessibility to the CBD). The notion of price-dependent supply and demand functions is one of the most basic concepts of economics, and it has proved invaluable in analyzing a host of problems. In the case of housing, however, it is difficult to compare houses with regard to price and quantity, and even abstract definitions are not straightforward. Nevertheless, before proceeding with an analysis of housing, the meanings of *price* and *quantity* must be sorted out.

The nature of the problem is easy to state: what is the difference between a $100,000 house and a $50,000 house? Is the price of the first house twice as high, is the price the same and the quantity twice as great, or something in between? Asset value, rather than price or quantity, is directly observed. Perhaps the $100,000 house is higher priced than the other one because it is more accessible to the CBD. Then again, it might simply be "more housing" sold at the same price per "unit."

The measurement problem is further complicated by the durability of housing and the existence of both rental and homeowner markets. Who is paying a higher price for housing—an owner of a $50,000 house or a renter paying $300 per month for an identical house?

The first task of this chapter is to sort out these price and quantity concepts and to use the concepts to present a coherent model of the housing market.

☐ QUANTITY AND PRICE MEASURES FOR HOUSING

Quantity

Economists have defined a standard *unit of housing* by various statistical techniques. If we think of housing as comprised of floor space and something that will be called *quality* (in general measured by such variables as number and quality of kitchen appliances, type of heating system, number of rooms, and structural integrity), in principle we can define a "one-unit" house, consisting of a certain number of square feet of a given quality. If consumers are willing to trade off floor space for quality, there is an *isoquant* of the type in Figure 10.1.[1] All combinations of floor space and quality on the isoquant are equally desirable (that is how the isoquant is defined), and each, by definition, is said to contain one unit of housing.

This reference isoquant provides a consistent method of measuring the quantity of housing in any house. Consider the house labeled *H* in Figure 10.1, which contains the quantities of floor space and quality indicated by its coordinates in the graph. Passing a line between *H* and the origin shows that *H* is twice as far from the origin as the reference isoquant; thus, *H* is a two-unit house.[2] That is, it represents twice as much housing as a house on the reference isoquant.

This method of measuring the quantity of housing in any given house (relative to some standard) requires that the reference isoquant be correct. The technique for establishing reference isoquants is called *hedonic price index analysis,* and it is beyond the scope of this book. Suffice it to say that the technique is both widely used and widely criticized. There is even debate as to whether the reference isoquant is a meaningful concept. Nevertheless, despite the statistical and conceptual difficulties, it is the only available method for measuring the quantity of housing.[3]

Price

Having measured quantity (relative to some norm), price now can be measured by dividing house value (total expenditure) by quantity. This number is a price measure in the following sense: it captures the variation in house value that remains after correcting for differences in quantity. Returning to the example of the $100,000 and the $50,000 houses, if the quantity measures showed that the first had twice as many units as the second, division would show that $100,000/2 = $50,000/1; that is, the price per unit of the two houses is the same. More specifically, this measure is defined as the *value price,* as it is found by dividing house value by quantity.

---

1. An isoquant is the locus of all input combinations that yield the same amount of output. The housing isoquants, of course, have many dimensions—floor space, lot size, quality of appliances, conditions of walls, and so on. Note that for some of these inputs, such as quality of walls, it makes no sense to talk about returns to scale. (What is the result when all inputs are doubled, including wall quality?)

2. Rosen (1974) has an excellent, although challenging, discussion of what can and cannot be learned from this approach. A pragmatic application, which is easier to follow, is that of King and Mieszkowski (1973).

3. This technique was introduced by Griliches (1971) to disentangle price and quality changes in automobiles.

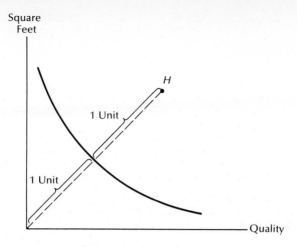

Figure 10.1 *Measuring "Units" of Housing*

By similar means, a *rental price* can be found by dividing monthly (or annual) rent by quantity. The rental price tells how much it would cost to rent a "standard" house, that is, one with characteristics lying on the reference isoquant.

Both value prices and rental prices, of course, may vary from time to time and from place to place. Chapter 6 introduced the possibility of spatial variation in housing prices, and this chapter will look at variations over time. The reason for going through the previous analysis is to be sure we are observing *price* in the sense that economists and others generally use the term.

Relationship Between Value Price and Rental Price

The market relationship between value price and rental price is probably the most important concept in the analysis of housing markets. Confusion over these concepts has led to significant errors in analysis and policy.

In principle, the relationship is straightforward: *value* is the present value of rent less the present value of costs of operation.[4] In fact, the relationship is rather complicated because of considerations of taxation, capital gains, inflation, maintenance, and depreciation, as well as interest.

The starting point is the simple case where rent and value are linked only via the interest rate. Assume in this simple model that housing lasts

---

4. The remainder of this discussion will use the terms *value* and *rent* rather than the more cumbersome *value price* and *rental price*. This will cause no problems so long as the reader remembers that *value* and *rent* each refer to the same-size house.

forever, with no depreciation, maintenance, capital gains, or taxes. In this case, if rent is to cover the landlord's costs,

$$R = iV, \tag{10.1}$$

where R is rent, i is the interest rate, and V is value. Given the simplifications assumed, the landlord's only cost is the annual interest payment on the investment (V). If the housing market is assumed to be competitive (and therefore the landlord makes no profit), annual rent (R) just covers annual cost (iV).

Note that the relationship between R and V has been described in two equivalent ways: R is the annual cost of holding a house of value V, embodied in Equation (10.1), or V is the present value of future R (assumed to be a constant stream forever). This version of the relationship can be found by rearranging Equation (10.1):[5]

$$V = \frac{R}{i} = \sum_{\tau=1}^{\infty} \frac{R}{(1 + i)^{\tau}}. \tag{10.2}$$

The rental price is the annual rent that a competitive landlord charges a tenant for the right to occupy a standard-sized dwelling for one year. The rental price, then, is the relevant price term when a renter's demand function for housing is considered. It is important to note that *the rental price is also the price a homeowner faces for the right to occupy housing.* This can be seen in two ways. First, note that the homeowner's annual cost is iV.[6] Second, the opportunity cost of occupying a house is obviously the annual rent the homeowner could charge if he or she were to move out and put the house on the rental market.

Thus, just like the renter's, the homeowner's cost of housing is the rental price, and it is the rental price—not the value price—that enters the homeowner's demand function and governs the amount of housing he or she consumes. The value price makes no difference either to the homeowner or the renter except through its influence on the rental price (via Equation [10.1] or [10.2]). By way of example, if the value price rises 10 percent and the interest rate falls 10 percent, the rental price does not change, and neither the owner-occupant nor the renter is induced to change behavior.

---

5. τ is a variable indicating the year number. This is a shorthand expression for the discounted sum of future rents:

$$\sum_{\tau=1}^{\infty} \frac{R}{(1 + i)^{\tau}} \equiv \frac{R}{(1 + i)} + \frac{R}{(1 + i)^2} + \frac{R}{(1 + i)^3} + \cdots + \frac{R}{(1 + i)^{\infty}}.$$

6. It does not matter how much of the house is financed by a mortgage. That which is not financed by the mortgage is the homeowner's equity. By having some of this wealth tied up in the house, the homeowner is forgoing interest that could be earned by selling the house and investing the equity at the market rate of interest. "Interest" includes interest paid on the outstanding mortgage plus forgone interest on the homeowner's equity.

☐ COST OF CAPITAL: COMPLICATIONS

The coefficient linking R and V is known as the *cost of capital,* because it measures the cost of holding a unit of capital for a year. In the previous case, the only cost is interest; if the interest rate is 10 percent, the cost of holding \$1 of capital for a year is \$0.10. This section's task is to modify the cost-of-capital term to account for costs other than interest associated with holding housing capital.

If the house is subject to a property tax at the tax rate T, depreciation and maintenance at the rate d, and expected capital gains at the rate g—and if it is recognized that management of a home requires some entrepreneurial effort (e, assumed proportional to house value)—the rental price becomes

$$R = iV + TV + dV - gV + eV$$

$$= (i + T + d - g + e)V. \tag{10.3}$$

Each of the terms multiplied by V is an item in the landlord's cost (negative in the case of capital gains) and is assumed to be proportional to the value.[7] To repeat, the way to read the expression is as follows: for a house of value V and unit costs given by i, T, d, g, and e, R is the rent that must be charged to cover costs. R is the total cost incurred by holding the house for a year, regardless of whether the owner occupies the house or rents it out. If the owner rents it out, he or she must recover these costs in rent; if the owner occupies it, he or she incurs these costs for housing.

Inflation

The incorporation of inflation into Equation (10.3) is a bit tricky, but it is critical to understanding the housing market in the 1970s and 1980s. Incorporating inflation requires an understanding of the relationship between interest and inflation.

Ignoring federal income taxes, the true cost of borrowing is the interest payment less the inflation that occurs between the time of borrowing and repayment. The reason for this is that inflation renders the repaid dollars less valuable than the borrowed dollars. Thus, the repayment of principal does not return to lenders all the purchasing power they originally lent out. To maintain the real value of the borrowed principal outstanding, or keep the principal whole, competitive markets tend to tack on an *inflation premium* to interest rates.

Expressing this observation in terms of rates of inflation and interest,

$$i = r + \pi, \tag{10.4}$$

---

7.   This assumption clearly is justified in interest, taxes, and capital gains, but depreciation and entrepreneurial costs might not vary proportionately with value.

where i is the interest rate, π is the inflation rate, and r is the true cost of borrowing in terms of purchasing power, called the *real interest rate*.[8] For concreteness, suppose there is 5 percent inflation, and a lender demands a 2 percent return on investment. The "nominal" interest rate (i) must be 7 percent (2 percent + 5 percent) in order to keep the capital whole and yield 2 percent.[9]

Suppose now that the nominal interest rate rises one percentage point for each percentage point of inflation and that the rate of capital gains does likewise. That is, suppose the real interest rate and real rate of capital gains are independent of the rate of inflation. This can be represented by replacing i by $(r + \pi)$ and g by $(g^r + \pi)$ in Equation (10.3) (g^r stands for real capital gains). How does this influence the cost-of-capital expression? It gives the following:

$$R = [(r + \pi) + T + d + e - (g^r + \pi)]V$$
$$= [r + T + d + e - g^r]V. \tag{10.5}$$

Since there is the same inflation premium on interest and capital gains, inflation cancels and the cost of capital is unaffected by inflation. This "pure" inflation is neutral to the rental price of housing, just as pure inflation is neutral with respect to all relative prices.

This result is important. It says that a rise in the interest rate brought about by a rise in inflation expectations does not depress the demand for housing. In other words, a 10 percent mortgage when inflation is 8 percent is no more costly than a 2 percent mortgage when inflation is zero. In the former case, the homeowner anticipates an 8 percent capital gain (due to the 8 percent inflation), which can be used to pay all but two percentage points on the mortgage. Of course, if the mortgage rate is 10 percent and inflation is zero, the true cost of borrowing is the full 10 percent. Many people express surprise over the fact that the high interest rates of the 1970s failed to choke off housing demand. An important part of the reason is that interest rates were not high after accounting for inflation, as will be shown.

Federal Income Taxation*

The next step is to introduce federal income taxation. Since the federal tax law treats owner-occupied and rental housing differently, this must be done in this section as well. This section begins with a

---

8. Equation (10.4) is not quite right, as it does not allow for continuous compounding. The correct expression is $1 + i = (1 + r)(1 + \pi)$. Multiplying out the righthand side yields $i = r + \pi + r\pi$, though the product ($r\pi$) can be ignored unless either r or π is very large.

9. This would be a "fair" inflation premium in the sense that the borrower would be paying, and the lender receiving, the same real interest rate regardless of the rate of inflation. See Tanzi (1980) for an empirical investigation of the relationship between interest rates and expected inflation.

* This section is fairly difficult and can be skipped without loss of continuity.

discussion of owner-occupied housing, but much of what is said will carry over to rental housing. If the homeowner pays federal income taxes and itemizes deductions,[10] the rental price is further modified:

$$R = [i(1 - t) + T(1 - t) + d - g + e]V \qquad (10.6)$$

where t is the marginal income tax rate. This expression recognizes that interest payments and property taxes are tax deductible (thus, the consumer's cost is interest payments plus property tax payments less the income tax reductions resulting from the deductions) and that interest income is taxable. Thus, for both the mortgage payment and the forgone interest on homeowner equity, it is the aftertax rate that is important to the homeowner.

Inflation and Income Taxation Combined*

The neutrality (the cancellation of inflation from the cost-of-capital expression) disappears when the interaction of inflation and taxes is considered. The problem arises because the federal tax law treats the two inflation entries in Equation (10.5) differently, thus creating a situation where inflation is not cancelled out in the rent/value equation. To see this, note that capital gains and interest have both an inflation component and a real component.

Capital gains—both the real and inflation components—generally escape federal income taxation altogether, or at most they are taxed at a very low rate for owner-occupied housing.[11] Interest, however—whether the real or the inflation component—is subject to taxation (and, of course, interest payments are deductible). Thus, the final form of the rent/value equation, incorporating all the assumptions discussed, is as follows:[12]

$$R = [(r + \pi)(1 - t) + T(1 - t) \\ + d + e - (g^r + \pi)]V. \qquad (10.7)$$

Combining the terms containing π,

$$R = [\underline{(r + \pi)(1 - t) - \pi} + T(1 - t) + d + e - g^r]V.$$

Look at the term in the underlined bracket. This expression is called the *real aftertax interest rate,* as it is the interest rate that must be paid

---

10. If the homeowner does not itemize, the appropriate expression is not found by striking out $(1 - t)$ everywhere it appears. The appropriate adjustment is rather complicated but not terribly important quantitatively (see Dynarski, 1981).

11. The details of the tax law covering owner-occupied housing can be found in Pechman (1982).

12. The symbols, whose definitions are scattered throughout the text, are all defined here: R = rental price; r = real interest rate; π = expected inflation; t = federal income tax rate; T = local property tax rate; d = depreciation rate; e = competitive return to landlord entrepreneurship; g = expected rate of capital gains; and V = value price.

* This section is fairly difficult and can be skipped without loss of continuity.

(or can be received) after accounting for both inflation and taxes. The crucial observation here is the following: *if the (nominal) interest rate rises one percentage point for each additional percentage point of inflation, the real aftertax interest rate (the true cost of borrowing) actually declines as inflation rises.* The reason for this is that the federal tax law makes no distinction between real interest and the inflation premium that is a part of nominal or market interest. Since both the real and inflation premium components of interest are tax-deductible, and since the inflation premium grows with inflation, the real interest rate after taxes and inflation falls as inflation rises.[13]

Further complications of the cost-of-capital expression will not be considered prior to the discussion of legal distinctions between owner-occupied and rental housing. The easiest way to think of the cost of capital is that it is interest and other interest-like cost items. These costs are incurred by all landlords and represent the true annual cost of occupying housing. One of the important observations from this section is that the real aftertax cost of capital tends to decline as inflation increases, given the institutions and federal tax laws of the United States.

☐ THE MARKET FOR HOUSING

The cost-of-capital expression, despite its tedium, is the crucial link between the supply and demand sides of the market for housing, and it is apparent that the market for housing cannot be analyzed without an understanding of the cost of capital. The following section will designate the cost of capital as ρ, recognizing that it incorporates all the terms in the brackets in Equation (10.7).

Demand for Housing

It has been emphasized that the demand for housing—whether by owner-occupants or renters—is influenced by the rental price, in addition to income and demographics. In deciding on the level of housing services to consume, a household is concerned with the monthly or annual cost of occupancy. Even an owner-occupant, in the role of occupant, cares about the rental price, not the value price. The value price matters, of course, but only because the value price times the cost of capital is the rental price. The demand curve (D) for housing should be downward sloping in a graph with axes labeled Q for quantity and R for rent, as in Figure 10.2.

---

13. Of course, if the inflation premium on mortgage rates were larger than one point of interest for one point of inflation, the real interest rate after taxes would not fall with rising inflation. Historically, however, for reasons that are beyond the scope of this book, inflation premiums have been large enough to offset inflation, but not inflation and taxes.

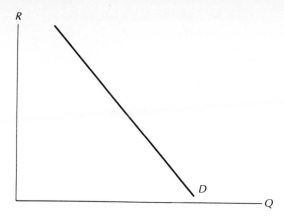

Figure 10.2 *Demand Curve for Housing Services*

Empirical Estimates of Demand Functions

Economists' quantitative knowledge of the determinants of the demand for housing has improved dramatically during the past thirty years with improvements in statistical techniques, basic economic concepts, data, and computing. The best current evidence is from Ellwood and Polinsky (1979), who report that the price elasticity is somewhere between 0.75 and 1.20 and that the income elasticity is about 0.75. Thus, it appears that the share of income spent on housing should fall with income and that expenditure might increase a bit as the price rises. There is some evidence that the demand is much less elastic with respect to both price and income for low-income people.

It might seem that it should not be difficult to estimate the parameters of the demand function for housing (that is, to learn how elastic the demand is with respect to income and price). Begin by assuming a specific functional form, say, linear: $Q = a_o + a_1 y + a_2 p$. Q is the quantity of housing demanded, y is income, p is price, and the a's are the coefficients. For example, a_1 tells how much Q rises as income rises by \$1. With data on Q, y, and p, a computer can estimate the a's (see Appendix B). It has already been noted, however, that disentangling price and quantity is difficult.

Strangely enough, even income is difficult to measure properly. Reported annual income ("current" income) is not the proper income measure for the demand function. The reason is quite simple: income fluctuates from year to year because of, among other things, such random shocks as unemployment and unexpected inheritances. It would not be sensible to change housing consumption every year in response to random and temporary changes in annual income. Instead, households base their housing and other consumption decisions upon a longer term expected or average income, known to economists as *permanent income*. Another way to state this is that permanent income is a better measure of a household's budget constraint, and it is, of course, the budget constraint that belongs in the demand function.[14]

Not surprisingly, it is difficult to get data on permanent income, so the temptation is to use current income and hope for the best. The best is not very good, however, as the careful studies of Muth (1960) and Ellwood and Polinsky (1979) demonstrate. The various means that have been employed to estimate price, quantity, and permanent income are beyond the scope of this chapter. (The paper by Muth, however, is quite readable.) In any case, this is the major source of difficulty in estimating the demand for housing.

Housing Supply

The dominant feature of housing supply at any point in time is the standing stock. The stock is altered only very slowly through construction, demolition, alteration, and conversion between housing and non-housing uses of buildings. These components of supply will be explored later in this chapter. This section offers only a caricature of this sector in order to get a supply curve to use in supply-and-demand analysis.

In any year, think of the standing stock as being sold to the highest bidder (typically the current occupant). As a result of this "auction," there is an equilibrium rental and value price for each dwelling unit. If it is possible to construct some type of house at a cost less than this value price, entrepreneurs are expected to add to the stock. Given the magnitude of the stock relative to the rate of construction, however, any move from short-run to long-run equilibrium takes place rather slowly.[15]

Thus, the supply curve of housing is quite inelastic in the short run. In the long run, however, the supply is surely quite elastic. If it is possible to build one house of a given type for $75,000, then given enough time it is surely possible to build a large number at the same cost.

For a given level of construction cost, a greater stock of housing is expected to be forthcoming the greater the value price. In particular, note that producers care about the value price rather than the rental price. Contractors do not care what the rental prices of houses are; their only concern is whether they can sell them for more than construction cost. Thus, the supply curve (S) appears as depicted in Figure 10.3; it is upward sloping, with axes labeled Q for quantity and V for value.

---

14. The idea of looking at permanent income as a proper measure of the household budget constraint originated with Milton Friedman (1957). Muth (1960) has an excellent discussion of the use of permanent income in housing demand studies.

15. In a typical year, the number of new units constructed is equal to about 2 percent of the stock, and about one-third of new construction replaces houses that are retired.

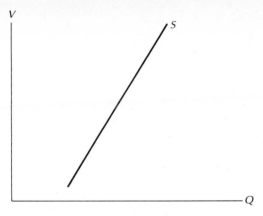

Figure 10.3 *Supply Curve for Housing Services*

Market Equilibrium

A supply curve relating value price to quantity and a demand curve relating rental price to quantity have now been established. Market equilibrium cannot be determined in the ordinary way—by drawing supply and demand curves on the same graph—because the price concepts are different for suppliers and demanders. Suppliers care about the value price and demanders about the rental price. However, since it is known that $R = \rho V$, for any given level of ρ the supply curve can be plotted on the demand curve graph or vice versa.[16] For example, at Q^* in Figure 10.4, V on the supply curve equals 100. If $\rho = 0.10$, $R = 10$ is consistent with $V = 100$. Hence, the point $(Q^*, 10)$ is a point on the supply curve plotted on the rent/quantity graph. By this technique the whole supply curve can be plotted in the rent/quantity space of the demand curve. This is done in Figure 10.4, which combines Figures 10.2 and 10.3, lined up one above the other so that Q is in the same units in both panels. Using the relationship between R and V, the supply curve is mapped onto the demand curve space and vice versa. Ignoring the dashed supply and demand curves for a moment, the equilibrium quantity can be read as (Q_1), value price (V_1), and rental price (R_1). This must be an equilibrium, because (V_1, Q_1) is on the supply curve, (R_1, Q_1) is on the demand curve, and $R_1 = \rho V_1$.

What happens when ρ changes? The demand curve in the rent/quantity graph does not change (the relationship between rental price and quantity demanded is unaffected by ρ), nor does the supply curve

16.   Recall that ρ is the summary variable for the cost of capital. It includes interest, taxes, depreciation, and capital gains. This section asks what happens in the market for housing when the cost of capital changes. Mostly it concerns the effect of changes in the real aftertax interest rate and capital gains.

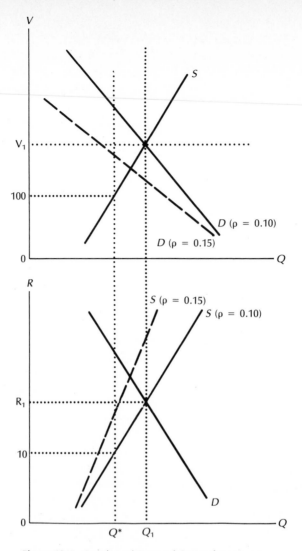

Figure 10.4 *Supply and Demand Curves for Housing*

in the value/quantity graph. The mapping of the supply curve into the rent/quantity space assumed a specific level of ρ, however, and with a new level the mapping must be redone. Returning to the previous numerical example, suppose ρ rises from 0.10 to 0.15. On the supply curve at Q^*, V is still 100, but the R that is required to cover the cost is now 15. Thus, when the supply curve is mapped into rent/quantity space, it is shifted upward and to the left. This reflects the fact that with a higher cost of capital, rents must be higher in order to bring forth any given supply.

Similarly, the demand curve must shift when mapped into value/quantity space, in this case downward and to the left. The rationale is the same: a given rent implies a lower value if the cost of capital is higher. The new equilibrium (Q_2, V_2, R_2) can now be read, and it reveals just what it should: a rise in the cost of capital leads to a reduction in value, a rise in rent, and reduced quantity.

Some of this is apparent without recourse to the supply and demand curves. If $R = \rho V$ and ρ rises, clearly some combination of rent increase and value decline is going to occur. If the shapes of the supply and demand curves are known with certainty, this analysis would tell how the effect of an increase in ρ is divided between a value decline and a rent increase; that is, it would tell the *incidence* of a change in the cost of capital. For example, if the supply curve were perfectly elastic, value could not change (since the supply curve is horizontal), and the entire effect of a change in ρ would be borne by rent.

A means for describing the market for housing has now been established. To reiterate, it is assumed that demand depends on the rental price, supply depends on the value price, and value and rental prices are linked by the cost of capital.

☐ THE MARKET FOR HOUSING IN THE 1970s

This section could well have been titled "Economics of Housing and Inflation," because the most significant force acting upon the housing market during the 1970s was the almost decade-long acceleration in inflation. Does this theory of the housing market correctly predict inflation's effect?

Response to Inflation

It is well known that the value price of housing rose dramatically during the 1970s, and this is documented in column A of Table 10.1. This column shows the price index of new one-family homes sold relative to the overall price level (as measured by the Consumer Price Index, or *CPI*) in each year. The index has been set equal to 100 in 1965. By 1970, for example, the value price of housing had risen 1.6 percent more than had the overall price level since 1965. So long as this index stays near 100 (up to about 1972), it can be said that the value price of housing has moved roughly in concert with other prices in the economy, or that the *real* value price has remained constant. Real value prices were quite stable from 1965 to 1971. By 1979, however, the value price of housing had outstripped overall inflation by 26.6 percent (since 1965). The rise in the relative price of housing began in earnest around 1972, with a particularly large spurt in 1977.

It is also well known that mortgage interest rates rose throughout the 1970s. Column B shows that the average mortgage rate rose from 5.83 to 11.15 percent between 1965 and 1979. These are the figures underlying frequent newspaper accounts that state that only the rich can afford housing. It will be seen that the house value and mortgage rate numbers, by themselves, are misleading. Even before turning to

Table 10.1 *Movements in Value Prices, Rental Prices, Real Interest Rates, and Nominal Interest Rates, 1965 to 1985*

	Value Price	Average Mortgage Rate	Rental Price	Real Interest Rate	Real Aftertax Mortgage Rate
	(A)	(B)	(C)	(D)	(E)
1965	100.0	5.83	100.0	5.09	3.63
1966	101.4	6.40	98.5	5.24	3.64
1967	101.4	6.53	97.5	5.19	3.56
1968	102.3	7.12	95.8	5.03	3.25
1969	104.6	7.99	93.9	5.88	3.88
1970	101.6	8.52	92.3	5.88	3.75
1971	102.7	7.75	92.6	4.64	2.70
1972	105.9	7.64	92.8	4.40	2.49
1973	108.6	8.30	91.1	5.05	2.98
1974	107.0	9.22	86.2	4.85	2.55
1975	107.8	9.10	83.0	5.17	2.90
1976	110.5	8.99	82.8	4.08	1.83
1977	127.1	8.95	82.4	3.68	1.44
1978	123.7	9.68	81.8	4.58	2.16
1979	126.6	11.15	79.0	5.27	2.48
1980	123.7	12.25	75.7	5.43	2.37
1981	121.2	16.52	74.5	9.78	5.65
1982	118.4	15.79	75.8	9.90	5.95
1983	118.1	13.43	76.8	8.15	4.79
1984	117.6	13.80	78.0	8.80	5.35
1985	n.a.	12.28	n.a.	8.80	5.73

Notes: Column A shows the real value price of housing: the price index of new one-family homes divided by the *CPI* and set equal to 100 in 1965.
Column B shows the average conventional new home mortgage rate.
Column C shows the *CPI* rent component divided by the *CPI*, set equal to 100 in 1965.
Column D shows the estimate of the real mortgage rate.
Column E shows the estimate of the real aftertax mortgage rate.
Sources: Data from U.S. Bureau of Labor Statistics, *Federal Reserve Bulletin*, and Hulten and Schwab (1987).

the analysis, however, it is worth pointing out that in 1980 just over one-quarter of home buyers had household incomes of less than $25,000. The median income for home-buying households was $33,100, as compared with a median for all households of $17,650.

Equally dramatic but less well known is the movement in the rental price of housing over this period. The rental price (relative to the *CPI*) fell from 100 to 79 between 1965 to 1979. Again, much of this 20 percent decline in the real rental price of housing occurred from 1973 to 1979.

Based on the theory of the previous section, these movements appear paradoxical. Surely an increase in interest rates should depress house values and raise rents. The numbers begin to make more sense, however, after looking at column D, an estimate of the real interest rate previously described. The real interest rate is the market interest rate (column B) less expected inflation. Hulten and Schwab (1987) have estimated expected inflation for each of the years in the table, and these estimates were used in calculating the real interest rate of column D. The column reveals that the rise in interest rates during the 1970s was not sufficient to offset the rise in expected inflation. The real interest rate in 1965 was 5.09 percent; by 1977 it had fallen to a low of 3.68 percent. After 1977 interest rates (after inflation) gradually began climbing back to the levels of the late 1960s and then, in the 1980s, to unprecedented levels.*

This pattern of falling real interest rates during the 1970s is even more striking when the real *aftertax* mortgage rate, an estimate of which appears in column E, is examined.[17] After accounting for both taxes and inflation, mortgage rates were extremely low in 1977 and 1978 and did not rise to their 1960s level until the 1980s. Finally, by 1982, President Reagan's tight money policy, coupled with declining inflation, caused the real aftertax mortgage rate to jump to 5.95 percent. This had the predicted chilling effect on the value price of housing, as can be seen in column A. Construction also declined dramatically, as revealed in Table 10.2.

Somewhat contrary to prediction, the rental price did not increase with the rising real interest rates of the late 1970s and only started to increase in 1982. Part of the reason for this is that the stock is fixed in the short run. Rents cannot be raised until some of this stock is retired.

The theory of the housing market, then, does predict correctly its response to the inflation of the 1970s and the declining inflation of the early 1980s. The pattern of rising value price and declining rental price is exactly what would be expected given a decline in the appropriately measured cost of capital. The decline in the cost of capital was a boon to housing, and the incidence of this boon appears to have been divided about evenly between capital gains and rent decreases.[18]

Capital Gains Component of ρ: The Investment Motive

Column A of Table 10.1 indicates that holders of the housing stock reaped large real capital gains during the 1970s. The truth of this observation can be confirmed by talking to anyone who owned housing

---

17. The first step in this calculation is to take 75 percent of the market mortgage rate (column B), giving the aftertax mortgage rate assuming the borrower is in the 25 percent marginal tax bracket. Schwab's expected inflation is subtracted from this number, yielding the real aftertax mortgage rate.

18. Note that this analysis relies heavily on the assumption that all demanders (both owner-occupants and renters) are concerned with the rental price of housing. To repeat, in the case of owner-occupants the rent is implicit.

* The following paragraph deals with the interaction between inflation and income taxes. Readers who skipped the previous starred sections also should skip this paragraph.

Table 10.2 *Housing Starts by Year (Millions of dwelling units)*

1959	1.55	1973	2.06
1960	1.30	1974	1.35
1961	1.37	1975	1.17
1962	1.49	1976	1.55
1963	1.63	1977	2.00
1964	1.56	1978	2.04
1965	1.51	1979	1.76
1966	1.20	1980	1.31
1967	1.32	1981	1.10
1968	1.55	1982	1.07
1969	1.50	1983	1.71
1970	1.47	1984	1.76
1971	2.08	1985	1.75
1972	2.38	1986	1.81

Source: Data from U.S. Department of Commerce, Bureau of the Census. *Construction Reports,* various issues.

during that time. Noting that capital gains enter negatively into the cost of capital, it is tempting to argue that rising capital gains also imparted downward pressure on the value of ρ and that this further contributed to rising values and declining rents. Capital gains cannot influence housing decisions, though, unless they are *anticipated* at the time of the decision. Unanticipated capital gains are merely a happy surprise. Although there is no way of knowing how much of the capital gains of the 1970s was anticipated, it is unlikely that market agents anticipated all the capital gains that occurred. (People who correctly anticipated the numbers in Table 10.1 should have put all the money they possibly could borrow into housing. The fact that most people did not do this indicates either that the capital gains were not anticipated or that the agents were not willing to take the risk of being wrong.)

The anticipation of capital gains is frequently referred to as the *investment motive* for owning housing. It is important to note that this investment motive is just like interest and maintenance—it is an element in the cost of capital (a negative element, in the case of positive capital gains). Regardless of the expected rate of capital gains, the decision as to how much housing to *own* always can be thought of as an investment decision: where will the highest rate of return on equity be earned—in housing or in something else? How much housing to own and how much to occupy are not the same decision, however. If housing is a good investment, it does not follow that everyone occupies a large amount of housing. That depends on the rental price.

☐ INFLATION AND HOUSING FINANCE

Many of the effects of inflation on the housing market operate through financial markets, and several of these effects will now be considered. This section begins with a discussion of the "standard" mortgage—the type of mortgage instrument that until about 1980 was almost the only kind of loan used to finance housing purchases.

With the standard, or level payment, self-amortizing mortgage, a given principal is borrowed and then repaid in equal monthly installments over a fixed period (usually twenty to thirty years). The monthly payment is calculated in such a way that the present value of the stream of payments, discounted at the mortgage rate of interest, is equal to the borrowed principal. It is possible to break down each payment into principal and interest, so at each point in time the outstanding principal can be calculated.

The standard mortgage is an excellent vehicle for financing housing during a period of low and stable inflation. It enables homeowners to make housing payments at roughly the same time they receive the services. Furthermore, a mortgage is a secure loan, since the collateral can easily be seized if payments are not made. As will be shown, however, there are serious problems with standard mortgage finance when inflation is even as high as 5 to 10 percent and when there is variation from year to year in the inflation rate of more than one or two percentage points.

Inflation and Homeowner Cash Flow Problems

Despite favorable movements in capital gains and real aftertax mortgage rates, the inflation of the 1970s that brought about these changes was a mixed blessing for some homeowners. Given the way both traditional and new mortgages work, inflation and the consequent rise in nominal interest rates tilt the time stream of mortgage payments toward the early years of the mortgage. The problem is brought about by the *existence* of inflation and the attendant inflation premium on interest rates; it is unrelated to problems of changing inflation, which will be discussed later.

One of the features of a level-payment mortgage, obviously, is that the same *nominal* mortgage payment is made in each year until the mortgage is paid off. In a period of inflation, however, a constant nominal payment stream implies a declining real stream paid by the borrower to the lender. The problem is illustrated in Figure 10.5. Each line in the graph shows the time path of *real* mortgage payments under the indicated regime. (The horizontal line shows the real payment path with no inflation; the downward-sloping curve shows the real payment path with 10 percent inflation.) For concreteness, assume the mortgage principal to be $50,000. At no inflation and a 3.5 percent, twenty-five-year

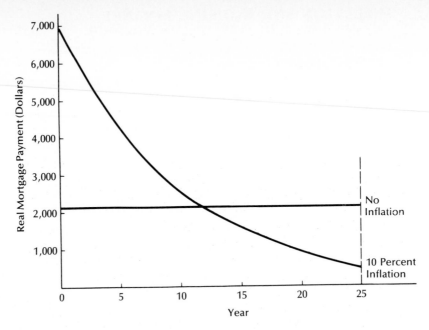

Figure 10.5 *Effect of Inflation on Real Mortgage Payments*

mortgage, real annual payments would be $2119.91 in each of the twenty-five years, depicted by the horizontal line labeled "no inflation."

Suppose there is 10 percent inflation and a "fair" inflation premium on the mortgage interest rate, giving a nominal mortgage rate of 13.5 percent.[19] In the initial year, the mortgage payment is much higher than it is with the inflation-free 3.5 percent mortgage. In fact, annual payments are $6993.86, or over three times as high as in the first example.[20] Ten percent inflation will rapidly erode the real value of these payments, however. In fifteen years the real payment will have fallen to $1674.27, and real payments in the twenty-fifth year will be only $645.51. These numbers are plotted as the downward-sloping line in Figure 10.5. The inflation premium is fair in the sense that the present values of the two payment streams, both discounted at 3.5 percent, are the same ($50,000).

The tilted payment stream in the inflationary world can cause severe cash flow problems for some homeowners, however. Suppose, for example, that in the inflation-free world the $2119.91 annual mort-

19. Taxes are ignored here, because that would complicate the story without substantially changing the outcome.

20. These numbers, which can be calculated from a standard mortgage table, were obtained from Rosen (1979).

gage payment is 20 percent of a homeowner's annual income. In the first year of the mortgage in the 10 percent inflation world, the same homeowner, buying the same house, would be using a staggering 66 percent of income for mortgage payments. Of course, twenty-five years later the payments would have fallen to 6 percent of income as a result of the effect of inflation upon the constant nominal stream. In the short run, however, with inflation rates well within recent experience in the United States, extraordinary cash flow problems can arise. Anyone with accumulated assets or access to a secondary borrowing market can smooth out the payment stream, for example by borrowing to finance the high-payment years and offering the promise of low-payment years as collateral. It seems reasonable to believe, however, that many first-time home buyers are unable to engage in this secondary borrowing. Indeed, when Schwab (1983) investigated this problem empirically, he found that high nominal interest rates did depress housing consumption of young households with few nonhousing assets, but not older ones.

Unanticipated Inflation

There is strong evidence that at least one important type of institution in the housing market was surprised by the persistent acceleration of inflation during the 1970s, namely, mortgage lending institutions. Savings and loans (S&Ls) and other mortgage lenders provided a large volume of mortgage credit during the 1970s at interest rates that turned out to be substantially negative after inflation and taxes. To see this, consider the case of a mortgage offered in 1965 at 5.83 percent. By 1978 inflation was 7.6 percent, so homeowners found themselves borrowing not at the anticipated real rate of about 3.5 percent after taxes, but rather (assuming a 25 percent tax rate) at the astonishing rate of -3.2 percent.[21] The average homeowner in the 1970s, in addition to facing a low *anticipated* rate of interest, became the recipient of unanticipated real capital gains; also, unanticipated inflation reduced the real interest rate below even that low rate the homeowner had anticipated. It is important to reiterate that these benefits accrued not only to owner-occupants, but also to owners of rental housing. Also, the available evidence indicates that competition forced landlords to pass some of these benefits on to renters in the form of lower real rents.

This happy surprise for owners of the housing stock was a most unhappy surprise for the lending industry. It was this disaster, as well as the desire to prevent its recurrence, that led to many legal and in-

---

21. A 5.8 percent mortgage after taxes is 4.4 percent, which is 3.2 points less than the 7.6 percent inflation of 1978.

stitutional changes in the lending industry around 1980. In large part, the lending industry's problem has been due to the fact that it borrows short (ordinary time deposits, largely) and lends long (mortgages of 20 to 30 years' maturity, although most mortgages are not held to maturity). Thus, the industry must pay the current interest rate to obtain funds, whereas the rates on its mortgages may have been set years ago. In a period of rising interest rates, this puts an obvious squeeze on balance sheets. According to one estimate (Carron, 1982), the aggregate net worth of thrift institutions fell from $23.4 billion in 1977 to – $44.1 billion in mid-1981.

Due-on-Sale Clause and Lock-in

Prior to the mid-1970s, many mortgages were *assumable,* meaning that upon sale of a house, the purchaser may take over responsibility for making monthly payments. The purchaser receives what amounts to a credit on the home purchase price equal to the outstanding balance on the mortgage. Assumable mortgages are a bad deal for lenders in an era of unanticipated inflation, however. If a homeowner has a below-market mortgage (issued when inflation was lower), the S&L is in a financial squeeze and would like to have the mortgage repaid. But if the mortgage is assumable, it almost surely will not be repaid, even when a homeowner sells. (Why pay off a 7 percent mortgage if current rates are 12 percent?)

To protect themselves against the risk of unanticipated changes in interest rates, S&Ls stopped issuing assumable mortgages in the mid-1970s. Now all standard mortgages are "due on sale." The mortgage must be paid off to the S&L when the house is sold. Some mortgages have even more stringent clauses, requiring repayment if owners move out, even if they intend to rent the house instead of selling it. The benefit to S&Ls is obvious. At least they have the option of calling the mortgage if interest rates have changed unfavorably when the house is sold.

Although it offers a measure of protection to S&Ls, the due-on-sale clause has created a problem for homeowners: lock-in. If homeowners have taken out a 7.5 percent mortgage and the current mortgage rate is 14 percent, they can retain the benefit of the below-market interest rate only so long as they continue to own their current house. To be concrete, suppose a homeowner has a $50,000 mortgage at 7.5 percent. The annual mortgage payment is roughly $3,800. Were the homeowner to pay off the mortgage and buy another house with another $50,000 mortgage, the annual mortgage payments would double. (Were it not for the due-on-sale clause, the homeowner could pass on the low-rate mortgage to the buyer *and* raise the sale price of the house accordingly.) The present value of the loss associated with prepayment of a below-market mortgage easily can amount to between $20,000 and $30,000. It is difficult to feel sorry for homeowners as a result of this "problem"; they are locked in because this is the only way they can take full advantage of an unanticipated windfall.[22] The inefficiences resulting from lock-in, however, may be quite important: basically, lock-in inhibits mobility.[23]

Recent Changes in Mortgage Finance

Two major changes have been instituted in the housing finance industry to deal with the problems associated with variability of market interest rates. The first is the phaseout of Regulation Q, and the second is the introduction of various new mortgage instruments.

Regulation of S&Ls. Prior to the Monetary Reform and Decontrol Act of 1980, S&Ls—the primary mortgage lenders in the United States—were subject to several legal restrictions. They were allowed to issue only certain types of deposits (essentially, passbook time deposits) at interest rates controlled by the government (Regulation Q), and they were required to invest a certain fraction of their assets in home mortgages. They were permitted to pay depositors 1 percent higher interest than commercial banks on their time deposits. The idea, which dated back to the 1930s, was to channel money into the housing market at favorable interest rates to promote home ownership, but a period of unstable interest rates caught S&Ls in the trap of borrowing short and lending long. When the regulated deposit rate became too unfavorable, S&Ls were unable to attract any deposits at all. Beginning in 1981, S&Ls have been permitted to issue longer-maturity savings certificates, and deposit rate ceilings ended in 1986.

These changes enable S&Ls to compete more fully for funds, thus avoiding the periodic shortages in loanable funds that have plagued the mortgage industry. Furthermore, the ability to issue certificates of deposit to some extent addresses the problem of borrowing short and lending long. With S&Ls issuing twenty- to thirty-year mortgages, however, they still face a substantial risk of being caught with low-interest mortgages in a period of high borrowing costs. This risk and the demonstration of its importance during the 1970s led to the introduction of new mortgage instruments.

New mortgage instruments. The inflation of the 1970s gave rise to two financial problems—the lenders' borrow short/lend long risk position and the homeowners' cash flow or tilt problem depicted in

---

22. It is plausible but not verified that part of the decline in real rents noted in Table 10.1 may result from this.

23. Chapter 8 showed that efficiency is enhanced when (among other things) workers seek the jobs with the highest wage offers. But lock-in can cause the following problem. Workers would not accept job changes if they also required that the workers move and thus pay off their mortgages, unless the wage premium were sufficient to compensate for the lock-in loss ($3800 per year in the previous example). In other words, lock-in may inhibit labor mobility.

Figure 10.5. Each of these problems has spurred the development of a new type of housing finance instrument.

Beginning about 1980, lenders began offering several versions of the *variable interest rate mortgage*. This is very much like the level-payment mortgage previously described, except that the mortgage interest rate is altered at prespecified time intervals (for example, annually to three years) according to some index of market interest rates. The advantage to S&Ls that issue these mortgages is that they are protected against future increases in interest rates.[24]

The other new set of financing instruments is called *shared equity,* or shared capital gain. It offers homeowners a way around the cash flow problem of Figure 10.5 (although at a cost). Typically, shared-equity financing involves a third party in addition to the lender and the homeowner—an investor who agrees to pay a part of the monthly mortgage payments (and sometimes part of the down payment as well) in exchange for a share of the capital gains at the time of sale of the house. The homeowner, in effect, issues an equity share of the house, reducing the monthly payments with the proceeds and offering part of any capital gain as a return to the share owner. It is important to note that this system works even if neither the homeowner nor the investor expects *real* capital gains, but only nominal capital gains as house values keep up with inflation (recall that the tilt problem arises only when inflation is expected and mortgage rates contain an inflation premium).

Housing and the Biased Consumer Price Index

In 1983 the housing component of the *CPI* was changed. According to the old way of calculating it, the owner-occupant component was badly biased during any period of changing inflation. The true cost of home ownership, as we have seen, is ρV, where ρ is the housing cost of capital. The proper interest component of ρ is the real aftertax interest rate. The *CPI,* however, until 1983, did not use the real interest rate; it used the nominal pretax interest rate. Using the numbers underlying Figure 10.5, it is easy to see that this can lead to wild swings in the apparent cost of housing. In going from zero inflation to 10 percent, the nominal interest rate goes from 3.5 to 13.5 percent. As interest is approximately one-third of the cost of capital ($\rho = 10$ percent), the rise in the mortgage rate raises the apparent cost of capital from 10 to 20 percent. That is, the *CPI* would report that the cost of housing doubled, when in truth it did not rise at all.

---

24. It may seem that homeowners get a reciprocal advantage—assurance that if interest rates in general fall, so will the mortgage rate. In fact, however, homeowners already have a considerable measure of this kind of assurance. If market mortgage rates fall, the homeowner always has the option of refinancing—prepaying the current mortgage and taking out another. Refinancing is fairly expensive but worthwhile whenever interest rates fall more than about one percentage point under typical conditions.

The problem is that the old method treats changes in the nominal rate as changes in the true cost of borrowing. In fact, however, most such changes are simply changes in the inflation premium. This bias overstates the rate of inflation during a period of rising inflation, as well as the rate at which inflation is declining during a period of declining inflation. According to one estimate, improper measurement of the housing component caused the *CPI* to overstate aggregate inflation between 1967 and 1979 by roughly 20 percent (Dougherty and Van Order, 1982). Since 1982, the housing cost component of the *CPI* has been linked closely to estimated rents which, as already seen, are little affected by inflation.

Even with the housing component of the *CPI* based upon the (correct) rental price concept, there are severe measurement difficulties. In comparing the price of housing from one period to the next, it is important to be sure that the sampled rental units are comparable from one period to the next. This can be very difficult, however, as has been shown. Even if the same rental units are sampled each year, the question arises as to how much the units have depreciated, and whether there have been physical changes in the structures or neighborhoods which have caused the rent changes.

The issue is of considerable importance. As of 1982, housing comprised over 41 percent of the *CPI;* thus a 2 percent rise in the (measured) price of housing adds almost one percentage point to measure inflation. It is unfortunate that the fundamental measure of inflation depends so crucially upon a price which is inherently almost unmeasurable.

☐ HOUSING WHEN INFLATION DECLINES

The dominant force affecting housing in the 1970s was the continual acceleration of inflation and the low real aftertax interest rates that accompanied the inflation. Cheap money made housing a very good investment; it was, in fact, one of the few good investments during the 1970s. To a substantial extent, people put their savings into housing rather than the more traditional savings instruments such as time deposits, stocks, and bonds. By some estimates, roughly half of household saving during the 1970s was in the form of increases in home equity.

The situation has changed dramatically during the 1980s. Although money interest rates have fallen with the inflation rate, real interest rates have increased, as column D of Table 10.1 shows. This has resulted from the national government's monetary and fiscal policies. Column E of Table 10.1 shows that real aftertax mortgage rates have risen dramatically. This has resulted partly because other interest rates have been high, partly because financial market deregulation has provided alternative high yield investments to savings and loan depositors and has permitted savings and loans to provide competitive returns to depositors, and partly because successive tax reductions have reduced the spread between other interest rates and aftertax mortgage rates (effectively reducing the part of mortgage interest that is paid by federal income tax deductions).

Yet housing construction has been strong following the 1982–83 recession. Real incomes have risen during the protracted recovery and many baby boomers have entered family formation and home buying years. Although real earnings per worker have risen little, employment grew twice as fast as the population from 1982 to 1986.

For the foreseeable future, it is likely that real interest and mortgage rates, and the capital cost of housing, will remain high. Nor would the resumption of rapid inflation[25] result in large windfall capital gains for many homeowners. Many mortgages are now of the adjustable rate variety, and most new ones would be if inflation resumed. Thus, resumed inflation would not result in large numbers of homeowners with mortgages whose interest rates were less than the inflation rate. Homeownership may remain a good investment, at least in rapidly growing sections of the country, but the experience of the 1970s is unlikely to be repeated.

Housing, Savings, and Investment

All capital investment is financed out of personal, corporate, or government savings. Anything that encourages one form of investment necessarily discourages other forms, as all potential investment activities compete for the same pool of savings. It has already been seen that the 1970s represented an attractive period for investment in housing and households channeled a very large fraction of their savings into housing. The tax law of 1981, however, created substantial incentives for corporate investment in plant and equipment, and these changes enhance the ability of corporations to compete for funds.

The Tax Reform Act of 1986 removed most of the tax shelters for both industrial capital and for income-producing real estate. Indeed, owner-occupied housing is almost the only tax shelter that survived intact. If Congress permits the provisions of the 1986 law to remain in effect for a few years, the result will almost certainly be a shift from rental status to owner-occupancy. The next chapter's discussion of filter-

---

25. Many economists believe that the large federal budget deficits of the 1980s have caused the high real interest rates. Government borrowing has traditionally run at about 1 to 2 percent of GNP, which constitutes about 15 percent of loanable funds. During the first years of the Reagan Administration, government borrowing rose to almost 6 percent of GNP (about 75 percent of loanable funds). This created fierce competition for loanable funds, and forced interest rates up. If this is the current explanation, real interest rates should not be expected to return to historical levels until federal borrowing returns to historical levels.

ing and abandonment will investigate the relationship between investment in new housing and use of the standing stock.

Differential Treatment of Renters and Homeowners

So far this chapter has emphasized the similarity between the decisions faced by owners and those faced by renters (in part because the similarities are important and in part because they are poorly understood). It is time, however, to recognize that there are differences. One such difference already has been noted: the cash flow problem previously described is peculiar to homeowners. Renters escape this problem, because in a competitive market they pay the true capital cost. Cash flow problems are not binding for landlords.

The other major difference results from the fact that owner-occupied and rental housing are treated differently in the federal tax code. The result is that the cost of capital differs between the two types of housing.

At this point a commonly held misconception must be put to rest: homeowners do not benefit relative to renters because of the tax deductibility of mortgage interest. During an inflationary period this deductibility does lead to a tax break for a noncost item (the interest inflation premium). As we saw, this led to a decline in the housing cost of capital during the 1970s. Owners of rental housing also deduct mortgage interest, however, and generally at a higher marginal tax rate than do owner-occupants. In a competitive environment this is passed on to tenants, and the evidence from Table 10.1 indicates that this has occurred.

The tax break that does accrue to owner-occupants results from the fact that, unlike owners of rental housing, owner-occupants are not required to report the income they earn as housing entrepreneurs. Owners of rental housing own an asset, collect the rent, pay the bills, and manage the buildings. The income from the rental property, of course, is the rent less the bills. On his or her tax return, the landlord reports gross rental receipts, deducts expenses (including mortgage interest), and pays income tax on the difference. Owner-occupants also pay the bills and manage the building—and earn income from doing so. The income they earn is the rent they would charge a second party for living in their house—the rent they forgo by occupying the house themselves. This income, however, since it involves no cash transaction, is not taxable. The point is easiest to see by way of example. Suppose two owner-occupants live in identical houses, each incurring $5000 per year in mortgage interest and other bills. For one year they swap houses, each charging the other $6000 rent. The extra $1000, they agree, is fair pay for the time and worry involved in being a landlord. That is, each does $1000 of work and rightly insists on being compensated. Unlike the year before the swap, when each homeowner faced the same bills and did the same entrepreneurial work, both now must report

$6000 of rental income. The difference, of course, is that in the previous year they were renting to themselves, thus the rental income escaped taxation.[26]

Not all the tax breaks go to owner-occupants, however. Owners of rental property are permitted to take depreciation deductions as a business cost, whereas owner-occupants are not. The 1981 tax law made the rules governing depreciation of rental housing among the most imaginative in the federal tax code.

It permitted accelerated depreciation of rental properties over the artificially short life of fifteen years (later changed to eighteen years). Rapid depreciation means that landlords are able to report expenses (the wearing out of capital) before they occur. In many cases, tax losses could be reported for several years on rental property and could be subtracted from other income before computing tax liability. Typically, part of the excess depreciation was recaptured by the IRS upon sale of the building. Part was not, though, and even the part that was recaptured was really an interest-free loan from the IRS to the landlord. The 1986 tax law eliminated accelerated depreciation and roughly doubled the number of years over which the dwelling had to be depreciated. This is the reason for the statement at the end of the previous section that the 1986 tax law will probably cause a shift from rental to owner-occupied housing. For owner-occupied housing no depreciation deduction is allowed; however, owner-occupants almost completely escape capital gains taxation.[27] Although the debate within the profession continues, it appears that the net effect of all these special provisions is that the rental price of owner-occupied housing is about 10 percent less than that of rental housing (Aaron, 1972; Peterson, 1980).

☐ CONSTRUCTION INDUSTRY

The construction industry is the final component of the housing supply sector. This industry, of course, is ultimately responsible for additions to the stock of housing. In 1978, 65 percent of the standing stock of housing was owner occupied; the bulk of it was single family units. A similar fraction—71 percent—of new dwelling units was single family. The vast majority of these units is built by small contractors that build a few to at most a hundred or so units per year. The industry is extremely fragmented, particularly by modern American standards.

---

26. Although implicit rental income is the largest example, the notion of implicit income's escaping taxation is quite general. Do-it-yourself production—other things being equal—is a better aftertax deal than working for pay on Saturday, paying income taxes, and using aftertax income to hire a plumber.

27. Owner-occupants pay no capital gains upon the sale of a house if they purchase another house within eighteen months of at least the same value as the sale price of the first. Furthermore, if people sell an owner-occupied house after they are fifty-five years old—even without purchasing another house—a substantial capital gain is tax exempt.

The first step in building a house is to obtain a parcel of properly zoned land, a building permit, and a construction loan. Until the extremely volatile times around 1980, many S&Ls would issue a promise of mortgage funding with the construction loan. Thus, the contractor would obtain working capital and a guarantee that if a buyer could be found, mortgage money would be available.[28]

Construction then begins. Some of the larger contractors have specialists—plumbers, electricians, and so on—on the payroll. Many do not. They hire only carpenters and laborers directly, and they subcontract for the specialty work, trying to get by with a minimum of permanent staff and financial commitments.

Without question, this organization adds to the cost of construction. The timing of the various stages of construction is important—excavators must arrive before the masons who lay the foundation, plumbing and wiring must be done before the drywall contractor installs the interior walls, and so on—and yet the general contractor has incomplete control over when the various subcontractors arrive. This can lead to delays and possibly a failure to integrate the various construction phases properly.

Despite the costs, however, there are reasons for the fragmented, low-capital organization of the industry. Most importantly, housing construction is the most volatile of the major sectors in the American economy. Table 10.2, which shows housing starts by year, emphasizes that the housing industry has grown and then shrunk by as much as 50 percent within periods of only two years. Clearly, in such an environment it is not wise to have a large labor force on retainer or to own a large amount of fixed capital.

A major reason for the cyclical nature of housing construction is that housing is very sensitive to credit conditions, although variations in the demand for new housing also may contribute. At various times the government and the Federal Reserve find it necessary to engage in restrictive monetary policy, generally for the explicit purpose of curtailing demand. The sector most sensitive to monetary restriction is housing construction, although this special role for construction may change with the repeal of Regulation Q. Monetary restrictions tend to raise interest rates. As has been seen, however, the deposit rates that S&Ls can offer are regulated. Therefore, during periods of tight money, mortgage and building loan money is often unavailable at any interest rate, because S&Ls are unable to attract funds at the regulated rate. In some states this problem has been compounded by usury laws that set ceilings on mortgage interest rates.[29]

28. Some homes are built on contract with the ultimate occupant, although most are built on speculation, in hopes of finding a buyer.

29. Most state usury laws were weakened or eliminated in the face of persistent high nominal interest rates during the late 1970s.

It frequently is argued that policies should be established to make the housing industry more stable—that the construction industry could do its job more efficiently if demand were more stable. So long as the government engages in stabilization policies, however, the output of some industry or industries must fluctuate in response to the policy initiatives. For two reasons, construction might be a good candidate. First, as has been shown, the industry has evolved in such a way that entry and exit are relatively easy. Second, in any one year, new construction contributes relatively little to the stock of housing, and thus even large swings in construction result in quite small swings in the size of the available housing stock. In the 1970s, for example, housing starts averaged 1.79 million per year, or roughly 2.6 percent of the stock. A 50 percent decline in construction in one year means that the stock is just over 1 percent less than it would otherwise be. Imagine, by contrast, the problems that would arise if stabilization policy worked largely by generating large swings in food production.

Technical Change in Housing Construction

One of the complaints concerning the housing industry is that innovation has been slow or nonexistent. The argument is straightforward: no single contractor, building an infinitesimal fraction of the nation's new housing units, has an incentive to seek more efficient construction techniques, since most of the benefits would accrue to the contractor's competitors and to buyers.

In fact, however, there has been rapid innovation in the way houses are built. Much of the innovation has been carried out by suppliers of building materials—generally firms much larger than building contractors and therefore more able to internalize the economic benefits of innovation. Although there are no good estimates of the rate of technical progress in home building (in part because of the difficulty of measuring the output), a few observations make it clear that the industry has been far from stagnant. The overwhelming majority of home construction cost occurs after the basic shell (foundation, framing, siding, and roof) has been put in place. Construction of the shell is only about one-sixth of the total, and developed land is about one-fifth (Kaiser Committee, 1969). The remainder, something over three-fifths, is interior finishing work (both labor and materials). And in this area—the biggest cost item—progress has been the most obvious. The following is an incomplete list of examples:

1. Thermal insulation. Prior to the 1950s, the spaces in exterior walls were not insulated. The value of insulation goes far beyond energy savings. Insulated houses can be heated and cooled much more evenly, and humidity can be maintained at comfortable levels. In addition, insulation gives a significant measure of fire protection.
2. Plumbing. The introduction of copper and plastic supply and drain pipe provided two advantages over galvanized pipes. It is easier

to install and the supply pipes are more durable and less prone to leaking and clogging.

3. Wiring. The introduction of circuit breakers and plastic-insulated wire has made wiring easier to install and safer to use.

4. Cabinetwork and molding. The construction and installation of doors, windows, stairways, and cabinets is the most exacting carpentry work in home building. In the last two or three decades, much of this work has been shifted from on-site production to a mill, where scale economies from the use of precision power tools can be realized. Modern contractors simply order doors and windows complete with molding from the mill, and they nail them to the framing.

It is clear that there has been steady technical progress in home building over the postwar era, although it is impossible to tell how rapid this has been compared with the rest of the economy.

Despite these observations, there is a widespread belief that standards of housing construction have declined over the years: "They don't build them like they used to." In fact, the opposite is true. The average quality of houses built in the 1980s is far higher than that of houses built in the past. The average 1890s or 1920s house *standing today* is a very good house, but most of the housing from that era has long since been demolished for a variety of reasons. One is that the old housing simply was not built for a society as rich as today's. Rooms were small, construction was shoddy, plumbing was nonexistent, and heating plants were inadequate (by modern standards). The surviving old houses have been preserved precisely because they were the best of their generation.

Stock of Housing

The stock of housing is the legacy of past construction, alteration, depreciation, and retirements. The stock depreciates quite slowly, probably about 1 percent per year (Chinloy, 1980). Furthermore, alterations are a relatively minor source of changes in the housing stock. Home improvement expenditure runs about 1 percent of the value of stock, but this figure overstates the volume of upgrading; much of this expenditure should properly be called *maintenance*. Thus, the most important means of altering the housing stock are construction and retirement, and even these processes operate on the massive housing stock rather slowly.

To get an idea of the quantitative impact of construction and demolition on the housing stock, consider the data in Tables 10.3 and 10.4 for the seven-year period 1973–1980. These remarkable data provide a complete picture of changes in the housing stock between 1973 and 1980. Much more detailed data are available in the source. The first column in each table shows the total number of dwellings that existed in the year and places indicated. The second columns show the parts

Table 10.3 *Sources of 1980 Housing Stock (Thousands of dwelling units)*

	1980 Stock	Same in 1973	Total Additions	New Construction
United States	89,292	70,725	17,174	13,119
SMSA	58,904	48,338	9,632	7,921
Central City	25,836	22,451	2,825	2,104
Outside	33,067	25,886	6,807	5,817

Source: *1980 Census of Housing: Components of Inventory Change.*

of the stock that existed in both years. The third column is the difference between the first two in each table, except that the data are all estimates from samples, so the arithmetic is inexact. For example, the first row of Table 10.3 shows that there were 89.3 million dwellings in 1980, of which 70.7 had existed in 1973. These two numbers imply that 18.6 million units were added to the stock between the two years, whereas the third column records additions of only 17.2 million. Thus, there is a discrepancy of 1.4 million units.

Of the 17.2 million additions reported, 13.1 million were constructed during the seven-year period. The remainder were conversions from nonhousing uses (hospital to apartments, warehouses to residential lofts in Greenwich Village in New York City) and separation of one dwelling unit into two or more (a three story town house is converted to three apartments). Table 10.3 shows that new construction provided 13.1 million of the 17.2 million dwellings added to the stock during the seven years. Thus, although construction accounted for more than 75 percent of additions to the stock, more than 4 million dwellings were added by conversion and separation. Such nonconstruction additions are sometimes an important source of growth in the supply of low-income housing, and are entirely separate from the filter-down source to be discussed in the next chapter.

Table 10.4 shows that 6.5 million dwellings disappeared from the 1973 stock by 1980, but that only 1.8 million had been demolished (including disasters, such as fire and flood, which often precede demolitions). The remaining 4.1 million units of the 1973 stock that had dis-

Table 10.4 *Disposition of 1973 Stock*

	1973 Stock	Same in 1980	Total Losses	Demolition and Disaster
United States	77,246	70,725	6,520	1,808
SMSA	51,819	48,338	2,586	1,044
Central City	24,471	22,451	1,410	709
Outside	27,348	25,886	1,176	335

Source: *1980 Census of Housing: Components of Inventory Change.*

appeared by 1980 were converted to nondwelling uses (such as stores and offices), or merged (gentrification may result in the merger of the three apartments in a townhouse into one dwelling). Thus, for the country as a whole, additions to and subtractions from the housing stock by conversion and merger and separation just about balanced at about 4 million units during the seven years. In net terms, construction less demolitions accounted for virtually the entire growth of the stock, about 11.3 million units.

☐ Summary

The unifying theme of this chapter is the relationship between the value and rental prices of housing. The rental price is the price of occupying a standard-size house for one year; the value price is the price of the permanent ownership right. Consumers care only about the rental price, and suppliers care only about the value price, making analysis of the market somewhat complicated. In this chapter recent movements in value and rental prices of housing were also traced, and the reasons for these movements examined.

Questions and Problems

Questions and problems for this chapter are included at the end of the following chapter, on pages 248–49.

References and Further Reading

Aaron, Henry. *Shelter and Subsidies* (Washington, D.C.: Brookings, 1972). A very good review of housing policies (including the tax law) and the relative costs for homeowners and renters.

Becker, Gary. *The Economics of Discrimination* (Chicago: University of Chicago Press, 1971). A classic analysis of discrimination.

Berry, Brian. "Ghetto Expansion and Racial Residential Segregation in an Urban Model." *Journal of Urban Economics* 3 (1976): 397–423. A statistical study of blacks' and whites' housing costs in Chicago.

Carron, Andrew. *The Plight of the Thrift Institutions* (Washington, D.C.: Brookings, 1982).

Chinloy, Peter. "The Effect of Maintenance Expenditures on the Measurement of Depreciation in Housing." *Journal of Urban Economics* Vol. 8 (1980): 86–107.

_____. "Estimation of Net Depreciation Rates on Housing." *Journal of Urban Economics* Vol. 6 (1979): 432–43.

deLeeuw, Frank. "Demand for Housing." *Review of Economics and Statistics* 53 (1971): 1–10. A careful survey of housing demand studies.

Dougherty, Ann, and Robert Van Order. "Inflation, Housing Costs, and the Consumer Price Index." *American Economic Review* Vol. 72 (1982): 154–64.

Dynarski, Mark. "The Economics of Community: Theory and Measurement." Ph.D. diss., Johns Hopkins University, 1981.

Ellwood, David, and A. Mitchell Polinsky. "An Empirical Reconciliation of Micro and Grouped Estimates of the Demand for Housing." *Review of Economics and Statistics* Vol. 61 (1979): 199–205. The best and latest evidence on the parameters of the demand function for housing.

Friedman, Milton. *A Theory of the Consumption Function* (Princeton, N.J.: Princeton U. Press, 1957). Contains the original discussion of permanent income.

Griliches, Zvi. *Price Indexes and Quality Change* (Cambridge, Mass.: Harvard University Press, 1971). A detailed discussion of hedonic price indexes.

Hulten, Charles, and Robert Schwab. "Income Originating in the State and Local Sector." University of Maryland, working paper, 1987.

Kain, John, and John Quigley. *Housing Markets and Racial Discrimination* (New York: Columbia U. Press, 1975). A thorough analysis of effects of racial discrimination on blacks' housing.

Kaiser Committee. *A Decent Home.* Washington, D.C.: Government Printing Office, 1969. A good summary appears in Kaiser Committee. "The Nation's Housing Needs." *Readings in Urban Economics,* eds. M. Edel and J. Rothenberg (New York: Macmillan, 1972). Has fair amounts of detail on the housing inventory and the character of construction and operating cost.

King, A. Thomas, and Peter Mieszkowski. "Racial Discrimination, Segregation, and the Price of Housing." *Journal of Political Economy* Vol. 8 (1973): 590–601. A very careful study of race differences in housing costs. Chapter 11 will refer to this work; it is cited here as a readable example of the use of hedonic price analysis.

Muth, Richard. "The Demand for Nonfarm Housing." *The Demand for Durable Goods,* ed. A. Harberger (Chicago: University of Chicago Press, 1960). One of the first studies of housing demand to use the permanent income concept. It makes excellent reading, as it is easy to see the mechanics of the research strategy.

Pechman, Joseph. *Federal Tax Policy* (Washington, D.C.: Brookings, 1982). An annual publication giving a careful description of the federal tax law.

Peterson, George. "Federal Tax Policy and the Shaping of Urban Development." *The Prospective City,* ed. A. P. Solomon (Cambridge, Mass.: MIT Press, 1980).

Polinsky, Mitchell. "The Demand for Housing: A Study in Specification and Grouping." *Econometrica 45* (1977): 447–462. An abstract conceptual analysis of housing demand that requires considerable knowledge of econometrics.

Rosen, Kenneth. "The Affordability of Housing in 1980 and Beyond." University of California at Berkeley, working paper, 1979.

Rosen, Sherwin. "Hedonic Prices and Implicit Markets." *Journal of Political Economy* 82 (1974): 34–55. A fundamental theoretical contribution to hedonic price analysis that requires advanced economics knowledge.

Schwab, Robert. "Real and Nominal Interest Rates and the Demand for Housing." *Journal of Urban Economics* Vol. 13 (1983): 181–95. This paper estimates the effects of both the cash flow tilt effect and real interest rates on the demand for housing.

Sternlieb, George. *The Tenement Landlord* (New Brunswick, N.J.: Rutgers University Press, 1969). A study of slum landlords in Newark, New Jersey.

Tanzi, Vito. "Inflationary Expectations, Economic Activity, Taxes, and Interest Rates." *American Economic Review* Vol. 70 (1980): 12–21.

U.S. Department of Commerce, Bureau of the Census. "Components of Inventory Change." *Census of Housing* (Washington, D.C.: Government Printing Office, 1970) Table HC(4).

11

Housing Problems
and Policies

☐ Major housing problems—slums, low quality and high prices for poor people, abandonment, and race segregation—are apparent to everyone. Before looking at these and other problems, however, it is important to put the matter into perspective.

Americans are housed better than at any time in our history, and surely better than the citizens of almost any other country. The available statistics, summarized in the following two tables and figures, indicate truly remarkable improvement in the quality of housing since 1940. Note, for example, that in 1940, 55.4 percent of dwelling units lacked at least one component of basic plumbing (usually a toilet or hot water, and sometimes both). By 1980 the incidence of incomplete plumbing had fallen to 2.7 percent.[1] In 1940, 9 percent of the units had more than 1.5 persons per room; by 1980 this figure had fallen to 1 percent, and even the number of units with more than one person per room was 4.1 percent. In fact, by 1980, 60 percent of the units had fewer than 0.5 person per room (up from 50 percent in 1970).

Blacks lag behind whites, but they also have made rapid improvements. The fraction of units with more than 1.5 persons per room fell between 1970 and 1980 from 6.9 to 2.2 percent (roughly the same improvement achieved by the population at large between 1950 and 1970).

As can be seen in the table, the obvious and easily quantifiable indices of housing quality—crowding and plumbing deficiency—have been virtually eliminated by 1980. This means, among other things, that measurement of subsequent changes in housing quality will be more difficult. The nation is now eliminating structural and other defects that are less easily measured. But even taking into account these problems,

1. It sometimes is argued that these figures overstate the improvement in the quality of plumbing because of frequent breakdowns. For 1978, however, only 2.8 percent of all households reported at least one breakdown of water supply, 0.8 percent reported sewer breakdowns, and 7.5 percent reported heating system breakdowns. Although earlier data are unavailable, it is unlikely that they would show recent deterioration.

Table 11.1 *Housing Characteristics, 1940 to 1980*

Characteristic	1940	1950	1960	1970	1980
Percentage of stock lacking complete plumbing	55.4	34.0	14.7	5.5	2.7
Percentage of stock with					
More than 1.5 persons per room	9.0	6.2	3.8	2.0	1.0
Blacks only	n.a.	n.a.	14.1	6.9	2.2
1 to 1.5 persons per room	n.a.	9.4	7.9	6.0	3.1
Blacks only	n.a.	n.a.	14.3	12.5	6.9
0.5 to 1 person per room	79.8[a]	82.9[a]	46.6	42.0	35.0
Blacks only	n.a.	n.a.	40.9	40.5	41.8

[a]Percentage for fewer than 1 person per room.

Source: Data from U.S. Department of Commerce, Bureau of the Census. *Census of Housing.* Washington, D.C.

the best available evidence shows that the quality of housing has continued to improve during the early '80s. In particular, it appears that the quality of low-income housing has continued to improve. Figure 11.1 shows the fraction of the housing stock (respectively all occupied units, moderately low-income units, and very low-income units) judged to be inadequate. As can be seen, for both moderately and very poor households, the incidence of inadequate housing fell by about 25 percent during the period covered by the figure. As the figure shows, this trend continued in the early '80s. (See Clemmer and Simonson [1983] for detailed discussion of the variables and trends.)

Now turn to Table 11.2, which shows that renters, including low-income renters, have been beneficiaries of the improvement in housing quality over the past decade. A somewhat longer, if less quantitative, perspective can be obtained from the *First Report* of the Tenement Housing Commission of New York (1903). They estimate that New York City's 82,000 tenements housed some 3 million people—about 88 percent of the city's population. Although the report lacks statistical summaries, it has vivid descriptions: ". . . conditions . . . so bad as to be indescribable in print, . . . sewer gas throughout houses . . . rooms so dark one cannot see the people in them. . . ." (In a later section they report filthy conditions the tenants were unaware of because of a complete lack of light.) They continue: ". . . [dirt floor] cellars occupied as sleeping quarters, . . . [sinks and cellars] with garbage and decomposing fecal matter. . . ."

Whatever else can be said of housing in the United States, conditions have improved dramatically within the last several decades. If the 1903 Tenement Housing Commissioners could see the housing stock today, they surely would be happy beyond their wildest dreams.

The picture which emerges from these facts is one of dramatic improvement in housing quality over at least the past eighty years, with strong evidence that the quality improvement has continued through the early 1980s. This raises the obvious question—what caused this almost continuous rapid improvement?

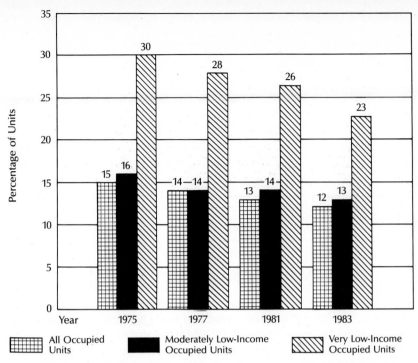

Source: Data from "Low and Moderate Income Housing: Progress, Problems and Prospects" (1986), National Association of Home Builders, Washington, D.C.

Figure 11.1 *Percentage of Units Which Are Inadequate, by Year and Income Level*

During most of the twentieth century real income per capita rose about 2 percent per year, and much of the improvement in housing quality is certainly the result of growth in housing demand caused by rising real incomes. Starting about 1973, however, real earnings growth ceased in the United States. By 1986, real earnings per worker were well below levels in the early 1970s. Why would housing continue to improve if income growth has ceased?

The basic answer is straightforward, although not widely understood. Although real earnings per worker have not grown since the early 1970s, real income per capita has continued to grow. The explanation of this paradoxical pattern is the rapid increase that has occurred in the fraction of the adult population that is working. Millions of young women whose mothers stayed home at similar ages are out working. That, combined with steady decreases in fertility, has caused income per capita to rise almost as fast as it did earlier, even though earnings per worker have been flat.

What about the relative price of housing? In the last chapter, it was suggested that the net capital cost of housing has risen during the 1980s because of the rise in real mortgage rates. The result has been as would be predicted from the price inelasticity of housing demand—an increase in rents paid, but little effect on housing consumption. Remember that

Table 11.2 *Characteristics of Rental Units by Household Income 1974 and 1983*

Income in 1983 Dollars	Median # Rooms		Percentage of Units with:							
			Complete Kitchen		Complete Plumbing		More than One Bath		Air-conditioning	
	1974	1983	1974	1983	1974	1983	1974	1983	1974	1983
3,000 – 6,999	3.6	3.7	91.9	96.7	88.8	94.4	4.3	8.0	28.5	37.3
7,000 – 9,999	3.8	3.9	94.4	98.0	92.5	96.1	5.7	11.5	32.8	45.9
10,000–14,999	3.9	4.0	95.8	98.7	95.4	98.3	8.7	15.2	41.2	51.5
15,000–24,999	4.1	4.1	97.7	99.1	97.6	98.7	13.2	20.3	48.8	58.7

1974 incomes adjusted to 1983 basis using the GNP deflator for personal consumption expenditures. Linear interpolation used to assign households to 1983 brackets.
Source: Annual Housing Survey, Part C, *Financial Characteristics of the Housing Inventory*, 1974 and 1983. National Association of Home Builders, Washington D.C.

rent is the product of price and quantity, so it increases as the price increases if demand is inelastic. Rents paid by renters rose from 20 percent of income in 1970 to 29 percent in 1983. This dramatic increase probably results in part from rising real rents per unit of housing, but also from the fact that the percentage of housing that is owner-occupied has increased somewhat during the period. That has meant that renters are increasingly concentrated at the low end of the income distribution. Since, as was suggested in the previous chapter, the income elasticity of housing demand is somewhat less than one, then low-income people spend a larger fraction of incomes on housing than do higher-income people. An increase in owner-occupancy reduces the average income of renters.

A final factor involved in the rising rent-income ratios is suggested by Figure 11.2. Many people probably realized that the income decreases suffered in the 1980–83 period were temporary. Anticipating that incomes would rise again, they may not have reduced their housing consumption. The flatter plot in Figure 11.2 shows median rent as a function of income, based on 1983 rents and incomes. The steeper plot shows rent as a function of income, based on rent and income averaged over 1980–83. The average plot shows lower rents for low income people than does the 1983 plot. It was indicated in Chapter 10 that housing decisions are almost certainly based on permanent income, not annual income. Since a four-year average of income is a better approximation of permanent income than a one-year figure, the rise in rent-income ratios of the poor in the early 1980s may be somewhat illusory.

☐ HOUSING PROBLEMS

None of these statistics or descriptions is intended to convey the impression that the United States has no housing problems. However, we should remember—even as we hope for improvement in the

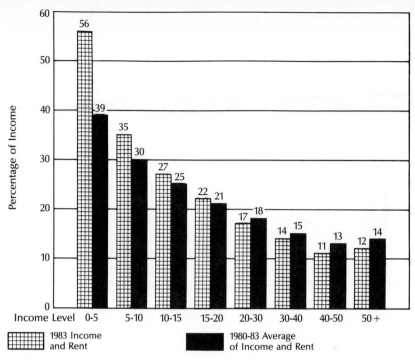

Source: Data from "Low and Moderate Income Housing: Progress, Problems and Prospects," (1986), National Association of Home Builders, Washington, D.C.

Figure 11.2 *Rent-Income Ratios, by Income Level: 1983 and 1980-83*

future—that we are in a much better position than we were a generation or two ago.

Many of the important social problems surrounding housing—abandonment, slums, displacement, and segregation—are linked with two peculiarities of housing. The first is that housing is the most durable capital asset. On the average, housing appears to depreciate less than 1 percent per year,[2] and under the right circumstances a well-constructed house can last indefinitely (many houses in this country are well over a century old, and show no signs of imminent retirement). The second peculiarity is that a dwelling unit, once constructed, is quite inflexible. It is very expensive to physically move a house, and it is also very costly to alter the quality of an existing house—in particular, it is difficult to upgrade a house.

Individual dwelling units may be inflexible, but demands are not. As society becomes richer, the demand for housing services increases; this means there is constant pressure to improve the quality of the housing stock.

Although some upgrading of individual units occurs, the least expensive way to improve the quality of the stock is generally to retire

2. Margolis (1982) estimates that housing depreciates at 0.39 percent per annum.

the old low-quality housing and build new. To see why this is so, recall that the shell of a dwelling unit represents only about one-sixth of the cost. Upgrading frequently means putting a new interior into an old shell. This involves replacing plumbing and wiring, removing walls to make bigger rooms, modernizing the kitchen and bathrooms, upgrading the heating plant, and installing air-conditioning and thermal insulation. Often the cost of working around the existing structure—for example, stringing wiring, pipes, and air-conditioning ducts through interwall spaces—makes this finishing work far more costly in an existing house than a new one.

If a building needs a complete rehabilitation job (known as "gut-rehab"), the cost per square foot is at least 80 percent that of new construction. If the foundation or exterior walls need work, gut-rehab may be no cheaper than starting from scratch (assuming the start from scratch takes place on vacant land and entails no demolition cost).[3]

The last chapter concluded by discussing the notion that construction and retirement form the major mechanism whereby the housing stock is upgraded. In the United States and other developed countries, the demand for this upgrading comes largely from income growth and from the fact that the demand for housing rises with income.[4]

Durable, hard-to-alter houses and growing incomes, however, result in an excess supply of low-quality housing and an excess demand for high-quality housing. Figure 11.3 illustrates this. The solid line depicts the size distribution of income at an initial time (a small number of very poor people, a large number of middle-income people, and a small number of very rich people). If the housing stock is tailored to satisfy the demands of these people, there are a small number of very low-quality houses, a large number of middle-quality houses, and a small number of very high-quality houses. At a later time, the size distribution of income has shifted to the right (the dashed curve in Figure 11.3), reflecting secular income growth. Now there is an excess supply of low-quality houses and an excess demand for high-quality houses. Note that this pattern of excess supply and demand is chronic in a society with secularly rising incomes. Put slightly differently, the quality of the housing stock inherited from the 1930s, 1940s, and 1950s inadequately satisfies current demands, because today's society is wealthier and our housing demands have grown accordingly. Bringing the housing stock inherited from past decades up to current standards (governed by current demand, which in turn is governed by current income) will require either upgrading existing dwelling units or retiring them and replacing them with better ones.

3. The gut-rehab numbers were provided by Macy Whitney of Knott Remodelling, Washington, D.C.

4. In the United States the replacement process may also have been accelerated by price declines and special tax advantages to new housing. Surely, for example, the decline in the real aftertax interest rate during the 1970s led to increased housing demand and therefore to an increased demand for upgrading the stock.

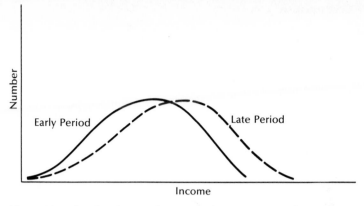

Figure 11.3 *Size Distribution of Income and Housing Demand*

The end of Chapter 10 noted that about two-thirds of housing construction accommodates population growth, with the other one-third serving as replacements for units retired from the stock. It is now easy to see why there is a steady stream of retirements from the housing stock at the same time as new housing is constructed—the more rapid the pace of construction, the more rapid the pace of retirement (holding the number of households constant). It is entirely plausible that much of the retired housing is perfectly sound and inhabitable. Many people express surprise and dismay over the fact that houses are retired from use before they wear out. At least part of this phenomenon, however, is a natural consequence of the durability and inflexibility of the housing stock, along with rising incomes.

☐ ABANDONMENT

In every major American city there are some abandoned dwelling units for which no one claims title. As cited elsewhere in this book, Baltimore has about 7000 abandoned units; Philadelphia, about 30,000; and New York City, about 100,000. Each case represents about 3 to 5 percent of the stock. Why this abandonment occurs and what might be done to prevent it are important policy and research questions.

The previous section discussed housing retirement, not abandonment. Abandonment, of course, is one of the ways to retire a dwelling unit—the other being reuse of the site for some other purpose, either through conversion of the house to a nonresidential use or demolition of the house and sale of the vacant land to another user. Unlike these other methods of retirement, abandonment essentially means throwing away the title—simply relinquishing all rights and responsibilities to the property. This involves concealing ownership to keep the tax collector and code enforcer away, but that is not difficult to do.

An Economic Decision

Why do property owners abandon title? Stated in its most sterile form, they do so whenever (1) income from the property cannot cover operating costs and (2) the value of the cleared land is less than demolition cost. The negative effect of abandonment on neighbors and the possibility that abandonment begets more abandonment will be discussed later. For now, however, it is important to recognize that even in the absence of slum externalities, it may be possible that demolition costs are sufficiently high and urban land values sufficiently low for abandonment to become the most economical way for a landlord to retire property. The discussion at the end of Chapter 7, culminating in Table 7.3, demonstrates that demolition is frequently not economically justified—even for worthless buildings.

One thing that adds to the relative attractiveness of abandonment is the administration of the property tax in many cities. The typical annual central-city property tax liability is about 2 percent of true market value, but low-quality housing tends to be overassessed, while high-quality housing tends to be underassessed. Although this regressive assessment policy may be deliberate on the part of local governments, at least part of the cause is that reassessments occur, on the average, only every three to five years. Infrequent reassessment while low-value houses are declining in value (because of the effects of excess supply depicted in Figure 11.3) and high-value houses are appreciating or holding their own means that low-quality houses tend to be overassessed.

In many cities it is possible to escape property taxation for a few years in anticipation of abandonment. A property tax of about 3 percent for low-income housing represents a substantial fraction of the operating cost of a dwelling unit—about one-third of the total, if the cost of capital is 10 percent. Landlords make a decision several years before they anticipate retiring buildings as to whether the better means of retirement is demolition and sale or abandonment. If they plan to sell sites, they must keep up on their property taxes to retain clear title. If they intend to abandon sites, they stop paying property taxes, immediately reducing their operating expenses by roughly one-third. Closer to the expected abandonment date, they completely stop maintenance, reducing costs by another one-third. Finally, they stop paying bills altogether and stop attempting to collect rent. Over a period of five years, it is possible for a landlord to save approximately 25 percent of the initial value of the property in operating expenses, as compared with the demolition and resale strategy.

Another contributor to the attractiveness of the abandonment option, particularly in old eastern cities, is the gradual decline in central-city land values.[5] In eastern cities, housing ripe for retirement is at least

---

5. Recall from Chapter 6 that transport improvements can be expected to erode the land value premium of central locations. This occurs because improvements in transport make city and suburb more alike in terms of accessibility.

several decades old and built on land near the CBD. At the time the housing was built the land was quite valuable, so the development was at relatively high density. High density means high demolition cost per acre (and, of course, it is the per-acre cost that matters, since the end product to be reused is vacant land). In the meantime, however, the land has lost some of its accessibility value, reducing the benefit of demolition and increasing the attractiveness of abandonment. A major component of urban renewal in the 1960s was slum clearance. The strategy was to acquire large tracts through eminent domain, clear the land, and sell it to a private developer.[6] To the surprise of the agencies involved, these programs invariably lost money.[7] But in light of this discussion it should be expected that slum clearance would be a money-losing proposition, independent of whether it is a good idea.

Finally, consider the effect of the federal tax code, which subsidizes owner-occupied housing relative to rental housing. It also subsidizes new rental housing relative to used, largely by permitting more rapid tax depreciation (relative to the actual useful lives) of new structures. The Tax Reform Act of 1986 improved the situation, but depreciable lives are still shorter relative to economic lives for new than for old rental dwellings. This provision increases the attractiveness of new housing relative to old, which in turn encourages replacement construction—construction beyond that which is required by increases in the number of households. For every unit of replacement construction, a unit must be retired. Subsidies to new housing, by simple logic, bring about retirements from the stock.[8] In an economic environment where abandonment is a viable retirement strategy, these subsidies lead to increases in the rate of housing abandonment.

Using regression analysis, Peterson (1977) has concluded that for every 100 replacement units constructed in the suburbs, about 10 units are abandoned in the central city. Thus, if the number of households increases by 1000 and there are 1500 housing starts in the suburban ring (1000 housing starts for net growth and 500 for replacement), there will be 500 retirements of units. According to Peterson's estimates, of the 500 retirements, fifty will be central-city abandonments. Peterson counted a unit as abandoned if the Census Bureau classified it either as "standing, uninhabitable" or "vacant, dilapidated." This, of course, means that 450 units were retired by demolition, merger, or conversion to other use.[9]

6. See Chapter 13 for a discussion of eminent domain.

7. For a more complete discussion of urban renewal, see Rothenberg (1972).

8. There is one missing link in this logic. Subsidies to new construction could encourage household formation. In this case, there would be less than one retirement for each subsidy-induced housing start. This housing price-induced household formation, however, is surely small, at least over substantial time periods.

9. Always bear in mind that regression analysis demonstrates correlation, not causation. It is possible that at least some of the causation works in the other direction: the abandonment of dwelling units itself leads to further abandonments because of the unattractiveness of neighborhoods with abandoned housing. This, in turn, leads to an increase in replacement construction in the suburbs.

In a recent study of New York City, White (1986) provides important evidence on two other policy questions surrounding abandonment.
White begins by noting that properties ripe for abandonment are generally declining in value, and therefore are typically overassessed (since
assessments are done only every few years). As a consequence, property taxes represent a very large portion of the operating cost of low-
income housing.[10] If taxes fail to decline with property values, the tax
burden enhances the incentive to abandon. Exploring the empirical relationship between the likelihood of abandonment and property tax assessments, White concludes that the relation between the assessed and
market property values is an extremely strong determinant of the rate
of abandonment, and that a policy of speedy reassessment in blighted
neighborhoods, coupled with quick foreclosure on properties in arrears
on taxes, would lead to very large reductions in abandonment. In her
analysis of the Brownsville section of Brooklyn, White predicts that a
6 percent reduction in assessed value would reduce abandonments by
13 percent. Approximately 80 percent of the property tax revenue lost
by the rollback of assessments would be made up by increased collections from the properties which are saved from abandonment. The other
20 percent of lost revenue is more than made up by reduced administrative cost of handling abandoned buildings.

This suggests a policy whereby cities can reduce abandonments and
make money too. White's policy advice is surely sound, and it is encouraging to see that the statistical relationship is so strong. It is not
clear, however, that the results would be as striking as they appear on
first examination. It may be that White's proposed tax cut would actually reduce abandonment, but another possibility is that it would simply *relocate* abandonment. An examination of abandonment across
neighborhoods within a city cannot shed any light on the determinants
of abandonment for the city as a whole. To see this, suppose that local
actions (tax assessments and speedy foreclosure) have no effect on the
total number of abandonments in the city, but determine *only* where
the abandonments take place. A study such as White's would still show
a strong relationship between abandonment and tax assessment, since
the observations are individual neighborhoods. The way to learn
whether tax assessment can reduce the overall rate of abandonment
in a city would be to carry out an analysis like White's using a cross-
section of cities (or SMSAs), to see whether cities with low tax rates
on low-income housing fare better than cities with higher tax rates (and
less aggressive foreclosure policies).

To an important degree the replacement of old housing with new
is stimulated by income growth. Abandonment occurs because replacement construction stimulates housing retirement and because, under
some conditions, abandonment is the most profitable retirement
strategy. In many cases the administration of the local property tax adds

10. For low-income housing in Newark, N.J., in 1971, Sternlieb and Burchell (1973)
estimated that property taxes accounted for 33 percent of rent.

to the profitability of abandonment relative to demolition or conversion. And the federal tax code, with its relatively favorable treatment of new housing, gives an additional impetus to the replacement cycle and, indirectly, to abandonment. This suggests two urgent policy questions. First, after considering all the costs and consequences, is it advisable to subsidize new housing relative to old; that is, to artificially speed up the replacement cycle? Perhaps instead the replacement cycle should be slowed down. In principle, the correct policies are taxation of implicit rents on owner-occupied dwellings and the requirement that depreciable lives equal economic lives for all dwellings. A less drastic policy change would be to give tax incentives for rehabilitation. Second, given that some significant rate of replacement is an almost inevitable (and desirable) consequence of secularly rising incomes, what is the most efficient mechanism for retirement of old housing and re-use of the land?

Some Effects of Abandonment

So far our discussion of abandonment has focused on a narrow issue: the abandonment method of retirement is a profitability decision, and retirement itself is the natural consequence of rising incomes. Abandonment, however, has enormous adverse external effects on the neighborhood containing the abandoned property. For example, Sternlieb and Burchell (1973) note that abandoned residential buildings accounted for 21.2 percent of all severe fires in Newark, New Jersey, in 1970 and 1971. Although it is difficult to quantify, it is easy to see how the problem feeds upon itself. Abandoned houses reduce the safety and attractiveness of a neighborhood (most likely, a neighborhood that contains a good deal of housing ripe for retirement), which in turn depresses property values. This property value deterioration increases the relative profitability of abandonment for the houses that are the next candidates for retirement by reducing the value of cleared land relative to the cost of demolition. In addition, residents are encouraged to move out of the neighborhood, implying that the retirements (which will occur somewhere) are likely to be concentrated in the neighborhoods where abandonment first took root. In a few cases such as the worst slums of New York City and Chicago, the externalities are so damaging that even completely cleared land has no market value, even though land a few miles away is worth several hundred thousand dollars per acre.

Indeed, there exists the logical possibility that the cycle will become even more vicious. Abandonment, through its effect on the neighborhood amenity level, reduces the quality of neighboring dwellings. This quality reduction stimulates the demand for new housing in suburbs and further increases the rate of retirement. Some of this abandonment-induced retirement will be in the form of abandonment.

The preceding two paragraphs are more a statement of concern and a research agenda than a description of economists' knowledge about the links among abandonment, neighborhoods, and cities. In fact, there is very little quantitative knowledge about the interaction between abandonment and neighborhoods.

☐ FILTERING

The notion of *filtering* in the housing market is basically the observation that most people—and particularly most poor people—live in hand-me-down housing. As every younger sibling knows, hand-me-down consumption is a mixed blessing. So it is with housing.

Figure 11.3 shows how filtering works. As a dwelling ages, the rent it can command falls. Partly, the reason is that old houses produce fewer housing services than new houses, simply because of the ravages of time. More importantly, as the discussion of abandonment emphasized, income growth means that people demand better and larger housing as time passes. Thus, rents of old houses must fall to levels that induce people to occupy them. The lowest quality houses, as has been seen, cannot be rented at any rent that covers costs, and they are retired. Filtering is a natural consequence of deterioration and income growth. Filtering helps explain several important phenomena.

First, it makes clear why almost all unsubsidized construction is of high-income housing. Rents and values are, of course, related by Equation (10.3) for both new and old housing. As was seen in Chapter 10, dwelling value must equal the present value of its rents during its remaining economic life. Values of old dwellings decline for two reasons. First, as noted in the previous paragraph, rents decline. Second, the remaining economic life is shorter for old than for new housing. For these reasons, values of filtered dwellings are far below construction costs. Thus, new housing cannot compete with filtered housing in supplying the low-income market.

Second, the housing cost savings imparted by the filtering mechanism mean that low-income people, to avail themselves of this savings, must live where the used housing is. Old, low-quality (and thus filtered-down) housing is generally located in the central parts of cities, for the simple reason that cities were built sequentially from the center out. The housing that was built earliest is generally of the lowest quality (here *quality* means the number and size of rooms, in addition to other amenities). According to one recent estimate (Cooke and Hamilton, 1982), the tendency of old, low-income housing to be located in central cities can fully account for the observed tendency for the poor to live closer to the CBD than the rich. In other words, filtering and the location patterns it implies are a sufficiently powerful means of income segregation to explain the entire city-suburban income discrepancy for Baltimore and Houston, the two cities Cooke and Hamilton examined. Nevertheless, some segregation results from the fact that blacks are frequently offered suburban housing only on worse terms than whites. Since blacks have lower incomes than whites, racial segregation is related to income segregation. This issue will be discussed more fully later in the chapter.

☐ NEIGHBORHOOD EFFECTS

Slums and Neighborhood Effects

So far housing has been discussed as if the quality of housing services was definable solely by the characteristics of the dwelling unit and its proximity to the city center. In fact, however, the quality of life offered by a dwelling unit depends to an important degree on the character of the neighborhood in which it is located. The economic theory brought to bear on this problem is that of externalities, and qualitatively the proposition is straightforward: the utility that housing occupants derive from their homes depends in part on the actions of their neighbors—whether they maintain their properties and whether they generate noise, crime, or fire hazards. Particularly in high-density (generally low-income) neighborhoods, residents are keenly aware of the actions of their neighbors. In such a world, suboptimal maintenance of structures is expected, since some of the benefits of maintenance accrue to neighbors.

If these neighborhood effects are quantitatively important (a topic that will be discussed later), they are likely to have the most serious consequence in the lowest-income neighborhoods. First, if anything generates adverse neighborhood effects, abandonment does. It has been seen that abandonment is concentrated in the lowest-income neighborhoods and probably spawns more abandonment. Indeed, abandonment may be the catalyst that transforms a stable low-income neighborhood into a slum in which the social fabric comes unwoven. Abandoned housing attracts the most hopeless of any city's destitute population, and it is easy to imagine how the social contract governing rights of property and person would break down under such circumstances.

The second reason for the importance of neighborhood effects in slums is that much of the low-income housing stock is destined for retirement in the near future. Even if the landlord does not intend to abandon it, the imminence of retirement means that maintenance is reduced, ultimately to the vanishing point. This makes good sense from the perspective of the entrepreneur: if the roof leaks and the building is to be demolished in five years anyway, buckets are cheaper than shingles and clear plastic is cheaper than new windows. The problem is that these visible signs of poor maintenance may depress the value of the whole neighborhood and may signal that the neighborhood is on the way down. This, in turn, depresses maintenance on neighboring houses, and tenants who can afford to move out do so. In this view, slums, like abandonment, are the messy end product of filtering.

Among the general public, the importance of these neighborhood effects is almost beyond dispute. Everyone has seen neighborhoods in which they would not wish to live, even in a mansion. Nevertheless, attempts by economists to document the quantitative significance of neighborhood effects have been largely unsuccessful.

The first attempt to quantify these neighborhood effects statistically was by Crecine, Davis, and Jackson (1967). They reasoned that if certain activities are harmful to neighbors, the existence of these activities in a neighborhood should have an adverse effect on property values. To test for this, they regressed sale prices of single family homes in Pittsburgh on several variables that described the character of the neighborhood (the *neighborhood* was defined as the block on which the sold house is located). By including appropriate variables and grouping observations, they corrected for other determinants of house value, such as accessibility and the characteristics of the house itself. Their findings were surprising. The presence of "undesirable" neighboring land uses, such as row and multiple family housing, parking lots, light industry, wholesaling, and railroad lines had no systematic effect on the sale prices of single family homes. Both the magnitude and direction of the effect shifted from one part of the sample to another, and in general the magnitude of the effect was small.

This finding has proved to be remarkably robust. Other researchers, using more detailed samples and more powerful statistical techniques, have almost uniformly failed to find significant and consistent effects of neighboring activities upon property values.

Another branch of neighborhood research provides at least a partial answer to the puzzle presented by the lack of empirically observable neighborhood effects. The answer, it seems, is that most neighborhood effects are extremely localized geographically. Tideman (1969) estimated the probability of affected parties attending a local rezoning hearing. He found that the probability of attending declines by 50 percent with each additional 80 feet of distance from the site of the proposed rezoning. This suggests that even if houses next door to one another are strongly affected by the externality, households a couple of doors away will be almost indifferent. If neighborhood effects are so localized, it is not surprising that statistical studies have failed to uncover systematic effects on property values.

Another reason for the failure to find quantitative evidence of neighborhood effects may be that none of the studies uses slums as its primary data base. As has been shown, these effects are likely to be the most important in slums. Neighborhood effects might be unimportant in stable and moderate-to-low-density neighborhoods because of the low density itself, as well as the absence of the worst kinds of neighboring disamenities, such as abandoned and badly deteriorated housing. In the same context, property value might be the wrong dependent variable in these regressions. Neighborhood effects may work as follows: an abandoned building reduces the value of a neighboring building, which in turn is allowed to deteriorate. In this case, the adverse neighborhood effect has revealed itself not in reduced house value (holding quality constant), but rather in reduced quality (and attendant reduced value). If house value is regressed upon quality and neighboring land use, quality explains everything and neighboring land use, nothing. Researchers interested in neighborhood effects and slums must take these interactions into account, although they have not yet done so.

Neighborhood Effects in Stable Neighborhoods

Even in stable, middle-class neighborhoods, there is reason to believe that neighborhood effects are of more importance than property value studies indicate. Recently, researchers have begun to explore the possibility that nonconforming uses have little effect upon property values for the simple reason that not everyone has the same attitude toward a nonspecific set of neighborhood uses. What matters for property value determination is not whether most people find a neighboring activity distasteful, but whether the marginal bidder finds it distasteful. To take a concrete example, consider a neighborhood through which a railroad runs. Even if 90 percent of the population detests railroads, there is no effect upon property values so long as it is possible to sell all the affected houses to the remaining 10 percent who likes or is indifferent to railroads. If tastes are sufficiently diverse, the lack of association between property values and neighborhood characteristics is not surprising, and does not imply that people are generally indifferent to characteristics of their neighborhoods.

Thornton (1978) obtained interesting evidence supporting this view. He examined several neighborhoods in which high-rise apartment buildings were constructed; in some cases the construction caught the neighbors by surprise, while in others the construction was probably anticipated (since the land had been zoned for apartments for a long time). In the cases where the apartment buildings were not anticipated, Thornton found that homeowners who lived within 250 feet of the apartment building were about 40 percent more likely to move within the next eight years than were homeowners who lived beyond 250 feet from the new building. Interestingly, the difference in the probability of moving did not emerge until about five years after the apartments were constructed. This suggests that, whereas the apartments did encourage people to move, they tended to wait until the move made sense for other reasons, such as a change in household structure (children moving away, for example) or job location. The evidence also indicates, however, that the nonconforming use (a relatively innocuous one in this case) was distasteful to a significant portion of the population. Presumably, the people who were induced to sell found buyers who were less concerned with the existence of the new apartment building.

Given this view, as it stands now, there is little reason for economists or policymakers to be concerned about neighborhood effects, except in slums. People who do not like apartment buildings do not live near them. If one is built in a neighborhood, such people sell and move out; they suffer no capital loss, because there are enough people who do not dislike apartments. The market mechanism, according to this story, leads to an efficient sorting-out of people according to tastes.

Neighborhood Attachment

Many of the economic problems that arise as a result of neighborhood effects occur when there is change in the character of a neighborhood. If a new land use comes in and some residents find it distasteful, they either have to suffer the consequences or move. Even if it possible to move out without suffering a capital loss on the house, as suggested by the empirical evidence, these moves frequently impose high costs on households. People form emotional attachments to their neighborhoods, and moving away to avoid a new neighboring land use necessitates the breaking of these attachments. Obviously, the buyer of the house is willing to compensate the seller for the value of the property, but not for the psychic losses involved in moving away from friends and familiar surroundings.

There is accumulating evidence that many people place a high value on the familiarity and attachments of their neighborhoods and are willing to endure substantial capital or income losses to avoid moving to a strange new neighborhood. The Roskill Commission (1970), studying the possibility of a third London airport, conducted a survey in which they asked people how large a premium over the fair market value of their homes they would insist on before moving voluntarily. The mean value was just under 40 percent; that is, they would not willingly leave their neighborhoods unless they were paid 140 percent of the value of their houses. A similar result was reported by Dunn (1979), who found that residents of a small town in the rural South, on the average, were willing to accept a 14 percent wage reduction (after the local mill went bankrupt) rather than move to another town and avoid the wage reduction.

Using a more complicated statistical technique, Dynarski (1981) also estimated the amount of money people were willing to forgo to remain in their neighborhoods. Unlike the other authors, he was able to examine the variation in this community attachment among types of people. He found that this "value of community," or value of familiar surroundings, is relatively high for older people (over age 56), blacks, low-income people, and people with friends and relatives in the neighborhood.

This set of findings is important because it tells us that *change* in the location of various activities imposes serious adjustment costs on people, and these adjustment costs are not recovered in the sale prices of houses. None of this constitutes an apology for the status quo, however. Change, including change in the character of neighborhoods, is the major vehicle by which progress arrives. In any event, it is inevitable. Nevertheless, the external costs associated with change are important.

☐ RACIAL SEGREGATION AND DISCRIMINATION

Racial segregation and discrimination are quite different from one another. *Segregation* refers to a physical separation of the races—the tendency of both blacks and whites to live in racially homogeneous neighborhoods. *Discrimination* refers to a situation in which housing is offered on different terms to blacks and whites—or not at all to blacks. Segregation, of course, might be a consequence of discrimination, but it also might be a consequence of benign forces, such as the preference of both races to live among others of the same race. An important observation in this context is that even people's mild preferences for living with their own race can lead to extreme segregation. Suppose, for example, that everyone was racially tolerant but did not want to live in a neighborhood in which he or she was actually in the minority. The only outcome that would satisfy this rather weak version of racial preference would be complete segregation by neighborhood. With anything less, someone would be in the minority.

Segregation

It is obvious that urban housing markets are highly segregated by race; typically, blacks occupy enclaves in central cities, and whites are distributed between all-white areas of central cities and suburbs. Some of this segregation occurs because blacks tend to be poorer than whites and because there is income segregation for the reasons discussed in Chapters 6 and 7. Racial segregation, however, is far greater than could be explained by income differences alone, as Taeuber and Taeuber (1965) have shown. They constructed an index of actual racial segregation (to be discussed below) and a similar index of the segregation that would emerge just because of income segregation and interracial income differences. By comparing the two indexes, they concluded that in 1960 only about one-third of actual race segregation was due to income differences.

This segregation, even if it is voluntary and a reflection of blacks' preference for living among other blacks, imposes significant costs upon the black populations of our cities. Black neighborhoods are located almost exclusively in central cities rather than suburbs, and they frequently are located downtown. Manufacturing jobs have suburbanized rapidly during the postwar era, as has already been shown. A central-city residential location, however, diminishes blacks' access to suburban jobs and, of course, precludes access to suburban schools. This problem will be explored in some detail at the conclusion of Chapter 15.

Measuring Segregation. For a variety of reasons it is important to be able to measure the extent of segregation. In part this is necessary in order to do quantitative research on the subject, and in part it is useful to have an objective measure of whether patterns of segrega-

tion are changing over time. Measurement of segregation is more difficult than it might seem, though, as will be seen.

The most frequently employed measure is the so-called segregation,
or dissimilarity, index:

$$D = \frac{\sum_0 N_0 |(b_0 - b)|}{2Nb(1 - b)} \cdot 100, \tag{11.1}$$

where D is the value of the dissimilarity index, N is the urban area population, and b is the fraction of the population which is black. The urban area is divided up into areas (census tracts, blocks, or whatever),
and the population of each area and the fraction of the population which
is black are now measured. These are respectively N_0 and b_0. For each
tract $_0$ the variable $N_0(b_0 - b)$ is constructed. If $b_0 = b$, the fraction
of the tract that is black is identical to what it is for the entire urban
area. For that tract, the variable $N_0(b_0 - b) = 0$. If this variable equals
zero for each tract, then the whole index equals zero, meaning that there
is no racial dissimilarity among tracts. This is, of course, the lowest value
the index can take on. A value of zero for the index means no segregation (that is, blacks have the same representation in each tract).

As an alternative, suppose each tract is either all black or all white.
For each tract, the numerator takes on the value either of $N_0 b$ or
$N_0(1 - b)$. This situation gives the largest possible value for the index,
namely $D = 100$.

This is the most widely used index for measuring discrimination.
Though there are a variety of problems with it, it is useful to point out
two in particular. The first concerns the selection of the entire reference area, and the second concerns the selection of the subareas.

As regards the selection of the entire reference area, standard practice is to construct an index either for a legal city or for an entire SMSA.
For either definition, one purpose of constructing the index is to determine whether segregation has increased or decreased over time. If
the index is defined for a legal central city, measures of changes in segregation can be badly distorted by migration between the city and
suburbs. To take an extreme case, suppose that in 1970 the city has
two tracts—one all black and one all white. The value of D is 100—
complete segregation. By 1980 all the whites have moved out of the
central city to the suburbs. Both city tracts are now all black—the same
as the city-wide total. D has fallen to 0—no segregation *within the central city* at all. The result which emerged from this example does not
require the extreme assumptions made here. It is quite easy for a city's
segregation index to decline simply as a result of the movement of
whites out of the city. In general, comparisons of segregation indexes
over time are valid only if the race mix of the entire area remains roughly
the same. This of course means that SMSA segregation indexes are much
more informative than central-city indexes.

The value of the index is also strongly affected by the way in which
the city is divided into subareas. To see this consider the following ex-

ample. Every city block is all black or all white, and the blocks are arranged checkerboard fashion—the "black" squares are black and the "red" ones, white. If blocks are used as units of observation in constructing the segregation index, $D = 100$ (complete segregation). If, however, the units of observation are two-block areas, $D = 0$, since each subarea contains the same racial mix as the whole urban area. In general, the smaller the subarea chosen, the higher the value of D.

It must be kept in mind that there is no "right" way to divide a city into subareas for purposes of constructing a segregation index. As a practical matter, most segregation indexes are constructed on the basis of census tracts (typical population about 3000) or blocks.

It has already been noted that one of the prime findings to emerge from the study of segregation indexes is that the distribution of blacks in metropolitan areas is far from random. Furthermore, by comparing actual values of D with those which would emerge if low-income people were randomly assigned to low-income housing (and vice versa) it can be determined what percentage of black segregation is due to the fact that low-income housing is segregated. The answer, as noted, is that only about 30 percent of racial segregation can be explained by geographical segregation of housing by quality.

In 1980, Chicago's segregation index was 91.9 (based on blocks) and 86.3 (based on census tracts), giving it a position it had long held—the most segregated city in the nation, though Cleveland was almost identical. Even this extremely high value showed a slight decline from 1970 (93.0), though this may have been solely due to white suburbanization, as discussed above. (By contrast, San Francisco's block index was 68.2.) All of these numbers are reported by Kain (1984).

The general pattern is that dissimilarity indexes have shown at least modest declines in American cities and SMSAs during the past forty years. Scholars, however, have calculated remarkably few dissimilarity indexes based on the 1980 census, so there is little concrete information on recent trends. (Calculation of these indexes is straightforward; students who wish to do research projects might find this a fruitful area for study.)

Discrimination

A naive interpretation of the standard microeconomic model would lead to the prediction that race discrimination cannot exist in a competitive economy. The reason is simple: discrimination is costly. In the labor market, an entrepreneur who refuses to hire blacks would be driven out of business. In the case of housing markets, a person who refuses to sell or rent to blacks would suffer an economic loss. The naive model is clearly inadequate, however: blacks and other minorities obviously do face discrimination in housing, job, and other markets.

Before exploring problems with the microeconomic model, it is worth noting that there is an important element of truth in the observation that competitive forces place restraints on the practice of discrimination. If black-white housing price differentials become large enough, there is profit to be made in arbitrage (blockbusting), and this reduces the price difference. If wage differences are sufficiently large, nonbigoted entrepreneurs (or at least entrepreneurs whose greed exceeds their bigotry) can hire black labor at a lower wage than can their bigoted competitors, thus achieving a competitive advantage.[11] A side effect will be the reduction of the wage spread. Nevertheless, there are important reasons to believe that competitive forces will not completely eliminate discrimination.

One of the problems with the microeconomic model in this context is its assumption of perfect information. Information is not perfect, however, and its acquisition is expensive. In the housing market, this can make a major difference. A potential homeowner must be found creditworthy, and a landlord must judge whether a potential tenant can pay the rent and keep down wear and tear on the property. For whatever reason, blacks *on the average* have more unstable income prospects, and larger families with more children and fewer adults, than white families. They are worse risks as both tenants and homeowners. Judgments about creditworthiness and likely treatment of the property must be made by landlords and lending institutions if they are to remain in business, yet the information required to make these judgments is difficult and expensive to obtain. A proxy for the information—race— is readily observable, however. Profit-maximizing entrepreneurs would be throwing away free information if they were blind to the race of prospective borrowers or tenants, and if the entrepreneurs' competitors are not blind to race, the entrepreneurs will be driven out of business. That is, competitive forces may place a lower limit, as well as an upper limit, on the price discrimination faced by blacks.

Probably the most blatant and pervasive forms of discrimination occur not because of the weakness of the competitive antidote to discrimination, but because of the active participation of government, with its court and police power. Such was the case in this country— particularly in the South—up to at least the mid-1950s, and it appears to be true in other countries as well. (Government racism clearly still exists in the United States, particularly at the local level, though it is greatly diminished relative to its position ten to twenty years ago.)

The evidence on segregation indicates that blacks and whites can be thought of as facing two separate housing markets. Both generally restrict their search for housing to neighborhoods of their own race. Predictions can be made about black-white housing price differences based on hypotheses about the interactions between the segregated neighborhoods.

---

11.   There is direct evidence of this in major league baseball. When the color barrier was broken in 1947, most teams began recruiting black players, but a few remained all white for several years. The teams that recruited blacks (most notably the Dodgers, of course) showed a quite significant improvement in their won-lost records as compared with the teams that were still segregated.

The easiest case to deal with is the one in which there are no interactions: blacks live on one island and whites on another. In this case, the price depends on the interaction of supply and demand on each island, and there is no reason to expect a price premium for one race or another. In a more realistic model, however, there is no moat separating the neighborhoods. Rather, there is a thin boundary—a street or a block—and depending on the institutions and the forces, the boundary can move.

The first formal model of housing markets with a boundary is that of Bailey (1959), who postulated that blacks are willing to pay a premium to live near whites, but that whites are willing to live near blacks only if they get their housing at a discount. Despite the chauvinistic assumptions concerning preferences, the model is important and revealing. Figure 11.4 shows the price of housing in two neighborhoods and at the boundary under the Bailey assumptions. It depicts the assumption that blacks pay a premium, and whites a discount, to live at the boundary. As depicted, the prices in the interiors of the two neighborhoods are the same.[12]

The price is higher on the black than the white side of the boundary, however, and this difference generates an incentive to convert housing at the boundary from white to black occupancy, that is, to shift the boundary to the right. Ignoring conversion costs of any sort, this incentive to shift is eliminated only when prices are the same on both sides of the boundary, as depicted in Figure 11.5. Now, of course, blacks in their interior receive their housing at a discount as compared with whites in their interior.

Putting aside the assumption that everyone wants to live near the whites, this model properly focuses attention on the boundary and what happens at the boundary. If prices are higher on the black side, will conversion occur until the differential is eliminated? If so, how quickly? A number of general observations can be made:

1. The stronger white neighborhood attachments, the greater the sustainable cross-border price difference. In fact, ethnic neighborhoods have been found to be much more resistant to conversion than nonethnic ones.

2. The greater the difficulty of physically altering the housing to satisfy black demand (probably to lower quality, given the tendency for blacks to have lower income), the greater the sustainable price difference.

3. The greater the rate of population growth in the ghetto, the greater the boundary price pressure. Even if boundary shifts completely eliminate any price difference in the long run, the adjustment process might be slow enough that it fails to keep up with popula-

12. Remember that this is price per standardized unit—roughly per square foot—rather than house value.

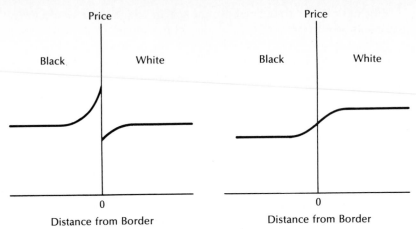

Figure 11.4 *Housing Price in Black and White Neighborhoods: Disequilibrium*

Figure 11.5 *Housing Price in Black and White Neighborhoods: Equilibrium*

tion growth. Conversely, the faster the rate of white departure, the more readily prices are equalized.

The standard method of testing empirically for the existence of housing price discrimination is to use regression analysis. Monthly rent, or house value, is regressed upon a variety of characteristics of the house, of the neighborhood, and of the household itself. The main purpose of the multiple regression is to "hold constant" other determinants of rent (or value) so as to isolate the effect of race. The major difficulty is in gathering a sample with reliable data and making sure that all important determinants of rent variation have been accounted for. There are a number of such studies, and the pattern that emerges from them is interesting.

Studies from the late 1960s and early 1970s tend to find blacks paying rent premiums of 10 to 15 percent.[13] More recent studies, however, drawing their samples from the mid to late 1970s, have failed to find consistent evidence of a housing price markup for blacks.[14] Perhaps the cessation and partial reversal of black migration to northern cities from the South, beginning about 1970, has reduced ghetto growth rates sufficiently that boundary adjustments have had a chance to reduce or, in some cases, eliminate the substantial price premiums that blacks surely were paying in the late 1960s.

None of this indicates that race-related housing problems are solved, or even that price discrimination has disappeared. First, the finding of a declining or disappearing racial housing price premium continues to be the subject of research and dispute. Second, other aspects of hous-

13. In one such study, King and Mieszkowski (1973) also found that both blacks and whites prefer to live in homogeneous rather than border or mixed neighborhoods.

14. For a good review of this literature, see Yinger (1979).

ing discrimination are important and appear to still be in place. Third, it is important to realize that this discussion does not touch on the important questions of job market discrimination and race differences in access to quality schooling.

An important type of discrimination that would not show up in any price index study is geographic—the exclusion of blacks from white neighborhoods except through expansion of the ghetto boundary. It has long been claimed that banks and real estate agents tend to direct clients to neighborhoods of like race, and anyone who has been given a tour of houses for sale by a real estate agent knows this to be true (Wienk, Reid, Simonson, and Eggers 1980). Whether this represents discrimination or an assumption on the part of real estate agents that clients prefer to live with their own race is difficult to know. Probably, some of each occurs. The observable outcome, of course, is race segregation. As has been noted, several researchers have showed that even a mild tendency by realtors to steer customers can lead to extreme patterns of segregation (Courant 1978; Yinger 1979). Despite the difficulty of quantitatively sorting out the difference between discrimination and segregation by choice, it is apparent that in general a black who wants to live in a white neighborhood needs, at a minimum, a very thick skin.

One important source of information on the extent of housing discrimination comes from a study (Wienk et al., 1979) sponsored by the Department of Housing and Urban Development (HUD) in 1977. Three hundred teams (one white and one black per team) responded to for-sale and for-rent advertisements placed in newspapers in various cities. The black and white team members applied for housing separately and compared notes on treatment (availability of housing, courtesy, credit check, and so on). In response to a given advertisement, the majority of teams found that blacks and whites received identical treatment. In about 20 percent of the cases, however, blacks were treated less favorably than whites.

☐ HOUSING POLICIES

Owner-Occupied Housing

Quantitatively, the most important housing program is the tax subsidy to owner-occupied housing already discussed in the previous chapter. Aaron (1972) estimates that this subsidy reduces the rental price of owner-occupied housing by some 10 percent relative to rental housing, and Peterson (1979) believes that the tax subsidy is directly responsible for raising the owner occupancy rate by about 15 percentage points.[15] White and White (1977) estimate that the tax subsidy to owner-

15. In 1940 just over 45 percent of housing was owner occupied; by 1970 the figure had risen to 65 percent. Some of this increase is due to rising incomes, but most of it appears to be due to tax advantages of owner occupancy, which became important only after personal income tax rates were raised substantially during World War II.

occupied housing cost the U.S. Treasury about $10 billion in 1970. A major consequence of this program has been to divert investment from other activities into housing, and indeed this was seen as a major objective during the 1950s. Savings and loans were created and given special privileges precisely to help channel money into owner-occupied housing.[16] Many observers feel, however, that this has gone too far in the 1980s—noting that the diversion of investment to housing has been diversion of the same investment *from* the manufacturing and other sectors. The 1970s was a decade of very low productivity growth in the United States (and in the rest of the industrialized world, which might indicate doubt that housing is the only culprit), and many have argued that some of the investment that went into housing could more usefully have gone into plant and equipment. Also, recall the Peterson argument that the encouragement of housing investment decreases our incentive to preserve the standing stock. A recent paper (Mills, 1987) has estimated, however, that the gap between social returns to other investments and those to housing, although still substantial, is becoming smaller.

Other important housing programs exist, and many have been designed explicitly to address the problems discussed in the first part of this chapter. The following sections will look at some of these programs and at empirical estimates of their effectiveness in light of the discussion of the problems in the first part of this chapter. Federal housing programs over the postwar era have been directed largely at three goals: (1) the improvement of the quality of housing for low-income people, (2) the removal or improvement of blighted or slum neighborhoods, and (3) the elimination of racial discrimination in the housing market.

Housing the Poor

Programs designed to improve the housing of the poor have been of two types. The first type approaches the problem by increasing the supply of low-income housing and the second, by increasing the ability and willingness of poor people to demand higher-quality housing.

Supply subsidies. The oldest and best known of the programs to supply low-income housing is public housing, first instituted in 1937. The federal government provides subsidies to state and local housing authorities, who own and operate the units, renting them out (below cost, because of the federal subsidy) to low-income people. Eligibility requirements, which change from time to time, are established by Congress.

Public housing is not an entitlement program, which means there is no requirement that a unit be provided to every eligible applicant.

---

16. Another stimulus to owner occupancy, instituted in the mid-1930s, was federal mortgage insurance. This led to the introduction of the "standard" mortgage described in Chapter 10.

This, of course, means that the housing authorities have discretion over which applicants they accept as tenants. The authorities frequently have been taken to court over their use of this discretion, however; their response typically has been to reduce the income limits (thus reducing the pool of applicants). The result, contrary to congressional intent, has been that public housing has been occupied only by the poorest households.

It is clear that much of the political support for public housing has come from the construction industry. In fact, the whole program has been terminated more than once, only to be revived during the next downturn in construction activity. For example, the Nixon administration cancelled the public housing program in 1973 (a boom year in housing and a year of highly publicized public housing failures), and it was reactivated in 1976 (by which time the bottom had fallen out of construction). In 1982 there were 1.2 million public housing units, just a bit over 1 percent of the stock. The average annual federal subsidy in 1979 was about $2000 per unit. The Reagan administration has proposed no more public housing construction, and in fact it recommends the sale or demolition of some of the highest-cost units (HUD Subsidized Housing Overview 1982).

By contrast, Section 236 of the 1968 Housing and Urban Development Act made interest subsidies available to private developers of low-income rental housing. This provision was replaced by Section 8 of the 1974 Housing and Community Development Act. Again, rent limits and quality standards are imposed by the federal government. The subsidy for this program has run about $4000 per unit.

Supply-side programs, almost of necessity, are not entitlements. It is hard to imagine that public housing will be built for every eligible person who might apply. The only way the programs can benefit the poor in general (as opposed to those who just happen to get into the subsidized units) is through the effect of increased supply on the price of available units. In fact, however, these benefits should be quite modest; the price of low-income housing is already well below replacement cost as a result of the filtering process. It is possible that public housing does not reduce the price of existing units to any substantial degree, but only increases the rate of retirement from the stock. Some of this retirement surely takes the form of abandonment, if Peterson's estimates are roughly correct. And in a few famous cases, the public housing units themselves were retired within a few years.

Demand subsidies. A combination of high cost, highly publicized failures, and doubts about effectiveness led people to look for alternatives to the supply-side approaches to low-income housing problems. This reexamination culminated in the Housing and Community Development Act of 1974. It has already been noted that Section 8 of this law provided subsidies to private developers of low-income rental housing. The major departure, also funded through Section 8, was the initiation of rent subsidies for low-income households. The first step in the calculation of the subsidy is the determination of market rent for a "standard" (as opposed to substandard) dwelling in the urban area. If this figure is more than 30 percent of the income of an eligible household, the government makes up the difference with a payment directly to the household.[17] The subsidy is tied to the household—not to the unit—and is designed to stimulate consumption rather than production of new units.

For a household that would have lived in a standard unit anyway, the subsidy program is a pure income transfer. For others, however, the income transfer is conditional upon the applicant's moving into a standard-quality unit. One benefit of this program is that it encourages participants to seek out the cheapest available housing. The tenants are the ones who save if they are able to find a housing bargain.

As of 1983, the Reagan administration has proposed cancellation of the Section 8 New Housing Program. Under this proposal, almost all subsidized-housing money would go into a modified Section 8 demand-side program, known as the Housing Certificate Program. The administration anticipates supporting almost one million housing certificates at a cost of $2000 each by 1988.[18] As of 1987, Congress has not enacted a new housing program.

Housing allowances. Housing allowances do not exist in this country except for very limited experiments in a few localities. As most frequently proposed, there are two differences between housing allowances and the Section 8 rent subsidy. The first is that the housing allowance program would be an entitlement. It thus could improve the housing standards of all eligible households, not just those whose applications were accepted. The second difference is that the subsidy formula might be somewhat different. Under some proposals, the housing allowance program would pay a certain fraction of rent to an eligible household rather than the difference between "fair market rent" as determined by the authority and 30 percent of income. This difference is important. Under Section 8, the subsidy does not vary with housing consumption, except for the fact that eligibility is contingent on the household's satisfying minimum quality standards. Thus, it provides no special incentive to increase housing consumption once the minimum standard has been met.[19] The "fraction of rent" housing allowance sub-

17. Actually, the subsidy is paid by the federal government to the local housing authority, which in turn pays it to the landlord. The subsidy goes with the tenant, not the unit, however, in the event the tenant moves.

18. For a more complete discussion, including the rationale for various policy changes, see "HUD Subsidized Housing Overview" (1982). For an excellent survey, along with a good background discussion see National Association of Home Builders, "Low- & Moderate-Income Housing" (1986).

19. In the absence of a requirement that the recipient live in adequate housing, the Section 8 rent subsidy does not differ in concept from an NIT. The cost of adequate housing is analogous to the intercept in the NIT formula—the subsidy payment if the family has no income. The percentage of income deemed reasonable to spend on housing is analogous to the marginal tax rate in the NIT; each dollar of additional income reduces the subsidy by that amount.

sidy is a pure price reduction, however, thus encouraging housing consumption even after the standard has been met. A national housing allowance program could employ either formula.

Housing allowances, or an entitlement version of the Section 8 rent subsidy program, would be an important step in providing consumer sovereignty to recipients of federal housing subsidies. For that reason, they are opposed by spokespeople for builders, banks, and local governments, all of whom now share in government programs to subsidize low-income housing.[20] Housing allowances would circumvent such groups, placing money directly in the hands of intended beneficiaries and encouraging them to spend the money to their best advantage, subject only to the restriction that they inhabit housing deemed adequate. Since only the poor would benefit, the proposal is opposed by groups that are traditional lobbyists for government housing programs!

Effectiveness of the programs.

In some ways, any program targeted at a specific good is less efficient than a cash-grant program costing the same amount of money. To see this, suppose that the government decides to give a $1000 housing subsidy to a poor person in the form of a rent rebate conditional on the person occupying some minimum quality of housing. If the person were simply given the $1000 in cash, he or she could buy that minimum house quality, or, if he or she preferred, could buy something else. Thus one of the costs of a housing subsidy program is that it causes people to spend their money differently from how they would if given complete freedom of choice.

Perhaps this consumption distortion should not be counted as a cost, since the objective of the program is to induce more housing consumption. But two other types of cost are unambiguous. The first is administrative and needs no further explanation. The second, particularly for supply-side programs, is production cost. This is the difference between the cost the government incurs by producing new or rehabilitated subsidized housing and the cost of acquiring the same quality of housing on the open market.

Mayo (1980) has discovered that supply-oriented programs are almost twice as expensive as demand-oriented programs. With new construction and public housing, it costs about $2 to provide a unit with a market value of $1, whereas the same $1 worth of services can be provided through a housing allowance or Section 8 rent subsidies for approximately $1.15. Therefore, if the objective is to provide housing services to poor people, a given budget will go much further (almost twice as far) if it is devoted to demand-oriented programs.

This should come as no surprise, given what is already known about the housing market. In most cities there is a surplus, not a shortage, of low-income housing. The available housing stock, as a result of this

---

20. The opposition of builders has a somewhat different basis. Public housing and the supply-side Section 8 programs do stimulate housing production, to the obvious benefit of the building industry.

surplus, already sells for low prices. Not surprisingly, a major effect of new construction of low-income housing is that this glut becomes more serious, and the new units provide housing services worth only a fraction of the construction cost. As was noted, the construction probably also aggravates the abandonment problem and certainly hastens housing retirement in other neighborhoods.

By contrast, the various rent subsidies address the true problem—poverty. Improving the ability of people to buy housing does improve housing consumption, and it does so in a reasonably efficient manner.[21]

Rent control. Another program, or rather a series of local programs, designed to help low-income renters is *rent control*. Rent control generally takes the form of a statutory ceiling on annual rent increases, sometimes with allowances for extraordinary cost increases such as fuel, major repairs, and taxes. New York City has had rent control, with various exemptions, throughout the postwar era. Many other cities adopted rent control measures during the mid-1970s.

The benefit of rent control seems obvious: some citizens get housing more cheaply than they otherwise would, though, as will be seen, it is not as straightforward as that. The cost is the adverse effect on the supply of rental housing. If government simply controls rents by edict, it ultimately reduces the supply of rental housing. If the supply of rental housing is fairly elastic in the long run, even a modest price reduction leads to a substantial decline in quantity.[22] If the supply elasticity is equal to 2 (a conservative estimate), a 10 percent price reduction ultimately will lead to a 20 percent decline in available supply! This problem, recognized by both proponents and opponents, must be addressed if rent control is to be effective. The possibilities for maintaining supply are fiat or subsidy, and localities have relied almost exclusively on fiat. It is extremely difficult to enforce such a fiat, however. It is hard to prevent a landlord from inadequately maintaining a building, and laws that prohibit conversion to condominiums and other uses are troublesome to enforce and of questionable constitutionality.

Much of the support for rent control apparently comes from the belief that landlords make large profits and that the principal effect will be to remove these profits (with little effect on supply). There is little evidence for this view, and little reason to believe it to be true. In every American city, landlording is a highly competitive business, and it is hard to imagine how entrepreneurs would be able to keep prices above costs.

Another element of support for rent control results from some highly publicized episodes of "regentrification" of inner city neighbor-

---

21. A high elasticity of supply for housing in general would be expected, since it appears to be produced under roughly constant returns. The elasticity of supply of rental housing should be higher yet, because it is easy to shift resources between rental and owner-occupied housing.
22. See the discussion of the rental price of housing in Chapter 10.

hoods. One of the results of this process has been a rapid increase in both property values and rents in the redeveloped neighborhoods. Rent control is seized upon as a tool to prevent this displacement, but it probably will not prevent the displacement in any case. Conversion to owner occupancy or, in some cases, demolition and sale of the vacant land becomes a viable option if rents are kept below market levels.

It is curious that rent control became popular during the 1970s, a decade when rents fell relative to the cost of living. Perhaps people have "money illusion"; rapid nominal rent increases, even though they failed to keep up with inflation and income growth, aroused their ire.

If rent control is effective, rents are driven below market-clearing levels (that is, below the levels the units could command in the absence of rent control). This brings up a difficult policy question: is the landlord permitted to raise the rent to the market-clearing level when the tenant moves out? As will be seen, each answer leads to unsatisfactory consequences.

If rent adjustment is permitted when a new tenant moves in, the landlord has an incentive to force the current tenant out as soon as the controlled rent falls below market rent. If that does not work, the tenant can agree to move out on the condition the landlord pays him or her off. Of course, it is possible (but unlikely) that adequate law enforcement will prevent either the tenant or the landlord from holding the other hostage. If so, one of the main consequences of rent control is that the current tenant has a strong incentive not to move (since he or she will be unable to replicate the controlled rent after moving). In this event, (1) the benefits of rent control accrue only to those who occupy units at the time the law is passed, and (2) rent control diminishes mobility, because tenants cannot take the benefits with them.

If the landlord is not permitted to raise rent for the next tenant, however, then the tenant can frequently collect a finder's fee, called key money, from the next tenant. As an example, suppose market rent is $800/month, and controlled rent is $500/month. By gaining access to a rent-controlled apartment, the prospective tenant expects to save the present value of $300/month forever.[23] This present value is the maximum amount he or she is willing to pay for access to a rent-controlled apartment, and any renter moving out of a controlled apartment will be sure to charge this amount.

In light of this discussion of key money, a surprising consequence of rent control can be seen. The only beneficiaries of rent control are those who have leases at the time the law is adopted. To the extent key money represents the present value of savings, all subsequent

---

23.   It may seem that the prospective tenant would pay key money only equal to the present value of rent savings during his or her own expected period of occupancy. But this is not the case. One of the benefits the new tenant acquires upon getting a rent-controlled apartment is the right to charge key money when he or she moves out. This key money in turn represents the present value of rent savings after the new tenant moves out.

tenants pay not the controlled rent, but rather the market rent. (Of course the market rent is higher than it would be in the absence of rent control, because rent control depresses the supply.) Seen in this light, rent control is a law which transfers part of the ownership rights of a rental property from the landlord to the original tenant. Among other things, this ought to make it clear that any income redistribution emanating from rent control bears little resemblance to the income redistribution that would emerge from a conscious policy to help the poor. Even if all renters are poor, rent control helps the first generation of renters at the expense not only of landlords but also of subsequent generations of renters.

Of course, the institutions and facts are not as simple as the foregoing conceptual discussion, though the distortions from rent control are not small. In New York City, rent control has caused a massive transfer of assets from owners to early tenants, many of whom pay rents of a fraction of market rents and retain legal tenant status long after they vacate the dwelling, renting it at about market rate.

Why Subsidize Housing?

All the programs discussed so far—the tax subsidy for owner-occupied housing, public housing and construction subsidy programs, rent supplement programs and rent control—take as given the notion that consumption of housing should be subsidized. Indeed, to many this seems self-evident. Housing satisfies a basic need, like food and clothing, and it is one of the most visible indicators of standard of living. Also, without question, too many people live in housing that is deplorable by modern standards.

The economic question, however, is not whether it's preferable to see poor people live in better housing, but whether housing warrants favorable treatment *relative* to other goods. Subsidization of housing encourages housing consumption *at the expense* of something else. For low-income housing programs, the best way to pose the question is: why subsidize housing rather than just redistribute income directly and let people choose how they want to spend their money? The answers that suggest themselves follow:

1. The donors would rather give their money for housing than for income transfers.
2. Poor people somehow undervalue housing when making their consumption decisions.
3. The market does not work smoothly, probably because of capital market imperfections. Subsidies are required to restore the efficiency conditions that would exist in a perfect market.
4. There are externalities associated with housing consumption (neighborhood effects, essentially) that imply that individual households spend too little on their housing.

5. Particularly in the case of the supply-side programs, donors are simply unaware of the high cost of these programs.
6. Again in the case of supply-side programs, as has already been noted, the housing industry is an important beneficiary and lobbyist on behalf of programs.

Economists can say little about donor preferences for housing, except to note that if that is what donors want to do, that is what they will do. Still, it is a little implausible to believe that donors have specific preferences for supporting housing unless it is because they believe that the second through fourth reasons are important. Economists also have little to say about the second possibility—that poor people "should" want more housing relative to other goods. This seems impossible to measure and impossible to know. The only thing to point out is the obvious, but frequently forgotten, fact that more housing means less of something else.

Market imperfections abound in housing in the form of imperfect access to borrowing and rental markets and extremely imperfect information regarding housing prices in various parts of a city.[24] The subsidization of housing does nothing to eliminate these imperfections, however. Open housing laws have helped promote equal access to capital and real estate markets and could help more if governments enforced them, but there is no reason to believe that subsidization of housing can redress these inequities.

Neighborhood effects certainly exist, although, as previously noted, they are extremely difficult to measure. Again, housing subsidies do not seem to be the answer. Indeed, it can be argued that subsidies only make the problem worse. As already seen, one of the major effects of public housing or construction subsidies is to create vacancies and retirements, as well as to put downward pressure on the value price of low-income housing. It has also been pointed out that it is plausible that the retirement process—the awkward end product of filtering—is responsible for the most deleterious neighborhood effects. There is no reason to doubt that every unit of public housing or subsidized private construction generates at least as much abandonment as does any other type of housing.

The point applies not only to construction-side subsidies. Demand subsidies also speed up the filtering process and increase the pace of retirements. Unlike supply-side subsidies, however, demand-side subsidies do not necessarily create new low-income dwellings. They may simply help finance existing housing that can be maintained at a sufficiently high quality to avoid adverse neighborhood effects and aban-

---

24. Among other researchers, deLeeuw and Struyk (1975) have found that substantial housing price differences among neighborhoods can exist and be maintained for long periods of time. Perhaps these differences reflect genuine differences in the attractiveness of the neighborhoods, or perhaps a lack of information inhibits migration among neighborhoods so as to eliminate the price difference.

donment. Even if housing subsidies improve housing for the recipient and improve the neighborhood for the neighbors, the same subsidies surely leave a wake of abandonment and decay elsewhere in the city.

To address the problem of neighborhood effects in the areas where the problems are most serious, it is necessary to look for a more efficient mechanism for retirement or reuse of housing than a consumption or production subsidy program.

☐ Summary

This chapter has shown that an important contributor to many housing problems is the extreme durability of the housing stock, and that both demolition and modification are quite expensive. This makes it hard to adjust the stock to new conditions.

Questions and Problems

1. Suppose a house costs $100,000. Inflation is 5 percent, the mortgage rate is 7 percent, and property taxes are 2 percent. Depreciation and maintenance are 1 percent each. There are no expected capital gains.
   a. What rent must the owner of this house charge to cover expenses?
   b. If inflation remains at 5 percent and the mortgage rate rises to 9 percent, what changes would you expect in rent or house value?

2. What do you think is the reason for the enormous variation in housing cost in the following table? Can you think of a way of testing whether your ideas are right?

Metropolitan Area Housing Costs (Detached Single-Family Home)

Metropolitan Area	Cost per Square Foot	Metropolitan Area	Cost per Square Foot
San Francisco	$105	Baltimore	$47
Los Angeles	89	Cleveland	45
Oakland	82	Pittsburgh	44
Miami	58	Nashville	42
Seattle	56	Atlanta	42
Chicago	55	Tampa/St. Petersburg	41
Dallas	51	All surveyed metropolitan	
Boston	50	areas	55

Source: Reprinted with permission from National Association of Realtors. *Real Estate Status Report* (March 1982): 4.

3. This chapter discussed some peculiarities of the housing market when income is growing and population is fairly stable (as in the

United States during the latter half of the twentieth century). How would the housing market be different if population were growing quickly and income were stationary (as in many developing countries)?

4. What do you think is the explanation for the patterns in the following table?

Median Home Size by Type (Square Feet)

Type	New	Existing	All
Detached single family	2,000	1,640	1,700
Apartment condominium	1,100	1,020	1,020
Townhouse	1,620	1,430	1,500

Source: Reprinted with permission from National Association of Realtors. *1980; National Homebuyers Survey.* (Washington, D.C.: National Association of Realtors, 1981): 13.

5. The following graph shows almost a 60 percent decline in existing home sales between September 1980 and February 1982. Why do you think this happened? Now note that private housing starts displayed roughly the same pattern. Would you generally expect these two series to move together, or is this a coincidence that would not be repeated in other periods?

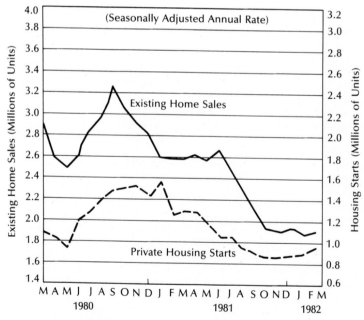

Source: Adapted with permission from National Association of Realtors. *Real Estate Status Report,* March 1982.

Existing Home Sales and Private Housing Starts

References and Further Reading

Aaron, Henry. *Shelter and Subsidies* (Washington, D.C.: Brookings, 1972).

Bailey, Martin J. "A Note on the Economics of Residential Zoning and Urban Renewal." *Land Economics* Vol. 35 (1959): 288–92. The original presentation of the housing-price boundary effects discussed in this chapter.

Clemmer, Richard B., and John C. Simonson. "Trends in Substandard Housing." *AREUEA Journal* 10 (Winter, 1983): 442–464.

Cooke, Timothy, and Bruce W. Hamilton. "Evolution of Urban Housing Stocks: A Model Applied to Baltimore and Houston." *Journal of Urban Economics* Vol. 17 (1984): 317–338.

Courant, Paul. "Racial Prejudice in a Search Model of the Urban Housing Market." *Journal of Urban Economics* Vol. 5 (1978): 329–45. An interesting discussion of the manner in which reasonable house search strategies might lead to extreme segregation.

Crecine, John, Otto Davis, and John Jackson. "Urban Property Markets: Some Empirical Results and Their Implications for Municipal Zoning." *Journal of Law and Economics* Vol. 10 (1967): 79–100. The original study of the relationship between neighboring land uses and land values. This paper spawned a great deal of subsequent research because of its surprising finding that deleterious neighboring land uses do not depress property values.

deLeeuw, Frank, and Raymond Struyk. *The Web of Urban Housing* (Washington, D.C.: Urban Institute, 1975). A simulation model of the urban housing market that takes into account the durability of housing.

Dunn, L. F. "Measuring the Value of Community." *Journal of Urban Economics* Vol. 6 (1979): 371–82.

Dynarski, Mark. "The Economics of Community: Theory and Measurement." Ph.D. diss., Johns Hopkins University, 1981. Discusses and measures the economics of attachment, current residence, and the inertia caused by limited willingness to move.

"HUD Subsidized Housing Overview." *Major Themes and Additional Budget Details: 1983 Budget of the United States Government* (Washington: GPO, 1982). A detailed discussion of current progams, proposed changes, and rationales.

Kain, John F. "Black Suburbanization in the Eighties: A New Beginning or a False Hope?" (Presented at Conference: The Agenda for Metropolitan America, 1984, Sponsored by the Center for Real Estate and Urban Economics, University of California at Berkeley.)

King, A. Thomas, and Peter Mieszkowski. "Racial Discrimination, Segregation, and the Price of Housing." *Journal of Political Economy* Vol. 8 (1973): 590–601.

Margolis, Stephen. "Depreciation of Housing: An Empirical Examination of the Filtering Hypothesis." *Review of Economics and Statistics* Vol. 64 (1982): 90–96.

Mayo, Stephen K., Shirley Mansfield, W. David Warner, and Richard Zwetchkenbaum. *Housing Allowances and Other Rental Assistance Programs—A Comparison Based on the Housing Allowance Demand Experiment* Revised (Cambridge, Mass.: Abt Associates Inc., 1980). A very thorough study comparing the various housing programs that have been either employed or seriously considered in the United States during the last decade.

Mills, Edwin. "Dividing Up the Investment Pie: Have We Overinvested in Housing?" *Business Review* (March–April 1987): 13–23.

Peterson, George. "The Effect of Federal Taxes on Urban Form." *The Prospective City,* ed. A. Solomon (Cambridge, Mass: MIT Press, 1979). Discusses several ways in which peculiarities of the federal tax code influence the housing market. Its topics include abandonment and suburban sprawl.

Peterson, George, and George Reigeluth. "Conservation of the Central City." Urban Institute working paper, 1977.

Roskill Commission. *Report on the Third London Airport* (London: Government of Great Britain, 1970). A Royal Commission report on the feasibility, and possible location, of a new London airport.

Rothenberg, Jerome. "The Nature of Redevelopment Benefits." *Readings in Urban Economics,* eds. M. Edel and J. Rothenberg (New York: Macmillan, 1972).

Sternlieb, George. *The Tenement Landlord* (New Brunswick, N.J.: Rutgers University Press, 1966). An analysis of the economics of tenement ownership.

Sternlieb, George, and Robert W. Burchell. *The Tenement Landlord Revisited* (New Brunswick, N.J.: Rutgers University Press, 1973).

Taeuber, K. E., and A. F. Taeuber. *Negroes in Cities* (Chicago: Aldine Publishing, 1965). One of the first careful and detailed studies of residential segregation patterns. It continues to be a valuable source despite the fact that the data are a bit old.

Tenement Housing Commission of New York. *First Report* (New York: Tenement Housing Commission, 1903). Little statistical analysis, but vivid descriptions and photographs of housing conditions in New York City's tenements at the turn of the century.

Thorton, Craig. "Zoning, Apartments, and Land Use Interactions." Ph.D. diss., Johns Hopkins University, 1978.

Tideman, T. N. "Three Approaches to Improving Urban Land Use." Ph.D. diss., University of Chicago, 1969. Three very readable and provocative essays on the land market and land use interactions.

Weicher, John. *Housing: Federal Policies and Programs* (Washington, D.C.: American Enterprise Institute, 1980). An excellent historical summary of federal housing programs.

Wheaton, William C. "Housing Policies and Urban 'Markets' in Developing Countries: The Egyptian Experience." *Journal of Urban Economics* Vol. 9 (1981): 242–56. A fascinating discussion of the effects of rent control upon the housing market in Cairo.

White, L. J., and M. J. White. "The Tax Subsidy to Owner-Occupied Housing: Who Benefits." *Journal of Public Economics* Vol. 7 (1977): 111–26.

White, M. J. "Property Taxes and Urban Housing Abandonment." *Journal of Urban Economics* Vol. 20 (1986): 312–330. A study of housing abandonment in New York City.

Wienk, Ronald, Clifford Reid, John Simonson, and Frederick Eggers. *Measuring Racial Discrimination in American Housing Markets: The Housing Market Practices Survey* (Washington, D.C.: GPO, 1980) Department of Housing and Urban Development, 1980. A compendium of the results of the survey described in the text.

Yinger, John. "Prejudice and Discrimination in the Urban Housing Market." *Current Issues in Urban Economics,* eds. P. Mieszkowski and M. Straszheim (Baltimore: Johns Hopkins, 1979). A survey article describing current research in the field.

12

Urban Transportation

☐ The theoretical analysis in Part 2 showed that the function of an urban area is to facilitate the exchange of goods and services by proximate locations of diverse economic activities. Firms whose products are exported from the urban area have an incentive to locate near ports, railheads, highway interchanges, or other places from which intercity trade can be conducted economically. Households that provide the work force in export industries or that consume goods imported into the urban area have a similar incentive, as do firms that produce inputs for the export industries or consumer goods for local residents. Thus an urban area consists of large numbers of specialized economic institutions that produce goods and services with large ratios of other inputs to land, and that locate close to each other to facilitate exchange.

The exchange of goods and services entails the movement of goods and people. Thus, the size, structure, and efficiency of an urban area are influenced by the transportation system on which goods and people are moved. *Commuting*—that is, the transportation of people for the exchange of labor services—is the most studied kind of urban transportation. Households also use the urban transportation system for noncommuting trips for shopping, recreation, and social activities. The movement of goods, or freight, within urban areas has been studied much less than the movement of people. Many writers assume explicitly or implicitly that an urban transportation system adequate for commuting is also adequate for all other demands made on it. Although this assumption may be justified for the analysis of an overall urban transportation system, it is not necessarily valid with respect to all the details of the system.

There is a substantial body of engineering research on urban freight transport, but economists have given the topic little attention. Therefore, the bulk of this chapter concerns personal transport (with emphasis on commuting). Following this discussion is a brief section on freight transport.

☐ PERSONAL TRANSPORT

Commuting constitutes about 25 percent of personal urban travel (in miles), with shopping, recreation, and personal trips (largely visiting friends) making up the bulk of the remainder. Commuting is important, however, because it is so concentrated during the morning and evening rush hours. It is commuting that strains the capacity of the transport network, and it primarily is commuting needs that dictate the extent of our road and public transit capacity.

Urban transportation is one of the most interesting examples of a mixed public-private sector in the American economy. The supply side is clearly a public sector responsibility. Streets and highways are constructed, maintained, and owned by governments. Public transit facilities such as buses, subways, and commuter trains are either owned or regulated by governments.

The demand side is more complex. Trucks and cars are privately owned and pay to use the public streets with user fees, such as taxes on motor vehicle fuel and tires, and vehicle registration fees. Public transit riders pay fares. To the extent that both are available, urban residents choose without coercion between private cars and public transit, depending on the combination of fares or fees and service they prefer. In contrast public education (for example) is supplied with an important element of coercion. Children are forced to go to school, and public schools are financed by tax revenues. Thus, parents cannot avoid paying for the public service, even if they refuse to consume it and instead send their children to private schools.

The difference is important. As bad as public education may be, large numbers of people consume it just because they cannot afford to pay for both the public and the private service. The use of private cars (either traveler owned or taxicabs) is generally a viable alternative to the use of public transit systems, however. As will be seen in detail in Chapter 15, central-city poor represent an important exception to this statement regarding the availability of automobiles. If the combination of fares and service is sufficiently bad in public transit systems, many people simply refrain from buying the service and use cars instead. Of course, governments can greatly influence the attractiveness of alternative modes of urban travel by the policies they follow. For example, public transit in the form of a subway system is relatively attractive if it provides frequent, economical service. Likewise, automobile travel is attractive if a system of urban expressways and adequate parking are available.

Thus the basic decisions about the supply of urban transportation modes are the responsibility of the public sector. Consumers, however, choose among available modes according to the terms on which the modes are made available and according to their needs and tastes. The public sector's task is to provide the urban transportation system that best serves the community. An important constraint on the public sector is that transportation services are bought by the public, and they can register dissatisfaction with one mode by purchasing the services of another.

A great debate regarding urban transportation has been under way since the 1960s. The issue is whether public policy should encourage the use of automobiles or public transit for urban commuting. One school of thought believes that only large public investment in mass transit facilities can save central cities from strangulation by congestion and pollution. Rapid inflation of fuel prices in the 1970s provided ammunition for transit advocates. Another school of thought believes that the advantages of the automobile to relatively high income commuters are so great that no viable alternative to investment in urban expressways exists. A third school of thought advocates a balanced urban transportation system, normally interpreted to mean substantial investment in both public transit and urban expressways. Almost inherent in this position is the advocacy of carefully planned and sophisticated pricing schemes to guide choices among modes.

The issues are complex. In part, the complexity results from the availability of several related alternatives. Streets and highways must be available in urban areas, because movement by motor vehicles of practically all intraurban freight is by far the cheapest mode. The same is true for at least some intraurban passengers. To some extent, automobile commuters can share these facilities, as can at least one major form of public transit: buses. The other important kinds of public transit— subways and commuter railroads—require their own rights-of-way, which is impractical for intraurban freight movement, given the great cost advantage of the truck. General railroad rights-of-way, however, can be shared among commuters, interurban freight, and interurban passengers. This debate will be discussed further in the "Cost and Supply of Urban Transit" section.

The details of urban transportation investments must be tailored to the size, structure, and existing transportation facilities of each urban area. For example, transportation investments that are optimum for the Philadelphia metropolitan area may not be appropriate for Los Angeles or Albuquerque. This chapter, therefore, explores the implications of pervasive characteristics of America's urban areas for transportation policy and surveys systematic procedures for evaluating the benefits and costs of alternative transportation systems.

☐ TRENDS IN URBAN TRANSPORTATION

Overall travel in American urban areas has increased rapidly since World War II. Rapid increases in urban population, incomes, automobile ownership, and suburbanization inevitably have led to a rapid growth of both passenger and freight transportation in urban areas. By

Table 12.1 *Urban Travel, 1940 to 1985*

| Year | Public Transit Passengers (In Millions) | | | | | Automobile[b] (In Billions of Vehicle Miles) |
	Railway	Subway[a]	Trolley	Bus	Total	
1940	5,943	2,382	534	4,239	13,098	129.1
1945	9,426	2,698	1,244	9,886	23,254	109.5
1950	3,904	2,264	1,658	9,420	17,246	182.5
1955	1,207	1,870	1,202	7,240	11,529	224.5
1960	463	1,850	657	6,425	9,395	284.8
1965	276	1,858	305	5,814	8,253	378.2
1970	235	1,881	182	5,034	7,332	494.5
1975	124	1,673	78	5,084	6,972	609.6
1980	133	2,108	142	5,837	8,567	671.0
1985	135	2,297	139	6,024	8,948	n.a.

Notes: 1985 data are preliminary.
[a]Includes elevated railways. Data for 1975 and later refer to reclassification as "heavy rail."
[b]Includes taxicabs and motorcycles.
Sources: Data from American Public Transit Association, *Transit Fact Book, 1987,* Washington, D.C., and *Statistical Abstract of the United States,* Washington, D.C.: Government Printing Office, 1987.

far the most dramatic change in urban travel has been the changing mix of modes, however.

Table 12.1 summarizes data on urban travel modes from 1940 to 1985. Public transit and passenger car figures cannot be added, however. The transit data refer to total passengers, while the automobile data refer to vehicle miles. The ideal figures to have would be passenger miles, but they are not available. Automobile travel data for 1985 are not available at all, since the source no longer distinguishes between rural and urban travel. Trip length per transit passenger and passengers per car probably have changed relatively little, so passenger miles today are about proportionate to the figures shown. The factors of proportionality differ among modes, however. Another problem is that the 1945 figures are badly distorted by the effects of World War II. The suspension of automobile production and gasoline rationing caused many travelers to use public transit during the war. The 1940 figures, therefore, are a better base for postwar comparisons.

The stark message of Table 12.1 is that urban automobile travel in 1980 was 5.3 times its 1940 level.[1] Thus the postwar growth of urban travel has been accompanied by a massive shift from public transit to private cars. Data from metropolitan transportation studies suggest that there are about 1.5 passengers per car on an average urban passenger car trip, and the average transit trip is about 5 miles (Tittemore et al.

---

1. Note the 18 percent rise in public transit ridership between 1975 and 1980.

1972). If those averages are applied to the 1980 data in Table 12.1, they indicate that more than 95 percent of passenger miles traveled were by car. Popular writers do not exaggerate when they emphasize the dominance of the automobile in urban travel in the United States.

The postwar decline of public transit travel has been accompanied by shifts in the vehicle mix. Railroads and trolleys have nearly disappeared as modes of urban travel in all but a few American cities. Subway travel declined only moderately from 1940 to 1960, increased somewhat during the 1960s, and grew more rapidly from 1975–85, primarily because of the opening of BART (Bay Area Rapid Transit) in San Francisco and Metro in Washington. Bus travel has been greater since World War II than in 1940. Although still far below its early postwar level, it has increased about 20 percent since bottoming out in 1970.

Much of the urban transportation problem is a peak-load problem resulting from concentration of travel at morning and evening rush hours. (See Figure 12.6 and the accompanying discussion in a later section.) Most rush hour travelers are on their way to or from work, and much concern with urban transportation, therefore, is focused on work trips. Chapter 4 showed that rapid suburbanization of both employment and residences has occurred in the postwar period. Considerable diversity, therefore, should be expected in origins and destinations of work trips. Table 12.2 presents comprehensive data for the ten largest SMSAs as of 1980 with respect to destination by place of residence.

Approximately 26 percent of suburban dwellers commute to the central city (including 6.1 percent who commute to the CBD), as compared to the 28 percent of city dwellers who commute to the suburbs. Many people who live and work in suburbs, and some who live and work in central cities, commute crosstown (for example, around a circumferential highway) instead of toward or away from a CBD. The section in Chapter 7 on "Commuting Patterns" showed that about 87 percent of commuting (for a different sample of cities) is either in the reverse direction or circumferential, rather than toward the CBD. Beyond a doubt, the growth of automobile ownership and improved urban expressways have contributed greatly to the diversity of origins and destinations since World War II. Not only are American suburbs low in density compared with metropolitan areas in other countries, but workplace destinations are also more diverse here than elsewhere. All discussions of public transit must take into account the fact that public transit is relatively inconvenient for reverse-direction and circumferential commutes.

Note that blacks, both city and suburban dwellers, are much more likely to work in the central city than the population as a whole. Almost half of black suburbanites commute to the central city.

Modal choices (that is, decisions about which modes to use) for work trips are somewhat different from modal choices for other kinds of urban travel. Table 12.3 presents some data from 1980. From data in Table 12.1 and facts presented in the text, it can be seen that 95 per-

Table 12.2 *Commuting Patterns in Ten Largest SMSAs*

| | Percent of all People who . . . | | | Percent of all Blacks who . . . | |
	Live in Central City	Live in Suburbs		Live in Central City	Live in Suburbs
Destination			Destination		
CBD	15.4	6.1			
Central City	55.7	20.8	Central City	99.0	49.7
Suburbs	28.8	73.0	Suburbs	1.0	18.6

Source: Calculated from U.S. Department of Commerce, Bureau of the Census. *1980 Census of Population and Housing; Census Tracts.* Tables P-9 and P-14.

cent of urban travel is by automobile, but Table 12.3 shows that slightly less than 60 percent of work trips originating in central cities were by automobile in 1980, and approximately 85 percent of suburb-originating trips were by car.[2] Public transit is much more heavily used by blacks than by the population as a whole, though the difference is much less striking for suburbanites than central-city dwellers. Thus, automobile travel dominates metropolitan commuting, but less than it dominates other urban travel. Within metropolitan areas, the vast majority of those who commute by public transit either live or work, or both live and work, in central cities.

The data presented in Table 12.3 suggest that the major use of public transit is for commuting to (or, at least, toward) the CBD. For other commutes and for nonwork travel, the automobile is the overwhelming mode of choice. The reasons for this will be examined when discussing cost and supply.

In most metropolitan areas, the worst road congestion is in central cities. As can be calculated from Table 4.4, central-city employment has increased only slightly in the postwar period. Congestion, however, has become worse, at least according to popular accounts. It seems paradoxical that central-city congestion should worsen during a period when its employment has hardly changed.

Part of the resolution of the paradox is in the data in Table 12.1. To the extent that congestion has worsened, the cause has been the massive switch from public transit to automobile travel in urban areas. Trains and subways do not use streets and highways, and trolleys and buses use them much more passenger-intensively than do cars. Thus, the switch from public transit to cars increases travel on urban roads, and it changes use to a mode that generates more congestion. Urban road capacity has increased since the early 1950s, mainly as a result of

---

2. If the sample underlying Tables 12.2 and 12.3 were expanded to include some smaller cities, the relative importance of public transit would decline somewhat, even for the central cities.

Table 12.3 *Commuting Mode in Ten Largest SMSAs*

| | Percent of all People who . . . | | | Percent of all Blacks who . . . | |
	Live in Central City	Live in Suburbs		Live in Central City	Live in Suburbs
Mode					
Drive alone	44.6	70.2	Drive alone	42.5	63.4
Carpool	15.3	19.1	Carpool	16.1	22.0
Bus	15.0	3.7	Public transit	41.4	14.6
Subway	16.7	3.0			
Walk	8.4	3.9			

Source: Calculated from U.S. Department of Commerce, Bureau of the Census. *1980 Census of Population and Housing; Census Tracts.* Tables P-9 and P-14.

the construction of urban parts of the interstate highway system. The increased capacity has not kept pace with the rapid increase in urban automobile travel, however.

The same data in Table 12.1 suggest that, even in the absence of shifts in government policy, urban road congestion may have passed its peak. With 95 percent of urban passenger travel already by car, it is impossible that the percentage will increase much in coming years. If, in addition, central-city employment continues to grow only slightly, it seems likely that demands placed on central-city streets and highways will grow little. If public transit use increases even moderately, congestion may decrease. In addition, it will soon be seen that there is substantial room for improvement in the efficiency with which existing facilities are used. If some of these potential gains are realized through changes in pricing and other policies, congestion also may be expected to fall.

☐ DEMAND FOR URBAN TRANSPORTATION

Concern about energy and environmental problems increased the intensity of the debate about urban transportation during the 1970s. Many people believe that high prices and unreliable supplies of gasoline, as well as pollution problems resulting from urban automobile driving, imply that more use should be made of public transit and less of automobiles in urban transportation. This is a complex matter that cannot be settled in this chapter. It is possible, though, to indicate what is known and what needs to be studied to obtain answers.

As with the market for any commodity or service, there is a demand side and a supply or production side to the market for urban transportation services. Basic transportation facilities typically are constructed and owned by governments, and cost data are made available by engineering studies undertaken to plan new facilities. The demand side, however, is subtle, because of the complex interaction between government and private decision making. Only in the 1970s have economists undertaken high-quality demand studies.[3] The analysis will be couched in terms of **work trips,** since that is the subject of most available studies, although the analysis that follows also applies to nonwork trips.

It is useful to divide work trips into three parts, referred to as suburban collection, line haul, and downtown distribution. **Suburban or residential collection** refers to the trip from the residence to the vehicle on which the longest part of the trip is made, regardless of where the worker lives. If the trip is by car, suburban collection entails no more than a walk to the garage or street. If the trip is by bus, suburban collection refers to the walk to the bus stop. If the trip is by rail, suburban collection may consist of a walk or a car or bus ride to the station at which the worker boards the train or subway. **Line haul** refers to the trip by car, bus, subway, or train from the suburban collection point to the downtown distribution point. **Downtown distribution** refers to the part of the trip after departing the line haul vehicle. It usually involves walking, but it may entail a bus or taxicab ride for some workers.[4]

Modal choice refers to choice of line haul vehicle. In contemporary American urban areas, the realistic choices are between car, bus, and subway. The mode chosen by a worker, however, depends on characteristics of all three parts of the trip. Ignoring this fact is the cause of much confusion in thinking about urban transportation. People sometimes conclude that subways are better modal choices than cars because subways are both faster and cheaper than cars. Whether they are faster and cheaper will be analyzed later. The point to be made here is that subway commuting entails suburban collection and downtown distribution trips that may be much longer or more irksome than those entailed by automobile commuting. If so, it will affect the modal choice of a rational commuter.

Trip characteristics that appear to have the greatest influence on modal choice are the time and money costs and comfort of each part of the trip. Certain modal characteristics, such as privacy and comfort, also may affect modal choice. In many studies, such data are either unavailable or indicate little effect on modal choice. They will be ignored here, but they easily can be included in Equation (12.1) in the next paragraph. In addition, certain characteristics of the worker, such as age, sex, and income, may affect modal choice. Once again, other variables can be included; however, income has been shown to be important, and only it will be included here.

---

3. Good references are Domencich and McFadden (1975) and Mohring (1976), on which much of this section is based.

4. A few commuting trips do not fit easily into this classification. Some workers walk or ride bicycles from their residences to their workplaces. Readers can make the necessary changes in the text to cover these possibilities.

What variable should be used to represent modal choice? There are advantages to the use of q_{ij}, the probability that a person of characteristics i chooses commuting mode j. Then the modal choice equation can be written as follows:

$$q_{ij} = f(pS_{ij}, pH_{ij}, pD_{ij}, tS_{ij}, tH_{ij}, tD_{ij}, y_i). \tag{12.1}$$

S refers to the suburban collection part of the trip; H, to the line haul; and D, to the downtown distribution. The symbol p refers to the money cost of the part of the trip indicated by the subscript, and t refers to the time cost. The symbol pS might be bus fare for getting to the suburban rail or subway stop. The symbol pH is the fare on a line haul public transit vehicle or the cost of operating a car. Transit fares are set by transit companies. Operating costs of cars are the sum of depreciation, fuel, and other costs, and they might be $0.20 per mile in the mid-1980s. The symbol y refers to income.

Care must be taken at this point. If the household would own the car anyway, interest and most depreciation should not be assigned as components of commuting cost. For such households, $0.20 per mile overstates the true operating cost by as much as 30 percent. For the other case, where the car is needed only because of commuting, properly calculated operating cost is closer to $0.30. The $0.20 figure stated here is a rough average. Of course, a unique suburban collection or downtown distribution mode does not correspond to a line haul mode. For example, it might be possible to drive a car to a suburban railway station and leave it there or to take a bus there. For simplicity, Equation (12.1) ignores such choices.

Each p and t depends on both i and j. They depend on the person (i), because commuters have different origins and destinations, so the money and time cost of the trip varies from person to person, as well as by mode. Income (y) depends only on the person.

Domencich and McFadden (1975) have shown how Equation (12.1) can be used to analyze modal choices. In a large sample q_{ij} can be replaced by N_{ij}/N_i, where N_i is the number of people in group i (they live and work in similar areas and have similar incomes), and N_{ij} is the number of them who choose mode j. Thus N_{ij}/N_i is the fraction of the people in group i who choose mode j.

Estimates of equations similar to Equation (12.1) have taught economists important lessons about modal choice. Most important is that people make substitutions between fares and travel time. Suppose, for example, that commuters who earn $10.00 per hour are observed to switch from bus to car if the time saving is ten minutes, even though the car trip costs $0.50 more than the bus trip. Then the commuters are observed to value travel time at about $0.05 per minute, or at $3.00 per hour. In fact, this result is typical. Commuters typically value travel time in line haul vehicles at between one-third and one-half their wage rates.[5] Several studies, however, have shown that time spent walking

5. See Hensher (1977) for a discussion of estimation techniques and evidence.

to or waiting at transit stops is valued at two to four times the value placed on line haul travel time. Exposure to weather, noise, and fatigue probably account for the high value placed on such suburban collection times. Presumably, the same is true of downtown distribution times, although evidence is lacking.

☐ CONGESTION AND PRICING

Controversy surrounds the pricing of both automobile and transit use in urban areas. Most controversy pertains to whether one mode or another is or should be subsidized. To understand these issues, it is necessary to investigate the effect of congestion on optimum pricing policy.

It has already been noted that congestion slows travel. The theoretical analysis is the same for all modes. There are many cities in the world in which buses congest streets, but in the United States, emphasis is properly placed on congestion from cars.[6]

The basic theoretical issue can be posed in a simple example. Consider a divided, multilane road stretch with no access or exits between points A and B. Suppose cars enter the road at A at a uniform rate per hour. Even if the rate is small, a maximum travel speed is imposed by legal speed limits and safety considerations. Associated with the maximum speed is a cost per vehicle mile of travel. It includes both time and operating cost, and it depends on the maximum travel speed and on the characteristics of the vehicle. Now suppose there is an increase in the rate at which vehicles enter at A. When the number of vehicles entering per hour becomes great enough, congestion occurs and travel speed falls.

The critical rate of entry at which congestion begins depends on characteristics of the road such as its width, grade, curves, and surface. On any road stretch, however, congestion occurs if the number of vehicles is great enough, because there are too many cars to permit the headway necessary for safety at high speeds, and cars must slow to a speed consistent with the available headway. Automobile operating costs are relatively insensitive to speed, but time costs are inversely proportional to speed. Thus, slow travel caused by large numbers of cars entering at A increases the cost per vehicle mile of travel from A to B.

The foregoing ideas are illustrated in Figure 12.1, where T is the number of vehicles entering per hour at point A, and $AC(T)$ is the average cost per vehicle mile of travel between points A and B. $AC(T)$ is constant for values of T up to T_0, which can be called the *design capacity* of the road. Beyond T_0, $AC(T)$ rises rapidly with T. Economists have estimated several specific forms of $AC(T)$.

---

6. It will be shown that trucks also add a substantial amount to urban congestion.

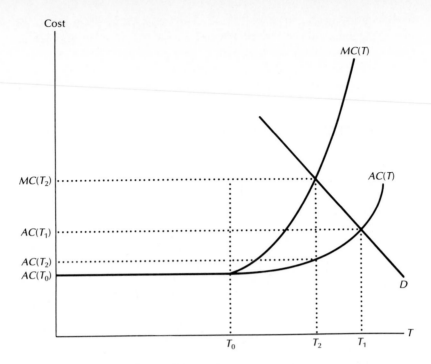

Figure 12.1 *Transport Cost and Demand*

Now suppose, in the spirit of Equation (12.1), that the number of users of the road from point A to point B depends on the cost of travel. If travel on the road is too costly, people use a different route or mode, alter travel time, or alter their places of work or residence to avoid the trip. The number of people who make the trip as a function of the travel cost is the demand curve for travel on the road from A to B, designated D in Figure 12.1. The equilibrium travel on the road is then T_1 vehicles per hour—the number of travelers willing to pay the cost of the trip. The equilibrium cost per vehicle is $AC(T_1)$. $AC(T_0)$ is the cost per vehicle in the absence of congestion, and $AC(T_1) - AC(T_0)$ is the congestion cost per vehicle.

With a constant rate of entry at point A, all vehicles travel at the same speed and incur the same cost, or $AC(T_1)$. Thus, $AC(T_1)$ is the total cost of travel for those making the trip divided by the number of travelers, or the average cost per traveler. Elementary price theory textbooks show that if an average cost curve is rising, the corresponding marginal cost curve must be above it. In the present context, *marginal cost* means the increase in travel cost to all travelers resulting from an increase in the number of vehicles using the road. In Figure 12.1, marginal cost is the curve designated $MC(T)$. It is important to understand exactly why $MC(T)$ is above $AC(T)$. If T exceeds T_0, speed decreases with increases in T, and $AC(T)$ therefore exceeds $AC(T - 1)$. Since everyone travels at the same speed, however, everyone goes slower if T cars enter per hour than if $T - 1$ enter. Thus the addition of a Tth user imposes costs on all T users because of the reduced speed. $MC(T)$ exceeds $AC(T)$ by the amount of the increased costs imposed on other travelers by the Tth entrant.

Expressing this in an equation,

$$MC(T) = AC(T) + [AC(T) - AC(T - 1)] \times (T - 1). \quad (12.2)$$

Recall that the marginal cost is the increase in the total cost resulting from one additional road user. The right-hand side of Equation (12.2) gives the components of this increase in total cost. First, the marginal user himself or herself incurs the cost of the trip, or $AC(T)$. In addition, the marginal user raises the trip cost of other users by slowing traffic. The total additional cost is the amount by which each other traveler's cost is increased, or $AC(T) - AC(T - 1)$, times the number of affected travelers, or $(T - 1)$. Clearly, the gap between average and marginal costs widens as the number of travelers (victims of congestion) increases. Thus Figure 12.1 is realistic; as T increases, so does the spread between average and marginal costs.

The excess of $MC(T)$ over $AC(T)$ is an external diseconomy of the type defined in Chapter 8. Each traveler perceives and bears the average cost, or $AC(T)$. Travelers have no reason to consider the cost their travel imposes on others. Therefore, the equilibrium number of travelers (T_1) equates average cost to the price of the trip. As Chapter 8 showed, the situation represents an inefficient allocation of resources in that too many people use the road and there is too much congestion. T_2 entrants per hour, which equates marginal cost to price, represents efficient road use. Of course, if D intersects $AC(T)$ to the left of T_0 in Figure 12.1, there is no congestion and no misallocation of resources.

This analysis implies that a special method of rationing the use of the road is needed. How can it be done? Ignoring collection costs, efficient road use would be restored by charging a road-use toll equal to $MC(T_2) - AC(T_2)$ per vehicle mile in Figure 12.1. The appropriate toll equals the excess of social marginal cost over the cost perceived by the traveler, at the optimum use (T_2).

The actual collection of an efficient congestion toll is extremely difficult politically, and it poses some technical difficulties as well, for reasons that will be discussed. The nature of the argument on efficient tolls is important, however, so for the moment the discussion ignores the problems associated with toll collection.

The congestion toll is efficient, because it discourages the use of a scarce resource; it encourages either doing without altogether or substituting other means of achieving the same end (other routes or modes, or other times, in the case of urban travel).[7] This means that it is impor-

---

7.   In the long run, efficient transport pricing also shifts the location of some economic activities away from the most congested areas.

tant for a congestion toll to vary with time of day (since congestion varies with time of day), as well as with location (since congestion is worse in some places than others). To state it differently, one of the important roles of an efficient congestion toll is to discourage people from taking shopping trips during rush hour. Only if tolls decline (or are removed) during off-peak hours do they properly encourage substitution between peak and off-peak travel times.

Congestion Tolls and Efficient Highway Investment[*]

It has been argued that the role of efficient pricing of road capacity is to internalize the congestion externality. Among noneconomists, however, there is a widespread view that the use of tolls (or any prices, for that matter) is justified only to pay for the facility. Tolls, according to this view, should only cover interest, depreciation, and maintenance on the road itself.

In an important set of cases, there is a neat reconciliation between these two views, and the reconciliation is contained in the following statement: under constant returns to scale in transport, if the economically efficient level of road capacity has been built, the optimum congestion toll is just sufficient to cover the cost of the facility (interest, maintenance, and depreciation).

To see this, look at Figure 12.2, which is a reproduction of Figure 12.1 with some extra cost curves included. In going from Figure 12.1 to Figure 12.2, the first thing to note is that the average cost curve of Figure 12.1, $AC(T)$, is labeled in Figure 12.2 as the average *variable* cost curve, $AVC(T)$. It is so labeled in recognition of the fact that the cost it depicts does not include the cost of the road capacity, but only the (variable) costs incurred by the users themselves. The cost of the road capacity is depicted as a standard average fixed cost curve, or $AFC(T)$. The curve shows how the average fixed cost varies with the number of users; it declines as a rectangular hyperbola, because with a rise in T, fixed cost per user declines. The vertical sum of $AVC(T)$ and $AFC(T)$ gives the U-shaped average cost curve, $AC(T)$. This curve is the standard U-shaped *short-run* average cost curve of producer theory.

If the demand curve is D, it has already been seen (using Figure 12.1) that the optimum congestion toll is t. This will bring in revenue of $t \times T_2$. The total cost of financing and maintaining the road is $AFC(T) \times T_2$, which is the shaded box between the $AVC(T)$ and the $AC(T)$ curves. As drawn, the toll revenue exceeds the cost of the road.

With the realization that road capacity can be changed through investment, it now can be asked whether society would be better off with an expansion of road capacity; in other words, do the benefits of in-

---

[*] This section is fairly difficult, and some readers may want to skip it. The theory in this section is based on work done by Herbert Mohring (1965).

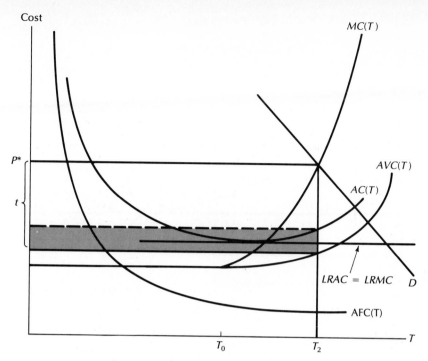

Figure 12.2 *Road Cost and Demand, Showing Capital Cost*

vestment exceed the costs? Under constant returns to scale, the long-run average cost curve, $LRAC(T)$, is horizontal, depicting the fact that expanding road capacity and users by the same percentage leaves the average cost unchanged. Thus, the $LRAC(T)$ curve is also the long-run marginal cost curve, $LRMC(T)$.[8]

The height of the $LRAC(T)$ curve—which is equal to the $LRMC(T)$ curve—measures the cost of an increment of urban travel, assuming that it is done using the optimum amount of road capacity; the height of the demand curve measures the willingness to pay for an increment of urban travel. In the situation depicted in Figure 12.2, at the level of demand chosen with an optimum toll, the willingness to pay (P^*) is greater than the long-run marginal cost (which equals the long-run average cost), so expansion of capacity is socially desirable. This excess of willingness to pay over the long-run marginal cost will prevail until arriving at a position like that depicted in Figure 12.3, which looks

8. In terms of the curves of Figures 12.1 and 12.2, the upward-sloping portions of the $AC(T)$ and $MC(T)$ curves are shifted to the right, and the $AFC(T)$ curve is shifted away from the origin, yielding a new $AC(T)$ curve that is shifted to the right. Under constant returns, the minimum point on the new $AC(T)$ curve has the same height as the minimum point of the old one. As the $LRAC(T)$ curve is the envelope of these $AC(T)$ curves, it will be horizontal under constant returns. The horizontal $LRAC(T)$ curve coincides with the $LRMC(T)$ curve, since the marginal is always pulling the average toward it.

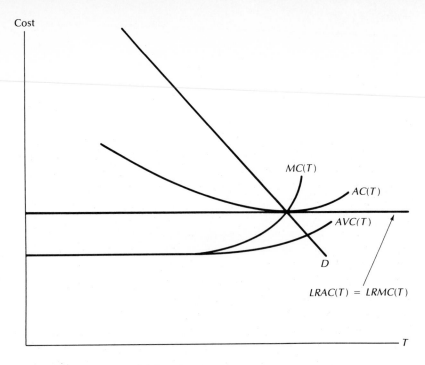

Cost

MC(T)

AC(T)

AVC(T)

D

LRAC(T) = LRMC(T)

T

Figure 12.3 *Optimum Road Capacity*

like the (efficient) zero-profit, long-run equilibrium of a standard competitive firm.

Now capacity expansion has caused a move along the demand curve to the point where willingness to pay no longer exceeds long-run marginal cost. Thus, further investment would not be socially justified. As can be seen, this is precisely the point at which the congestion toll just equals the average fixed cost; that is, toll revenue covers the cost of the facility and no more. This same result can be stated somewhat differently: under constant returns to scale, when capacity investment has been carried out to the optimum level, the optimum congestion toll is also a fair market rent for the use of the facility.[9]

Spatial Variation in Optimum Congestion

Every observer knows that congestion tends to be worse in central cities than in suburbs and worse in suburbs than in the countryside. What is less well appreciated is that congestion *should* be worse in central cities. Congestion is the substitution of the commuter's time

---

9. Of course, things do not work out so neatly if the *LRAC(T)* curve is not horizontal (that is, if there are not constant returns to scale). Scholars disagree on this point. Keeler et al. (1975) found constant returns for highways; Vickrey (1963) and Walters (1961) found decreasing returns; and Meyer, Kain, and Wohl (1965) found increasing returns. Advanced students might want to explore the relationship between capital cost and long-run optimum tolls under these alternative assumptions regarding returns to scale.

Cost

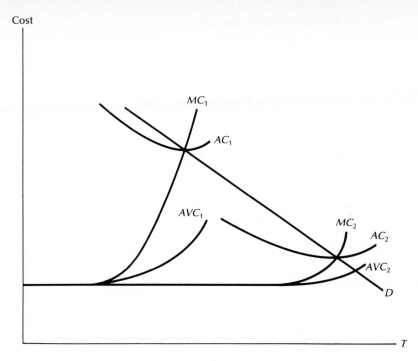

Figure 12.4 *Variation of Optimum Congestion with Land Cost*

for land; it is the commuting analogue to the substitution of capital for land as represented in tall buildings. In short, congestion is one way of economizing on land when it is scarce, and, as already seen, it is more scarce in central than in remote locations.

The relationship between congestion and distance from the CBD can be seen by studying the result previously derived: the optimum congestion toll is a fair market rent for the facility. Since land is an important component in a road network, the cost of the road rises with proximity to the CBD. Hence, a toll sufficient to cover road costs also must be higher close to the CBD. Since this is the same as the congestion toll, however, it means that the congestion toll also must be higher. Figure 12.4 depicts the optimum toll-and-investment outcome (for a given demand curve) where land is cheap (AC_2, MC_2, and AVC_2) and where land is expensive (AC_1, MC_1, and AVC_1). Clearly, the optimum decision where land is expensive is to have more congested roads and less capacity.

Keeler et al. (1975) used this theory to estimate the optimum rush hour toll for suburban roads ($0.09 to $0.25 per vehicle mile, depending on details of assumptions) and for central-city freeways ($0.32 to $0.91) for San Francisco.[10] (These figures have been converted into 1987 dollars.)

10. San Francisco is more congested than many cities of comparable size and has higher land value, presumably because of its topography. Thus, optimum congestion fees in other large cities probably would be somewhat lower.

Realistic Pricing Possibilities

Subject to the uncertainties inherent in the estimates, the Keeler et al. findings tell us that suburban road users impose congestion costs on others of about $.10 to $0.25 per mile on the average, and up to $0.90 per mile at the most highly congested times and places. It would be worthwhile to charge tolls to force consumers to recognize these costs so long as the act of collecting the tolls is not more expensive than the original damage.

Tolls. As noted, the ideal congestion toll should vary with time of day to encourage people to travel during off-peak times. It also should vary by location to encourage people to use less congested routes. The standard mechanism for collecting tolls is the familiar tollbooth, but this is impractical for most urban congestion pricing. Tollbooths use a large amount of land and disrupt traffic (and may well be more disruptive than the inefficient congestion they are trying to alleviate). In addition, they should be fairly closely spaced to allow for geographic variation in tolls. The ideal condition for using tollbooths to collect congestion tolls that vary by time of day is a fairly heavily traveled limited-access highway or a bridge. Here tolls can be collected cheaply and, using modern technology, with a minimum of traffic disruption. For many routes, however, the benefits do not justify the costs of administration and traffic disruption.

The major proposed alternative to tollbooths is automatic vehicle identification (AVI)—an electronic device on each vehicle that registers travel past certain points on a road network equipped with sensing devices. At the end of the month all vehicle owners are sent statements of urban travels by location and time of day, and they are billed accordingly. Of course, there are many problems with such a proposal, but resource cost is not among the major problems.[11] One study estimates the total cost per one-way trip at $0.007.[12]

It would be quite feasible in many cities to establish time-of-day pricing for congested roads.[13] For whatever reason, however, time-of-day pricing for urban travel seems to have little political support. This

11. How to deal with occasional visitors (and, for that matter, how to apprehend operators without metering devices) and whether the system would be mandatory (some people object, on privacy grounds, to the creation of a record of travel patterns) are two problems that have been discussed.

12. For a detailed discussion of congestion pricing possibilities and problems, see Bhatt (1976).

13. In the United States there is no use of AVI and essentially no use of pricing of any sort to discourage road use during congested times and places. Such pricing is used, however, in other countries. Beginning in 1975, Singapore doubled its daytime parking fees and required a special license to enter the downtown area during the peak period. The plan is discussed briefly by Bhatt (1976) and in more detail by Holland and Watson (1978). In addition, time-of-day pricing exists in the United States for many goods other than urban transport, such as restaurants, theaters, telephone service, and, in some cases, electricity.

has led to a discussion of other pricing policies that would approximate the efficient pricing previously discussed.

Gasoline taxes. In general, urban roads are more congested than rural, so some people propose higher gasoline taxes in urban areas. The optimum gasoline tax would be very large by current standards. At an average congestion cost of about $0.20 per mile under optimum conditions and average gas mileage of about 15 miles per gallon, the optimum tax would be $3.00 per gallon, or about $45 per tank.[14]

The problem with this approach is that it discourages all urban automobile travel, not just the roughly 25 percent that takes place under congested conditions. This could be quite important. The demand for nonwork trips is much more price elastic than that for work trips. Therefore, a gasoline tax might result in a drastic reduction in nonwork trips (when roads are uncongested anyway) and leave work trips relatively unchanged. Also remember that an efficient price structure would (among other things) encourage people to shift travel to less congested times of day. A gasoline tax obviously cannot do this.

CBD parking taxes. It is possible to impose a tax on CBD parking that would vary with time of day in such a way that all-day parking would be much more expensive than evening or midday parking. Clearly, this discourages driving to the CBD for work and encourages car pools and public transit.[15] With a 16-mile round-trip commute and an optimum toll of $0.20 per mile, the optimum parking tax would be about $3.20. The advantage of this system over the gasoline tax is that it can be restricted to the highly congested CBD and to people who travel during rush hour. Thus, unlike the gasoline tax, this system encourages at least some types of efficient time and route substitution. A disadvantage is that it does not vary with length of commute. This disadvantage is not particularly serious. The greatest unpriced congestion is generally on routes fairly near the CBD. Long-distance commuters accumulate most of their long distance on relatively uncongested suburban roads; hence, failure to charge for this is not of great consequence. Another disadvantage is that the parking tax has no effect on drivers who simply pass through the CBD during rush hour. (During the morning rush hour, about one-third of vehicles traveling on Baltimore CBD streets are simply passing through, according to the Baltimore City Planning Department Traffic Study of 1983.)

Public transit subsidization. For public transit, it is fairly easy to charge tolls that vary with time and place, since the collection of the tolls is an integral part of providing the service anyway. Another problem arises in this instance, however. In the absence of efficient road

---

14. If the difference in gas prices was too great, it would pay city residents to drive to the country to buy gas. At $30 per tank, this is a real possibility for some drivers.

15. It also might encourage firms to relocate in the suburbs.

pricing for automobile users, congestion tolls for public transit might cause the wrong kind of substitution—namely, toward automobiles rather than toward different routes or times of day. In other words, a move toward marginal cost pricing for one mode might not lead to an efficiency gain. It is not certain that marginal cost pricing improves efficiency except when all modes of travel at all times of day are subject to marginal cost pricing. Therefore, many observers believe that rush hour public transit fares should be below marginal cost so long as rush hour highway pricing is below marginal cost to avoid distorting the modal choice decision.

Although this may well be better than marginal cost pricing of public transit and a subsidy to automobile travel (through the lack of a congestion toll), further welfare gains could be realized if it were feasible to have marginal cost pricing for all modes. With no congestion toll for automobiles and with subsidized prices for transit, all (rush hour) travel is priced below cost. The first result of this is that people travel too much. The second result, as Chapter 15 will discuss, is that urban areas are more decentralized than they otherwise would be. (This effect, as will be seen, is rather modest.)

☐ COST AND SUPPLY OF URBAN TRANSIT

Nearly all people in the United States get to work by automobile, bus, or subway. An important question for planners is this: which systems, if properly designed, would do the job most economically? In addressing this question it is important to consider all costs, including out-of-pocket, time, and pollution costs. There are obvious trade-offs among these elements of cost; out-of-pocket and pollution costs would be very low if everyone walked to work, but the average commute would take about two hours. Thus, the now-standard procedure for comparing costs among modes begins with an assignment of dollar values to time and pollution costs, based on available statistical evidence. Then all costs are denominated in dollars, and the least expensive mode can be arrived at more straightforwardly.

Urban travel analysis examines the cost of travel along a *corridor*—basically, an artery from a suburban region into the CBD. The cost comparison then looks at the full costs of travel along the corridor via each mode, assuming the optimum use of available technology for that mode.

Automobile

The cost of an automobile trip is made up of the following components: operating, time, roadway, pollution, and parking costs.[16] For a

---

16. Recall that with an efficient system, the proper charge for the roadway is also a proper congestion toll, and congestion need not be listed as a separate cost.

given number of users per hour, the only important trade-off is between time and roadway costs (with more roadway, people can drive faster). For a given amount of traffic, engineering studies tell how much extra speed can be obtained with any extra investment in road capacity. This gives sufficient information to calculate the cost-minimizing way of carrying out automobile-based commuting. Empirically, the most important feature of an automobile-based system is that there are *no scale economies* beyond very modest densities of travel.

Bus and Subway

The analyses for bus and subway systems are similar to each other, although obviously the numbers are different.[17] As in the case of automobiles, the cost components are operating, time, roadway, and pollution costs (but no parking costs). The relationship among operating, time, and roadway costs is much more subtle, however. Consider what is involved in a bus trip when there is a given volume of demand for travel along the corridor. Suburban collection requires that people first get to the bus stop and then wait for the bus; the cost of this phase depends on the distance to the bus stop and the headway, or time, between scheduled buses. More closely spaced stops reduce distance to the bus stop, but they increase the number of times the bus stops and, therefore, increase the time cost once the riders get on the bus. Running buses more frequently reduces headway but increases the number of stops a bus makes before it gets full (or increases the fare it must charge to compensate for running half-full).[18]

After the line haul part of the bus trip, which occurs as the full bus travels along a freeway to the CBD, downtown passenger distribution takes place. Costs of downtown distribution are much like residential collection costs; there is a trade-off among the number of stops, travel speed, and the required walk.

The suburban collection and downtown distribution portions of bus and subway trips are subject to an important element of *scale economies*.[19] As demand increases, buses can be filled by making fewer residential stops or running with closer headways. Either of these reduces the time cost of this portion of the trip (and, as will be seen, the time cost of this portion is a major component of the total cost of a bus or subway trip).

17. One difference between bus and subway systems is that a bus system can use a road network that also can be used by others (cars and trucks). This does not mean, however, that there are no road capacity costs associated with a bus system.

18. Walters (1982) states that this problem can be overcome in large measure by using smaller buses.

19. Obviously, a bus has scale economies in that the demand must be sufficient to fill the bus (a subway also has these economies, although on a larger scale). As will be seen, however, the scale economies associated with the mode extend far beyond this very modest size.

Buses and subways are inherently inferior to the automobile in the residential collection and downtown distribution portions of the trip because of the necessity of making several stops and the imposition of waiting costs upon riders. The automobile is inferior as a line haul vehicle, however, because subways (sometimes) travel faster, and buses have lower operating and roadway costs per passenger. Public transit's scale economies in residential collection and downtown distribution suggest the possibility that beyond some scale, these modes can offer cheaper overall transport than the automobile.

With available technological information, it is possible to calculate the minimum possible total per-passenger cost of a bus or subway trip for any given density of travel demand. Unlike automobile travel, the cost for buses and subways depends on the number of people per hour demanding travel in the corridor because of scale economies in suburban collection and downtown distribution.

Comparative Costs

Among the most careful cost comparisons is that of Keeler et al. (1975); Figure 12.5 depicts a representative set of their conclusions. For a 6-mile line haul trip (the average one-way commute in major American cities is just over 8 miles), the automobile is the most economical mode at demand densities of less than 2000 passengers per hour, but at any greater density a bus network is cheaper. A subway (San Francisco's BART, in this case) is competitive with automobile travel when demand along the corridor reaches a bit over 20,000 passengers per hour. Even at 30,000 passengers per hour, however, the subway mode is about three times as expensive as a bus system.[20]

In the early 1960s, only New York City had an average corridor density of greater than 40,000 passengers per hour, and only Chicago was between 30,000 and 40,000. Five cities were between 13,000 and 30,000 (Philadelphia, Boston, Washington, Los Angeles, and San Francisco). Thirteen more cities had corridor densities in excess of 6000 passengers per hour (Meyer, Kain, and Wohl [1965], Table 25). Since that time, corridor travel densities have fallen significantly because of employment decentralization. For these twenty cities and possibly a few more, a cost-minimizing bus system is cheaper than an optimum automobile system *for persons who work in the CBD*. For all but New York City and Chicago, travel densities are generally not great enough to make bus service competitive for non-CBD workers.

The conclusion is that for roughly the top twenty urban areas (basically those with populations larger than one million), an optimum bus system is the cheapest way to deliver workers to the CBD. Except un-

---

20. Different assumptions regarding the interest rate, the opportunity cost of time, and the dollar cost of air pollution have only modest effects on the curves; the overall conclusions do not change.

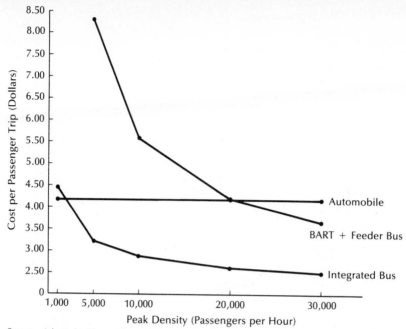

Source: Adapted with permission from Keeler, Theodore; Small, Kenneth; Cluff, George; Finke, Jeffrey; Merewitz, Leonard; Pozdena, Randall, *The Full Costs of Urban Transport*, (Berkeley, Ca.: Institute of Urban and Regional Development, University of California, Berkeley Monograph No. 21, Part III, 1975):128.

Figure 12.5 *Comparative Costs of a Six-Mile Line Haul Trip Plus Collection and Distribution (Interest = 12 percent; Time Value = $3 in Vehicle, $9 in Walking and Waiting)*

der special conditions, the automobile is a cheaper mode for smaller cities, for nonwork travel, and for non-CBD work travel.

These calculations are slightly biased in favor of mass transit. They assume that the systems studied will be used only for work trips and will remain idle for the remainder of the day.[21] As Figure 12.6 demonstrates, this assumption is more valid for public transit than for automobiles. Almost all nonwork trips are made by automobile for a variety of reasons. First, origins and destinations are much more diverse than for work trips, so public transit routes rarely are convenient. Second, as the density of demand drops during nonpeak hours, the optimum service frequency declines, which increases waiting time for public transit. Third, the automobile is used to transport purchases of shopping trips. Fourth, many nonwork trips are made by families. The cost of operating an automobile does not rise with the number of passengers, but bus fares are charged per passenger.

The peaking problem revealed in Figure 12.6 is the source of one of the major financial difficulties facing public transit. Most transit sys-

---

21. Actually, Keeler et al. (1975) do assign a bit of the capital cost of the road-based and subway systems to nonpeak users.

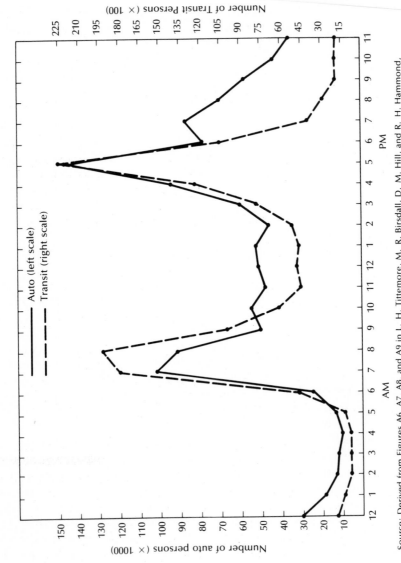

Source: Derived from Figures A6, A7, A8, and A9 in L. H. Tittemore, M. R. Birsdall, D. M. Hill, and R. H. Hammond, *An Analysis of Urban Area Travel by Time of Day* (Boston: Peat, Marwick, Mitchell and Co., 1972).

Figure 12.6 *Number of Auto and Transit Persons in Motion: St. Louis, 1970*

tems are required to operate close to twenty-four hours a day, even though they run nearly empty during nonrush hours. It is possible to cut service frequency during off-peak times, but this further discourages demand by increasing waiting time. For a transit system to operate without a subsidy, it must cover its capital costs (and even much of those operating costs that arise from off-peak operation) from its rush hour traffic.

Subway versus bus. Keeler et al. (1975) found a bus system less costly than a subway system even for corridor densities of 30,000 passengers per mile (the highest density studied).[22] The conclusion is that subway construction is not economically justified; it does not follow that cities should stop using the subways that are already in place (although, in some cases, this also may be true). The studies do indicate—quite forcefully—that none of the subways constructed in the 1960s and 1970s operates with a cost even approaching that of a well-designed bus system.[23]

Numerical example. The following example shows why it is so difficult for mass transit to compete with automobile travel except under ideal conditions. First, calculate the cost of a rush hour automobile trip to a CBD (the left side of Table 12.4) and then the cost of a bus trip (the right side of Table 12.4). The automobile is assumed to carry 1.5 people on the average. The average automobile commute in major American cities takes just under twenty minutes and, as was already noted, is about 8 miles long. Based on numbers already referred to, the optimum toll for this trip would be about $1.50; the value of the commuter's time, at $3.00 per hour, would be about $1.00.[24] Vehicle operation costs about $1.20, and parking, $1.50 (parking at $3 per day is split between the morning and afternoon trips). Multiply toll, operating, and parking cost by two-thirds to convert them from per-vehicle to per-capita costs. This gives a trip cost of $3.80.

The bus trip begins with a walk to the bus stop and a wait, totaling ten minutes ($1.25 at $8.00 per hour for walking and waiting time). On-bus time is assumed to be thirty minutes at $3.00 per hour—ten minutes longer than in-car time to account for the fact that the bus must make other stops and take a somewhat circuitous route to pick up and dis-

22. As can be seen, the dominance of bus over subway will continue well above 30,000 passengers per mile unless subway costs begin to decline very rapidly at higher densities.

23. The Keeler et al. (1975) work and other studies by economists ask how to most efficiently use existing technology. The studies, by necessity, ignore the possibility that current subway systems (basically, BART and Washington's Metro) have not been engineered efficiently. Vickrey believes that subways could be constructed much more cheaply than they are, and that taking this into account would tip the balance in favor of subways in a substantial number of cases.

24. Evidence cited by Keeler et al. (1975) indicates that commuters value time spent in an automobile at about one-third of their hourly wage, and they value time spent waiting for the bus at well over two-thirds the wage.

Table 12.4 *Full Cost of an Eight-Mile Urban Rush Hour Trip*

| | Automobile | | Bus | |
Cost	Per Vehicle	Per Passenger		
Toll	$1.50	$1.00	Walk and wait	$1.25
Time (at $3 per hour):				
20 minutes		1.00	On-bus time	1.50
Operation ($0.15 per mile)	1.20	0.80	Fare and toll	1.00
Parking	1.50	1.00	Walk to work	0.62
		$3.80		$4.37

charge other passengers. The value of this time is $1.50. Assume a fare of $1.00 and a five-minute walk downtown for another $0.62, giving a total cost of the bus trip of $4.37.[25] In this example, the automobile trip is a bit cheaper than the bus trip, although that conclusion could be reversed by a plausible change in the underlying assumptions. If a trip has a destination other than the CBD, however, it is virtually impossible for a bus trip to be competitive with an automobile trip. Such a non-CBD trip generally would require a transfer, adding perhaps ten minutes to waiting time at $1.25 and five to twenty minutes to on-board time. It is apparent that mass transit has trouble competing with the automobile on routes that involve transfers.

The obvious way to make buses more competitive with automobiles is to reduce the time cost of bus travel, since it is in the dimension of time cost that the automobile soundly beats the bus. For a given volume of demand, however, time cost can only be reduced by increasing money cost—basically by running buses more frequently and making fewer stops. This is why scale is so important. High-density demand permits reduced headway and fewer stops to fill a bus.

Example: The Washington, D.C., subway.

The first segment of the Washington, D.C., Metro opened in 1976; by 1981 it had six major lines running from the suburbs into the CBD. According to Keeler et al. (1975) estimates, such a system would be economically viable *compared with automobiles* at a peak corridor volume of at least 20,000 passengers per hour, for a total of 120,000 passengers per hour for the six lines. It is easy to see that such volumes are not feasible for Washington. The District of Columbia has about 670,000 jobs (about 15,600 of them in the Federal Triangle, a restrictive definition of the CBD). If all central-city workers rode the subway to work, there would be about 110,000 riders per corridor, or about 55,000 per hour over a two-

25. Fares are generally less than $1.00, but bus operations almost always are subsidized, both because they receive cash subsidies to cover operating costs and because they (like automobiles) are not required to pay optimum road-use tolls.

hour rush hour. Many central-city jobs and many homes (both city and suburban) do not have easy access to subway lines, however; only about 7 percent of the residential land area is within 1 mile of a subway stop. Also, a subway is superior to an automobile only on the line haul portion of the trip. Clearly, for many people who both live and work in the central city, the line haul will be relatively short. The prime population for subway commuting is persons who live in the suburbs and work in the city. In Washington, 21.2 percent of suburban residents work in the city. The conclusion is that Washington cannot have a subway that is as efficient as automobile travel.

Washington did not, in fact, build an economically viable subway system. In 1981 the average weekday ridership was 290,000 (145,000 each way). Capital cost through 1981 was $4828 million; at a 10 percent cost of capital (interest and depreciation), the annual capital cost is $483 million. Dividing the capital cost by 250 (workdays per year) gives the daily capital cost of $1,932,000. Dividing by 145,000 riders gives an interest and depreciation cost of $13.32 per round trip.

Operating expenses were $94,200,000 for fiscal year 1981, which comes to $2.60 per round trip. Capital plus operating cost was $15.92 per round trip. To break even, the one-way fare would have had to be over $8.00. The total cost of the trip is, of course, much higher; we have ignored time costs and the commuters' out-of-pocket costs associated with residential collection and downtown distribution. These might add about $2.50 to the total (one way).

Could a rebuilt Washington, D.C., support a subway? As shown, Washington's Metro is not economically viable; that is, there are much cheaper ways of providing the same bundle of services. Some observers conclude from this type of evidence that subway transit should not be used except in the very largest cities in this country. Others, however, argue that the evidence is flawed. Washington, D.C., was built as an automobile-based city; in addition, the city of Washington has a building height restriction of ten stories. If Washington had always had an efficient subway system (and no height restriction), the pattern of development and commuting would have been much different than it is now, and corridor densities might have been sufficiently high to tip the economic balance in favor of subways. This section asks what Washington, D.C., would look like if it were built to make subway travel viable.

To be competitive with automobiles, a subway system must carry about 20,000 passengers per rush hour per corridor, or about 240,000 each morning on a six-corridor route (assuming a two-hour peak). To be competitive with an efficient bus system, it must carry at least twice this volume, or 480,000 passengers per peak period. This latter figure is about 70 percent of the central-city work force. Currently, only about 2 percent of the central-city labor force works in the Federal Triangle; a broader definition of the CBD would perhaps include 15 percent of the central-city work force, or about 6 percent of the SMSA work force. The first step toward making Washington viable for subways would be to relocate almost all jobs into the CBD, increasing employment density there by some sevenfold.

In addition, residential patterns would have to be changed. The subway would be viable hauling 480,000 workers per day. These workers would come from households with a total population of 1.2 million (assuming 40 percent of the population were in the labor force). When the system is completed, there would be sixty-two subway stops in basically residential areas and 194.7 square miles of land within walking distance of a residential subway stop, assuming people would be willing to walk up to 1 mile to a stop.[26] To house 1.2 million people, the population density within the mile-radius circles surrounding the stops would have to average 7,200 persons per square mile,[27] or about five households per residential acre.[28]

If the city were to be rebuilt according to these specifications, subway travel (to the CBD) would be somewhat cheaper than automobile travel and about competitive with bus travel. The benefit would be a very modest saving in total travel cost as compared with the present system, and the cost would be a substantial reduction in average lot size and a great increase in the density of CBD development.

☐ EFFECTS OF TRANSPORTATION ON URBAN STRUCTURE

Most of the foregoing analysis has taken as given the origins and destinations of work trips. In other words, it has assumed that the locations of residences and workplaces are unaffected by the urban transportation system. The assumption cannot literally be true. Indeed, the analysis in Chapter 6 showed that the residential density pattern is affected by the relationship between housing prices and transportation costs. Thus, it is inevitable that a major transportation investment, such as the construction of a transit system, would have at least some effect on the locations of residences and workplaces. Some writers take the view that the effect of transit systems on urban structure is profound.

---

26. This is a generous assumption; a 1-mile walk takes about fifteen minutes. Added to even a modest wait, the residential collection portion of the trip becomes almost twenty minutes.

27. Presently, the average population density for the Washington, D.C., urban area is roughly 1900 persons per square mile.

28. If it is assumed that the maximum walk to a subway stop is 0.75 miles, the average population density rises within the circles to about nine households per residential acre. If the maximum walk is a more realistic 0.5 miles, the density must be about twenty households per acre.

It is frequently maintained that a modern transit system would stop or reverse the alleged decay of downtown business areas, eliminate urban sprawl, and solve the unemployment problem in urban ghettos.

The effects of transit systems on urban structure depend on the system and the metropolitan area in question. It is easy, however, to see that the strongest claims are exaggerated. Even the best-designed and best-operated public transit system could have only a moderate effect in reducing the total time and money costs of commuting. Although there has been underinvestment in public transit in America's urban areas, the existing—mainly automobile based—transportation system is simply not much more costly than one with a better mix of public transit and automobiles.

The purpose of a radial transit system is to make radial travel economical. With public transit improvement, people already employed in the CBD would find it advantageous to live farther out, on the average, to take advantage of low land (and therefore housing) prices. Chapter 6 showed that a decrease in transportation cost would flatten the population density function of CBD workers.

The transit system would make the CBD more attractive for firms, because it would be more accessible to their employees. Thus, CBD employment would increase at the expense of suburban employment, making the employment density function steeper. The transit system might also attract CBD employment that would not have located in the SMSA at all in the absence of the transit system. Construction of the subway system in San Francisco was accompanied by a surge of downtown skyscraper construction. San Francisco was growing rapidly even before construction of the subway system, however. It is unlikely that large transit investments would have a significant effect on total employment and population in the SMSA.

Furthermore, it is unlikely that transit improvements would result in a large number of new CBD jobs for the central-city unemployed. The main effect of the transit system is to increase accessibility to the CBD from suburbs. Thus, most jobs created probably would be for predominantly well-educated and well-paid suburbanites. The central-city unemployed already have access to the CBD, and a transit system would hardly increase the attractiveness of the CBD as a place of employment for them.

Based on the analysis of Chapter 6, this transit improvement would be expected to increase suburban residential property values and depress central-city residential property values. Given this, it is interesting (and disturbing) that the nonfederal share of Washington, D.C., subway deficits is distributed as shown in Table 12.5.

In conclusion, major transit improvements would slow, but probably not reverse, employment decentralization, nor would the effect on total SMSA employment be large. Transit investments would hasten the flattening of population density functions.

Table 12.5 *Distribution of Nonfederal Share of Washington Subway Deficits*

Jurisdiction	Percent of Subsidy
District of Columbia	44
Montgomery County	13
Prince George's County	14
Arlington County	10
Fairfax County	13
Alexandria	5

☐ TRANSPORTATION AND URBAN POVERTY

Urban poverty enters into the consideration of urban transportation in two ways. First, low-income housing sometimes is displaced by the construction of urban transportation facilities, especially expressways. In some ways, the problem is similar to the displacement of low-income housing by slum clearance projects. Unlike slum clearance, however, urban expressways are not restricted to poor parts of central cities. In fact, much of the postwar construction of urban highways has been of circumferential roads (which pass only through suburbs) and radial expressways (which pass through both low- and high-income areas).

The problem is similar to that of slum clearance in that low-income people are affected differently by conventional compensation procedures than are high-income people. High-income residents tend to be owner-occupiers, and compensation of the property owner is therefore equivalent to compensation of the resident. Low-income residents, however, tend to be renters, and therefore do not benefit when property owners are compensated under condemnation proceedings. Moreover, renters may suffer—whether they are displaced by slum clearance or by highway construction—if their homes and neighborhoods are destroyed. It seems indisputable that renters should be compensated for such losses, be they financial or psychic. The determination of psychic losses is not easy, but it is done in other equity proceedings. The cost of such compensation is a cost of the facility constructed, and it should be borne by those who benefit from the facility. Some federal programs now assist renters in finding places to live.

The second way in which urban poverty enters into consideration of urban transportation is more complex: an automobile-based urban transportation system has an *income bias* in that the poorest people cannot afford cars. The problem is especially acute among blacks confined to central-city ghettos because of racial discrimination in housing markets. Some people advocate the construction of public transit systems in order to improve the access of ghetto residents to suburban employment centers.

It can hardly be doubted that the problem is real. Many labor specialists believe that ghetto unemployment rates are high partly because blacks who live there lack access to suburban jobs. Even if housing segregation was not a major cause of ghetto unemployment, segregation would nevertheless impose costs on blacks in the form of excessive commuting to suburban jobs, as Chapter 11 discussed.

The problem is not basically one of transportation. If ghetto residents are deprived of access to suburban jobs because of housing segregation, the obvious answer is to open up suburban housing to blacks on the terms under which it is available to others. Special provisions for the transportation of ghetto residents to suburban jobs might be viewed as a way of maintaining all-white suburbs.

In addition, little is known about what transportation system would be best for ghetto residents. The mass transit systems now being planned clearly are designed to bring suburban residents to central cities rather than to bring central-city residents to the suburbs. This is at least suggested by the proposed locations of radial rights-of-way and of suburban line haul stations. It is also clear that suburban bus systems are planned to bring suburban residents to line haul stations, not to bring central-city residents from suburban line haul stations to suburban employment centers.

It is possible that the diversity of origins and destinations of ghetto residents who would commute to suburban jobs is such that an automobile-based system would be better for them than a transit system. If so, that the poor cannot afford automobiles implies that they are even less able to afford transit transportation. The foregoing comments are meant to raise questions rather than provide answers. The special transportation needs of the urban poor are simply not known.

☐ URBAN FREIGHT TRANSPORT

Almost all intracity freight is carried by truck.[29] Much interurban freight, of course, is carried by other modes—train, pipeline, water transport, and a small amount by air—but much of this freight is delivered to its ultimate urban destination by truck.[30] Hence, the analysis of urban freight transport has concentrated on the truck.

A few basic facts underlie the discussion of the economics of urban truck travel. First, truck miles make up about 20 percent of total

29. This excludes, of course, drinking water and sewage, as well as items purchased on personal shopping trips.

30. Examples are gasoline, home heating oil, new cars, and some department store merchandise.

urban vehicle miles (Tittemore et al. 1972). Second, terminal costs typically constitute over two-thirds of urban truck travel cost.[31] Third, transport represents only about 10 percent of the total cost of producing and distributing goods in the United States.

The economic analysis of urban truck transport has concentrated on two questions: first, does industry minimize private truck costs, and if not, what could be done about it? Second, are there important externalities that warrant government intervention?

Private Costs

Casual examination strongly suggests the existence of important inefficiences in the trucking sector, although a closer look leaves more doubt. Trucks in the United States average less than three hours on the road out of every twenty-four, and in New York City about one-third of all trucks do not move at all on a given weekday. In addition to a large amount of idle time for a rig, trucks generally haul much less than a full load when on the move. In fact, survey numbers from Chicago and Columbus, Ohio, indicate that average urban truck cargoes are less than 20 percent of capacity. Obviously, with more intensive use of the nation's truck fleet, the same freight could be delivered with many fewer trucks and probably with fewer miles driven.

There are important reasons to doubt, however, that this more intensive use of the truck fleet would make economic sense. Running trucks fuller and more hours per day involves extra costs of handling, coordinating, and warehousing. In addition, it would surely increase time in transit. Imagine, for example, a retailer receiving shipments from three different wholesalers. It may be more efficient to dispatch three different trucks to the three different warehouses rather than hire one to make a circuit of all three. (In the latter case, for example, all three deliveries must be made on the same day, which may cause logistic problems.) In addition, given the high cost of terminal handling, it sometimes may be cheaper to use a truck trailer as a storage facility for a few days if the alternative is to unload the cargo into a warehouse and then reload it for shipment to its final destination.

The important point is that the line haul represents a minority of urban freight-shipping cost; although the cited numbers indicate substantial room for line haul cost savings, such savings surely would be at the expense of further increases in terminal costs. In short, although doubts persist, there is no strong reason to believe that the freight transport sector fails to minimize private cost.

31. See Hicks (1976). Much of the material on freight transport comes from his discussion, and all numbers, unless otherwise noted, are from his work.

External Costs

As seen in the "Personal Transport" section, the most important external cost of urban transport is congestion. Although trucks constitute about 20 percent of urban travel, they may contribute more than this share to total congestion. Trucks are larger and more unwieldy than cars, and they are more likely to obstruct traffic when loading and unloading.

Truck drivers, like car passengers, have no incentive to modify their behavior to reduce the congestion costs they impose on others. As noted, a truck imposes much higher congestion costs than a car; thus, its optimum congestion toll is higher as well. There are apparently no estimates of the optimum congestion toll for trucks, but it seems apparent that it would be several times that for cars, probably in the range of $1 to $5 per mile of downtown streets during rush hour. If trucks faced this rush hour road-use price, they would have an added (efficient) incentive to avoid the use of downtown streets during rush hour. Some shifting to other times or fuller loads would probably result.

Although time-of-day pricing would set up the incentives described, there is no evidence on how much adjustment in fact would occur, nor on how much congestion would be reduced as a result of any adjustment. As Figure 12.7 shows, truck travel even now is not particularly concentrated during rush hour (although the figure does show that there is a substantial amount of truck travel during rush hours).[32] There is reason to believe, however, that there would be substantial response to an efficient toll. A toll of $3 per mile (taking the middle of the wide range of plausibility) at 10 miles per hour is a toll of $30 per hour, or roughly a doubling of operation cost. At this cost, many operators might find it worthwhile to incur the inconvenience (and possible overtime pay) associated with making midday or nighttime deliveries. More information on this point would be extremely valuable.

Much (although no one knows how much) of the congestion caused by trucks is created when they stop for unloading. At least part of the solution to this problem may be changes in law and stricter enforcement of existing laws. A study of Toronto's city center noted that 19 percent of all recorded freight vehicle stops were at office buildings with "good off-street facilities with good loading/unloading facilities" (Hicks 1976), yet 90 percent of these stops made no use of the facilities. Almost certainly these instances of street unloading represent a mild increase in convenience for operators at the expense of a substantial increase in congestion faced by others.

---

32. In St. Louis (the city underlying the data in Figure 12.7), trucks account for 15 percent of vehicle miles during the morning rush hour, 18 percent during the evening rush hour, and 21 percent over the whole day.

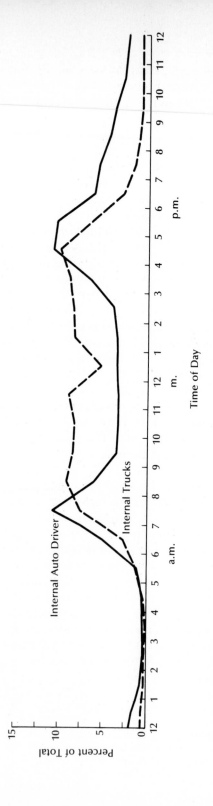

Source: Reprinted from Tittemore, et al. (their figure 10)
Note: "Internal" means either origin or distribution in metro area.

Figure 12.7 *Hourly Distribution of Auto and Truck Volume, St. Louis, 1970*

The efficient pricing of trucking road use—both for driving and unloading—possibly could lead to quite substantial improvements in the efficiency with which the urban transportation network is used. Hard evidence is simply not available, however.

☐ Summary

The purpose of an urban transportation system is to facilitate the exchange of goods and services in the urban area. The optimum transportation system for an urban area depends on the area's size and structure, as well as its historical development.

Since 1940 the volume of urban transportation has grown rapidly, and there has been a massive shift from public transit to private automobile transportation. Total commuting in an urban area depends on locations of employment and residences. A person's choice of mode depends on time and money costs of alternative modes, with time likely to be the dominant consideration. Any mode becomes congested if used by enough passengers. Congestion costs are an important element in planning and pricing urban transportation systems. Both public transit and private automobile transportation are typically underpriced in America's metropolitan areas, at least during rush hour.

The major policy debate in urban transportation concerns the benefits and costs of public transit versus automobile travel in medium-sized metropolitan areas. The decision depends mainly on whether a combination of fares and conditions of service can be offered by public transit that would be attractive to enough commuters to make public transit economical. Subway systems surely cannot be economical for any but the largest metropolitan areas.

There is considerable doubt about the effects of urban transportation systems on the structure of urban areas. Public transit systems would probably increase CBD employment, but it is unlikely that the effect would be large. Very little is known about the urban transportation needs of the poor, but it is unlikely that the public transit systems being designed for many metropolitan areas will be valuable for low-income residents.

Questions and Problems

1. It is frequently proposed that New York City's subways and buses be free to all passengers. Evaluate the proposal on the grounds of efficiency and equity.

2. Suppose technological improvements made it possible for helicopter buses to carry fifty commuters each at 60 miles per hour and a fare of $0.20 per mile. What would be the effect on location of

employment and housing in metropolitan areas during the re-mainder of the century?

3. Do you think it might be desirable to have one or more circum-ferential subway lines in large metropolitan areas at a future date?

4. Do you think low-income workers spend more or less time com-muting than do high-income workers in metropolitan areas? Which group do you think commutes longer distances? Can you recon-cile your answers with the theoretical analysis in Chapter 6?

5. Give the economic analysis underlying the following quotation, at-tributed to Yogi Berra: "Nobody goes to that restaurant anymore; it's too crowded."

6. Tittemore et al. (1972) studied traffic patterns on radial expressways for four cities (Boston, St. Louis, Seattle, and Louisville), and dis-covered the following: between 6:00 and 9:00 A.M. about 70 per-cent of the traffic was going toward the CBD, whereas between 4:00 and 6:00 P.M. less than 40 percent of the traffic was flowing toward the CBD.
   a. Does this traffic pattern suggest anything to you about efficient design and use of roadway?
   b. Do you see any problems with the road-use plans you discussed in part a?
   c. The data from Tittemore et al. are from 1970. How do you think the numbers have changed since then, and what are the impli-cations for efficient road use?

7. Suppose all transportation in the urban area were priced at peak-period pricing. If landlords could rent by the minute, what would happen to the rent gradient? What would happen if landlords could not rent by the minute?

8. Evaluate the effect of the following policies on equilibrium traffic flow:
   a. "High-density vehicle" lanes, for example, traffic lanes open only to buses and cars carrying four or more passengers. (For an analysis of priority bus lanes, see Mohring [1979].)
   b. Traffic information, for example, radio broadcasts from helicopters.

9. (The authors thank Molly Macauley for this question.) In March 1986, a Staten Island congressman succeeded in obtaining Congres-sional legislation that eliminated the toll for vehicles crossing the Verrazano-Narrows Bridge in the eastbound direction, from Staten Island into Brooklyn. Instead, a double toll was imposed in the re-verse direction. (After the change, tolls were $3.50 for cars and from $8 to $24 for trucks, depending on size.) The aim was to cut travel time for peak morning commuters traveling into Brooklyn and Man-hattan, and to reduce the buildup of carbon monoxide on Staten

Island from emissions generated by vehicles waiting in line to pay tolls.

a. One year after the legislation, annual toll revenue on the Verrazano-Narrows Bridge had declined by $7 million. Would you have predicted this decline in toll revenue? Why or why not?

b. Annual westbound traffic declined by about 1.2 million cars and 200,000 trucks. Where do you think all this traffic went?

c. Evening travel times increased an average of three to six minutes along the New Jersey-bound lanes of the Holland Tunnel. What does this reveal about commuters' value of time?

d. By March 1987 there was a proposal to rescind the original change in the toll collection. How would you vote if you lived on Staten Island? How about Brooklyn, Manhattan, or New Jersey?

References and Further Reading

American Public Transit Association. *Transit Fact Book of 1981* (Washington, D.C., 1982). A good annual publication giving data on public transit.

Baltimore City Dept. of Planning. *Traffic Study* (1983).

Bhatt, Kiran U. *What Can We Do About Urban Traffic Congestion? A Pricing Approach* (Washington, D.C.: Urban Institute, 1976, Paper 5032-03-1). A discussion of congestion pricing problems and possibilities.

Domencich, Thomas, and Daniel McFadden. *Urban Travel Demand* (Amsterdam: North Holland, 1975). A definitive technical study using the probabilistic approach to travel demand.

Hensher, David. "Valuation of Journey Attributes: Existing Empirical Evidence." *Identification and Valuation of Travel Choice Determinants,* ed. D. A. Hensher and M. Q. Dalvi (New York: McGraw-Hill, 1977). A very good source on consumer valuation of the time devoted to various aspects of travel, including a discussion of how economists estimate such things.

Hicks, Stuart. "Urban Freight." *Urban Transport Economics,* ed. David Hensher (New York: Cambridge University Press, 1976): 100–30. The basis for most of the discussion on freight transport; it includes substantially more detail.

Holland, E. P., and P. L. Watson. "The Design of Traffic Pricing Schemes." *Transportation Engineering* Feb. (1978): 32–38. A good review of pricing possibilities, including a discussion of experiences outside the United States.

Keeler, Theodore, et al. *The Full Costs of Urban Transport* (Berkeley, Calif.: Institute of Urban & Regional Development, 1975). Monograph No. 21.

Meyer, John, John Kain, and Martin Wohl. *The Urban Transportation Problem* (Cambridge, Mass.: Harvard University Press, 1965). A thorough analysis of the benefits and costs of alternative transportation modes.

Meyer, John, and John Kain. "Transportation and Poverty." *Urban Economics: Readings and Analysis,* ed. Ronald Grieson (Boston: Little, Brown, 1973).

Mohring, Herbert. "Urban Highway Investments." *Measuring Benefits of Government Investments,* ed. Robert Dorfman (Washington, D.C.: Brookings, 1965).

————. *Transportation Economics* (Cambridge, Mass.: Ballinger, 1976). A survey of transportation economics.

Quandt, Richard, ed. *The Demand for Travel: Theory and Measurement* (Lexington, Mass.: D.C. Heath, 1970). Technical papers on travel demand.

Tittemore, L. H., M. R. Birdsall, D. M. Hill, and R. H. Hammond. *An Analysis of Urban Area Travel by Time of Day* (Boston: Peat, Marwick, Mitchell and Co., 1972). An excellent source of information on temporal variation in travel patterns.

Vickrey, William. "Pricing in Urban and Suburban Transport." *American Economic Review* Vol. 53 (1963): 452–65. One of the original discussions of innovative road-pricing mechanisms: very enjoyable reading.

Walters, Alan. "Theory and Measurement of Private and Social Cost of Highway Congestion." *Econometrica* Vol. 29 (1961): 676–99. A very good discussion on how to estimate real values for optimum tolls.

———. "Externalities in Urban Buses." *Journal of Urban Economics* Vol. 11 (1982): 60–72. Explores the possibility that smaller buses would be more efficient than larger ones, and has important implications for cost comparisons between cars and buses.

13

Local Government

☐ In the United States, state and local governments provide most of the government services that have a direct and immediate impact on people's lives and welfare. A large part of the federal government's budget is devoted to national security and other activities that affect the country's relationships with the rest of the world. Another part of the federal budget finances programs that affect the public only indirectly, such as research and space exploration. A third use of federal funds is to help finance programs that are the direct responsibility of state and local governments. State and local governments administer almost all government services provided directly to the people, however. Important examples are public education, public health and welfare programs, police and fire protection, public transportation, and water supply and sanitation.

☐ SYSTEM OF STATE AND LOCAL GOVERNMENTS

Under the Constitution, sovereignty is shared between federal and state governments. Local governments are the creations of state governments. A characteristic of our federal system is that state governments have created a bewildering variety of local governments. Although this subject is mainly the concern of political science rather than of economics, some understanding of the system of local government is a prerequisite to understanding problems of local governments.

In 1977 there were nearly 80,000 local governments in the United States, almost all having limited power to levy taxes and spend the revenues collected. The best known of these governments are the 3000 counties that nearly blanket the country and the 19,000 municipal governments. In addition, there are about 19,000 townships, 15,000 school districts, and 25,000 special districts. School districts are ordinarily empowered to levy property taxes to support public education. Special districts are established for specific purposes—most commonly water supply and waste disposal—and they levy taxes to finance their activities.

The functions assigned to particular governments vary greatly from state to state. Some state governments perform functions that county or municipal governments perform in other states. In some states municipal governments provide public education, whereas school districts provide it in other states. Furthermore, there is little coincidence among boundaries of jurisdictions. School and special district jurisdictions may overlap municipal and county boundaries. Thus, it is very difficult to obtain comparable data on state and local public finance. For example, the fact that one state government has a much smaller budget than another may simply mean that municipalities in the first state finance services financed by the state government in the other.

As a result, many citizens are within the jurisdiction and taxing power of several local governments. Furthermore, an integrated economic area, such as an SMSA, may contain an extraordinarily large number of local governments. The Chicago SMSA has more than 1100 local governments, and the New York City, Philadelphia, and Pittsburgh SMSAs have more than 500 local governments each.

Political scientists tend to be critical of the complex system of local governments from the point of view of governmental operations. Although the issues go beyond the scope of economics, it is difficult not to conclude that the system is cumbersome and unwieldy. Some implications for government resource allocation are explored later in the chapter.

There has been a tendency to reduce the number of local governments during recent decades, although the reduction results entirely from school district consolidation. In 1952 there were almost 117,000 local governments in the United States, including 67,000 school districts. The number of special districts has more than doubled since the early 1950s, however.

☐ FINANCE

Trends in State and Local Finance

Table 13.1 summarizes twentieth-century trends in government expenditure. Overall, government has been a major growth industry both in dollar expenditure and as a fraction of the GNP. In 1929 government expenditure at all levels accounted for 9.9 percent of the GNP. Almost 60 percent of government expenditure was incurred by local governments; the federal government accounted for less than a quarter of the

Table 13.1 Twentieth Century Trends in Government Expenditure

Year	1 Total Government Expenditure — As a Fraction of GNP	1 Total Government Expenditure — Per Capita In Constant (1972) Dollars[b]	2 State Government Expenditure[a] — As a Fraction of GNP	2 State Government Expenditure[a] — Per Capita In Constant (1972) Dollars[b]	3 Local Government Expenditure — As a Fraction of GNP	3 Local Government Expenditure — Per Capita In Constant (1972) Dollars[b]	4 Grants from Federal to State and Local Government — As a Fraction of GNP	4 Grants from Federal to State and Local Government — Per Capita In Constant (1972) Dollars[b]
1929	9.9	$ 258	1.6	$ 42	5.9	$153	0.1	$ 3
1939	19.2	472	3.3	81	7.3	178	1.1	26
1949	23.0	757	3.0	98	4.8	160	0.9	29
1954	26.4	999	2.9	110	5.3	200	0.8	30
1959	26.8	1,090	3.4	138	6.2	252	1.4	57
1964	27.6	1,262	3.8	172	7.0	319	1.6	74
1969	30.4	1,630	4.5	243	8.0	432	2.2	115
1974	32.1	1,872	5.3	308	9.0	524	3.1	178
1975	34.5	2,026	5.8	342	9.2	538	3.5	207
1976	33.5	1,996	5.4	322	9.2	550	3.6	211
1977	32.5	2,060	5.6	357	8.5	535	3.5	223
1978	31.6	2,034	5.1	330	8.6	558	3.6	231
1979	31.2	2,031	5.4	349	8.1	527	3.3	217
1980	33.1	2,139	5.2	336	8.3	540	3.4	218
1981	33.3	2,186	5.0	331	7.9	519	3.0	195
1982	35.5	2,236	5.2	332	8.1	517	2.7	174
1983	35.3	2,312	5.1	336	8.0	524	2.6	171
1984	34.3	2,379	n.a.	n.a.	n.a.	n.a.	2.5	176
1985	35.4	2,491	n.a.	n.a.	n.a.	n.a.	2.5	180

[a]Including transfers from federal and excluding transfers to local governments.
[b]One 1972 dollar equals $2.69 1987 dollars.
Source: Data from Advisory Commission on Intergovernmental Relations. *Significant Features of Fiscal Federalism, 1985–86 Edition,* Washington, D.C.: Government Printing Office, 1986.

total. Thus, state and local government together spent 7.5 percent of the GNP.

The Great Depression and World War II reversed this pattern. By 1949 government spent 23 percent of the GNP, and federal expenditure was almost twice as large as state and local combined. From this point, total government expenditure grew fairly steadily, temporarily peaking at 34.5 percent of the GNP in 1975, declining mildly for the next five years, and rising to 35.5 percent by 1982. During this period, state and local expenditure growth modestly outstripped federal; by 1975 state and local expenditure was about 70 percent as large as federal.[1] During this period, state and local expenditures rose from 7.8 percent of the GNP to 15 percent, thus representing one of the major growth sectors of the postwar economy.

The figures in columns 1 through 3 of Table 13.1 appear to point to a resurgence of state and local government in the postwar era, following the federal dominance from 1929 through 1945. To a degree this is true, but the role of the federal government at the state and local level has grown dramatically during this period, as is apparent from column 4, showing federal aid to lower levels of government as a percentage of the GNP. Federal aid rose from 0.9 percent of the GNP in 1949 to a high of 3.6 percent in 1976 and 1978. Thus, over one-third of the postwar rise in state and local expenditure (columns 2 and 3) was financed by grants from the federal government. Although it is difficult to sort out state and local finances, it appears that substantially more than half of the postwar growth in local expenditure has been financed by growth in federal aid.

Much of what was just discussed is more or less well known. Table 13.1, however, also reveals something much less well known: the middle 1970s witnessed the end of the postwar growth of government, particularly at the local level. As a fraction of GNP, local government expenditure peaked in 1976 and has been declining more or less steadily ever since.[2] State expenditure followed the same pattern, except that it peaked a year earlier, in 1975. Federal aid continued to grow modestly for a few more years, peaking in 1978 and registering a fairly steep decline thereafter. By 1985, federal grants to state and local governments were only 78 percent as high as in the peak year of 1978. Since the 1950s at least, the pattern of growth and decline of local expenditures has closely tracked the progress of the baby-boom generation through the educational system. This topic will be returned to later in this chapter.

Revenue. Table 13.2 presents a detailed picture of the sources of state and local government revenue. The percentages refer to amounts the governments raise from their own sources. Intergovernmental transfers appear at the bottoms of the columns. Transfers to state governments are from the federal government. Transfers to local governments may come directly through state governments, or from funds raised by the state governments.

State governments raise 30 percent of their revenues from sales taxes. Personal income taxes are the second-largest source of state government revenue, yielding about 60 percent as much revenue as

---

1. In all of these discussions and in the figures in columns 1 through 3 in Table 13.1, federal aid to state and local government is excluded from federal expenditure but included in state and local expenditure.

2. The rise in federal government expenditure in 1981 (and 1982 and 1983) is partly because of the Reagan military buildup, but it is partly countercyclical.

the sales tax. Of state government revenue, 16.6 percent comes from charges such as tuition at state universities and license fees. (This is up dramatically from 1976–77, when this source yielded only 12.5 percent of revenue.) The "other taxes" category, which accounts for 7.2 percent of state government revenues, includes motor vehicle taxes, death and gift taxes, severance taxes, and several other taxes.

Local governments receive about 39 percent of their revenue from property taxes (down from 50 percent in 1976–77). Many also are permitted to levy sales taxes, and a few have income or payroll taxes. The dependence of local governments on property taxes is great and of long duration, however. No other tax yields nearly as much revenue. Local governments also raise substantial amounts of revenue from such charges as water bills, tuition at community colleges, parking fees, transit fares, and license fees. Table 13.2 shows that nearly half of all taxes and charges collected by state and local governments are collected by local governments.

Expenditure. What do state and local governments do with the money they collect? Some comprehensive data appear in Table 13.3. Expenditures in the table refer to direct expenditures for the purposes indicated. For example, state governments finance substantial parts of local government expenditures on public welfare. Such expenditures show up as a direct expenditure of local governments in the table and as an intergovernmental grant of state governments at the bottom of the table. It is important to recognize that these are expenditures made by the indicated level of government, with no presumption about the source of the funds. In the case of welfare, local expenditure frequently constitutes little more than local administration of a program financed at the state and federal level.

Education now constitutes 20.1 percent of state government expenditure—mostly higher education in state colleges and universities, which has grown rapidly in recent years. Many state governments also finance substantial parts of the cost of local elementary and secondary education, but this is included in intergovernmental transfers in the state government budgets. State transportation expenditure is mainly construction and maintenance of state highway systems. Public welfare and health expenditures together account for roughly 29 percent of state budgets and grew very rapidly during the 1960s and 1970s.[3]

Local governments spend 36.6 percent of their budgets on education. Aside from utilities and liquor stores, the second-largest item is health and hospitals, consuming 6.9 percent of local expenditure. Note that welfare makes up 4.7 percent of expenditure, but remember two things in interpreting this number. First, it fluctuates substantially over the business cycle, and second, at least half of this figure is financed

---

3. Much of this is federally mandated state expenditure on Aid to Families with Dependent Children.

Table 13.2 *State and Local Government Revenue Sources, 1983 to 1984 (In Millions of Dollars)*

Source	State		Local		State and Local	
Property tax	$ 3,862	1.2%	$ 92,595	38.7%	$ 96,457	17.4%
Sales and gross receipts tax	95,801	30.4	18,296	7.6	114,097	20.6
Individual income tax	58,942	18.7	5,680	2.4	64,622	11.6
Corporate income tax	15,511	4.9	1,535	0.7	17,046	3.1
Other taxes, including licenses	22,679	7.2	5,293	2.2	27,972	5.0
Charges and miscellaneous	52,495	16.6	73,105	30.5	125,600	22.6
Utility and liquor store revenues	5,397	1.7	35,217	14.7	40,614	7.3
Insurance trust revenue	60,950	19.3	7,704	3.2	68,654	12.4
Total	$315,637	100.0%	$239,425	100.0%	$555,062	100.0%
Intergovernmental transfers	$ 81,362	–	$126,708	–	$ 97,081	–

Sources: Data from *Statistical Abstract of the United States*, Washington, D.C.: Government Printing Office, 1987, and Advisory Commission on Intergovernmental Relations, *Significant Features of Fiscal Federalism, 1985–86*. Washington, D.C.: Government Printing Office, 1986.

by the state government in most states (New York is the major exception, as will be seen). Of the other expenditure items, only transportation exceeds 5 percent (it is 5.9 percent). It is important to note how heavily education dominates local budgets.

The dominance of education has diminished in recent years with the decline in the school-aged population. In 1971 to 1972, 41.2 percent of local, and 34.5 percent of state and local, expenditure was for education. This decline is entirely due to the decline in the school-age population. As will be seen, the last decade has witnessed substantial increases in expenditure per pupil.

Table 13.2 shows that state and local governments collect roughly equal amounts of taxes from their residents. Table 13.3 shows, however, that local governments spend about 50 percent more than state governments. The disparity between local government expenditures and tax collections is mainly financed by grants from federal and state governments.

Although total state and local government expenditures have grown rapidly since World War II, the proportions spent on important categories have changed relatively little. Contrary to much popular opinion, the proportion of state and local government expenditures used for health and welfare has changed little since the war. As Chapter 9 showed, almost all income redistribution is carried out by the federal

Table 13.3 *State and Local Government Expenditures, 1981 to 1982 (In Millions of Dollars)*

Function	State		Local		State and Local	
Education	$ 42,448	20.1%	$113,848	36.6%	$156,296	29.9%
Transportation	21,178	10.0	18,284	5.9	39,462	7.5
Welfare	41,513	19.6	14,704	4.7	56,217	10.7
Health and hospitals	19,398	9.2	21,483	6.9	40,881	7.8
Public safety	9,825	4.6	24,969	8.0	34,794	6.7
Parks and natural resources	6,527	3.1	7,543	2.4	14,070	2.7
Sanitation	359	0.2	14,581	4.7	14,940	2.9
Housing and community development	488	0.2	8,096	2.6	8,584	1.6
Administration and interest	19,601	9.3	24,971	8.0	44,572	8.5
Utilities and liquor stores	6,138	2.9	42,274	13.6	48,412	9.3
Insurance trust	34,730	16.4	4,779	1.5	39,509	7.6
Other	9,412	4.4	15,883	5.1	25,295	4.8
Total	$211,617	100.0%	$311,415	100.0%	$523,032	100.0%
Intergovernmental transfers[a]	$ 98,743	–	$ 1,957	–	–	–

[a]Transfers to other governments *from* the government level indicated at the top of the column.
Sources: Data from U.S. Department of Commerce. Bureau of the Census. *Census of Governments*, Washington, D.C.: Government Printing Office, 1982.

government. Among major expenditure categories, only education has increased substantially as a fraction of total state and local government expenditure since the war. As noted, this trend has been reversed as a result of the maturing of the postwar babies.

Systematic data do not exist for local government expenditure before 1929, but it is clear that the century from 1820 to 1920 constituted a period of rapid growth in the scope and cost of the responsibilities of local government. In 1820, New York City's budget was approximately $1.00 per capita (and this figure was probably the highest in the country). At that time government did not provide sewer and water service, police and fire protection, or education. The increasing complexity of cities which began in earnest in about 1820 placed new demands upon the public sector in all of these areas.

To take one example, the increasing density of cities increased the risk of catastrophic fire, and indeed most major cities had several major fires during the nineteenth and early twentieth centuries. Many cities found volunteer brigades inadequate beginning in the 1840s, and took on fire prevention as a government task.

Public provision of water and sewer service also became fairly widespread before the Civil War, and the discovery that proper attention to clean water and proper sewage disposal reduced epidemic diseases added impetus to the movement.

The increasing scope of activity is reflected in the cost of government. New York's per capita expenditure, for example, was up to $6.53 in 1850 and $27.31 in 1900.

Overview of Big City Finances

Table 13.4 presents data on per capita revenues and expenditures for central cities and the entire SMSA in six SMSAs for which comprehensive data are available. The SMSAs were chosen partly because they are representative of conditions in older, predominantly eastern, SMSAs, but primarily because their local government structures are sufficiently simple to permit tabulation of data.

The top lines of the table show that central cities raise more revenue both from local taxes and charges and from intergovernmental transfers (provided by federal and state governments) than do suburbs in five of the six metropolitan areas. The only exception is New Orleans, where the central city raises slightly less revenue per capita from local sources than do suburban governments. On the average, the six central cities raise about 15 percent more from local sources and 25 percent more from all sources, on a per capita basis, than do all local governments in the SMSAs.

It is well known that income is greater in suburbs than in central cities. In fact, per capita income is about 16 percent greater in suburbs than in central cities, a smaller spread than many people think. As Chapter 15 will show, however, other measures reveal a much greater city-suburb spread in economic well-being. Per-household income is about 39 percent higher in suburbs than central cities, and for northeastern cities the spread is even larger—63 percent. (That is, in the Northeast, suburban per-household income is 1.63 times that of central cities.) Furthermore, the incidence of poverty is much higher in central cities. The central-city poverty, relative to suburbs, explains why central cities receive more intergovernmental aid than suburbs, but it does not explain why they raise more revenue from their own sources. A poorer jurisdiction would be expected to spend less on both public services and private goods.

There appear to be three reasons why central cities tax themselves more heavily than do suburbs. First, central cities are relatively well endowed with nonresidential property. If half of the tax base is nonresidential, every dollar of property tax paid by a household is matched by a dollar paid by nonresidents. This effectively cuts the price of public expenditure by 50 percent, which in turn stimulates demand. Of course, the fiscal benefit of nonresidential tax revenue is reduced if the government makes expenditures explicitly for the benefit of nonresidential taxpayers. Most observers believe nonresidential taxpayers pay much more in taxes than the cost of the services they receive from local governments, however.

Second, many of the grants to local governments have *matching provisions* (although this practice is less prevalent today than in the early 1970s). Under these matching conditions, receipt of grant money is conditional upon some expenditure ("matching") of local funds. These matching provisions have the same stimulative effect as nonresidential taxable property.

Third, many services are apparently more costly to provide for poor central-city residents than for rich suburban residents. The prime example is education, which will be discussed in detail later. The basic point is that a given level of service quality (educational attainment, fire protection, and safety) requires more expenditure if the population is poor and the housing is high density.[4]

As Table 13.4 shows, central cities tend to outspend suburbs in almost all categories of expenditure. The only important exception is education, where the central cities in the sample spend about 90 percent as much as the whole SMSA. Even this figure is deceptive, however, because the numbers are per capita. A smaller fraction of central-city populations is made up of school-aged children, and a larger fraction of central-city children go to private schools. For these SMSAs, the central cities have about 8 percent fewer school-age children than their suburbs. In addition, about 20 percent of central-city children use private schools, as compared with 10 percent in the suburbs. Making these adjustments reveals that per-pupil expenditure is approximately the same in these central cities as in their suburban rings.

Reasons for Central-City Fiscal Problems

The fiscal problems of central cities—rising taxes, taxpayer revolts, bankruptcies, and general perceptions of declines in service quality—received a great deal of attention during the 1970s and early '80s. A substantial portion of these problems can be traced to five causes. The first, already discussed (and which will be further explored in Chapter 15), is that central cities have increasingly become the home of low-income households for whom the provision of services is inherently expensive. The other four major causes are discussed here.

Declining economic importance of central cities. The improvement in intraurban transportation—both of people and goods—has led to a decline in the location advantage of central cities as compared with their suburbs. The result of this has been a decline in central-city land rents relative to suburban, as Figure 13.1 depicts. (See Chapters 6 and 7 for a full development of this point.)

---

4. Oates (1977) presents a very good discussion of the evidence on this point.

Table 13.4 Local Government Finance in Six SMSAs, 1981 to 1982 (Dollars per Capita)

	New York City		Philadelphia		Baltimore		New Orleans		Richmond		Roanoke	
	Central City	Suburban Ring	Central City	Suburban Ring	Central City	Suburban Ring	Central City	Suburban Ring	Central City	Suburban Ring	Central City	Suburban Ring
Revenues												
Intergovernmental	$1,037	$ 439	$ 718	$ 364	$1,109	$322	$ 547	$ 329	$ 467	$303	$ 424	$276
Own source	1,580	1,107	920	695	693	658	768	766	889	539	724	443
Total	$2,617	$1,547	$1,638	$1,059	$1,802	$980	$1,315	$1,095	$1,356	$842	$1,148	$718
Expenditures												
Education	$ 487	$ 713	$ 398	$ 513	$ 437	$517	$ 385	$ 412	$ 453	$435	$ 354	$449
Transportation	118	58	69	52	306	64	111	66	97	32	76	11
Public welfare	469	144	48	56	6	1	16	1	158	33	74	21
Health and hospitals	219	86	66	31	131	8	12	191	25	13	6	0
Police, fire, and correction	215	132	226	74	198	89	152	98	174	106	117	70
Parks and natural resources	29	33	36	11	48	24	67	60	43	25	32	13
Sanitation	56	29	39	13	31	21	24	19	32	11	19	27
Housing and community development	187	17	99	16	193	9	69	5	49	3	46	4
Administration and interest	160	101	195	113	169	88	135	122	173	115	164	74
Utilities	320	21	528	32	43	37	57	45	399	71	52	111
Liquor stores and insurance trust	195	0	77	3	41	13	38	2	30	0	60	0
Other	278	214	239	119	153	114	212	57	83	140	201	70
Total	$2,732	$1,547	$2,020	$1,033	$1,756	$986	$1,275	$1,078	$1,716	$985	$1,202	$851
1980 population (in thousands)	7,072	2,048	1,688	3,029	787	1,887	558	629	219	413	100	124

Note: Suburban-ring numbers calculated by the authors from published central-city and SMSA numbers. First column is SMSA per capita. Second and third are calculated CC and SMSA totals; form basis for calculation of suburban per capitas in Table.
Source: Data from U.S. Department of Commerce, Bureau of the Census. Census of Governments, vol. 5. Washington, D.C.: Government Printing Office, 1982, table 5.

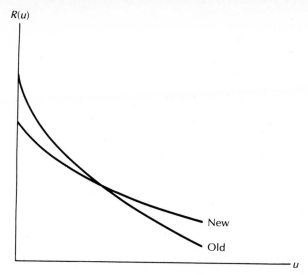

Figure 13.1 *Change in Land Rent Function Over Time*

The flattening land rent gradient (see Chapter 6) depicted in Figure 13.1 indicates that firms' preferences for central locations are less strong than in the past. This lack of strong preference for central location means that firms cannot be taxed too heavily, or they may leave the city. Back in the days when the CBD was the only feasible location for many activities, this was not a serious concern. Recently, however, nonresidential activity has decentralized more rapidly than residential. As a result, the nonresidential fraction of a city's tax base has declined over the past few decades. As previously noted, the higher the nonresidential fraction of the tax base, the lower the effective price of public services. Thus, the decline in nonresidential property has increased the price of public services to residents.

Historically, central cities have had higher property values and a higher ratio of nonresidential to residential tax bases than have their suburbs. This pattern continues today, although in a much diminished form relative to twenty or thirty years ago. This city-suburban difference gives rise to the pattern of budget constraints depicted in Figure 13.2. The steeper budget constraint (line *A*) is faced by a central-city voter and reflects the fact that public services are relatively cheap and housing is relatively expensive. The flatter, suburban constraint (line *B*) shows that public services are relatively expensive and private goods are relatively cheap. As it is drawn, both constraints are tangent to the same indifference curve (*I*), which is to say that the price structure is such that it is possible to achieve the same utility in either place. Indeed, if all households were identical, that is the expected result. The argument is identical to that used to derive the land rent gradient in Chapter 6. If, at the given price structure, everyone prefers the suburbs, the price of central-city housing falls. This decline continues until house-

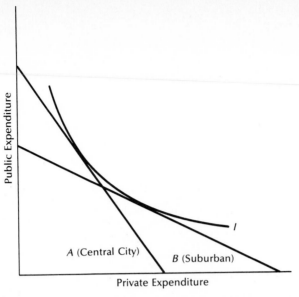

Figure 13.2 *City-Suburb Difference in Public Versus Private Expenditure*

holds are again indifferent between living in the city and the suburbs. This is simply a generalization of the observation that a land rent gradient soaks up any geographic utility differences that otherwise would exist. Thus, the difference between city and suburb is depicted in Figure 13.2 as a combination of a high central-city price for housing and a low central-city price for public services.

Clearly, public expenditure would be higher in the central city, ceteris paribus, than in the suburbs. As Table 13.4 shows, this prediction is borne out empirically. Per-capita expenditure is about 15 percent higher in central cities than in their suburbs.[5]

The gradual erosion of central cities' comparative advantage, particularly in the Northeast, has caused central-city budget constraints to become more like the suburban constraint depicted in Figure 13.2. With the shift to the constraint shown by line *B,* a given tax effort by a voter-taxpayer brings forth a smaller level of service than before. This, not surprisingly, leads to voter pressure to cut taxes, as well as to complaints about service declines. The problem is that central cities put many plans into effect a few decades ago, when public expenditure was cheap (for voters). The dismantling or scaling-down of these programs, now that tax dollars are more expensive, is a painful and difficult process.

---

5. The price differential that this section has discussed is by no means the only reason for this expenditure gap. For reasons that will be explained later, production costs are higher in central cities than in suburbs, so a given level of service costs more dollars. If demand is inelastic, this gives rise to higher expenditures. Also, as will be shown, federal aid has been targeted disproportionately to central cities, which has had a highly stimulative effect.

Central-city population decline.   Chapter 15 will discuss the reasons for central-city population decline and document its occurrence. At this point the only concern is the effect of population decline on central-city government. For this purpose it need only be noted that, for whatever reasons, central-city population decline went from being rare in the 1950s to being commonplace in the 1970s. A typical population loss for a northeastern central city during the 1970s was about 10 percent.

It might seem that declining population would not impose a financial burden on a municipality—if population declines, there are fewer people demanding service, and it should be possible to cut costs. This is particularly sensible in light of the strong empirical evidence that most local public services are produced under constant returns to scale (see Chapter 13, "Goods Provided by Local Governments"). The problem, however, is that returns are not constant in the *short run*. If the sewer and water systems were built for a city of one million, and population falls to 800,000, it is not possible to immediately reduce the stock of water mains, hookups, and treatment plants by 20 percent. The same point applies to streets and, to a lesser degree, to police and fire protection and to schools.

Notice that the problems caused by population decline are quite different from those caused by economic decline (discussed in the previous section). The erosion of the central-city comparative advantage causes a permanent shift in the ability to finance local public services. Population decline, in contrast, generates a temporary effect—the spreading of temporarily fixed costs over fewer people. In the long run these costs become variable, and the problem can be expected to go away. One of the cost items that must be cut, of course, is labor—either through layoffs or (real) salary reductions. The real question that arises is, how quickly and to what degree can the local government transform its fixed costs to variable (cuttable) costs and therefore return to production at minimum average cost?

Peterson (1976) has gathered a substantial amount of evidence on all these problems. He has obtained spending figures for all central cities (except Washington, D.C.) where population exceeded 500,000 either in 1960 or 1970. As compared with growing cities, the cities that were losing population from 1960 to 1973 spent almost 75 percent more per capita.[6] Cities that were growing between 1960 and 1970, but were declining after 1970, spent 28 percent more than growing cities. These figures are particularly striking because growing cities must, by virtue of their growth, make capital expenditures that frequently are not fully

6.   It is clear that only a part of this expenditure difference is due to the phenomenon of fixed costs and declining population discussed here. If the population had declined even 30 percent recently and expenditure remained unchanged, it would raise the per-capita expenditure by 43 percent—just over half the observed difference between growing and declining cities.

amortized. Clearly, something associated with decline greatly increases per-capita expenditure. Most of this expenditure difference, according to Peterson, is due to differences in the per-capita number of public employees.

Thus, it appears that declining cities have had more trouble cutting back on employment than on capital expenditures. This is not surprising; most capital expenditure of a declining city is for maintenance and repair, and in bad times the easiest thing to do simply may be to let the capital deteriorate. The public sector labor force, however, is not as easy to cut. Public employee unions are frequently strong in large cities, and public employees frequently represent a major segment of voter turnout in local elections.

In the latter half of the 1970s, and more dramatically in 1980 to 1982, the employment differences between growing and declining cities narrowed (see Table 13.5). Though data are incomplete, this narrowing was apparently accelerated during the early 1980s. In part, this may be the kind of adjustment that would be expected after some lag. Part of it also is surely due to the shift in the focus of federal aid to cities. As the next section will show, prior to Revenue Sharing (which began in 1973), this aid was heavily targeted to declining cities. Relative to prior programs, however, the revenue sharing program is more generous to growing cities. This also may explain the narrowing of the expenditure gap.

In addition to its effect on short-run average cost, population decline has a temporary adverse effect on revenue. If a city suffers a substantial population decline, almost of necessity it will be left with surplus housing. The existence of this surplus will put downward pressure on housing values. The depression of housing values will continue until the excess stock has been removed—a process that could take many years. According to one estimate (Hamilton and Schwab, 1983) a decline of 1 percent in population growth leads to a 0.65 percent decline in the rate of increase of housing values. The effect on the property tax is obvious.

Thus, the process of population decline has serious adverse *short-run* consequences for local governments. Note that being small is not disadvantageous fiscally; rather, it is the process of converting from being a big city to a smaller one that is painful. Once the adjustment has been made, there is every reason to expect currently declining cities to be as viable as they ever were. The short run, however—the period of adjustment between a city's being big and small—may be quite long. In large measure the adjustment process is one of retiring and refitting a capital stock—and a very durable capital stock, at that.

Although it is not clear what this means operationally, the role of the federal government should be one of easing the adjustment from big to small. As will be shown, however, federal aid over the past twenty-five years has had quite the opposite effect: it has made the adjustment much more painful.

Table 13.5 *Central City Public Employment Patterns*

Type of City	Employees per 1,000 Population			Percentage Change in Total Employees	
	1964	1973	1980	1973 to 1975	1975 to 1980
Growing	22.2	24.0	23.4	+11	−13.5
Growing to 1970; declining thereafter	22.5	30.6	26.5	+ 4	−17.4
Declining	25.4	35.8	31.9	− 9	− 1.9
New York City	35.3	51.6	45.1	−13	+ 0.4

Note: The sample cities are those used by Peterson (1976). Three of the cities in his "growing to 1970; declining thereafter" category ultimately recorded positive population growth in the decade from 1970 to 1980. The inclusion of these cities in the "growing" category changes the numbers only modestly.
Sources: Data from George E. Peterson. "Finance." In *The Urban Predicament*, eds. W. Gorham and N. Glazer. Washington, D.C.: Urban Institute, 1976, table 6; U.S. Department of Commerce. Bureau of the Census. *Local Government Employment in Selected Metropolitan Areas and Large Counties.* Washington, D.C.: Government Printing Office, 1980.

Intergovernmental aid.   The period from 1960 to 1976 witnessed rapid increases in federal aid to cities, sometimes administered directly and sometimes through state governments. Until 1973 much of this money was awarded in response to competitive applications and had rather specific strings attached. Some aid required either local matching or a specific level of tax effort on the part of the locality. On both counts large declining central cities had an advantage relative to suburbs and small cities. For reasons already stated, large cities were already taxing themselves rather heavily. Furthermore, large city bureaucracies, by virtue of their size, had an advantage over smaller governments in applying for federal grants. The result was that a large share of grant money went to big cities, and thus the period from the early 1960s to the mid-1970s was one of extremely rapid growth in big-city expenditures. Peterson (1976) reported that between 1962 and 1972, big-city expenditure rose 198 percent, whereas spending by all local government rose by only 142 percent. He further reported that almost two-thirds of this increase was financed directly by federal aid.

Beginning in 1973, the diverse set of federal transfers to states and cities was phased out, to be replaced by Federal Revenue Sharing. This shift diminished cities' competitive advantage in attracting funds. Revenue-sharing money is passed out according to a completely mechanical formula, with few strings attached and with only small weight given to tax effort. There is no longer any great advantage to skill at manipulating the federal bureaucracy. Revenue-sharing money sometimes is targeted to poorer jurisdictions, but this is blunted by an upper limit on the per-capita revenue-sharing grant.

The move to Revenue Sharing itself signaled a shift of grants away from big declining cities. (Peterson reports that Boston suffered a 20 percent decline in federal aid between 1971 and 1975.) In fact, however, the change was bigger than just this program shift would indicate. Shortly after the introduction of Revenue Sharing, the growth of total federal aid to cities and states came to a halt (adjusting for inflation). In more recent years it actually has declined. Column 4 of Table 13.1 shows that real per capita aid to state and local government peaked in 1978 at $231 and declined by 25 percent by 1983.[7] This decline represents about 6 percent of state and local expenditure.

The effect of the growth and subsequent decline in federal aid on state and local expenditure is enormous. In 1954 state and local expenditure was 8.2 percent of the GNP; by 1974 it had risen to 14.2 percent. For local governments alone, some 35 percent of 1972 expenditure came from intergovernmental grants (not all was from the federal government, but many of the state grants were pass-throughs from the federal government). About 25 percent of state government expenditure came from the federal government. Thus, roughly 30 percent of 1972 state and local expenditure came from the federal government. Eliminating this source of funding and assuming that state and local tax efforts would not be any different, state and local expenditure in 1972 would have been 10 percent of the GNP—a modest increase over the actual figure for 1954 of 8.2 percent. It is fair to say that the explosion in state and local expenditure—and particularly big-city expenditure—is due mostly to the growth in intergovernmental aid.[8]

Whatever the growth of federal aid during the 1960s and early 1970s may have done, it certainly did not ease the transition of declining cities. During precisely the period when population declines were becoming commonplace and the need to adjust to smaller size was becoming apparent, federal aid programs were put in place that encouraged local governments (particularly large central cities) to expand programs and offer expensive wage and benefit packages to their employees. When the decline in aid to big cities began in about 1975, the required adjustments were more painful than they otherwise would have been because of the extra expenditure programs cities had undertaken over the previous decade.

Sensitivity to economic cycles.   The fourth financial problem local governments face is that their fiscal health is extremely sensitive to the business cycle. Almost unique among economic agents, state and local governments are constitutionally forbidden to run a current-account deficit during a recession.[9] The federal government, private businesses, and individual households can borrow (or increase borrowing)—with varying degrees of difficulty—to tide them over hard times.

7.   The $179 is in 1967 dollars, or about $540 in 1982 dollars.

8.   Intergovernmental aid, because of its matching provisions, may have stimulated local tax effort as well, but the evidence on this is less complete.

9.   The other major institution that is forbidden to run a deficit during a recession is the social security system. As with state and local government, every recession brings cries of imminent bankruptcy for social security.

This is not true of state and local governments. They are required to run a balanced current-account budget every year. Although they can engage in financial balancing acts to some extent, the constraint is quite rigid.

The restraint is a burden, because a recession has a strong tendency to increase local government expenditures and reduce their revenues. On the revenue side, only property taxes are relatively unaffected by business cycles (although delinquency tends to rise in a recession). Income and sales taxes, fees, and user charges all decline. On the expenditure side, welfare, health, police, and housing expenditures all rise as unemployment rises. Thus, a locality that was running a healthy surplus in one year can find itself in a badly strained position one to two years later. During a recession it is necessary either to cut expenditures or raise taxes. Whatever effect these acts may have on the quality of public services, they do balance the books during a recession. They also set the stage for a very healthy fiscal recovery during the next boom. With high taxes and lean expenditures, the government will run a large surplus during the next expansion.

Summary. Given this list of central-city financial problems, it is not surprising that the 1970s witnessed some highly publicized state and local fiscal upheavals. The decline of central-city population, which began in earnest in the 1960s, continued (and, in some cases, accelerated) in the 1970s. The economic importance of central cities relative to their suburbs declined, which reduced the tax bases of central cities. The growth of federal aid, which began in the early 1960s, came to a halt in the mid-1970s and then actually declined through 1983. The economy was unusually prone to recession. Finally, the reversal of the decade-old pattern of growing federal aid to big central cities coincided with the recession of 1975, making that episode especially painful for city governments.

New York City Bankruptcy and Proposition 13: Case Studies or Special Cases?

The two best-known episodes in state and local finance in the 1970s are New York City's brush with bankruptcy and California's Proposition 13. At the time, each was cited as merely the first in a long line of either fiscal crises or tax revolts, as the case may be. In fact, although each episode was caused in part by the general fiscal conditions already described, each is also sufficiently unique to provide no real basis for making more general predictions.

New York City.[10] New York City's fiscal problems are like those of other large eastern cities in the following sense: had it not been for

---

10. This section is based largely on Reischauer, Clark, and Cuciti (1975).

the city's economic and population decline, as well as the rise and subsequent fall in federal aid, New York City probably would not have been in much financial difficulty. Furthermore, had it not been for the recession, the city probably would not have been pushed to near-default in 1975.

There were some important peculiarities as well. New York City's fiscal health is probably more sensitive to business cycles than that of any other major city. On the revenue side, only 43 percent of New York City's tax receipts in 1972–73 came from the relatively recession-proof property tax, as opposed to 62 percent for metropolitan local governments nationwide. (The city was forbidden by the state to levy a property tax of more than 2.5 percent.) On the expenditure side, the combination of state and federal law required (in 1974) that the city cover 23 percent of Aid to Families with Dependent Children Cash Assistance and Medicare payments. By comparison, Minnesota required its localities to pay 21.8 percent and California, 14.5 percent. For all other states with even moderate-sized cities, the local contribution was less than 10 percent; for most, it was 0 percent. Largely as a result of this unique law, New York City's welfare-related expenditures in 1974 were about $3.5 billion, or one-third of the total current-account budget. On the average, local governments spent only about 7.5 percent of their budgets on welfare at that time. (Welfare expenses, of course, rise dramatically during a recession.)

Thus, New York City was legally prevented from increasing property taxes, as well as required to spend about one-third of its revenue on welfare. This combination has made the city very sensitive to the business cycle and has left it with strictly limited funds for common urban services during normal economic times. In addition to this, New York City has an unusually large system of hospitals and universities, which were begun when the city could finance a large public sector from taxes on high nonresidential property values.

The problems faced by New York City in the late 1960s and the early 1970s, then, were a combination of problems unique to that city and common to other old cities. However much the problems had in common, though, New York City's approach was unique. Year in and year out, almost for a full decade, the current-account deficit was not closed through tax increases or expenditure reductions, but rather through borrowing, mostly in the short-term market. Borrowing to finance the current account is illegal in New York, as in other states, but borrowing to finance capital expenditures or in anticipation of revenue is not. Thus, many current-account functions were transferred to the capital account (for example, bridge painting, which must be done every three years, and salaries of vocational school teachers, on the grounds that they were producing human capital). Anticipation bonds were issued in anticipation of revenues that never would be received. One-year bonds were issued in anticipation of revenue-sharing money that had not even been authorized by Congress. By mid-1975 the city had $56.3 billion of short-term debt—29 percent of the national total.[11]

Astonishingly, New York City apparently accumulated this huge debt with neither hope nor plan for repayment. It simply treated borrowing as a source of funds like any other. At this time the stage was set, and all that remained was for the bubble to burst. That happened in April 1975. There is no question as to why banks stopped issuing credit to New York City; the city was a terrible risk. The real question is why they allowed the city to borrow so much before closing the credit window. Indeed, one reason the New York City situation got so serious is simply that the financial community failed to make any judgment on the creditworthiness of its customer (the city). Perhaps the lenders felt—almost correctly, as it happened—that either the state or the federal government would honor the debt.

By various mechanisms, state and federal guarantees have been placed behind the city debt, along with loans from the federal government. In exchange, the city is required to make a strict accounting of its expenditures and was required to embark upon a strict austerity program. City employment fell from 375,000 in 1970 to 319,000 in 1980, partially in response to this pressure.[12]

New York City was not the only city to suffer financial hardships in the 1970s. Indeed, six cities were widely regarded as being close to New York City in distress (Newark, Detroit, Buffalo, Boston, Philadelphia, and Cleveland). Five of these recovered fiscal health with economic recovery; only Cleveland ultimately went into bankruptcy. (For a nice discussion of Cleveland's predicament and its causes, see Humphrey, Peterson, and Wilson, 1979).

Proposition 13.[13]   In 1978 California voters enacted the tax limitation Proposition 13 by almost a two-to-one majority. The law (1) rolled back property taxes by 57 percent; (2) placed a 2 percent ceiling on annual reassessments, except at time of sale; and (3) required that any other tax increase receive a two-thirds approval of the legislature or the electorate, depending on whether the tax is state or local. This represented a 20 percent reduction in total revenue received by state and local government, as well as a 37 percent reduction in own-source revenues of local governments.

11.   New York City also had $9.4 billion of long-term debt, a much more reasonable 6 percent of the national total. An important source of borrowing—not covered in these figures—emerged from a dramatic rise in unfunded pension liability. When workers are granted pension increases and funds are not set aside to cover these future liabilities, it is an act of borrowing to cover current (labor) costs.

12.   This 15 percent decline in payroll employment is in contrast to the national trend. Nationwide, local government employment rose by 29 percent between 1970 and 1980 (about two-thirds of this growth occurred in the first half of the decade).

13.   This section is based largely on Oakland (1979).

Table 13.6 *State and Local Taxes as a Percentage of Personal Income, 1957 to 1978*

Year	United States[a]	California	California-United States
1957	8.14	9.31	1.17
1962	9.32	10.46	1.14
1963–1964	10.13	12.07	1.94
1964–1965	10.24	11.98	1.74
1965–1966	10.43	12.47	2.04
1966–1967	10.32	11.98	1.66
1967–1968	10.49	13.37	2.88
1968–1969	10.91	13.71	2.80
1969–1970	11.44	13.38	1.96
1970–1971	11.66	13.73	2.07
1971–1972	12.42	14.94	2.52
1972–1973	12.71	14.91	2.20
1973–1974	12.16	14.01	1.85
1974–1975	12.00	14.59	2.59
1975–1976	12.17	14.89	2.72
1976–1977	12.38[b]	15.78[c]	3.40
1977–1978	12.11[b]	15.96[c]	3.85
1978–1979	11.93[d]	15.97[c] (12.64)[e]	4.04 (0.71)[e]

[a]Excluding California.
[b]Based on estimates of U.S. Department of Commerce as reported in the *Survey of Current Business.*
[c]The 1976 to 1978 tax receipts were based on the author's estimates using California state comptroller reports. Personal income for 1978 was taken from *Economic Report of the Governor,* Sacramento: State of California 1978.
[d]Same as b, but the first quarter of 1978 was used to project the entire year.
[e]After Proposition 13.
Sources: Adapted with permission from William Oakland. "Proposition 13: Genesis and Consequences." *National Tax Journal,* June 1979, 387–409; after U.S. Department of Commerce. Bureau of the Census. *Government Finances.* Washington, D.C.: Government Printing Office, selected years.

Proponents claimed that similar measures would be enacted throughout the country, that American citizens were overtaxed, and that Proposition 13 was the first victory in a national tax revolt. As Oakland (1979) clearly shows, however, Proposition 13 passed not because American citizens were overtaxed, but because Californians were overtaxed relative to other people in the United States. The most important cause of voter discontent, and therefore of Proposition 13, was the very rapid growth of the tax burden on Californians during the mid-1970s. Table 13.6 shows state and local taxes as a percentage of personal income for various years in California and the rest of the nation. Although California always has been ahead of the rest of the nation, the real gap began to open up in the early and mid-1970s. By 1975 to 1976, per capita California taxes were 32 percent above the national average, and California's taxes as a fraction of personal income were 19 percent above the national average.

California was overtaxed relative to the rest of the nation because of a combination of design and accident. The state income tax was highly progressive and therefore highly responsive to the inflation-induced income increases of the 1970s. Property values were growing rapidly because of net immigration and the inability of construction to satisfy demand immediately. Thus, property tax receipts grew rapidly as a result of fair reassessments.[14]

Oakland (1979) estimated that from 1975 to the enactment of Proposition 13, the income elasticity of tax revenue was 1.75, meaning that a 1 percent rise in income—whether it be real or inflation generated—brings forth a 1.75 percent increase in tax receipts.[15] The result of this very high revenue elasticity during a period of rapidly increasing nominal income was that the state began accumulating huge surpluses (at the rate of $3.3 billion per year at the time of Proposition 13). The total accumulated surplus by 1978 was $7.1 billion.

Not all the increased revenue went into accumulated surpluses, however. Some of it undoubtedly went into increased services, and a substantial portion went to wage increases. California public sector wages were 23 percent above the national average, whereas manufacturing wages were only 9 percent higher. If the manufacturing wage is taken as a rough measure of the cost of living, the real wages of California public sector workers were 13 percent above the national average. Since wages are 55 percent of the public budget, expenditure was 7 percent above the national average simply because of the higher real wages received in California.[16]

According to Oakland's (1979) estimates, Proposition 13 required a 9.5 percent reduction in expenditure the first year, after accounting for the release to local government of accumulated state surplus money. All but about 2.5 percent could be realized simply by bringing the (real) California pay scale in line with the rest of the nation's. In fact, progress in that direction has been made; in the first year after Proposition 13, no cost-of-living pay increases were permitted for public employees.

The unique feature of California in 1978 was its huge accumulated surplus and its highly elastic tax structure during a period of rapidly increasing house values and money income. The vote for Proposition 13 was not a vote for a cut in services (or at least this was not the outcome). Rather, the major financial effects were to get the state out of the business of accumulating budget surpluses and to bring its public

---

14. This is just the opposite of the short-run population loss problem faced by declining cities that has been discussed. When population increases, excess demand pushes property values above their equilibrium level. If assessments keep up, this yields a temporary windfall of tax receipts.

15. The elasticity of revenue with respect to real income was even larger, since most of the income growth over this period was due to inflation.

16. The tendency to increase wages when funds are plentiful is by no means unique to California. Inman (1979) reports that as much as 80 percent of increases in federal aid are spent on public sector wage increases.

employee pay in line with the rest of the nation's.[17] Like New York City's situation, California's story has enough important unique features that it would be very dangerous to make general predictions about other times and places based on this experience.

☐ GOODS AND SERVICES

The "Finance" section of the chapter was concerned largely with the effects of various external forces on the ability of state and local government to obtain revenues. This section examines the services local governments perform for their citizens. It is concerned largely with the nature of the goods provided—who receives them and who pays for them. Among other things, it discusses economic efficiency and income redistribution.

Goods Provided by Local Governments

One starting point is an examination of the goods local governments provide, beginning with reference to Table 13.3. Just under 40 percent of local expenditure is for education (almost entirely primary and secondary). Most of the remainder of the budget is split among transportation, police, fire, water, sewers, parks, hospitals, and welfare services. None of these items amounts to as much as 20 percent of the typical local budget. Putting aside welfare for later discussion, first the goods local governments provide to their citizens will be examined.

For a variety of reasons, the technology for producing many of these goods has not improved very much over the past few decades.[18] Unlike manufactured goods, the production of many local public services is not amenable to mass production, and therefore it is not particularly amenable to technological improvement. Typically—although not universally—more rapid technological progress in goods than in service production is expected. The failure of technological progress in the local public sector to keep up with that in manufacturing means that the relative price of local public services has been rising and will probably continue to rise.

17. Many other states considered fiscal limitation statutes in the late 1970s. Indeed, California was presented with Proposition 9 in 1980—a proposal that would have cut income tax rates in half. It was rejected by over a 60 to 40 majority. Of the laws that passed, only Massachusetts's Proposition 2½ (a 2.5 percent ceiling on property taxes, passed in 1980) and, to a lesser degree, Michigan's Headlee Amendment (a measure that limits the growth of state and local revenues but does not roll back current taxes) have been restrictive enough to have any real effect upon expenditure. Prior to Proposition 2½, Massachusetts residents were taxed almost as heavily as California's. The Massachusetts tax revenue relative to personal income was 23 percent above the national average in 1979. See Oates (1981) for a more complete discussion of fiscal limitation movements.

18. There have been important technological improvements in some services such as fire protection (see Getz 1979) and police, but many services are provided with roughly the same technology as they were twenty years ago.

The second and most important observation about the common services is that they are not pure public goods in the sense, say, of national defense. In other words, it is not true that a police force, water or sewer system, or school system of a given size can deliver the same quality of service to a city of 200,000 that it can to a city of 100,000. Unlike the case of pure public goods, additional residents do add to the cost of a given level of service. In fact, empirical evidence suggests that beyond a modest city size (say, around 10,000 population), local public services are produced under roughly constant returns to scale.[19] In other words, a population increase of 10 percent requires an expenditure increase of 10 percent if services are to be maintained at a constant quality.[20]

If these goods are produced under constant returns to scale, why are they provided through the public sector rather than through private production and marketing as are food, housing, medical care, and a long list of other essential and nonessential goods? The answers vary from good to good.

In the case of most road networks, any method of collecting tolls to finance a for-profit firm would be so unwieldy that it would defeat the purpose of having an efficient network of streets.[21] In the terminology of public goods, even though roads are rival (one person's consumption reduces the amount available for others' consumption), they are nonexcludable, or at least exclusion is very costly. This means that the very act of collecting a price from users would be extremely costly. Such "nonexcludable" goods are distinguished from the goods which usually appear in economics models as a result of this cost-of-pricing feature. Typically such goods are provided by government and are financed not through the collection of an unwieldy fee but rather through taxation. This is the reason most roads are provided through the public sector, and why they are financed through taxes rather than tolls. But as seen in Chapter 12, collection of tolls on some busy roads would yield benefits in terms of reducing congestion.

19. Inman (1979, 296–98) notes that the evidence supporting the constant returns claim is not fully convincing. Nevertheless, there is no evidence to contradict constant returns, nor any inherent reason to believe that there would be important scale economies or diseconomies for most public services. (Mass transit is an important exception; see Chapter 12.)

20. Some people have argued that local public goods are unique because they can be congested, yet they have some of the characteristics of public goods. Up to some class size in a school, additional students do not diminish the quality of instruction; beyond some point, however, congestion sets in. This observation, although basically correct, in no way distinguishes local public goods from private goods. In the short run, output can be increased up to some point with no strain on fixed capacity. Eventually, the law of diminishing returns (that is, congestion) takes over, and costs begin to rise. In fact, however, the same argument applies to any plant operating with short-run fixed capacity. When the capacity constraint becomes binding, the prescription is the same in both private and public sectors: build a bigger plant.

21. See Vickrey (1963) for a contrary view.

In the case of police protection, the problem is somewhat different. Police protection involves coercion (apprehension of criminal suspects and the like). If the coercive power is not to be enforced by terror, it surely must be granted by the public sector.

Water, sewers, and fire protection, however, are like neither coercive police protection nor nonexcludable roads. It is easy to exclude someone from water service by shutting off the valve. The appropriate model here is *natural spatial monopoly,* and it is best illustrated by way of example. Clearly, it is more efficient for the residents of one street to be served by one water main than two. Thus, it is hard to imagine a competitive water supply industry. Even if it were imaginable, it would be inefficient, since it would involve duplication of water mains. Note that the existence of this natural spatial monopoly is consistent with constant returns to scale; the extension of water service to 10 percent more people might increase the total cost by 10 percent, while serving one street with two water mains is twice as expensive as serving it with one. The natural spatial monopoly does not arise from increasing returns, but rather from the avoidability—through monopoly—of duplication of capital. There are, of course, other natural spatial monopolies, such as telephone service and electric power supply. The public has responded to these latter cases by regulating private industries, but in the other cases the most frequent (although by no means the only) response has been direct government takeover of the functions. Although this approach has disadvantages that will be discussed, it has the advantage of eliminating concern that the public will have to pay monopoly prices for services.[22]

Education is the most important and difficult case. Education is not a natural monopoly, nor does it involve the police power of coercion.[23] It is both rival (able to become congested) and excludable (unlike roads). There is no reason to doubt that education could be provided efficiently through the private sector; indeed, in most cities private education exists and is a thriving and competitive industry.

The rationale for the public provision of education seems to be more philosophical and constitutional than economic. It derives from notions of equality as expressed in the Declaration of Independence and the Constitution. More explicitly, most state constitutions require their subdivisions to operate "thoroughgoing and equal" primary and secondary education systems. The purpose is that whatever else *equality* might mean in the constitutional sense, it surely means at least some approximation of equal access to the basic skills needed for functioning in the adult world. If education were left to an unregulated private

22. Government operation is by no means the only approach that offers at least some hope of competitive (average cost) pricing. For an excellent discussion of options, see Ely (1888).

23. It is true that education is compulsory; unlike police protection, however, this does not prevent it from being provided in the private sector.

sector, the quality of education surely would vary significantly according to both the income and tastes of parents. Unequal access to education—particularly inequality based on parents' income—would serve as a significant barrier to upward mobility.

If the rationale for providing education is to achieve some measure of equality in access, however, it must be asked how well this objective is met through our current educational system. The best way to address this question is to look for a realistic theoretical model of the local public sector. The best-known and most complete model is known as the *Tiebout hypothesis.* The following section is a discussion of this model and an examination of its implications and realism. Some special problems of providing education will be discussed further later in the chapter.

Tiebout Hypothesis

In 1956 Charles Tiebout put forward a provocative hypothesis about the interaction of government and private decision making in the context of America's local government system. Since then dozens of books and papers have elaborated, criticized, and tested the theory. No one can understand local government in the United States without understanding the Tiebout hypothesis.

In essence, the Tiebout hypothesis argues that "shopping" for a jurisdiction and its attendant offerings of education and other services is much like shopping for other goods. According to this model, competition fosters efficiency in the local public sector much as it does in the private sector. A crucial feature of this shopping model is the availability of a wide variety of jurisdictions offering different mixes of public services. In general, the better the services, the higher will be the cost in terms of taxes and housing cost (as will be seen). Thus, choice of jurisdiction represents choice of public service offering, along with an obligation to pay the cost. In the next several pages, the details of this model will be worked out, and its realism and implications examined.

Chapter 4 showed that American metropolitan areas have been decentralizing for decades. In the nineteenth century, decentralization typically was accompanied by the outward movement of central-city boundaries. Since World War II, decentralization has occurred on a massive scale, but movement of central-city boundaries has become the exception rather than the rule.

Chapter 7 discussed the tendency for high-income residents to live farther from metropolitan centers than low-income residents, even in the absence of local governments. Consider a typical postwar metropolitan area that is growing and decentralizing rapidly. People with average or above-average incomes are moving into areas outside the central city in large numbers. At this point one of three things must happen: these residents must petition to be annexed to the central city, new local government jurisdictions must be formed, or rural governments must be made into suburban governments. The central city is being populated with low-income people, crime and tax rates are rising, and public schools are deteriorating. The new suburban residents perceive that they would be better off having their own local government instead of being annexed to the central city. It is most advantageous if a group of perhaps 10,000 to 100,000 people with similar incomes and demands for local public services form a new jurisdiction. There they can vote the bundle of local government services and the real estate taxes to pay for them that best suit their needs and tastes. In this way several suburban governments are formed, within each of which live a few tens of thousands of people who are similar in income and family composition. Family composition is an important determinant of the demand for the most expensive local government service—public schools. The advantage to groups of people with similar demands for local government services in locating in the same jurisdictions is the essence of the Tiebout hypothesis.

The American tradition of financing local governments by locally levied real estate taxes complicates the analysis in the last paragraph. As Chapter 10 showed, the income elasticity of housing demand is not far from 1. Thus, the relatively high-income residents of a particular suburb own relatively expensive homes. The real estate tax rate is set so that tax payments on the homes yield the revenues needed to finance the chosen bundle of local government services. However, a low-income family with a correspondingly modest housing demand would be tempted to move to the community. Every resident pays the same tax rate, so the total taxes on a modest home would be small. Thus, the low-income family could obtain the local government services at a relatively small cost. Such a family is referred to as a "free rider," in that its share of local taxes is smaller than the share of local government services it consumes.

Communities have perceived that they can exclude free riders by land-use controls. The ostensible justification for land-use controls is to protect residents from nuisances such as noise, pollution, and congestion. State governments and courts, however, have given local governments wide latitude in choosing land-use controls. In the 1950s, 1960s, and 1970s, a common justification for land-use controls became "to protect the character of the community," which often means "to prevent free riders." Local land-use controls frequently specify minimum lot sizes and square feet of floor space, prohibit multifamily housing, and so on. A long list of such requirements effectively excludes from a community those whose homes would not pay the residents' shares of the cost of local government services. Tiebout did not emphasize land-use controls to exclude free riders, but subsequent writers have.

A large metropolitan area might have many suburban jurisdictions. Some might be inhabited by very high-income residents and have stringent land-use controls and very high-quality government services.

Others might be inhabited by people with more modest incomes and have correspondingly modest government services and land-use controls. As an illustration, suppose there is a rich jurisdiction and a poor one—Jurisdiction A and Jurisdiction B, respectively. All houses in Jurisdiction A are worth $100,000, and the jurisdiction provides $2000 per year in public services. The property tax rate is 2 percent. In Jurisdiction B every house is worth $50,000, and the community provides $1000 in public services. Thus, Jurisdiction B's tax rate also is 2 percent. Obviously, all residents get what they pay for. The "price" of public services is equal to average cost, which in turn is equal to marginal cost if there are constant returns. Equally obvious is the fact that there is no income redistribution.

For households that demand a $50,000 house and $1000 in public services or a $100,000 house and $2000 in public services, the consumption bundle in this primitive public economy is exactly what it would be if there were no taxes and people bought public services at a store. If a sufficiently rich variety of communities exists, every household receives the bundle it would demand in a private market, and the competitive (efficient) outcome is mimicked perfectly. Notice that a low-income person would rather live in Jurisdiction A than in Jurisdiction B; property taxes are the same in both jurisdictions, and public services are twice as high in Jurisdiction A. Of course, if all low-income people moved to Jurisdiction A, its tax base would be diluted, and taxes would have to be raised or services reduced. This is why voters in Jurisdiction A would be expected to erect zoning barriers that prevent the construction of $50,000 houses (or, for that matter, houses worth anything less than $100,000).

Capitalization. This model is unrealistic; jurisdictions are far from homogeneous with regard to house value, and therefore with respect to tax payment. The result that there is no income redistribution also seems to be an overstatement. It is true that there is no redistribution between the rich suburbs and the poorer central city. Surely, however, the poor who are in the suburbs are beneficiaries of public sector redistribution, and surely there is redistribution between central-city rich and poor.

In the case of a representative suburb, the poor do pay less in taxes than do the rich, and they probably have almost equal access to the public services. Precisely because of this apparent redistribution, however, the few low-income houses in the otherwise rich jurisdiction are unusually valuable. Suppose the suburb is Jurisdiction A of our previous example, and Jurisdiction B is the central city. Jurisdiction A is now dotted with a few low-income houses, although not enough to have any noticeable effect on the tax base. One of the low-income houses, which is physically identical to the $50,000 houses in Jurisdiction B, comes on the market. If poor people attach any value to the extra $1000 of services offered in Jurisdiction A as compared with Jurisdiction B, the house sells at a premium above $50,000. If they value the service at the full $1000, the premium is equal to the present value of this extra $1000 of services ($10,000, if the interest rate is 10 percent).[24] Thus, in this case the house sells not for $50,000, but rather for $60,000. This house value premium—the present, or capitalized, value of the extra services (or, in some cases, the tax savings)—is called *capitalization*. Once the housing market is in equilibrium, capitalization effects eliminate any utility differences that otherwise would exist between city and suburb. It is one more application of the land rent gradient principle: if geographic differences in attainable utility exist, the tendency of people to migrate to the high-utility region will bring about housing price differences sufficient to soak up the utility differences.

The striking and important conclusion from this analysis is the following: if a poor household wants to become a beneficiary of income redistribution by moving into a rich suburb, it must purchase this right at a fair market price. What the tax-expenditure bundle gives, the housing market takes away.[25] Table 13.7 clearly illustrates this point (Hamilton, 1977). The numbers are for fairly centrally located plots of vacant land in Toronto. Substantial effort was made to obtain data from parcels that are identical except for their zoning restrictions. The R-2 zoning category permits two dwelling units per acre, and RM-2 permits 12. Clearly, R-2 houses will be nicer and more expensive than RM-2 houses. This is why the city anticipates $1210 in tax revenue from an R-2 house and only $361 from an RM-2 house. At an annual per-house public sector cost of $800, it appears that rich people are subsidizing the poor. At a 10 percent interest rate, the present value of the extra taxes paid by an R-2 as compared with an RM-2 house is $8490. This conclusion, however, is contradicted by the last column, which reveals that rich people pay a much lower price for the land on which their housing sits than do poor people. An R-2 lot (one-half acre) sells for $45,000,

24. This calculation is not quite right; with the house value increase the taxes will go up, and this will slightly depress the premium.

25. There is a potentially important qualification to this finding, namely that supply adjustments may bring about some redistribution after all. This issue is treated only briefly here, because it is somewhat technical and because empirical evidence suggests that the account in the text is basically correct. The supply adjustment works as follows: in Jurisdiction A, a house otherwise worth $50,000 sells for $60,000 because of the fiscal advantage in Jurisdiction A. Since it only costs $50,000 to build, there is extra profit to be made in building low-income housing in Jurisdiction A. This extra incentive remains until the price in Jurisdiction B has been driven back to $50,000 (at which time the same housing in Jurisdiction A will cost only $40,000 so as to be competitive with the $50,000 house in Jurisdiction B). Now low-income people get their housing plus public services at below cost throughout the urban area. This is financed by high-income people paying more than cost for their services, and the end result is a measure of true income redistribution. In fact, as will be shown, this supply adjustment does not appear to take place to any important degree. The reason is that every jurisdiction—in an effort to protect or enhance its tax base—passes zoning ordinances that restrict the supply of low-income housing high enough to undo the redistribution through local taxation and expenditure.

Table 13.7 *Toronto Zoning and Land Values*

Zoning Category	Units per Acre Permitted	Tax Revenue per Unit	Public Sector Cost per Unit	Land Price per Acre
R-2	2	$1,210	$800	$90,000
RM-2	12	$361	$800	$150,000

Sources: Data from B. W. Hamilton. "Local Government, the Property Tax and the Quality of Life: Some Findings on Progressivity." In *Public Economics and the Quality of Life*, eds. L. Wingo and A. Evans. Washington, D.C.: Resources for the Future, 1977; after Peter Mieszkowski.

while the same quantity of land zoned RM-2 costs $75,000—a premium of $30,000. This makes the RM-2 tax break of $8490 (present value) look like it is not such a good deal after all.

In the Toronto example, the zoning law restricts the supply of low-income housing. Many people are surprised to learn that land zoned for low-income housing sells at a premium as compared with land zoned for high-income housing. The pattern has been observed in many cities, however, and in many cases the price differences are greater than those reported for Toronto. On reflection, the pattern of land-price differentials is what would be expected. In residential zoning, low-income (high-density) housing is always the excluded activity. If land were more valuable when devoted to high-income housing than low-income housing anyway, zoning would be superfluous.

If the poor are to be kept out, zoning is needed precisely because, in many circumstances, the poor would be able to outbid the rich for land in an unrestricted market. In the Toronto case, twelve poor households obviously can outbid two rich households for land. Zoning keeps the price of high-income housing low (and the price of low-income housing high) by setting aside a large amount of land for high-income development and preventing poor people from bidding on the land. It is a bit like passing a law that sets aside a certain portion of total food output for rich people.

The net effect of property taxation (which tends to redistribute from the rich to the poor) and zoning (which redistributes from the poor to the rich) is that there is little or no income redistribution at the level of local government. People receive public services from local government and pay for them with a combination of taxes and house-value premiums. Therefore, people generally get what they pay for in the way of public services.

Not only do people get what they pay for, there is considerable evidence that they get roughly what they demand. Statistical studies have shown that expenditure on both education and other public services rises with average income and the fraction of the tax base that is nonresidential, and that it falls with the relative cost of providing the service. This pattern is just what would be expected in analyzing the market demand for an ordinary good. Based on these estimates, demand appears to be mildly inelastic with respect to both price and income.[26]

Realism of the Tiebout hypothesis.
Is the Tiebout hypothesis realistic? Its preconditions are a substantial number of suburban governments in a metropolitan area, each with considerable local control over taxes, service provision, and land-use controls. Its implications are that such communities vary, but that within a community there are people with similar incomes, houses, and demand for local government services.

No one can drive through typical metropolitan suburbs and believe there is no truth to the Tiebout hypothesis. Many observers have commented—sometimes sarcastically—about the homogeneity of suburban communities. In addition, statistical studies have shown that there is more homogeneity by income and house value within suburban than within central-city neighborhoods, and more than would be expected in the absence of the motivations in the Tiebout hypothesis (Hamilton, Mills, and Puryear, 1975).

Another set of statistical studies pioneered by Oates (1969) shows that property values are higher in jurisdictions with high public expenditure than in low-expenditure jurisdictions, other things being equal. Similarly, low-tax jurisdictions have high property values. Interestingly, Oates found that property values are about $12 higher for each extra dollar of annual public expenditure. This would appear to be about the present, or capitalized, value of the extra expenditure. This is strong evidence that the *foot-voting* (deciding where to live based on public service offerings and taxes) that is the heart of the Tiebout model really does occur, since it is hard to imagine how property values would be affected by public expenditure levels except through people's tendency to migrate from low- to high-expenditure jurisdictions. To state it a bit differently, high-expenditure jurisdictions are more valuable than low-expenditure jurisdictions because the high expenditure makes them more desirable. The previously postulated capitalization really does occur, and it is reasonable to believe it is part of the mechanism that ultimately stems the flow of migration to high-expenditure jurisdictions.

Of course, there is variety within suburban communities. People's choices of residential location depend on many things other than local taxes and government services provided. Suburbs are by no means as homogeneous as they would be if the Tiebout mechanism were the only force at work. Recall, however, what has been shown: communities need not be perfectly homogeneous for the Tiebout hypothesis to work. Certainly the Tiebout hypothesis contains important variables without which the residential pattern of America's suburbs cannot be understood.

---

26. Inman (1979) provides a good summary of this evidence.

Welfare economics and the Tiebout hypothesis. What about the normative characteristics of the Tiebout hypothesis? Do suburbs organized along Tiebout lines promote efficiency and equity in resource allocation? The question is important. Local government expenditures account for more than 10 percent of personal income in the United States. It is important that they satisfy the conditions for efficient and equitable resource allocation discussed in Chapter 8.

Many people are surprised to learn that a world like that in the Tiebout model might allocate resources efficiently to local governments. If there are enough local government jurisdictions, each person can live in a community that provides the optimum bundle of local government services and corresponding taxes. By choosing the right community and voting for officials who favor the appropriate services and taxes, each person can consume the quantity and quality of local government services he or she would consume if the services were sold on competitive markets. The requirement is that there be enough communities to provide each desired bundle of local government services, houses of a particular value, and location relative to workplaces. Of course, no metropolitan area has enough jurisdictions to satisfy this requirement. The Tiebout hypothesis, however, provides an approximation of both reality and efficient resource allocation.

An important corollary to the efficiency characteristic of the Tiebout hypothesis is that there be no resource misallocation from local real estate taxes. Shopping among different communities for the right bundle of local government services is just like shopping among car dealers for a car that combines the optimum combination of quantity, quality, and price for the customer. In both cases, the market satisfies the conditions for efficient resource allocation presented in Chapter 8.

This efficiency result must be qualified. First, the limited number of metropolitan jurisdictions available means that the efficiency result is at best an approximation. That is, there simply is not enough variety so that all consumers are precisely on their demand curves. (Of course, there is also a limit to the number of available automobile types, as a result of scale economies. So many customers are not able to find precisely the car they would like to buy either.) Second, local governments must be free to choose their bundle of services and tax rates. In Europe, local governments are financed or tightly controlled by national governments. The Tiebout hypothesis cannot work there. It has been seen that in the United States, local governments are increasingly financed by grants from state and federal governments. This prevents the Tiebout-like world from working efficiently. Third, some government services cannot be provided by fragmented local governments, for example, metropolitan areawide public transit and water supply systems. Such services must be provided by state governments or by agreements among local governments.

Fourth, it is unlikely that competition among jurisdictions offers the same technological discipline as does competition in the private sector. In the perfect-competition model of the private sector, each firm earns zero profit; failure to operate with the best available technology results in bankruptcy. Thus, any technological improvement penetrates the industry relatively quickly. Since the method of shopping for local public services is so indirect, however, it is unlikely that any discipline imposed on inefficient producers would be either as swift or as certain in the public sector as in the private sector.

As will be discussed, technological progress tends to be relatively slow in the public sector (basically because it is not amenable to mass production techniques to which technological improvements can be readily applied). The lack of market discipline noted above, however, may bring about a worse record on efficiency gains than is required by the nature of the product. Hulten (1982) has estimated that there actually has been negative technological progress in the provision of state and local services over the past twenty years—that more physical inputs are used now to produce the same output.

Finally, the Tiebout hypothesis cannot ensure efficient resource allocation to local governments in metropolitan central cities. One reason is that most central cities were built before land-use controls became important, so land-use controls cannot perform their function of excluding free riders in central cities. Another reason is that central cities are too big and diverse for the Tiebout mechanism to work. In most metropolitan areas it is not possible to find enough people with similar demands for local government services and location to populate a central city. This implies that real estate taxes have a much greater effect in distorting resource allocation in central cities than in suburbs.

To be specific, consider the following example. Suppose a worker is promoted, raising his or her take-home pay 25 percent. As a result, the worker's family wants a better house and better public education. If the family lives in a suburb, it can move to another suburb better suited to its higher economic status. If it moves from one house to another in the central city, it may obtain a better house, but the quality of public education is unlikely to be much better at one school than another within the central city (with the exception of so-called *magnet schools,* which cover large districts anyway). Thus higher taxes paid on the better house represent no higher-quality local government services. Such taxes distort resource allocation.

If the family does not like the central-city schools and taxes, why does it not move to a suburb? One reason may be that the central city is a much better location for it, given the breadwinner's workplace. Another reason may be that its income is not yet high enough to get the family over the barrier raised by the exclusionary land-use controls in suburbs. A third reason may be that the family is black and is excluded from or made unwelcome in suburban communities by racial prejudice.

It is unfortunate that the efficiency characteristics of the Tiebout hypothesis are unavailable precisely where residents can least afford the loss of welfare caused by distorting real estate taxes—the central city. That is not the end of the story, however. From an equity view-point, the basic purpose of people's "voting with their feet" is to avoid paying more in real estate taxes than the local government services are worth to them. In other words, in a Tiebout world, local governments cannot redistribute income. If a suburban jurisdiction is homogeneous, there is no one within the jurisdiction to whom income must be redis-tributed. If the local government did levy significantly higher taxes on more valuable homes, either the residents would move to a jurisdic-tion in which local taxes reflected their demand for local government services or their houses would become cheaper. Given the approxi-mate nature of the Tiebout hypothesis, local governments can engage in a small measure of income redistribution; given the mobility of upper-income households, however, this redistribution cannot be substantial.

The final aspect of the equity issue is that, in the postwar United States, land-use controls that excluded low-income central-city residents from suburban residences by and large exclude blacks and other minori-ties. The police power of suburban governments thus is added to other forms of discrimination against minorities in the United States. (See "In-efficiencies in Private Land Markets" for a discussion of police power.)

One possible reaction to these equity issues is to decide that in-come redistribution should continue to be left to the federal govern-ment, as it mostly has been. Once that view is taken, along with the view that the enforcement of open housing laws makes the racial ex-clusion unimportant, approval can be given to Tiebout-like suburbs. This is a case in which, for many people, there is strong conflict be-tween efficiency and equity considerations.

Federal and state legislatures have shown little hostility to exclu-sionary suburbs. Strong attacks in the courts have been partially suc-cessful, however. Some have contended that exclusionary zoning deprives central-city residents of access to government services—especially education—that are guaranteed by state or federal constitu-tions. Other attacks have been more broadly based, claiming that all residents have a right to live wherever they can bid successfully, and that land-use controls artificially raise housing costs beyond the reach of many (Mills, 1979; Rubinfeld, 1979).

Many attacks have not survived appeal. Some have, however, and courts are increasingly sympathetic to plaintiffs as their understanding of the implications of the Tiebout hypothesis improves. What influence the courts have is another matter. Courts do not build houses. They can say that a certain pattern of controls is unconstitutional and must be redone within certain guidelines. Local planners then redo the con-trols, and a new set of legal procedures is required to test their con-stitutionality. The point is that the courts have permitted local governments to have a wide range of land-use controls. To distinguish between constitutional and unconstitutional uses of those controls is a difficult task.

Summary of the Tiebout hypothesis. The basic conclusions that emerge from the Tiebout model are (1) that it describes a mechanism for promoting economic efficiency (although surely quite an imperfect one) and (2) that it severely limits the ability of local government to redistribute income. Although the Tiebout model was introduced to examine education, the results apply across the whole range of local government activities, including welfare. If a jurisdiction has a particularly generous welfare program, the value of low-income housing can be expected to be relatively high and the value of high-income housing to be relatively low. The poor must pay (in higher housing costs) for the welfare they receive, and the rich are compensated (with below-market housing) for contributing to the welfare programs. It is easy to see why this result is so general: if there is perfect mobility between jurisdictions, it is impossible for the poor in one jurisdiction to be better off than those in another.

Some Special Problems of Education

As already noted, it is quite feasible to provide education in a purely private market, and there is every reason to believe that such a market outcome would be competitive rather than monopolistic. The public provision of education seems to rest on the view that people would not like the private market outcome for philosophical reasons.[27]

An examination of the actual outcome of the public education delivery system, however, shows that it is very much like a market outcome. Parents with a strong demand for education provide high-quality education for their children, and parents with lower demands actually provide their children with lower-quality education. Both types of parents pay about what it costs to educate their children. In other words, the Tiebout mechanism has given us an elaborate and cumbersome mimic of the outcome that would have emerged if education had been left in the private sector. If society retains the view that the market outcome in education is undesirable, people should be just as unhappy with the Tiebout outcome.

Displeasure with the Tiebout outcome has led to a number of proposals to reform education. The primary proposals are education vouchers and increased centralization (involvement of state and federal government) in the provision of education. Before examining these proposals, it is important to note one special feature of the technology for providing education—namely, the role of students, parents, and peers in the production of education.

So far education has been discussed as if it were produced according to a technology just like any other good. Inputs (teachers, books,

---

27. Some have argued that education is provided publicly because of the external benefit of having an educated populace. This does not require public provision, however; it merely dictates a subsidy.

and buildings) are purchased, and they produce an output (which might be imperfectly measured as improvements in the cognitive skills of students). A large body of evidence, however, indicates that education is not enhanced by purchasing more teachers and capital (Summers and Wolfe, 1977). Universally, researchers have found that the characteristics of students, peers, and parents are among the most important determinants of education quality.

Centralization.   This finding has important and disturbing consequences. It means that educational opportunity cannot be equalized by giving compensatory aid to low-income school districts, and it further means that the centralization of education finance (complete takeover by the state, for example) will not eliminate the incentive of rich people to keep poor people out of their school districts (Oates, 1977). So long as private schools are a viable option, the centralization of the public school system probably will cause an increase in upper-income attendance at private schools. In other words, preventing rich parents from fleeing to Tiebout suburbs is likely to induce a flight to private schools instead.

Rich parents who do not want to leave the central city already are faced with this choice. Not surprisingly, private-school patronage is much higher in central cities (particularly in the Northeast) than elsewhere. As shown in Table 13.8, in northeastern central cities, 20.3 percent of students were enrolled in private schools in 1979; the analogous figure for northeastern suburbs was 10.3 percent. In nonmetropolitan areas the analogous figure was 7.1 percent (Current Population Reports 1982). Although this hypothesis has not been tested statistically, it appears that school districts with heterogeneous populations tend to drive a substantial number of their students into private schools.[28]

In turn, this increased reliance on private education results in reduced expenditure in public schools. One study (Brown and Saks, 1975) reports that a 10 percent increase in the fraction of children in private schools results in a 4 percent decline in the public school expenditure.

For these reasons, the centralization of finance and administration is at best a highly imperfect way to address the adverse distributional consequences of the Tiebout model. Even if everyone stayed within the public school system, the equalization of expenditure would go only a modest way toward equalizing quality. Furthermore, with the viability of private schools, an attempt to provide the same quality of public education to rich and poor could result in an exodus of the rich from the public system, as well as decreased financial support for public schools.

---

28.   For a more complete discussion see Hamilton and Macauley (1988).

Table 13.8 *Public and Private Elementary/Secondary School Enrollment by Region and Metropolitan Status, October 1979*

Region Metropolitan Status	Total Enrolled, (In Thousands)	Enrolled in Public Schools	Enrolled in Private Schools (Percentage)			
			Total	Religiously Affiliated	Unaffiliated	Affiliation Not Reported
All regions:						
Total, all students	42,981	90.2	9.8	8.2	1.4	0.2
Metropolitan	28,435	87.7	12.3	10.4	1.6	0.3
Central city	11,106	84.0	16.0	13.5	2.1	0.4
Outside central city	17,329	90.0	10.0	8.4	1.3	0.2
Nonmetropolitan	14,546	95.0	5.0	4.0	0.9	0.1
Northeast:						
Total, all students	9,734	87.5	12.5	11.1	1.2	0.3
Metropolitan	7,476	85.8	14.2	12.6	1.2	0.4
Central city	2,894	79.7	20.3	18.6	1.2	0.6
Outside central city	4,582	89.7	10.3	8.9	1.2	0.2
Nonmetropolitan	2,259	92.9	7.1	5.9	1.1	0.1
North Central:						
Total, all students	11,198	88.5	11.5	10.4	0.9	0.3
Metropolitan	7,352	85.7	14.3	12.7	1.3	0.3
Central city	2,768	82.7	17.3	15.2	1.5	0.5
Outside central city	4,584	87.5	12.5	11.2	1.2	0.2
Nonmetropolitan	3,846	93.9	6.1	5.9	0.0	0.2
South:						
Total, all students	14,482	92.2	7.8	5.7	1.9	0.1
Metropolitan	7,887	89.3	10.7	8.3	2.3	0.2
Central city	3,450	87.6	12.4	9.2	3.1	0.1
Outside central city	4,437	90.6	9.4	7.5	1.7	0.2
Nonmetropolitan	6,595	95.8	4.2	2.6	1.5	0.1
West:						
Total, all students	7,567	92.1	7.9	6.2	1.4	0.3
Metropolitan	5,721	90.5	9.5	7.4	1.8	0.3
Central city	1,994	86.0	14.0	10.9	2.7	0.4
Outside central city	3,726	92.9	7.1	5.5	1.3	0.3
Nonmetropolitan	1,846	97.2	2.8	2.4	0.3	0.1

Note: Details may not add to totals because of rounding.
Sources: Adapted with permission from National Center for Educational Statistics, table 2.3, p. 62; after U.S. Department of Commerce. Bureau of the Census. Current Population Survey, unpublished tabulations.

Vouchers. Some economists, most notably Milton Friedman, have argued for a system of education vouchers. The parents of each child would receive vouchers which could be redeemed at any accredited school, with no distinction between public and private. Schools would have to compete for students, and this competition would provide a healthy discipline. All students would be able to afford education up to the value of the voucher, so there would be a floor under expenditure, if not quality. Whether this system would lead to more racial and socioeconomic integration or equality is not clear, however. The effect on education quality also is unclear, given the demonstrated importance of peers and parents in the education process.

The quality of education. There is widespread concern that the quality of education is bad and getting worse in the United States. The most frequently cited evidence is a steady decline in test scores, as well as a decline in the relative pay of teachers.

All of the popularly employed standardized tests began to show declines beginning sometime between the late '60s and 1970. But what is less well known is that after reaching a trough in the mid-'70s, all of the tests have shown a recovery approximately as rapid as the original decline. If the data are plotted by birth date, an interesting pattern emerges. At all grade levels, pupils who were born between about 1962 and 1964 perform worse than those who were born either before or after this period. The most recent data, for fifth graders born in 1974, show scores higher than at any previous time. Thus the decline in test scores seems to have been fairly short-lived, and largely concentrated among children born between 1962 and 1964. This characterization of the facts is pervasive—it applies to blacks, whites, segregated and integrated school districts, and to all regions of the country.

There are two significant but quantitatively small qualifications to this pattern. First, black students showed smaller declines than whites; their scores stopped declining earlier; and the upturn in black scores was sharper than that of whites. Thus during the period 1975–1984 the gap between black and white performance narrowed by about 20 percent. (The same is true for Hispanics.) Second, this narrowing of the gap in test performance took place both for blacks in integrated and heavily segregated schools.[29] These trends raise fascinating and troublesome questions: what went wrong with the birth cohorts of 1962–64, and what can be done to prevent a recurrence? To date there is no research even directed toward these questions, let alone answers.

The second concern regarding education quality concerns expenditure levels in general and teachers' salaries in particular. Real expenditure on education has declined steadily since 1978, though not as quickly as school enrollment. This, of course, means that real expenditure per pupil has risen (see Table 13.9). On the other hand, it is true that teachers' salaries have declined, both in purchasing power and relative to all full-time employees, in the past fifteen years, as shown in Table 13.10. Paul Peterson, who gathered these data, offers a straightforward economic explanation for the patterns: the rapid decline in the supply of school-age children led to a reduction in the demand for teachers, driving their salaries down. Governments responded by hiring more teachers and reducing class size.

Of course this explanation does not address the fundamental question concerning the future: will the decline in teachers' salaries reduce the quality of people going into the teaching profession in the next generation? Alternatively, the salary decline might influence the num-

---

29. These facts on educational achievement come from "Trends in Educational Achievement," Congressional Budget Office, 1986.

Table 13.9 *Current Education Expenditure (Per Pupil in 1987 Dollars)*

Year	Expenditure
1970	$2,234
1975	2,688
1980	3,033
1985	3,580
1986	3,677

Source: Data from *Statistical Abstract of the United States*. Washington, D.C.: Government Printing Office, 1987.

ber, rather than the quality, of teachers. In this case salaries should ultimately be bid back up.

The dropout problem.   One crucial measure of the success of a school system is its ability to produce high school graduates. Many central-city schools report dropout rates in excess of 25 percent, and some cities report dropout rates approaching 50 percent. This strongly suggests that the minimal standard (production of high-school graduates) is frequently not met. There is particular concern that ghetto schools are producing a generation of blacks who will be unable to cope with the modern labor market. Upon careful examination, the facts show a more hopeful picture. In particular, there is a striking discrepancy between the data on dropout rates and independent data on the education status of adults. Table 13.11 gives data since 1940 on the percentage of young adults (age 25–29) who have completed high school, for the population as a whole, and for blacks. In 1940, only 11.6 percent of young black adults had completed high school (median number of years completed was 7). By 1985, 80.6 percent had completed high school (as compared with 86.1 percent of the population as a whole). Note that the percentage of young black adults who failed to complete high school in 1980 is comparable to the percentage who failed to complete the fifth grade as recently as 1950.

Two questions emerge from this table. First, what has caused the dramatic rise in completion rates for blacks, and second, why are the completion rates so strikingly at odds with dropout rates?

Regarding the first question, there seem to be two forces at work. As can be seen in the table, there has been a tendency for high-school completion to rise among the population at large, and blacks have simply been part of this trend. Second, the rise in black completion rates coincides closely (with about a ten-year lag) with the wave of black migration to the urban sector.

The discrepancy between completion and dropout rates also appears to come from two sources. First, the dropout statistics are not very accurate (students who transfer to another school are sometimes

Table 13.10 *Teacher Salaries as Compared to Average Employee Earnings in All Industries*

Year	Elementary and Secondary Teacher Salaries	Average Earnings of Full-time Employees in All Industries	Percent Above Average Received by Teachers
1929–30	$ 1,420	$ 1,386	2.4%
1939–40	1,441	1,282	12.4
1949–50	3,010	2,930	2.7
1959–60	5,174	4,632	11.7
1969–70	8,840	7,334	20.5
1975–76	13,120	11,218	16.9
1980–81	18,409	16,050	14.7

Source: National Center for Education Statistics, *Digest of Education Statistics*. Washington, D.C.: Government Printing Office, 1982.

listed as dropouts), and second, many students who drop out eventually return and complete high school.

In summary, it is clear that the quality of black inner-city schools is much worse than that of white suburban schools. It is important to recognize, however, that the opportunities faced by inner-city blacks are strikingly better than those faced by their sharecropper parents or grandparents.

What produces quality education?   In the preceding sections it was noted that research has shown that the quality of education depends crucially upon the characteristics of parents and peers, and that variation in expenditure has relatively little influence on educational

Table 13.11 *Educational Attainment of 25–29-year-olds*

Year	All Persons		Blacks	
	Less Than 5 Years of School	High School Graduates	Less Than 5 Years of School	High School Graduates
1940	5.9	38.1	27.7	11.6
1950	4.7	52.8	16.8	22.2
1960	2.8	60.7	7	37.7
1970	1.7	73.8	3.2	55.4
1980	1.1	84.5	1.1	75.2
1985	0.7	86.1	0.4	80.6

Source: Data from *Statistical Abstract of the United States*. Washington, D.C.: Government Printing Office, 1987.

outcomes. In this section the research techniques employed in arriving at this conclusion are discussed.

Suppose there is a sample of school districts, and for each district some measure of education outcome (such as test scores or percentage completing high school) is available; call this measure Q. In addition, there is data on purchased inputs (possibly expenditure or teachers per pupil); call this variable E. Finally, there is data on the average socioeconomic characteristics (SEC) of people who live in the district. It is now a simple matter to run a regression of a form such as

$$Q = a_0 + a_1E + a_2SEC, \tag{13.1}$$

where, for example, a_1 gives the statistical relationship between E and Q. In the simplest (and least satisfactory) education studies, a_1 is taken as the *effect* of E on Q. In such studies, expenditure is uniformly found to be unassociated with Q.

In all likelihood, the failure of equations such as (13.1) to show any effect of E on Q is due in part to a subtle but important statistical phenomenon known as the *identification problem*. The identification problem is perhaps one of the most frequent sources of misinterpretation of statistical relationships, so it is worth exploring, even aside from its relevance to our current discussion.

To see how the identification problem arises in the current context, it is necessary to consider a more complete description of the determination of education quality. Suppose that education is "produced" according to a relationship that looks very much like (13.1):

$$Q = \alpha_0 + \alpha_1E + \alpha_2Y, \tag{13.2}$$

where for simplicity Y (income) is now used as the only SEC. The interpretation of (13.2) is that increasing E by one raises Q by α_1. Now invoke ordinary demand theory and assume that the quantity of education which will be demanded (voted for) by the electorate depends upon the cost (that is, E) and upon the voters' income Y:

$$Q = \beta_0 + \beta_1E + \beta_2Y. \tag{13.3}$$

Before proceeding, it is useful to compare both (13.2) and (13.3) with (13.1). Is the a_1 coefficient in (13.1) an estimate of α_1 or β_1? The answer, in general, is that it is not an estimate of either α_1 or β_1; that is the identification problem. Since there are two different causal relationships between E and Q (namely the production and demand functions), any observed statistical association generally cannot be identified as either the production or the demand coefficient.

The identification problem arises because the observed Q,E pairs are intersections of production and demand functions, and it is not known which is being traced out by the various pairs.

There are various statistical techniques that at least to some degree address this problem. Most of these techniques involve estimating an equation much like (13.1), but choosing the observations in such a way that there is reason to believe that the relationship observed is the production rather than the demand function. In almost all of these studies there is at least some question as to how successfully the researcher has sorted out the effects, however.[30] This possible problem should be recognized when looking at the findings. Bearing this caveat in mind, most studies find the following pattern:

1. Purchased inputs—teachers' salaries, teachers per pupil, and the capital plant—appear to have little or no influence on educational attainment.
2. On the other hand, educational attainment is very strongly related to parental background (including education and income) and the parental background of classmates.
3. Despite the first finding cited, there is strong evidence that the characteristics of the classroom environment matter. Some individual teachers consistently outperform others; similarly with some principals and schools. In other words, purchased inputs do matter after all, but the desirable purchased inputs generally do not cost any more than the undesirable ones.

If good teachers can improve the quality of education (and this finding exists virtually whenever anybody has tested for it), it seems strange that expenditure differentials between districts produce no observable effects. Perhaps this is a manifestation of the identification problem. Or perhaps it is so difficult for administrators to distinguish between the better and the worse teachers that there is no way for pay scales to reflect this quality variation. A final possibility is that teachers demand premium pay to go to "bad" school districts. If this happens, "good" school districts can get quality teachers cheaper than "bad" districts, and expenditure differences between districts do not measure differences in the quality of purchased inputs.

If education is produced by a combination of purchased inputs, parents, and peers, then the Tiebout model of education takes on some strange new twists (the twists are particularly important if peers play a crucial role in the education process). If peer group effects are significant, some important things happen. Various exclusionary practices, such as zoning, must be viewed as much more important policy tools available to jurisdictions. Exclusion of poor children from a rich dis-

30. Dynarski, Schwab, and Zampelli (forthcoming) have made a particularly careful attempt to disentangle the roles of parents as productive inputs and demanders, relying on a sample of California school districts where expenditure was out of the control of the parents (because of Proposition 13). School districts were forbidden from raising taxes, and therefore from raising expenditures. Presumably in this case variation in expenditure is independent of demand, and its role in the production process can be isolated. Even here, though, the evidence is not conclusive. Perhaps it works as follows: parents demand a given quality of education. Forbidden by Proposition 13 from raising taxes to improve schools, they devote extra parental time to their children to make up the difference. (Despite the existence of this possible alternative explanation for their findings, the Dynarski-Schwab evidence is the latest and most convincing in a long line of findings that strongly indicates that parental and peer characteristics are much more important than expenditure levels in determining education quality.)

trict becomes valuable not only because the rich are saved from having to subsidize the poor, but also because the rich are saved from having low-achievement pupils reduce the quality of their schools.

The same forces which make exclusion so attractive for the rich make it particularly sinister from the perspective of the poor. The one thing that would most effectively raise the quality of education for low-income children appears to be inclusion with higher-achieving students (recall that increasing expenditure appears to have only limited effectiveness). It must be noted that this achievement gain that would be obtained by more mixing carries a cost—reduced attainment of higher-achieving children.

Finally, it should be noted that the efficiency claim of the Tiebout hypothesis no longer holds if parents are inputs in the education process. The efficiency claim of the Tiebout hypothesis is quite simple. If all people vote with their feet, and if a sufficient range of choice emerges, all people will be on their demand curves and all public services will be produced at minimum cost. In the presence of peer-group effects, though, migration does more than match up offerings with demand. If the cost of providing a given quality of education varies with where people live, then the location outcome that emerges from foot-voting may well not minimize the cost of education.

☐ REGULATION

In addition to levying taxes and providing public services, local governments regulate private activities. The regulations are of two basic kinds. First, some natural spatial monopolies generally are regulated rather than publicly owned; second, the use of land for any purpose is regulated through zoning ordinances and building codes.

Regulated Enterprises

There is little difference between the economics of the provision of water and electric power, yet the former is generally a public enterprise and the latter a regulated private enterprise. For no obvious reason, local governments have tended to deal with some natural monopolies through public ownership and to deal with others through regulation. Among the more recent regulated industries is cable television.

As compared with completely free enterprise, the regulation of a monopoly has the obvious advantage of preventing monopoly pricing. The disadvantage, however, is that the regulator must monitor both the production and the pricing policies of the firm. Furthermore, the firm under regulation generally has an incentive to behave in an inefficient manner (see Averch and Johnson, 1962).

Perhaps a more important cost of regulation is that its scope has extended to industries for which there is no economic justification. In many cases, regulation is a blatant anticompetitive device enacted at the behest of the regulated industry. For example, local governments often regulate the number of taxicabs, with the result that the supply becomes restricted and the price is raised.[31]

Land-Use Regulation

Almost all local governments regulate the use of land with building codes and zoning ordinances. This section will explore the economic rationale for each of these types of regulations and then discuss some of the actual economic consequences of these regulations. Land-use controls as a fiscal tool have already been discussed—essentially, as a means for protecting the tax base. These controls also have other purposes and consequences, however.

Building codes. Building codes generally specify materials to be used in wiring and plumbing, as well as such things as the configuration of windows and some aspects of interior wall location. They sometimes also specify standards for framing, foundation, and external building materials. The economic rationale for building codes is to protect the public from invisible defects in homes and other buildings (although the code generally covers visible aspects of the buildings as well). The notion is that a buyer cannot readily examine wiring, plumbing, and some aspects of structural integrity, and the code is required to keep the builder honest.

Many people object to codes as they are now generally constituted, because they require the use of specific materials rather than performance standards. If performance standards were imposed instead, builders would have an incentive to look for the least expensive way of satisfying the standard. For example, most codes specify a certain thickness of fiberglass insulation. Frequently, however, proper caulking and weather stripping would be a more productive way of achieving the same thermal resistance.

Zoning. A zoning map specifies which types of structures and activities can take place on each parcel of land. Sometimes, zoning is hierarchical: land uses are ranked from most to least noxious. All activities are permitted on land zoned for the most noxious use. Moving up the hierarchy, the more noxious uses are excluded. Thus, for example, single-family homes can be built on land zoned for row houses, but not vice versa. More frequently, however, zoning is *exclusive use,*

---

31. See the "Licensing Taxicabs" problem in Milton Friedman's *Price Theory* (1973, 282).

meaning that the land can be used only for the activity permitted on the zoning map. Broadly speaking, the economic justification for zoning rests on the notion that there are inherent inefficiencies in an unregulated land market. For a thorough discussion of both the institutions and economics of zoning, see Fischel (1985).

Inefficiencies in private land markets. The most obvious potential inefficiency in an unregulated land market is the existence of externalities from neighboring uses. For example, many industrial plants generate air, water, and noise pollution, as well as visual disamenities. Restricting the number of households exposed to the disamenities can mitigate their deleterious effects. This is a major justification for segregation of residential from various types of nonresidential activities. Although private market forces probably generate a fair amount of segregation of uses, the externalities may be sufficiently important that government intervention is appropriate.

Chapter 11 showed that the statistical evidence for neighborhood effects is very weak and that any externalities that do exist appear to be quite limited geographically. This raises doubts about the value of zoning to internalize neighborhood effects. The measurement of these neighborhood effects, however, as well as people's attitudes toward them, is far from perfect. Thus, care should be taken in concluding that these externalities do not generate important land market imperfections. By the same token, however, it might be asked what zoning officials will base their decisions about how to segregate land uses on if there is no hard evidence on the magnitude (or even the direction, in some cases) of these externalities.

Some experts claim that externalities exist among various types of residential land uses. Apartments, rowhouses, and other high-density dwellings are said to create traffic, noise, and visual disamenities justifying their separation from lower-density housing.

If high-density and low-quality housing impose costs on neighbors, however, zoning does not eliminate the problem; it just concentrates it in one place. The problem still exists, but the rich do not have to see it. An appropriate response to this type of neighborhood effect problem would be to subsidize the consumption of low-income housing.

Also, some believe there is value to maintaining farmland and open spaces, largely for the visual amenities they produce.[32] This is tricky; within the boundaries of an urbanized area, the preservation of farmland also can be labeled *sprawl*.

---

32. Some also argue that a policy of preserving farmland is needed specifically because of the value of the agricultural output. There seems to be little substance to this argument, however. In a competitive land market, land would remain in agricultural production so long as the value of its marginal product were higher there than in urban uses. In the United States, the market value of agricultural land probably exceeds its social agricultural value, because the massive agricultural price support system raises farmland values.

Ecological reasons for land-use controls also exist, the most prominent being watershed management. As more land in the upstream part of a drainage area is covered with buildings and concrete, the ability of the land to absorb rainwater is diminished, which leads to increased flooding downstream. Private developers tend to ignore these external costs, and some form of regulation is called for.

The final justification for zoning involves planning. Once local governments became the main providers of streets, sewers, and water, they faced the problem of predicting land-use density to determine street, water, and sewer main capacity requirements. Making the correct prediction is extremely valuable; once buildings are in place, the cost of widening streets and laying bigger water mains can be very high. One solution to the prediction problem is to mandate—by zoning ordinance—that the prediction come true. Historically, this was one of the motivations behind zoning.

Most economists agree that there would be important inefficiencies in an unregulated private land market. The lack of evidence in support of neighborhood externalities may be due to difficulties in measuring the variables. Even if these externalities are unimportant, however, the problems of planning for roads, water, sewers, watershed management, and, possibly, the preservation of farmland and areas of scenic beauty raise doubts about the efficiency of a private market.

There are important reasons, however, to doubt that the cure is an improvement over the problem. First, it is unlikely that zoning officials can determine the best locations for all economic agents. It may be necessary to distinguish between such matters as watershed and floodplain management on the one hand and neighborhood externalities on the other. The costs of increasing flooding downstream are demonstrable and reasonably easy to document, but the segregation of economic activities within an urban area might be another matter. It is hard to know which rules to apply in establishing zoning guidelines.

Second, and more important, the actual objectives of zoning officials may go far beyond correcting market failures, and the pursuit of these other objectives may have some undesirable consequences from both the efficiency and equity perspectives. Zoning officials are either elected or appointed by elected officials. In either case, the constituency is the people who are eligible to vote in the jurisdiction. Therefore, the officials have an incentive to maximize the welfare of the current residents of the jurisdiction. They have no reason to be concerned with the welfare of nonresidents, yet zoning actions frequently have important consequences for nonresidents. Before exploring this further, the legal environment in which zoning takes place must be examined.

Under America's constitutional system, government has two sources of power to regulate private activity, aside from the power to tax. The first is called *eminent domain,* the power to seize private property for public purposes, such as road building. The Constitution forbids the seizure of private property without just compensation. The sale of property can be forced at a court-determined price, however, even if the landlord does not wish to sell. Thus, for example, it is impossible for one landowner to prevent a road from being built.

The other source of power over the private use of property is the *police power of the state*. Actions under police power do not require compensation. For example, if motorists are stopped at a roadblock checking for drunk drivers, the state is not required to compensate them for their time.

Under current Supreme Court rulings, almost all local land-use regulations are acts of police power rather than eminent domain, so the government is not required to compensate the property owner for costs imposed by regulation. This has important economic consequences.

Assume that zoning authorities act selfishly, or rather that they act on behalf of the selfish interests of residents. In standard microeconomic theory, selfish behavior is guided by the invisible hand to yield an efficient outcome. When one of the selfish agents has the power to seize property without compensation, however, the invisible hand does not work. For example, suppose a plot of vacant land in a jurisdiction would be worth $100,000 in the absence of zoning. The land commands this price because of its valuable access to the CBD. The present value of commute saving is roughly $100,000 if development occurs on this parcel rather than at the urban fringe (where land value is zero). In other words, the market price of the land is a good estimate of the social value of using the land for urban development. Costs associated with using the land also exist, however, in the form of lost visual amenities and increased traffic congestion. If the costs exceed the benefits, efficiency dictates that the development not take place.

The problem with zoning is that our current institutions do not induce officials to weigh the costs as well as the benefits of development of a parcel of land. Instead, the zoning board is likely to ask a much simpler question: will any costs be imposed on current residents if the parcel is developed? If so, they are likely to deny permission to develop. Even if the benefits of development are $100,000 and externality costs are only $1000, the zoning board has an incentive to deny the right to develop.

What has all of this to do with police power and eminent domain? Basically, in the previous example the problem arose because the benefits of development were ignored in the zoning board's decision-making process; this was due to the zoning board's indifference to the effects of its actions on the value of the parcel of land. The parcel was worth $100,000 in the absence of zoning restrictions; with restrictive zoning, the value might fall to $20,000. The $80,000 in lost property value is a measure of the (gross) social cost of the restriction. The authorities, however, have no reason to care whether the restriction reduces the value by $1, $100, or $100,000. From an economist's perspective, the zoning restriction in this example is equivalent to the seizure of $80,000 worth of property rights. On efficiency grounds, this seizure should take place only if the benefits of the restriction are worth at least $80,000. If the authorities respond to the wishes of the electorate, however, the property rights will be seized so long as the benefits are positive at all.

This example is not farfetched. As already shown, land values can vary widely according to how the land is zoned. The power of the local zoning board to take and give valuable property rights to citizens (all without compensation) is very great indeed. The possibilities for abuse, including unwarranted seizure and bribery, are obvious.

If zoning were an exercise of eminent domain, this problem would not arise. The $80,000 of property rights in the example still could be seized for the public benefit, but only with just compensation; that is, only by paying the owner $80,000. Then the authorities would have to decide whether they wanted the property rights badly enough to pay for them; in other words, there would be a market test governing the use of land.

☐ Summary

Total government expenditure grew dramatically over the past half-century, rising from 9.9 percent of GNP in 1929 to 35.4 percent in 1985. Local government expenditure rose from 5.9 percent of GNP in 1929 to a high of 9.2 percent in 1975, falling to 8 percent in 1983. In the first part of this chapter these trends and their causes and consequences were examined. The 1970s and early 1980s created particular financing problems for many central-city governments. Several of the reasons for these difficulties were discussed.

The second part of this chapter was concerned with the nature of the goods provided by local governments, and the efficiency and distributional consequences of the current means of providing these goods. Of particular interest, it was shown that the amount of income redistribution that goes on at the local-government level is much less than is commonly believed.

Questions and Problems

1. What would be the effect on central-city government finances of an NIT? of a housing allowance?

2. The federal government can redistribute income by taxing high-income people and providing transfers either to low-income people or to local governments with large low-income populations. Which do you prefer?

3. What would be the effect of metropolitan areawide local government on local taxes paid and government services received by poor central-city residents?

4. The tax revolt of the late 1970s was a revolt of middle-class suburban residents against local governments. Transfers to the poor appeared to be the object of their hostility, yet suburban governments transfer little money to the poor. How do you explain this?

References and Further Reading

Averch, Harvey, and Leland Johnson. "The Behavior of the Firm Under Regulatory Constraint." *American Economic Review* Vol. 52 (1962).

Babcock, Richard F. *The Zoning Game* (Madison: University of Wisconsin Press, 1966). A highly readable book on the legal and political environment in which zoning takes place.

Baumol, William. "The Macroeconomics of Unbalanced Growth: The Anatomy of Urban Crisis." *American Economic Review* Vol. 5 (1967): 414–426. A study of the long-run implications of low productivity growth in the government sector.

Brown, B., and D. Saks. "The Production and Distribution of Cognitive Skills Within Schools." *Journal of Political Economy* Vol. 83 (1975): 571–594.

Coleman, James, and Sara Kelly. "Education." *The Urban Predicament,* eds. W. Gorham and N. Glazer (Washington, D.C.: Urban Institute, 1976). A review of the state of our knowledge regarding education.

Dynarski, Mark, Robert Schwab, and E. Zampelli. "Community Characteristics and Educational Production Functions." *Journal of Urban Economics,* forthcoming.

Ely, Richard. *Problems of Today* (New York: Crowell, 1888).

Fischel, William. *The Economics of Zoning Laws: A Property Rights Approach to American Land Use Controls* (Baltimore: Johns Hopkins University Press, 1985). Fischel provides a detailed discussion of the fact that zoning is an act of taking property rights without compensation.

Frieden, Bernard J. *The Environmental Protection Hustle* (Cambridge, Mass.: MIT Press, 1979). A provocative book on the forces underlying the environmental movement; it is rather one-sided, as the title suggests.

Friedman, Milton. *Price Theory* (Chicago, Aldine, 1973).

Getz, Malcolm. *The Economics of the Urban Fire Department* (Baltimore, Johns Hopkins Press, 1979).

Hamilton, B. W. "Capitalization of Interjurisdictional Differences in Local Tax Prices." *American Economic Review* Vol. 66 (1976): 743–753.

_____. "Local Government, the Property Tax and the Quality of Life: Some Findings on Progressivity." *Public Economics and the Quality of Life,* eds. L. Wingo and A. Evans (Washington, D.C.: Resources for the Future, 1977). A discussion of capitalization with empirical evidence.

Hamilton, B. W., E. S. Mills, and D. Puryear. "The Tiebout Hypothesis and Residential Income Segregation." *Fiscal Zoning and Land Use Controls,* eds. E. Mills and W. Oates (Lexington, Mass.: Heath, 1975). An empirical examination of the link between local government structure and residential income segregation.

Hamilton, B. W., and Molly Macauley. "The Determinants and Consequences of the Public/Private School Decision." Johns Hopkins University working paper, 1988.

Hamilton, B. W., and Robert M. Schwab. "Expected Appreciation in Urban Housing Markets." *Journal of Urban Economics* Vol. 18 (July, 1985): 103–118. An examination of the determinants of actual and predicted capital gains for residential property.

Hulten, Charles. "A Method for Estimating Public-Sector Productivity Change." Urban Institute working paper, 1982. A clever but difficult paper that estimates the rate of technological progress in the state and local public sector.

Humphrey, Nancy, George Peterson, and Peter Wilson. *The Future of Cleveland's Capital Plant* (Washington, D.C.: Urban Institute, 1979). Chapter 1 gives an excellent summary of Cleveland's financial plight.

Mieszkowski, P., and M. Straszheim, eds. *Current Issues in Urban Economics* (Baltimore: Johns Hopkins, 1979). A series of detailed up-to-date literature reviews. This is the first source to turn to for more advanced discussions of both local public finance and other branches of urban economics. Especially useful are chapters by Inman, Oakland, Clotfelter, Mills, and Rubinfeld.

Oakland, William. "Proposition 13: Genesis and Consequences." *National Tax Journal* Vol. 32 (June 1979): 387–409. The discussion of Proposition 13 on which the section in this chapter is based.

Oates, W. E. "The Effects of Property Taxes and Local Public Spending on Property Values: An Empirical Study of Tax Capitalization and the Tiebout Hypothesis." *Journal of Political Economy* Vol. 77 (1969): 957–970. The original study of the effects of property taxes and expenditure on property values.

————. "On the Use of Local Zoning Ordinances to Regulate Population Flows and the Quality of Local Services." *Essays in Labor Market Analysis,* eds. O. Ashenfelter and W. Oates (New York: Wiley, 1971) 201–219. A very good discussion of some interesting, but subtle, aspects of the Tiebout hypothesis.

————. "Fiscal Limitations: An Assessment of the U.S. Experience." Sloane working paper no. 5-81 (July 1981), University of Maryland.

Peterson, George E. "Finance." *The Urban Predicament,* eds. W. Gorham and N. Glazer (Washington, D.C.: Urban Institute, 1976). An excellent review of local government finance; it is more detailed than the first section of this chapter.

Reischauer, Robert, Peter Clark, and Peggy Cuciti. *New York City's Fiscal Problem* (Washington, D.C.: Congressional Budget Office, 1975). Has much more detail than this chapter's discussion of New York City's financial crisis.

Summers, A. S., and B. L. Wolfe. "Do Schools Make a Difference?" *American Economic Review* Vol. 67 (1977): 639–652. A careful examination of the determinants of educational attainment.

Tiebout, Charles. "A Pure Theory of Local Public Expenditure." *Journal of Political Economy* Vol. 64 (1956): 416–424. The original statement of the Tiebout hypothesis.

U.S. Department of Commerce, Bureau of the Census. *Current Population Reports: Private School Enrollment, Tuition and Enrollment, Trends: October, 1979.* Series 23, No. 121 (1982). Detailed data on private schools and enrollment trends.

Vickrey, William. "Pricing in Urban and Suburban Transport." *American Economic Review* Vol. 53 (1963): 452–465.

14

Pollution and Environmental Quality

☐ Public and private concern with pollution have increased enormously since World War II. Before the war, concern with pollution was mostly restricted to small groups of conservationists, who sometimes appeared to be urging society to adopt the irrational policy of not using depletable natural resources. All that now has changed. Opinion polls show environmental problems to be high on the list of public concerns. Articles on the despoliation of the environment fill newspapers and magazines. Officials pollute the media with statements on pollution. Dozens of laws have been passed by federal, state, and local governments with the purpose of abating pollution. Although the intensity of concern with environmental problems has slackened during the 1980s, they still rank high among people's concerns.

The reasons for increased concern are not hard to find, although no one can work long with environmental problems and not realize the inadequacies of the data base. First, there can be no doubt that the volume of wastes discharged into the environment has increased in recent decades. At a given state of technology and with a given mix of inputs and outputs, waste generation is about proportionate to the production of goods or to the level of real income. In 1986 real income and output were almost five times their 1940 levels. Improvements in technology and public policy undoubtedly imply that waste generation increased by less than output during this interval, but it cannot be doubted that the increase was substantial. Furthermore, modern technology produces some particularly persistent and harmful wastes that were unknown a few decades ago. Atomic radiation and pesticides are good examples.

The second reason for increased concern is that pollution is more bothersome than it used to be. Popular writers refer to the revolution of rising expectations regarding the environment. It is a short step from that view to the position that a worsening of pollution is partly a matter of perception. Widespread prosperity has provided the income and leisure necessary to enjoy the environment through boating, camping, swimming, hiking, and skiing. Income elasticities of demand are high for such activities. Somewhat more subtle, but closely related, is the fact that people become much more concerned with the effects of pollution on health and mortality when urgent problems of massive unemployment and poverty have abated. Such concerns, however, are neither irrational nor frivolous.

Third, the rapid urbanization of the country makes pollution worse than it used to be. Despite some views to the contrary, harmful waste discharges per capita are not greater in urban than in rural areas. The opposite actually is true, since some large waste-producing activities, such as agriculture and mining, occur predominantly in rural areas, and more resources are devoted to careful waste disposal in urban than in rural areas. The environment has the capacity to assimilate wastes. If that capacity is not exceeded, environmental quality remains intact. Large concentrations of people and economic activity, however, place great stress on the environment. Thus, the most serious deterioration in air and water quality has occurred in large metropolitan areas such as New York City, Chicago, and Los Angeles.

As with poverty, poor housing, and inadequate financing of local public services, pollution is by no means exclusively an urban problem. Some of the worst open dumps and littering of landscapes are in rural areas. Rural lakes and streams are frequently polluted. Even though urban areas have more than their share of air and water pollution, rural pollution is of concern to urban residents.

☐ FACTS, INSTITUTIONS, AND BASIC ECONOMICS

What Is Pollution?

Although illustrations have been given, no limits have yet been placed on the concept of pollution. As pollution abatement has become an accepted goal, people have tended to include a variety of odious activities under the rubric of pollution. Air and water pollution are familiar concepts. Most people are used to describing as pollution the littering of the landscape with solid wastes. Some people would include excessive noise under the pollution heading. Others would include a range of issues that relate to the beauty of urban and rural areas, social tensions, and other problems.

The term will be used narrowly in this chapter. Economic activity requires the withdrawal of materials from the environment. Most materials are eventually returned to the environment in ways more or less harmful to the environment. The term *pollution* will be used to describe the impairment of the environment by the return or discharge of materials to it. The definition includes the usual categories of air, water, and solid waste pollution, but it excludes a wide variety of social and aesthetic issues sometimes classified as environmental. The reason for limiting the subject is not that the included problems are necessarily more important than the excluded ones, but that waste disposal problems have important elements in common that are not shared by the excluded issues, and that can be analyzed in certain ways. Air, water, and solid waste pollution result from waste disposal, and they mainly involve materials that have potential economic value. These characteristics are not shared by an inadequate architectural environment, for example.

Materials Balance

The first step in thinking systematically about environmental problems is to place them in the context of the materials balance. This leads to some of the fundamental insights regarding environmental problems.

All commodity production consists of the application of other inputs—labor, capital, and so on—to materials extracted from the environment in order to transform them from their natural states into useful products. As materials are extracted and processed, large amounts of unwanted materials are separated and returned to the environment. Once the completed commodities lose their economic value, they too must be returned to the environment or be recycled back into the productive process. The **materials balance** is an identity that equates exhaustive lists of sources and dispositions of materials. In its simplest form, it can be stated as follows: materials extracted from the environment during the year must equal those in the system at the end of the year plus those returned to the environment during the year. Additions to the stock of materials in the economic system are *capital accumulation*. Thus, the materials balance also can be stated as follows: in any year, materials extractions from the environment equal discharges to the environment plus capital accumulation.

The materials balance bears the same relationship to the national materials accounts that the identity between sources and dispositions of income bears to the national income accounts. Unfortunately, only fragmentary data are available concerning the components of the materials accounts. Capital accumulation is 10 to 15 percent of total production and is probably about the same proportion of materials output in the United States. Thus, returns to the environment in the United States now equal about 85 to 90 percent of withdrawals from the environment.

Table 14.1 shows some private estimates of materials extraction plus net imports in the United States for 1965. The volume of extraction is enormous. The total in Table 14.1 comes to about 70 pounds of materials extracted from the environment per person per day; and that excludes masses of construction material that are merely moved from one place to another without being processed. Of the total in the ta-

Table 14.1 *Weight of Basic Materials Production in the United States Plus Net Imports, 1965 (In Millions of Tons)*

Material	Weight
Agricultural	
Crops	364
Livestock	23.5
Fisheries	2
Subtotal	389.5
Forestry products	
Sawlogs	120
Pulpwood	54
Other	42
Subtotal	218
Mineral fuels	1,448
Other minerals	
Iron ore	245
Other metal ore	191
Other nonmetals	149
Subtotal	585
Total	2,640.5

Source: Adapted with permission from Allen Kneese, Robert Ayres, and Ralph D'Arge. *Economics and the Environment* (Baltimore, Johns Hopkins University Press, 1970): 10.

ble, more than half is fuels. The remainder is divided about equally between nonfuel minerals and agricultural, forestry, and fishery products. Unfortunately, the numbers in the table are dated. For the mid-1980s, 120 pounds per person per day is probably a good estimate of total withdrawals. The relationships among the numbers are probably as accurate today as they were in 1965.

Form of discharges. The materials balance tells us that approximately 85 percent of the roughly 120 pounds per person per day of materials withdrawals is returned to the environment. What happens to this enormous volume of discharges? Of the large volume of withdrawals in agriculture and minerals extraction industries, much is returned to the environment on the site from which it was extracted. Some such returns do no harm to the environment, but most extractive industries do great environmental damage unless materials are returned with care. Strip mining of coal is currently a controversial example in this category.

Smaller, but still large, parts of withdrawals are processed and incorporated in products. All such materials eventually are returned to the environment as discharges into air, water, or land. The nature of the media waste discharged depends on the technical characteristics of products and production processes and on economic variables. For example, fuels are burned, discharging some materials to the air and leaving some as solid waste. The energy released is converted to heat, which eventually is discharged into the air. Solid waste from fuel results in part from noncombustible impurities, but also in part from incomplete combustion. The amount of such waste to be disposed of depends in part on the relative prices of fuels and high-quality combustion systems.

Most liquid waste, both in industry and households, is really solid waste that is either dissolved or conveniently floated away in water. For example, kitchen garbage appears as solid waste if it is put in the garbage can and as liquid waste if it is ground in the disposal and washed down the drain.

Thus, many wastes can be discharged as liquid, airborne, or solid wastes, depending on the products produced, the production processes, and the treatment processes employed to convert wastes from one form to another. The effects of waste discharges on people and the environment depend crucially on the form in which they are discharged. The materials balance states that most materials withdrawn must be returned to the environment, but it does not tell the form in which they are returned or the medium to which they are returned. These depend on technical, economic, and government policy variables.

Amount of discharges. The materials balance states that, except for the capital accumulation, materials discharges equal materials withdrawals. If the production of commodities and services were proportionate to materials inputs, the only way to reduce withdrawals and discharges would be to reduce production and, therefore, living standards. Some environmentalists indeed have urged governments to reduce living standards systematically to preserve environmental quality. If that were the only way to achieve a livable environment, it would be justifiable. In the last part of the twentieth century, however, it is a counsel of despair. The previous subsection showed that environmental damage depends on not only the amount, but also the form, of returns.

In addition, it is in fact possible to reduce the withdrawals and discharges necessary to achieve a given living standard. Indeed, that is a normal characteristic of technological progress. For 150 years or so, the total output per unit of materials extraction has risen gradually in the United States. This is because an important characteristic of technological progress is learning how to make more efficient use of materials. For example, in the early years of the century, much of the content of crude oil was returned to the environment after fuel had been refined out. Now a wide range of products—plastics, chemicals, and medicines, for example—is made from previously discarded materials.[1]

---

1. Chapter 2 discusses another example—steel.

Another way to reduce the materials withdrawals and discharges necessary to produce a given living standard is to reuse materials. For example, trees are felled and processed into newspapers, and petroleum is pumped from the ground and processed into fuel for thermalelectric generators. Newspapers usually are returned to the environment by placing them in landfills. (A day or so after publication, a newspaper's consumption value is gone, although its physical condition is unchanged by consumption.) Petroleum is mostly returned to the environment in the form of heat and gases released by combustion. The production and consumption of newspapers and electricity can be maintained, while reducing the withdrawal and discharge of petroleum, by burning used newspapers as fuel in thermalelectric plants. The return of newspapers to the environment is thereby unchanged, but the form of the return is altered.

Thus, materials reuse depends on both technical and economic variables. Many materials can be reused, but some only at great cost. The cost depends on the nature of the material and on the nature of the product in which it is incorporated. Other materials are easy to reuse and are reused in large quantities. The greater the reuse of materials, the smaller is the volume of materials withdrawal and discharge required to maintain given living standards.

Absorptive capacity of the environment. Finally, every aspect of the environment has a considerable capacity to absorb waste and regenerate itself. A stream can dilute any waste, and it can degrade and render organic wastes innocuous. If a stream is overloaded with organic wastes, however, it loses its capacity to degrade organic material. Extreme overloading occurs when so much organic material is discharged into the stream that it becomes *anaerobic* (that is, it loses all its dissolved oxygen). Its regenerative capacity is then virtually destroyed and may take a long time to return. An anaerobic stream cannot support fish life, and it stinks from the hydrogen sulfide gas it produces.

Chemical and other processes in the atmosphere also permit the absorption of limited amounts of waste without damage. For example, much of the sulfur discharged into the atmosphere eventually is converted to sulfuric acid and other compounds and is returned to the earth by precipitation. Particles discharged into the air eventually settle back onto the earth's surface. Much less is known, however, about the chemical and other processes by which air restores its quality than about those by which water restores its quality. Although hydrocarbons from automobile exhausts certainly seem to be a major factor, it is still not known, after many years of intensive study, just how smog is produced in Los Angeles and other cities. This is unfortunate, since, as Allen Kneese—the leading economist specializing in environmental problems—put it, "We are in somewhat the same position in regard to polluted air as the fish are to polluted water. We live in it" (Kneese, cited in Wolozin, 1966, 33).

The environment also can degrade limited amounts of solid waste. Organic materials eventually rot, and ferrous metals rust. Problems arise, however, when the environment is overloaded, and modern technology produces materials such as glass, pesticides, and plastics that do not degrade.

Unfortunately, it is not known how large parts of the materials withdrawn from the environment are returned. Most are returned as solid wastes, but most environmental damage is done by the relatively small amounts returned to air and water environments.

Pollution of all forms is most serious in urban areas, because the overloading and subsequent impairment of the environment are most serious there. The concentration of people and affluence produces much more waste than the environment can absorb.

Amounts and Effects of Pollutants

Air pollution.   Some materials discharged to the atmosphere are innocuous, at least in the short run. Most important is carbon dioxide, which is discharged in large volumes by the combustion of fossil fuels. Combustion has measurably increased the carbon dioxide content of the atmosphere during the twentieth century. Further increases may have adverse influences on weather and vegetation, but there is no evidence that present levels are harmful. Of the materials discharged to the atmosphere, five are likely to have adverse effects on people and property: particulates, sulfur oxides, carbon monoxide, hydrocarbons, and nitrogen oxides. Table 14.2 shows sources and amounts of these discharges for 1980; for each pollutant it also shows 1980 and 1950 emissions as a percentage of their 1974 level. All except nitrogen oxides show some improvement since 1974. Note that the final column, 1950 emissions as a percentage of the 1974 level, reveals that air quality deteriorated between 1950 and 1974, except for the particulates category.

The total discharges in Table 14.2 are nearly a ton per capita. About half is carbon monoxide; sulfur oxides, nitrogen oxides, and hydrocarbons are about 15 percent each; and particulates are about 5 percent. Most of the carbon monoxide comes from automobile exhaust. Diesel engines, used in some trucks, buses, and cars, produce negligible amounts of carbon monoxide. Most sulfur oxide discharges are from the combustion of fossil fuels in electric power plants, factories, and homes. Hydrocarbons are discharged by many industrial processes, but nearly half comes from automobile engines. Particulates are small bits of solid matter, such as dust and ash, which come mostly from industrial processes. Nitrogen oxides come mainly from combustion in vehicles and stationary combustion systems.

What are the effects of these pollutants on people and property? Property damage by pollutants can be studied in laboratory experiments, but health damage must be inferred from laboratory experiments on

Table 14.2 *Air Pollution Emissions, 1980 (In Millions of Metric Tons Per Year)*

Pollutants and Sources	1980	1980 as a Percentage of 1974 Level	1950 as a Percentage of 1974 Level
Particulates			
Transportation	1.4		
Fuel combustion in stationary sources	1.4		
Industrial processes	3.7		
Solid waste disposal	0.4		
Miscellaneous	0.9		
Total	7.8	64	192
Sulfur oxides			
Transportation	0.9		
Fuel combustion in stationary sources	19.0		
Industrial processes	3.8		
Solid waste disposal	0.0		
Miscellaneous	0.0		
Total	23.7	88	73
Carbon monoxide			
Transportation	69.1		
Fuel combustion in stationary sources	2.1		
Industrial processes	5.8		
Solid waste disposal	2.2		
Miscellaneous	6.2		
Total	85.4	83	83
Hydrocarbons			
Transportation	7.8		
Fuel combustion in stationary sources	0.2		
Industrial processes	10.8		
Solid waste disposal	0.6		
Miscellaneous	2.4		
Total	21.8	92	74
Nitrogen oxides[a]			
Transportation	9.1		
Fuel combustion in stationary sources	10.6		
Industrial processes	0.7		
Solid waste disposal	0.1		
Miscellaneous	0.2		
Total	20.7	103	46

[a]The failure to reduce emissions of nitrogen oxides is noteworthy. Airborne nitrogen and sulfur oxides are the main contributors to acid rain (Council on Environmental Quality, 1981, 45–48).
Source: Data from Council on Environmental Quality. *Environmental Quality*. Washington, D.C., 1981, p. 246.

small mammals or from data on the health of people variously exposed to the pollutants in their normal lives. Lave and Seskin (1977) have undertaken the best of the second kind of study. Most of the substances in Table 14.2 are deadly in high concentrations, but average exposures are far below such levels; the challenge is to estimate chronic health effects of low-level exposures.

Evidence of chronic health effects is strongest for sulfur oxides and particulates. Lave and Seskin estimate that 50 percent reductions in ambient concentrations of these pollutants from their 1970 levels over the average metropolitan area might add a year or so to life expectancy there. It is a striking conclusion and, if correct, justifies a large government air pollution abatement program. Health effects from the other three pollutants, for which the automobile is the main culprit, are much less well established.

Carbon monoxide appears to do no property damage at existing concentrations. Hydrocarbons and nitrogen oxides probably do no more than slight property damage. They interact to form smog in the presence of sunlight. Although smog has no discernible long-term health effects, it irritates and annoys people.

Most estimates place the benefits of the air pollution abatement mandated by existing laws at about $25 billion per year 1980 or thereabouts. About $20 billion of the total was health benefits. This was a substantial total, approaching 1 percent of GNP. Although the methods and data employed in most estimates can be severely criticized, the frequency of such results suggests that this estimate of total benefits is at least in the ball park.

The costs of abating polluting discharges by a specified change in production technology are relatively easy to estimate. For example, a frequently used air pollution abatement strategy has been substitution of oil for coal in thermalelectric plants. It is not difficult to calculate the costs of such a substitution. The difficult task is estimating what changes in technology will be required to accomplish mandated discharge abatements. Both government and private estimates of the costs of achieving the discharge abatement mandated by existing laws are available. For the years around 1980, they clustered around $20–$25 billion per year—about half for motor vehicles and half for stationary sources.

Putting together benefit and cost estimates suggests that benefits probably exceed costs for existing air pollution control programs. This by no means proves that the programs are the best that can be devised, but it suggests that they aim at roughly the right amount of abatement.

Water pollution. Humans have no feasible alternative to breathing air, so all of it should be fit to breathe. They drink only a small part of the available water, however, so not all of it needs to be fit to drink. When lay people think of water shortages and water pollution, they think of water for drinking and other domestic purposes. Domestic use, however, is only a small part of the water story.

The most important distinction regarding water use is between in-stream and withdrawal uses. *In-stream uses* are those for which the water remains in its natural channel. The most important examples are commercial and sport fishing, pleasure boating, navigation, swimming, hydroelectric generation, and aesthetic use. The last example refers to the fact that many recreational activities—especially hiking, picnicking, and camping—are enhanced by proximity to bodies of water.

Withdrawal uses are those that require water to be withdrawn from its natural channel. The major purposes of withdrawal are municipal use, industrial processing, cooling, and irrigation. Water withdrawn by municipalities for public water supply is for domestic, commercial, and public (for example, fire protection) uses. *Industrial processing* refers to a variety of industrial uses, many of which involve the washing away of wastes. *Cooling* means the use of water to dissipate heat, by far the most important example being thermalelectricity generation. *Irrigation* refers to the withdrawal of water for farm animals and crops.

Water quality is a complex notion with many dimensions, and quality requirements vary enormously among the many uses of water. For pleasure boating and aesthetic uses, the major quality requirements are the absence of odors, discoloration, and floating solids. Quality requirements vary among industrial processing uses, but for most, the major requirement is the absence of salts that corrode pipes. Noncorrosive properties are also important for cooling uses, as is temperature. Different kinds of fish can live in water of different qualities, and much is known about the effects of water quality on game fish.

The highest quality requirements are for municipal water, since it must be fit to drink. Public health authorities in the United States set stringent quality standards, although there are many unanswered questions about the effects of relaxing one or more standards. The United States, however, has largely avoided waterborne diseases endemic in countries that apply less strict standards for drinking water.

Swimming water is something of an enigma. Authorities set the same requirements for swimming as for drinking water, although swimmers need not drink the water they swim in, and many people swim in water they should not drink. Various afflictions can result from swimming in poor-quality water, but little is known about the likely incidence at different quality levels. Chlorine used to purify water in swimming pools may cause ear and other problems. With swimming, as with other water quality requirements, there is an important subjective element, in that people simply find it distasteful to swim in dirty water.

The subjective element in water quality standards causes much confusion. It often is claimed that people do not like to drink reused water, regardless of its quality. To the extent that the reason is a misunderstanding about its quality, presumably people's feelings can be changed by education. To the extent that subjective feelings represent genuine tastes, however, they should not be ignored. The fact that some people pay $100 more for color television than for black and white is not ignored, although the preference is certainly subjective. With water use, however, people often want someone else to pay the cost. For example, New York City has long urged the federal government to build it a plant to desalt sea water so that New Yorkers can avoid reusing Hudson River water. No New York mayor has yet seen fit to ask the city's residents whether they are willing to pay for high-cost desalted water. If they are, outsiders should not object.

Not only do the various water uses have different quality requirements; they also have various effects on water quality. In the course of using water, humans discharge an enormous variety of wastes into streams and estuaries. The most important and best-documented category of waste discharge is organic material. Although there are many kinds of organic materials, most share the important characteristic of using dissolved oxygen in the water as they are degraded. The dissolved oxygen content determines the kind of fish and other life that can survive in the water and affects virtually every use of water. An anaerobic stream is useless for almost all the purposes that have been discussed. Thus, the most significant measure of water pollution is the rate at which organic discharges use oxygen, referred to as *biochemical oxygen demand* (BOD). The quality of the water in a stream is determined by the BOD of wastes discharged into it and by the rate at which the stream can replenish its oxygen from the atmosphere, called its *reaeration rate.*

Table 14.3 shows estimates of BOD discharges into water bodies in the United States in 1973. The table includes only wastes actually discharged into bodies of water. Thus, it excludes BOD wastes that were generated but then removed from waste water by treatment. It also excludes wastes discharged directly into the ground, as in septic tanks. Most of the municipal and industrial waste in Table 14.3 is urban. Some of the *nonpoint sources* (that is, sources that cannot be traced to a specific site) are urban, for example, pollutants washed off city streets into nearby streams. Most wastes from nonpoint sources are agricultural, however.

Table 14.3 shows that more than 80 percent of organic waste discharges are from nonpoint sources. The national pollution control program has greatly reduced organic waste discharges from municipal and industrial sources since the 1960s. Further progress will require reductions from nonpoint sources, however. Wastes from city streets can be collected and treated, although only at considerable cost; however,

Table 14.3 *Organic Waste Discharges in the United States, 1973 (In Billions of Pounds of BOD)*

Source	Waste
Municipal	5.6
Industrial	4.3
Nonpoint	45.0
Total	54.9

Note: These numbers were not updated in the 1981 issue of *Environmental Quality.*
Source: Data from Council on Environmental Quality. *Environmental Quality.* Washington, D.C., 1976, p. 257.

organic wastes from fertilizer and other agricultural sources cannot. For these, discharge reduction requires either erosion control or a reduction in the organic wastes produced.

Suspended solids such as salts and silt are the second important type of water pollutant. Salts are corrosive and affect fish life in streams. Irrigation leaches salts from the soil, and irrigation return flow is the major source of harmful salts in western rivers. Silt is mainly runoff from farmland and construction projects. Slowly moving water allows silt to settle, and it fills up navigational channels and water supply reservoirs. Silt also changes the color of water, affecting its aesthetic use. Most importantly, it reduces light penetration in water, impairing its ability to degrade organic materials.

Heat is another major polluting waste. A large thermalelectricity plant may withdraw most of the water in a moderate-sized stream and raise its temperature 10 or more degrees. Atomic plants tend to be larger than the largest conventional plants, and they operate at lower efficiency levels. They therefore discharge enormous amounts of heat. Water temperature affects fish life. In winter, fish that have disappeared from other parts of streams can be caught near the outfalls of electric plants. In summer, however, heat discharge may raise water temperature above the survival level. Most importantly, high temperature speeds the process of organic degradation, thus reducing the stream's ability to cope with organic pollutants. (The more rapid degradation speeds the depletion of oxygen.)

Nutrients, such as phosphates and nitrates, are an increasingly serious source of water pollution. Nutrients are the major constituents of agricultural fertilizer and an important ingredient in detergents. They are produced by the degradation of organic material, whether it takes place in a body of water or in a sewage treatment plant. Nutrients thus enter bodies of water by the degradation of discharged organic material, by the effluent from municipal treatment plants, and by runoff from fertilized farmland. Nutrients fertilize water as they do land. In water, fertilization causes algae growth, which affects the appearance, taste, and odor of the water. Fertilization, or *eutrophication,* of the water from treatment plants is most common in estuaries or downstream from large cities. Eutrophication from agricultural runoff is, of course, most common in rural areas.

A large variety of long-lived chemicals is discharged into water bodies by chemical and other industries. Chemicals also enter water bodies inadvertently. Powerful pesticides such as DDT enter water from agricultural runoff. A particularly perplexing problem is acid drainage from mines. When coal mines are abandoned, they usually fill with water. As ground water passes through them, sulfuric and other acids are formed. Some of the acid eventually seeps into streams. The effects of chemical discharges vary from chemical to chemical. Some are poisonous to fish, wildlife, and humans. Others cause odors and discoloration.

Solid waste pollution.   By volume, most of the materials in Table 14.1 are returned to the environment as solid wastes, and about 90 percent are discharged at the point of extraction. This subsection will focus on solid wastes that are wholly or partly processed into products. Most such solid wastes are discharged in urban areas.

Table 14.4 shows data on solid waste discharges. The total comes to more than 10 pounds per person per day. A bit less than half the total is collected by government and private municipal refuse collection agencies. About 80 percent of the collected refuse is combustible, consisting of paper, cardboard, garbage, wood, leaves, and grass. The remainder is mostly glass, metal, and plastic. Industrial solid waste is known to be more variable than domestic waste. Much is either noncombustible or releases toxic fumes when burned.

About 75 percent of collected solid waste is disposed of in nearby open dumps. About 13 percent is placed in sanitary landfills, where each day's waste is covered with a layer of soil to prevent odors, fires, eyesores, and vermin. About 8 percent is incinerated, thus converting solid waste into airborne waste and an unburned residual solid waste.

What harm is done by the various means of solid waste disposal? The question is surprisingly difficult to answer. Most sources present lists of qualitative and potential damages, but quantitative evidence is almost nonexistent. The most prominent effect of poor solid waste disposal is aesthetic. Open dumps are terrible eyesores, as are the bottles, cans, and papers discarded on streets, parks, and beaches. Much of the harm from open dumps, however, comes from the air and water pollution they cause. Dumps frequently burn, causing air pollution. In addition, organic wastes leak into streams, adding discharges from other sources to the BOD.

Alternative Government Environmental Policies

It is easy to understand the fundamental reason for the pollution problem. Polluting discharges to the environment are an *external diseconomy,* as the term was defined in Chapter 8. As has been shown, many kinds of production can use combinations of inputs that generate a range of kinds and amounts of waste.

In many cases, productive techniques that generate large amounts of harmful wastes are cheaper than other techniques. Furthermore, wastes can be discharged to the environment in many forms, depending on the ways they are treated. All forms of treatment require valuable resources, however. Finally, the extent to which used products are recycled or discharged into the environment depends on the relative costs of new and used materials. As also has been seen, people value a high-quality environment for health, aesthetic, and recreational reasons.

Table 14.4 *Solid Waste Discharges in the United States, 1977 (In Millions of Tons)*

Source	Waste
Municipal[a]	
Residential/commercial/industrial	145
Sewage sludge	5
Junked automobiles,	
construction/demolition	45
Industrial	
Nonhazardous	323 to 342
Hazardous	38 to 57
Radioactive	0.04
Total	556 to 594

[a]Does not include "uncollected," which was about one-quarter of the total in 1969.
Source: Data from Council on Environmental Quality. *Environmental Quality.* Washington, D.C., 1981, p. 92.

Producers can keep costs low by large and relatively harmful discharges to the environment. The cost of the resulting deterioration in environmental quality is borne by those whose use of the environment is impaired, but those who make the decisions regarding harmful discharges fail to take account of the costs that discharges impose. Although a high-quality environment is valuable, its value does not get counted in market transactions. Thus, too few resources are devoted to the reduction of waste discharges by recycling and to the treatment of wastes.

Why do producers and users of the environment not make private agreements to optimize discharges? Sometimes they do. Many agreements are made regarding waste disposal on private land. Air and flowing water, however, are *fugitive resources:* their movements are hard to predict, and it is extremely difficult to compute the damage done to them by each discharger to the environment. The transaction costs of private agreements are so great for many environmental problems that private agreements are rare. The history of government policy toward the environment has been a history of a search for policies that regulate discharges to the environment without large transaction costs to the government and private sectors.

It has never been legal to discharge wastes freely into the air and water. The common law has long restricted activities that create nuisances. State water-rights laws always have provided some protection for the rights of downstream users, and public health laws have long imposed stringent restrictions on discharges into water used for domestic water supply. These laws have been important, especially in protecting public health. From the point of view of optimum resource allocation, however, they are a patchwork created at different times and for many purposes, and they are extremely resistant to change. In the postwar period, the need for special laws aimed squarely at pollution has become clear.

Government collection and disposal.   The most straightforward government antipollution policy is government construction and operation of facilities to collect, treat, and dispose of wastes. Public facilities are the predominant method of handling household and commercial sewage and solid wastes. Scale economies make it desirable for a single organization to perform these services for an entire metropolitan area. Such an organization should be either publicly owned or privately owned and publicly regulated. Both methods are employed in the United States, but the former predominates.

Regulation and enforcement.   Aside from the construction and operation of disposal facilities, the most common government antipollution program in the United States is discharge regulation. After more than a decade of experimentation with alternative approaches, the present program was laid down in laws passed in the early 1970s. These laws established the Environmental Protection Agency (EPA) and empowered it to control air, water, and solid waste discharges.

For air and water discharges, the procedure is similar. The EPA is instructed to regulate total discharge volumes into a stream or into the air over a metropolitan area, keeping environmental quality at levels that protect public health and welfare. This is an enormous task, especially for the large numbers of wastes discharged into water. Any firm or municipality that wants to discharge wastes into air or water must apply to the EPA for a permit to do so. The EPA attempts to restrict the total allowed by the permits issued to discharge volumes that meet its ambient environmental quality goals.

For motor vehicle emissions to the air, the procedure is somewhat different. Unlike other environmental provisions, the automobile pollution law enacted in 1970 specifies permitted automotive discharges; permitted discharges were to decrease gradually until, in 1976, discharges per car would be no more than 5 percent of discharges by the last uncontrolled cars, made in 1967. The goals have since been postponed several times because of energy crises and other events, but standards in effect in the mid-1980s entailed about 85 percent abatement from 1967 discharge levels.

Control of solid waste discharges is still mainly the responsibility of states, which delegate most responsibility to local governments. The federal program is restricted to research and development, data collection, and encouragement to state and local governments to upgrade disposal facilities.

There can be no doubt that the government program has improved environmental quality since the early 1970s.[2] Air discharge volumes

2.   For a sample of cities, the number of "unhealthful" and "very unhealthful" days (defined by an index of pollutant concentrations) fell by about 30 percent (Council on Environmental Quality, 1981, 32).

shown in Table 14.2 are smaller than those in earlier years, and ambient environmental quality measures show improvement. Nevertheless, almost all economists who have studied the programs are highly critical of them. They are very expensive, and economists conclude that the benefits could have been obtained at lower cost.

The permit systems have become extremely complex. The EPA is now our largest regulatory agency, with more than 10,000 employees. The law requires the EPA to issue permits fairly, but literally every industrial, commercial, and government discharge facility is unique. The result is that there are rooms full of regulations about what facility can discharge what wastes. Inevitably, permit levels are negotiated between industrial and government officials. This means that government officials become partners in major business decisions about new plant construction, expansion or redesign of existing plants, design of new products, and important changes in industrial technology. As a result, business decision making is slower, more bureaucratized, less innovative, and less responsive to market signals.

Inevitably, the EPA ends up issuing permits if specific devices have been installed, for example, secondary treatment plants, catalytic converters on cars, and so forth. The procedure emphasizes known and conventional devices, not devices designed to optimize a particular situation. Most importantly, it emphasizes installation instead of operation of abatement devices. Two examples will illustrate.

For the most part, the EPA issues organic waste discharge permits to municipalities if they construct secondary treatment plants, which can remove about 90 percent of organic wastes before discharge. Municipalities are happy to construct such facilities: most of the money is provided in grants by federal and state governments, and local governments win the favor of construction contractors and unions by the resulting business. Municipalities have no incentive to operate the treatment plants efficiently once they have been built, however, so many are operated at about half their potential effectiveness.

New cars must meet stringent discharge limits stipulated in the law. Once cars are on the road, however, emissions are not checked except in a few states (notably New Jersey) that check emissions at annual safety inspections. Emission control devices do not continue to function properly longer than two or three years unless they are serviced and maintained. Furthermore, the car owner has a disincentive to maintain the devices, since the car's fuel mileage improves if the devices fail. The result is that new cars have technically sophisticated and expensive emission control devices, but most cars on the road do not meet the legal standards. Much of the money spent to make a car meet extremely high standards when new is wasted.

Economists believe that the federal discharge abatement program should encourage flexibility and innovation in the means by which discharge goals are met and in the precise times at which they are met. Most importantly, they believe the program should permit decentralized and market-oriented decision making, in which businesses can make discharge decisions on the basis of economic criteria and without negotiating every major decision with government officials.

Subsidies. A federal grant program to subsidize the construction of municipal sewage treatment plants is a major part of the nation's pollution abatement program. Annual appropriations were in excess of $4 billion in the late 1970s, but have fallen during the 1980s. The program has resulted in treatment plant construction all around the country and certainly has reduced the volume of organic discharges to streams and estuaries by municipalities. It already has been pointed out that the discharge abatement program places too much emphasis on facility construction and not enough on operation. The purpose of the subsidy program is political. In principle, the federal government should issue discharge permits, and the required abatement should be at the expense of those who generate the wastes. In the case of municipal sewage, the expense would be borne by local taxpayers. In fact, the federal government has almost no way to force local governments to comply with permits it issues. Local officials cannot be fined and jailed. About the only possibility is for the federal government to withhold grant funds for other purposes, such as housing subsidization, in the event of noncompliance. Such funds are given for urgent purposes—mostly to benefit the poor—and to withhold them would be unpopular. In the absence of large federal construction subsidies, many hard-pressed local governments probably just would not comply with federal permits.

Public officials frequently propose broad-based discharge abatement subsidies. The proposal most often studied is simple: a payment to all dischargers proportionate to the amount by which they abate discharges. Economists oppose such proposals on both efficiency and equity grounds. On efficiency grounds, subsidies do not achieve desired abatement economically. Subsidization would reduce discharges per unit of output, but the firm's improved revenue position would motivate it to increase output. The net effect could be an increase in polluting discharges. On equity grounds, subsidies are, in effect, payments to those who pollute by the remainder of society. This hardly seems like a desirable way to redistribute income.

Such a subsidy scheme also would be an administrative nightmare. It would require the estimation of discharge volumes in the absence of subsidy payments. Dischargers would be motivated to exaggerate the volume of discharges they would have had. Especially with new or expanded production facilities, or new or modified products, estimation would be extremely difficult.

Effluent fees. Almost all economists who have studied the subject favor a partial or total dismantling of the permit program and its replacement by an *effluent fee*. Effluent fees are extremely simple: dischargers are permitted to discharge whatever quantity of wastes they wish, but they must pay the government a fee per unit of waste discharged. The fee for each major waste would be set by the government at the level it estimates would result in discharge volumes that equate marginal social benefits and costs of abatement.

Setting effluent fees requires the same data and calculations that issuing permits requires—no more and no less. The government must estimate the benefits and costs of abatement for either program, and it must meter actual discharges, at least on a sample basis. The great advantage of effluent fees over the permit program is that the government would be removed from business decision making, with environmental decisions placed within the market context that firms are motivated to use and are experienced in using. Firms could design whatever abatement devices appeared to them to be the most economical means of achieving each abatement level. They would not need to obtain government permission for devices or discharge volumes.

Dischargers would be motivated to seek economical means of abatement as long as they discharged any wastes. Under a permit system, dischargers have no incentive to discharge less than the level provided by their permit.

Effluent fees have been better studied than almost any actual or potential government program. Their advantages in comparison with alternatives are overwhelming. They have been advocated by economists, business groups, and environmental groups. Other countries, especially West Germany and France, have tried them successfully. Why have they not been tried in the United States? The existing environmental program was put in place during the zenith of the environmental movement in the early 1970s. The mood of the country was similar to that of a crusade—not a time when politicians want to listen to economists talk about the dangers of government intrusion into business. Since then, an enormous amount of human and physical capital has been invested in the permit program: designing it, implementing it, and learning to live with it. Furthermore, attention has shifted to fuel and other materials shortages.

In fact, interest in introducing economic incentives into the environmental program is growing. Government officials are more interested in economic arguments now than they were a decade ago; the problems with the permit program have become more obvious, and more is known about the practical aspects of effluent fee programs. The EPA is moving to introduce better economic incentives into the program.

Marketable pollution rights. The notion of marketable pollution rights, worked out in some detail by Coolinge and Oates (1982), is an interesting variant of effluent fees. First, a state or local government decides that the total amount of pollution (usually just point-source pollution) to be permitted in an area shall be X percent of the current level of pollution. Each existing fixed-site polluter then is granted a license to dump X percent of its current level of pollution. The final step allows holders of these pollution permits to buy or sell them at whatever price the market will bear. Once the "market" for pollution has cleared, the outcome will have the following features: (1) pollution will be X percent of its original level, just as the government had wanted, and (2) every firm will face the same price of pollution, namely, the market price of pollution coupons.

This proposal has two advantages over the standard effluent fee system. First, the government would know in advance how much pollution will be reduced; with effluent fees it can do little more than guess. Second, the redistribution of wealth and the resistance to the plan would be much more modest under the marketable pollution rights scheme. Under the effluent fee system, many firms would be driven out of business because they were unable to pay the fees (for several steel mills, this is a real possibility). The hardship under the marketable pollution rights system would be much less severe. Suppose efficiency calls for a pollution reduction of 50 percent. Under an efficient effluent fee scheme, a firm would be induced to reduce pollution by 50 percent, but it still would have to pay a fee on the other 50 percent. Under the marketable pollution rights scheme, the same (efficient) 50 percent pollution reduction would be achieved without forcing the firm to pay a fee on the remaining 50 percent.

As this discussion makes clear, the difference between the programs is basically a difference in ownership of the property right to environmental quality. As such, many people argue that the marketable pollution rights scheme passes out property rights to the wrong group of people—those who have polluted the environment in the past. The dispute is over a fair redistribution of property rights.

Materials reuse. Although air and water pollution control is a cooperative federal-state program, its basic characteristics have been federal initiatives since the 1950s. Solid waste disposal, and hence reuse, is still mainly a state and local responsibility, however. Furthermore, most of the used products from which reusable materials come are in urban areas. Thus, solid waste disposal and materials recovery are of great interest to urban governments.

Materials reuse responds strongly to prices of new materials. During times such as the early 1970s, when newly extracted materials—from food to metals to fuel—are scarce and expensive, recovery and reuse flourish. When new materials become relatively less costly, as they did in the mid-1970s and especially in the early 1980s, recovery and reuse languish.

Some materials are much easier to recover and reuse than others. Virgin copper is expensive, and much of it is used in such products as copper wire, from which the copper can be recovered easily. An automobile, by contrast, is a complex product containing many materials, and materials recovery and reuse require sophisticated technology.

Many government actions—mostly having to do with the tax system—favor the use of virgin instead of used materials. There is justification for government programs to promote reuse. Unfortunately, no one knows how much bias toward virgin materials is introduced by governments. In addition, solid waste disposal is a chronic problem for local governments in metropolitan areas. Especially in central cities, land that can be used for landfills is almost nonexistent. Furthermore, local governments appear to be unable to contract with each other so that, for example, central-city governments can dispose of solid wastes in distant suburbs.

During the 1970s several cooperative federal-state-local solid waste recovery and disposal experiments were carried on. Typically, a central facility was established to which municipal and industrial wastes could be brought. At the facility, materials would be separated and processed for reuse. Those for which there was no demand would be disposed of in landfills or incinerators. A typical activity of such facilities was the preparation of organic wastes to be used as fuel in thermalelectric plants. Such experiments have met with mixed success, but experience and high fuel prices presumably will guarantee eventual success. Experiments with "trash-to-stream" continued in the 1980s, but success has been remarkably elusive.

A special local government solid waste problem is presented by sludge from municipal treatment plants. Traditionally, sludge has been burned, disposed of in landfills, or hauled to sea and dumped there. Dumping at sea has been banned, however, creating a crisis in coastal cities. Promising experiments have processed sludge into fertilizer that can be used on farms and lawns. Easy processing results in an inexpensive and high-quality fertilizer. The biggest problem, however, is caused by heavy metals that are discharged into the sewage system by industry and remain intact through treatment. Heavy metals in sludge that is processed into fertilizer may be taken up by plants and ingested by people or animals who eat them. People in the United States, fortunately, have been free of heavy metals poisoning, but experience elsewhere—especially in Japan—shows that heavy metals poisoning can lead to incurable illnesses and death.

Many questions are raised about cooperative solid waste recovery and disposal facilities. Are they successful? To what extent is success the result of the large subsidies that facilities receive, and to what extent is it the result of their innovative activities? Should they be government-run? It is too early to answer such questions.

☐ ENVIRONMENTAL AMENITIES AND URBAN ECONOMICS

So far this discussion of the environment and pollution has had little to do with urban economics per se, that is, with the workings of cities and their economies. Environmental economics, however, is legitimately a branch of urban economics in two important respects.

High Density

The first "urban" observation is that many environmental problems are not problems at all when population densities are small. High density creates a problem by increasing the number of victims of any environmental degradation. If air quality reduction imposes a cost of $100 per year per exposed resident, it is of much more quantitative importance in a city of two million than in a town of 5000.

Second, in addition to increasing the number of pollution victims, and therefore the social costs of pollution, a concentration of people and economic activity generally increases the density of pollutants as well. This is important, because damage generally rises more than proportionately with the volume of discharges—particularly when the pollutants are degradable. For example, up to a point, a stream is capable of degrading organic wastes with little adverse effect on water quality. Once the oxygen is gone, however, the stream cannot support fish life, and further decomposition of organic materials is anaerobic. This anaerobic decomposition causes the foul smell of some sewage-laden streams. Thus, it is frequently large volumes of pollutants that give rise to environmental damage. The same applies to air pollution; many effluents are innocuous at low densities.

These two uniquely urban components of the pollution problem—large numbers of victims and damage that rises more than proportionately with discharges—mean that the per capita cost of pollution is likely to rise with city size. This, of course, means that the marginal cost of pollution is higher than the average cost. That is, the increase in total pollution damage that results from the arrival of a new resident in a city is greater than the per capita pollution damage before the resident's arrival. The new resident pulls up total pollution cost because (1) he or she represents an additional victim of the existing level of pollution, and (2) the resident's presence adds to the existing level of pollution, imposing additional costs on others.

The economic analysis of this situation is much like that of road congestion. The marginal resident, in deciding where to live, takes account of the current pollution level in the city but ignores the effect his or her presence will have on the pollution endured by current residents. Some have argued that this makes major cities too large in a market economy, since households do not face the proper migration incentives. The next chapter will return to this question in considering pollution and congestion problems at the same time.

Amenities, Rents, Wages, and Location

To implement an efficient system of effluent fees (or direct regulations), authorities must determine how much people are willing to pay for environmental improvement. This is the crucial missing information when it comes to deciding how vigorously to pursue pollution abatement. How can the value of air quality improvement be determined?

Urban economics provides one of the few reasonably reliable ways of answering this question. Through their behavior in urban land and labor markets, people provide a substantial amount of evidence regarding their demand for environmental quality.

Intraurban amenity variations. Although there are important qualifications, the basic principle to be explored is that intraurban differences in the value of environmental amenities (including, for example, air quality) are reflected in differences in property values. This principle already has been applied several times in this book—the land market, through spatial variation in rent, soaks up any geographic differences in attainable utility, regardless of whether these differences result from variation in access to the CBD, school quality, taxes, neighborhood amenities, or air quality.

As seen when discussing neighborhood effects, however, the conditions under which property value differences can simply be used as pure measures of amenity differences are quite stringent. Most importantly, it must be assumed that all households have the same demand for the amenity. If demands vary among households—as a result of either income or taste differences—property value differences generally yield an underestimate of the value of environmental quality. For example, suppose there is a city with two households (A and B) and two houses (a and b). Household A has a stronger demand for clean air than does Household B, and the air over House a is cleaner than that over House b. Household A will outbid Household B for House a, with clean air. In equilibrium, however, House a will command a rent premium equal only to the extent of Household B's preference for House a over House b, because this is all that Household A need offer in order to outbid Household B for the house with clean air. Notice that Household A would have been willing to pay a greater premium, but the market did not require it. In other words, the land market reveals Household B's willingness to pay for clean air, but it reveals nothing about Household A's (greater) willingness to pay.[3] So it always is with auctions: the winning bid is the maximum price the second-highest bidder is willing to pay. Obviously, this is less than what the highest bidder is willing to pay.

Despite these caveats, variations in property values contain much information about people's willingness to pay for environmental ameni-

3. It may seem that this example works because of the small number of participants, but that is not so. The market clean air premium generally will be smaller than the willingness of the high-demand people to pay, so long as demands vary. See Polinsky and Rubinfeld (1977) for a thorough, but difficult, discussion of this problem.

ties. Polinsky and Rubinfeld (1977) use the property value method to estimate the value to consumers of a 50 percent reduction in suspended particulates and sulfur dioxide for the St. Louis SMSA. They calculate the present value of the benefit to be about $900 per capita, which gives an annual benefit of roughly $90.[4]

Interurban amenity variations. Researchers have looked at the effects of amenity variations among urban areas for a variety of reasons. One reason is that there is more variation among than within urban areas, so estimation possibilities are richer. Another reason is that the data needs are more modest, as will be shown.

As has been noted at several points, studies of the determinants of rent (or value) variation are hampered by the difficulty of disentangling price from quantity. To examine the effects of amenities on rents, data on rents of dwelling units must first be collected. This is a difficult data-gathering and data-processing task.

Most of these problems do not arise in studies of interurban amenity variations, because the value of these variations reveals itself not in land markets, but rather in labor markets. (This discussion is based upon analysis in Chapter 6.) It works basically as follows. Suppose two urban areas are identical to one another in size, air quality, and all other relevant characteristics. The land rent gradient is the same in both cities, and so are the wage rates. Now air quality over one urban area is improved, making it a more desirable place to live. In the short run, this raises property values (that is, it shifts the land rent gradient up) in the clean city sufficiently to leave people indifferent between the two cities. The clean urban area's land rent gradient now appears as curve B in Figure 14.1. It is not an equilibrium gradient, however; land rent at the edge of the urban area does not fall to zero (or to the exogenous value of agricultural land). Thus, developers have an incentive to increase the size of the urban area by converting land from agriculture to suburbia. In the process, land-market equilibrium is restored; the "tail" is added to the land rent gradient in Figure 14.1. The land rent gradient is still higher in the clean (curve B) than the polluted (curve A) urban area.

Thus, it might appear that a regression of property values on air quality and other determinants still would find an association between air quality and property values. This is not true, however, if population is included in the regression, as it should be. Chapter 6 showed that large urban areas should have higher land rent gradients than small urban areas, and Chapter 7 provided evidence to support this prediction. In fact, in equilibrium, the height of the land rent gradient is de-

---

4.   This is roughly the per-capita cost of today's automobile emission standards. Since automobiles contribute substantially less than half of all forms of air pollution except carbon monoxide (see Table 14.2), this estimate raises some doubt as to whether the benefits of the more stringent automobile emission standards are worth the costs, at least in St. Louis.

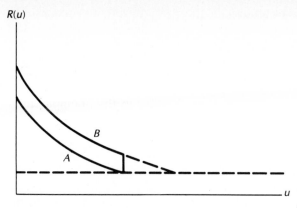

Figure 14.1 *Behavior of Land Rent Function When Air Quality Improves*

termined *only* by population and the amount of available land. There may be irregularities in the shape of the land rent gradient due to within-urban area variations in amenities of various sorts. Aside from these "blips," however, the height must be governed only by population. The reason for this is that rent must fall to zero (or to the exogenous agricultural rent) at the edge of the city to preserve equilibrium between rural and urban land users. The only observable statistical association is between population and land value, not between air quality and land value. Two urban areas of equal size, but different levels of air quality, have identical land rent gradients. And two urban areas with different populations and the same air quality have different land rent gradients.

Returning to the two-urban area example, the clean urban area is now larger and has a higher land rent gradient than the smaller one, and the land market is in equilibrium. What about the labor market? Chapter 6 showed that workers insist on wage premiums to live in a large urban area (to compensate them for the greater commuting or land rent that life in the large urban area entails). Would such a wage premium exist in the large urban area with clean air? If it did, workers would prefer to live there rather than in the small, polluted urban area. It is true that the urban area is bigger and more costly to live in, but the wage premium compensates for this. In addition, the air is cleaner, so the net effect is that everyone prefers living in the large urban area rather than the small, polluted one. This is a situation that cannot persist in equilibrium.

The final equilibrium condition needed is this: after correcting for other determinants, interurban area wage differences must compensate workers for interurban area differences in amenities.

If wages vary among urban areas to compensate for variations in amenities, regression analysis should be able to estimate the size of the compensation workers require to endure various environmental disamenities.[5] Rosen (1979, 100, 101) carried out such a study, which determined the following wage premiums:

$15   per rainy day,

$136   per 10 percent increase in suspended particulates,

$50   per 10 percent increase in the crime rate,

$290   per 1 percent increase in the unemployment rate,[6]

$120   per 10 percent *decrease* in population density, and

$48   per 10 percent increase in population.

Chapter 7 noted that the wage premiums for large population and low population density closely agree with the values predicted by theory. The other numbers above are plausible and interesting, and they tend to confirm that the labor market works basically in the previously indicated way. Rainy days, particulates, crime, and unemployment all are associated with wage premiums, indicating that workers must be compensated for enduring them. The effect of particulates is somewhat larger than that estimated by Polinsky and Rubinfeld (1977). If a 10 percent reduction in particulates results in a wage reduction of $136, a 50 percent reduction in particulates would yield a $680 compensating wage reduction. With about 40 percent of the population in the labor force, this translates to $272 per capita, as compared with the $90 per capita estimated by Polinsky and Rubinfeld.[7] At this stage, these techniques for evaluating environmental amenities are not as refined as might be hoped, although it is encouraging to see that the studies yield plausible results.

Firm location.   Chapter 2 discussed several determinants of firm location. It noted the historical importance of regional variations in input and output prices, as well as in the costs of transporting both inputs and outputs. It also showed, however, that both transport orientation and production cost orientation have declined over the past two centuries as a result of declines in transport costs and reductions in regional input cost variations. Increasingly, firms are footloose—not strongly tied to any location, at least for the traditional reasons. This, it has been argued, has led to an increase in amenity orientation—the tendency for firms to seek locations where working and living are en-

5. As is always the case with regression analysis, it is necessary to include other determinants of wages (such as education and experience) in order to isolate the effects of amenities.

6. It might seem that high unemployment—indicating a depressed labor market—would be associated with low wages. Apparently, however, the compensation effect predominates; if an urban area has a reputation for high unemployment, workers insist on a wage premium to live there. In developing countries this effect (originally observed by Harris and Todaro) is associated with an urban/rural wage ratio of as much as 3.

7. One problem might lie in the assumption that a 50 percent reduction in particulates is five times as valuable as a 10 percent reduction. As has been noted, the benefits of additional pollution abatement probably diminish rapidly as air quality improves.

joyable. However, it can now be seen that, at least in part, amenity orientation is labor cost orientation. Firms may not be attracted to high-amenity regions at all (it is hard to imagine why they would be, if they want to maximize profit); rather, they may be attracted to low-wage regions. In the past, low-wage regions were regions with a temporary surplus of labor, such as the South. These disequilibriums have largely disappeared as a result of massive migration of both firms and workers, however.[8] Most of the rather modest wage variations that remain appear to be compensation for amenity differences.[9]

☐ Summary

Pollution is defined as environmental deterioration resulting from the return of materials to the environment. The materials balance is an exhaustive list of sources and dispositions of materials used in economic activity. The practical ways to abate polluting discharges are to recycle more materials and alter the form of discharges by process changes and by treatment of wastes.

Pollutants are discharged to the environment as gases, liquids, or solid wastes. There is considerable evidence that air pollution affects mortality and morbidity, as well as property. Water pollution affects a large variety of water uses. Inadequate methods of solid waste disposal mar the landscape and impair many uses of land.

Economic theory shows that excessive pollution results unless discharges are controlled by government policy, because pollution costs are not borne by those who discharge wastes. Government policies to abate pollution may entail the public collection and disposal of wastes, regulation of discharges, subsidies for waste treatment, or fees for the discharge of wastes. In the United States, government pollution abatement programs consist mainly of government collection, treatment, and disposal of wastes, as well as an elaborate permit program to regulate discharges. Only recently have governments shown interest in introducing economic incentives into pollution control programs.

Solid waste recovery and disposal are mainly local government responsibilities. Implementing effective recovery programs is a challenge to both government and private sectors.

8.   In Rosen's (1979) sample of nineteen cities, the spread between the highest- and lowest-wage city was about 30 percent.

9.   In another study of intercity wage variation, Hoch and Drake (1974) found that variation in environment, city size, and the like accounted for about 75 percent of the intercity variation in wages for several predominantly male occupations (janitor and mechanic, for example). The same variables, however, explained only about 40 percent of the wage variation for predominantly female jobs (accounting clerk, stenographer, and typist, for example). This suggests that males are better able to move in response to intercity wage differences than are females.

Questions and Problems

1. What effects would more stringent controls on air and water pollution have on income distribution between rich and poor?

2. How would the following be affected by a fee levied on the discharge of sulfur to the atmosphere?
   a. Regulated electric utilities
   b. Manufacturers of atomic reactors
   c. Sulfur-mining companies

3. Evaluate the contention that polluters should be jailed as common criminals instead of being slapped on the wrist by effluent fees.

4. *Depletion allowances* are percentages of gross revenues that mining firms are permitted to subtract before computing federal corporate profits taxes. Suppose that, instead, they were required to depreciate their holdings like any other capital asset. What would be the effect on materials reuse?

5. How would you modify the materials balance to account for material and commodity imports and exports?

6. Suggest a method to measure the value of weather information to consumers when its predictability is observed to vary in a cross section of urban areas.

References and Further Reading

Baumol, William, and Wallace Oates. *The Theory of Environmental Policy* (Englewood Cliffs, N.J.: Prentice-Hall, 1975). A technical, theoretical analysis of environmental economics.

————. *Economics: Environmental Policy and the Quality of Life* (Englewood Cliffs, N.J.: Prentice-Hall, 1979). A nontechnical and practical analysis of environmental programs.

Coolinge, Robert, and W. E. Oates. "Efficiency in Pollution Control in the Short and Long Runs: A System of Rental Emission Permits." *Canadian Journal of Economics* Vol. 15 (1982): 346–354.

Council on Environmental Quality. *Environmental Quality* (Washington, D.C., 1981). The annual report of the federal executive office agency that advises the president on environmental issues.

Harris, J. R., and M. Todaro. "Migration, Unemployment and Development: A Two-Sector Analysis." *American Economic Review* Vol. 60 (1970): 126–142. An early model in which the market compensates for high urban unemployment with high wages.

Hoch, Irving, and Judith Drake. "Wages, Climate and the Quality of Life." *Journal of Environmental Economics and Management* Vol. 1 (1974): 268–295.

Kneese, Allen, Robert Ayres, and Ralph D'Arge. *Economics and the Environment* (Baltimore: Johns Hopkins Press, 1970). A basic data source for the materials balance.

Kneese, Allen, and Charles Schultze. *Pollution, Prices and Public Policy* (Washington, D.C.: Brookings, 1975). A careful analysis of the use of economic incentives in government policy making.

Lave, Lester, and Eugene Seskin. *Air Pollution and Human Health* (Baltimore: Johns Hopkins Press, 1977). A careful statistical analysis of the health effects of air pollution.

Mills, Edwin, and Philip Graves. *The Economics of Environmental Quality, Second Edition* (New York: W. H. Norton, 1986). A textbook on environmental economics.

Polinsky, A. M., and D. Rubinfeld. "Property Values and the Benefits of Environmental Improvements: Theory and Measurement." *Public Economics and the Quality of Life,* eds. Lowdon Wingo and Alan Evans (Baltimore: Johns Hopkins Press, 1977) 154–180. An early use of property-value data to evaluate the demand for environmental quality.

Rosen, Sherwin. "Wage-Based Indexes of Urban Quality of Life." *Current Issues in Urban Economics,* eds. Peter Mieszkowski and Mahlon Straszheim (Baltimore: Johns Hopkins Press, 1979). An estimate of the determinants of interurban wage differences.

Wolozin, Harold, ed. *The Economics of Air Pollution* (Morristown, N.J.: General Learning Press, 1974).

15

Sizes and Structures of Urban Areas

☐ Part One presented historical data on the sizes and shapes of America's urban areas, with particular emphasis on the size distribution of cities and urban areas, the relationships among regions, and the degree of suburbanization of both residences and jobs. Now, with the benefit of intervening material, this chapter returns to these topics and discusses a number of related questions. Is population excessively concentrated in the country's largest urban areas; that is, are large cities too large relative to smaller ones? What have been the recent patterns of population movement between cities and suburbs, as well as between urban areas? What have been the causes of these movements, and is there evidence of market failures (leading, say, to excessive suburbanization)?

It is invariably contended that the largest urban areas are too large and the smallest are too small. This may be the most widely held belief regarding social problems. It is held by city planners, government officials, journalists, and scholars. It is held in rich and poor countries and in capitalist and socialist countries; it is held in African countries, where the largest urban area has only a few hundred thousand people, as well as in Japan, which has the world's largest urban area (some 25 million people). Many countries in Europe and Asia have official, although mostly ineffectual, policies of discouraging growth of the largest urban areas (Sundquist, 1975).

Also widely held is the view that metropolitan areas in the United States are excessively spread out or suburbanized. Chapter 4 showed that suburbanization proceeded rapidly and far after World War II. Most metropolitan suburbs are dominated by single family houses on large lots. Journalists and planners complain that such low-density suburbs make wasteful use of land and fuel for heating, cooling, and transportation, while also leading to undesirable lifestyles. The phrase "slums and suburban sprawl" conveys the feeling of antipathy held by many toward suburbs. Most literature on the subject, however, leaves unclear whether the alleged deficiencies of suburbs are matters of efficiency or equity, or whether they result from market failure, from preferences of which authors disapprove, or from misguided government policies.

Although the beliefs analyzed in this chapter are widely held, they are less coherent than the problems analyzed in earlier chapters. An important task of the chapter will be to ask exactly what the alleged problem is; why it is a problem; and, finally, what—if anything—should be done about it.

☐ SIZE DISTRIBUTION OF URBAN AREAS

Theory

Chapter 4 presented data and analysis on the size distribution of urban areas. What reasons are there to believe that the size distribution resulting from residents' and firms' location decisions might not represent an efficient use of productive resources? Mainly as a result of work by Tolley (1974), a coherent analysis of this subject is now available. Much of the following is based on this analysis. It relies on the notion of market failure because of external diseconomies. The basic theoretical analysis of market failure was presented in Chapter 8. Chapter 14 applied the analysis to pollution problems. To build on that analysis, this chapter will introduce the urban size distribution problem in the context of environmental problems. It then will show how the analysis can be applied to other causes of market failure.

As Chapter 2 pointed out, input productivity varies among urban areas because of differences in comparative advantage and other considerations. If the sizes of urban areas matter, it means that input productivity also depends on the size of the urban area. Some inputs, notably labor, are mobile among urban areas. Massive urban migrations observed in the United States and elsewhere, discussed in Chapter 2, represent input movements to the most advantageous locations.

The simplest situation to analyze is one in which there are two urban areas—one large and one small. The same product is produced in each urban area. A given labor supply consisting of N identical workers is to be allocated between the two urban areas. In Figure 15.1, A is the large, and B the small, urban area in equilibrium. The number of workers in A is measured on the horizontal axis, with the origin at the left vertical axis. Since N is fixed, N_B, the number of workers in B, is $N_B = N - N_A$. The length of the horizontal axis is N, so N_B is the distance from the right vertical axis to N_A. $MP_{NA} \times P_A$ measures the value of the marginal product of workers in A, and $MP_{NB} \times P_B$ measures the value of their marginal product in B. Each MP is labor's marginal product, and each P is the local product price. $MP_{NB} \times P_B$ is measured from the right vertical axis, so it falls to the left. Assume that the labor market is competitive within and between urban areas. As Chapter 5 showed, the wage rate equals the value of the marginal product in com-

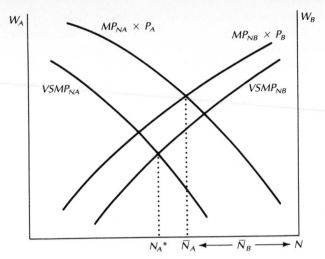

Figure 15.1 *Assignment of Population to Big and Small Cities*

petitive equilibrium. Assume for the moment that workers care only about the local wage rates, W_A and W_B, respectively, in choosing between A and B. Then the labor force is in *locational equilibrium* when the wage rate is the same in both urban areas.[1] That occurs when $\overline{N}_B$ workers work in B.

Now suppose that not only commodity production, but also pollution discharges (say, to the air), increase as employment increases in each urban area. Assume for the moment that each firm's discharge damages the plants of other firms in the same urban area. (For example, discharges may peel paint from walls.) Then, as Chapter 14 showed, the social value of extra production from each firm is worth less than its market value; *from the market value of the marginal product must be subtracted the market value of the resulting additional pollution.* $VSMP_A$ and $VSMP_B$ show the social value of the marginal product of labor in A and B as functions of N_A and N_B. $VSMP$ is below $MP \times P$ at each value of N_A, and $VSMP_{NB}$ is below $MP_{NB} \times P_B$ at each value of N_B, showing that additional polluting discharge is harmful.

Now make the crucial assumption that incremental damage from additional discharges is an increasing function of total discharges and, hence, of total output and labor input. For example, the incremental damage of the third ton per day of sulfur oxide discharge might be slight, but the incremental damage of the tenth ton per day might be much greater.[2] The assumption implies that the vertical distance between

---

1. This discussion abstracts from any wage premium that may exist in one city or the other to compensate for differences in costs or amenities. It is the real wage, not the money wage, that is equalized across urban areas.

2. One plausible way to get this result, in the spirit of Equation (12.2), is to note that a large city has more victims of an increment to environmental degradation than does a smaller one. Hence, the pollution externality will be more severe in a large city than in a small one, regardless of whether the tenth ton of pollutant deteriorates the environment more than the third ton.

$MP_{NA} \times P_A$ and $VSMP_{NA}$ increases with movement to the right, and that the distance between $MP_{NB} \times P_B$ and $VSMP_{NB}$ increases with movement to the left. Furthermore, at $\overline{N}_A$, $VSMP_{NA}$ is further below $MP_{NA} \times P_A$ than is $VSMP_{NB}$ below $MP_{NB} \times P_B$. A socially efficient labor force allocation between the two urban areas requires that $VSMP_{NA} = VSMP_{NB}$—that the value of the social marginal product of labor be the same in the two areas. This follows from the result, established in Chapter 8, that social efficiency requires the (social) marginal product of an input to be the same in all uses. This occurs when N_A^* workers live and work in A in Figure 15.1. If $N_A^* \neq \overline{N}_A$, it follows that efficient labor allocation requires a movement of workers from A to B—that workers be shifted from the large to the small urban area.

This result is based on common sense: *if incremental pollution damage increases with the size of the urban area, then market equilibrium causes too many workers to locate in the large urban area and too few to locate in the small urban area.* Before discussing the implications of the analysis for government attempts to improve resource allocation, it is important to explore the limits of the formal model in a less formal fashion.

First, the theoretical model does not apply only to pollution. Suppose, for example, that road congestion is an increasing function of an urban area's population. The analysis in Chapter 12 makes that a plausible assumption. Then assumptions analogous to those previously made imply that *unpriced congestion also causes large urban areas to be too large and small urban areas to be too small.* Certain other types of market failure may have similar implications for the relative sizes of urban areas. The possibility will be explored later.

Second, the formal model assumed that the polluting discharges did not directly affect residents' welfare. It might be thought that since polluting discharges do reduce residents' welfare, the fact that the large urban area is more polluted than the small one would prevent excessive population in the large urban area. The congestion example, however, shows that this conclusion is false. Chapter 12 showed that congestion is not adequately deterred by the fact that underpriced travel causes travelers direct welfare loss. Even though congestion hurts only those who travel in congested conditions, underpricing nevertheless causes excess crowding on roads. Likewise, in the pollution example, the fact that the large urban area is more polluted than the small urban area deters some, but not enough, people from living in the large urban area. To induce workers to live in the large urban area, equilibrium wages are higher in the large than in the small urban area, inducing more production to locate in the small urban area than if pollution did not affect wages. This does not, however, cause an optimum distribution of population between the two urban areas any more than the disutility of congested travel prevents congestion.

Third, the analysis does not depend on there being only two urban areas. Imagine an entire distribution of urban sizes, as discussed in Chapter 4. Then, if the marginal damage from increased pollution in an urban area increases with the population of the urban area, it follows that a set of the largest urban areas is too large, and the remaining smaller urban areas are too small. In practice, damages from pollution are by no means uniquely correlated with the size of the urban area. They also depend on natural conditions (such as weather), on the industrial structure of the urban area, and on other variables. Nevertheless, there is a tendency for large metropolitan areas to be more polluted than small metropolitan areas.

The analysis so far, even in the light of the qualifying comments, suggests that externalities related to urban size render large cities too large and small ones too small. One more observation casts crucial doubt upon the basic conclusion, however. One of the reasons for concentrating production in cities is the existence of agglomeration economies: other things being equal, a firm's production costs are lower in a large city than elsewhere, essentially because a large city offers easy (that is, inexpensive) access to a rich variety of specialized inputs and markets. This is an external economy of large city size. A firm that locates in a city increases the size of the city and, in the process, reduces production costs for other firms in the city. This cost reduction accrues to the incumbents—and not to the entrant—with the result that the potential entrant has an insufficient incentive to migrate to the city. The conclusion that emerges from looking only at this externality is that large cities are too small.

Unfortunately, no one knows the net effect of these external diseconomies and economies on the relative sizes of cities. As already seen, there are forces working in both directions. The problem is that the magnitude of these externalities (particularly agglomeration economies) is particularly difficult to measure. As the next section will show, however, even if it was known that the net effect of these externalities were to make large cities too large, the appropriate policy would not be to discourage people from living in large cities.

Policy Questions

What can governments do to remove the resource misallocation that results in an inappropriate urban size distribution? The immediate reaction of many people is to urge government to undertake a variety of ad hoc programs to deter growth of large metropolitan areas. Many such programs would do great harm. In fact, the policy analysis is complex and must be undertaken with care.

If an external diseconomy were *technologically* linked to population, the policy solution would be simple. Suppose, for example, that pollution discharges were proportionate to population in an urban area. Then the correct government policy would be a tax on each resident in each urban area equal to the difference between $MP_N \times P$ and $VSMP_N$, evaluated at the optimum population (N^*). The tax would be higher in larger urban areas, given the assumptions made in Figure 15.1.

Even in this simple situation, inappropriate policies frequently are urged on governments. The most common error is to urge taxes or other controls only on newcomers, say, on those who come to reside in the urban area after its population passes N*. *Newcomers, however, are no more polluting than older residents; pollution is proportionate to total population.* The tax should exclude those to whom residence in the urban area is least valuable, and it should be levied on all residents. Taxes for the privilege of residing in large urban areas are understandably unpopular. Thus, government officials commonly think of indirect ways of discouraging growth of large urban areas. For example, steering federal defense and other contracts away from large urban areas frequently is proposed. All such proposals interfere with the optimum distribution of particular industries among urban areas and are therefore undesirable.

A crucial point, which is misunderstood in almost all discussions of government policies to change the urban size distribution, is that *external diseconomies are by no means technologically linked to urban population.* Chapter 14 showed that polluting discharges depend on how resources are allocated, not just on total population. Wastes can be treated before discharge, production processes and products can be modified so as to produce less waste, wastes can be transported to discharge points where they do less harm, and so forth. The appropriate government policy toward polluting discharges is controls or, better yet, effluent fees, on discharges.

Effluent fees should probably be higher, or controls more stringent, in large urban areas than elsewhere. The result may indeed be to shift population and employment somewhat from large to small urban areas. The main result, however, would be to reduce the polluting discharges resulting from a given total population and employment in an urban area. Any effect on total population in an urban area would be incidental and probably small. In fact, as Table 15.1 shows, air pollution tends to be worse in big urban areas than in small ones, but the table also reveals a substantial variation in pollution that is unrelated to population. It would take an enormous cut in the population of the New York City metropolitan area to improve its air quality much. Population redistribution is about as costly a pollution control program as could be imagined.

If the analysis is taken a step further, it even becomes unclear that an optimum pollution control program would shift people and jobs from large to small urban areas. Figure 15.1 assumed that polluting discharges affected production costs in the urban area but did not directly affect residents' welfare. In fact, pollution affects both people and property, but the most important effects are on health. Consider a large, badly polluted urban area, and suppose an optimum effluent fee is levied on discharges in the urban area. The effluent fee has two effects. First, it makes living and working in the urban area more expensive, inducing people to live and work elsewhere and thus shifting population to

Table 15.1 *Air Pollution and City Size*

Severity Level (Days with PSI Greater Than 100)	SMSA	Unhealthful, Very Unhealthful, and Hazardous (PSI > 100)	Very Unhealthful and Hazardous (PSI > 200)	1980 SMSA Population (In Thousands)
More than 150 days	Los Angeles	231	113	7,478
	San Bernardino, Riverside, and Ontario, Calif.	174	89	1,557
100 to 150 days	New York	139	6	9,120
	Denver	130	36	1,620
	Pittsburgh	119	18	2,264
	Houston	104	23	2,905
50 to 99 days	Chicago	93	14	7,102
	St. Louis	89	19	2,355
	Philadelphia	74	6	4,717
	San Diego	72[a]	8[a]	1,862
	Louisville	70	4	906
	Phoenix	70[a]	6[a]	1,508
	Gary	68	33	643
	Portland	62	11	1,242
	Washington	62	3	3,060
	Jersey City	58[b]	0[b]	557
	Salt Lake City	58	18	936
	Seattle	52	3	1,607
	Birmingham	50[b]	8[b]	847

smaller urban areas. Second, it makes the urban area more attractive as a place to live. In fact, an optimum set of effluent fees probably would improve the environmental quality in large urban areas relative to that in small urban areas. This second effect tends to increase population and employment in the large urban area. Thus, the two effects are offsetting, and it appears to be impossible to predict their net effect on the urban area's population without detailed data for the particular urban area.

The same analysis applies to every alleged external diseconomy. Chapter 12 showed that road congestion depends not only on the total population of an urban area, but also on the allocation of resources in the urban area. Congestion depends on the mix of automobile and public transit investments, on charges that discourage urban travel, and on locations of residences and workplaces. As with environmental problems, a government policy to reduce congestion by reducing the total population of an urban area would be about the most inefficient policy imaginable to reduce congestion. Appropriate programs to control congestion are directed at transportation resource allocation, not at the ur-

Air Pollution and City Size (continued)

Severity Level (Days with PSI Greater Than 100)	SMSA	Unhealthful, Very Unhealthful, and Hazardous (PSI > 100)	Very Unhealthful and Hazardous (PSI > 200)	1980 SMSA Population (In Thousands)
25 to 49 days	Cleveland	46	11	1,899
	Detroit	39	4	4,353
	Memphis	37[b]	3[b]	913
	Baltimore	36	2	2,174
	Indianapolis	34	2	1,167
	Cincinnati	28	1	1,401
	Milwaukee	28	2	1,397
	Kansas City	28[b]	1[b]	1,327
0 to 24 days	Sacramento	22	1	1,014
	Dallas	21	1	2,975
	Allentown	21	2	637
	Buffalo	20[a]	4[a]	1,243
	San Francisco	18	0	3,253
	Toledo	15	2	792
	Dayton	15	1	830
	Tampa	8	1	1,569
	Syracuse	7	1	642
	Norfolk	6[a]	0[a]	807
	Grand Rapids	6[b]	0[b]	602
	Rochester	5	0	972
	Akron	4	0	660

[a]Based on two years of data.
[b]Based on one year of data.
Sources: Data from Council on Environmental Quality. *Environmental Quality.* 1981, p. 33; and U.S. Department of Commerce, Bureau of the Census. *Census of Population.* Washington, D.C.: Government Printing Office, 1980.

ban area's total population. As with environmental programs, appropriate transportation programs to control congestion may affect the total population of an urban area, but the effects would be incidental and probably small.

The implication of this section can be summarized briefly: *if an activity distorts urban sizes, the activity should be controlled directly.* Urban size distortions are no more than symptoms of resource misallocation. To attack the urban size distribution directly is to attack the wrong variable. Tolley, Graves, and Gardner (1979) analyze a variety of causes of urban size distortions and propose remedies for some.

It is useful at this point to recall the discussion of central-place theory in Chapter 1. In particular, recall that there is an important economic rationale for the emergence of a few large cities. Some goods have scale economies associated with their production sufficient to make them inefficient to produce except at a small number of locations. According to the central-place theory, the disparity among goods in the degree of scale economies leads to a disparity of city sizes and, in particular, to a large number of small cities and a small number of large cities. At least roughly, this skewed size distribution of cities minimizes the sum of production and transportation costs for the goods people consume. Although there are clearly market failures of various sorts in any complex economy, the theoretical and empirical case that large cities are too large is a modest one, at best.

☐ SUBURBANIZATION

In Chapters 2 through 4, changes in the percentage of metropolitan residents living or working in central cities or suburbs were employed as measures of suburbanization. It was pointed out that the measure is a poor one, because central-city boundaries are moved occasionally, and because independent suburban local government jurisdictions are virtually unknown in most countries.

The analysis in Chapter 7 and Appendix A suggests a measure of suburbanization that does not depend on locations of local government jurisdictional boundaries. It shows that urban population density can be approximated by an exponential function,

$$D(u) - D_o e^{-\gamma u}, \tag{15.1}$$

where $D(u)$ is population per square mile u miles from the urban center, e is the base of the natural logarithm, and D_o and γ are constants to be estimated from the data for each urban area. Equation (15.1) is an exact density function in special circumstances and an approximation otherwise. Putting $u = 0$ shows that D_o is the density at the urban center. This is an artificial notion, since few people live within a short distance of most urban centers, where most land is used for employment. For most urban areas, however, Equation (15.1) is a good approximation for distances more than half a mile or so from the center, as noted in Chapter 7. The term γ is positive if density increases with distance from the urban center. Equation (15.1) has the general shape shown in Figure 7.1. The density function is flatter at each u the smaller is γ. It can be shown by differentiating Equation (15.1) with respect to u that 100γ is the percentage by which population falls per mile of distance from the urban center. For example, a γ of 0.3 implies that density falls 30 percent per mile of movement from the center.

A final property of Equation (15.1) shows the relationship between the exponential density function and suburbanization. If an urban area's population grows by increasing D_o, leaving γ unchanged, the whole gradient shifts up, and the percentage of the urban population living within a fixed distance of the center remains unchanged. For example, the percentage living within the central city remains unchanged. It is therefore natural to say that, of two exponential density functions, that with the smaller γ represents the more *suburbanized* urban area. The basic advantage of using γ as estimated from Equation (15.1) as a measure of suburbanization is that the measure does not depend on the location or movement of central-city boundaries.

As Chapter 7 discussed, Equation (15.1) has been estimated for many dozens of metropolitan areas in several dozen countries, some for years as long ago as the early nineteenth century.

As Table 7.2 noted, the available evidence indicates that residential density gradients have been getting flatter, at least since 1880. Surprisingly, there is no evidence of an acceleration of suburbanization in more recent decades. Indeed, in the era from 1880 to 1920, the density gradients for the four metropolitan areas with available data were falling about 50 percent faster than for the period from 1920 to 1963. Fragmentary evidence indicates that European metropolitan areas have been decentralizing since the early nineteenth century. Much more plentiful evidence indicates that the trend toward decentralization has been pervasive in noncommunist developed and developing countries during the post-World War II period. Decentralization has gone less far in other countries, but the speed of decentralization is greater in many countries—including Japan—than in the United States. Racial and school-related tensions and the widespread use of automobiles may play an important role in present-day suburbanization. If so, however, this is a case of new causes bringing about the continuation of a very old trend.

It is logical to ask what the determinants of suburbanization are, by examining the determinants of residential density gradients. This suggests running a regression like the following:

$$\gamma = \beta_1 X_1 + \beta_2 X_2 + \ldots + \beta_n X_n, \tag{15.2}$$

where γ is an urban area's density gradient (see Chapter 7), Xs are variables thought to influence the gradient, and βs are the estimated coefficients that reveal how Xs influence γ.

A study of this sort is useful for examining the causes of interurban differences in the degree of suburbanization, but it sheds little light on possible causes (such as the automobile) common to all urban areas. The broad historical pattern of suburbanization, revealed in Table 7.2, is not really amenable to detailed statistical analysis. Thus, attention now turns to determinants of interurban variations in suburbanization (as measured by interurban differences in density gradients), as well as to what is known about the historical determinants of decentralization.

Interurban Variation

The most important variable governing the steepness of a city's density gradient is the city's age. Old urban areas have much higher density central cities and steeper density gradients than do newer ones. Using a regression like Equation (15.2), Muth (1969) found that each decade of additional age of a city increased the steepness of its density gradient by 0.08 (about 20 percent of the average value of the density gradients he estimated).[3] In other words, a fifty-year-old SMSA would have a density gradient about twice as steep as would an urban area of age zero.[4]

The next finding that emerges from studies such as Muth (1969) and Macauley (1984) is that large urban areas have flatter gradients than small ones. This finding is contrary to the predictions of the model analyzed in Chapters 6 and 7, and in Appendix A. In that model, the steepness of the gradient is independent of population. The discrepancy between model and fact may be due to the importance of subcenters in larger urban areas.

The other variable that is consistently associated with the steepness of the density gradient is the racial mix of the central city. If a large fraction of the central city's population is black, the density gradient tends to be flatter (that is, more suburbanized).

In addition to this information on the determinants of the steepness of density gradients, something is known about the manner in which urban areas' density gradients change through time. Bradbury, Downs, and Small (1982) found that city population growth (from 1970 to 1975) relative to suburban growth was influenced in the following ways: cities grew slowly relative to the SMSA if:

1. old housing was more concentrated in the city than the suburbs,
2. the city had a high percentage of black population relative to the suburbs,
3. the suburban ring had a large number of municipalities, and
4. city taxes were high relative to the suburbs.[5]

The first finding suggests that SMSAs with old central cities are suburbanizing more quickly than those with newer central cities. It has been noted already that old SMSAs have steeper gradients than newer ones, as well as that cities of the past had steeper gradients than do today's cities. It appears that old cities carry a legacy of the past in the form of steep density gradients. Not surprisingly, this legacy is being diminished with the passage of time, and its gradual disappearance can be seen in the more rapid suburbanization of old cities.

The same pattern was observed by Macauley (1984), who noted that density gradients that were steeper in 1948 tended to flatten more quickly over the next thirty years than did gradients that were relatively flat in 1948. Thus, there was much less variation among urban areas' density gradients in 1980 than in 1948. This convergence can readily

3. Specifically, Muth's (1969) variable was the number of decades since the SMSA attained a population of 50,000.

4. Despite the large magnitude of this effect, Muth (1969) did not find the coefficient to be very significant statistically.

5. This finding should be interpreted with caution. It already has been seen that population loss might lead to higher taxes. It is not clear which way the causation is going in this case.

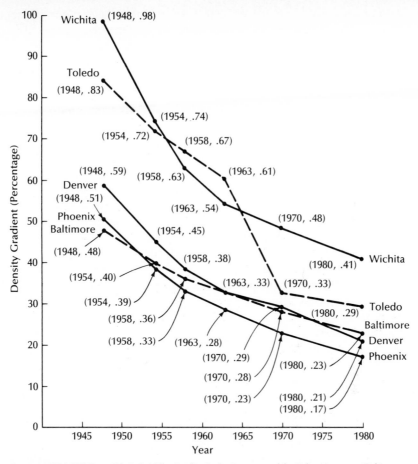

Sources: 1954-1963 Data, Edwin S. Mills, *Studies in the Structure of the Urban Economy* (Baltimore: Johns Hopkins University Press, 1972), p. 40.
1970-1980 Data, Molly Macauley, "Recent Behavior of Urban Population and Employment Density Gradients," Johns Hopkins Working Paper no. 124, 1983.

Figure 15.2 *Density Gradients for a Sample of Urban Areas, 1948 to 1980*

be seen in Figure 15.2. Old urban areas are apparently gradually converting from high-density housing to lower-density, automobile-age housing.[6]

The second finding is straightforward: racial antipathies cause more than one white person to leave the central city for every black entrant. This may be a purely race-related phenomenon, or it may be due to such variables as income and income instability, which are statistically correlated with race.

6. This does not necessarily mean that the housing stock is of lower density. Part of reduced population density takes the form of a reduction in the number of persons per room.

The third finding provides some support for the Tiebout hypothesis discussed in Chapter 13. A large number of suburban jurisdictions implies a rich variety of public service offerings, which seems to attract people from the central city. The fourth finding also supports the Tiebout hypothesis, subject to the caveats in footnote 5.

Historical Trends and International Comparisons

The historical pattern of a gradual flattening of density gradients is not amenable to regression analysis. As will be seen, the most plausible causes of flattening gradients are rising incomes and falling transport costs. Since, however, the trends in income, transport cost, and density all have occurred together (for example, there are no important episodes of rising income, but constant transport cost), statistical analysis cannot be used to infer anything about the causes of decentralization. Note, though, that decentralization is what would be predicted as a result of rising income and falling transport cost. Chapter 6 showed that the price gradient becomes flatter with a fall in transport cost and possibly with a rise in income. Since it is the rising price of housing (as the CBD is approached) that brings about higher density, it follows that a flattening of the price gradient leads to a flattening of the density gradient.

Population density gradients for most other developed countries are much steeper than for the United States. Chapter 7 noted that Japanese urban areas have gradients over twice as steep as those in the United States. To a lesser degree, the same is true in western Europe. Gradients aside, urban density is higher in western Europe and Japan because land is much more scarce than in the United States. Table 15.2 gives average population densities for several countries in 1980. The stark fact emerges that land (relative to people) is very plentiful in the United States. In fact, the only nations with lower population densities than the United States are those with large tracts of virtually uninhabitable land. Western Europe and Japan have average densities roughly ten times that of the United States.[7]

One of the consequences of the scarcity of land in western Europe and Japan is that land is much more costly there than in the United States. It has been estimated that the market value of land in Japan is more than three times GNP, as compared with about two-thirds GNP in the United States (Mills and Ohta, 1976). In relation to incomes, land values are five times as high in Japan as in the United States. Inevitably, the result is that Japanese economize on urban land. Homes, factories, and offices are built on tiny lots, so metropolitan areas are much higher in density and less decentralized than in the United States. Typical conditions in northern Europe are probably somewhere between those in

---

7. Alaska contributes relatively little to this gap. The population density for the contiguous forty-eight states is about seventy-five persons per square mile.

Table 15.2 *Average Population Densities, 1980 (In Persons Per Square Mile)*

Country	Population Density	Country	Population Density
Mongolia	2.76	Austria	231.97
Libya	4.39	France	252.19
Australia	4.93	People's Republic of China	278.24
Iceland	5.79	Czechoslovakia	310.30
Canada	6.10	East Germany	413.32
Congo	11.66	Italy	490.44
Bolivia	13.20	India	519.13
Argentina	25.46	United Kingdom and Northern Ireland	592.48
U.S.S.R.	30.83	West Germany	642.49
Finland	36.74	Japan	810.97
Brazil	37.44	Belgium	842.18
United States	62.43	Taiwan	1,181.00
Spain	192.06	Singapore	10,575.22

Source: Data from *1983 World Almanac and Book of Facts* (New York: Newspaper Enterprise Association, 1982).

Japan and those in the United States. The only industrialized countries in which densities and land values are as low as in the United States are Canada and Australia.

Density gradients are steeper in other countries partly because transport cost tends to be higher (high land values result in the economical use of land for transport, among other things). Also, in many of these countries, income is lower than in the United States.

Racial mix, school quality, taxes, and demographics (see the "Return-to-the-City Movement" section later in this chapter) all have been statistically linked to suburbanization. Despite the importance of these phenomena, it is important to remember that the trend toward suburbanization is worldwide and at least a century old. The causes that have been noted in this paragraph are quantitatively insignificant in light of the broad historical experience.

Market Failure?

There is a widespread feeling in the United States that suburbanization is excessive. In part, this view rests on the accurate observation that suburbanization occurs at the expense of both central-city and rural land. Given a fixed population and land area, suburbanization does reduce the stock of rural land, and it does provide an alternative to central-city living that reduces the demand for central-city housing. Suburbanization does have benefits, however. Many households—

particularly those with children—prefer low-density suburban living. Also, despite the pain of adjustment to lower density, current density levels of central cities may be higher than optimum, given the low cost of land and transportation. For an economist, the major question is whether there are inefficient market (and nonmarket) signals that have led to more suburbanization than would have occurred in a regime in which everyone faced efficient prices. An annotated list of possible causes of excessive suburbanization follows.

Pollution. Pollution is the easiest kind of market failure to analyze as a cause of excess decentralization. Suppose that air-polluting discharges are concentrated near the centers of urban areas, which is certainly true of discharges from motor vehicles and from combustion from space heating. Pollutants diffuse throughout the metropolitan area according to wind patterns. They become less concentrated farther from discharge points, though, so air quality tends to improve somewhat with distance from the CBD in most urban areas.

If air quality improves with distance and if people prefer clean to polluted air, the land rent gradient that equalizes utilities between central and suburban locations is flatter than it would be otherwise. To understand this, recall the role of the land rent gradient: to soak up the utility gain associated with living close to the CBD. People gain utility by living close to the CBD as a result of reduced commuting needs. If air quality improves sufficiently with distance from the CBD, however, the utility differences between city and suburb are relatively small before accounting for land rent differences. Therefore, in the presence of pollution that declines with distance from the CBD, a relatively flat land rent gradient will be sufficient to equalize utilities between locations. As discussed in Chapters 6–7, the flatter the land rent gradient, the flatter the density gradient. This is the mechanism through which pollution might lead to a flattening of density gradients. This flattening is inefficient only to the extent that the pollution is inefficient. Even in an optimum world, pollution is probably higher in CBDs than suburban locations because of the higher concentration of economic activity. Only if the tendency for pollution to be worse in central locations is excessive will the resulting suburbanization be excessive.

The decentralizing effect of air pollution probably is not very important. The United States now has stringent controls on air-polluting discharges. Discharges are nevertheless somewhat greater near urban centers than in suburbs. It seems unlikely, however, that the difference in air quality is great enough to have much effect.

Transportation underpricing. Chapter 12 suggested that urban transportation—especially during rush hour, when optimum congestion tolls are highest—is consistently underpriced in the United States. This means that the housing price gradient, Equation 7.1, is flatter than it would be under efficient pricing. From this observation it follows that the density gradient is flatter than it should be.

It is easy to calculate roughly how important this underpricing is. Chapter 7 argued that under reasonable assumptions, the density gradient would be about five times as steep as the housing price gradient (with about the same steepness as the land rent gradient). Suppose the price gradient is 0.04, giving a density gradient of 0.20. Further, suppose that transportation is underpriced by 25 percent (the optimum congestion toll of Table 12.4 is 26.3 percent of full automobile transport cost, though it is approximately 35 percent of the full cost exclusive of parking). Under both optimum and inefficient transport pricing, the density gradient is about five times greater than the housing price gradient. Thus, if the density gradient under inefficient pricing of transport were 0.20, the imposition of efficient congestion tolls would raise the gradient by 25 percent, to 0.25. The effect of such a change would be fairly modest; the difference between a gradient of 0.20 and one of 0.25 represents roughly the amount of flattening that takes place every five years. To state it differently, consider an urban area with a central-city radius of 8 miles. With a density gradient of 0.20, 47.5 percent of the population lives inside the central city; with a gradient of 0.25, the percentage living in the city rises to 59 percent.

It was noted that the optimum congestion toll appears to be more than 25 percent of marginal commuting cost, suggesting that these calculations have understated the centralizing effect of efficient pricing. There is, however, an important offsetting effect—under efficient pricing, congestion, and hence time cost, would decline. Thus, 25 percent may be approximately right after all.

Of course, all changes in density gradients are long run in nature, requiring the construction and alteration of dwellings. Presumably, the effect of an increase in urban travel cost to correct underpricing would be to slow down the decreases in gradients that occur for market reasons. No one should think, however, that even drastic increases in urban travel costs would dramatically reverse the long-term trend toward decentralization.

Land-use controls. Chapter 13 discussed land-use controls for fiscal or exclusionary purposes. Although a wide range of such controls exists, zoning is perhaps the most important. An important zoning provision is the exclusion of all dwellings except single family detached houses on lots no smaller than a stipulated minimum. Frequent minimums are 1 or 2 acres, but some are much larger. One purpose of such controls is to exclude dwellings whose real estate taxes would not pay the cost of local government services provided to their residents. Their mechanism is to require all residents' housing to be of as high a quality and as low a density as is appropriate for a group of residents able to control zoning provisions. The typical procedure is for the initial residents to have relatively high incomes and to establish zoning provisions appropriate to their housing demand. As the metropolitan area grows and decentralizes, however, lower-income residents who would move in if the zoning provisions were absent are precluded from doing so. This inevitably causes suburbs to be of lower density than they would be in the absence of zoning.

How large is the excessive decentralization resulting from low-density zoning? No one knows. Beyond a doubt, suburban zoning provisions are consistent with the housing demands of most people who would live there even in the absence of zoning restrictions. A sudden removal of all controls on the types and densities of suburban housing probably would slow the speed of metropolitan decentralization, but it would not reverse the direction.

The most important evidence that distortions from land-use controls are of modest proportions is that urban density functions show little evidence of discontinuity as central-city boundaries are crossed. As was seen in Chapter 13, zoning controls on dwellings are much less important in central cities than in suburbs. If low-density zoning caused large resource misallocation, discontinuities in density functions would be expected at central-city boundaries. Such discontinuities appear to be either nonexistent or small, however.

Subsidization of owner-occupied housing. It is frequently claimed that government actions make owner-occupied housing less costly than it should be. The two government programs most frequently referred to are Federal Housing Administration (FHA) and Veterans Administration (VA) mortgage insurance and the federal income tax treatment of mortgage interest and real estate taxes. The latter was discussed in Chapters 10 and 11.

The FHA and VA mortgages certainly place emphasis on owner-occupied housing, yet the effect on housing prices and demand is small. The tax reduction resulting from the deductibility of real estate taxes and mortgage interest is large, but there is probably only a modest differential effect between owner-occupied and rental housing. Furthermore, real estate taxes in suburbs more nearly approximate prices paid for local government services than do such taxes in central cities, as the discussion of the Tiebout hypothesis in Chapter 13 showed.

Energy costs. The latter part of the 1970s was a period of rapidly rising fuel costs. Many people are deeply concerned that low-density suburbs may be an inappropriate form of urban resource allocation in a period of high energy costs. The issue is not one of market failure, but rather one of adjustment from a form appropriate for low-energy costs to one appropriate for high-energy costs. The issues fall into three categories.

First is heating and cooling costs. It requires only about one-third as much energy to heat and cool a high-rise apartment as it does to heat and cool a single-family detached house. Of course, energy requirements are less the better constructed and insulated any dwelling is, but the two-thirds savings is about the same for all construction materials, insulation types, regions of the country, and fuel types, provided similar dwellings are compared. For example, the two-thirds saving is about the same in the cold North as in the warm South. Heating and cooling are lost through outside walls, windows, doors, and roofs. The saving in high-rise buildings comes from shared walls, ceilings, and floors. Other housing types, such as garden apartments, are between the extremes for high-rise apartments and single-family detached houses.

The large fuel saving is no argument for requiring or subsidizing attached dwellings or for taxing or preventing detached dwellings. Provided fuel prices are at equilibrium levels, markets provide adequate incentive for fuel-efficient dwellings. However, *high fuel prices are a powerful reason for local governments to abolish land-use controls that prohibit multifamily housing.* As Chapter 13 showed, the main purpose of land-use controls is exclusionary and of doubtful social benefit. In an era of high fuel prices, restrictions on multifamily housing are unforgivable.

The second issue in discussing energy costs is gasoline consumption from automobile use. Low-density suburbs probably entail somewhat longer trips for work and shopping. The fact of low density, however, does not necessarily mean that jobs and shops are far away. It has been shown that jobs are almost as suburbanized as residences. If households were to choose their homes and jobs *from the existing stock of homes and jobs* with more attention to the required commute, it would be possible to greatly reduce total commuting without recentralizing our cities. If gasoline prices rise sufficiently to cause a major change in consumer behavior, it is not clear that the change will take the form of high-density living.

Two other observations should temper any conjecture that rising gasoline prices will halt the suburbanization of the last 100 years. First, in real terms the price of gasoline has not risen nearly as much as most people think; in fact, it has fallen since 1950, with peaks never reaching the 1950 level (see Table 15.3). Second, there is substantial evidence that the most important *long-run* response to a rise in the price of gasoline is the use of more fuel-efficient cars, not a reduction in the number of miles driven.

Even if the gasoline price increase had been large (or if subsequent increases are large), the effect on location decisions is likely to be small for two reasons. First, gasoline is a small part of commuting cost, as Table 12.4 showed. Second (related to the first reason), the total amount of money involved is fairly modest. Consider a household that drives 10,000 miles per year (somewhat above the average). Total gasoline consumption is about $500; however, probably no more than about 25 to 30 percent of this is consumed for CBD-bound trips, so the gasoline cost of trips toward the CBD is about $150. Even a doubling of this figure will have no important effect on a household earning $20,000 with a definite preference for the suburbs.

The third and most complex issue in energy costs is public transit. Beyond doubt, buses and subways require less energy per passenger

Table 15.3 *Retail Price of Gasoline, Including Tax in Constant 1987 Dollars and Average Vehicle Gas Mileage*

Year	Price	Automobile Gas Mileage	Gas Cost Per Mile (Cents)
1950	$1.249	14.95	8.35
1955	1.221	14.53	8.41
1960	1.182	14.28	8.28
1965	1.109	14.15	7.84
1970	1.032	13.58	7.60
1972	0.971	13.67	7.10
1973	0.981	13.29	7.38
1974	1.194	13.65	8.74
1975	1.194	13.74	8.69
1976	1.164	13.93	8.36
1977	1.152	14.15	8.14
1978	1.125	14.26	7.89
1979	1.136	14.49	7.84
1980	1.133	15.32	7.39
1981	1.121	15.68	7.15
1982	1.101	16.25	6.77
1983	1.056	16.81	6.28
1984	1.043	17.05	6.12

Sources: From "Energy," by Milton Russell in *Setting National Priorities: The 1978 Budget;* U.S. Department of Commerce, *Statistical Abstract of the United States,* Government Printing Office, 1975, 1980, 1987; U.S. Department of Labor, *Monthly Labor Review,* June, 1983; U.S. Department of Energy, *Monthly Energy Review.*

mile than do cars. A passenger mile of car transportation requires at least ten times as much fuel as a passenger mile in a nearly full bus. Thus, the higher motor vehicle fuel prices are, the lower the relative price of public transit compared with automobiles and the greater the shift of demand to public transit travel.

Once again the magnitudes are important. Return to the example of Table 12.4. Even at a price of $1.00 per gallon, the gasoline required for the 8-mile trip considered costs only about $0.40, or $0.05 per mile (assuming 20 mpg). Suppose fuel prices rose by 50 percent. That would raise the costs of the trip by automobile by $0.20, to $4.00. It might raise the bus fare by $0.09, increasing the cost of the bus trip to $4.46. (Energy consumption per bus passenger mile is about 45 percent of energy consumption per auto passenger mile.) It is clear that even a drastic increase in fuel costs would have only a modest effect on modal choice; only those travelers who are almost indifferent would switch modes.

There can be no doubt that low-density suburbs make it difficult to operate economical public transit systems. Chapter 12 showed that public transit systems require large numbers of travelers between particular origin-destination pairs. The relaxation of land-use controls on multifamily housing and small lots would help. However, a modal shift toward public transit commuting will be a gradual process in American metropolitan areas in any case, barring catastrophic fuel shortages.

☐ CITY-SUBURBAN INCOME DIFFERENCES

It has already been noted at several points that income tends to rise with distance from the CBD, giving rise to the familiar pattern of suburbs' having higher incomes than their central cities. This observation, along with other relevant information, is summarized in Table 15.4. First, note that on the average, central-city per capita incomes are only modestly smaller than entire-SMSA incomes. Second, income disparities are much larger in the Northeast and the north-central United States than in the South and West. Third, it is clear that the per-capita income comparisons overstate the economic well-being of central-city residents. Per-household incomes are substantially lower in central cities, particularly in the Northeast and north-central United States, reflecting the fact that family sizes tend to be smaller in cities than in suburbs. Also, the incidence of poverty (as of 1979) was 2.18 times higher in cities than their suburbs (again more so in the Northeast and the north central region).[8] The final section in the table reveals that old housing is concentrated in central cities in the Northeast and the north-central region, but not in the South and West; in other words, where old housing is concentrated, so is poverty.

The cause of this pattern continues to be subject to some dispute, with leading theories being the following:

1. The rent offer curve for high-income people is flatter than that for low-income people; hence, the low-income outbid the high-income people for central locations (see Chapter 6). Chapter 7 noted that the empirical evidence for this is weak.
2. Urban areas have been gradually built from the center out, so the old (lower-quality) housing is concentrated in the central city. That is the housing low-income people can afford, so that is where they live (see Chapter 7).
3. Various exclusionary activities have prevented low-income people from moving into the suburbs.

The correct explanation is surely a combination of the second and third of these possibilities, and possibly the first as well. Little is known about the relative importance of these forces, though the dramatic difference between old frostbelt cities and new sunbelt cities, as revealed in Table 15.4, lends considerable support to the second of these explanations.

---

8. The figures are 15.7 percent low-income people in central cities and 7.2 percent in suburbs.

Table 15.4 *City-Suburb Income Comparison by Region*

	1980			1970
	Central City	Suburbs	Central City/ Suburbs Ratio	Central City/ Suburbs Ratio
Average per-household income				
United States	$14,600	$20,260	0.721	0.768
Northeast	12,840	20,910	0.614	0.733
North central	14,290	20,930	0.683	0.756
South	14,660	19,470	0.753	0.824
West	17,180	19,890	0.864	0.844
Average per-capita income				
United States	$6,627	$7,669	0.864	0.947
Northeast	5,309	7,870	0.675	0.781
North central	6,477	7,677	0.844	0.954
South	6,426	7,107	0.910	0.926
West	7,934	8,059	0.984	1.019
Fraction of housing stock built before 1940				
United States	0.417	0.207		
Northeast	0.635	0.393		
North central	0.530	0.224		
South	0.240	0.099		
West	0.282	0.115		

Source: Data from "Federal Housing Characteristics for the United States and Regions: 1980." *Annual Housing Survey.* Washington, D.C.: U.S. Dept. of Commerce, Bureau of the Census, 1980, part A.

☐ RETURN-TO-THE-CITY MOVEMENT

Beginning in the mid-1970s, a widely proclaimed return-to-the-city movement received substantial attention. The most exuberant reports suggested a massive influx of middle- and upper-income households to old city neighborhoods, resulting in a widespread revitalization of housing and improvements in central-city tax bases. In addition, the unhappy side effect of displacement received a substantial amount of attention.

Understanding of the causes and future course of this movement is modest, at best. The patterns to date, however, give some evidence on both the causes and the future of the movement. The most important characteristic of the back-to-the-city movement is that it is quantitatively very small. By one estimate, the average major city witnessed about 1600 substantial renovations of dwelling units over the decade from 1968 to 1978 (with the bulk of the redevelopment coming in the last half of this period). For a typical major city, this constitutes about 1 percent of the housing stock, or a rate of redevelopment of about 0.1 percent per year. By way of contrast, in 1982 Baltimore had an es-

Table 15.5 *Characteristics of Mount Pleasant and Capitol Hill Reno-vators Compared with All District of Columbia Residents*

Characteristic	Renovators		D.C. Residents	All First-Time Home Buyers
	Mount Pleasant	Capitol Hill		
Have children under 19 years old	37%	21%		29%
White	77	94	25%	
Earn income over $15,000	87	90	25	
Have college degree	86	97	17	
Aged 30 to 34	44	48	11	34[a]

[a]The National Homebuying Survey does not use the "age 30 to 34" category; it reports 68 percent between the ages of 25 and 34. Probably more than half of these are 30 to 34 years old.

Sources: Data from Gale, pp. 98–99, in Shirley Laska and Daphne Spain, eds. *Back to the City: Issues in Neighborhood Renovation.* New York: Pergamon, 1980; and National Association of Realtors. *National Homebuying Survey.* Washington, D.C.: National Association of Realtors, 1981., p. 6.

timated 7000 abandoned dwellings; Philadelphia, 30,000; Detroit, 12,000; and New York City, 100,000.[9]

Comprehensive data on the characteristics of urban renovators are unavailable, but a common pattern emerges from surveys of renovated neighborhoods. The renovators typically are young (twenty to thirty-five years old), white, well-educated, high-income, and typically either single or childless couples.[10] Table 15.5 summarizes the characteristics for the Mount Pleasant and Capitol Hill sections of Washington, D.C. To the extent that the data permit comparisons, the renovators are similar to all first-time home buyers, except renovators are more likely to be white and well-educated.

The attraction of the central city for young whites is not a new phenomenon, as Figure 15.3 illustrates. In the 1960s the migration flow of whites between the ages of about twenty and thirty was to central cities (in the cases of New York City, Boston, and Washington, D.C.) and, of older whites and their children, out of central cities.

The big change in the 1970s was probably not in the inherent attractiveness of central cities, but rather in demographics. As can be seen in Figure 2 (inside front cover), in this decade the first postwar babies became first-time homeowners. In addition, the young adults in the 1970s had lower fertility than their predecessors, further increasing the pool of people looking for the kind of housing central cities have to offer.

9. These numbers were provided by Richard Davis of the Baltimore Department of Housing and Community Development.

10. This pattern has been observed in Washington, D.C., New Orleans, and Philadelphia, among other cities. Case studies for all these cities are discussed in Laska and Spain (1980).

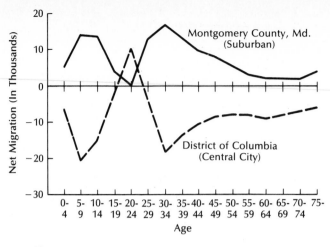

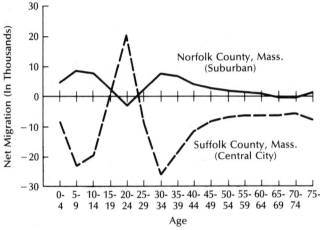

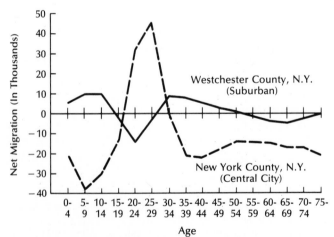

Figure 15.3 *Net Migration of White Population, 1960 to 1970, for Washington, D.C., Boston, Manhattan, and Selected High-Income Suburban Counties, by Age*

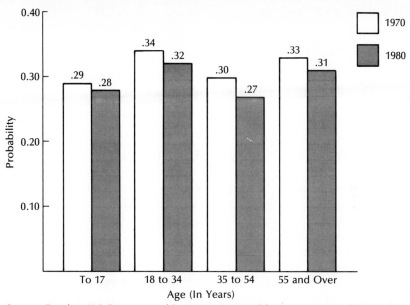

Sources: Data from U.S. Department of Commerce. Bureau of the Census. *State and Metropolitan Area Data Book*. Washington, D.C.: Government Printing Office, 1982; and U.S. Department of Commerce. Bureau of the Census. *Statistical Abstract of the United States*. Washington, D.C.: Government Printing Office, 1980.

Figure 15.4 *Probability of Living in U.S. Central Cities, Given a Person's Age, 1970 and 1980*

Figure 15.4, showing the probability of a person's living in the central city—by age group, for 1970 and 1980—strengthens the view that there has not been a dramatic shift in preferences toward central-city living. For every age group, including young adults, the fraction living in central cities declined over the decade. Combining Figure 15.4 with Figure 1 (inside front cover), it can be seen that the maturing of the baby boom generation in the 1970s led to a temporary bulge in the population most likely to live in central cities (young adults).

The cash flow problems facing first-time home buyers in the latter half of the 1970s (discussed in Chapter 10 and depicted in Figure 10.5) also may have contributed to the attractiveness of renovation. One way to reduce both the down payment and the monthly mortgage payments is to purchase a home in need of renovation and invest what has come to be called "sweat equity."

The meager evidence supports the notion that the upsurge in central-city renovation that began in the mid-1970s is largely or entirely a demographic phenomenon, possibly augmented by the cash flow problems that first-time homebuyers faced in that period. As can be seen in Figure 1, Census Bureau projections indicate a rapid increase in the proportion of young adults up through the early 1990s, after which the low fertility of the 1970s (one of the apparent contributors to the present-day return-to-the-city movement) will bring about a dramatic decline in the proportion of young adults. By that time, the young adult urban homesteaders of the 1970s and 1980s will be middle-aged. Whether they still will be childless and still city dwellers are matters for speculation. So far, the behavior of this cohort is not strikingly different from that of previous cohorts at the same stage in life (except for the postponement of childbearing). If this cohort continues to adhere to the migration patterns depicted in Figure 15.3, the 1990s promises to be a big decade for the suburbs.

☐ CENTRAL CITY POPULATION LOSS

Despite the publicity surrounding urban homesteading, it was quantitatively insignificant compared with the massive migration out of many central cities. The magnitude and causes of central-city population loss will now be examined.

Until the 1960s it was extremely rare for a central city to lose population. During the 1960s, however, population declines in central cities became commonplace; by the 1970s, entire SMSAs were losing population. Of the 153 cities with more than 100,000 population in 1970, 95 lost population between 1970 and 1975,[11] as compared with 59 during the 1960s. Among the cities in this sample, the average population loss was not large—2.51 percent over the decade of the 1970s[12]—but the average population loss among cities that lost population (that is, excluding cities that gained population) was over 6 percent for the decade. And for the 34 cities that suffered the most rapid decline, the average decline was 13 percent (following an average decline of 6 percent for the same cities during the 1960s). Thus, there is a relatively new phenomenon of a substantial number of cities losing a significant portion of their populations.[13]

The SMSA population losses are more recent and much smaller. Twenty-four SMSAs lost population beginning in 1970, and none did before that. The average population loss over the decade for these twenty-four SMSAs was about 1.5 percent. As will be noted, the decline in average household size over the 1970s is more than sufficient to account for this loss in SMSA population.

What is the cause of central-city population loss, and what do these trends foretell? The first step in addressing this question is to catalog the possible sources of central-city population change.

First, a city's population can change, even if the SMSA population does not, as a result of redistribution of people between city and suburbs—suburbanization or the return-to-the-city movement, as the case may be. Second, a city's population can change as a result of natu-

---

11. Two other cities would have lost population, except for annexation.

12. The rate of loss was twice as high in the first half of the decade as in the second half.

13. The material in this paragraph and much of the subsequent material comes from Bradbury, Downs, and Small (1982).

ral increase—an excess of births over deaths—in the current population. Third, a city's population can change as a result of migration to or from the outside world. This migration might be between the city and the rural hinterland, between cities, or between the city and foreign countries.

If a city's population declines, it must be because the net effect of these sources of population change is negative. This became commonplace during the 1960s and 1970s. Examining each of these sources of population change will reveal why many cities began to lose population during the 1960s and 1970s. Before doing that, however, it is important to know which cities are concerned. Of the thirty-four cities that suffered substantial population losses in the 1970s, twenty-five were in the Northeast or the north-central region.[14] In contrast, of the forty-four cities that gained population from 1970 to 1975, only five were in the Northeast or the north-central region. Decline is almost exclusively the domain of the Northeast and the north-central region, and city growth is restricted to the South and West.

One of the causes of city decline has been suburbanization, yet suburbanization—the flattening of population density gradients, essentially—has been going on since at least the 1880s, as already seen. On the average, the pace of suburbanization did not increase in the 1960s or 1970s as compared with previous decades. It is true that in the absence of suburbanization there would have been only trivial city population loss (since SMSA population loss was trivial), but it is not true that an upsurge of suburbanization is responsible for central-city losses.

For the nation as a whole, population growth through natural increase and immigration from abroad fell from 19 percent during the 1950s to 11.4 percent during the 1970s. Thus, total population increase as a potential source of city growth was much smaller in the 1970s than in the 1950s.[15] Migration from farms essentially came to a halt after the great wave of black migration from the rural South in the 1950s and 1960s, as Chapter 2 noted. Quite simply, the reason is that there is hardly anyone left on farms. Thus, the traditional sources of urban population increase essentially disappeared beginning about 1970. Thereafter, any major changes in central-city populations have resulted from flows between city and suburbs, or between cities.

Chapter 2 discussed population flows between regions, noting that population has flowed from the Northeast and the north-central region to the West for many decades. These flows continued into the 1970s,

14. Bradbury, Downs, and Small (1982) define "substantial" loss to be more than 6.5 percent between 1970 and 1975. Since the average household size declined by 6.5 percent over this period, a population loss of less than that amount probably implies an increase in the number of households. (During the second half of the decade, average household size declined by another 5.8 percent.)

15. In fact, it was smaller than in any decade in our history except the 1930s.

becoming more visible because of the virtual cessation of natural increase, international immigration, and rural-urban migration.

In large measure, cities of the Northeast and the north-central region began losing population in the 1960s and 1970s for two reasons. First, the long-standing flows of population from these regions to the South and West were no longer offset to any important degree by the traditional sources of replacement—natural increase, rural-urban migration, and international migration. Second, northeastern and north-central cities, on the average, are much older than southern and western cities, and it has been shown that older cities have been suburbanizing more quickly than newer ones.

Paradoxically, the same demographic forces that led to the (modest) return-to-the-city movement also contributed to central-city population decline. With the population age distribution bulging with young adults, and with the postponement of childbearing, the average household size fell by 12.4 percent between 1970 and 1980. This means that, on the average, an urban area's population could decline over this period by 12.4 percent, with no reduction in the number of dwelling units occupied. In fact, the average household size was pulled down by the large weight given to young childless adults (or young adults with few children), not by a reduction in household size in other adult age groups. As already seen, this young adult group is the age group most attracted to the central city, so the reduction in household size should be most pronounced in central cities. For many cities, this fall in household size is the sole cause of population decline.

There is some reason to believe that this emptying out of old cities has about run its course. It already has been shown that the interregional wage differences of the past two centuries largely have been eliminated. This should diminish the rate of interregional migration. Also, the above-average suburbanization of older cities probably will slacken off, as population declines of the 1960s and 1970s have brought the population density levels of these cities fairly closely into line with those of new cities. Thus, the pattern of faster-than-average suburbanization in older cities probably will not continue very much longer. Finally, the wave of black migration to old northern cities—which has been linked to central-city population loss—has halted and, in fact, reversed in recent years. Preliminary evidence indicates that the pace of the population shift between regions already may have slowed. Bradbury, Downs, and Small (1982, 35) reported that "growing cities are growing more slowly, and most declining cities are declining more slowly" in the period from 1975 to 1980 than in the previous five years.

☐ THE ECONOMIC DECLINE OF CENTRAL CITIES

The longstanding trend of suburbanization of both residences and jobs, and the concentration of poverty in central cities, have already been discussed. This section builds upon much of the preceding material in this book to explore some of the causes and consequences of these central city problems.

The economic problem can be seen most clearly by looking more closely at the economic condition of central-city residents. In 1982, the central-city unemployment rate for black males was 23.4 percent; for whites it was 9.5 percent. (Both of these figures are raised somewhat from their typical levels by the effects of the 1980–81 recession.) Furthermore, black male unemployment rates were very high in central cities for all education levels and in all regions (though less severely so in the West). What is less well appreciated is that the unemployment picture has gotten much worse in central cities for both blacks and whites over the past fifteen years (and on some measures the gap between blacks and whites has increased). In 1969 black male central-city unemployment was only 5.4 percent (4.1 percent among high-school graduates).

Dramatic as it is, the fifteen-year rise in unemployment understates the erosion of economic opportunity. For both blacks and whites, the proportion of central-city males not even in the labor force (and therefore not counted as unemployed) rose by approximately 60 percent from 1969 to 1982.

Thus, the underlying facts are (1) things have gotten worse very quickly in the central-city labor market, and (2) though blacks have fared much worse than whites, the deterioration has been severe for both groups. Any explanation of this phenomenon must account for both of these facts.

One possible explanation can be ruled out very quickly. The deterioration is not due directly to black migration from the South at a time when there were not enough jobs in northern cities. First, the employment malaise has hit whites as well as blacks. Second, as noted, the wave of black migration stopped in the early 1970s—shortly after the onset of the upturn in central-city unemployment, but well before it reached today's proportions.

The spatial mismatch hypothesis. The most plausible explanation begins with an idea put forth by John Kain in 1968. Kain argued that much black unemployment was caused by the fact that blacks were restricted to confined ghettos and that job opportunities were dispersed. He pointed out that postwar suburbanization had seriously aggravated this problem. (Since the publication of Kain's paper, the disappearance of entry-level jobs from central cities has accelerated, as already seen.) He demonstrated empirically that the percentage of employees who are black (particularly in customer-contact jobs) declined dramatically with distance from the nearest black ghetto.

As an explanation for the trends noted above, Kain's hypothesis has some problems. First, the fact that black employment declines with distance from a ghetto may reflect nothing more sinister than the notion that blacks, like whites, prefer to work near their homes. Second, Kain's theory does not explain the deterioration in black employment over the past fifteen years (this is not surprising; his paper was published in 1968). Third, his paper does not explain why white males have suffered unemployment increases recently.

Kain's central idea is that for some groups of people, jobs and homes are sufficiently remote from one another that the costs of job search and commuting present serious obstacles to employment. So it is appropriate to ask whether this geographic mismatch has become more severe over the past fifteen years, and whether it is likely to have affected both blacks and whites. If it has, then the mismatch hypothesis takes on considerable additional plausibility.

The first piece of this puzzle is to note that central cities have disproportionately been the home of blacks and other minorities, and the poor. It has already been pointed out that there is a combination of benign and discriminatory explanations for this phenomenon. To reiterate briefly, the benign part of the explanation is that cities were built from the center out. Particularly in older cities, this means that the center was built at a time when society as a whole was poorer. A consequence is that central-city housing tends to be small and lacking in amenities that the modern middle class is willing to pay for. The central city is thus the location at which old, relatively inexpensive housing is available (through the filtering process) for today's poor and disadvantaged. This benign, or natural-forces, explanation is augmented by a host of discriminatory practices which artificially depress the supply of moderate-income housing in the suburbs, and particularly discriminate against blacks.

Though the geographic spread between rich and poor has increased over the past fifteen years, the patterns of home location by quality have existed since the first wave of upper-class suburbanization following the development of the streetcar. But there is one crucial reason for a pattern of increasing income segregation of American urban areas—the slowdown in the growth of urban population.

If filtering is the primary means of providing housing to low-income people, then the poor are geographically restricted to the places where old housing is abundant. New housing will be built for the rich where vacant land is abundant. Thus, the poor are confined to the central city, while wealthier families reside in the suburbs. Up through the 1920s, and again right after World War II, American urban areas were growing sufficiently rapidly that new housing was constructed for people fairly far down the income distribution (there was not enough old filterable housing to satisfy demand). In such a world, residential location is not so tightly tied to the location of the existing housing stock, and more randomness in income-location patterns would be expected. (To take the extreme case, when Chicago grew from nothing to a population of one million in fifty years in the nineteenth century, virtually everybody lived in new housing.) Thus, the slowdown in urban population growth over the past two decades naturally leads to intensified patterns of segregation.

There are several ways students might want to test this theory. With available census data, students might want to determine whether residential segregation by income and race is more intense in urban areas which (a) are older, and (b) have been growing more slowly in recent years.

The location of jobs will now be examined to show that employment location patterns have undergone a change at least as dramatic in the past two decades as have residential patterns. The overall pattern is this:

1. manufacturing has declined in relative importance throughout the American economy;
2. manufacturing has shown a modest movement out of larger SMSAs in general, and
3. there has been a massive exodus of manufacturing from old central cities.

As noted at the end of Chapter 4, the major growth industry in old central cities has been professional services (following Kasarda, this sector is called "information processing"). Chapter 4 documented the reasons for this employment shift; now it is time to discuss the consequences.

The most significant consequence is also the most obvious: entry-level jobs, for which high-school education is sufficient, have been leaving central cities at a massive rate over the past two decades; there has been a dramatic (but only partial) replacement of these jobs with more education-intensive professional jobs.[16]

The specialty product of the modern city core is massive personal contact. This is precisely the type of activity which "ought" to take place in an urban core. The activity is not particularly space intensive, and vertical transportation is probably at least as efficient as horizontal. Thus expensive land can be used to its fullest, with high-rise office buildings. Once it became economically possible for manufacturing to leave the urban core—with the development of electric power, the automobile, and the truck—the urban core became available for office buildings.

By chance, the concentration of high-education jobs downtown and the suburbanization of entry-level jobs occurred just as the preexisting location pattern of the housing stock was increasingly concentrating poor people in central cities. This set of events appears to be the primary reason for the massive increase in central-city unemployment (particularly but far from exclusively among blacks) over the past two decades.

This proffered explanation of the rapid increase in central-city un-

---

16. Though this case appears to be unique, the total number of jobs in New York City actually increased by 167,000 between 1977 and 1981 (see Kasarda, 65).

employment must be regarded as both incomplete and tentative. It is tentative because it has not been thoroughly examined by scholars.[17]

The mismatch hypothesis is incomplete because it leaves unexplored another crucial question. Have these jobs requiring low educational attainment merely suburbanized, or have they been disappearing from the national economy altogether? In the case of total manufacturing jobs, it is known that employment in the United States has been rising (slowly), suggesting suburbanization rather than total disappearance. The same appears to be true of entry-level service, retail, and wholesale jobs. Essentially what has happened with these jobs is that they have suburbanized along with population. These jobs have followed middle-class whites to the suburbs, and for central-city blacks without cars, they are virtually inaccessible.[18]

It appears that the most viable solution to the mismatch problem is increasing suburbanization of blacks and other victims of the mismatch (precisely as Kain advocated as early as 1968). Not only will this increase access of low-skill people to jobs, but it also is probably the most promising way of increasing educational attainment. The return of entry-level jobs to the central city does not seem to be the answer. The CBD's comparative advantage for the foreseeable future will be in information processing, requiring the employment of well-educated people. Employment opportunities for people with modest education will be in manufacturing and those services associated with shopping, home maintenance, and the like. Each of these activities seems to have irrevocably moved to the suburbs or beyond.

Recognizing that it is the residences and not the jobs which must move does not provide a solution, however. Movement of poor and minority households to the suburbs involves the breakdown of discriminatory barriers. In addition, it may involve construction of new housing for low-income families. The latter will surely be a more costly way of providing low-income housing than the filtering mechanism that now provides most low-income housing. Perhaps a solution will be found through a combination of training, housing location, and transport policies.

Black suburbanization. If it is true that the crisis of black central-city unemployment is due in part to spatial mismatch, then it seems clear that suburbanization of blacks must be at least an impor-

---

17. One recent careful study finds little support for the geographic mismatch hypothesis. Ellwood (1983) has examined the location patterns of black residences and jobs, and his empirical findings tend to refute the mismatch hypothesis. In particular, he finds that blacks who live near large concentrations of jobs do not fare much better than blacks who live far away from such concentrations.

18. Kasarda has calculated the fraction of black and Hispanic city households with no automobile or truck in 1980 for Philadelphia, Boston, and New York. For Boston and Philadelphia, approximately half lacked cars. For both groups, approximately 70 percent of New York City dwellers lacked private transport.

tant part of the solution. The Civil Rights Act of 1968 prohibits virtually all discriminatory acts with respect to both owner-occupied and rental housing. Until only a couple of decades before that date, government was frequently an active participant in residential discrimination. Racial covenants were legally enforceable until 1948 (zoning until 1917).

Since 1968, there have been substantial increases in black representation in American suburbs. According to calculations by Kain (1984) 18.1 percent of blacks in SMSAs of more than one million population lived in suburbs in 1970; by 1980 the figure had risen to 25 percent. He shows that the vast bulk of this suburbanization merely represents an expansion of the ghetto across the city-suburban boundary, rather than true dispersal and mixing at the neighborhood level. He notes, however, that the number of all-white suburban jurisdictions declined markedly during the 1970s. Typical is the suburban ring around Chicago. In 1970, sixty-nine of 117 suburban communities had fewer than five black households; by 1980 the figure had fallen to fifteen. The general pattern appears to be emerging in most suburban rings; formerly all-white suburbs almost everywhere have been acquiring small numbers of black households.

Kain makes two crucial observations about these new black suburbanites. First, the number of blacks living in largely white suburban communities is very small (well under 5 percent of the black population of the SMSA). But second, it is no longer true, as it was two decades ago, that the arrival of a few black households portends the switching of an entire neighborhood or jurisdiction to black occupancy. The reason is very simple. There are not enough blacks to "tip" even a small fraction of the suburban communities which now have a small number of black households. Thus these influxes must remain fairly small. This is much different from the entry of a few blacks into a neighborhood in 1960 or even 1970, because (1) urban black populations are not growing as they were two decades ago, and (2) there have recently been so many small inroads made that they cannot all be followed up by massive flows. It is impossible to know yet whether this optimistic interpretation is correct, but recent changes in black residential location may be the first step in dramatic changes in both location patterns and attitudes.

It has been emphasized that the deterioration of economic opportunity for central-city dwellers extends beyond the black (and growing Hispanic) population, but even a cursory examination reveals that minorities bear the brunt of the social burden. The trend toward high black central-city unemployment has been accompanied by many indications of severe stress in black urban social and family life, including dramatic increases in female-headed households and teenage pregnancy.

There is some reason to believe that these problems have been exacerbated by the fact that blacks migrated so quickly and massively to cities. There has been remarkably little time for the development of stable community relationships, and urban black communities have been severely lacking in the presence of an older generation capable of providing stability and leadership.[19] With the end of black migration (a young-adult activity, largely) and the passage of time, the age distribution of blacks will become more like that of other residents. Many researchers believe that a part of the problem facing urban black America is related to the turmoil brought about by the continuous wave of migration which ended in the early '70s.

☐ Summary

There is widespread concern among government officials, scholars, and the public that the largest metropolitan areas are too large and that most urban areas are excessively decentralized. In both cases, much of the concern is misplaced. It is unlikely that any appropriate government intervention would have much effect on urban sizes or structures.

Large metropolitan areas are thought to be too large because environmental, congestion-related, and other externalities increase in importance with urban size. It does not follow, however, that appropriate intervention to solve the underlying problem would reduce the sizes of the largest urban areas. Whether government attacks on the problem would reduce the sizes of large urban areas or not, changes in urban sizes would be incidental to the solution of the problem. The effect of government actions would be to alter resource allocation in metropolitan areas of a given size.

Suburbs in the United States are thought to be excessively decentralized for several reasons: centrally concentrated pollution discharges, underpricing of urban transportation, land-use controls, subsidization of owner-occupied houses, and high energy costs. Thinking is confused on several issues, and a resolution of the problems probably would not have large effects on urban densities. Urban areas have decentralized in the United States and elsewhere for decades because of powerful market forces. To reverse the process would be unjustified and probably impossible.

Questions and Problems

1. In most countries, the share of the urban population living in the largest urban area falls as real income rises. Why do you think that is?

2. During the 1970s and early 1980s, the share of the urban population in the East and the north-central region decreased, and the share in the South, the West, and the Rocky Mountain region increased.

---

19. William Wilson (1985) notes that the median ages of blacks and whites, respectively, in central cities in 1977, were 23.9 and 30.3.

What effect has the regional shift had on the size distribution of urban areas? What effect has it had on energy use?

3. Suppose all residential land-use controls were abolished. How many more people would live in multifamily housing by the end of the century? How much energy would be saved?

4. Suppose government programs returned typical American density functions to their 1960 levels by the end of the century. What would be the percentage saving in energy use?

5. Do you think density gradients will continue to decline until metropolitan densities are uniform at all distances from the city center?

References and Further Reading

American Public Transit Association. *Transit Fact Book* (Washington: American Public Transit Association, 1981).

Beckmann, Martin, and John McPherson. "City Size Distributions in a Central Place Hierarchy: An Alternative Approach." *Journal of Regional Science* 10 (1970): 25–77. A theoretical model of urban size distribution.

Bradbury, Katharine, Anthony Downs, and Kenneth Small. *Urban Decline and the Future of American Cities* (Washington, D.C.: Brookings, 1982). A careful and thoughtful study on the causes and consequences of central-city population loss.

Ellwood, David T. "The Spatial Mismatch Hypothesis: Are There Teenage Jobs Missing in the Ghetto?" National Bureau of Economic Research working paper no. 1188, 1983.

Gale, Dennis E. "Neighborhood Resettlement: Washington, D.C."*Back to the City: Issues in Neighborhood Renovation,* eds. Shirley Laska and Daphne Spain (New York: Pergamon, 1980). An analysis of neighborhood revitalization in Washington, containing a large amount of information on the characteristics of renovators and the types of houses involved.

Henderson, J. Vernon. *Economic Theory and the Cities* (New York: Academic Press, 1977). An advanced theoretical treatise on urban economics including an analysis of distortions within and among urban areas.

Kain, John F. "Housing Segregation, Negro Employment, and Metropolitan Decentralization." *Quarterly Journal of Economics* (May 1968). This very readable classic paper was the first to carefully analyze the relationship between residential location and unemployment.

————. "Black Suburbanization in the Eighties: A New Beginning or a False Hope?" (Presented at Conference: The Agenda for Metropolitan America, 1984, Sponsored by the Center for Real Estate and Urban Economics, University of California at Berkeley.)

Laska, Shirley, and Daphne Spain, eds. *Back to the City: Issues in Neighborhood Renovation* (New York: Pergamon, 1980). An excellent series of essays on several aspects of the return-to-the-city movement.

Long, Larry H. "Back to the Countryside and Back to the City in the Same Decade." *Back to the City: Issues in Neighborhood Renovation,* eds. Shirley Laska and Daphne Spain (New York: Pergamon, 1980). A good discussion of the demographic aspects of the back-to-the-city movement.

Macauley, Molly. "Estimation and Recent Behavior of Urban Population and Employment Density Gradients." *Journal of Urban Economics* (1985) 251–

260. An updating of Edwin S. Mills's *Studies in the Structure of the Urban Economy* density gradients, along with new analysis and correction of some statistical flaws.

Mills, Edwin S., and Katsutoshi Ohta. "Urbanization and Urban Problems." *Asia's New Giant,* eds. Henry Rosovsky and Hugh Patrick (Washington: Brookings, 1976). A study of urban problems in Japan.

Muth, Richard. *Cities and Housing* (Chicago: University of Chicago Press, 1969). Contains a careful analysis of density functions.

National Association of Realtors, *National Homebuying Survey* (Washington, D.C.: National Association of Realtors, annual) A good annual source of data on the housing market, including detailed characteristics of homebuyers and homes bought.

Peterson, Paul E., ed. *The New Urban Reality* (Washington: Brookings, 1985). A collection of scholarly interpretive essays on several aspects of the current urban scene. Of particular relevance to this chapter are the following: "Urban Change and Minority Opportunities," by John Kasarda. The discussion in the section "The Economic Decline of Central Cities" draws on this work. "Islands of Renewal in Seas of Decay," by Brian Berry. "The Urban Underclass in an Advanced Industrial Society," by William Wilson.

Real Estate Research Corporation. *The Costs of Sprawl* (Washington, D.C.: Real Estate Research Corporation, 1974). A study of costs—government and private—of suburban developments at various densities.

Sundquist, James. *Dispersing Population* (Washington, D.C.: Brookings, 1975). An analysis of European population-dispersal programs.

Tolley, George, Philip Graves, and John Gardner. *Urban Growth Policy in a Market Economy* (New York: Academic Press, 1979). Technical analyses of distortions in urban sizes.

Tolley, George. "The Welfare Economics of City Bigness." *Journal of Urban Economics* Vol. 1 (1974): 324–345.

Yinger, John. "Measuring Racial Discrimination with Fair Housing Audits." *American Economic Review* (December, 1986): 881–893. This paper reports finding extensive housing discrimination, discovered through the employment of an audit, in which black and white auditors pose as prospective buyers or renters.

16

Urbanization in Developing Countries

☐ Until 200 to 300 years ago, only a tiny fraction of people—rulers, courtiers, large landowners, and a few merchants—were able to achieve over sustained periods living standards substantially above the minimum required to subsist and reproduce. Then in England, much of northern Europe, and later, North America, important economic changes culminated in sustained rises in real incomes for a widening circle of ordinary people. By the early twentieth century, such economic growth had spread to a few places—notably, Japan—outside northern Europe and its former colonies in North America. Since the middle of the twentieth century, this growth has spread to many other countries—mostly former colonies in which almost everyone had lived at near subsistence living standards throughout history.

The high-income countries of northern Europe and North America have had high growth rates of per capita income for 100 to 200 years, averaging 2 to 3 percent annual real per capita growth during much of the period, interrupted by occasional devastating wars. Japans's rapid growth started late in the last century, but its people were reduced to near-subsistence living standards by World War II.

Since World War II, a moderate number of countries—most starting at near-subsistence levels—has achieved growth rates that were previously unknown as sustained experiences. During the remarkably peaceful period from 1960 to 1980, among the world's growth leaders were Japan (7.1 percent), Rumania (8.6 percent), Singapore (7.5 percent), South Korea (7.0 percent), Hong Kong (6.8 percent), and Greece (5.8 percent). An even larger group of countries achieved growth rates between 3 and 5 percent.

At the other extreme, a moderate number of countries has achieved little or no growth. Living standards for Bangladesh's 90 million people were no higher in 1980 than in 1960. The same is true for much of sub-Saharan Africa and much of Southeast Asia.

The questions of why and how economic growth occurs and what private groups, governments, and international organizations can do to foster it have attracted the attention of some of the world's best economists, and several Nobel Prizes have been awarded for the results. Introducing economics students to the complexities of economic development requires a book of its own.[1] This chapter has the more limited purpose of analyzing the link between economic development and urbanization, as well as of analyzing a few of the problems that accompany urbanization in developing countries.

☐ CHARACTERISTICS OF DEVELOPING COUNTRIES

A few common features of developing countries play crucial roles in urbanization. Table 16.1 quantifies these characteristics for a sample of nations.

Income

As Table 16.1 reveals, per capita GNP is some fifty times higher in rich countries than poor ones, and relatively few countries have what might be called middle levels of GNP.[2] A per capita GNP of $1000 is roughly equivalent to that of the United States in the early nineteenth century.[3]

Income Growth

Some developing countries have fairly rapid rates of growth of GNP.[4] Much of this is eaten up in population growth, however, so GNP per head is growing only very slowly (generally, not fast enough to make substantial gains upon developed countries). This pattern appears quite starkly in column 8.

Differences in observed growth rates of per capita GNP produce enormous differences in living standards during short periods. A 7 percent growth rate doubles income in ten years. In less than half a century, a 7 percent growth rate raises living standards from among the lowest to among the highest in the world. A 3 percent growth rate mul-

1. Findlay's (1973) is a respected introduction to the subject.
2. Almost 70 percent of the nations listed in the original World Bank table have per capita incomes below $1000 or above $7000.
3. GNP comparisons probably overstate international differences in standard living, because low-income countries conduct more of their economic activities outside the realm of organized markets and, thus, much economic activity escapes inclusion in GNP. Also, GNP overstates income in all countries, because it includes expenditures required to replace depreciated capital. Despite these imperfections, GNP per capita is the most reliable and readily available measure of living standards.
4. Developing countries, like the rest of the world, generally suffered a slowdown in GNP growth in the 1970s.

Table 16.1 Characteristics of Nations at Various Stages of Development

Country	GNP Per Capita RANK 1977	GNP Per Capita RANK 1984	GNP Per Capita 1984	Average Percentage Rate of Population Growth 1965–73	Average Percentage Rate of Population Growth 1973–84	Percentage Urban 1984	Rural Population Density (Per Square Mile)[a] 1984	Average GNP Per Capita Growth Rate 1965–84	Calculated Growth Rate of Urban Population[b] 1984	Adult Literacy Rate (%) 1984
	(1)	(2)	(3)	(4)	(5)	(6)	(7)	(8)	(9)	(10)
United Arab Emirates	1	1	$21,220	11.8	10.7	79	8.43	—	—	21
United States	7	4	15,390	1.1	1.0	74	17.07	1.7	1.35	99
Canada	10	6	13,280	1.4	1.2	75	1.63	2.4	1.60	98
Finland	20	11	10,770	0.2	0.4	60	15.08	3.3	0.67	100
Singapore	30	21	7,260	1.8	1.3	100	—	7.8	1.30	75
Portugal	40	40	1,970	−0.2	1.0	31	198.37	3.5	3.23	70
Panama	50	38	1,980	2.8	2.3	50	35.36	2.6	4.60	78
Syria	60	48	1,620	3.4	3.4	49	72.20	4.5	6.94	53
Peru	70	60	1,000	2.8	2.4	68	11.75	−0.1	3.53	72
Bolivia	80	78	540	2.4	2.6	43	8.34	0.2	6.05	63
Ghana	90	94	350	2.2	2.6	39	81.41	−1.9	6.67	30
Central African Republic	100	105	260	1.6	2.3	45	5.72	−0.1	5.11	—
Sierra Leone	110	97	310	1.7	2.1	24	101.27	0.6	8.75	15
Chad	120	—		1.9	2.1	21	—	—	10.00	7

[a]Calculated agricultural population density is discussed in the text.
[b]Assumes no growth in rural population; Column 5−Column 6.
Source: Data from World Banks, *1986 World Development Report*, Baltimore: Johns Hopkins University Press.

tiplies income almost twenty times in a century. It does not take long, at even modest growth rates, to raise living standards dramatically.

Population Growth

Columns 4 and 5 of Table 16.1 give annual rates of population growth between 1965 and 1973 and between 1973 and 1984, respectively. There is a strong tendency for growth rates to be higher in lower-income than higher-income countries, as well as a modest pattern of increase in the rate of population growth in developing countries during recent years.[5] The initial reason for this is the decline in mortality because of improvements in sanitation, nutrition, and medical care. Birth rates have not dropped as quickly as death rates, and in some cases they have risen. In fact, the decline in mortality has contributed to a rise in birth rates in some places. The biggest improvements in mortality have been among infants and children, and this improvement soon yields a large cohort of adults of childbearing age. Even with declines in average family size, the age distribution of the population in many developing countries is such that birth rates surely will remain high for many years. Average completed family size has begun to decline in some developing countries, however, as will be discussed. This may be due in part to improved educational attainment of females.

Agricultural Population Density

Column 7 estimates agricultural population density.[6] Developing countries generally have agricultural population densities between ten and thirty times higher than developed countries. The reason is straight-forward: average farm size is much smaller in developing countries as a result of population pressure and the fact that there is much less agricultural mechanization than in developed countries.[7] Thus, when the population explosion began in the 1960s, agricultural population density was already high. Population growth added to this density.

Level of Urbanization

The final important characteristic of developing countries is that they are inevitably less urbanized than developed countries, as column 6 reveals. The reason for this is that urbanization is a concomitant of

5.   Consider Panama and poorer nations as "developing." For this sample the average population growth rate was 2.42 percent in the 1950s and 2.7 percent from 1970 to 1977.

6.   Agricultural population density is calculated as the fraction of the labor force in agriculture times the total population density, which is correct if the urban land area is negligible and if the labor force participation rates are the same in the rural as in the urban economy. This clearly understates the agricultural population density, since not all land is under cultivation. The same point, however, applies to developed as to developing countries, so the relative farm size calculation should be close.

7.   In part this relative lack of mechanization may be due to the fact that developing (typically tropical) countries produce crops that are naturally more labor intensive. Note, however, that capital-intensive rice cultivation exists in the southern United States.

development. A less-developed country is almost necessarily one with a predominantly agricultural economy.

It is no great mystery why the urban share of the population correlates so strongly with the level of economic development. The basic pattern was seen in Chapter 3, which outlined the urbanization of the American economy, and it is being repeated in presently developing countries.

Food is the prime requirement for life, and in the poorest countries, most production effort is devoted to agriculture. As economies develop, inputs and outputs shift from agriculture (the primary, or extractive, sector, sometimes including mining) to manufacturing (the secondary, or processing, sector, sometimes including construction) and services (the tertiary sector). In 1980 low-income countries had a weighted average of 72 percent of their labor forces in agriculture; in middle-income countries, the percentage was 43; and in industrial market economies, the percentage was 7 (World Development Report, 1987). Labor force percentages in industry (manufacturing, mining, construction, electricity, water, and gas) and services, respectively, were as follows: low-income economies, 13 and 15; middle-income economies, 23 and 34; and industrial market economies, 35 and 58. Over the entire range of development, the percentage of the labor force in agriculture varies from 75 to 93 in the lowest-income countries (Nepal, Ethiopia, and many African countries) to 3 to 6 in the highest-income countries (United States, Belgium, and West Germany).

Why does the massive shift out of agriculture and into industry and services occur during economic development? One important reason is that demand shifts. At low-income levels, most income is spent on food; however, the income elasticity of food demand is low and probably falls as income rises. The income elasticities of demand for manufactured products and services are larger, and income shares spent on them rise with income. Thus, the ten- or twenty-fold increase in income that occurs during development causes a massive shift of demand from food to manufactured products and services. Employers in the growing sectors offer relatively high wages and other input prices, and labor and other inputs move in directions of relatively high returns.

In addition, product prices of manufactured goods and services may fall relative to those of agricultural products. Technical progress may be faster in industry and services than in agriculture, and the accumulation of both physical and human capital may favor industry and services relative to agriculture. The relative price effects depend on whether the commodities are traded internationally and on the extent to which the economy is open. The more tradeable a commodity and the more open the country, the more cost decreases result in production increases—with resulting labor and other input shifts—and the less the cost decreases result in price decreases.

Since the beginning of this book it has been shown that there are powerful reasons for industries and services to be located in urban areas: large markets permit scale and agglomeration economies to be exploited;

production can locate where comparative advantage dictates and near water, road, and rail transportation facilities so that inputs and outputs can be shipped cheaply; and proximity to inputs produced in the same urban area permits savings on transportation costs.

☐ IMPLICATIONS OF URBANIZATION

Growth of Urban Population

Equation (16.1) expresses the accounting link among the total population growth rate (g_t), the rural and urban population growth rates (g_r and g_u, respectively), and the fraction of population that is presently urban (U/P):[8]

$$g_t = [g_u \times U/P] + [g_r \times (1 - U/P)]. \qquad (16.1)$$

The equation states that the growth rate of the entire population is equal to the urban growth rate times the fraction of the population that is urban plus the rural growth rate times the fraction of the population that is rural. Rearranging, the growth rate of the urban population can be expressed as a function of the other variables:

$$g_u = \frac{g_t}{u/p} - g_r \frac{1 - u/p}{u/p}. \qquad (16.2)$$

Reference to the g_t (column 5) and U/P (column 6) numbers from Table 16.1 shows that it is almost inevitable for developing countries to have extremely rapid rates of urban population growth. If the rural population growth rate is zero, the urban population growth rate is the national growth rate divided by the fraction of the population that is urban.

Of course, the rural population is growing in many developing countries. As will be shown, however, this must be due in large measure to the lack of absorptive capacity of the cities.

Returning to Equation (16.2), it now can be asked what the prospects for urban population growth are, since there may be little room for rural population growth. The calculated annual growth rate of the urban population, on the *assumption of zero rural population growth,* is reported in column 9 of Table 16.1. It is found by setting g_r equal to zero in Equation (16.2).

For the developing countries in Table 16.1 (Panama and below), the average annual rate of urban population growth—assuming no growth of rural population—is 6.5 percent, *a growth rate that would double the urban population every eleven years.* By stark contrast, the

---

8. The reader can readily verify that this expression is correct. Clearly, Δpopulation = Δurban + Δrural. If this expression is divided through by total population, the left-hand side becomes g_t. Multiplying Δurban/population by urban/urban and rearranging terms gives $g_u \times u/p$. In a similar way (multiplying by rural/rural), the last term is converted to $g_r \times (1 - u/p)$.

average annual calculated urban population growth rate for the sample of developed countries is 1.63 percent, which doubles the urban population every forty-two years.

Even if total population growth in developing countries were to stop tomorrow, extremely rapid urbanization would continue for some time because of the high density of agricultural population. Suppose modern farm technology, when fully employed in developing countries, eliminated 80 percent of farm jobs. This would cut agricultural density by 80 percent—still leaving it roughly twice as high as in developed countries, on the average. This emptying of farms into cities would leave the urban population 2.6 times greater than today's. In other words, the backlog of potential urban dwellers currently living on small-plot farms is sufficient to sustain a roughly 5 percent annual growth in urban population for about twenty years, even if total population growth completely stops.

The inescapable conclusion is that urban populations in developing countries will grow extremely rapidly for the next several decades. This is probably the central feature distinguishing urban economics in developing countries from urban economics in developed countries.

There are several additional valuable observations regarding the current urban population explosion in developing countries. First, the same thing happened in currently developed countries in the nineteenth century, although on a more modest scale.[9] Second, many observers believe this rapid urbanization carries the seeds of its own end. As the urban population segment expands, the rate of urban population increase declines, as shown in Equation (16.2). In addition, completed family size tends to be smaller in urban than in rural areas, so the shift to an urban population reduces the growth rate of the total population (once the effects of the skewed age distribution have been eliminated).

Size of the Urban Sector

The high calculated rates of potential urban population growth have not been realized in any nation, although a few cities have achieved growth rates approaching 10 percent during brief periods. For the developing countries in Table 16.1, the average actual rate of urban population increase was 4.31 percent over the period 1973–84—considerably below the 6.5 percent calculated by assuming zero rural population increase. This means that urbanization is proceeding more moderately than the calculation suggests (although urban population still doubles every fourteen years). This means, however, that agricultural population density is being pushed still higher, as well as that the period of rapid urbanization will continue for a longer period after the total population increase slows down.

9. The urban population of the United States grew at about 5 percent per year for the century between 1790 and 1890, but during this period the physical extent of the nation also was increasing rapidly. No single region realized a 5 percent annual growth of urban population for more than a few decades.

The extremely rapid rate of urban population growth previously discussed has led many observers to conclude that urbanization is proceeding too quickly. A frequent component of these arguments is that urban growth is excessively concentrated in large cities (that there is excessive *primacy,* which will be discussed later), that it is too concentrated in prosperous regions, and that it requires excessive expenditure on local government services. A related belief is that concentrations of low-income people in urban slums are undesirable and that cities are, in some ways, parasites living off the efforts and production of rural workers.

The belief that urbanization is proceeding too quickly seems to come from three sources. First, as Chapter 14 showed, externalities (pollution and congestion, basically) may imply that the equilibrium level of urbanization is excessive. Second, many argue that urbanization should proceed more slowly on the grounds that rapid growth toward a given target is more costly and disruptive than slow growth. And third, rapid urbanization always has been accompanied by nostalgia for the bucolic life left behind.[10]

Migration to the urban sector is obviously migration from the rural sector, so the first task in understanding the phenomenon is to discuss the relationship between these two sectors.

Link between rural and urban sectors.   In most developing countries, the product of marginal labor in agriculture is not far above zero. Since farming is frequently a cooperative family operation rather than an enterprise with wage labor, the marginal product requires careful definition. The relevant concept is the marginal product of a *laborer,* that is, what happens to total output if the number of working household members changes. Typically, the loss of a working member of a farm household results in little output loss, because the same work load is shared by fewer workers.[11] When the farm household makes a family decision about whether to send one of its members to the urban market, it will compare the worker's *expected real wage* in the urban sector with the *VMP* in the rural sector. In the case of nearly zero agricultural marginal product, total household income rises if a migrant to the city can expect to make even a modest real wage.

The expected real wage is the wage paid in the urban sector less any urban wage premiums reflecting the costs of urban life (urban housing cost and commuting, for example) and the risk of unemployment. Suppose, for example, that annual commuting cost is $50. Just as in the open city model of Chapter 6, the urban labor market must offer a wage premium of $50 to attract workers. In equilibrium this premium covers all costs and disamenities associated with urban life. Thus, the equilibrium urban wage is equal to the rural *VMP* (that is, the *VMP* of

10. For a particularly poignant statement of this nostalgia, see Oliver Goldsmith's "The Deserted Village," a classic English poem on rural life after the Enclosures.

11. For a fuller discussion, see Sen (1968).

a farm worker, which is sometimes not far above zero in developing countries) plus this wage premium that compensates for associated costs and disamenities. If the actual wage exceeds this compensation, workers migrate from the rural sector. In the typical case, where the rural marginal product is close to zero, the migration of a family member to the urban sector raises total family income, even if the expected real urban wage is small.

Under what circumstances does the movement of a worker from the rural to the urban sector raise total welfare, in the sense of Chapter 8? Ordinarily, welfare is increased whenever the worker shifts from a low-*VMP* job to a high-*VMP* job. The case of rural-urban migration, however, must also take into account the fact that there are costs associated with urban life (and employment) that are largely absent in rural life. The prime example is commuting, although in fact there are many such costs. Since commuting uses resources, welfare maximization requires that the gain in output resulting from migration be weighed against the increased demand on resources. In other words, optimality dictates that the flow of workers to the urban sector stop when the *VMP* of the urban worker exceeds the *VMP* of the rural worker, and this gap between the urban and rural *VMP*s is equal to the resource cost required by the last migrant. To return to numbers analogous to those in the previous paragraph, suppose that total commuting costs (including those of the migrant) rise by $50 per year by the entry of one more worker to the city. Optimality dictates that the urban *VMP* exceed the rural *VMP* by $50. Otherwise, the gain in output would be offset by the increased commuting requirement. Assuming wages are equal to the *VMP* in both rural and urban sectors, efficiency requires that there be an urban wage premium (of $50, in this example).

Markets give correct migration signals when the actual wage premium equals the optimum wage premium. This occurs whenever migrants are forced to pay all the costs (including congestion costs, in this example) associated with their move to the city. In other words, real wage differences serve as efficient signals about labor movement so long as there are no externalities associated with urban population growth.

This is the same argument made in Chapter 14's discussion of environmental quality. It argued that whatever externality problems exist can be more efficiently handled with pricing methods than with controls on urban populations. In any case, it is not clear that the externalities are quantitatively important in developed countries. In developing countries the situation is less straightforward. First, in societies with a high level of illiteracy and an urban population made up largely of recent immigrants from farms or peasant villages, it may be difficult to impose efficient externality fees. Second, the extremely high density of many cities suggests that externalities may be more severe in developing countries. The dollar value of the externalities, however, is likely to be low. The demand for environmental amenities is highly income elastic (not surprisingly, at low incomes people prefer income to a nice environment). Similarly, the congestion externality is the imposition of time cost upon others. When the opportunity cost of time is low, however, so is the money cost of congestion. To summarize, there is no evidence to suggest that urban externalities are sufficiently important to justify restrictions on labor mobility, even if direct pricing policies are unavailable. Although facts on the magnitude of urban externalities in poor countries are scarce, there is no reason to believe that the equilibrium level of urbanization is nonoptimum.

Knowledge about a related topic is even sketchier. Suppose the notion that unrestricted migration ultimately leads to an efficient level of urbanization is accepted. At the same time, it might be true that efficiency would be enhanced if the society approached that level of urbanization more slowly. The argument is that a given amount of growth can be accommodated at less cost if the growth takes place slowly rather than quickly. This might be true for a number of reasons. First, urban life is quite different from village or farm life in the complexity of its rules and interactions. It is plausible that the city functions more smoothly and with fewer bottlenecks if the proportion of people new to urban life is relatively small.[12] Second, the construction of housing and other capital probably occurs under a special kind of increasing cost such that the total cost of building a housing (or transport, water, or sewer) stock can be reduced if the construction is spread over several years.[13]

Although no quantitative information has been gathered, there may be some truth to these arguments. It does not follow, however, that governments should limit migration to cities. A decline in the rate of urban population growth implies an increase in the rate of rural population growth. For the sample of developing countries in Table 16.1, rural population growth is currently about 1.9 percent (doubling farm population in about thirty-five years). For each 1 percent decline in urban population growth, the rural growth rate rises by about 0.5 percent. Since there is already surplus labor in the rural sector, any slowdown in the pace of urbanization would be harmful to the rural sector.[14]

12. Recall that, at current population growth rates, half of the population of a given city will have lived there for less than fourteen years.

13. In the investment literature, this is the distinction between the marginal efficiency of investment and the marginal efficiency of capital. At a rapid pace of investment, the marginal efficiency of investment falls below the marginal efficiency of capital, because rapid investment is more expensive (for a given amount of total capital produced) than slower investment.

14. Some researchers argue that rural development does not receive the attention it deserves in many national development strategies. This argument, however, is that the return to capital investment in the rural sector would be high. It is plausible that such capital investment would be a substitute for labor, thus increasing the surplus of farm labor and increasing the pressure to migrate to the urban sector. Empirically, it appears that some types of rural development—especially irrigation and the introduction of more productive plant strains—increase the demand for rural labor. The mechanization of planting, cultivating, and harvesting clearly displaces rural labor, however (see Ishizawa, 1978).

The net effect of these considerations is that there is no basis for a presumption that slowing the rate of urbanization would be beneficial, once the effects of this policy on the rural sector have been accounted for. There is also an equity issue here. All government programs to slow rural-urban migration inevitably slow migration of predominantly poor people. High-income urban residents designing these programs benefit at the expense of poor people who are precluded from migration.

Primacy. The term *primacy* refers to the size, or allegedly excessive size, of the largest metropolitan area in a country. More generally, the term sometimes refers to the claim that several of the largest metropolitan areas are too large.

The percentage of the urban population living in the largest metropolitan area or areas varies enormously among countries. There is, however, a definitional issue. A country must have at least one urban area—its capital. If the country consists of sufficiently little additional territory, the share of its urban population living in the largest urban area is inevitably large. Singapore and Hong Kong are the extremes, being little more than city-states. Some small African countries are almost in the same situation. Mozambique and Guinea, containing 10 and 5 million people respectively, have 83 and 80 percent of their urban populations living in their national capitals, respectively.

The definitional problem is more severe than the existence of national capitals. From an economic point of view, national boundaries are frequently arbitrary. A given distribution of population between farms, villages, and cities can yield vastly different primacy rates, depending on where the national boundary is drawn. Taking an example from the United States, the New York City SMSA's population is 7.2 percent of the national total. Were New York State, Connecticut, and New Jersey to secede from the Union, however, this new nation would have a primacy ratio of 57.5 percent.

Among countries with large populations, Thailand—with 52 million people—is the most primate, with 69 percent of its urban population in its largest metropolitan area. Mexico and the Philippines, with 32 and 30 percent of their urban populations living in their capitals, respectively, are among the more primate developing countries. At the other extreme, India and China have only 6 percent each of their urban populations living in their largest metropolitan areas.

As a rule, large countries tend to be less primate than small countries (partly for the reason illustrated in the New York example), and high-income countries tend to be less primate than low-income countries. Beyond that, there are few regularities.

Most developing and many developed countries have policies to curtail the growth of their largest metropolitan area or areas. Mechanisms vary from requirements that people have permits or licenses to live or produce in the largest metropolitan area, to subsidies to firms that produce elsewhere, to policies to locate government-owned firms outside large metropolitan areas. Several countries—notably, Brazil and the United States—have moved the national capital to get it away from a large city or metropolitan area. Countries vary greatly as to the firmness with which such policies are applied.

The excessive primacy argument has the same basic components as the excessive urbanization argument just discussed: it maintains that some externality causes the private benefits of moving to the largest cities to exceed the social benefits. As in the case of excessive urbanization, the argument cannot be completely dismissed, although it should be recalled that there are external economies of large city size as well. The gap between marginal and average congestion cost may well be somewhat wider for large cities than small, and the same may be true of pollution costs. There is no evidence, however, regarding the quantitative importance of these considerations and no strong reason to believe they are large. It is known on the one hand that policies to reduce the sizes of large cities have a cost (productivity is higher in large than small cities);[15] on the other hand, given the state of current knowledge, any benefit of shifting population (and employment) from large to small cities is conjectural.

There is one key empirical finding on this subject, however. Henderson (1982) and others have found that, other things being equal, countries with centralized or unitary governments have much more primate size distributions of urban areas than countries with federal systems of government. Brazil, India, and Malaysia have federal systems and dispersed size distributions of urban areas, whereas South Korea, Thailand, and the Philippines have centralized governments and highly primate city size distributions.

The explanation is easy. In federal systems, states or provinces have some constitutional autonomy and can raise their own taxes to provide the local government services (transportation, basic education, water supply, waste disposal, and so on) needed to make urban areas grow. In centralized governments, state or provincial and local governments receive their spending instructions, as well as much of their revenues, from the central government. National governments in such countries invariably pour money into the national capital to the neglect of other urban centers. The national capital is likely to have the best universities, public transit system, museums, convention centers, hospitals, and other services—provided, at least in part, with central government money.

Thus governments in many developing countries try to undo with one hand what they have done with the other. Economic growth and

---

15. According to one estimate for the United States (Sveikauskas, 1975), a doubling of city size is associated with a 5.98 percent increase in labor productivity. It is an open question whether the same result would hold for developing countries, although there is surely some increase in labor productivity as city size increases. Big-city employers are willing to pay the wage premiums that have been discussed rather than move their operations to small cities or villages, presumably because labor is more productive in large cities.

social welfare inevitably suffer from such contradictory policies. The solution is also clear: permit local governments to raise taxes locally and spend the money for the benefit of their constituents. Local autonomy would relate local government spending more closely to the needs and wishes of the local populace, introduce competition among local governments, and disperse political power. These are essentially the Tiebout model benefits discussed in Chapter 13.

Not all local government spending should be financed by locally raised taxes. Some regional and national considerations are involved. Nevertheless, local governments should have much more autonomy than they have in most developing countries. In most countries, the third benefit of local autonomy is precisely the reason central governments do not permit it. Most central governments in developing countries are autocratic and are unwilling to share power with local governments or voters.

Much of the opposition to urbanization in general and the growth of large cities in particular is surely an expression of the subconscious wish that total population growth would slow. Urbanization probably could proceed more smoothly if urban populations were growing more slowly. It is inappropriate to cite this fact in isolation, however; slowing the pace of urbanization would be detrimental to the rural sector, as has been explained. The case for slowing the pace of urbanization is further weakened once it is recalled that urbanization is among the effective means of curbing population growth.

Poverty and Income Distribution

Low-income countries contain mostly low-income people. In 1985 GNP per capita was $150 in Bangladesh, $110 in Ethiopia, and $310 in China. No income distribution can permit lives of dignity for the majority of people if average incomes are at these levels. Economic growth is a prerequisite to decent living standards for most people in all low-income countries. Nevertheless, income distribution differs greatly among countries, and most governments in low-income countries make more or less strong efforts to change the distribution. As was shown for the United States, poverty and income distribution are not inherently urban issues; as in the United States, however, they mostly arise in the context of urbanization.

The distribution of income varies considerably among countries whose income averages fall within a narrow range. Change in income distribution, however, follows a characteristic pattern as countries develop. The pattern was first perceived by Kuznets and has been studied by many economists during the 1970s and 1980s (Chenery, 1979).

Before discussing this pattern, some explanation of measures of inequality is needed. The best graphic representation of income distribution is the Lorenz curve, shown in Figure 16.1. To obtain the data on which this curve is based, make a list of people's incomes in a country, going from the person with the lowest to the person with the highest

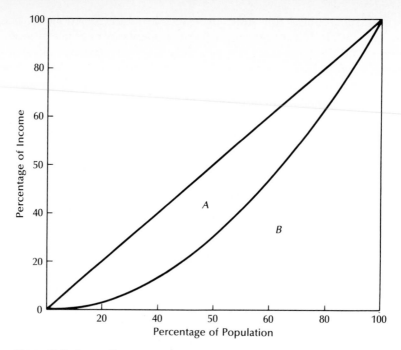

Figure 16.1 *Lorenz Curve*

income. The poorest person has a certain share of total income; the next poorest, a larger share; and so on. The Lorenz curve is a graph of population shares against these income shares, ordered from poorest to richest.

Since 0 percent of the people have 0 percent of income and 100 percent of the people have 100 percent of income, the Lorenz curve touches the lower left and upper right corners of the square. If everyone had the same income, x percent of the people would have x percent of the total income for any x between 0 and 100. Thus, the Lorenz curve would be the straight line shown in Figure 16.1. If there is any inequality, the poorest x percent of people must have less than x percent of the income for $0 < x < 100$. The smaller the income share of the poorest x percent of the people, the farther is the Lorenz curve below the straight line. Thus the area between the straight line and the Lorenz curve, A in Figure 16.1, is a measure of inequality. Typically, A is divided by the total area under the straight line, $A + B$. Thus the measure of inequality is

$$G = \frac{A}{A + B},$$

where G is called the *Gini coefficient*.

The larger is G, the greater is inequality. If G is 0, everyone has the same income. If G is 1, the highest-income person has all the income. For most countries, G is in the interval $0.3 \leq G \leq 0.6$.

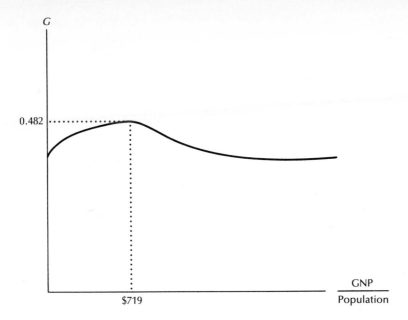

Figure 16.2 *Kuznets Curve*

The pattern perceived by Kuznets is that G is small in very low-income countries, increases as average income rises from low levels, and decreases after average income passes some modest level. Figure 16.2 shows an estimated Kuznets curve. Its characteristics are typical of recent estimates of Kuznets curves.[16] The income levels in Figure 16.2 are in Kravis-adjusted 1970 American dollars.[17] The $719 income level at which the Gini coefficient peaks must be about doubled to place it in 1980 prices. The Kuznets curve in Figure 16.2 implies that more than half the people in the world live in countries in which further growth means increased income inequality. It is not difficult to understand why people become agitated about this.

If the Kuznets curve were steep enough at low-income levels, as average income rose, the income shares of low-income people would fall so rapidly that their per capita incomes would decrease. This is a subject of intense concern in developing countries, and some scholars believe that low-income people do not benefit from economic growth. In fact, no careful estimate of the Kuznets curve implies that per capita incomes fall in any segment of the distribution as average income rises. There is no documented case in which the average income of a low-income segment has fallen as the overall average income increased. The average income of a particular low-income group may fall as the over-

16. This estimate is taken from Becker (1981).

17. The Kravis adjustment converts domestic monetary figures into American dollars, taking into account exchange rates, foreign currency restrictions, and nontradable goods (see Kravis, Heston, and Summers, 1982).

all average income increases, however. For example, the average incomes of low-income small farmers might fall if mechanization—which favors large farms and drives down crop prices—occurred during development.

The Kuznets curve still is not understood in detail, but the basic explanation appears to be as follows. At very low income levels, economic growth means that opportunities open up in particular places (mostly cities and particular industries—the modern manufacturing sector, in particular). Small groups of people are best placed to take advantage of these opportunities. A few entrepreneurial people may have money to invest, and small groups of workers have the education, skills, and health to take part in the growing sectors. The incomes of such people rise well above the average, increasing inequality. Indeed, these are the reasons that incomes are not only higher, but are also more unequal, in urban than rural areas in low-income countries. At later stages of development, a much larger segment of the labor force acquires the skills, health, and education needed to benefit from economic growth, so inequality decreases. Likewise, physical capital becomes plentiful relative to labor, and capital's share in the GNP falls. Property income is always more concentrated than labor income in high-income groups, so the decrease in the share of property income reduces inequality. In addition, inequality of property ownership probably falls as more people reach income levels at which they can save.

To summarize briefly, at very low-income levels, human capital, and probably physical capital, become more unequally distributed as the economy develops; at higher developmental levels, however, both become less unequally distributed, and the share of relatively equally distributed human capital increases.

The possibilities for government intervention to redistribute income to low-income people are quite different in character in developing, as opposed to developed, countries. Traditional cash redistribution is difficult, in large part because record keeping and control are not well developed. In any case, such programs would have to be financed, probably through progressive taxation. Nations that desperately need investment funds are concerned about the effect of progressive taxation on the rate of saving.

In contrast, several types of in-kind transfers may offer important benefits.[18] Many of these in-kind transfers are aimed directly at increasing the productivity (and thereby the incomes) of low-income people. Health and education services are the best examples. In the lowest-income countries, half the adults typically are illiterate, and many more are only barely literate. Many studies show that the returns to basic education are very high in these countries; however, children often obtain little or no education because there is no school in the town or

18. Of course, in-kind transfers must be financed, too, so the adverse effect on savings remains.

village, schools are inconveniently located relative to residences of the low-income people in cities, families cannot afford books or uniforms, or parents are unable or unwilling to send children to school.

Henderson (1982) found (for Brazil) that education programs can improve the incomes of uneducated, as well as educated, workers. According to his estimates of the urban production technology, educated labor is complementary to uneducated labor. In other words, the limited supply of educated people is a bottleneck that limits (for example) the level of manufacturing activity, in turn limiting employment opportunities for the uneducated. Thus, an expansion in the supply of educated labor raises the productivity (and hence the wage) of uneducated labor (as well as that of people who receive the education).

Health is a serious problem in all low-income countries. Neighborhood or village clinics, ''barefoot'' (partially trained) doctors, and other health-related programs can improve the health, and thus the income-earning ability, of low-income people.

These productivity-enhancing redistributive programs are attractive in that they offer the possibility of raising total income at the same time they equalize the distribution.[19] In developed countries, productivity-enhancing opportunities are less effective, since the least expensive (most cost effective) of such activities already have been carried out. Illiteracy, chronic preventable disease, and malnutrition are rare, so the most obvious opportunities for simultaneously redistributing income and improving productivity are unavailable.[20]

The most widely publicized form of income redistribution in developing countries is land reform. Some researchers feel this is another case of productivity-enhancing redistribution, but the argument is inconclusive. Proposed reforms entail the seizure of large landholdings, their division into small plots, and the granting of ownership to peasants. If the original landlord is not fully compensated, or if the peasants receive title at below market price, land reform involves redistribution. Nevertheless, as an income redistribution vehicle it tends to be haphazard. The beneficiaries are the peasants who are awarded title; in realistic programs, this involves only a minority of peasants. In an important sense, the beneficiaries are chosen at random.

In a low-income country, a major land reform program can have a large effect on the distribution of income, though, because the share of property income is high in very low-income countries. The main reason is that in these countries most income originates in agriculture, and the share of property income is higher in agriculture than in manufacturing and services. Several South and Central American and

19. Remember, however, that the programs must be financed through taxation. This taxation distorts incentives, which in turn tends to depress total income. Nevertheless, the return to education, for example, is probably sufficiently high to offset this.

20. This is not to say that no such opportunities exist in developed countries. The remaining such opportunities are likely to be fairly expensive, however, and hence less cost effective than those of developing countries.

African countries have some of the world's most unequal income distributions, and they have been subject to bloody civil wars in the 1970s and 1980s. The main reason for their extreme inequality of income is the concentration of landownership in the hands of a few high-income people. Technically, government land redistribution programs are not difficult, and several governments have carried them out successfully. In some countries, however, land redistribution is nearly impossible without bloodshed. Land redistribution can dramatically redistribute income to low-income peasants in low-income countries, but it also can be politically and economically disruptive if attempted by a weak government.

Is land reform a pure exercise in income transfer, or does it also enhance agricultural productivity? There is no theoretical basis for predicting whether farm productivity will increase or decrease. The conversion of peasants from sharecroppers or wage laborers to entrepreneurs enhances their incentive to work efficiently; however, the subdivision of a large landholding may result in the loss of scale economies. In keeping with this ambiguous theoretical prediction, the evidence is mixed. The answer almost surely varies from country to country.

Land reform policies may affect the rate of urbanization. Sen (1968) found that labor use per acre is higher on small plots than on large ones, suggesting that the diversification of landownership may retard urban migration.[21] In the long run, however, any effect of land reform (the creation of small owner-farmed landholdings) upon fertility also must be considered.

Housing

Chapter 11's discussion of housing problems in the United States emphasized the durability of housing. In an urban area with roughly constant population and steady income growth, this durability and non-malleability of housing leads to the situation depicted in Figure 11.3; there is a chronic surplus of low-income housing and a chronic shortage of high-income housing. This creates benefits for the low-income people (housing is available at a low price), as well as a cost (housing is available only at certain locations and, frequently, in declining neighborhoods). Indeed, problems of decline and abandonment were seen to be due in part to the high cost of demolishing or renovating surplus low-income housing.

Cities in developing countries, by contrast, are characterized by a rapid population increase and very low (in some cases, zero or negative) growth of per-household income. Figure 16.3 is the analogue of Figure 11.3 that captures the underlying facts for developing countries.

---

21. Sen also found that small holdings had higher crop yields per acre, although this finding is subject to some dispute, as noted. For a recent discussion, see Rudra and Sen (1980).

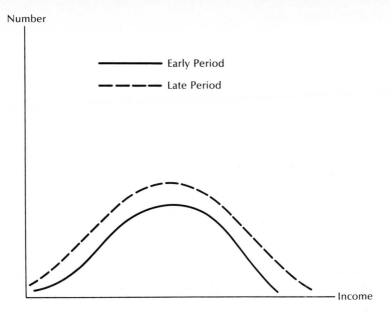

Figure 16.3 *Size Distribution of Income and Housing Demand*

With the passage of time, the size distribution of income (and therefore of housing demand) shifts from the solid to the dashed curve. For most developing countries, this shift is basically straight up (a rise in numbers) rather than to the right (a rise in per-capita income, but little change in numbers). In the case of developing countries, the dynamics of income and population change do not create surpluses of low-income housing; rather, there is a chronic shortage throughout the quality range.

Important observations emerge from the difference between Figures 11.1 and 16.3. The most obvious is that filtering is almost nonexistent in developing countries. Low-income people generally do not live in hand-me-down housing and are not able to acquire their housing at a price below construction cost. Low-income people in developing countries generally live in new housing (with the population's doubling every fourteen years, almost everyone lives in new housing), frequently in illegal squatter settlements (to be discussed). In developed countries, low-income people can be found where there is old housing, frequently in the most central parts of the city.[22] In developing countries, by contrast, low-income people can be found where there is vacant land available for either legal or illegal development, which is frequently at the periphery.

22. Many developed countries do not exhibit the pattern discussed in Chapter 11. In Japan, for example, income does not show much variation with distance from the CBD. There are apparently three reasons for this: (1) a substantial amount of Japanese housing was destroyed during the war; (2) there was extremely rapid migration into Japanese cities after the war; and (3) Japanese housing traditionally has not been as durable as American housing.

Slums and Squatters

In all countries, housing quantity and quality vary greatly among residents. Slums exist in almost all countries, yet most low-income countries have a special problem almost unknown in high-income countries. There are millions of *squatters* in low-income countries. Bombay and Calcutta alone have at least one million each, and they are present in almost every city in South Asia, South America, and Africa.

A *squatter* is an illegal settler, almost always in an urban area. In fact, the term covers several distinct activities. Settlers may be illegal because they have no legal right to use the land (they neither own it nor have permission from the owner to use it); because it is not legal to build on the land (for example, because of land-use controls), although they have the legal right to use it; or because the structures in which they live are illegal (for example, they do not meet housing or building codes).

Typical squatters are low-income and relatively recent migrants to the urban area who cannot afford legal housing. They squat on government or privately owned land and build on the land whatever shelter they can, mostly with used or scrap materials and frequently with the help of friends.

Persons often squat on riverbanks, railroad rights-of-way, wide sidewalks, parks, land too hilly for normal development, land private owners have not developed, or simply open spaces surrounding apartment houses. In South America squatters often settle on hills that are undeveloped because they are too steep to build on safely or too high for water and sewage service. In India they may be on riverbanks or sidewalks.

Not all squatters are low-income newcomers. Some are there because ownership rights are confused, because the government lacks the physical or political will to remove them, or just because squatting provides cheap housing. In some cases, squatters have constructed substantial dwellings and improved them over the years.

There are good reasons why squatting is peculiar to developing countries. First, as Table 16.1 shows, urban population is growing rapidly, and as Figure 16.3 reveals, this leads to a chronic shortage of existing low-income housing, so slums must be built new on vacant land. This pattern continues until per capita income growth accelerates and population growth slackens. It does not follow from Figure 16.3, however, that newly built slums are illegal and lack the benefits of basic public infrastructure (such as a layout of lots and streets, or some sort of water supply and sewage disposal). The development frequently occurs illegally because governments lack the power to enforce property rights.

Squatters are controversial wherever they are found. They may live in unsanitary and often dangerous places, many are unemployed and frequently politically troublesome, and some settlements harbor criminals. Like other migrants, however, many squatters come to cities from the countryside in search of better living standards, education, and employment for themselves and their families. Surveys in several countries show that many urban squatters lived in much worse conditions in the rural villages they left.

What should governments do about squatters? Government policies fall into four categories, often followed approximately in sequence and with little consciousness of the evolution taking place.

First, governments ignore squatters. They do not appear on master plans or housing registers. They may not be permitted to remain long in their illegal residences, so they do not get counted in censuses and other data. They are not provided educational, health, water, sewage, street, or transportation services.

Second, governments try to remove squatters, often under pressure from owners of land on which squatters have taken up residence; nearby legal residents; or government agencies charged with health care, maintaining building codes, and administering public land on which squatters have located. In the 1960s pictures appeared in American newspapers of South American governments destroying squatter settlements with bulldozers marked "Gift of the Alliance for Progress" (the U.S. government's foreign aid program for Latin America). Of course, squatters removed from one location frequently turn up in another, usually in the same city.

Third, governments try relocation. Land is set aside (usually on the outskirts of the city where vacant land is available), and public housing is built (usually relatively high quality, high-rise, slab concrete apartments). The squatters then are evicted from their illegal residences and offered the new apartments at subsidized rents or purchase prices. Generally, relocation has not worked. The housing may be more costly than residents can afford, even with subsidized rents or purchase plans. Relocated squatters often resell or sublet their new quarters at market prices and end up back in slums, a little richer. More often, the new quarters are in the wrong places—far from places where residents find work—because public housing usually ignores the intimate relationship between work and residence of low-income people. Many low-income people—particularly recent migrants—work in the "informal sector," providing small services such as repairs, transportation of goods, and retail sales of food. Typically, some family members process or repair goods in the residence while an adult buys, sells, seeks customers, and so on. Indeed, this informal sector self-employment is traditionally the first type of job for the rural migrant. It provides subsistence income to new residents while they look for wage employment. For this purpose, the home must be where the business is carried on, and it must be close to customers. Public housing in some distant suburb satisfies neither of these requirements.

The fourth government policy is legalization. If the squatters are not too dangerously located—say, on a hillside subject to landslides or a riverbank subject to floods—the government gives the land or, more likely, sells it on concessionary terms to the residents, usually on the condition that the residents construct dwellings that meet minimum standards. Sometimes the government helps provide materials, and usually it provides "sites and services," meaning that the government lays out orderly plots and constructs paved paths, public latrines and water pumps, and some street lighting. The procedure often entails a modest subsidy to the residents, but it dramatically improves their incentives. They know they will own and can inhabit, rent, or sell whatever they build. A means test is required to prevent large numbers of people from squatting somewhere and demanding that the land be given or sold cheaply to them, and the program usually requires that the recipient live on the plot for several years. Legalization generally takes place only after some years of squatters' having lived in squalor, and the plots offered are often so small that only genuinely poor people would want them.

From an economist's perspective, squatting and the evolution from illegal to legal status have two important aspects: wealth redistribution and resource allocation. The legalization or toleration of the permanent occupancy of squatter settlements involves a wealth redistribution from the former owners to the new de facto owners. Almost invariably this is pro-poor redistribution with compassion on its side.[23] The resource allocation effects are more troublesome. With squatting, the allocation of land to low-income housing passes no market or analogous efficiency test. Thus, there is no presumption that land goes to its best use. Second, if existing squatter settlements are periodically legalized, with title given either free or at subsidized prices, the incentive to squat is enhanced. In addition, squatters frequently spend many years on their plots before it is clear that title will be recognized by the authorities. During this time the original legal owners cannot sell the property, since they cannot assure the buyer that occupancy will be physically possible. The squatters have limited incentive to build substantial durable structures because of the possibility that they will be evicted and their structures either repossessed or, more likely, destroyed.

Urbanization and Capital Investment Needs

Urban life requires much more physical capital than does rural life. Water provision and sewage disposal can be managed with only primitive capital in a rural setting, but the same service quality requires much more elaborate and expensive investment in an urban area. Similarly, urban housing tends to be more costly than rural because of the substitution of capital for land. Formal education is more important in an urban than a rural setting (in a developing country), and it requires the expenditure of resources. Finally, commuting and goods shipment require investments in road and rolling stock capacity that are largely un-

---

23. Many observers, however, feel that a more equal distribution of income—particularly in poor countries—reduces the total volume of saving. This reduces investment, which retards development.

necessary in rural life. Of course, there are economic benefits to urbanization (such as the realization of scale economies), but the costs must be incurred before the benefits accrue (that is, the costs represent investments). All this means that a nation undergoing rapid urbanization is committed to a high level of investment in urban infrastructure. In other words, rapid growth in urban population places a heavy burden on investment funds and of necessity reduces the funds available for plant and equipment, as well as agricultural modernization.

Lewis (1977) argues that it is the pace of urbanization, rather than poverty, that gives rise to the standard pattern of developing nations' borrowing heavily from developed nations. He points out that the same pattern existed in the middle of the nineteenth century, when the United States, Canada, Australia, and Argentina (the rapid urbanizers of that era) were heavy borrowers from France, England, and Germany (nations whose cities were already in place and that had excess loanable funds). These nineteenth-century debtor nations were in fact richer than were the lending nations (and they had real income levels comparable to those of many developing countries today).

The cash flow problems associated with the costs of rapid urbanization can be severe, particularly when it is realized that the period of rapid urbanization typically precedes the period of rapid industrialization and income growth.[24] This means that the cost occurs well before rising incomes enhance ability to pay.

☐ Summary

Though sharing many features with the urbanization process in currently-developed countries, developing countries have enough unique characteristics to ensure that urbanization is quite different from, say, nineteenth-century America.

Developing countries are, of course, much poorer than industrialized nations, but not substantially poorer than the United States and western Europe before industrialization. The most striking feature of urbanization in developing countries is the speed with which it is taking place, and the near-certainty that very rapid urbanization will proceed for several decades. This rapid growth of population, coupled with widespread poverty and illiteracy, causes urbanization in developing countries to have a different character from that in developed countries. There is essentially no filtering and abandonment of housing, since such a small fraction of the housing stock is old and low-quality (relative to demand). The poor are not concentrated in central cities, but

---

24. To get a visual representation of this fact, see Figure 3 on the inside back cover. It shows a large increase in urbanization associated with a rise in per capita GNP in the $100-to-$1000 range, but a rather modest further increase in urbanization associated with GNP growth from $1000 to $8000. The same pattern can be seen over time in the United States. The period of most rapid urbanization was from 1820 to 1860, whereas the period of most rapid industrialization was the latter half of the nineteenth century.

more typically form squatter colonies on vacant land. A very large fraction of the cost of providing public services must continually go to the development of infrastructure (streets, lighting, water, and sewers). These durable investments place a serious drain on scarce funds, a problem which is much less significant in a society which is not undergoing rapid change.

It is relatively easy to see, in broad outline, how urbanization in developing countries differs from that in developed countries. It is much more difficult to determine appropriate urbanization policies for developing countries. These policy problems offer one of the most important challenges facing urban economists.

References and Further Reading

Becker, Charles. "Urban Sector Income Distribution and Economic Development." *Journal of Urban Economics* Vol. 21 (March 1987): 127–145. An analysis of urban and national income distribution as countries develop.

Beier, George, Anthony Churchill, Michael Cohen, and Bertrand Renaud. "The Task Ahead for Cities of Developing Countries." *World Development* Vol. 4 (May 1976): 363–409. A discussion of the problems facing cities in developing countries.

Chenery, H. *Structural Change and Development Policy* (New York: Oxford, 1979). A careful study of all aspects of developing policy.

Findlay, Ronald E. *International Trade and Development Theory* (New York: Columbia University Press, 1973). A textbook on economic development.

Henderson, J. Vernon. "The Impact of Government Policies on Urban Concentration." *Journal of Urban Economics* 12 (1982): 280–303.

_____. "Urban Development: City Size and Population Composition." Brown University working paper, no. 82-12, 1982.

Ishizawa, S. *Labour Absorption in Asian Agriculture* (International Labor Organization, 1978). A discussion of the relationship between agricultural employment and several other aspects of the production process.

Kravis, Irving, Alan Heston, and Robert Summers. *World Production and Income* (Baltimore: Johns Hopkins, 1982).

Lewis, W. Arthur. *The Evolution of International Economic Order* (Princeton University Press, 1977). A monograph of twentieth-century economic development.

Rudra, Ashok, and A. K. Sen. "Farm Size and Labour Use." *Economic and Political Weekly* Vol. 15 (February 1980): 391–94. A brief discussion of farm size and labor productivity.

Sen, A. K. *Choice of Technique* (Oxford: Blackwell, 1968). An examination of the determinants of the input combinations used in the agricultural sector of developing countries.

Sveikauskas, Leo. "The Productivity of Cities." *Quarterly Journal of Economics* Vol. 89 (August 1975): 393–413. An estimate of the relationship between productivity and city size.

World Bank. *World Development Report* (New York: Oxford University Press). Published annually.

Appendix A

*Simplified Mathematical
Model of Urban Structure*

☐   This appendix introduces some of the mathematical techniques that
have proved useful to urban economists, as well as to researchers in
other specialties. One of its purposes is to prove some of the statements
made in the text. A much more important purpose is to show that mathematics is a useful tool in understanding urban processes and problems.
The fundamental characteristic of an urban area is that many forces interact to determine land rents, land uses, and other interesting urban
characteristics. In other words, an urban area is a system with a large
amount of simultaneity. Mathematics is indispensable in analyzing such
systems.

    It is not necessary to be a professional mathematician to be an ur-
ban economist. In any specialty in economics, it is desirable to have
a mixture of scholars with different levels of mathematical interest and
background. A specialist in any branch of economics should be able
to follow the relevant literature, however. For that purpose the minimum requirement is a knowledge of elementary calculus. That background is sufficient to follow this appendix and, indeed, practically all
the important work in urban economics. Anyone lacking that background should try to understand the assumptions and conclusions in
this appendix but should not be concerned with derivations.

☐   MODEL OF URBAN STRUCTURE

    The model analyzed here is mainly concerned with the urban area
residential sector.[1] It is the most important urban sector and the one
that has been studied most carefully. Most models that include more

---

    1.   The model analyzed in this appendix is a simplified version of those analyzed
by Mills (1972) and Muth (1969).

than one sector are too large to present here and require the help of a computer to solve.

Assume that the urban area has a predetermined center, perhaps at a port or railhead. At each distance from the center, ϕ radians of a circle are available for urban uses. Since a circle has 2π radians, ϕ must not exceed 2π. The rest of the land, $2\pi - \phi$ radians, is either unavailable for urban use (perhaps because of topographical characteristics) or is used for transportation, parks, and other public purposes.

Assume that all the urban area's employment is located in a semicircular CBD with a radius of $\underline{u}$ miles. Thus, the CBD has an area of $(\phi/2)\underline{u}^2$ square miles, and it is assumed that N people work there. The terms ϕ, $\underline{u}$, and N are given from outside the model.

The available land outside the CBD is used for housing as far away from the center as is necessary to house the N workers employed in the CBD. The total amount of land available for housing within u miles of the city center is $(\phi/2)u^2 - (\phi/2)\underline{u}^2$.

Housing Supply and Demand

Equations expressing the conditions for location equilibrium in the residential sector now can be introduced. It is assumed that commuting cost depends only on the straight-line distance between place of residence and the city center. It follows that land rent and the intensity of land use also depend on straight-line distance, so all the land u miles from the center commands the same rent and is used with the same capital/land ratio. This is an important simplification in urban models, since it implies that activities can be located with only one variable (distance from the center) rather than two (distance and direction). The value of each variable at a distance u miles from the center is designated with a u in parentheses following the variable. For example, $K(u)$ and $L(u)$ represent inputs of capital and land in the production of housing services u miles from the center. This notation shows that the variables are functions of u, and solving the model consists of deducing from the equations in the model the functional relationship between the variables and u.

It is also assumed that housing services are produced with land and capital inputs. The production function is assumed to be the *Cobb-Douglas production function,* which economists have used to study many production activities. Using this function, the output of housing services at u, $X_s(u)$, depends on the inputs of land and capital employed at u in the following way:

$$X_s(u) = AL(u)^\alpha K(u)^{1-\alpha}, \tag{A.1}$$

where A and α are constants. A is a scale parameter and depends on the units in which inputs and output are measured. The term α is called the *distribution parameter,* and it must lie in the interval $0 < \alpha < 1$. (It is discussed later.) It can be verified that Equation (A.1) has constant returns to scale, so competitively priced input payments exhaust firms' revenues.

It is assumed that input and output markets are perfectly competitive, so firms use amounts of inputs equating the *VMP* to input rental rates at each u. It is assumed that the market for housing capital is national, so its rental rate, r, is independent of both u and the amount used in the entire urban area. Land rent, $R(u)$, and the rental rate for housing services, $p(u)$, are determined by the model and, of course, depend on u.

If Equation (A.1) is differentiated, it is seen that the *MP*s of land and capital are

$$MP_{L(u)} = \alpha AL(u)^{\alpha-1}K(u)^{1-\alpha} = \alpha X_S(u)/L(u)$$

and

$$MP_{K(u)} = (1 - \alpha)AL(u)^{\alpha}K(u)^{-\alpha} = (1 - \alpha)X_S(u)/K(u).$$

Therefore, the equations relating factor *VMP*s to their rental rates are

$$\frac{\alpha p(u)X_S(u)}{L(u)} = R(u) \tag{A.2}$$

and

$$\frac{(1 - \alpha)p(u)X_S(u)}{K(u)} = r. \tag{A.3}$$

If Equations (A.2) and (A.3) are multiplied by their respective input amounts and divided by $p(u)X_S(u)$, they show that the ratio of each input's remuneration to total revenue equals the input's exponent in Equation (A.1). These ratios are the shares of the inputs in housing rental revenues; thus, it can be seen why α is called the *distribution parameter*. The value of α determines the distribution of housing rental revenues between the two inputs. A typical house may be worth four times the land it occupies, which suggests that α might be about 0.2.

It is assumed that all workers receive the same income, w, determined outside the model, and that all have the same tastes. The demand function for housing services per worker living at u, $x_D(u)$, is assumed to be

$$x_D(u) = Bw^{\theta_1}p(u)^{\theta_2}, \tag{A.4}$$

where B is a scale parameter and depends on the units in which housing services are measured. The terms θ_1 and θ_2 are the income and price elasticities of demand for housing, respectively, as can be verified by computing the elasticities from Equation (A.4). Unlike other demand functions, Equation (A.4) assumes the elasticities to be constant, and it has been used in many applied studies of demand theory. Housing per worker depends on u, as Equation (A.4) indicates. Housing is not an inferior good; hence, $\theta_1 > 0$. The housing demand function slopes downward; hence, $\theta_2 < 0$. Recent studies of housing demand suggest that θ_1 may be about 1.0 and θ_2, about -1.0. $X_D(u)$, the total housing demand at u, is housing demand per worker multiplied by $N(u)$, the number of workers living at u:

$$X_D(u) = x_D(u)N(u). \tag{A.5}$$

In equilibrium, housing demand and supply must be equal at each u:

$$X_D(u) = X_S(u). \tag{A.6}$$

In addition, the text showed that locational equilibrium in housing requires that Equation (6.6) be satisfied. That equation can be written as follows:

$$p'(u)x_D(u) + t = 0. \tag{A.7}$$

Here, $p'(u)$ is the slope of $p(u)$, and t is the cost per 2 miles of commuting. Equation (A.7) says that families are unable to increase utility by moving their households if the change in the cost of housing from a move is just offset by the change in commuting cost.

Other Equilibrium Conditions

It already has been assumed that ϕ radians of land are available for housing at each u, so ϕu is the length of the semicircle available for housing u miles from the city center. Land used for housing cannot exceed what is available, and no available land can be left unused out to the edge of the urban area. Thus,

$$L(u) = \phi u. \tag{A.8}$$

It is assumed that nonurban uses of land command a rent, $\overline{R}$. Therefore, the urban area can extend only as far as households can bid land away from nonurban uses. Thus the distance from the center to the edge of the urban area is $\overline{u}$ miles, where

$$R(\overline{u}) = \overline{R}. \tag{A.9}$$

Finally, the land available for housing must house all N workers in the urban area. If $N(u)$ workers live u miles from the center, the total number of workers in the urban area is the sum, or integral, of $N(u)$ for values of u from $\underline{u}$ to $\overline{u}$; that is,

$$\int_{\underline{u}}^{\overline{u}} N(u)du = N. \tag{A.10}$$

The model is now complete. The first eight equations relate the eight variables—$X_S(u)$, $L(u)$, $K(u)$, $p(u)$, $R(u)$, $x_D(u)$, $X_D(u)$, and $N(u)$—at each value of u. Their solution provides the value of each variable at each u between $\underline{u}$ and $\overline{u}$. Equation (A.7) contains a derivative of $p(u)$ with respect to u. A differential equation, its solution requires a predetermined value of the variable at some u. It will be shown how Equation (A.7) can be expressed as a differential equation in $R(u)$. Equation (A.9) then provides the required value of $R(u)$ at $\overline{u}$, known as an initial condition for the differential equation. Finally, Equation (A.10) can be solved for the variable $\overline{u}$.

Once the model is solved, it shows a complete picture of the housing sector of the urban area. For each value of u, it shows land rent and the rental rate of housing services. From the solution for $K(u)$ and $L(u)$, it is easy to compute the capital/land ratio at each u. From the solution of $N(u)$, population density can be computed at each u.

☐ SOLUTION OF THE MODEL

The land rent function is the key to the foregoing model. Once it has been found, all the other variables can be calculated easily. The first step in solving $R(u)$ is to derive a well-known relationship between input and output prices for the Cobb-Douglas production function. Solving Equations (A.2) and (A.3) for $L(u)$ and $K(u)$ gives

$$L(u) = \frac{\alpha p(u) X_S(u)}{R(u)} \text{ and } K(u) = \frac{(1 - \alpha) p(u) X_S(u)}{r}.$$

Substituting these expressions for $L(u)$ and $K(u)$ in Equation (A.1) and rearranging terms gives

$$p(u) = [A\alpha^{\alpha}(1 - \alpha)^{1-\alpha}]^{-1} r^{1-\alpha} R(u)^{\alpha}, \qquad (A.11)$$

which shows that $p(u)$ is proportionate to $R(u)$ raised to a power between 0 and 1. Thus, housing prices are high wherever land rents are high, but housing prices rise less than proportionately with land rents because of input substitution. If α is 0.2, a 10 percent rise in land rent will lead to a 2 percent rise in housing prices.

The derivative of Equation (A.11) with respect to u is

$$p'(u) = A^{-1} \left\{ \frac{\alpha r}{1 - \alpha} \right\}^{1-\alpha} R(u)^{-(1-\alpha)} R'(u), \qquad (A.12)$$

where $R'(u)$ is the slope of $R(u)$. Now substitute Equation (A.4) for x_D (u) in Equation (A.7), substitute Equation (A.11) for $p(u)$, substitute Equation (A.12) for $p'(u)$, and collect terms. The result is

$$E^{-1} R(u)^{\beta-1} R'(u) + t = 0, \qquad (A.13)$$

where E and β stand for collections of constants,

$$E^{-1} = \alpha\beta w^{\theta_1} [A\alpha^{\alpha}(1 - \alpha)^{1-\alpha}]^{-(1+\theta_2)} r^{(1-\alpha)(1+\theta_2)}$$

and

$$\beta = \alpha(1 + \theta_2).$$

Equation (A.13) expresses the differential Equation (A.7) in terms of $R(u)$. Using the initial condition of Equation (A.9), the solution is

$$R(u) = [\bar{R}^{\beta} + \beta t E(\bar{u} - u)]^{1/\beta}, \text{ if } \beta \neq 0, \qquad (A.14a)$$

and

$$R(u) = \bar{R} e^{tE(\bar{u}-u)}, \text{ if } \beta = 0. \qquad (A.14b)$$

In Equation (A.14b), the term e is the base of the natural logarithm. This equation therefore indicates that, when β is 0, land rent decreases exponentially as u increases. Both equations indicate that $R(u)$ equals $\bar{R}$ when u equals $\bar{u}$. Both have the characteristic shape established in the text and illustrated in Figure 6.1. It can be seen from the definition of β that $\beta = 0$, and Equation (A.14b) thus applies, when $\theta_2 = -1$. It was indicated earlier, however, that θ_2, the price elasticity of demand for housing, is probably about -1, and the exponential function of Equation (A.14b) therefore should be a good approximation of urban land rent functions. The term β is positive if $\theta_2 > -1$, that is, if housing demand is price inelastic. Regardless of the sign of β, $R(u)$ is steep at small values of u and flat at large values of u.

Equations (A.14a) and (A.14b) contain the variable $\bar{u}$, representing the radius of the urban area. So far, Equation (A.10) has not been used, and $\bar{u}$ has not been computed. Using the equilibrium condition of Equation (A.6), Equation (A.5) can be written as follows:

$$N(u) = \frac{X_S(u)}{x_D(u)}.$$ (A.15)

Taking the ratio of Equation (A.2) to Equation (A.3), $K(u)$ can be expressed in terms of $L(u)$:

$$K(u) = \frac{1 - \alpha}{\alpha r} R(u)L(u).$$

Now substitute this expression for $K(u)$ in Equation (A.1). The result is

$$X_S(u) = A\left\{\frac{1 - \alpha}{\alpha r}\right\}^{1-\alpha} R(u)^{1-\alpha}L(u).$$ (A.16)

Substitute Equation (A.11) for $p(u)$ in Equation (A.4). Then, in Equation (A.15), substitute Equation (A.4) for $x_D(u)$ and Equation (A.16) for $X_S(u)$. Rearranging terms gives

$$\frac{N(u)}{L(u)} = ER(u)^{1-\beta}.$$ (A.17)

If both sides of this equation are multiplied by $L(u)$, Equation (A.8) is substituted for $L(u)$, and the result is integrated from $\underline{u}$ to $\bar{u}$, an expression for the left-hand side of Equation (A.10) results. Equating it to N provides the equation from which $\bar{u}$ can be calculated. The result, however, is cumbersome and so is not presented here.

Equation (A.17) shows how the number of resident workers per square mile varies with u. Except for a multiplicative factor equal to the reciprocal of the labor force participation rate, it is the same as population density, and it will be referred to as *population density* from here on. Equation (A.17) expresses a remarkable result: *population density is proportionate to land rent raised to the power $1 - \beta$*. The $1 - \beta$ must be positive, since θ_2 is negative. Thus, as would be expected, population density is high wherever land rent is high. More importantly, if $\beta = 0$, so Equation (A.14b) applies, and population density is proportionate to land rent and therefore declines exponentially with u, just as land rent does. Exponential functions have been used in many applied studies of urban population density (some of which are reported in Chapter 15) and have been found to fit the data very well. Thus Equation (A.17) provides a link between theory and observation.

A universal conclusion of urban population density studies is that density functions become flatter through time. Many writers have speculated that increasing incomes and falling commuting costs cause density functions to flatten. The mathematical model here shows that the speculation has a theoretical basis. The population density function of Equation (A.17) will be flatter the larger the coefficient of u in Equation (A.14a) or (A.14b); that is, the closer the coefficient is to 0. Both increases in w and decreases in t flatten the density function by increasing the coefficients of u in Equations (A.14a) and (A.14b).

It is easy to see that finding $R(u)$ is the key to solving the mathematical model. Many of the other variables already have been expressed as functions of $R(u)$; the term $p(u)$ can be calculated from Equation (A.11); the term $L(u)$ is given by Equation (A.8); the term $X_s(u)$ can be calculated from Equation (A.16); and the term $N(u)$ can be calculated from Equation (A.17). As an exercise, calculate $x_D(u)$, which shows how housing demand per worker varies with u, and prove that it is exponential if $R(u)$ is exponential.

☐ TWO HOUSEHOLD SECTORS

This section generalizes the mathematical model to study the effects of income differences on the household location pattern. In particular, it provides a proof for the statement in the text that, under realistic conditions, high-income households live farther from the city center than do low-income households.

Until now, the time cost of travel simply has been included in t. This section assumes that commuters value travel time proportionately to the wage rate, w. Thus t is written

$$t = t_0 + t_w w, \qquad (A.18)$$

where t_0 represents the operating cost per 2 miles of travel (about $0.25 to $0.35 if travel is by automobile); t_w represents the time cost or disutility of 2 miles of travel per dollar of income; and t_w is inversely proportional to travel speed. For example, suppose commuting speed is 25 miles per hour. Then 2 miles of travel requires $2(1/25) = 0.08$ hours (4.8 minutes). If travel time is valued at the wage rate, $t_w = 0.08$. If the wage rate is $7.50 per hour, the time cost of 2 miles of commuting is $0.60. If t_0 is $0.30, 2 miles of commuting have a total cost of $0.90. In this example, location equilibrium requires that the workers' housing expense fall by $0.90 per day, or about $20 per month (assuming a 22-day working month), if they move 1 mile farther from the city center.

If travel time is valued at less than the wage rate, t_w is less than in the example. If commuting speed is faster than 25 miles per hour, t_w is also less than in the example. As the text indicated, the assumption that the marginal disutility of commuting is independent of commuting distance is a special case. It is shown later that the assumption is crucial to the results obtained here.

Suppose there are two household sectors, distinguished only by income. Household Sector 1 has income w_1, and Household Sector 2 has income w_2. All households have the same tastes and therefore the same housing demand function, but the amount of housing demanded differs from one sector to another.

For convenience, the household sector closer to the city center is designated Sector 1, and its rent offer curve, as $R_1(u)$. The sector farther from the center is Sector 2, and its rent offer curve, $R_2(u)$. Then the two rent offer curves must be as shown in Figure A.1. If Sector 1 is to be close to the center, its rent offer curve must be above that of Sector 2 for small values of u. Household Sector 1 occupies the available land at values of u between $\underline{u}$ and u_0, and Sector 2 occupies the land between u_0 and $\bar{u}$. Suppose u_0 and $\bar{u}$ satisfy all the equilibrium conditions.

$R_2(u)$ has the initial condition $R_2(\bar{u}) = \bar{R}$, and its solution is Equation (A.14a) if $\beta \neq 0$; that is,

$$R_2(u) = [\bar{R}^\beta + \beta t_2 E_2(\bar{u} - u)]^{1/\beta}, \tag{A.19a}$$

where w affects E and t, but not β. Therefore, E_2 and t_2 designate the values of E and t when the wage rate is w_2.

$R_1(u)$ has the initial condition $R_1(u_0) = R_2(u_0)$, and its solution is

$$R_1(u) = [\bar{R}^\beta + \beta t_2 E_2(\bar{u} - u_0) + \beta t_1 E_1(u_0 - u)]^{1/\beta}. \tag{A.19b}$$

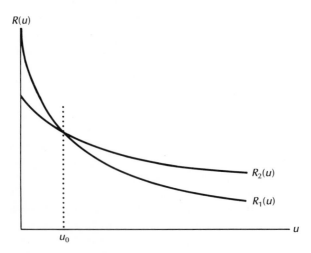

Figure A.1 Equilibrium with Two Sectors

It can be verified that Equation (A.19b) satisfies its initial condition and that $R_1(u)$ and $R_2(u)$ can have only one intersection.

Is Sector 1, close to the center, the high-income or the low-income sector? The condition that $R_1(u)$ be greater than $R_2(u)$ at values of u less than u_0 is

$$[\bar{R}^\beta + \beta t_2 E_2(\bar{u} - u_0) + \beta t_1 E_1(u_0 - u)]^{1/\beta}$$
$$> [\bar{R}^\beta + \beta t_2 E_2(\bar{u} - u)]^{1/\beta} \tag{A.20}$$

for $u < u_0$. If β is positive, Inequality A.20 reduces to the condition that the term in square brackets on the left-hand side exceed the term in square brackets on the right-hand side; that is,

$$\bar{R}^\beta + \beta t_2 E_2(\bar{u} - u_0) + \beta t_1 E_1(u_0 - u) > \bar{R}^\beta + \beta t_2 E_2(\bar{u} - u)$$

for $u < u_0$, or

$$t_1 E_1 > t_2 E2. \tag{A.21}$$

If β is negative, Inequality (A.20) reduces to the condition that the term in square brackets on the left-hand side be less than the term in square brackets on the right-hand side; that is,

$$\bar{R}^\beta + \beta t_2 E_2(\bar{u} - u_0) + \beta t_1 E_1(u_0 - u) < \bar{R}^\beta + \beta t_2 E_2(\bar{u} - u).$$

Canceling terms and remembering that $\beta < 0$, this inequality also reduces to Inequality (A.21).

Thus, it is only necessary to establish the relationship between w_1 and w_2 that is equivalent to Inequality (A.21). The following theorem provides the key relationship: if $\theta_1, \geq 1$, then Inequality (A.21) holds if and only if $w_2 > w_1$. To prove the theorem, first note that E is w^{θ_1} multiplied by terms that cancel on both sides of Inequality (A.21), which therefore can be written

$$\frac{t_0 + t_w w_1}{t_0 + t_w w_2} > \left(\frac{w_1}{w_2}\right)^{\theta_1} \tag{A.22}$$

by substituting Equation (A.18) for t.

1. Suppose $w_2 > w_1$. Then Equation (A.22) holds for $\theta_1 = 1$, since

$$\frac{t_0 + t_w w_1}{w_1} = \frac{t_0}{w_1} + t_w > \frac{t_0 + t_w w_2}{w_2} = \frac{t_0}{w_2} + t_w$$

reduces to $w_2 > w_1$. The right-hand side of Inequality (A.22) becomes smaller as θ_1 becomes larger than 1, however. Therefore, $w_2 > w_1$ implies Inequality (A.22).

2. Suppose $w_2 < w_1$. The left-hand side of Inequality (A.22) has a maximum value of w_1/w_2 when $t_0 = 0$, and it decreases asymptotically to 1 as t_0 becomes large. The right-hand side of Inequality (A.22) exceeds w_1/w_2 if $\theta_1 > 1$, however. Therefore, Inequality (A.22) cannot hold.

This proves the theorem. Using Equation (A.14b), the theorem can be verified if $\beta = 0$. Thus, in this model, an income elasticity of demand for housing of at least 1 implies that low-income workers live closer to the city center than high-income workers. Generally, any number of household sectors, differing only in income, will be ranked by distance from the city center inversely to their rank by income.

The theorem proves that low-income groups live close to the city center only if $\theta_1 \geq 1$. It does not prove that they will live elsewhere if $\theta_1 < 1$. Inequality (A.22) may still hold for $w_2 > w_1$ even if $\theta_1 < 1$. For example, suppose that t_0 and t_w have the values 0.30 and 0.08 used in the foregoing example. Suppose further that $w_1 = \$2$, and $w_2 = \$4$. Then Inequality (A.22) holds if $\theta_1 \geq 0.54$.

It is easy to see that the theorem may not hold if high-income workers value travel time higher in relationship to the wage rate than do low-income workers, or if the marginal disutility of commuting increases with the amount of commuting. In the former case, t_w is larger for the high-income group than for the low-income group. In the latter case, t_w is larger for the sector residing farther from the city center. It can be easily verified that the theorem does not hold if either change is made in the model. It is still true, however, that a sufficiently large income elasticity of housing demand results in the location pattern implied by the model.

References and Further Reading

Brueckner, Jan. "A Note on Sufficient Conditions for Negative Exponential Population Densities." *Journal of Regional Science* 22 (1982): 353–359. A criticism of the model in this Appendix.

Mills, Edwin S. "An Aggregative Model of Resource Allocation in a Metropolitan Area." *American Economic Review* 57 (1967): 197–210. Presents the mathematical model upon which the model of this Appendix is based.

Muth, Richard. *Cities and Housing* (Chicago: University of Chicago Press, 1969). A detailed theoretical and empirical study of urban form. The theoretical structure, though much more elaborate, is in the same spirit as that of this Appendix.

Appendix B

Regression Analysis

☐ Economists frequently refer to the notion that a change in one variable will bring about a change in another variable. A rise in income causes an increase in housing expenditure; an increase in distance from a CBD causes a decline in residential density. It is often important to make quantitative statements about these associations based on real-world observations, both to test theories and to make predictions. The standard statistical tool for making these quantitative statements is *regression analysis.*

Suppose the hypothesis that Y depends on X (say, housing expenditure depends on income) has been formed. The first step in any statistical study, obviously, is to gather the data. A sample of X and Y is depicted in Figure B.1. Each point in the scatter diagram is called an *observation;* it is a matched set of values of each of the variables. For example, an observation would be the income and the housing consumption of a household.

The next step in a regression study is to choose a *functional form* for the regression equation; for example, the hypothesis that the relationship between X and Y is linear might be formed. A *linear regression* is the straight-line equation which most nearly passes through all the points on the scatter diagram; the equation of this best possible approximation is

$$Y = a_0 + a_1X, \qquad (B.1)$$

and it is drawn in Figure B.1.[1] Many computer programs have been designed to find the straight line that gives the best fit to the observations. Finding the best fit entails finding the optimum values for the parameters a_0 and a_1; the computer gives us these parameters.

---

1.   Formally, the *best possible approximation* generally means the line that minimizes the sum of the squares of the (vertical) distances of the observations from the regression line. These distances are known as *errors;* one such error is labeled ϵ in Figure B.1.

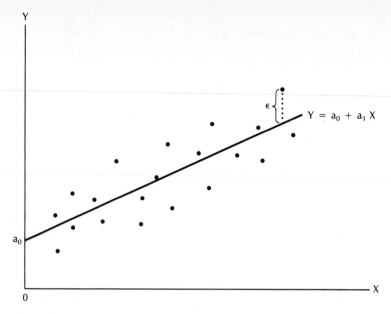

Figure B.1 *Scatter Diagram and Regression Line*

Notice that a_1 is equal to $\Delta Y/\Delta X$. Thus, for example, if X and Y are income and housing expenditure, respectively, it is possible to look at the results from a regression equation and know immediately how much (on average) housing expenditure goes up with income.

How much Y goes up with X on the average is only part of the answer, however. It is also important to know how much confidence to place in this "on average" statement. Suppose, for example, that on average, housing expenditure goes up $0.20 for every $1.00 of extra income; $a_1 = \$0.20$. Is the expenditure change always between $0.19 and $0.21, or does it range anywhere between $-\$0.80$ and $+\$1.20$? How close do the points in a graph like Figure B.1 lie to the regression line? The first piece of information on this "goodness of fit" question is R^2, the fraction of the variation in Y explained by the variation in X. Since it is a fraction, it must lie between 0 and 1. If R^2 is 1, all the observations lie on the regression line; there are no errors. If R^2 is 0, knowledge of X is useless in predicting Y.

Sometimes there is reason to believe that Y depends on more than one variable; for example, urban land value might depend both on SMSA population and air pollution. Just as before, observations are gathered (matched data on land value, city size, and air pollution) and a functional form, say, linear, chosen:

$$Y = a_0 + a_1X_1 + a_2X_2, \tag{B.2}$$

where Y = urban land value; X_1 = SMSA population; and X_2 = level of air pollution.

Once again the computer finds the best-fit values of the parameters a_0, a_1, and a_2. The term a_2 tells how much land value changes as air pollution rises, *holding city size constant.* To determine the effect of air pollution on land value, it is important to include city size in the regression equation, even if this effect is not considered important. To see why, consider what would happen if it were left out and a regression of land value on level of air pollution were run. Furthermore, suppose the following to be the true state of the world: land value rises with city size but is unaffected by air pollution, but air pollution tends to be worse in big cities than small. In such a world, air pollution is correlated with land value, simply because both are correlated with city size. Thus, a regression like Equation B.1, where Y is land value and X is air pollution, will lead to the erroneous belief that high air pollution causes high land value. With a regression like Equation B.2, however, with city sizes being the other right-hand variable, the effect of city size on land is accounted for, and the regression correctly finds that air pollution and land value are not correlated. The inclusion of other variables in the regression holds constant their effect, providing isolation of the effect of the variable of interest.

If two or more variables appear on the right-hand side, the equation is called a *multiple regression.* With a multiple regression, R^2 continues to measure the fraction of the variation in Y explained by variation in the Xs. It gives no information, however, on the contribution of the individual variables to the explanation of the variation in Y. Returning to the previous example, suppose land value is regressed upon city size and air pollution. As Chapter 14 discussed, air pollution is not expected to be associated with land value, after holding constant city size. Regression analysis can be used to see whether this is true. Basically, this means doing the following. Regress land value on just city size, and write down the R^2. Now regress land value on city size and air pollution. R^2 is not expected to rise significantly by including air pollution, since the theory says air pollution adds nothing to the explanation of rent differences between cities, after city size is corrected for.

The usual measure of whether R^2 rises significantly with the addition of another variable is the t-statistic. There is a t-statistic associated with each variable in the regression; its interpretation is as follows. If the t-statistic is greater than about 1.9 (in absolute value), the variable is of statistical significance. In the above example, the prediction is that the coefficient on the air-pollution variable will have a t-statistic smaller than about 1.9.

Acknowledgments

p. 133: From *Industrial Real Estate Market Survey* (Washington, D.C.: Society of Industrial Realtors, Spring 1982). Reprinted by permission of the National Association of Realtors; p. 179: From *Setting National Priorities: The Next Ten Years,* edited by Henry Owen and Charles Schultze. (Washington, D.C.: The Brookings Institution, 1976). Reprinted by permission; p. 181: From *Public Expenditures, Taxes, and the Distribution of Income* by Morgan Reynolds and Eugene Smolensky. Copyright © 1977 Academic Press, Inc. Reprinted by permission of Academic Press, Inc. and Morgan Reynolds; pp. 219, 221: From "Low and Moderate Income Housing: Progress, Problems and Prospects." (Washington, D.C.: National Association of Home Builders, 1986). Reprinted by permission; p. 220; From *Annual Housing Survey, Part C.* (Washington, D.C.: National Association of Home Builders, 1974 and 1983). Reprinted by permission; pp. 248, 249: From *Real Estate Status Report.* (Washington, D.C.: National Association of Realtors, March 1982). Reprinted by permission; p. 249: From *National Homebuyers Survey.* (Washington, D.C.: National Association of Realtors, 1981). Reprinted by permission; p. 273: From *The Full Costs of Urban Transport* by Theodore Keeler et al. Reprinted by permission of the author; p. 303: Data from "Finance" by George E. Peterson in *The Urban Predicament,* edited by W. Gorham and N. Glazer. (Washington, D.C.: Urban Institute, 1976, table 6). Reprinted by permission; p. 308: From "Proposition 13: Genesis and Consequences." Adapted with permission from William Oakland; p. 317: From "Local Government, the Property Tax and the Quality of Life: Some Findings of Progressivity" by B. W. Hamilton in *Public Economics and the Quality of Life,* edited by L. Wingo and A. Evans. Copyright © 1977 by Resources for the Future, Inc. Reprinted by permission; p. 341: From *Economics and the Environment* by Allen Kneese, Robert Ayres and Ralph D'Arge. Copyright © 1970 by Resources for the Future, Inc. Reprinted by permission; p. 377: From *Studies in the Structure of the Urban Economy* by Edwin S. Mills. Copyright © 1972 by Johns Hopkins University Press. Reprinted by permission; and from "Recent Behavior of Urban Population and Employment Density Gradients," Johns Hopkins Working Paper No. 124, 1983 by Molly Macauley. Reprinted by permission; p. 379: From *The World Almanac & Book of Facts,* 1983 edition. Copyright © 1982 by Newspaper Enterprise Association, Inc., New York, NY 10166. Reprinted by permission; p. 384: From "Energy" by Milton Russell in *Setting National Priorities: The 1978 Budget,* edited by J. Pechman. (Washington, D.C.: The Brookings Institution, 1977). Reprinted by permission; p. 387: From *National Homebuyers Survey.* (Washington, D.C.: National Association of Realtors, 1981). Reprinted by permission; p. 388: From "Back to the Countryside and Back to the City in the Same Decade" by Larry Long in *Back to the City: Issues in Neighborhood Renovation,* edited by Shirley Laska and Daphne Spain. Copyright © 1980 by Pergamon Press, Inc. Reprinted by permission; p. 403: From *1980 World Tables.* Copyright © 1980 by Johns Hopkins University Press. Reprinted by permission.

Photo Credits

cover photo: © Santi Visalli; p. 1: New York Manhattan traffic tie-up, AP/Wide World Photos; p. 84: Oak Street Beach and North Lake Shore Drive traffic in Chicago, © Santi Visalli

Index

Aaron, Henry, 210, 239

Abandonment of housing, 223–28. *See also* Demolition of housing; Slums

Absorptive capacity of environment, 343–44

Agglomeration economies of urban areas, 19–20, 113, 116, 370

Agricultural population densities, 403, 404, 407

Agricultural revolution, 56

Agriculture. *See also entries beginning with* Rural
  in developing countries, 404–05
  and industries, labor distribution between, 55–57
  land for, 139, 332
  technological progress in, 55–57

Aid to Families with Dependent Children, 177, 179, 306

Air pollution, 344–46, 352–53, 360n, 371–73, 380

Alonso, William, 12n

Amenities, environmental, 357–63, 409

Amenity orientation of firms, 37–38

Annexation of land by cities, 72

Apgar, William, 121n

Assumable mortgages, 204

Automatic vehicle identification (AVI), 268

Automobile pollution, 344–46, 352–53, 360n

Automobile travel:
  in city growth, 29
  congestion caused by, 261–71
  costs of, 262–78, 383–84
  versus public transit systems, 253–58, 383–85

Average cost in automobile travel, 262–63

Average population densities, 4, 378–79

Averch, Harvey, 330

Ayres, Robert, 341

Bailey, Martin J., 237

Balloon (frame) construction technique, 26

Basic (export base) employment, 15, 45

Basic welfare theorem, 149

Beach, Alfred Ely, 27n, 28n

Becker, Charles, 415n

Beer industry, 35

Bessemer process, 25

Best possible approximation in regression analysis, 435–37

Bhatt, Kiran U., 268n

Biochemical oxygen demand (BOD), 348, 350

Birch, David, 122n

Black Americans:
  in central cities, 256, 280–81, 376–78
  discrimination against, 102, 236–39, 280–81, 321
  reduction of discrimination, 182–83
  migrations of, 45, 48–49, 238
  poverty of, 170–174, 182–83
  prejudice against, 377
  segregation of, housing, 233–36
  suburban job access of, 280–81
  suburbanization of, 396–98
  urbanization of, 171–73

Bobrick, Benson, 27n, 28n

Bradbury, Katharine, 376, 390n, 391n, 392

Break-even point for pretax and aftertax income, 176–78

rehabilitation of, 222, 386–90
rental, 191, 192, 207,
209–10, 225, 244–46. *See
also* prices of, rental, *above*
retirements of, 213, 222–28
in slum areas. *See* Slums
stock of, 194, 213–15, 222–32
subsidies for, 225, 240–44,
246–48, 382
suburban, 104–07, 225,
280–81
supply of, 194–97, 244,
426–29
units of, determining, 185–86
as urban externality, 159
value, 186–88, 192, 197–99
Housing allowances for low-
income households, 242–43
Housing and Community De-
velopment Act of 1974,
241, 242
Housing and Urban Development Act of 1968, 241
Housing markets:
analyzing, 185–215
construction industry in,
210–15, 241–43. *See also*
Housing, construction of
cost of capital in, 189–97,
199–200
discrimination in, 102,
236–39, 280–81, 321
equilibrium in, 195–97
filtering in, 228–29, 419
and income taxes, 102,
190–92, 209–10, 225,
239–40, 382
inflation in, 189–92,
197–210
interest rates in, 189–90,
197–99, 211. *See also*
Mortgage interest, tax
deductibility of; Mortgage
interest rates; Mortgages
measures in, 185–88,
197–99, 240
in 1970s, 197–200

racial segregation in, 233–36.
See also discrimination in,
above
supply and demand analysis
of, 192–97. *See also* Housing, demand for; stock of;
supply of
Housing price functions,
105–07, 117–20
Housing price gradients,
125–26, 130–31, 381
Hoyt, Homer, 132
Hulten, Charles, 320

Import substitution by cities, 15,
23, 39
Improved land values, 86–87
Income distribution. *See also* Income redistribution pro-
grams; Incomes
in developing countries,
413–18
efficient, 156
by race, 173–74
Income-maintenance policies,
175–83
Income redistribution programs,
175–83
in developing countries,
416–18
versus housing subsidies,
246–48
in-kind, 180, 416
in local jurisdictions, 314–17,
321
and taxes, 161–62, 182–83
transfer payments in, 162
Income segregation, 118, 138–39
Income taxes:
excess burdens of, 162
federal, and housing market,
102, 190–92, 209–10,
225, 239, 382
local, 293, 294. *See also* Local governments, taxes of
negative, 175–78, 243

state, 292–93, 294. *See also*
State governments, taxes of
on wages, 93
Incomes. *See also* Income distribution; Income redistribution programs
city-suburban differences in,
296, 385–86. *See also*
Suburbs, household in-
come in
current, 193–94
decentralization related to, 378
in home buying, 117–18
in-kind, 167, 180, 416
land values related to, 378
local taxes as percentage of,
308
low. *See* Low-income households; Low-income hous-
ing; Poverty; Poverty
income, computing
money, 167
of developing countries,
402–04
permanent, 193–94
postfisc, 181
poverty, computing, 168. *See
also* Low-income house-
holds; Low-income hous-
ing; Poverty
state taxes as percentage of,
308
wage, 93
Industrial processing, water in, 347
Industrial sites, prices for,
132–33
Industrialization, history of, 54–57
Industry(ies). *See also* Firms
and agriculture, labor distribution between, 56–57
beer, 35
construction in housing markets, 208, 210–15, 241–42
in developing countries, 405
footloose, 37. *See also*
Production cost orientation
of firms

government classification of,
62–66
inside and outside standard
metropolitan statistical
areas, 58–66
in urban areas, 97–101,
108–12
land demand by, 89. *See also*
Industrial sites, prices for
land rents offered by, 108–10
lending, 203–06, 211, 240
location of, 96–101, 108–15.
See also Industrial sites,
prices for
manufacturing, 38–39, 42,
48, 58–66
market-oriented, 63
materials-oriented, 63
rent functions of, 108–12
scale economies in, 8–20.
See also Scale economies
single industry model for,
96–101
steel, 36–37
textile, 34
two-industry model for,
108–10
Inefficiency in private land markets, 332–35. *See also*
Efficiency
Inflation in housing markets,
189–92, 197–210
Information processing, 80
Ingram, Gregory, 121n
In-kind income redistribution
programs, 180, 416
In-kind income versus money
income, 167
Inner city neighborhoods, renovation of, 245, 386–90
Input markets, competitive, 87, 98
Inputs:
marginal product of, 88–89
purchases of, 19
Insurance, mortgage, 240n, 382
Interest, mortgage, tax deducti-
bility of, 209

and wages, analogy between, 93–94

welfare and ethical aspects of, 90–94

Land use:
boundaries in, rural-urban, 139
controls on, 314, 320–21, 331–35, 381–82
externalities in, 332, 333
models of, 96–122

Land values, 86–87, 119–20, 126–27. *See also* Property values

Laska, Shirley, 387

Lave, Lester, 345, 346

Least squares regression in estimating Pareto distribution, 74–75

Leisure, value of, 154–55

Lending industry, 203–06, 211, 240

LeRoy, Stephen, 25n

Level payment, self-amortizing mortgages, 201–04

Lewis, W. Arthur, 423

Line haul, 259, 271, 282

Linear regression, 435

Lipsey, Richard G., 18n

Livestock, transport and slaughter of, 35–36

Living standards, 167–68, 172–73, 342–43, 401–04

Local governments. *See also* Government(s)
antipoverty efforts of, 180
of developing countries, 413
efficient resource allocation to, 319–21
expenditures of, 293–300, 304–05
financing, 290–310, 313–14, 318–21
goods and services provided by, 295–96, 310–15
jurisdictions of, 3–4, 313–21
labor in, cutting back on, 301–02

pollution abatement proposals for, 356–57
racism by, 236
regulation by, 330–35
revenue sources of, 292–93, 296–98, 302, 306
solid waste responsibility of, 352, 357
and state governments, overlapping functions of, 290
taxes of, 293, 294, 308
types of, 289–90

Location equilibrium condition:
defined, 105
of firms, 115
of households, 105–06, 117–20. *See also* Housing price functions
of labor force, 368

Location in urban areas:
economic theory of, 8–20
of firms, 32–38, 112–16, 362–63, 370
of households, 101–07, 110–16, 431–34
of industries, 96–101, 108–15

Location models:
firm, 112–16
household, 101–07, 110–16, 431–34
open city, 115–16
patterns of, 121–22, 431–34
several sector, 107–12
single industry, 96–101
two industry, 108–10

Lock-in as homeowner problem, 204–05

Long, Larry H., 388

Lorenz curve for income distribution, 413–14

Lösch, August, 10, 12n

Low-income households, 168, 240–48, 280–81, 313–21, 385. *See also* Poverty

Low-income housing, 229–30, 317, 321

Walters, Alan, 266n, 271n
Washington, D.C., subway system, 276–78
Wastes in environment. *See* Discharges into environment, characteristics of; Pollution
Water:
quality of, standards for, 347–48
uses of, 346–47
Water pollution, 346–49
Water service:
in early nineteenth century, 21
as local government service, 310–11
Watson, P. L. 268n
Welfare:
in developing countries, 409, 416–17
and land rent, 90–94
Welfare economics:
criteria in, 147–56. *See also* Efficiency; Equity
defined, 145
and Tiebout hypothesis, 319–22

and urban problems, 145–62
value judgments in, 145–47
Weight-gaining products, 35
Weight-losing products, 35–36
Wheaton, William C., 118
White, L. J., 239
White, M. J., 136, 226, 239
Wienk, Ronald, 239
Withdrawal uses of water, 347
Wohl, Martin, 266n, 272
Wolfe, B. L., 323
Work trips, 112–15, 256–61, 270–78. *See also* Commuting

Yinger, John, 239

Zampelli, E., 329n
Zoning:
in local government regulation of land use, 331–35
low-income housing restrictions of, 317, 327
suburbanization related to, 381–82

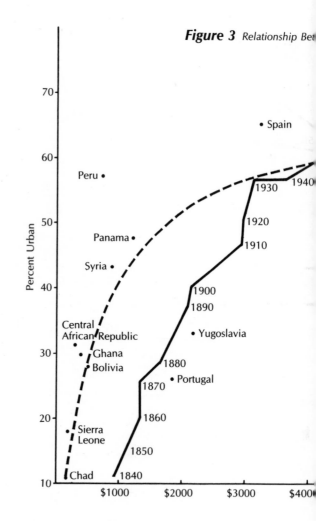

Figure 3 Relationship Bet